D0832919

PORTRAIT

OF

SHELLEY

WATER–COLOR PORTRAIT BELIEVED TO BE THE
LOST MINIATURE OF SHELLEY
BY EDWARD ELLERKER WILLIAMS

Here published through the generosity of the owner, Mrs. W. Murray Crane

PORTRAIT

OF

SHELLEY

BY

NEWMAN IVEY WHITE

ALFRED A. KNOPF : *NEW YORK*

1968

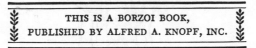

THIS IS A BORZOI BOOK,
PUBLISHED BY ALFRED A. KNOPF, INC.

COPYRIGHT 1945 *by* ALFRED A. KNOPF, INC. *All rights reserved. No part of this book may be reproduced in any form without permission in writing from the publisher, except by a reviewer who may quote brief passages in a review to be printed in a magazine or newspaper.* Manufactured in the United States of America. Published in Toronto, Canada, by Random House of Canada Limited.

PUBLISHED MARCH 19, 1945
SECOND PRINTING, DECEMBER 1959
THIRD PRINTING, MAY 1968

PR 5431
W 52
c. 2

Preface

THIS BOOK is a condensation of my *Shelley,* which appeared in two heavily documented volumes in 1940. So many possible readers have urged the need of a shorter and less expensive edition that my publishers and I have been convinced of a real demand for the present volume. Since the appearance of *Shelley* some of the errors which it corrects have been repeated in popular and semi-popular books, leading me to the conclusion that popular misapprehensions can only be corrected with reasonable promptness and finality (if at all) through a popular or semi-popular medium. An additional motive, frankly vainglorious, was a long-cherished, consuming desire to write a book without a footnote.

The present volume achieves its condensation by the omission of notes, appendices, and the final, summary chapter, and by the condensation throughout of style and of numerous incidents and episodes. No incident of general significance has been omitted, and no discussion has been omitted other than those specified above. Many passages have been entirely rewritten, but the language remains in general that of the original. Some slight minor errors, mainly typographical, have been silently corrected, and a few slight details, unknown to me in 1940, have been silently included. The whole depends for its authority on the fully documented work.

Thus, if any academic reader still pines for footnotes, he may consider my original *Shelley* as one prodigious footnote to this volume.

For reading and editorial assistance I wish to thank my colleagues C. Richard Sanders and Helen Bevington.

DURHAM, N. C.
September 30, 1943

N. I. W.

NOTE

The cover stamp, an emblem used by King Christian II of Denmark, embodies Shelley's symbol of conflict between the serpent of good and the eagle of evil. With King Christian, and possibly with Shelley, it had its origin in Pliny.

808266

PORTRAIT

OF

SHELLEY

Chapter I

IN THE YEAR 1792 the people of Sussex, as now, were averse to change and excitement. One of their folk-sayings was: "We won't be druv." Sussex yeomen had been among the last in England to embrace Christianity or to accept the Reformation; the ancient sport of bear-baiting, which vanished generally in England during the eighteenth century, continued in Sussex until 1814. Sussex took no very tense interest, therefore, in the tremendous disruption of the old order across the Channel in France. Let the frog-eaters have their revolution if they liked, and let the squire and his guests discuss it at dinner; it was of small concern to the Sussex farmer or sheep-raiser. All sorts of battered refugees from France were landing at the Sussex ports from smugglers' packets, open boats, or anything that would sail, and were making their way inland on horseback, in carts, and afoot. Most of them went toward London, sustained as they went by the conviction that the good old days would soon return – the oldest and falsest of human illusions.

Near the Surrey border on the London road, still thirty-five miles southwest of London, these fugitives passed by the town of Horsham, a quaint market town on the lazy little Arun River, with stone-flagged, tree-lined streets, and seven or eight hundred houses picturesquely roofed with stone slabs from neighboring quarries. On any Saturday they would have seen a bustling corn-market in progress there, or a poultry-market on Tuesday; or they might also have shared the roads with sheep and cattle being driven to the thriving cattle-market held the last Tuesday of each month. If any of these refugees paused for refreshment in the tap-room of Horsham's principal inn they probably noticed a handsome, slovenly-looking man of about sixty, usually sitting by himself and listening with pleasure to the hard, realistic talk of prices and property transfers.

This man was Squire Bysshe Shelley, the richest man and probably the most extraordinary man of the town. He traced his ancestry through six generations of undistinguished squires and country gentlemen, all of whom had married wives of good, well-to-do country families, back to Henry Shelley, Esquire, of Worminghurst, who died in 1623. They were very probably a younger branch of the Michelgrove Shelleys, a family of real distinction since the time of Edward I.

3

Bysshe Shelley possessed characteristics of boldness, ambition, and imagination suggestive more of the older than the younger branch of the Shelley family. His father, Timothy Shelley, was a younger son, who had emigrated to Newark, New Jersey. Here he had made a moderate living as a merchant until his older brother was declared insane and he inherited the family estate in England, except for a part which was devised to his younger son, Bysshe.

Young Bysshe was then a tall, straight youth, with regular features, large brown eyes, wavy brown hair, and a distinguished manner. He had not waited to inherit the family estate at Fen Place, but had set out at once to capitalize his own natural endowments. At the age of twenty he had increased his fortune by eloping with a sixteen-year-old orphan heiress. She had borne him two daughters and a son before her death, nine years after her marriage. At thirty-eight, Bysshe Shelley had married Miss Elizabeth Jane Sidney Perry, a descendant of Sir Philip Sidney's younger brother and of the Earls of Leicester, and also the mistress of a large fortune. She had died in 1781, leaving him seven children, the eldest of whom was to become a baronet in 1818.

Since the death of his second wife Bysshe Shelley had been devoting himself entirely to increasing his wealth, which was already considerable even before the Fen Place and Field Place estates of the Shelley family came to him by inheritance. Field Place he had turned over to his oldest son, Timothy. He himself lived somewhat meanly at Horsham while awaiting the completion of Castle Goring, a magnificent country seat that was being built as the future home of the family he was so determined to aggrandize. He was in alliance with the Duke of Norfolk, leader of a liberal wing of the Whig Party, who controlled the parliamentary elections of the district, and he was hoping for a baronetcy to go with his Castle Goring estate.

His son Timothy, to be sure, was not the ideal foundation for the dreams of family grandeur cherished by Mr. Bysshe Shelley. After a respectable, undistinguished career at Oxford he had married Elizabeth Pilfold, of Effingham, Sussex, a beautiful and sensible woman of slightly better family than his own. Timothy was a good farmer, a conscientious, sympathetic landlord, and rather liberal in politics and religion – to about the same extent as the Duke of Norfolk, whose influence had sent him to Parliament in 1790. But he lacked completely the enterprise and imagination of his father, and old Squire Bysshe was at times openly and profanely scornful of his humdrum virtues.

4

In August 1792, at the age of forty, Mr. Timothy Shelley was expecting the birth of his first-born. A male heir, gifted with some of
his grandfather's imagination and hard-headed enterprise, could con-
solidate and carry forward the family fortunes. It was a boy, born
in a small upstairs bedroom on August 4, 1792, and named Percy
Bysshe.

On the very day the boy was born the French National Assembly
was confiscating all church property, the grenadier guards of France
were protesting against the indignity of guarding the King, and the
allied monarchs across the Rhine were threatening dire vengeance
on Paris. The refugees drifting like dead leaves down the Sussex
highways were dreaming their futile dream of a quick return to the
old order. They could scarcely have dreamed, however, that the boy
then being born at Field Place would keep alive for generations the
echo of that great cataclysm which they regarded so confidently as
a passing shock.

Young Bysshe, as he was called, learned in early boyhood that he
could rely on old Bysshe, his grandfather, for support in his boyish
enterprises. Old Bysshe, growing richer and more secluded and
miserly, and some said just a trifle daft as young Bysshe passed
through his early boyhood, saw the youngster developing some of
the very qualities he had hoped for. Sitting in his inn tap-room, listening to the market talk he loved, he dreamed his dream of family
grandeur founded on the boy. He entailed his estate so that young
Bysshe would inherit it through his father and pass it on to his own
son. Young Bysshe would grow up, go to Oxford, enter Parliament
under the Norfolk interests, marry the right sort — of course with
money — and beget sons to establish the family on new heights.

Chapter II

As YOUNG Bysshe gradually passed from babyhood to boyhood and youth he was joined by five sisters and a brother: Elizabeth (born May 10, 1794), Hellen (born January 29, 1796, died four months later), Mary (born June 9, 1797), Hellen (born September 26, 1799), Margaret (born January 20, 1801), and John (born March 15, 1806). Naturally there were other small boys of his own age in the neighborhood, but there is no record of his early association with any of them. He was the natural protector and leader of his sisters from the first. With them his word was law; he was a dictator, but always a benevolent one.

At the age of six he was sent daily to be tutored by the Reverend Mr. Edwards, an elderly Welsh parson at Warnham. He was a good Latin student and showed at once that he had a remarkable memory. Not only did he recite long Latin passages to his father, but once, after hearing Gray's poem "On the Death of a Favourite Cat," he was able to repeat the whole poem from memory.

When he was ten years old the boy was sent to Syon House Academy, at Islesworth, near Brentford, then six or seven miles out of London. It was a fairly good school for the sons of middle-class parents and must have been chosen with an eye more to Squire Timothy Shelley's moderate means at the time than old Bysshe Shelley's ambition. The choice may have been influenced by the fact that an older cousin of Bysshe's, Tom Medwin of Horsham, was already a student there. Dr. Greenlaw, the master, had a touch of that irritable, brutal tyranny too common among schoolmasters of the day. He was liberal in his politics, however, as befitted the instructor of one intended to become a liberal member of Parliament; and he was a fair scholar and teacher who deserves the credit of having given young Bysshe a good start in his studies.

The subjects taught were reading, writing, arithmetic, Latin, French, geography, and astronomy. The students numbered about sixty, aged eight to sixteen, and were housed and taught in a substantial brick building, surrounded by high walls, with excellent gardens and an enclosed playground adjoining. Beyond were the dirty streets and mean houses of Brentford.

The sensitive and slightly built boy of ten had been poorly pre-

6

pared by his previous experience for the world he was now entering. He did not even know enough to laugh with counterfeited glee when Dr. Greenlaw occasionally offended his sensibilities with a coarse story at which the other small boys cackled manfully. His girlish looks and associations were fatal to any chance of happiness with his fellows. He had no interest in the usual boyish sports. He knew nothing whatever of either the technique or the ethics of giving or taking punishment. After a lapse of eighty years one of his school-mates clearly remembered that he was "like a girl in boy's clothes, fighting with open hands and rolling on the floor when flogged, not from the pain, but from a sense of the indignity."

Bysshe had been used to dominating his sisters at home. But at Syon House, where there was no fagging system to allot one a prin-cipal bully, all the older and stronger boys bullied all the younger ones. He had to chase hoops and balls for them until he was utterly exhausted. Occasionally Tom Medwin, playing with the older boys and noticing the wretched loneliness of Bysshe, would leave his play to walk and talk with him. The talk, he later remembered, was some-times far beyond the boy's years. Occasionally Medwin and Bysshe played truant and went in a boat to Richmond to see a play.

The boy found class-work so easy that it was sometimes rather a bore. Tom Medwin observed that he often sat idly at his desk gaz-ing out of the window or sketching pine trees on his papers, ances-tors of that trim procession of pines or firs that marches across the borders of Shelley's later manuscripts. Nevertheless, he was remem-bered by Sir John Rennie as a good scholar, proficient in writing both English and Latin verse. But the boy positively hated his dancing lessons and did his best to avoid them, with the result that his master soon pronounced him impossibly awkward.

The very qualities that made Bysshe miserable at Syon House also provided recompenses. Adam Walker, a self-taught natural philos-opher and inventor of scientific toys who occasionally lectured near by at Eton, was engaged by Dr. Greenlaw to lecture to the Syon House boys on some of the wonders of science. His scientific ap-paratus, his experience as a teacher of boys, and his wide scope of interest made him the ideal herald of a new wonderland. Young Bysshe heard and was entranced. It is very probable that Adam Walker was the starting-point for the electrical experiments, burn-ing-glasses, microscopes, Leyden jars, and chemical mixtures that Shelley toyed with for about ten years thereafter.

These lectures opened for the boy a new universe of speculations, especially in astronomy and chemistry. Walker demonstrated the wonders of telescope and microscope, and performed some simple scientific experiments. Either at Syon House or Eton (where he heard Walker again) Bysshe probably paid his eighteen pence for a pamphlet of eighty-six pages entitled *"Analysis of a Course of Lectures on Natural and Experimental Philosophy, viz. Magnetism, Mechanics, Chemistry, Pneumatics, Fortification, Optics, Use of the Globes, etc., Astronomy,* by A. Walker, Lecturer to his Royal Highness the Duke of Gloucester, to Eton and Westminster Colleges, and Member of the Dublin Society." There was also an eight-page syllabus listing the lectures, each of which was of two hours' duration. They covered every branch of science in which Shelley later showed any interest. There were two lectures on pneumatics, or "principles of the air," two on electricity, three on astronomy, and one on chemistry. Immediately after these lectures were delivered we begin to hear of chemical and electrical experiments at Field Place and Syon House and of excited speculations inspired by the possibilities of telescope and microscope.

The imaginative boy quickly adopted Adam Walker's convictions that the numerous worlds of stellar space were inhabited. Excitedly he urged upon Medwin the possibility that some of the celestial inhabitants were a higher race than ours and that in future existences mere mortals might be destined to pass through a series of stages on various planets that would ultimately make them more gods than men.

Bysshe had not been long at the school before he began reading books from the circulating library maintained at Brentford by Mr. P. Norbury. Most of the books so obtained were trashy thrillers of a very extravagant type, generally known as "blue books." Medwin describes them as "stories of haunted castles, bandits, murderers, and other grim personages." This is amply supported by the titles of several such books published during the two years Shelley was at Syon House; for example, *Don Algonah, or the Sorceress of Montillo; The Black Forest, or The Cavern of Horrors; The Subterraneous Passage, or Gothic Cell; The Cavern of Horrors, or Miseries of Miranda, a Neapolitan Tale.* Such books as these were greedily devoured by the Brentford schoolboys. On returning from holidays they brought in fresh titles, which circulated till worn out or discarded. Bysshe read scores of novels of this type. Several books of a more lasting quality known to have been read by him at this same

8

time are the novels of Mrs. Ann Radcliffe and "Monk" Lewis, and Robert Paltock's *Life and Adventures of Peter Wilkins*.

Syon House, obviously, was not a harmonious world for a slender, girlish-looking boy with a lively mind, an extraordinary memory and imagination, and no experience in the robust sports and petty brutal tyranny known to other boys of his age. From the brutal world of sordid reality he took refuge more and more in the glowing world of scientific imagination and the thrilling world of impossible adventure that had been made available by Adam Walker's lectures and the numerous novels he read. By a natural instinct he sought unconsciously to bring these two worlds into harmonious unity. One of his schoolmates (later famous as Sir John Rennie, who completed London Bridge) recalled that he often talked of "spirits, fairies, fighting, volcanoes, etc.," and that "not unfre quently" he blew up with gunpowder the boundary palings of the playground and even the lid of his desk. A legend was long current in Dr. Greenlaw's family that he poisoned the doctor's pigs as the result of an unfortunate experiment. On an Easter vacation visit to his Grove cousins, shortly before leaving Syon House, he persuaded them to turn woodsmen with him and cut down their father's young fir trees.

Yet somehow the physical world with which he was unreconciled would not blend itself harmoniously into the imaginative world he preferred. Many of the boys, as Sir John Rennie recalled, considered him "almost on the borders of insanity."

If Syon House furnished the young schoolboy with an inharmonious introduction to social life, Field Place in vacation was fortunately a partial corrective. Here, at least, he could establish a harmony of his own. As a leader and entertainer of his younger sisters Bysshe fancied himself tremendously. He told them tales of the legendary Great Tortoise that haunted Warnham Pond, where the family sometimes went for a picnic dinner; and of the Old Snake that had led a peaceful existence for many years in the Field Place grounds until accidentally slain by a gardener. He tapped the ceiling with a stick to discover to them a secret passage which must certainly be beyond; he drew graphic pictures of an old gray alchemist who dwelt in a garret that was closed against their explorations. Fantastic costumes were devised in which to personate spirits or fiends while Bysshe, as the arch-fiend, rushed through a passage with a flaming liquid in a portable stove.

According to neighborhood tradition he once set fire to a faggot-stack so that he might have "a little hell of his own." There were also chemical and electrical cures for chilblains. Like Franklin, he flew kites to catch electricity. The day he left home to enter Eton, the wash-room reeked with smoke from some experiment gone awry.

All this was not much more than a boyish effort to turn the vivid imaginative world into which he withdrew himself at Syon House into actual experience in the more friendly environment of Field Place. The device for conveying electric shocks and the flying of kites for electricity had both been described in detail in Adam Walker's lectures. No longer a slave in a world of tyrants, but a benevolent despot among adoring subjects, he could make the occasional innovations from the wilder world of his reading that his sister Hellen's recollections show he did make. Mystification, sudden surprise, and extreme benevolence and diabolism characterize both his reading and the exploits related of him at Field Place.

Tom Medwin remembered particularly Bysshe's delight in Robert Paltock's *Peter Wilkins*. Peter shaped first to his benevolent wishes a family and then a kingdom; two of his winged children were adopted by royalty. Straightway Bysshe "wished for a winged wife and little winged cherubs for children," contemplated adopting a vagrant child who occasionally came to the back door as a tumbler, and later scoured the near neighborhood on his pony seeking whom he could adopt.

When Bysshe returned to Syon House after such vacations, the impact of the discordant world into which he was again projected was sometimes frightful. Lacking a natural outlet or sympathetic audience for his highly excited imagination, driven in upon himself, he walked in his sleep and experienced severe nervous shocks when awakened. He was given to waking dreams in which he appeared unconscious of his surroundings. Afterwards "his eyes flashed, his lips quivered . . . his voice was tremulous with emotion, and he talked more like a spirit or an angel than a human being." John Rennie was particularly impressed with his violent and extremely excitable temper. "The least circumstance that thwarted him produced the most violent paroxysms of rage; and when irritated by other boys, which they, knowing his infirmity, frequently did by way of teasing him, he would take up anything, or even any little boy near him, to throw at his tormentors." Similar testimony was to come later from Eton. "Yet with all this," Sir John added, "when treated

10

with kindness, he was very amiable, noble, high-spirited and generous."

Nothing like this happened at Field Place; his willing subjects there remembered him later as unvaryingly sweet-tempered and kind. Nor was he always overwrought even at Syon House. Tom Medwin's older-boy friendliness offered some slight protection, though doubtless a somewhat puzzled and embarrassed one. There was also a nameless friend of his own age whom Bysshe either knew in the flesh or conjured into reality by the strong power of imagination to meet his desperate need for sympathy. In a later unfinished essay Shelley speaks of him as "generous, brave, and gentle" with "a delicacy and a simplicity in his manners, inexpressibly attractive."

The clashing, frustrating discord of his two worlds of imagination and reality soon led this tenacious, highly sensitive child to a truly amazing decision. For him the true world was that of his imagination and ideals; he would fight the false brutal world of reality and champion its victims. One fresh May morning, which he clearly remembered for years afterwards, young Bysshe walked forth upon the glittering grass, listening to the voices from the near-by schoolroom as "The harsh and grating strife of tyrants and of foes." With a sense of intolerable outrage he took his resolution:

> I will be wise
> And just, and free, and mild, if in me lies
> Such power, for I grow weary to behold
> The selfish and the strong still tyrannise
> Without reproach or check. . . .

The resolution tranquillized him, and from that hour he began consciously to prepare himself for the warfare he had undertaken.

Such was Shelley's later account of a scene that he claimed to remember well even to the day and hour. He described it both in his "Hymn to Intellectual Beauty" and in the introductory poem to *The Revolt of Islam;* and he referred to it in a letter to Leigh Hunt. There can be no doubt, therefore, of its reality. It may possibly have occurred a year or two later at Eton, for Shelley mentions no particular school, but such description as there is suits Syon House rather than Eton. Very probably such scenes occurred more than once, gathering maturity with repetition, but the first one remained vividly in his mind as perhaps the most decisive moment of his life. Years later, as a mature man fully launched on his career, he claimed that

11

he had kept his vow, and the claim is fully supported by all the records of his life from the time he was at Syon House.

Amazing as it seems that a whole career should be visibly governed by a precocious resolution taken at the age of eleven or twelve, it is little more amazing than other demonstrable relationships between this same boy and the mature man he became. The strong stimulus first applied by Adam Walker persisted to the end of his days in a love of scientific reading, and for some years in a love of sensational scientific experiment. Eight years later, when he wrote *Queen Mab*, Shelley's voice almost merges with that of Adam Walker in his picture of the plurality of worlds and of the earth as "the smallest light that twinkles in the heavens," insignificant among a million variously colored constellations. Fifteen years later, in "The Cloud" he was to describe the unending cycle of air, water and electricity pretty much as Adam Walker had done, even remembering in the lines

> I pass through the pores of the ocean and shores,
> I change, but I cannot die,

old Walker's description of the air as "so subtil that it pervades the pores of all bodies."

The habit of trying to re-enact books, seemingly confusing the planes of imaginary action and real action, reappeared at several points in Shelley's later life. The interest in adopting children, stimulated apparently by Robert Paltock's *Peter Wilkins*, did not end in childhood, but reasserted itself several times in later years. Peter Wilkins was the first Prometheus Shelley knew, the giver of arts and laws to the winged race of glumms and glowries. He purified their religion, which had degenerated through the selfishness of the priests. He, too, found priests the chief obstacles to progress. He was particularly a foe of slavery and abolished it everywhere he went. "Monk" Lewis's Ambrosio and Mrs. Radcliffe's Schedoni were early patterns on which Shelley formed his notions of priests, some time before he became antagonistic to their religion. If we pause to recall that the tyrannical father or guardian was a stock character in the books from which the boy's ideas and conduct were taking such a perceptible color, is it so strange that the respectable Mr. Timothy Shelley soon fitted into the pattern, or that he later felt that his son had been ruined by books?

With the prophetic power of aftersight, it is not difficult to see in

12

the boy Shelley amazing possibilities that could scarcely have been perceptible to the most sympathetic of contemporaries. Such a one, seeing him enter Eton College at the age of nearly twelve, would have said he lacked the appearance and much of the spirit of normal boyishness, that he was a good student through natural quickness of mind rather than industry and self-discipline, that his memory, his imagination, and his intellectual energy were most extraordinary; that he lived too much in his imagination to find easy common ground with his fellows; and that he was unusually sensitive, sweet-tempered, and generous, but capable of distressingly intemperate, helpless rage. Certainly he was a queer son for Timothy Shelley, and very possibly an insecure basis for old Bysshe Shelley's dreams of family grandeur.

Chapter III

ON JULY 29, 1804 Percy Bysshe Shelley, not yet quite twelve years of age, signed his name in the entrance book of the headmaster of Eton College. It was in some respects a new world he was entering. The venerable fifteenth-century brick structures just across the Thames from Windsor Castle represented a vast improvement in atmosphere and tradition over the respectable but gloomy-looking building on the edge of dirty, brawling Brentford. A similar change shortly took place in the worldly prospects of the young scholar. For whereas at the academy he had been merely the son of a local squire who would eventually inherit a considerable fortune, he was from the year 1806 heir to a baronetcy, his grandfather having been made a baronet in that year.

Dr. Goodall, Eton's headmaster in 1804, had already somewhat improved the general quality of the school over its low level of the eighteenth century; and during Shelley's residence the famous Dr. John Keate was to begin his rather misunderstood improvement of the discipline. " 'Blessed are the pure in heart,' " he quoted — "If you are not pure in heart I'll flog you"; or "Read your Bible, boy, or I'll flog you." The sober historical truth seems to be that there were many boys at Eton who were never flogged at all and that the victims were mostly habitual offenders. Keate was in fact one of the ablest of Eton headmasters, described by those who knew him best as generally kind-hearted and just. Though Bysshe was in his classes and was otherwise liable to unfavorable notice from him, there is no record of his having been flogged by the formidable, bushy-browed headmaster.

The rules under which the boys lived were enforced by the various masters and several monitors, or præposters, from the upper forms. The conduct of the boys toward each other was a matter of tradition and brute force. Under the fagging system upper-form boys could have from one to three "fags," who performed for them such personal services as preparing breakfast, brushing clothes, stopping balls at cricket, and running errands. As in all boys' schools, bullying and fighting were not unusual. On one occasion two boys fought for three hours, until stopped by the redoubtable Keate himself. One small boy was killed by fighting to exhaustion and then

14

swallowing the brandy with which his second had told him to rinse his mouth. Students who were sensitive or peculiar might expect to be treated intolerantly.

The life of the average Etonian in the early nineteenth century was very largely play. According to a critic in the *Edinburgh Review*, a boy about half-way through the school had about eleven hours a week of "school-time" without allowing for extra holidays. Except for preparation, which was rather a light matter, the rest of the time was largely for play. A list of games in vogue at Eton in 1766 includes cricket, fives, hoops, marbles, several top games, several ball games, several hunting games, football, leaping pole, and kites. Swimming and boating were quite popular in Shelley's day. Some of the more daring broke rules by driving, riding, hunting, coursing with beagles, attending races or fairs, or even poaching in the royal forest of Windsor. Boyish pranks, such as one or two related of Shelley, were not uncommon.

Studies were limited in scope and poorly directed. Greek and Latin and a smattering of divinity and geography were the only subjects taught regularly, though French, drawing, dancing, and fencing could be had outside of regular school hours, as extras. There was no modern history, no mathematical or physical science, almost no Greek drama, no Herodotus, Thucydides, Xenophon, Livy, Polybius, or Tacitus. The authors and books studied were mainly Homer, Virgil, Horace, Ovid, the Greek Testament, Cornelius Nepos, Cæsar, Terence, Æsop, Lucian, and the various scraps contained in *Scriptores Græci et Romani*. Lessons in construing included from sixteen to sixty lines at a time; Shelley must have got through some 75,000 lines of Greek and Latin prose and poetry during six years at Eton. Considerable memory work from the ancient classics was exacted, and considerable composition of Latin verses. Theoretically a boy might write as many as 10,000 lines of Latin verse during his whole career at Eton; but there existed a common treasury of such verses which, together with aid from other students, made the actual burden generally a rather light one. The proportion of masters to boys — about one to fifty or sixty in Shelley's day — made instruction largely mechanical and superficial, though this was less true for the boys who had private tutors.

Such was the situation into which Field Place's young Master of the Revels and Dr. Greenlaw's sensitive young schoolboy was introduced on July 29, 1804. It was a scheme that he was ill fitted for and had already learned to resent, and it was the longest and probably the strongest single environmental influence of his life. Yet it was not radically different from what he would have encountered at any of the other public schools, and it was practically the best school environment available.

Shelley entered Eton in the upper fourth form; next year he was in the next form, known as the remove. In 1808 he was in the upper fifth, and in 1810 he was in the sixth. Living in succession with two masters, one a domine and the other a tutor, he received better food and lodging and was thrown into less crowded contact with his fellow lodgers than the majority of oppidans, who lodged at the houses kept by dames. Hexter, with whom he first lodged, taught writing in the lower forms and was also a major in the militia; George Bethell, his tutor and second house master, was a genial, kindhearted gentleman, notoriously dull and inept as a teacher of the classics.

At Eton Bysshe's habits and associations were not very different from what they had been at Syon House Academy. He set fire to old trees with burning-glasses and was a foe to authority. Most of the boys thought him mad. He became known as "Mad Shelley," also as "Shelley the atheist," although "atheist" in this sense may have meant merely an opposer of the local powers rather than one who denies the existence of a God. His dress was careless — he was conspicuous for wearing his shoes without strings and dispensing with his hat entirely — and his lack of skill and interest in most of the popular games was obvious. Such facts as these, the basis on which all but a few of his schoolmates judged and remembered him, gave him no recommendation either to their favor or that of the masters, and he was rather generally unpopular with both.

His inability to fight was early recognized and long remembered by his schoolmates. It must have made him a convenient stepping-stone for younger boys desirous of rising by their fists. Thomas Style, a smaller and younger boy, thus achieved a place in Eton tradition by weathering two unfavorable opening rounds and putting the overconfident Bysshe to ignoble flight in the end. George Lyne, apparently a younger boy, also thirsted to build a reputation for prowess on Shelley's lack of it. His only record runs: "Son of a tailor in the Strand. He fought Shelley at school and was soundly beaten."

The nagging and teasing that had contributed to Bysshe's misery at the academy continued, but on a larger scale. The helpless, frustrated rage to which he had sometimes given utterance at Syon

House seemed to many of his schoolmates a show well worth promoting. "I have seen him surrounded," wrote one of them, "hooted,
baited like a maddened bull, and at this distance of time I seem to
hear ringing within my ears the cry which Shelley was wont to
utter in his paroxysm of revengeful anger." Sometimes he would find
himself surrounded and "nailed" with a muddy ball; at other times
his tormentors would beset him and yell his name, point, push his
books from under his arm, or pluck at his garments — anything to
produce the rage which "made his eyes flash like a tiger's, his cheeks
grow pale as death, his limbs quiver." Occasionally he could succeed in practically ignoring his tormentors. Once, however, he was
so maddened that he seized a fork and stabbed another boy in the
hand with it. These "Shelley-baits" were of almost daily occurrence
during Shelley's early years at Eton.

From all this the victim escaped in vacations to the warm, friendly
society of Field Place, where his two worlds of imagination and of
fact could be harmoniously blended. One of Bysshe's principal pleasures among his sisters was disguise, a pleasure he had many times
enjoyed vicariously in his reading. Sometimes he pretended to be a
fiend. Once he dressed himself as a countryman and paraded past
the nursery windows carrying a truss of hay to a lady in the village
so that she might make hay tea to relieve her chilblains. In the
guise of a country boy with a broad Sussex dialect he succeeded in
engaging himself to a Horsham lawyer as gamekeeper's boy. Riding
with a gentleman toward Horsham and concealing his own identity,
he brought the conversation round to Squire Shelley's son, at Field
Place, only to learn that there were some who considered him a
trifle insane. Some of his boyish adventures took place solely in his
own imagination, and were remembered later by his sister Hellen
as definitely "eccentric," the products of a mind "almost alone in its
peculiar nature."

The tricks and wild experiments that had already impressed those
who knew Shelley at Field Place and Syon House Academy continued at Eton. Some were tricks of a purely mischievous nature
such as are always recollected by former schoolmates, though not
always accurately. He was falsely given credit for putting a bulldog
in Dr. Keate's desk, and was also said to have suspended a stolen
inn-sign over the headmaster's door, where the doughty doctor col-
lided with it on rushing forth next morning.

Shelley's scientific exploits at Eton, which must have seemed to some to be mere willful pranks, are better authenticated and were much more numerous. He sent up fire-balloons, as other Eton boys were doing also. One Etonian remembered Shelley's interest in explosives as extending to the purchase at auction of a brass cannon, which was captured by the tutors before it went into action. He experimented with chemical brews and nearly blew himself up; and once he poisoned himself. In confederation with Edward Leslie, he electrified a tomcat. Striking higher, he even electrified "Butch" Bethell when that blundering tutor and landlord too hastily investigated a galvanic battery. At Field Place during vacations he was also demonstrating certain effects of powders and acids to his young sisters. He bought small electrical machines that were vended among the students by Adam Walker's assistant, and with the aid of a traveling tinker he constructed a steam engine that duly exploded.

Up to this point Shelley's scientific interests simply continued the enthusiasm for the mysteries and possibilities of natural science first aroused by Adam Walker. Two or three times, at least, the stimulus was renewed, for every other year Walker gave his lectures and demonstrations at Eton.

But young Shelley would not be confined within the very generous bounds of Walker's interests. Ranging from the physical to the metaphysical, he absorbed the scientific reveries of Albertus Magnus and Paracelsus with eager enthusiasm for new sensation. He sought out the lore of magic and witchcraft, and learned incantations for raising ghosts and devils. At Field Place he planned to gain entrance to the charnel house at Warnham Church and watch beside the bones of the dead. Once at Eton he stole forth at midnight fearfully intent on raising a ghost; he repeated his incantation, drinking three times from a skull, and when no ghost appeared he concluded that the fault lay in his magic formula. Well might Tom Medwin remember that Shelley's mind at this time "ran on bandits, castles, ruined towers, wild mountains, storms and apparitions — the terrific." Shelley himself recalls something quite similar in his "Hymn to Intellectual Beauty."

Abnormal as some of these activities seem, and intense as they surely were, they were not quite so abnormal as they appear in the recollections of his schoolfellows. Fireworks were a common passion at Eton, and attempts to raise the dead were not particularly remarkable in a generation of schoolboys who fed on horror-stories. Bysshe did not lose or flee from every fight, nor did he fail to enjoy boating and other boyish sports. Boating was one of his principal pleasures at Eton, nor was he averse to duck-spearing. Probably at Eton and certainly at Field Place in vacation he was often abroad with a gun. When he left Eton and went up to Oxford he was tanned and freckled from outdoor exercise.

One of Eton's most picturesque institutions was the "Montem" celebrations, during which the boys dressed themselves in fanciful costumes and marched in semi-military style to Salt Hill. In 1805 as a midshipman and in 1808 as a corporal, Bysshe took part in the only two processions that occurred during his six years at Eton. His only other public appearance was on Election Day, shortly before he entered Oxford, when he delivered an oration of Cicero against Catiline.

Young Shelley was certainly not as friendless at Eton as he had been at Syon House, but he was too unusual a lad either to seek many friends or to be sought by many. Among his first friends were Andrew Amos, one of the two other lower-form boys at Hexter's house, and Charles William Packe, who sat near him in Bethell's class and liked him for "a good, generous, open-hearted fellow." With Andrew Amos, Shelley used to enjoy composing and acting plays for the other lower-form boys at Hexter's. Later his list of friends widened to include Price (described as an excellent classicist), Rees Howell Gronow (later, as Captain Gronow, author of *Reminiscences and Recollections*), Edward (or Edmund) Leslie, to whom Shelley inscribed himself an "affectionate friend" in several gift-books, and Walter Halliday (later a country clergyman). One fellow student with whom he was intimate in 1808 and 1809 was Timothy Tisdall, a ward of Lord Charleville. His letters to Tisdall show Bysshe engaged in writing novels, poems, and letters, and also quite normally observant of "the Beaus and Belles of the Horsham Ball."

Shelley carried with him to Oxford a number of books given him by Eton schoolmates, and some of his former friends continued to call on him there. By the few who really knew him he was regarded with affection and respect. After fifty years Walter Halliday wrote glowingly of his "kindliness and affectionate ways . . . his marvellous stories of fairyland, and apparitions, and spirits, and haunted ground . . . his speculations . . . of the world beyond the grave," his excellence as a student, and his love of long country walks with a congenial companion.

The Shelley of Walter Halliday's remembrance is very similar to the older brother that Hellen Shelley recalled as she remembered his later vacations at Field Place. He enjoyed taking his sisters for walks through the country lanes or across the open fields. Sometimes he walked forth alone, at night, somewhat to his mother's uneasiness. But the servant who followed him reported merely that Master Bysshe had taken a walk and come back again.

Like any other son of a country squire, he knew the use of firearms. He also rode frequently about the country lanes on his pony. His mother, whether because she had grown up among horse-lovers herself or because she was disquieted by his hectic imaginative energy, did what she could to encourage this side of his development. She sent him abroad with the gamekeeper or went fishing with him herself. There can be little doubt that Squire Shelley, who was a good husbandman and a conscientious father, had occasional walks and talks with Bysshe in which he saw to it that his son and heir knew something of Field Place, its crops, its livestock, and its tenants.

The author in Shelley began stirring at an early age, probably before he entered Eton, but his first recorded poem belongs apparently to his later vacations at Field Place — five six-line stanzas on a cat. With his oldest sister, Elizabeth, he wrote a play which they seriously submitted to a producer and which was returned with equal seriousness. Certain verses of his own were printed at Horsham, and old Sir Bysshe is said to have paid the bills. For the delight of his sisters he wrote verses ridiculing their French teacher, which were so excitedly circulated that they eventually fell into the hands of the enemy. None of these early efforts survive except the stanzas on a cat, which conclude with a spirited reflection:

> But this poor little cat
> Only wanted a rat,
> To stuff out its own little maw;
> And 'twere as good
> Had some people such food,
> To make them hold their jaw.

During these vacations reading continued, father and son often reading together. Relations between the two were affectionate and unstrained. When Mr. Timothy Shelley was ill during Bysshe's second year at Eton, the son was distressed and sympathetic. There is no record of the boy's own illness during the six years he was at Eton except once when he was sent home to recover, and again during a vacation.

In the less congenial atmosphere of Eton what the youth most needed, and never had, was the sympathetic comprehension of a wise master. An intense craving for complete sympathy is deeply characteristic both of his feeling and behavior in childhood and youth and of his mature thought. It was instinctive long before it became conscious, and it drove him to seek its fulfillment. What Eton could not offer he found in Windsor, just across the Thames.

Here lived Dr. James Lind, physician to the royal household in Windsor Castle. He was an eccentric old man of over seventy, white-haired, tall, and thin, yet lively and energetic, full of odd bits of wisdom and experience from his early life on an East Indiaman. He was given to all sorts of curiosities and speculations and welcomed the same interests in others. Young Shelley often crossed over to Windsor to browse among his books, witness his little tricks of Eastern conjury, and hear exciting talk about the possibilities and bounds of knowledge and experience. To the eager, sympathy-starved youth he was "exactly what an old man ought to be — free, calm-spirited, full of benevolence and even of youthful ardour." There were long talks about everything under the sun, and the youth listened with shining eyes to "the spirit of kindest tolerance and purest wisdom."

Once, as Shelley told later, the youth was ill and delirious at Field Place and a servant told him that there was talk of sending him to a private madhouse. A desperate secret message brought Dr. Lind to his bedside, and the project was prevented by his fearless and peremptory opposition. Shelley's proneness throughout his whole life to confuse the reality of strong feeling with actual reality makes it possible that this story may have been only a permanent deposit from his delirium, but the fact that several years later his father actually called him mad makes it possibly true, and its psychological truth is indubitable and more significant than its actual truth. It shows that the boy's inner nature was imperatively demanding far more sympathetic comprehension than it was receiving and that the early affectionate bonds between father and son were weakening through lack of mutual sympathy. After Shelley left Eton Dr. Lind passed entirely out of his life, but not out of mind. Years later he talked of Dr. Lind with enthusiasm, and created upon his model two wise, stately old men in his poetry, the old philosopher who restored Laon to health in *Laon and Cythna,* and Zonoras, the high-minded preceptor of the Prince in *Prince Athanase.*

One of Shelley's most intimate friends during his last years at Eton was Edward Fergus Graham, whom he saw, not at Eton, but at Field

Place and in London. Young Graham was a protégé of Shelley's father, who was paying the expenses of his musical education in London. He was about five years Shelley's senior. Graham's London lodgings were usually Bysshe's town headquarters. He was Bysshe's agent and confidant in matters of all sorts, from receiving and holding correspondence and acting as London shopping agent, to seeing that the press took proper notice of his first publications.

Through Graham, Shelley met in London a young man who became for a while one of his intimate friends. Joseph Gibbons Merle was in 1809 a pupil of Graham's music master, the rather well-known Joseph Woelff. When Graham was shown one of Merle's poems, he remarked that his young friend Bysshe Shelley was also a poet, and undertook to make the two acquainted. Merle, a self-conscious youth, had expected his new acquaintance to be stiff or patronizing, but found him affable and enthusiastic. A rather close friendship developed between the two. Shelley visited Merle several times in London, and the two exchanged letters frequently. Within a few months Merle was visiting Shelley at Field Place and making the acquaintance of Sir Bysshe. Young Merle admired Shelley greatly for his intelligence, generosity, and sympathy, but he was disturbed by his antagonism to Christianity and felt obliged to remonstrate against his efforts to "convert" him.

This antagonism to Christianity was a new development toward the end of Bysshe's Eton days. It may have had its dim origin in the oppressive Catholic Church and wicked priests encountered in so many of the Gothic novels he had been reading for at least eight years. Tom Medwin, who, though no longer a schoolfellow, still saw Shelley frequently, traces the definite emergence of this idea to the influence of Pliny's chapter *"De Deo."* Shelley was so enthusiastic about Pliny's *Natural History,* containing this chapter, that he set about translating the whole. At the same time Lucretius, whom he admired as the greatest Latin poet, told him that there was no god other than blind chance, and that religion was an invention of selfish priests preying on human credulity.

Shelley read constantly and voraciously, finding still in books what was so largely denied in life. His pocket money went largely for books and scientific toys, and he began to complain that his father was stingy in not allowing him enough. An active mind devoted to reading can absorb a great many volumes in six years. Less than a dozen book titles and about half a dozen additional authors can be cited as belonging to his reading at this time, but the influence of hundreds of unknown books may be imagined from that of those known.

Between Pliny and Lucretius and a growing antagonism to Christianity the connection is plain. Charlotte Dacre's *Zofloya, or the Moor,* the only definitely known title among the scores of sensational novels he read, had a considerable effect on *Zastrozzi,* which Shelley wrote at Eton. Some modern books of chemistry which he had borrowed from the Medwin family library had to be returned because chemistry was "a forbidden thing" at Eton, but he read ancient books of chemistry and magic with credulous wonder and enthusiasm, among them the works of Albertus Magnus and Paracelsus. The works of Benjamin Franklin and Condorcet lent modern support to his belief in the wonderful powers of the human mind over matter. He quoted them to Medwin; they are credible sources for the glowing conversations his schoolmates remembered.

While Bysshe waxed enthusiastic over Franklin, Condorcet was silently preparing the ground for the imminent and much greater influence of Godwin's *Political Justice.* As yet Shelley knew Godwin only through the novel *St. Leon,* which mingled with other sensational fiction and miraculous science to help set the tone of his own *St. Irvyne.* Among poets, he was reading and imitating Scott with a qualified enthusiasm, reading and rejecting Wordsworth as too simple and unexciting, and reading Southey's *Thalaba* and *The Curse of Kehama* with intense admiration. He knew both poems almost by heart, went about declaiming them among his intimates, and showed plainly in *Queen Mab,* several years later, that they were still his ideal of great poetry.

Inevitably this keen intellectual excitement demanded expression, as it had done even in early boyhood. From the age at which his younger sister Hellen first remembered him, Bysshe had enjoyed telling fanciful stories. He had continued to compose poems and plays for his schoolmates even when some of them made boisterous fun of his efforts. As he neared the end of his career at Eton, Bysshe became almost feverishly eager to write and publish.

Before reaching this point, however, he was already in love with his cousin, Harriet Grove. Harriet's mother was a Pilfold, a sister of Shelley's mother. The Grove family had an estate called Ferne House in Wiltshire, also a Welsh estate at Cwm Elan in Radnorshire. For years the children of the two families had exchanged frequent visits.

23

As early as February 28, 1805 young Bysshe had written a poem containing an affectionate reference to Harriet. By about 1808 he and Harriet began to realize that they were in love with each other. It was understood in the two families that eventually they were to marry.

Harriet was then a strikingly beautiful girl of seventeen, one year older than Bysshe. The journal which she kept in 1809–10 reveals her as naturally good-tempered and somewhat naïve, fond of her family, her "Aunt Shelley," and her cousins. She was a moderate reader, and a fairly regular member of the Church of England — not unusually intellectual or sensitive, but well balanced both mentally and emotionally. She calls Shelley "Dear Bysshe," several times "Dearest Bysshe," but the same expressions are applied to her brothers, her Aunt Shelley, Elizabeth, and Field Place. During the first nine months of 1809 she recorded the receipt of forty-four letters from Bysshe and the writing of twenty letters to him. He was almost her only correspondent, except for his mother and his sister Elizabeth.

When Harriet went up to London in the spring of 1809 to visit her brother, Bysshe arrived four days later with his father. For four days Bysshe squired her about town, to the theater, to an exhibition of worsteds, to the Panorama of Grand Cairo, and to Clapham to see Shelley's younger sisters at school there. Harriet thought them "the Nicest Girls I ever saw." One of them preserved a glowing memory of the same visit. "How fresh and pretty she was," wrote Hellen Shelley many years later. "Her assistance was invoked to keep the wild boy quiet, for he was full of pranks, and upset the port wine on the tray cloth . . . then we all walked in the garden, and there was much ado to calm the spirits of the wild boy."

In September 1809, however, the correspondence between Bysshe and Harriet practically ceased. For fifteen months Harriet recorded only one letter from Shelley and two letters to him. Possibly Shelley was too busy writing books to write letters, or possibly there had been a change of mind in the family. Yet Harriet's less frequent references to Bysshe continued as affectionate as ever.

About this time Tom Medwin, taking long walks with Bysshe on his visits home, noticed a growing literary fever and became captive to it as listener and co-author. Before he had left Eton, Shelley was author or co-author — in the space of little more than a year — of four separate volumes, besides a wild, extravagant romance called

The Nightmare, begun with Medwin and left unfinished and unpublished. One of these works was published while he was still at Eton, one during the vacation between Eton and Oxford, and one after Shelley's death.

Either *The Nightmare* or *Zastrozzi* must have been the partly finished romance that the young author somewhat grandly offered Longman and Company on May 7, 1809. *Zastrozzi* was published anonymously in March 1810. Edward Graham, who was becoming a sort of literary agent for the budding author, received a letter early in March suggesting the necessity of impressing both publishers and critics in advance. The former were to be visited in a barouche and four "to shew them that we are no Grub Street garretteers," and the latter, as venal fellows, especially the *British Review,* were to be "pouched," i.e., bribed.

As a rather poor example of one of the poorest types of fiction ever evolved, *Zastrozzi* could have profited from a little puffing in exchange for "pouching." Zastrozzi is a fiery, terrible person revenging his mother's wrongs; Verezzi, his foil, is a mysterious, benevolent object of revenge; and there are two heroines, one beautiful and passionate, the other ethereally virtuous — all interacting on each other in a manner indicative of a very excited and nervous puppet-master. Pouching or no pouching, the *British Review* remained silent, but two other respectable journals took notice. The *Gentleman's Magazine* seriously characterized it as "a short, but well-told tale of horror . . . not from an ordinary pen." The *Critical Review* pounced upon it with almost ridiculous earnestness. Zastrozzi was "one of the most savage and improbable demons that ever issued from a diseased brain," and the book's "gross and wanton pages" were full of "open, barefaced immorality." But the undaunted author gave a celebration dinner to eight of his fellow Etonians, a "most magnificent banquet," as one of them recalled, paid for out of the proceeds of the book, understood to be forty pounds.

Within a few months appeared another volume that had been taking shape *pari passu* with *Zastrozzi. Original Poetry by Victor and Cazire* was a collection of poems, also mainly in the tradition of Gothic horror. Victor was Shelley, Cazire his oldest sister Elizabeth, a bright, lively girl who had become Shelley's confidante and helper in most of his schemes.

A printing firm at Worthing, near Horsham, had by September 6, 1810, printed a large number of copies, which it only remained for the enterprising author to dispose of in order to pay his printing bill.

25

John Joseph Stockdale, a London publisher who dealt in remainders, consented to publish them, received the surprising number of 1,480 copies on September 17, and immediately advertised the work in the *Morning Chronicle,* the *Morning Post,* and the *Times.*

Stockdale soon discovered (what all four reviewers of the volume overlooked) that one of the poems, entitled "Saint Edmond's Eve," was really "The Black Canon of Elmham, or Saint Edmund's Eve," from "Monk" Lewis's *Tales of Terror,* a well-used copy of which reposed in the Field Place library. When he communicated this embarrassing discovery to Shelley, the young poet seemed much surprised and expressed great indignation at having been victimized by his collaborator. He entreated Stockdale to destroy all remaining copies. Perhaps Stockdale did, since only three copies are extant today — and perhaps he did not, since he was exposed later as a somewhat unscrupulous publisher, and since he had his money in them.

At all events, the book was reviewed by four periodicals, the *Literary Panorama* for October 1810, the *British Critic* and the *Antijacobin Review* for April 1811, and the *Poetical Register* for 1810–11. Three of the reviews were rather rudely uncomplimentary; but the *British Critic,* sensing the youthfulness of the young poets, exposed the flimsiness of their volume with a patronizing, avuncular humor that is both amused and amusing. "Could anything possibly be finer — that is, more terrific — that is — ahem! — than the following?"

The volume contains seventeen poems, all dated from October 1809 to August 1810. The two first are assignable on internal evidence to Elizabeth Shelley and most of the rest to Bysshe. In poetic quality there is nothing to indicate Shelley's future eminence. Several of the sentimental poems were inspired by his love for Harriet Grove, and the Gothic horror of most of the poems provides yet another evidence of the food Shelley's mind was feeding on. Certainly there is nothing original about its black whirlwinds, yelling fiends, ghosts, goblins, sinking hearts, chilled souls, and frozen blood.

Bysshe had still another poem ready for the press at this time. It was on a subject that had only recently excited a lively interest in his mind — the legend of the Wandering Jew. He had already encountered this character in "Monk" Lewis's *The Monk.* Then, one day while he was walking with Tom Medwin in Lincoln's Inn Fields, one of them picked up a wind-blown scrap of paper identifiable now as from a contemporary monthly magazine, *La Belle Assemblée.* It contained a translation from the German of Christian Schubart's poem on the Wandering Jew. The two lads began a poem on the same subject, employing some materials from their unpublished novel *The Nightmare*, from Lewis's *The Monk*, and from a recent volume of Cambridge prize poems. It was finished and was sent to Thomas Campbell for an opinion — which was that there were only two good lines in it. Two publishers to whom it was sent — Ballantyne of Edinburgh, and Stockdale of London — were equally unimpressed. The poem remained in manuscript until some time after Shelley's death, when two different versions were published in the *Edinburgh Literary Journal* in 1829 and *Fraser's Magazine* in 1831.

"The Wandering Jew" is no better poetry than the poems by Victor and Cazire. Its verse is badly imitated from Scott, and its narration is bromidic and confused. The Wandering Jew himself is without real passion and conveys scarcely a hint of the definite symbolic character he was soon to assume in Shelley's poetry.

But the character he was to assume for Shelley is almost weirdly significant. A very brief forecast of his wanderings through Shelley's mind for the next twelve years throws an interesting light on the young poet's peculiar nature. In Schubart's poem the Wandering Jew was a tragic sufferer from the just vengeance of Heaven and was eventually pardoned. The pure sensationalism of his story made an astonishing impression upon young Shelley. He paraphrased a part of Schubart's poem in a note to his own poem. One of his first actions when he became a student at Oxford was to seek further information about Schubart's poem in the Bodleian Library. He made a manuscript copy of it to give to Thomas J. Hogg, his new friend at Oxford. The intensity of its language became unconsciously his own; a whole sentence of it appears as his own a year or so later, in a strong outbreak of rage and despair. Soon thereafter he quoted the translation almost entirely in a note to *Queen Mab* (1813), omitting the last sentence because he could not accept the reconciliation of Heaven with its victim.

The Wandering Jew became in *Queen Mab* a burning symbol of religious vengeance and intolerance. This conception probably colors a lost poem on the subject written at about the same time, as it does a strong allusion in *Alastor* (1815). One of the climaxes of the Wandering Jew's sufferings is expressed by Schubart: "that may be extended, may pant, and writhe, and die." From 1817 1821 this expression echoes consecutively in *Laon and Cythna*, "Constantia Singing," "Ode to the West Wind," "Indian Serena and *Epipsychidion*: "To see his enemies writhe, and burn, and ble "thus to be lost, and thus to sink and die"; "I fall upon the thor

27

life, I bleed"; "I die, I faint, I fail"; "I pant, I sink, I tremble, I expire."

By 1819, however, Shelley, had found in Prometheus a nobler symbol who combined the benevolence of Peter Wilkins and the heroic defiance of the Wandering Jew. Thereafter the Wandering Jew appeared once more in Shelley's poetry, in *Hellas* (1822), but metamorphosed into a wise, benevolent prophet, no longer either a rebel or a martyr. To such an extent may a scrap of paper carelessly salvaged from a dusty gutter have strange effects for years afterwards on the thoughts of a sensitive, sensational-minded youth of strong memory and persistent ideas.

It would seem that the literary works already enumerated were more than enough for Shelley's last year at Eton, but he was also engaged on another romance, *St. Irvyne*, which he completed soon after his arrival at Oxford. Also his letters to Edward Graham mentioned that he was working on a tragedy to be submitted to Covent Garden, and enclosed several short lyrics that he hoped Graham, or Graham's music teacher, would set to music.

At the same time the youth was becoming quite a letter writer. His unconventional friend Dr. Lind had maintained that there was no reason why one should not open correspondence with perfect strangers. Thus Bysshe wrote to the well-known preacher Rowland Hill, offering to fill his pulpit for him, to the poet Campbell and probably others on literary matters, and to various unknown persons (one of whom threatened to have him caned) raising scientific questions. In 1807 or 1808 Tom Medwin returned from a visit in Wales full of the praises of Felicia Dorothea Browne (later Hemans), then a promising young poetess of thirteen or fourteen. Young Bysshe immediately opened a correspondence which was ardent while it lasted, but was soon terminated. Two or three years later he could refer to her with quite casual distaste as "certainly a tigress."

Not long after this brief, obscure flurry, Bysshe's love for Harriet Grove appears to have flared up again. In April 1810 the Grove family spent a week at Field Place and its neighborhood. "Bysshe was at that time more attached to my sister Harriet than I can express," Charles Grove later revealed. "Bysshe was thoroughly happy and his spirits were high." When they visited the Duke of Norfolk's house at Horsham, Bysshe improvised a typical piece of dramatic humor by dressing as a workingman and starting off toward Field Place "with one of those very little chests of drawers peculiar to old houses like Hills." It made Elizabeth nervous, "but Bysshe had the power of entering so thoroughly into the spirit of his own humour that nothing could stop him when once his spirits were up, and he carried you along with him in his hilarious flight and made you a sharer in his mirth, in a manner quite irresistible."

These high spirits were not inconsistent with a certain luxurious gloom and desperation which his novel-reading indicated as the conventional mood for lovers. In a poem enclosed in a letter to Edward Graham dated April 22 he represented himself as a youth with "darkened brow," "torn soul," and "frail form," tortured by fiends, threatened by "dire Fate's terrific storm," the "frantic pain" of whose bosom only Harriet could soothe. Such phrases were certainly less true than prophetic, for only three days later Shelley, Elizabeth, and their mother set out to make a return visit to the Groves at their town house in Lincoln's Inn Fields, the home of John Grove, Harriet's older brother. In town they picked up Edward Graham, who had already received a most ebullient summons from Shelley:

. . . My Mother brings a blood-stained stiletto which she purposes to make you bathe in the life-blood of her enemy.

Never mind the Death-demons, and skeletons dripping with the putrefaction of the grave, that occasionally may blast your straining eyeball . . . the fiend of the Sussex solitudes shrieked in the wilderness at midnight. . . . DEATH + HELL + DESTRUCTION if you fail.

Charles Grove recorded of this visit that "Bysshe was full of life and spirits, and was well pleased with his successful devotion to my sister." Harriet's journal shows that she was at least comfortably happy in the attentions of Bysshe and in the congenial society of "dear Aunt Shelley" and the lively Elizabeth. But the poet in Bysshe had forebodings. A poem dated April 1810, in the very midst of these pleasures, paints a somewhat despondent picture and concludes:

> Then —— ! dearest farewell,
> You and I love, may ne'er meet again;
> These woods and these meadows can tell
> How soft and how sweet was the strain.

The Shelleys returned to Field Place and the Grove family to their estate at Ferne House, in Wiltshire. Like a character in Jane

Austen's novels, Harriet took up a leisurely round of occasional family dinners, county or regimental dances, and small neighborhood affairs. An occasional caller in whom her journal displays no special interest was Mr. William Helyar, scion of a near-by county family, whom Harriet had known since the previous October. Bysshe and Harriet exchanged a few letters, and her rather infrequent references to him continued as affectionate as ever. Bysshe continued to hope and to send her presents of art crayons, books, and his own compositions, published and unpublished.

On July 30, 1810 Shelley delivered at Eton his oration of Cicero against Catiline and returned to Field Place to await the opening of Michaelmas term at Oxford on October 10. The six years at Eton had done much for the twelve-year-old boy who had left Syon House Academy in 1804. The old character remained, but he was no longer to the same extent the fragile, self-conscious youngster, full of romantic ideas and living largely in an imaginary world, driven in upon himself everywhere except at Field Place. With all its faults, Eton had proved, as Medwin said, "a new and better world." The strangeness and brutality of the external world still made him suffer, but gradually he was learning enough of its ways to feel at home in it.

The old wild spirit of prankish self-assertion persisted in diminished form, perhaps as a defense mechanism. His health was better; he enjoyed several forms of physical exercise; he had learned how to make friends. He was definitely beginning to realize his superior mental and imaginative qualities. Already he was a great reader and a voluminous writer of letters, poems, and novels — all of which reflected an amazing mental life with an insufficient basis in human experience. Tom Medwin, several years older, had noticed in the vacations that each succeeding half-year produced a rapid mental development in him; much of his talk must have been over Tom's head already. Squire Timothy Shelley, still reading with his son in vacations, was already falling behind and was soon to be bewildered and distracted by a widening gap of which he was quite unconscious. Some of the "wild notions" that were to occasion later disasters were already present in the manuscript of *St. Irvyne.*

To an observer already acquainted with the future, most of the characteristics and many of the ideas, symbols, and even phrases typical of the mature Shelley would have seemed already startlingly apparent. In only slight variations did his later development violate the pattern already set. But the real indications were beneath the surface; superficially young Bysshe seemed to be developing fairly well in accordance with the family hopes. He himself still took it for granted that he would go through Oxford, marry, settle down on the family estates, and sit in Parliament as a liberal Whig under the banner of the Duke of Norfolk.

Chapter IV

THE UNIVERSITY which young Percy Bysshe was now entering, ostensibly for the next four years, was well equipped to thwart or divert most of the characteristics and tastes to which he was already committed. For the last hundred years complacency, intellectual and physical laziness, and conservative, reactionary dogmatism had characterized Oxford University as a center of "port and prejudice." There had been a few brief "golden periods" of intellectual activity in a few colleges, but the contempt expressed or shown by visiting foreign scholars, by Gibbon, Johnson, Chesterfield, Jeffrey, and De Quincey had been, and still was, well merited.

The second greatest library of Europe, the Bodleian, was closed at three in the afternoon. Examinations were private or semi-private and were farcically easy. Professors seldom bothered to lecture and could justify themselves reasonably enough by pointing out that students seldom came to listen. Attendance upon tutors was generally casual. The lax discipline and trivial penalties made little distinction between such offenses as slipping off to London, creating an uproar, and gross immorality. In most colleges the antiquated curricula consisted mainly of Greek, Latin, logic, and divinity, with a small list of required reading, and the writing of occasional papers. English literature and the physical sciences were ignored.

There had been some slight stir amid the general somnolence during the revolutionary ferment of the early 1790's. Young Robert Southey was certainly not the only one of his kind then at Oxford, but the burning of Tom Paine in effigy on the top of Carfax in 1793, though not by gownsmen, was probably more popular even then than the ideas cherished by young Southey and his kind.

As young Shelley entered Oxford the first note of public dissatisfaction with these conditions was becoming audible. The powerful *Edinburgh Review*, in four long articles from January 1808 to April 1810, charged that Oxford suppressed free inquiry, ignored all the scientific progress of the last three hundred years, and even forfeited through bad teaching most of the merits of its narrow Greek and Latin curriculum. Since most tutors were clergymen, "a genuine Oxford tutor would shudder to hear his young men disputing upon moral and political truth. . . . He would augur nothing from it but impiety to God and treason to kings."

Edward Copleston, Oxford's unusually young and vigorous Professor of Poetry, answered boldly that Oxford's primary duty was not utility or individual interests, but the preservation of an established system. She did not care to trouble herself "with every crude opinion or untried theory." Others might do so if they liked, but let them beware of tampering with the "sacred citadel" of religion. "The scheme of Revelation, we think, is closed, and we expect no new light on earth to break in upon us."

There was much talk of Oxford at Field Place during the summer of 1810, and very possibly young Bysshe read Professor Copleston's words. If so, he must have smiled scornfully, unaware that they were closely connected with his own future. But most of the talk then current about Oxford all over England had to do with the election of Lord Grenville as Chancellor of the university. He had been elected over Lord Eldon only after a lively contest. Catholic emancipation, which Lord Grenville favored, had been an indirect issue in the election and had made it a contest between liberals and conservatives. Field Place, following the Duke of Norfolk, was for Lord Grenville. Tom Medwin recollected later that young Bysshe even published a letter in one of the London newspapers, signing himself "A Master of Arts of Oxford" and recommending Lord Grenville.

The total membership of the university, including both dons and students, was about two thousand, which was about one fifth of the population of Oxford. University College, which Shelley was entering, occupied a fairly average position among the twenty colleges then included in the university. It was presided over by a dreamy, seclusive Master, Dr. James Griffith, who took little interest in anything except his hobby of portraits in burnt wood. The real executive was the Dean, George Rowley, bustling, officious, and repressive. The students were prankish and ill disciplined; the fellows were still disgruntled over the election of Lord Grenville over Eldon, a University College man.

Bysshe began residence at Oxford on or about October 10, 1810 as the holder of a Lord Leicester scholarship. Proud of his son's literary attainments, Mr. Timothy Shelley accompanied Bysshe to help get him well settled. During the several days that Mr. Timothy

Shelley lingered, savoring his own undergraduate days anew, anticipating a more brilliant scholastic career for his son, Bysshe's rooms were newly fitted up with excellent furnishings. One thing only remained. In renewing his old associations at Oxford Mr. Timothy Shelley found that Henry Slatter, the son of his former landlord, had just established a partnership with the Oxford bookseller and printer Munday. He took young Bysshe to their shop, introduced him, and proudly instructed the printers: "My son here has a literary turn; he is already an author, and do pray indulge him in his printing freaks." The youth was well launched, and the squire could return to his acres. Bysshe visited the Bodleian Library in a vain effort to discover the German author of his precious magazine fragment on the Wandering Jew, and began hunting up various fellow Etonians, some of whom were soon afterwards callers at his rooms.

Shortly after his father's return to Sussex, Shelley was eating his first dinner in hall. Near him was seated a rather remarkable young man, solid-looking and self-confident, named Thomas Jefferson Hogg, the son of a well-to-do barrister of Stockton-upon-Tees, near York. Hogg had been a student at University College since January. Cool, practical, and perhaps a little sardonic, he had already learned that his college lacked intellectual stimulus; but being determined to prepare himself for the law, he was undisturbed by what he later called the "total neglect of all learning," "the open and habitual drunkenness," and "universal laziness" of his environment.

Young Hogg noticed that his neighbor seemed thoughtful and absent-minded. A conversation opened so casually that neither could recall later how it began. They argued earnestly over the comparative originality and imaginative qualities of German literature versus Italian. The dons and dignitaries of the high table filed out; the uproar of undergraduate talk increased with the withdrawal of Dignity. Still they argued and discussed. The undergraduates gradually left the hall, and the servants began clearing off the table. The young disputants then adjourned to Hogg's rooms, where they calmly confessed to each other that they knew almost nothing of the languages and literatures they had respectively championed.

What did it matter, anyhow, said Shelley. Languages were nothing but words and phrases standing for things; the really important point was to understand *things* — whereupon, with increased ardor, he launched upon a eulogy of chemistry. Hogg kept him going with occasional questions and doubts. He was greatly impressed, but at the same time he was coolly appraising this slender boy whose small, animated features, tousled hair, odd gestures, and lively enthusiasm were so out of the ordinary. It seemed a pity that such a fine clever fellow had to express himself in a voice "intolerably shrill, harsh and discordant"; otherwise he would be a most desirable acquaintance. When Shelley suddenly remembered that he must go to a lecture on mineralogy, Hogg invited him to come back later for tea.

But all the lecturer would talk about was "stones! stones, stones, stones! nothing but stones!" How different it was from old Adam Walker's all-inclusive scientific magic at Eton! The outraged listener soon made an awkward escape and returned to conclude his own lecture in Hogg's rooms. Tea was consumed, and afterwards supper.

After supper Shelley proved himself a true disciple of Adam Walker in a glowing account of the blessings humanity would shortly inherit from sciences as yet only in their infancy. Synthetic foods and fertilizers, the discovery of new principles of heating and irrigation, the control of electricity, would render human life infinitely less toilsome and uncomfortable. Man had only just learned to lift himself from the earth in balloons, but eventually unexplored regions would be charted from the air. The shadow of the first balloons falling upon Africa would end slavery there and elsewhere, "for ever."

The talk swung to the moral sciences, in which Hogg, as a future lawyer, was more interested; then to mathematics, which Shelley scornfully dismissed. Metaphysics, proclaimed Shelley in the end, was the noblest of all studies, because it was the key to the mind itself, and not to mere matter. By this time the fire was out, and there was just enough virtue in the guttering candles to light the visitor downstairs.

The meeting, in its various phases, had lasted seven or eight hours. The two boys now learned each other's names, and Hogg promised to visit Shelley's rooms next day to see his scientific instruments. Already the irritating harsh voice seemed to him of little consequence.

The next afternoon, at two, Hogg kept his engagement. Shelley's rooms surprised him with their smart freshness. Paper, paint, curtains, carpets, and furniture were all new. More surprising, however, was their aspect of utter, careless confusion. Books and crockery, papers and shoes, clothes and scientific apparatus, were scattered anywhere and everywhere. Tables and carpets already showed damage from chemical experiments. There were traces of a recent party.

An experiment was in progress at the moment; an argand lamp was burning beneath a small retort supported by the fire-tongs placed across two piles of books. Hogg had scarcely seated himself before this experiment boiled over in a cloud of evil-smelling fumes.

While listening to another enthusiastic discourse on the possibilities of science, Hogg saw Shelley demonstrate his electrical machine, his galvanic battery, and other contrivances. After dinner the conversation was resumed and lasted until a late hour. This time there was much ardent discourse of poetry. Each had discovered in the other an intellectual liveliness and curiosity quite at variance with the general tone of the place. They were, in a sense, universities to each other. Hogg found the ardor he had previously missed, and Shelley, on his part, probably profited almost as much from the greater coolness, calmer judgment, and more methodical habits of his friend. From this time on, the two passed most of their time together, more often in Shelley's rooms than in Hogg's.

Shelley's interest in the physical sciences waned perceptibly after the first early meetings. Hogg had no enthusiasm for experiments with which to reinforce Shelley's. In fact, they made him nervous, both for himself and for his friend. He had almost imbibed aqua regia in Shelley's rooms out of a cup that should have contained only tea. Shelley was disorderly and impatient in his experiments; he lacked manual dexterity — and Hogg's calm failure to take him very seriously as a practical scientist gradually diminished his energies. His scout's persistent efforts to put the rooms in order further discouraged him by making it difficult to lay hands on a particular ingredient or piece of apparatus in any of the minor crises by which experiment seemed to proceed. The scout's son, a gawky boy who had unwittingly helped demonstrate the wonders of charged doorknobs, soon grew so wary that he yelled with alarm if Shelley approached him with apparatus in his hand.

The daily life of the two young men soon settled down to a fairly regular routine. Hogg rose early, at six or seven, attended college "lectures," read in private for several hours, and joined Shelley nearly every day at one o'clock. It is probable that Shelley did not rise regularly as early as Hogg or visit his tutor as regularly. Very likely he spent part of the four or five free hours of the morning in "scientific" tinkering and in attending to a correspondence that was at times considerable. But if he read as much as Hogg supposed, he too must have spent the larger part of this period in reading.

From one o'clock till six they were generally in Shelley's rooms, sometimes reading together, sometimes studying separately, eternally discussing, arguing, and speculating. Often they took long afternoon walks together, but at six, with reasonable punctuality, the scandalously unpunctual Shelley regularly went to sleep, either on the couch or curled up on the rug before the fire, with his head always in the hottest position. Hogg made tea, read, and wrote by himself until eight or ten o'clock, meanwhile keeping an eye on the sleeper, who sometimes rolled over and sometimes talked excitedly in his sleep. At eight or ten Shelley awoke. At ten they had supper together, after which they remained together, generally reading and discussing, until one o'clock.

This program was occasionally interrupted by callers. More than once Hogg met Etonians in Shelley's rooms. But though Bysshe always spoke of them kindly, he did not encourage their visits and they seem not to have entered very largely into his life at Oxford. Another friend, not an Etonian, was James Roe, of Trinity College, whom Shelley asked to criticize a "poetical scrap" for him, and who was invited at least once to an afternoon of "wine and Poetry."

One day, while taking shelter in a doorway during a sudden windstorm, Bysshe became engaged in a philosophical conversation with a young fellow of Wadham College, some five years his senior. Surprisingly enough he turned out to be George Marshall, whose father had been rector of Horsham since 1784. A friendship sprang up which led to several long conversations in George Marshall's rooms. Marshall's friend, Thomas Barnes, later editor of the *Times,* who happened to be paying him a visit about this time, was much impressed by the "frankness and uprightness" of character suggested by the young freshman's conversation.

When the weather was suitable, Shelley and Hogg often fared forth for long afternoon walks in the country around Oxford. These walks were no interruptions to the conversation, of course, nor did the walking entirely exclude reading. Shelley generally had a book in his hand or in his pocket. Only considerable experience could have developed the awkward agility by which with his attention fixed on anything except the course of travel Shelley dexterously and unconsciously avoided collisions and missteps.

Out they would sally, past the old porter and into the High Street, past the imposing fronts of colleges, past townsmen and gownsmen — the latter still scrupulously designated by their insignia accord-

37

ing to their various social ranks — out along the highways for several miles, and then across open country, crossing roads and lanes, skirting woods and enclosures or boldly walking through, until it was time to return to the college. It was Shelley's favorite recreation. The region around Shotover Hill pleased him most, because of a pond into which he loved to toss pebbles or on whose surface he skimmed flat stones, gleefully counting the number of skips.

On the earlier excursions, until dissuaded by the apprehensive Hogg, Shelley carried two dueling pistols, with which he demonstrated great accuracy at target shooting. Once during their rambles they were set upon by a dog which was beaten off only after the loss of Shelley's coat-tails. Again Bysshe became very angry at seeing a boy mistreat an ass. On another ramble he made generous efforts to relieve the distress of a small girl whom they found hungry and apparently deserted; and on another he stopped to engage in odd friendly pranks with some gypsy children whom they encountered. One of their excursions brought them suddenly upon a secluded garden whose desolate quiet stimulated Shelley's imagination wonderfully for the rest of the walk, and may in fact be an ingredient of "The Sensitive Plant," written nine years later in Italy.

The most extraordinary of these incidents, however, proceeded from Shelley's philosophic interests. One Sunday afternoon he and Hogg had been reading Plato and discussing with such interest the Platonic idea of immortality that it was rather late when they began their afternoon walk. In the middle of Magdalen Bridge, while Shelley's mind was still full of pre-existence, they met a woman carrying a young child in her arms. Bysshe suddenly seized upon the child and asked the mother most earnestly: "Will your baby tell us anything about pre-existence, Madam?"

The startled mother's assertion that the child could not yet speak seemed to Shelley an ignorant evasion. He urged that the child's reticence must be a whim, that no child only a few weeks old could have so soon "forgotten entirely the use of speech." But the child continued to withhold information, and Shelley sighed as they walked on, "How provokingly close are those new-born babes!"

Naturally young Shelley had interests and personal relations at Oxford other than those connected with the bland and self-confident Hogg. Such easy demands as his college made upon its students he probably met much more punctiliously than the average freshman. He duly visited his tutor and was told somewhat drearily that he must "read, read" — not the books that Shelley then and there produced to demonstrate his reading, but Æschylus, Demosthenes, Euclid, and Aristotle. All except possibly Euclid he did read, though perhaps not all at Oxford. The Aristotelian logic so dear to Oxford he took to with a relish that was eventually disastrous. Apparently he complied with the modest requirements for weekly written exercises. He wrote a number of voluntary argumentative essays which he may or may not have shown to his tutor.

For some time Shelley seems to have avoided major collisions with college discipline. Absences from chapel and from dinner in hall probably occurred, but they could be taken care of by paying small fees or by "pricking aeger" — reporting oneself officially ill. Dean Rowley was a petty disciplinarian who did not balk at cutting down Mrs. Griffith's favorite pear tree to prevent boys who were out late from returning over the college wall by its aid; but though Shelley still retained some of the monkey tricks of the schoolboy, he was apparently never caught in any specific dereliction that could not be passed off either by a fine or by one of his ludicrously humble apologies.

There are certain indications, however, that his college authorities regarded him with some misgiving. They suspected him as a principal mischief-maker. In a college with a total membership of only seventy persons he was much too fond of arguing his opinions for such a person as Dean Rowley not to have an inkling of what they were. Former Eton boys who had heard him curse father and King prodded him into repetitions and probably dropped a few words to other Oxonians. He was already engaging in anonymous publications which he imagined were secret, even while Charles Kirkpatrick Sharpe, a member of another college, was discussing them freely in his letters as matters of common gossip at Oxford. Both Medwin and Hogg believed that the Shelley championship of Lord Grenville in the elections for chancellor had seriously offended the authorities of University College, and Hogg even asserted later that from the beginning Shelley was on this account "regarded with a jealous eye" and that it was the main cause of Shelley's misfortunes at Oxford. Certainly both Shelley and Hogg were already generally unpopular in the college.

Yet despite his unconcealed disapproval of prevailing standards, Shelley was happy at Oxford. He wished to spend his whole time in reading, writing, and talking, with a dash of "scientific" experiment; and the university made it possible for him to do this with

39

practically no interference. He and Hogg often congratulated themselves on their opportunities. He particularly enjoyed the ease with which he could at any time deny himself to visitors by closing his outer door, known in Oxford parlance as "sporting his oak."

There was also a rather voluminous correspondence to be maintained. Mr. Timothy Shelley wrote letters that amused the two boys by their rambling, haphazard character. Bysshe's answers, sometimes innocently and sometimes by intention, occasionally provoked his rather irritable parent into an angry outburst. Letters from his mother and sisters were always received with pleasure. Elizabeth, who was his advocate with Harriet Grove, was his favorite. How fine it would be to bring about a union between this sister, a promising candidate for enlightenment, and the wonderful Jefferson, already enlightened! Jefferson must visit him at Field Place and fall in love with Elizabeth. Shelley was also in correspondence with Harriet Grove, who was growing farther and farther away from him, but of this he seems to have told Hogg little or nothing.

The bulk of his correspondence, however, was of the sort learned from Dr. Lind. His passionate fondness for arguing, and also for genuine enlightenment, could hardly be confined within oral bounds. Profiting eagerly by the university's emphasis on logic, he prepared analyses and briefs from his reading and solicited the opinions of others on the matter by correspondence. He used several assumed names and took the further precaution of giving a London address — that of Edward Graham, his patient London factotum. "If any letter comes directed to the Revd. Charles Peyton," he wrote Graham, "it is mine." Another of his pseudonyms was Jeremiah Stukely.

At times his correspondence of this sort was considerable. In the beginning the subjects were largely scientific, but science was soon entirely superseded by ethical and moral questions. Soon he found that by printing his abstract he could more readily elicit an answer. This abstract he would enclose as something he had found that unfortunately seemed unanswerable, and solicit his victim's comment. Then, as Hogg expressed it, "Unless the fish was too sluggish to take the bait, an answer of refutation was forwarded to an appointed address in London, and then in a vigorous reply he [Shelley] would fall upon the unwary disputant, and break his bones. The strenuous attack sometimes provoked a rejoinder more carefully prepared and an animated and protracted debate ensued." He was so fond of the debate that he sometimes argued more for "the shock of contending minds" than from immediate conviction of his own. The truth is that his motives were curiously mixed. He sincerely desired to get at the truth. He also loved intellectual activity and adventure as a form of excitement, and he was fascinated by the exercise of logic.

The business of becoming an author, which had resulted in two published volumes before he entered the university, continued unabated. Shelley was still seeking to publish *The Wandering Jew*. He had brought to the university his *St. Irvyne, or The Rosicrucian*, almost if not entirely complete. Stockdale, his publisher, had it printed and bound by December 10, a few days before its anonymous author returned to Field Place for the Christmas vacation. It was published anonymously as by a "Gentleman of the University of Oxford" and was somewhat brazenly advertised as "the University romance" in the *Times* for January 26 and February 2, 1811.

Like the young author's preceding volumes, *St. Irvyne* is worthless from a literary point of view. Its two hazily related plots are decidedly chaotic. It involves such standard Gothic ingredients as the elixir of life, a compact with the Devil, a band of brigands, free love, seduction, murder, suicide, beauty in distress, and a fatal duel to avenge an injured heroine. The tinkering that both Stockdale and Shelley bestowed on them failed entirely to bring these elements into logical or even interesting relation to one another. Nevertheless they do possess an interest of another sort. They show Shelley's mind still dominated mainly by his Gothic interests, combining them for the first time (except for a brief passage near the end of *Zastrozzi*) with revolutionary moral ideas. Also significant is the fact that *St. Irvyne* contains a passage of rather penetrating self-characterization.

With *St. Irvyne* the powerful stimulus given to Shelley's imagination by the terror school of literature reached its last full expression. At the same time that his passion for physical science was yielding to a developing interest in ethical and moral questions, his love for physical sensationalism was also giving way to an intellectual sensationalism which in turn was to be supplanted by moral fervor. But the literature of terror and wonder had already exerted a profound effect on the early thought and expression of a marvelously active and retentive mind, and from time to time throughout the rest of his life it was to lend a peculiar color to his poetic imagery, as in the opening lines of the "Ode to the West Wind."

St. Irvyne sold badly and was a financial loss to the publisher, though perhaps one or two sarcastic reviewers were mildly grateful for the opportunity it offered. The *British Critic* concluded with

41

suave sarcasm that the "Gentleman of the University of Oxford" must be a very young gentleman indeed, to whom better sense and taste would in due time be vouchsafed. The *Literary Panorama* condemned the romance more subtly by limiting its comment to three captions placed over four lurid excerpts: "How to Begin a Romance, A.D. 1811"; "How to End a Romance, A.D. 1811"; and "Conclusion." The *Anti-Jacobin Review,* however, matured its indignation for a year and then condemned the volume seriously and weightily, not merely as "enthusiastical and nonsensical," but as a reckless and dangerous assault on all ideas of decency and morality.

In Oxford *St. Irvyne* was on sale at Slatter and Munday's and was probably read by a number of people, since it was advertised as a university romance and might contain any amount of veiled reference to Oxford toasts and dons. Charles Kirkpatrick Sharpe, a brilliant young Tory who had been resident at Christ's Church for some years after obtaining his degrees, was one who had read it and knew a good bit about the author. He sent a copy of the volume to his friend Lady Charlotte Campbell, with a sarcastic description, and received from her an opinion not very different from his own.

While *St. Irvyne* was being printed Shelley was engaged upon another volume which actually preceded it from the press, as a rather handsome quarto containing twenty-two pages, entitled *Posthumous Fragments of Margaret Nicholson*. This volume was published pseudonymously by Slatter and Munday, as edited by John Fitz-Victor, signifying secretly the son of the Victor concerned in *Original Poetry by Victor and Cazire*. Margaret Nicholson, the ostensible author, was a mad washerwoman who had attempted to assassinate George III twenty-five years earlier. Mr. Munday was so taken in by this hoax that he asked and received permission to publish the book as his own financial venture. But though the poems were thus given a superficial appearance of burlesque – and though Hogg later described them as such – they are in reality no such thing. One of them, "Melody to a Scene of Former Times," expresses Bysshe's keen despair over the unsatisfactory course of his love for Harriet Grove. The two longest and most important poems are revolutionary attacks upon despotism that might well have got both publisher and author into trouble had not the name of Margaret Nicholson functioned efficiently as a burlesque cloak. According to Hogg, it became quite the fashion for a while to be seen reading the mad washerwoman's poems. But Charles Kirkpatrick Sharpe promptly attributed the volume to Shelley and characterized it to Lady Charlotte Campbell as "full of treason," but "extremely dull."

In most copies of the book, but not in the one sent to Shelley's mother, there is a warm, free-spoken bit of love-dialogue which Shelley said was "the production of a friend's *mistress*" and would make the book "sell like wild-fire." Not trusting entirely to this, he promised to send Edward Graham some abuse of the volume to be inserted in London papers. Nevertheless, the book was not noticed in London, nor, apparently, by Mr. Timothy Shelley at Field Place, for Shelley had warned Graham: "Of course to my Father, Peg is a profound secret."

At the same time Shelley was assisting Hogg with a novel called *Leonora*, which the Oxford printers refused to complete on account of its "free notions." His letters also refer somewhat obscurely to an unnamed novel of his own, which appears never to have been published. In addition he was writing a Godwinian poetic "Essay on Love" and a "Poetical Essay on the Existing State of Things," both of which seem to have been printed and subsequently lost.

Writing rapidly and carelessly, Shelley had plenty of time left for reading, and for encouraging other authors. A young poetess of Oxford named Janetta Phillips was bringing out a volume in which he took considerable interest and for which he obtained a number of subscriptions. There was also at Oxford a former naval officer named Browne, passing under the assumed name of Bird, and endeavoring to publish a book on Sweden. From his last year at Eton Shelley had become interested in him as the victim of alleged "oppression." He now undertook to help him. Almost his last act at Eton was the signing of a six-hundred-pound bond for the publication of Browne's book — a sum that Slatter and Munday, who had gone security for the bond, eventually had to pay.

By far the larger part of Shelley's time at Oxford — and indeed for most of his life — was spent in reading. Hogg asserted that he often spent two thirds of the day and night book in hand — "in season and out of season, at table, in bed, and especially during a walk," in the country, in the High Street of Oxford, and even in the crowded streets of London. Tom Medwin, who now saw Shelley too seldom to observe the great extent of his reading, was equally impressed with the manner of his reading and his amazing retentive powers. "He took in seven or eight lines at a glance, and his mind seized

43

the sense with a velocity equal to the twinkling of an eye. . . . His memory was prodigious." If the spirit of Oxford seemed exactly calculated to thwart all the growing tendencies of this particular youth, it furnished its own antidote by providing him with the best possible opportunity for extensive reading.

Bysshe was still reading science and Gothic romance, but both these lively earlier interests were now definitely quite minor ones. He read "with more than ordinary interest" books of Eastern travels and Oriental tales of wonder, and delighted in Greek tragedy and English drama, particularly Shakespeare. As yet he was reading Greek only in translation. Plato's *Phædo* and the *Republic,* together with other unnamed dialogues, he and Hogg read enthusiastically together. Walter Savage Landor's *Gebir* he read aloud so often that Hogg threw the book out of the window in self-defense, while Southey's *The Curse of Kehama* furnished some lines as a model for his lost poem on the "Existing State of Things" and considerably influenced his later *Queen Mab.*

A rapidly growing interest in society, politics, and religion probably accounted for most of Shelley's reading at Oxford. One particularly important book, William Godwin's *Political Justice* (1793), is almost the only title that has been recorded. Shelley had doubtless heard of this book at Eton and may even have dipped into it in the library of Dr. Lind, but only after his coming to Oxford did it have an appreciable influence on his writing and thinking. Within little more than a year he was to call it "the regulator and former of my mind." It opened his mind, as he soon acknowledged, to "fresh and extensive views," weaned him (as he thought) from romantic idealism, and "materially influenced my character."

Godwin, probably seconded by Hogg's preference for the social and ethical sciences, led to the reading together of a number of other writers on moral and social questions. Among these writers were Locke and Hume, both of whom influenced Shelley's writings shortly afterwards.

The Christmas vacation was now at hand, and Shelley returned to Field Place outwardly the same, but actually considerably changed. At the very time that Oxford's emphasis on logic was reinforcing his tendency toward oral and epistolary argument, the subject of his interests — and hence of the activities in which they were sure to find an outlet — had shifted largely from the relatively safe physical sciences to the dangerous social ones. William Godwin, abhorred of all safe and sane conservatives, was becoming his spiritual father.

The storm that was eventually inevitable broke at once. Stockdale, who had become alarmed by his young client's interest in anti-Christian literature, informed Mr. Timothy Shelley of his fears. Mr. Shelley immediately called upon him and learned that Hogg was aiding and abetting young Bysshe's worst tendencies. He started inquiries about Hogg and was not reassured.

It seemed to Mr. Shelley that prompt action was indicated. He had taken Bysshe with him to the House of Commons and had not been too disturbed by his disgust at the politicians he saw there. He had seen to it that the Duke of Norfolk liked Bysshe and was anxious to support his future political career. Was all this preparation to be endangered? He immediately wrote to the boy in no uncertain language, threatened to withdraw him from college, and forbade Hogg's projected visit to Field Place. It was a disappointment to be deprived of Jefferson, and the reproaches of his mother and sisters were not pleasant either. Bad as it was, however, the situation was not without dramatic possibilities which could be employed in a letter to Hogg: "I am reckoned an outcast; yet I defy them and laugh at their ineffectual efforts. . . . There lowers a terrific tempest, but I stand, as it were, on a pharos, and smile exultingly at the vain beating of the billows below."

Soon other informants persuaded Mr. Shelley that Jefferson was after all a solid young man, probably usable as a good influence. He came home and authorized Bysshe to invite Jefferson to Field Place for the Easter vacation. Both parents were still alarmed, however. Bysshe now tried to argue his father into his own point of view. Mr. Shelley listened and even agreed, until Bysshe thought him convinced. "But when I came to *apply* the truths on which we had agreed so harmoniously, he started at the bare idea of some facts generally believed never having existed, and silenced me with an Equine argument, in effect with these words: — 'I believe, because I do believe.'" Bysshe had sufficient respect for his father's stubbornness in these beliefs to give out at home that he would publish no more, even though he was at the moment preparing for the press a novel, about which all that is known is that it apparently contained views similar to those which were already disturbing his parents.

If Bysshe could stand "on a pharos" against parental pressure and disapprobation, there were other troubles at the same time against which he was less confident. News reached him that Harriet Grove

45

was soon to be married to Mr. William Helyar; in his agitation he seems to have considered that she was in fact already married. The slender hopes that he had allowed himself to cherish since the previous summer were now completely dissipated. "She is gone!" Shelley wrote to Hogg on January 11. "She is lost to me for ever! She is married! Married to a clod of earth; she will become as insensible herself; all those fine capabilities will moulder." He indulged in some rather remarkable talk of suicide. "I cannot avoid feeling every instant," he wrote Hogg, "as if my soul were bursting. . . . Is suicide wrong? . . . I slept with a loaded pistol and some poison last night, but did not die. . . . I never, never can feel peace again. What necessity is there for continuing in existence? Is she not gone? And yet I breathe, I live!" Bysshe "wandered in the snow," was "cold, wet, and mad," and spent most of one night pacing Warnham churchyard.

Elizabeth, who had been his abettor with Harriet in more hopeful days, was distressed by his wild talk, and whenever he took his gun and walked in the fields she always followed closely for fear that he might shoot himself. But even Elizabeth was beginning to desert the tight little world which he had imagined she and Hogg shared only with him. One of Bysshe's strongest desires was to see Jefferson and Elizabeth united in love. Elizabeth apparently did not know that he would have preferred this union (following Godwin's *Political Justice*) without the dubious "benefit" of clergy. Though impressed by Bysshe's account of Hogg, she disapproved of the religious skepticism which she assumed he shared with Bysshe. She returned his letters unread, despite Bysshe's passionate protests, but rather self-distrustfully than scornfully. Bysshe did his energetic best as intermediary, but feared that the case was desperate.

Wild and fevered as they were, self-confessedly "mad" and Gothic-novelized in their emotional passages, Shelley's thirteen letters to Hogg between December 20, 1810 and January 23, 1811 are the record of one of the great crises of his life. Like many another youth, he considered his life blasted, but unlike others, he did not blame Love. Even the emptiness of love, he assured Hogg, was better than the fullness of other states. He wove this conception of love into the philosophic arguments that he was conducting with Hogg in the midst of their miseries. "Do I love the person, the embodied entity, if I may be allowed the expression? No! I love what is superior, what is excellent, or what I conceive to be so; and I wish, ardently wish, to be profoundly convinced of the existence of a Deity, that so superior a spirit might derive some degree of happiness from my exertions: for love is heaven, and heaven is love." "Even if the Universe were created by mere fortuitous concourse of atoms," he continued, "that fortuity must have had a cause, and that Cause must be Deity. O that this Deity were the soul of the Universe, the spirit of universal, imperishable love! Indeed, I believe it is. . . ." A prophet might have seen here the promise of some of Shelley's most characteristic later poetry.

In the same letters Shelley accepted the imputation of skeptic. But in his moments of most intense feeling he believed in a God of Love. Christianity, however, he now hated as a system designed to frustrate Love. Long before this he had dedicated himself to warfare against oppression, but now for the first time he saw clearly and intensely his Enemy. Hogg's unhappiness, the defection of Elizabeth, his own deep dejection over Harriet, even his relatively petty domestic discomforts of the moment, all seemed to stem directly or indirectly from the pernicious doctrines of Christianity. "My unhappiness is excessive. . . . But that which injured me shall perish! I even now by anticipation hear the expiring yell of intolerance." "I know the cause of all your disappointment — worldly prejudice; mine is the same, I know also its origin — bigotry." On two separate occasions he solemnly swore vengeance.

"O! I burn with impatience for the moment of the dissolution of Christianity; it has injured me. I swear on the altar of perjured Love to revenge myself on the hated cause of the effect. . . . Indeed I think it to the benefit of society to destroy the opinions which can annihilate the dearest of its ties." This was on December 20, immediately after he had returned to Field Place. Two weeks later (January 3) he was even more vehement: "Yet here I swear that never will I forgive Christianity! It is the only point on which I allow myself to encourage revenge. . . . Oh! how I wish I were the Antichrist! — that it were mine to crush the demon; to hurl him to his native hell, never to rise again. . . . Oh Christianity! When I pardon this last, this severest of thy persecutions, may God (if there be a God) blast me! Has vengeance, in its armoury of wrath, a punishment more dreadful?"

The last sentence is particularly interesting, in that it is a literal quotation from the fragmentary translation of Schubart's *Wandering Jew* that Shelley has been treasuring for a year or two. Apparently without realizing it, Shelley identified himself with the greatest of all legendary victims of Christianity. Shelley's intense self-dedication to a warfare against Christianity was anything but the bit of Gothic fustian that a careless reader might suppose; it was more like Hannibal's vow against Rome. Two years later he was preparing its first powerful broadside, *Queen Mab,* prefaced by Voltaire's motto, *"Écrasez l'infâme,"* which is oddly reminiscent of the phrase, "crush the demon," in his letter of January 3.

While Shelley's letters from Field Place were tense with personal emotion, they also continued calmly, though rather briefly, to discuss philosophical questions of common interest and to refer occasionally to the long, argumentative correspondence on philosophical and theological questions that the two youths were conducting with a gentleman named Wedgwood, who amused Shelley by assuming that he was a clergyman.

During the last week in January Shelley returned to Oxford, thwarted in his own love and in his design of uniting Hogg and Elizabeth. For the latter, however, he had hopes from Hogg's expected visit to Field Place at Easter; meanwhile he continued earnestly to sing their praises to each other. Unwittingly he had also taken the first step toward replacing the faithless Harriet. In the midst of his troubles he had visited his younger sisters' boarding-school with a present from his sister Mary to her friend, a beautiful, fair-haired girl named Harriet Westbrook. The meeting impressed him sufficiently to cause him to send her a copy of *St. Irvyne.*

Once more in quiet Oxford after his unhappy vacation, Shelley addressed a very stiff letter to Stockdale, demanding a full and satisfactory explanation of his "scandalous" and "contemptible *attempts* at calumny" in his recent talks with Mr. Timothy Shelley. Then the old pleasant life of reading, writing, arguing, and strolling began again. "It would be impossible," Hogg asserted, "faithfully to describe the course of a single day in the ordinary life of Shelley without showing, incidentally and unintentionally, that his nature was eminently benevolent." He paints an attractive picture of Shelley's pawning his precious microscope in order to relieve the poverty of a man he had never seen before, and gives several other instances of his benevolence. His sympathies were theoretically so extensive that he already questioned the right of humanity to take animal life merely for pleasure, but he had not yet abjured hunting or the eating of flesh. Hogg insists specifically that "the purity and sanctity of his life was most conspicuous" and that he was offended by coarse jests.

Toward the end of February an occasion arose which called forth
his political sympathies. At this time, according to Hogg, Shelley
was "wholly republican," "entirely devoted to the lovely theory of
freedom," but in actual feelings and behavior often rather aristocratic through an inveterate fastidiousness. Peter Finnerty, an Irish
journalist, had been sentenced to eighteen months' imprisonment
for a published criticism of Lord Castlereagh. Liberals like Sir
Francis Burdett and Leigh Hunt rushed to his defense, meetings
were held, editorials written, and subscriptions taken.

The *Oxford University and City Herald* opened a subscription for
him. Shelley's subscription of one guinea, standing third on the
published list (March 2, 1811), probably pained the Tory officials
of University College. Shelley went further. He caused to be advertised in the same journal, for March 9, "A Poetical Essay on the
Existing State of Things, By a Gentleman of the University of Oxford, for assisting to maintain in Prison Mr. Peter Finnerty, imprisoned for a libel." Charles Kirkpatrick Sharpe mentioned the
poem and knew Shelley to be the author, but showed no knowledge
of it that could not have been gained from the *Herald*. In fact, there
is no evidence that anyone saw more than Sharpe, and it is quite
possible that the poem was prudently withdrawn at the last minute,
or even that it was never written, but was a fiction to support interest
in Finnerty's case.

At almost the same time Shelley became interested in Leigh Hunt,
editor of the *Examiner,* as another victim of government persecution. Hunt had already been twice prosecuted by the government for
his fearless editorials. He now emerged triumphant from a third
prosecution. Shelley wrote to him on March 2, 1811, to congratulate
him on his victory and to suggest the formation of an association
by which liberals could protect one another to some extent against
government prosecution. He concluded: "My father is in parliament,
and on attaining 21 I shall, in all probability, fill his vacant seat. On
account of the responsibility to which my residence in the University subjects me, I of course, dare not publicly to avow all that
I think, but the time will come when I hope that my every endeavour,
insufficient as this may be, will be directed to the advancement of
liberty."

Meanwhile Mr. Timothy Shelley's uneasiness was by no means
abolished. Just possibly he received a hint from Messrs. Slatter and
Munday, who had recently remonstrated with their young patron,

and had even called in a Mr. Hobbes to reinforce their arguments, but without effect. Soon Mr. Shelley was writing to his son urging the reasonableness of Christianity and the desirability of making the most of his opportunities at the university. Shelley answered reassuringly on both points. He was attending lectures in logic, was already prepared for his examiners in divinity, and was also working for the poetry prize, as his father had recommended. Even though he felt Christianity not established by the physical evidence, and hence not convincing for him, he agreed it was good for the uncritical majority, and promised to be circumspect in all his public utterances.

Shelley's letter sounds quite sincere, and yet at that very moment (February 17) he already had in his possession the printed document that was to bring this prudent resolve to naught. Some time earlier Shelley and Hogg had made synopses of much of their reading together, including Locke and Hume. From these synopses Shelley had prepared a brief abstract of arguments against revealed religion, for use as a handy tool in the pseudonymous epistolary arguments carried on by the two youths. Soon it seemed desirable to have it printed, still apparently only with the idea of convenience in discussions with correspondents. It was printed anonymously at the shop of C. and W. Phillips in Worthing.

On February 9 Shelley had caused this little essay to be advertised in the *Oxford University and City Herald* as soon to be published under the arresting title of *The Necessity of Atheism*. Four days later he was directing Edward Graham to advertise it in "eight famous papers" in London. But before Graham could execute his orders they were countermanded, very probably at just about the same time Shelley was reassuring his father.

For nearly two weeks publication was withheld. Then, knowing how Messrs. Munday and Slatter would regard the little volume, Shelley one day took advantage of their absence to strew their shop with copies of the book, instructing the shopman to sell them quickly at sixpence each. In about twenty minutes a fellow of New College, the Reverend John Walker, strolling past the shop, was smitten with the alarming title, *The Necessity of Atheism*. He entered, examined the book, and straightway took counsel with the proprietors. All agreed that the copies should be burned. They were collected then and there, carried into the back kitchen, and burned in the presence of the Reverend Mr. Walker.

The victimized publishers also wrote at once to the printers, warn-

ing them of the danger of prosecution and advising the destruction
of every vestige in their possession — books, manuscript, and type.
They then summoned to their support Councillor Clifford and held
a conference with the author, hoping apparently to persuade him
to destroy the copies still in his possession. All three entreated and
threatened, but "all seemed of no avail — he appeared to glory in
the course he had adopted."

There were in fact more grounds for Shelley's defending the
pamphlet than might be supposed from those who have read it only
by the deceptive title. In its seven pages of text it argued that belief
can come only from three sources: physical experience, reason based
on experience, and the experience of others, or testimony. None of
these, it argued, establishes the existence of a deity, and belief,
which is not subject to the will, is impossible until they do. Hence
the existence of a God is not proved.

The language was temperate and the conclusions were no more
than agnostic. Shelley's desire for the truth (which he maintained in
the document could not be harmful) was probably genuine. Only
two months before in his letters to Hogg he had been advancing
arguments for the existence of a deity. It was only "in the popular
sense of the word 'God,'" as he later wrote to Godwin, that he became an atheist at Oxford. Moreover, to argue on all questions was
his dominant passion. *The Necessity of Atheism* was really concerned
less with Christian theology than with the right to argue, even about
God.

On March 15 Charles Kirkpatrick Sharpe informed Lady Charlotte Campbell that Shelley had come out with "a prose pamphlet in
praise of Atheism." Shelley and Hogg continued mailing their
pamphlet as if nothing had happened or could happen. It was circulated largely among professors, heads of colleges, and bishops.
Even the sister university was not neglected. Dr. James Wood, Lady
Margaret Professor at Cambridge, received a copy which later went
into the library of St. John's College.

Still University College took no action. James Griffith, the Master,
absorbed in his avocation of burnt-wood portraits, may never have
heard of the book-shop incident; but the officious Dean, George
Rowley, must certainly have heard, and it is hard to imagine that
what was considered good enough Oxford gossip for Charles Kirkpatrick Sharpe to pass on to Lady Charlotte Campbell was not
mentioned at the high table of the culprit's own college. Quite probably the incident was known but was expected to blow over, now

that the offending books had been burnt. There was no proof that Shelley was the author, and an expulsion for atheism might cause unfavorable talk about the college.

Perhaps the affair would have blown over if Shelley had not made the mistake of sending a copy of the pamphlet to the Reverend Edward Copleston, Professor of Poetry and Fellow of Oriel. Like all the others it was accompanied by a polite letter in the author's own handwriting signed Jeremiah Stukely and inviting criticism and discussion. So vigorous a personality as Edward Copleston would certainly see that some action was taken. Necessity! — had he not written and published that "To make necessity the standard of what is praiseworthy or honourable is against the uniform judgement of mankind"? Had he not publicly served notice against the *Edinburgh Review's* criticisms that Oxford would tolerate no new discoveries in the field of religion — that "the scheme of Revelation is closed, and we expect no new light to break in upon us"? Who was this new light-bringer? Edward Copleston set out for University College with the pamphlet and the incriminating letter. The peaceful Master of University College was forced into action, and his subsequent uncharacteristic display of temper may have been due in part to this fact.

Immediately after breakfast on March 25, 1811 Shelley was summoned to the college common room. There he found the Master and two or three fellows, the former very short-tempered and peremptory. Producing a copy of *The Necessity of Atheism,* he asked Shelley if he was the author. Bysshe refused to affirm or deny authorship and demanded to know the evidence against him. When the Master insisted and Bysshe again refused to affirm or deny authorship, he was immediately expelled.

The almost inevitable climax had arrived and had taken Bysshe completely and utterly by surprise. He was aggrieved and deeply shocked. He returned to his rooms with the Master's words: "I desire you will quit the College early tomorrow morning at the latest," still ringing in his ears. Jefferson was waiting in Bysshe's room to read with him, and heard the news with astonishment and indignation. "Expelled, expelled!" Shelley kept saying over and over, shaking with emotion. Hogg immediately wrote a note to the Master and fellows, asking them to reconsider. Instead, he was summoned at once and subjected to a similar inquisition. He refused to admit or deny his guilt, but insisted that if Shelley was guilty, he was equally so. He was at once given a sentence of expulsion that was already made out. The official sentence in both cases was "for contumaciously refusing to answer questions proposed to them, and for also repeatedly declining to disavow a publication entitled *The Necessity of Atheism.*"

Oxford and University College felt no regrets. Miss Elizabeth Grant, a niece of the Master of University College who was living with her aunt and uncle at the time, thought of Shelley as an insubordinate ringleader in minor mischiefs, whose departure restored quiet to the college. Mr. C. J. Ridley, a member of the university at the time, believed that no one regretted the expulsion, and spoke of a general distrust of Shelley's strange conduct and opinions. Matthew Rolleston, a fellow of University College, wrote to a friend conveying the news and adding: "For Hogg I am sorry, not for Shelley." Charles Kirkpatrick Sharpe was sarcastically sympathetic and later recorded that Shelley was an altogether strange creature at Oxford, where he was thought insane. Jefferson Hogg's father, seeking inside information through a friend, was informed that both young men had made themselves unpopular by affecting to be different from and superior to their fellows, and that Shelley was suspected of insanity.

The amiable and studious qualities which should have made both young men, if properly understood, a credit to their college were almost completely unrecognized. For this their own singular behavior was perhaps as much to blame as their dull and uncomprehending environment. Both young men, and particularly Shelley, had set out to be singular and had been completely successful.

Before they left they were reported by unsympathetic witnesses to be strutting about the quadrangle behaving like heroes and talking of emigrating to America. Shelley called hurriedly on his Eton friend Halliday. "I am come to say goodbye to you, if you are not afraid to be seen with me." It was also necessary to call upon a Mr. Strong with whom Shelley had been associated in raising subscriptions for Miss Janetta Phillips's volume of poems. But that gentleman, when told that Shelley had just been expelled for atheism, fainted away, and when Shelley brought him to, had only strength to utter: "I pray God, sir, that I may never set eyes on you again."

The next morning, March 26, 1811, with twenty pounds borrowed hurriedly from the brother of Henry Slatter, Shelley and Hogg mounted to the top of the eight-o'clock stage and were soon on their way to London.

Chapter V

WHEN SHELLEY and Hogg arrived in London after their expulsion, they went first to a coffee-house near Piccadilly, whence they sallied forth to take tea with the Grove family in Lincoln's Inn Fields. Hogg thought the Groves seemed rather glum. Shelley was restless and excited long after leaving them. So at four o'clock in the morning Tom Medwin heard an insistent knocking at his door, then Shelley's well-known voice, cracked and high when excited: "Medwin, let me in, I am expelled!" The suddenly awakened Medwin absorbed the news rather slowly; Shelley laughed loudly and half-hysterically and repeated: "I am expelled — for atheism."

After breakfast at their coffee-house Shelley and Hogg set out to look for more congenial lodgings. In this matter Shelley proved obstructively fastidious. Places were rejected because fishmongers or carters could be heard outside, or because of the maid's nose or the mistress's voice. Then in Poland Street, whose very name suggested freedom, they engaged two bedrooms with a sitting-room beautifully papered in a grapevine design. "We must stay here," said Shelley, "stay for ever."

On March 29, four days after the expulsion, Bysshe wrote his father a brief, indignant account of his expulsion, apparently not doubting that his father would also resent such an unjustifiable interference with intellectual freedom. But University College had anticipated him. Two days before Bysshe wrote, Timothy Shelley took the initiative by writing a brief note to Hogg canceling the invitation to spend the Easter vacation at Field Place. This was the opening gun of a long, stiff battle between Shelley and his father, in which Hogg was to prove a more important issue than Oxford University.

The young liberty-lovers of Poland Street continued for a while to live as nearly as possible as they had done at Oxford. In the morning Shelley generally wrote, mostly letters, presumably. They took long walks, read and argued, dined generally at a coffee-house, and returned to have tea under their own brightly colored grapevines. They loved variety. Charles Grove, who was with them almost every day, recollected dining with them at almost every coffee-house in

London. One book, hot from the press, pleased Shelley immensely. It was Byron's *English Bards and Scotch Reviewers.*

Several times Shelley visited his sisters in Miss Fenning's school at Clapham Common. They felt much sympathy for Bysshe and tried to help him with little contributions from their pocket money. In these dealings they sometimes used as an intermediary their friend Harriet Westbrook, an older girl, who lived in London, and who had been acquainted with Bysshe since the Christmas holidays.

There were also occasional teas and dinners with the Grove family. John Grove introduced them to Kensington Gardens, whose quiet shady nooks became a favorite resort with them. He also took them to a bachelor dinner where there was port and much serious conversation on the subject of women. With Charles Grove, a medical student, Shelley attended a course of lectures on anatomy.

If all this was only a little less comfortable than Oxford, there was still an important matter to settle with Field Place. Timothy Shelley was an affectionate, stubborn father whose pride had been wounded. He had already come to regard Bysshe as odd, but he had built great hopes upon him. Considering himself a liberal, he had tacitly admitted Shelley's right to his own convictions, so long as he was prudent about uttering them. He now hated Shelley's opinions, but not so much in themselves as because they were injuring *him.* Mr. Timothy Shelley hurried up to London.

In an interview on March 31 Bysshe declined firmly to accept his father's views of meeting the situation. Six days later, from his London lodgings at Miller's Hotel, Mr. Shelley wrote a letter to his son laying down definite terms. Bysshe was to go at once to Field Place, abstain from correspondence with Hogg, and submit himself to a tutor of Mr. Shelley's choice. Otherwise "I am resolved to withdraw myself from you, and leave you to the punishment and misery that belongs to the wicked pursuit of an opinion so diabolical."

Bysshe remained unimpressed. Under no circumstances would he renounce Hogg. On the same day he answered his father briefly and almost tauntingly; he felt it his duty, he said, "decidedly to refuse my assent to both the proposals in your letter, and to affirm that similar refusals will always be the fate of similar requests." Mr. Shelley had threatened to return to Field Place, leaving Bysshe to his fate, but he lingered for another interview in London, with both boys.

According to Hogg's later account, both boys entered and left this interview in a spirit almost of mockery. Mr. Shelley, it would seem, had swung back once more to the necessity of meeting and confuting Shelley's arguments. He had copied a number of arguments out of Paley's *Evidences of Christianity*, but Shelley listened coldly and said he had heard the arguments before. Mr. Shelley argued incoherently; he scolded, wept, and swore by turns, but the interview ended where it began, and the two young men walked away laughing over his pronunciation of Paley as if it rhymed with Sally.

Mr. Shelley wrote to Hogg's father (who was already acting in the matter); then swearing: "I shall and will be firm," the vacillating, confused, and impulsive father began rather wildly to seek advice and help wherever he could find it. The family legal adviser, Mr. William Whitton, of Bedford Row, was drawn in; likewise a Mr. Hurst, who was a friend and neighbor; a Mr. Clarke, representing Hogg's father; John Grove; and two of Shelley's uncles, Mr. Robert Parker and Captain John Pilfold.

Mr. Whitton, a hard-headed lawyer, counseled firmness. Mr. Clarke communicated to Mr. Hogg Mr. Timothy Shelley's belief that Hogg was the original corrupter of his son's opinions and so caused Shelley to write to Mr. Hogg a letter denouncing his father's beliefs as totally false. The others all undertook direct negotiations with Bysshe, who rejected Mr. Hurst as an intruder, but treated the others with politeness. Their later reports to Mr. Shelley were in substantial agreement: Bysshe really desired a reconciliation but would not accept it at the price of abandoning Hogg or giving up his opinions until fairly persuaded that they were false. Another mediator entered the scene at Mr. Hogg's suggestion — no other than the same Reverend George Stanley Faber, vicar of Stockton-upon-Tees, whom the two young men had for some time been baiting in one of their epistolary adventures. Him they seem promptly to have insulted.

Two weeks of effort had produced no progress, and Mr. Shelley returned to Field Place on April 11. Writing to William Whitton, he placed the matter of "this young Lunatic" in his hands. Mr. Whitton showed his bias at once — and also his opinion of Mr. Shelley's firmness — by writing to old Sir Bysshe in condemnation of Shelley's conduct and hinting that Sir Bysshe would do well to stiffen Mr. Timothy's firmness. As the business was thus falling more and more under Whitton's harsh management, an effort was made by the boy's mother. Intercepting one of Bysshe's letters that would have irritated the father, she sent him the money to come home. But Bysshe returned the money and declined, very possibly out of loyalty to Hogg.

Then Bysshe, on April 12 or 13, unexpectedly offered a joint proposal that had already been approved by Mr. Hogg. They would apologize to Mr. Faber, refrain from expressing atheistical opinions, and separate and return home — Hogg to begin the study of law, and Shelley to select some profession or calling. They insisted only on the right of corresponding with each other. Shelley offered this "with a real and sincere wish for coming to an accommodation." It was all that his father could hope for, since there was no way of preventing a correspondence between the two — but it came too late. Mr. Shelley was too hurt and too stubborn to yield even on a condition he could not enforce. Characterizing Shelley's letter as a presumptuous effort to offer proposals, he turned the whole matter over to Mr. Whitton, with the comment that perhaps "the word of a person of such dreadful opinions could not be taken." In this he was supported by old Sir Bysshe, who also wrote to Whitton that the rebels deserved no terms except unconditional surrender — thus unconsciously administering the *coup de grâce* to his own dream of family grandeur.

Hogg and his father were now in agreement, and Hogg was leaving London on April 16 or 17. Whitton wrote to Shelley inviting him to an interview in which he doubtless expected a capitulation. At the same time Shelley was writing to Whitton with another proposal: he would resign all claim to the portion of Sir Bysshe's property entailed on him and accept an annuity of two hundred pounds.

This innocent (and legally impossible) proposal proved a perfect bombshell. Whitton characterized it as an insult and refused to transmit it; Shelley thereupon wrote Whitton such a haughtily furious letter that Whitton broke off negotiations, explaining to Mr. Shelley that otherwise he might have been compelled to turn Bysshe out of his house. Mr. Timothy Shelley was much more deeply shocked than he had been at the news of Bysshe's expulsion. This was not unnatural, for Bysshe's proposal to renounce the entail completely reversed the situation. *He* was proposing to throw the family overboard, to accept a severing of all formal connections. It is evident from Mr. Timothy Shelley's correspondence that up to this time he had regarded the matter as one that could be settled by parental discipline and threats he never anticipated having to carry out to the end. When the boy himself coolly proposed to throw away all the family hopes that were founded on him, Mr. Shelley realized for the first time something of the full gravity of the situation. He wrote two incoherent letters to Whitton, and himself arrived in London with the second, which he mailed from Miller's Hotel on April 23.

John Grove was the best source of information about Bysshe, so Mr. Shelley called at his home the morning after reaching town. Bysshe happened to be calling at the same time and met his father in the passage. "He looked as black as a thunder-cloud," Bysshe reported to Hogg, "and said, 'Your most humble servant!' I made him a low bow, and wishing him a very good morning — passed on. He is very irate about my proposals."

The Duke of Norfolk now stepped in as a friend of the family, invited Bysshe and his father to one of his dinners, and sought again to interest Bysshe in a political career. But Bysshe wanted no borough-mongering politics; he thought the suggestion an attempt to shackle his mind.

In Hogg's absence Shelley was beginning to feel a little lonely. Still John and Charles Grove were at hand, and there were Gibbons Merle, Edward Graham, and Tom Medwin. He saw the Groves nearly every day, and frequently walked with Medwin in Kensington Gardens, where he delighted in sailing paper boats on the Serpentine. He was reading books from the British Museum and keeping a notebook on his own dreams. He had a touch of fever, and Medwin noticed that his old sleep-walking habits were returning, and that he once wandered into Leicester Square in a fit of somnambulism. At this time also he became acquainted with the radical bookseller Rowland Hunter, and through him with Leigh Hunt. He had a very pleasant breakfast with the Hunts, but the acquaintance came to nothing at this time.

The absence of Hogg was a considerable deprivation. "Certainly this place is a little solitary," Shelley wrote to Hogg, adding that he made the time pass more quickly by going to bed at eight o'clock. But a solace was beginning to appear in the person of Harriet Westbrook, his sisters' friend whom he had met about four months earlier. Hogg had been gone only a day or two when Harriet and her older sister Eliza made Bysshe grateful by calling upon him — so much so that he, the foe of Christianity, took the sacrament with Harriet on the following Sunday and wondered whether it would be any real kindness to enlighten her. When she returned to school (which Shelley called her prison-house) he accompanied her, and visited her there later with her sister. She was, he confided to Hogg, "a most amiable girl"; her sister he thought "really conceited," yet "condescending."

Harriet was indeed a "most amiable girl," whose good sense and manners and frank, pleasant cordiality made friends for her wherever she went. She was sixteen at the time, the most beautiful girl in her school, with a fine pink-and-white complexion, hair described by Hellen Shelley as "like a poet's dream," well-modeled features, and a light, graceful figure. Her father, Mr. John Westbrook, of 23 Chapel Street, Grosvenor Square, was a retired, rather well-to-do tavern-keeper.

Mr. Shelley had returned to Field Place after having promised John Grove to allow Bysshe two hundred pounds a year and his freedom. A day or two later he annulled this agreement and returned to his hope that Bysshe would surrender unconditionally. He was still, for several weeks, extremely shocked and angry at Shelley's wish to resign his inheritance. Shelley, on his part, now wished to return to Field Place, principally to prosecute his design of a union between Hogg and Elizabeth. But Mr. Shelley had become at least partly aware of this design. He set himself against Shelley's return and resolved under any circumstances to remove Elizabeth from his influence.

Letters flew thick and fast between Hogg and Shelley. Philosophy — the old eager search for truth — holds an important place in Shelley's letters at the time, tinged somewhat incongruously with the sheer love of argument. Christianity, he asserted, was an unamiable religion because it insisted on faith as a moral duty, whereas faith can only be free. It might still be best for the ignorant, but the inquiring mind should reject it as odious, "the child of cold prejudice and selfish fear." Tom Medwin, hearing some of the same talk, was convinced that Shelley had now gone most of the way from mild agnosticism to militant atheism. Both Medwin and Hogg later regarded this as an indirect result of his expulsion from Oxford.

The same letters were full of the projected union of Hogg and Elizabeth Shelley. Hogg cherished a romantic despair which Shelley had to combat in the face of his own fear that Elizabeth was lost. "I will not deceive myself; she is lost, lost to everything; Intolerance has tainted her — she talks cant and twaddle." Even Hogg was beginning

59

to talk cant and twaddle by expressing a preference for matrimony over free love. Matrimony, Shelley argued earnestly, might do for the vulgar mass, already hopelessly corrupt, but was beneath men of virtue and honor. "For God's sake, if you want more argument, read the Marriage Service before you *think* of allowing an amiable, beloved female to submit to such degradation."

Meanwhile Harriet Westbrook, back in school at Clapham Common, was being persecuted for her friendship with Bysshe Shelley. She informed him that she was shunned and called an abandoned wretch, but that she accepted this treatment with calm contempt. Soon she was at home again, ill — and her sister Eliza sent for Shelley. Even Bysshe thought there was something a little odd about the grave courtesy with which Harriet's father and sister greeted him. Harriet lay on a couch, pale and suffering, while Eliza talked about love. Then Harriet said she had such a headache she couldn't bear conversation, and Eliza left her alone with Bysshe until twelve thirty. When Harriet was "compelled" to return to school, Bysshe accompanied her to Clapham. Any flitting half-suspicion that he was being managed vanished in the delightful discovery that both Harriet and her sister might make excellent crushers of intolerance. For the next two weeks he spent much of his time in Grosvenor Square, talking with Eliza and steadily improving his opinion of her.

When he returned to Field Place he was committed to a correspondence with both sisters. A letter from Eliza to Shelley urging that their friendship be kept secret from his father actually fell into the hands of Mr. Timothy Shelley. But if that gentleman read Eliza Westbrook's purpose between these lines, he made no comment as he sent the letter on to Whitton. Apparently he was too busy sniffing brimstone to be able to smell a mouse.

Bysshe actually re-entered Field Place via Cuckfield, Captain Pilfold's home, about seven weeks after his expulsion. That sympathetic uncle first had Shelley in his own home and then persuaded Mr. Timothy Shelley into an agreement. On May 15 Bysshe wrote to Hogg from Field Place and announced an agreement by which he was to receive two hundred pounds a year and the right to live where he chose. Rather airily he also informed Edward Graham that he had received two hundred pounds a year, "free agency etc.," adding: "he looks rather blue today but the Capt. keeps him in tol. order." To neither did he mention that he had agreed to enter some profession. He probably failed to realize that the profound uneasiness and distrust that the last three months had generated in his father, together with his own impulsive instability, rendered any agreement only a temporary one. Otherwise he would hardly have begun referring to his father, in letters to Hogg and Graham, as "old Killjoy," nor would he have written a rhymed letter to Graham making a coarse burlesque of a recent scurrilous anonymous letter received by his father accusing Mrs. Shelley of infidelity with Graham.

Bysshe found Elizabeth greatly changed — gay and worldly and practically dead to the cause, though just possibly capable of resuscitation. Mr. Shelley did all he could to keep them apart, but it was perhaps unnecessary, for Elizabeth actually jeered: "You and your mad friend! Those whom I have seen, and who have seen me, make but little excuse for your folly." When she condescended to say more, a few days later, it was to talk pointedly of matrimony and to reject Shelley's scorn of that institution with a scorn of her own: "This, then, is the honourable advice of a brother!" Hogg, too, still cherished the word "matrimony," in spite of the "ineffable, sickening disgust" with which Bysshe regarded "this most despotic, most unrequired fetter which prejudice has forged." All Bysshe could do was to urge a romantic plan by which Hogg was to make a secret visit to Field Place and get a glimpse of Elizabeth from Bysshe's bedroom window.

Life for the returned prodigal was dull and a little bitter. His father was still suspicious, Elizabeth flouted and avoided him, Mary and Hellen were in school at Clapham, and John and Margaret were too young to be enlightened. Even his mother, whom he regarded as at least partly unprejudiced, considered most topics unsafe with him except the weather. Hellen, had she been there, might have made "a divine little scion of infidelity," for had she not taken Harriet's part at school against her oppressors? At it was, he could only read and write.

Janetta Phillips, the Oxford poetess, was afraid to correspond with him. Even Harriet Westbrook was horrified at first by his opinions — but did not discourage argument about them. He wrote several times a week to Hogg and occasionally to the Reverend Mr. Faber, who never seemed to know when he had had enough. He continued, as in London, to write a few poems, which still gave no promise of future greatness. And of course he read. Field Place was far inferior to Oxford and London as providing the kind of books he most wanted. In Captain Pilfold's library he found (or kept) George Ensor's *Na-*

tional Education, which he read with approval. He became quite enthusiastic over the beauties of Miss Sydney Owenson's novel *The Missionary,* which has just been published by Stockdale, and he ordered Scott's latest poem, *The Vision of Don Roderick.*

Some of his time he spent with his genial uncle, Captain Pilfold, at Cuckfield, a short ride from Horsham. The Captain was a bluff, hearty fellow who had fought with distinction under Nelson. Of course Shelley "enlightened" him, and was immensely pleased when at dinner one day the Captain completely disabled a local "red-hot saint" with a broadside from *The Necessity of Atheism.*

It was during one of these stays with Captain Pilfold that Bysshe made the interesting acquaintance of Miss Elizabeth Hitchener, the twenty-nine-year-old mistress of a little school at Hurstpierpoint, near by. She was tall and thin, of a dark complexion, neither handsome nor absolutely homely, imaginative, impulsive, and quick-spirited. Her parentage was somewhat humble, but she enjoyed the esteem of the community and taught the children of some of the local gentry. In politics and religion her views were somewhat too advanced for her community. Bysshe perceived at once that she was an excellent candidate for enlightenment. His glowing arguments against Christianity failed to convince her, but she was at least willing to consider them. A correspondence sprang up immediately, and Bysshe sent her several books. In his letters he told her that he was now fully convinced that no personal God existed. Christian theology was insulting and intolerant, and Christianity was the great foe of genuine virtue. Elizabeth, ten years his senior, dropped easily and naturally into the position of respectful disciple. But she was still not ready to proclaim herself anti-Christian, chiefly because she might wound others by doing so, and because she felt that Christian literature strengthened her virtuous impulses.

Meanwhile Shelley was stirred to scorn and indignation by an incident which was receiving considerable condemnation from liberals and radicals all over England. The Prince Regent on June 19 gave an extravagant fête at Carleton House. In a letter to Miss Hitchener Shelley compared it with the corrupt luxury of Imperial Rome. He wrote, or planned to write, an ode, to be set to music by Edward Graham, satirizing the royal family. Either this poem or another — a poem of some fifty lines which he showed to Charles Grove — he actually printed and carried up to London. Here, according to Charles Grove, "he amused himself with throwing copies into the carriages of persons going to Carleton House after the fête."

Field Place, however, could never again be the happy little kingdom it had once been. Its atmosphere now was one of continued
boredom and frustration. Everyone was doubtful, or suspicious, or
afraid of him. "I am a perfect hermit: not a being to speak with!" he
wrote to Hogg:

> I sometimes exchange a word with my mother on the subject
> of the weather, upon which she is irresistibly eloquent; other-
> wise all is deep silence! I wander about this place, walking all
> over the grounds, with no particular object in view. I cannot
> write, except now and then to you — sometimes to Miss West-
> brooks. . . . My hand begins to hurry, and I am tired and en-
> nuied.

From his first week at home Bysshe had been planning to execute
a reunion with Hogg that had been decided upon when Hogg left
London. He had received two invitations, one of which could be used
as a cover for this design. Thomas Grove and his wife had invited
him to visit them at their home, Cwm Elan, in Radnorshire, and Mr.
Westbrook had invited him to accompany him and his family to their
house in Aberystwith, Wales. Mr. Timothy Shelley approved the first
invitation and was doubtless kept ignorant of the second. Bysshe's intention was to visit the Westbrooks a week in London and then join
Hogg at York instead of going to Wales. He did stop in London for
several days, but his father got wind of the design to visit Hogg and
informed him that no money would be forthcoming if he did. Somewhat unwillingly Shelley then proceeded to Cwm Elan, where he
arrived on July 14 or 15.

Thomas Grove's ten-thousand-acre estate was five miles southeast
of Rhayader, the nearest post office, in Radnorshire, South Wales.
Thirteen years before Shelley arrived, another poet, William Lisle
Bowles, had spent part of a summer there as the guest of Mr. William Grove, and had celebrated its wild beauty in one of the best
of his blank-verse poems, written on the spot. With feeling the Wiltshire parson described the deep, narrow glen through which the Elan
descends to join the Wye, the wild confusion of slate and limestone
crags, the waterfall, the thick woods of oak and ash, the green pas-
tures, and light blue smoke ascending from a quiet cottage.

Shelley noticed these natural beauties readily enough. "Here are
rocks, cataracts, woods, and Groves," was his first somewhat un-
awed impression. He wrote to Hogg that the scenery was divine —

and he was bored. Probably he was also pained by thoughts of Harriet Grove. For Harriet had been here before him; in the happiest spring of his life, during those long moonlight walks in which they had felt the quiet beauty of the Sussex countryside, she had filled him with the desire to see these wilder scenes — so proper, Shelley still thought, for Gothic-novel settings. That was little more than a year ago, and meanwhile Harriet Grove had been completely alienated from him; she could no longer correspond with him, and by October expected to be married to the "clod of earth" to whom she had become engaged.

It certainly never occurred to Shelley as possible that *he* would be married to another before Harriet Grove's marriage — though Hogg was evidently beginning to read the signs. Shelley set him straight:

> Your jokes on Harriet Westbrook amuse me: it is a common error for people to fancy others in their own situation, but if I know anything about love, I am *not* in love. I have heard from the Westbrooks, both of whom I highly esteem.

Cwm Elan did no more than Field Place to assuage Shelley's restlessness and boredom. "All very dull, stale, flat, and unprofitable," he complained to Hogg; "indeed, this place is a very great bore." "I am now with people who, strange to say, never *think*," he told Miss Hitchener; "I have however much more of my own society than of theirs." Almost every letter to Hogg reiterated his complaint: "I am all solitude, as I cannot call the society here an alternative of it." "I do not see a soul; all is gloomy and desolate. I amuse myself, however, with reading Darwin, climbing rocks, and exploring this scenery. Amusement!" Occasionally he rode to Rhayader with Mrs. Grove or, on Sunday, went to church, where the service was partly in Welsh and a christening was performed "out of an old broken slop-basin." Erasmus Darwin's combination of science with poetry impressed him quite sufficiently to leave its marks on *Queen Mab* (1813) and on his later poetry. He also re-read *The Missionary* and read the newspapers. He still planned to slip away and rejoin Hogg in York under the name of Peyton. But caution was necessary, for his father was alert. Also, until his finances were a little recruited — he had recently paid some bills — he *had* to remain at Cwm Elan.

Occasionally there were letters from his mother, Elizabeth, and probably Captain Pilfold and Edward Graham; more frequently he heard from Hogg, Harriet Westbrook, and Elizabeth Hitchener.

With Miss Hitchener the discussion had swerved, apparently at her desire, from religion to politics, and Shelley became eloquent on the subject of Equality. Hogg had actually visited Sussex, slipped into Warnham Church incognito, and obtained a glimpse of Elizabeth. He was now more in love than ever. Shelley continued to forward to Hogg all of Elizabeth's letters to himself, but he no longer had any hopes of a match and sought earnestly both to abolish Hogg's despondency and to persuade him that he was not genuinely in love. To J. J. Stockdale, who had been pressing him for the debt still due on *St. Irvyne*, Shelley imparted the news of further literary labors: "I am at present engaged in completing a series of moral and metaphysical essays — perhaps their copyright would be accepted in lieu of part of my debt?"

So far as may be inferred from Shelley's letters to Hogg, Harriet Westbrook occupied a place in his thoughts distinctly subordinate to his desire to rejoin Hogg and even to his waning hopes of rescuing his sister Elizabeth for Hogg from the "machinations of worldly interests." He mentioned Harriet a number of times, and still intended to visit the Westbrooks at Aberystwith, but he seemed genuinely amused at Hogg's jokes on the subject. No doubt his anti-matrimonial arguments contributed to his sense of security. All of Hogg's arguments in favor of matrimony had failed to convince him. If Hogg's jokes caused him to think again, he must have reflected that the Westbrook sisters were also perfectly acquainted with his anti-matrimonial views.

Nevertheless, he should have seen plainly that matters were becoming quite serious with Harriet. She wrote more and more often, and in an increasingly desperate and despondent mood, which he was becoming more and more interested to combat. Having been persecuted at school on Shelley's account, she was determined not to return, but her father insisted. He turned a deaf ear to Shelley's arguments on her behalf, and Shelley encouraged her to continue her resistance. She said she was totally useless and might commit suicide, that her family was unjust to her, and that it was sheer misery to continue "living where she could *love* no one."

In the midst of this correspondence Harriet sent Bysshe a novel and "earnestly" desired his opinion of it. Hogg had previously mentioned the same book, and Shelley now informed Hogg that he would read it that very night. The book was Amelia Opie's *Adelina Mow-*

bray, or the Mother and Daughter (1804). It was a very strange book indeed to crop up purely by accident just when it did. Harriet could never have read it without being strongly reminded of Shelley, nor could her older sister have read it – and known Shelley – without perceiving how strongly his immediate conduct toward Harriet might be affected by it. It would have been impossible for Shelley to have thrown the book aside after once starting to read it.

Glenmurray, the hero of *Adelina Mowbray*, was a very idealistic, high-minded young author of good family and moderate means who had become odious to the orthodox on account of his publications. His books had formed the social and moral opinions of Adelina, before she knew the author. She too was a very high-minded person, who fully shared his views on the evils of matrimony, but not on religion. When they met at Bath and fell in love, she was quite willing to unite her fortunes with his in a pure and constant free-love union. To protect her against the persecution of society, he was willing to flout his principles by a marriage, but she would not allow him to do so, as long as they both believed in the justice of the principles. Persecuted by a stepfather who was in love with her, and harshly treated by her mother, she was soon forced to flee abroad with Glenmurray. Up to this point the book described a situation that was almost literally identical with that of Shelley and Harriet. The remaining two thirds of the book emphasized the disastrous consequences of unmarried love until both Glenmurray and Adelina recorded their convictions that it is condemned by its results.

It would be a matter of great interest to know what comment Shelley made to Harriet on this story. All we know is that Harriet, persecuted at home, soon threw herself like Adelina on the protection of the man who had led her in persecution's way; and that Shelley for the first time expressed doubt of his anti-matrimonialism. Afterwards, though clinging to his general views, he twice justified his own marriage because of the disproportionate sacrifice entailed upon the unmarried wife. This was exactly the conclusion Glenmurray reached in *Adelina Mowbray*.

Before and after Harriet sent Shelley this book, her letters were consciously or unconsciously placing her in the position of its heroine. Shelley, who had before sought to duplicate life from books and was to do so later – the same Shelley who had just been laughing at the idea that he was in love – placed himself immediately in the role of Glenmurray. Within two weeks or less after receipt of the book he astonished Hogg with the following undated letter:

My dear Friend,

You will perhaps see me before you can answer this; perhaps not; Heaven knows! I shall certainly come to York, but *Harriet Westbrook* will decide whether now or in three weeks. Her father has persecuted her in a most horrible way, by endeavouring to compel her to go to school. She asked my advice; resistance was the answer, at the same time that I essayed to mollify old W[estbrook] in vain! And in consequence of my advice *she* has thrown herself upon *my* protection!

I set off for London on Monday. How flattering a distinction! — I am thinking of ten million things at once.

What have I said? I declare, quite *ludicrous*. I advised her to resist. She wrote to say that resistance was useless, but that she would fly with me, and threw herself on my protection. We shall have £ 200 a year: when we find it run short, we must live, I suppose, upon love! Gratitude and admiration all demand that I should love her *for ever*. We shall see you at York. I will hear your arguments for matrimonialism, by which I am now almost convinced. I can get lodgings at York, I suppose. Direct to me at Graham's, 18 Sackville Street, Piccadilly.

Whether the sending of *Adelina Mowbray* was the suggestion of a mature woman who had observed that Shelley's conduct was unusually influenced by books and whose actions for some time previous suggest matrimonial designs, or whether it was the independent idea of a schoolgirl desperately in love, who can say? At any rate it seems difficult to accept as pure coincidence. Charles Clairmont, who was told later the details leading up to Shelley's elopement with Harriet, described them as "so very peculiar as could never have happened to any but one of so very strange a turn of mind as himself."

Shelley hastened immediately to London, moneyless as he was, except for ten pounds just received from Hogg. He did not stay at Graham's lodgings in Sackville Street, where he had told Hogg to address him, but went direct to the Groves', at Lincoln's Inn Fields. Only Charles Grove, to whom Shelley had written from Cwm Elan of his "summons to link his fate with another," was taken into his confidence.

Shelley found Harriet very much depressed:

I was shocked at observing the alteration of her looks. Little did I divine its cause; she had become violently attached to *me*, and feared that I should not return her attachment . . . prejudice made the confession painful. It was impossible to avoid being much affected, I promised to unite my fate with hers. I staid in London several days, during which she recovered her spirits.

In the midst of the events themselves, there was the necessity of giving Hogg some account of them. From his two letters to Hogg we learn that Shelley considered Hogg's friendship his paramount interest; that he was giving Harriet's situation his whole time and thought; and that he still remained in London, "embarrassed and melancholy." Hogg had disapproved Shelley's intention, and Shelley assured him twice that he now accepted his arguments on the question of matrimony (which were the same as Mrs. Opie's in *Adelina Mowbray*). It would appear that Harriet, like Adelina Mowbray, had scruples about allowing him to sacrifice his principles and required argument. But Shelley was now "a perfect convert to matrimony." He was certainly not in love, in the full sense of the word, though his letters and conduct rather suggest that he was nearer being in love than he realized. Sympathy and chivalry, at war with an intellectual conviction, must have had several victories and defeats before the final decision was made.

But after a few days he made a trip to Field Place for the purpose of securing funds for an elopement. Hogg's ten pounds were probably exhausted, and a mail-coach trip to Edinburgh for two would cost about thirty guineas in fares and tips, with expenses after arrival still to be provided for. He applied to his uncle Thomas Charles Medwin, keeping him in ignorance of his purpose, and received a loan of twenty-five pounds. He expected his quarterly allowance of fifty pounds in a short time, probably on September 1, and he expected, vainly as it turned out, to borrow again from his uncle Thomas Medwin. These sums, if realized, would have been ample for his immediate needs.

These activities had not gone unnoticed by the poet's suspicious father. Returning from Field Place, Shelley had airily informed Hogg that Mr. Timothy Shelley also was in London "wondering, possibly, at my London business. He will be more surprised soon, possibly!" Shelley himself would have been surprised had he known that his father was investigating rumors that had reached him about Shelley and Harriet. He instructed Whitton to call on Mr. Grove (apparently John) and find out exactly what was happening. Whitton thought the matter very serious. However, since Mr. Grove was out of town, the inquiry had to be delayed until it was too late.

When he returned from Field Place, Shelley found Harriet still in a state of painful indecision. There were many meetings with Harriet, to some of which Charles Grove accompanied his friend. Finally the decision was reached; they would elope to Edinburgh. From a coffee-house in Mount Street, near Harriet's house, Shelley wrote a note appointing an hour at which he would have a coach waiting for her there. On the next day, August 25, Shelley and Charles appeared early at the coffee-house and ordered breakfast. They were far ahead of the appointed time, and as they waited Shelley threw oyster shells across the street and remarked nervously: "Grove, this is a *Shelley* business!" Soon Harriet appeared; they entered the coach. The Edinburgh mail coach did not leave until seven or eight in the evening, and for a whole day they all waited within the Bull and Mouth Tavern, sheltered behind its grotesque plaster sign of a gigantic open mouth holding a bull. Nevertheless Shelley was seen and recognized by a Mr. Dunn, an acquaintance of the family, who lent him ten pounds under the impression that he was arriving from Wales and continuing to Field Place.

Ahead for the fugitives lay two hundred miles of tiresome travel, a night and a day on the Great North Road, with little to break the monotony except stops in noisy inn-yards for meals or for a change of horses before they reached York, about midnight. During a pause at York Shelley wrote a note to Hogg, asking him to send ten pounds to Edinburgh at once. Leaving this note at the inn to be delivered next morning, they were off again, through Northallerton, Durham, with its memories of feudal warriors, and Newcastle-upon-Tyne, with its ugly reminders of modern industry. Near Durham Shelley posted a note to his father asking that his personal property be sent to Charles Grove – and saying nothing about Harriet.

The entrance to Edinburgh was through mean, narrow streets. The travelers had passed two nights in a mail coach, had suffered more than fifty hours of jolting, and were almost without money. Nevertheless, when Hogg found them a few days later – having been on the point of going somewhere on vacation when Shelley's note reached him, and deciding at once for Edinburgh – they were bright and happy. On the long journey Shelley had struck up a conversation with a young Scotch advocate who had explained how they might marry. A certificate was issued on August 28, and they were married either on that day or the next.

Meanwhile Mr. Timothy Shelley had received his son's letter

posted en route. He immediately hurried up to London and learned from Whitton that Bysshe could not be disinherited. Together with Whitton he had a long talk with Mr. Westbrook and Eliza. Next day there was a further conference, Eliza being absent and John Grove and Mr. Westbrook's solicitor present. Whether any common course of action was agreed upon is uncertain, but for himself Mr. Timothy Shelley resolved to stop his son's allowance and pay no attention to his letters. Mr. Westbrook seems also to have resolved to make no financial provision for his daughter, at least for the present.

Chapter VI

SHELLEY AND HARRIET took a comfortable ground-floor suite of rooms at 60 George Street, where Hogg joined them a few days later, taking an upstairs bedroom. Their landlord, a hostler named William Cumming, had listened sympathetically to Bysshe's story of present financial stringency and future expectations and had agreed to wait for his money. Hogg's advent was of little help financially, for he had only the funds that had been intended for his own vacation, and his father declined to send him any more when he learned through Mr. Timothy Shelley that the two young men were once more together.

Even Hogg, who cherished comfort, found the living arrangements quite pleasant. The food was abundant and excellent, particularly the shortbread — Hogg's preference — and the honey — which Shelley devoured almost gluttonously. The maid-of-all-work, named Christie, furnished considerable entertainment by her distracted dartings to and fro in response to frequent calls for the tea-"kittle," and by her naïve answers to questions. Discovering that her voice grated harshly on Shelley's supersensitive ears, Hogg and Harriet practiced quizzing her at length for his special benefit, until in real or pretended agony he would beg Harriet to send her out.

There was naturally a great deal of the long, ardent talk that had formerly been part of the joy of Oxford and of Poland Street, discussions in which Harriet's part, though unequal, was both interested and zestful. Bysshe frequently brought in whole armfuls of books secured from some library: modern French philosophy, novels, and some of the works of Buffon. In the mornings Bysshe worked on a translation of one of Buffon's treatises, while Harriet translated her favorite novel of the moment, Madame Cottin's *Claire d'Albe*.

Harriet, it turned out, was also a great reader, with a taste for works of a high ethical tone. Hogg doubted if he had ever met a girl who read so much, or who so enjoyed reading aloud. With her pleasant voice and unusually distinct utterance, she read aloud incessantly, almost mercilessly. Agreeable as it was, Hogg was sometimes tempted to nod, but dared not. The bridegroom, more secure, occasionally nodded openly, and was fiercely stigmatized as an inattentive wretch. Hogg admired her, "always pretty, always bright, always blooming; smart; usually plain in her neatness; without a spot, with-

71

out a wrinkle, not a hair out of its place." When Shelley was away, Hogg would have preferred conversation, for without realizing it, he was already becoming dangerously attracted to her. But always when Shelley left, Harriet began reading aloud.

Edinburgh, the "Athens of the North" and one of the handsomest cities of Europe, thrilled the young adventurers very little. Its recent associations with Hume, Burns, and Campbell, its present associations with Walter Scott and the great *Edinburgh Review*, appear to have evoked little enthusiasm. Harriet alone showed an interest in its historic scenes and insisted on an early excursion to Holyrood, after which she and Hogg climbed Arthur's Seat for the view, while Shelley returned home to write letters. Shelley's dominant feeling was one of scorn for the "filth and commerce of Edinburgh"; he felt himself "chained" there through lack of funds, and longed with a vast impatience to be gone.

The daily routine was simple, and as much as possible like that of the Oxford and Poland Street days: study and correspondence in the morning, walking in the afternoon, tea at dusk. Occasionally they went forth into Princes Street in the evening to gaze at the famous comet, from which the eyes of the poet wandered to the other starry systems with a speculative, imaginative delight. More often their evenings were spent indoors, the hours gliding smoothly toward bedtime as Harriet read aloud to them.

Sundays were then, as now, the longest days in Edinburgh. Shelley was once reproved by a grave citizen for laughing on the streets on the Sabbath. He felt terribly depressed by the relentless rigor of the Sunday services that he attended with Hogg. In no very reverent spirit he and Hogg accompanied the maid Christie to the Catechist and heard the dread question propounded: "Wha's the de'il?" Shelley burst into a wild laugh and rushed madly out of doors.

Shelley gave much of his time to a great mysterious correspondence about which his companions learned little. Three of these letters, to his father, are all that are now known. In the first of these, as in his letter written en route, he made no mention of Harriet, nor did Hogg mention her in his early letters from Edinburgh. After waiting for two weeks and learning in the meantime that his father knew all about the elopement and was deeply offended, Shelley wrote again to repeat his request for money and to deprecate his father's anger. His soothing admonitions, however, were slightly flavored with a very incautious sarcasm.

72

Hearing nothing in reply to this, Shelley waited almost another fortnight and then wrote once more, taking the precaution of having Hogg address the letter, lest his father send it on to Whitton unopened. Marriage, he asserted, was not a crime, and his secrecy, though possibly annoying, had been necessary. He then proceeded to lecture his father at length on the Christian duty of forgiveness:

> What! will you not forgive? How then can your boasted professions of Christianity appear to the world, since if you forgive not you can be no Christian — do not rather these hypocritical assumptions of the Christian character lower you in real virtue beneath the *libertine* atheist . . . ?

The letter concludes with a respectful request for the overdue quarterly allowance of fifty pounds. All three letters show an effort to avoid the appearance of disrespect while still cherishing its substance. What should have been the main purpose — to secure a desperately needed fifty pounds — Shelley jeopardized by a reckless desire to display technical skill in argument, to laugh in his sleeve at Christianity, and to convict his father of hypocrisy. His letters were far better calculated to win the approbation of Hogg than of Mr. Timothy Shelley. In a Gothic novel or an abstract epistolary warfare they would have served, but not in a personal crisis. In fact, they suggest that the author hardly saw his own predicament as an actual situation.

Mr. Timothy Shelley, however, was no romantic. He had already warned Hogg's father that Shelley was traveling north with a "young female" and might join Hogg at York, and he had duly apprised Mr. Hogg of the reunion at Edinburgh. Knowing that Mr. Westbrook would furnish the fugitives with no money and that Hogg's funds were sufficient only for himself, he made no answer to his son's letters. But he could not maintain even this position with dignity. The shock of Bysshe's flight, the painful interviews with the Westbrooks, and the unsatisfactory nature of his son's letters had thrown him into a state of anxiety and emotional distraction in which he talked loosely to friends and neighbors about his family misfortunes.

Had it not been for Captain Pilfold the culprits might have been starved into absolute surrender, or, more probably, into acts of reckless desperation. The genial Captain wrote frequent cheerful and lively letters and supported the garrison with cash. Somehow, after five weeks in Edinburgh the party felt rich enough to leave. They were off to York, to carry out the plan agreed upon before Harriet had entered into their schemes — a year at York together while Hogg finished his legal training there, and then London "for ever." The return to York was a leisurely three days' jaunt through mud and mist, while Harriet sought with indifferent success to spread cheerfulness by reading one of Holcroft's novels aloud.

Through York's crooked little streets in the mist and the dim twilight they sought lodgings, which were eventually found at No. 20 Coney Street. Hogg resumed his work in a conveyancer's office and was thereafter unavailable to his friends from nine to five, though he spent most of his evenings with them. The lodgings were dingy, and the beauties of York impressed Shelley very little. To him they were merely so many thousands of hours of human labor, misapplied to perpetuate human abuses.

Bysshe — or Percy, as Harriet preferred to call him — immediately resumed his effort to reach an agreement with his father. In answer to a letter of October 5 his father sent Percy's books, papers, and clothes to York, without comment. A week later a second appeal, somewhat chastened, but not altogether respectful, brought no reply, nor did a letter next day to old Sir Bysshe. With nerves already strained by his father's policy of aloofness, Shelley now heard of the letters in which Mr. Timothy Shelley had warned Hogg's father against him. From his point of view a cold, heartless silence on the part of his father was now aggravated by treacherous, stealthy persecution. Throwing all caution and tact to the winds, he wrote his father a furious letter accusing him of libel, treachery, persecution, and cowardice, ending:

> I shall take the first opportunity of seeing you; if *you* will not hear my name, *I* will pronounce it. Think not I am an insect whom injuries destroy . . . had I money enough I would meet you in London and hollow in your ears Bysshe, Bysshe, Bysshe . . . aye, Bysshe till you're deaf.

Meanwhile Shelley had reopened his correspondence with Elizabeth Hitchener. After a silence of about six weeks he wrote to her (probably Ocober 8) to announce his marriage and to justify it against the anticipated criticism that it violated his principles. He hoped that Elizabeth could pay him and Harriet a visit or even live with them, now that Harriet's presence would remove any notion of impropriety in their friendship.

74

The cordiality of Elizabeth's answer, contrasting with his father's hostile attitude, precipitated one of the most remarkable letters Shelley ever wrote. To this physically unattractive country school-teacher ten years his senior, whom he had known less than five months and with whom his previous relations had been almost impersonal, Shelley now expressed the most ardent devotion. She was the sister of his soul and was to share equally with his mother and sisters and Hogg (the brother of his soul) in any property he was to inherit. She was dearer to him than any of his blood kindred, being bound by a stronger tie than the mere accident of family relationship. This relationship he boldly called love, but he made it quite plain that to his mind it was a sexless love:

> Henceforth will I be yours — yours with truth sincerity and unreserve. Not a thought shall arise which shall not seek its responsion in your bosom, not a motive of action shall be unenwafted by your cooler reason . . . and, [by] so doing, do I not choose a criterion more infallible than my own consciousness of right and wrong . . . ? . . . I love you more than any relation, I profess you are the sister of my soul, its dearest sister, and I think the component parts of that soul must undergo complete dissolution before its sympathies can perish. . . .

Leaving Harriet in Hogg's care, Shelley set out for Sussex, very possibly on the same coach that carried the so radically different letters he had just written to his father and to the sister of his soul. After three days and nights on the outside of a coach he reached Cuckfield on Friday morning, October 18. His father refused to talk with him and referred him to Mr. Whitton in London, who in turn requested that Shelley deal with him by letter rather than seek a personal interview. Mr. Shelley even snubbed Captain Pilfold for entertaining Shelley at Cuckfield. Percy managed to see old Sir Bysshe, but only to be told that he must learn to be dutiful and obedient before his family could receive him.

Shelley was now violently angry with his mother, over a very different matter. He believed that she was promoting a match between his once perfect sister Elizabeth and Edward Graham, now scornfully referred to as "the music master Graham." Percy went to Field Place and raised such a scene that his mother and Elizabeth were very much frightened and even his father thought of hiring a bodyguard. He wrote his mother a violent abusive letter and to both

Elizabeth Hitchener and Charles Grove he condemned her "base conduct." His family never saw Shelley's furious letter to his mother, because Whitton withheld it, but they were nevertheless convinced that he was mad — not definitely and totally, but still dangerously so when under the stress of excitement. Within the next two weeks Mr. Timothy Shelley's letters to Whitton three times referred to Bysshe's "perturbed," "disordered," and "untoward" mind, which would "not stop at any abuse of his parents" and which might be worked up "to such a Pitch as to do mischief to himself or some others."

The visit to Sussex had left matters worse than they had been before. Shelley had talked with his uncle, Thomas Medwin, about the legality of his Scotch marriage and had made arrangements for a marriage settlement of seven hundred pounds a year on Harriet whenever the money became available. He had received some comfort from Captain Pilfold, who accompanied him to London in spite of Mr. Shelley's disapproval, and he had had an evening's conversation with Elizabeth Hitchener at the Captain's house. He had got nothing from either his father or Captain Pilfold and he had come to regard his mother almost as an enemy. After a tiresome and dispirited journey he was back in York by October 26. One of his first actions on arriving was to write a letter to his father complaining of the continued withholding of his allowance and boldly accusing him of several libels. He also wrote Whitton such a furious letter about his "impudence" that Whitton characterized it to Sir Bysshe as "the most scurrilous letter that a mad viper could dictate."

Shelley had intended bringing Eliza Westbrook with him from London to York, but he found Eliza at York ahead of him. He soon learned the probable reason. Harriet had summoned Eliza as a protection against Shelley's best friend, Thomas Jefferson Hogg, as much the brother of his soul as Elizabeth Hitchener was its sister! Hogg had fallen in love with Harriet in Edinburgh and had declared his love at York even before Shelley's journey south. Harriet had repulsed him and kept silence, hoping to hear no more of it. As soon as Shelley was gone he had renewed his suit, beseeching her with arguments some of which must have seemed dangerously similar to those she had heard Shelley approve. But Harriet only read aloud a little more insistently from what Hogg sneeringly called "staid and instructive books" and talked placidly of what Percy might be doing at the moment and of what a fine person her

76

sister Eliza was, who would be coming soon. Hogg still pressed his arguments, which she withstood with a fortitude that Shelley frankly marveled at when he heard the story later. Not only that, she turned upon him in the earnestness and strength of her bourgeois morality and convinced him of the utter unworthiness of his conduct. He proposed to confess to Shelley in a letter, but this Harriet forbade, fearing the effect on Shelley's nerves.

Whether or not Harriet told this story to Eliza on her appearance is uncertain, but there is nothing uncertain about the immediate dislike Hogg took to Eliza. In his later account (which of course suppresses his own misconduct) he mercilessly ridiculed both Harriet's subservience to Eliza and Eliza's solicitude for Harriet's "nerves." Harriet still wished to keep her story from Percy, but felt obliged to drop a number of vague hints that Hogg was unworthy of his friendship. Unwillingly, in response to his insistence, she finally came out with the full story.

Shelley was deeply shocked. He immediately sought out Hogg and took him for a long walk in the fields. Pale and remorseful, Hogg confessed everything. Whatever resentment Shelley may have felt at the insult and distress to Harriet was dwarfed by his profound disillusion in Hogg. He who had been "but little below perfection" was now revealed in all his baseness as "a mistaken man — vilely, dreadfully mistaken." Scorning as he did the conventional views of marriage and monogamy, Shelley did not find it so hard to pardon Hogg as might be expected; to Elizabeth Hitchener, his sole confidante at the time, he wrote:

> I told him that I pardoned him freely, fully, completely pardoned, that not the least anger against him possessed me. His vices and not himself were the objects of my horror and my hatred. I told him I yet ardently panted for his *real* welfare. . . . I engaged him to promise to write to me. You can conjecture that my letters to him will be neither infrequent nor short.

As soon as they could arrange to do so, Shelley, Harriet, and Eliza Westbrook left York, keeping Hogg ignorant of the time of their intended departure. One evening about November 1 or 2 Hogg turned up at their lodgings and found merely a note of farewell. Harriet and Eliza wished to go to the Lakes; Shelley, with no preferences of his own, listlessly agreed. To deceive Hogg, in case he should follow them, they pretended to be going to Richmond. After some days of weary traveling they arrived at Keswick, probably on November 5 or 6. Here they took lodgings temporarily with Mr. Daniel Crosthwaite, a portrait painter, at Town Head. A week later they were settled in a cottage known as Chestnut Hill Cottage.

For a month after the flight from York the mails were laden with agonized, partly incoherent letters between the two young men, whose ruptured friendship was the greatest agony that either of them had ever been called upon to endure. In his first letter Shelley wrote with a reasonable control of his own feelings. He assured Hogg that he deceived himself either by false reasoning or by real passions which obscured true reasoning — and in either event the result was "disgusting and horrid." He still doubted the genuineness of Hogg's professed conversion. Except for a promise to write again next day, it would almost appear that this letter was intended to be final.

Hogg's reply was evidently an impassioned one. He was suffering exquisite and undeserved misery; he protested how much he had "loved" and "adored" — apparently both Shelley and Harriet. Shelley answered that Hogg's love had really been only for himself, and that he was as wretched as Hogg, and undeservedly so. Growing suddenly impassioned, he argued earnestly with Hogg to desert his weakness, master himself, and become again the "superior being," the "best, the noblest of men," whom he had formerly known and loved. Acknowledging that he was "half-mad" and was writing wildly, he declined in one breath to see Hogg again until further convinced of his recovery; then invited him to "come . . . dearest, best-beloved of friends . . . share my fortunes, enter into my schemes." Changing swiftly once more, he hinted that their reunion might come only after death. "Oh how I have loved you. I was even ashamed to tell you how! and now to leave you *for ever*. . . . no not for ever."

Hogg's letters were no less emotional. Having failed to convince Shelley that he had mastered his passion, he argued that he could rejoin the Shelleys and control his love — while at the same time he was writing such fervid letters to Harriet that she was indignant and Shelley was more than ever convinced that only a separation for some time could meet the situation. Hogg even mentioned a duel — which Shelley ignored — and suicide — which Shelley pointed out had no value as argument.

Shelley based his position not on his views of matrimony, which remained the same, but on his duty to Harriet. He claimed to be totally free of a prejudice for exclusive cohabitation; it would not

78

disquiet him in the least to share Harriet's love with a friend. It was not a question of Harriet's love or Harriet's person, but of her "prejudice." She did not share his views on free love, and her whole happiness depended on his support of her views. So senseless seemed the world's opinions in such matters, and yet so binding upon him because Harriet shared them, that he hinted that he too thought of suicide.

While Shelley was thus conducting the most distracting correspondence of his whole life, he was also settling himself and his family in a new environment. Chestnut Hill Cottage, where they remained for the rest of their stay in Keswick, was comfortable and inexpensive. It stood on a hilltop a mile out of Keswick and commanded an excellent view of two lakes, Derwentwater and Bassenthwaite. All around were the cloud-capped mountains, not so wild as those to which Shelley had given only perfunctory admiration in Wales, but perhaps as beautiful. As the distress of his separation from Hogg began gradually to fade into the background of his thoughts, Shelley's letters to Elizabeth Hitchener show an increasing sensitiveness to the beauty and majesty of the region. On November 23 he wrote:

> These gigantic mountains piled on each other, these water-falls, these million-shaped clouds tinted by the varying colours of innumcrable rainbows hanging between yourself and a lake as smooth and dark as a plain of polished jet — oh, these are sights attunable to the contemplation. . . .

Again, on December 11:

> Oh how you will delight in this scenery! These mountains are now capped with snow, the lake, as I see it hence, is glassy and calm. Snow-vapours, tinted by the loveliest colours of refraction, pass far below the summits of these giant rocks. The scene, even in a winter sunset, is unexpressibly lovely. The clouds assume shapes which seem peculiar to these regions. What will it be in summer?

In contrast with the stimulating natural environment, Shelley found the people disappointing — humanity seemed debased by commerce even in rural Keswick:

> In fact, my friend, at this Keswick, though the face of the country is lovely, the *people* are detestable. The manufacturers with

79

their contamination have crept into the peaceful vale, and deformed the loveliness of Nature with human taint. The debauched servants of the great families who resort contribute to the total extinction of morality.

Harriet's continued worship of her sister as "more than Mother," to whom she owed everything, was still only a potential danger. Shelley regarded Eliza complacently enough as a prospective convert, a rather superior woman, prejudiced, but amiable, and definitely progressing in enlightenment. The usual reading aloud and the usual walking abroad continued, including sometimes a visit to the local museum of natural history or a stroll past the house to which the great Southey was expected soon to return. Shelley undertook to induct Harriet into his own pleasure in boating and on one such occasion incurred or barely escaped an accident.

Once it seemed as if they might have to seek new lodgings. Their landlord, Mr. Gideon Dare, appeared one day in late November to ask them to move elsewhere. "The country," he informed Shelley, "talks very strangely of your proceedings. Odd things have been seen at night near your dwelling." Mr. Dare was with some difficulty satisfied by Shelley's explanation that the "odd things" were really some experiments with hydrogen gas with which he had been entertaining Harriet and Eliza.

During most of their stay at Keswick the Shelleys were in an even worse state of finances than when they left York. Negotiations with the family stood at a stalemate. On November 26 Shelley wrote to his uncle Thomas Medwin to inquire if there was no possible way of raising money on his expectations; four days later he admitted desperately that he was now desirous of raising money even at the ruinous rate of seventy per cent. A small sum sent grudgingly by Mr. Westbrook would soon be exhausted, and they would lack the actual necessities of life.

But aid was already near at hand. The Duke of Norfolk, at the time of Shelley's flying visit from York, had become interested and had spoken to both Mr. Shelley and Mr. Whitton. He had hoped to see Shelley also, but had missed him. Hearing of this, Shelley had written him to express appreciation of his interest and to ask him to endeavor to influence Mr. Shelley toward a more tolerant attitude. Soon afterwards, on November 7, the Duke of Norfolk wrote to both Percy and his father, telling the former he would interfere, though with little hope of success, and asking the latter to discuss the matter with him at Horsham on the 10th. Then, on November 23, having conferred with Mr. Shelley, he wrote to invite Bysshe, Harriet, and Eliza to Greystoke, his northern seat, where he had recently taken up residence.

Shelley's little party was down almost to the last guinea when this invitation arrived, so that it was perhaps fortunate that Greystoke was only some eighteen miles distant, at Penrith. On December 1, in a storm of snow and sleet, Shelley, Harriet, and Eliza reached Greystoke and were made kindly welcome by the Duke, who was entertaining several other guests at the same time, including James Brougham, brother of the *Edinburgh Review* editor, and William Calvert, brother of Wordsworth's deceased friend, Raisley Calvert. William Calvert, a good friend of the Duke, lived at Windybrow, near Keswick. Almost certainly he had already been told of the Duke's friendly interest in Shelley. During the eight or nine days of the visit a friendship began which was to make Shelley's further stay in the region considerably more enjoyable.

His Grace also proved himself an able and successful mediator in the Shelley family troubles. Twice during the visit he wrote to Mr. Timothy Shelley, nor did he conceal from Percy his opinion that Mr. Shelley's grievances were to some extent just. He prevailed upon Percy to write his father a letter expressing genuine regret at the sorrow he had caused. Percy's letter, dated December 13, is in a dignified, earnest tone entirely free of the half-concealed jeers and mockery he had previously allowed himself. "Accept my apologies," he wrote, "for the uneasiness which I have occasioned; believe that my wish to repair any uneasiness is firm and sincere." He still insisted, however, but with becoming tact and deference, on his freedom of opinion.

To this letter his father replied somewhat stiffly that he was glad the Duke of Norfolk had convinced Bysshe that he had acted erroneously toward his parents. He could never admit into his family the principles that had caused Shelley's expulsion from Oxford, but he trusted everything would "in due time and proper Probation be brought to an excellent work." This seemed encouraging to Shelley. He wrote on December 23 to express his pleasure, and to inform his father that Mr. Westbrook was now allowing Harriet two hundred pounds a year. His own principles, he said, had not changed; he expressed them "with coolness and moderation" upon occasion, but he hoped his father would not object to his way of thinking. By January 26 Shelley's allowance of two hundred pounds had been restored. Perhaps Timothy Shelley was somewhat shamed by Mr. Westbrook's conduct, for he remarked ungraciously that he provided the money to prevent Bysshe's cheating strangers.

Shelley was now sure of an income, but he was also sure that he had hitherto been estimating his father's attitude much too lightly. For the first time he realized clearly that Field Place was definitely closed to him as long as he held the opinions that he knew he would never abandon. His father would take no chances of having the other children corrupted. Shelley wrote secretly to Hellen, begging her not to believe all she was told about him, but to continue to love him, and always — *always* — to think for herself. The letter was intercepted, but Hellen's later reminiscences show that at least her memories of her brother were affectionate.

After returning to Keswick the Shelleys saw a good deal of the Calverts, at Windybrow. Mr. William Calvert was both a liberal in politics and an amateur of the physical sciences, the owner of an electrical machine, a water-clock, and an instrument for measuring altitudes by triangulation. Between the Calverts, the Wordsworths, and the Southeys existed a close and friendly intimacy.

Shelley had long wished to meet Southey; it thrilled him even to contemplate Southey's house. He would certainly have introduced himself soon after reaching Keswick had he not been informed that Southey was out of town. Shortly after the middle of December Shelley met Southey at Windybrow and received at once a practical proof of his personal kindliness: Southey procured the reduction of his rent from two and a half guineas weekly, with linen provided, to one guinea, with linen provided by Southey.

A friendship sprang up at once. In spite of different opinions about the Irish, Catholic emancipation, and Parliamentary reform, Percy discovered that Southey was "great and worthy," "an advocate of liberty and equality" (but in the future), a professing Christian who was in reality a deist (a discovery not to be made from Southey's letters and publications of the period), "a man of virtue," a stubborn, inferior reasoner, but a great poet. He was somewhat impressed by Southey's belief that a revolution was inevitable; he even discovered that Southey's notion of Deity was quite similar to his own. "He says I ought not to call myself an atheist, since in reality I believe that the universe is God. I tell him I believe that God is another signification for the Universe. I then explain. . . . Southey admits and believes this." In politics and ethics they differed amicably over the place of expedience, Southey holding that it ought to be the ground for politics, but not morals, Shelley arguing that politics should be considered merely an extension of morals, an idea which he emphatically reasserted eight years later in the third chapter of his *Philosophical View of Reform*. On such occasions Southey generally concluded by assuring Shelley — who could see no logic whatever in the assertion — that "when you are as old as I am you will think with me." So ardent an idealist and so acute a reasoner as Shelley could not fail to perceive the strain of opportunism in Southey's views.

Although it was necessary for Southey to write systematically and incessantly, he gave Shelley generously of his time and lent him books from his excellent library. He tried to interest Shelley in Berkeley, but Shelley was as yet too much a disciple of Locke. It speaks well for Southey's kindly and genial interest in his young friend that Shelley at first judged Southey as leniently as possible and phrased his judgment with the sensitive sympathy he usually reserved for only those with whom he felt himself entirely *en rapport:*

> I am not sure that Southey is *quite* uninfluenced by venality.
> He is disinterested, so far as respects his family; but I question
> if he is so, as far as respects the world. His writings solely sup-
> port a numerous family. His sweet children are such amiable
> creatures that I almost forgive what I suspect.

The young radical affected Southey like his own ghost; he was "just what I was in 1794." Southey was pleased at Shelley's pleasure in meeting a man who, in his own too confident phrase, "perfectly" understood him and did him "full justice." To his friends Grosvenor C. Bedford and John Rickman, Southey wrote fully and enthusiastically about Shelley. Through Rickman he hoped indirectly to influence Mr. Timothy Shelley in his son's behalf. He even became in this letter the first prophet of Shelley's greatness. "Unless I am greatly deceived," Southey pronounced, "there is every reason to believe he will become an honour to his name and his country."

Relations between the Southeys and Shelleys continued personally cordial as long as the Shelleys remained in Keswick. Shelley, however, was becoming more and more convinced that Southey was merely a time-serving deserter from the only cause that mattered. To Elizabeth Hitchener he expressed himself with some feeling:

> I do not think so highly of Southey as I did. It is to be confessed
> that to see him in his family, to behold him in his domestic circle,

he appears in a most amiable light — I do not mean that he is or can be the great character which once I linked him to. His mind is terribly narrow, compared to it.

A fortnight later (January 20) his feelings were even more decided: "He has *lost* my good opinion. . . . I can only exclaim with Boling-broke, 'Poor human nature!' . . . Southey's conversation has lost its charm; except it be the charm of horror at so hateful a prostitution of talents."

To the several sharp personal disillusionments he had experienced in the last year — Harriet Grove, Elizabeth Shelley, Hogg — was thus added his first disillusion in a public character whom he had once regarded as a champion of virtue. Experience was beginning slowly to modify his views of human nature.

Even as he turned from Southey, Shelley was turning toward William Godwin, the philosopher of *Political Justice,* who since the stirring days of the 1790's had passed almost into obscurity. Shelley had admired him ever since leaving Eton, but had thought him no longer alive. Learning now that Godwin was living in London and conducting a modest publishing business in Skinner Street, Shelley wrote him a letter on January 3, 1812. Thus he began a long correspondence to last throughout life, and thus, unconsciously, he laid the foundation for a later series of events that was to alter the whole course of his life.

Shelley described himself to Godwin as an ardent young philanthropist who was the victim of persecution. He had long admired and reverenced the name of Godwin, he said, and now that he knew Godwin to be actually a living man he wished ardently to share the benefits of his intellect on a more intimate footing. Godwin was interested and wrote at once (January 6) to ask for more information about his proposed new disciple, to which Shelley replied promptly (January 10) with an autobiographical sketch and new professions of devotion. "To you, as the regulator and former of my mind, I must ever look with real respect and veneration."

On two points Godwin's reply to this letter must have rather surprised his young admirer. He expressed some doubts as to the wisdom of embarking on a campaign of radical action and publication too early in life. He also showed himself doubtful about Shelley's attitude toward his father. This, from the man who had taught him his scornful view of parental authority, must have been a mild shock

even to Shelley's adoration. Nevertheless, Godwin was genuinely
interested. He promised his help and friendship. The calm, passionless estimate of Shelley that was slowly forming in Godwin's mind
is implicit in this letter; he waited until he had received four letters
and then delivered his Olympian verdict with characteristic insensitive coldness:

> I have read all your letters (the first perhaps excepted) with
> peculiar interest, and I wish it to be understood by you un-
> equivocally that, as far as I can yet penetrate into your char-
> acter, I conceive it to exhibit an extraordinary assemblage of
> lovely qualities not without considerable defects. The defects
> do, and always have arisen chiefly from this source, that you are
> still very young, and that in certain essential respects you do not
> sufficiently perceive that you are so.

Coming from a supposedly purer fountain, this rather shrewd analysis did not irk Shelley as Southey's similar remarks had done.

Shelley immediately proceeded to amplify his previous effort at
self-analysis and to explain himself on the points that had aroused
Godwin's uneasiness. He was *not* angry with his father; on the contrary he had always desired a reconciliation if it could be obtained
without injury to the independence of his opinions. His father may
have *acted* for his welfare, but he had certainly not *felt* for it. "I
never loved my father — it was not from hardness of heart, for I
have loved and do love warmly." Godwin's implied fear that Shelley
was inculcating his beliefs too soon and too promiscuously elicited
the remark that between affectation and self-distrust there was a
genuine modesty which he hoped he did not overstep in advancing
his opinions. "I will not again crudely obtrude the question of
atheism on the world." He believed that he could at the same time
improve his own powers and "diffuse true and virtuous principles"
without being too forward or presumptuous. Above all, he was deeply
grateful that the man whose teachings had inspired him when those
of all other tutors and advisers filled him with disgust should now be
his friend and counselor. "That William Godwin should have a
'deep and earnest interest in *my* welfare' cannot but produce the
most intoxicating sensations."

There can be no doubting the genuineness of this intoxication; it
overflowed into his next letter to Elizabeth Hitchener. He quoted a
part of one of Godwin's letters and promised to send her the others:

Godwin has answered my letters, and he is now my *friend;* he shall be yours — share with me this acquisition, more valuable than the gifts of Princes. His letters are like his writings, the mirror of a firm and elevated mind. They are the result of the experience of ages, which he condenses for my instruction. It is with awe and veneration that I read the letters of this veteran in persecution and independence. He remains unchanged. I have no soul chilling alteration to record of his character. . . .

Shelley's stay at Keswick was far from being a simple round of afternoon walks, occasional social calls, and letter writing. The studies which he had transferred from Oxford to London and later to Edinburgh continued, mainly in the mornings and evenings. He was quite conscious of expanding intellectual powers. As he studied he sought to express these growing powers in prose and verse. Harriet feared that he was working too hard for his health and also that he might be writing himself into prison. From December 11, 1811 until the beginning of February he was engaged on no less than five literary projects, all but one of which were completed, or nearly completed, by the latter date.

The first of these projects he mentioned to Miss Hitchener only to say that he was laying it aside as not suited to the present temper of his mind. It was a poem to picture first "the manners, simplicity, and delights of a perfect state of society, tho' still earthly," to be followed by a picture of heaven — and Elizabeth Hitchener's aid would be necessary to make it all that it should be. The idea in whole or part is not unprophetic of the latter part of *Queen Mab* and of the spiritual paradise described first in *The Revolt of Islam* and most fully and triumphantly in *Prometheus Unbound.* Another project first mentioned along with the abandoned poem was a collection of his early verse. By January 2 it was presumably ready for the press and Shelley was looking for a printer. Since "the poor cannot understand and w[oul]d not buy my poems" Shelley proposed to print them "expensively" and use the anticipated proceeds to help finance his more popular radical productions. This volume he never published, but some of its contents later became known.

Shelley was still writing the "moral and metaphysical essays" he had offered to Stockdale on August 1. By January 2 he had written about a hundred and fifty pages. Since these essays were metaphysical and not likely to prove popular, he intended to print them "expensively," like the poems. What happened to them later is unknown.

Still another work that has been lost was the novel *Hubert Cauvin*, designed to "exhibit the cause of morals and opinions in France during the latter years of its monarchy." It was to deal with some of the leading passions, but would pointedly exclude sex. About two hundred pages had been written when Shelley first mentioned it to Miss Hitchener, on January 2. He expected to finish it early in February.

Except for a few scraps in his letters, and several poems reprinted by Professor Dowden, the only one of Shelley's literary undertakings at Keswick that has been published is his *Address to the Irish People*. It is the only one that he mentioned to Godwin, who disapproved of juvenile literary efforts. When he mentioned it first to Miss Hitchener on January 20 it was already sufficiently advanced for him to describe and quote from it. His design was to print it on rough, cheap paper so that it could be posted up on vacant walls, as Tom Paine's writings had been. The work would seem to have been practically completed at Keswick.

Under the sunshine of Elizabeth Hitchener's approval, "ideas, millions of ideas," crowded into Shelley's consciousness. His expression of a few of them to her furnishes the best available evidence of the state and growth of Shelley's mind during the period of their correspondence. There is a definite, increasing vein of hostility to soldiers and commerce, leading straight toward the denunciatory passages in *Queen Mab* in 1813. Shelley continued his attack on Christianity as immoral, incredible, and oppressive. "You seem to doubt Christianity," he wrote to the still hesitant Elizabeth on January 2. "I do not: I cannot conceive . . . even the possibility of its genuineness." His views of marriage were but slightly altered by his own experience. He still thought it "an evil — an evil of immense and extensive magnitude," "monopolizing, exclusive, jealous" — but an evil so ingrained in human nature by custom that the remedy would be difficult.

The changes that a few months had brought about in Shelley's relationships with Hogg, Miss Hitchener, and Harriet prompted several interesting comments on friendship and love, chiefly in relation to each other. Ordinary love, like marriage, Shelley characterized as selfish; it was inferior to friendship in that the essence of the latter was unselfish sympathy.

Consistent with what has previously been made evident about Shelley's youthful anticipation of some of the most characteristic ideas and expressions of his maturity, these letters contain some very suggestive passages. Thus, in a letter to Hogg (June 16, 1811) Shelley writes: "Perhaps the flowers think like this [i.e., that there is a future life]; perhaps they moralize upon their state, have their attachments, their pursuits of virtue; adore, despond, hope, despise. Alas! then do we, like them, perish; or do they, likewise, live forever?" Here obviously, is a reflection of recent reading in Erasmus Darwin's *Loves of the Plants*, and possibly of a similar passage in George Ensor — but, looking to the future, here also is the basic imagery of "The Sensitive Plant" (1820). A letter of June 20, 1811, when Shelley was reading and admiring Miss Owenson's *The Missionary*, contains the skeleton idea of *Alastor* (1816), which also owes other details to that novel. The idea of a golden age to be brought about by "the eventual omnipotence of mind over matter," which is a central idea of *Prometheus Unbound* (1819), occurs in a letter written to Elizabeth Hitchener on October 18, 1811. Similarly in a letter of October 15 or 16, 1811 the *Queen Mab* note on Necessity is clearly anticipated; the phrasing of the opening lines of *Queen Mab* and of "To Death" is suggested by a sentence in a letter of November 8, 1811 to Hogg, and the phrase "soul of my soul," employed in a letter of January 10, 1812 to Godwin, is only turned into Greek — *Epipsychidion* — nine years later to form the title of a poem containing some sentiments very similar to those expressed in 1811 to Elizabeth Hitchener.

Individually it would be easy to overstress the importance of any one of these, and similar, parallels, but collectively they indicate clearly enough that much of Shelley's most mature works grew slowly from seeds evident in his correspondence when he was a mere youth. Oddly enough, however, the fine musical and imaginative quality of Shelley's mature poety is by no means predictable from the mediocre poems he was enclosing with the same letters that contained so many prophetic ideas and phrases. The letters demonstrate a remarkable intellectual acuteness, and a real power of clear expression in prose, but not in poetry.

In the midst of these "millions of ideas" Shelley experienced, about the middle of January, a queer adventure that was also to be repeated, with variations, in later years. At this time he was suffering from nervous attacks severe enough to cause him to resort to laudanum for relief. Only a day before he recovered from one of these attacks he was the victim of a physical assault, either real or imaginary. At about seven o'clock on the evening of Sunday, January 19, Shelley stepped outside the door of their cottage to investigate an unusual noise. He was immediately knocked senseless by an unseen assailant. Fortunately he fell inside the cottage and the assailant was afraid to proceed with his supposed design of robbery. Mr. Dare, a near neighbor, was attracted by the commotion, snatched up a gun or pistol, and rushed upon the scene, whereupon the assailant or assailants fled into the night. There had recently been a number of robberies in Keswick, but the general impression among the neighbors was that Shelley had suffered an illusion rather than an attack.

By this time an idea that had been slowly developing in Shelley's mind since early December reached the point of definite decision. Even at Oxford he had become a champion of the oppressed Irishman Peter Finnerty, and soon thereafter he was reading the works of another Irishman, George Ensor, whose books on reform show an interest in Ireland's woes even when the general subject is English. The Irish question was one on which Shelley argued with Southey. As long as money was lacking, there was nothing to do but write and talk — and he was already writing an *Address to the Irish People*, which he hoped to take to Dublin and publish there. By January 20 Shelley's plans were definitely settled; he was "eager and earnest" to be gone; he viewed the state of Ireland as "a great crisis in opinions" where a young crusader could render the best service, particularly if aided, as he hoped and expected, by such a noble fellow laborer as Elizabeth Hitchener. Now, on January 26, his allowance of £200 was restored; there was another £200 allowance from Mr. Westbrook; Captain Pilfold promised £50; another £100 might be borrowed from the Duke of Norfolk; and the essays and poems recently written should swell the total.

The date of departure from Keswick was set for February 3. Godwin was uneasy about the project, but was assured that Shelley's *Address* could not "excite rebellion" or "widen the breach between the kingdoms." Elizabeth Hitchener declined a pressing invitation to join the party at once and betrayed some uneasiness for Shelley's safety. Shelley himself toyed with the idea that he might "go to prison" or meet "noblest success or the most glorious martyrdom," but ended by assuring her that Harriet and Eliza were not frightened, and that he proposed to be very careful and stay within the law's protection.

"We have but a certain time alloted us in which to do its [life's] business," he wrote. "How much does it become us to improve and multiply this time; and to regard every hour neglected, misspent, or unimproved, as so much lost to the cause of virtue, liberty, and happiness."

After three weeks of mounting enthusiasm Shelley, Harriet, and Eliza sailed from Whitehaven on the night of February 3, 1812. The last week in Keswick had been spent with the Calverts — a week of vile, stormy weather which was rendered less depressing by the cordial hospitality of Mrs. Calvert. Shelley found slight encouragement for his undertaking. The Calverts were all violently opposed except Mrs. Calvert, who heartily wished them success. Southey was sorry to see them go. But Shelley, keyed for action against wrongs that Southey's conduct encouraged, "passed Southey's house without *one* sting." In the letter he wrote to Elizabeth Hitchener while waiting for the tide at Whitehaven, he recorded his doubt even of Southey's private character, "stained and false as is his public one."

In the short space of five months Shelley had eloped with a girl he did not really love, married her against his own anti-matrimonial principles, acted with such mad frenzy at Field Place that his whole family were terrified of him, and separated from a friend he virtually adored to protect in the exercise of a "prejudice" a wife he was only beginning to love. At the same time he was experiencing his first disillusion with one "great man" and becoming the professed disciple of another. Such a series of occurrences would have seemed incredible in the wild novels of his boyhood reading, but in life they are fully verified facts.

The most significant of these recent occurrences, from the point of view of understanding Shelley's peculiar character, is the amazing flowering of his friendship with Elizabeth Hitchener following immediately upon the rupture with Hogg.

During the whole of the residence at Keswick, and in fact until the following autumn, Elizabeth Hitchener occupied the same high pedestal on which Shelley suddenly placed her shortly after his arrival at York. To others, even Godwin, he wrote with some restraint. Nothing of this sort could apply to Elizabeth, whom he called the "sister of *my soul*," "the friend of my heart," "my second self," even (in words anticipating his later doctrine of intellectual beauty) "the stronger shadow of that soul whose dictates I have been accustomed to obey." From her he proposed to conceal nothing; he would "pour out" his "whole soul" to her. Often he urged her to visit in his home, either temporarily or "for ever." He continually assured her of the high value of her friendship to his personal happiness and of her intellect and character to the great cause of truth and justice. The defection of Hogg, which he described as "indeed dreadful," so "terrible, dismaying" that his reason "almost withered"; the sickening discovery that Southey, once a great voice for freedom, had sold himself to the oppressors, seemed to him as trivial as "gnat-bites" against his confidence in Elizabeth and hers in him.

Shelley regarded Elizabeth as "one of those beings who carry happiness, reform, liberty, wherever they go." "Your pen . . . ought to trace characters for a nation's perusal." "That tongue of energy, and that eye of fire, would awe them [the Irish Tories] into native insignificance." "I perceive in you the embryon of a mighty intellect which may one day enlighten thousands." She whom he regarded as in many respects a superior was to be a necessary partner in his poems and essays. On these points the inferiority of the sixteen-year-old Harriet to the thirty-year-old Elizabeth was true and was tacitly acknowledged by all the parties — though Shelley's letters to Elizabeth show a growing respect for Harriet on this plane, as well as a growing love on the plane that "my dear Harriet" best understood.

Harriet loyally accepted Miss Hitchener at Shelley's estimate and welcomed her with cordial, admiring, little-sisterly letters. To her there seemed no difficulty in regarding Elizabeth as a coadjutor on a different plane rather than as a competitor for her husband's affections. Even Eliza Westbrook allowed herself to be referred to in Harriet's letters as Elizabeth's admirer.

Nor is Shelley's estimate of Elizabeth, exaggerated as it was by his peculiar psychological necessities, as absurd as it later appeared, even to Shelley. The suggestion that she was exploiting him from the first cannot survive any fair examination of their correspondence; it was Elizabeth, more than Shelley, who conferred financial benefits and suffered financial loss. She was undoubtedly a woman of more than commonplace intellectual strength. The woman she is sometimes described as being would not study and discuss Locke as intelligently as she did, nor would she suggest or inquire about Xenophanes or recommend Parkinson's three-volume *Organic Remains of a Former World*. Merely to stimulate and understand the philosophic and metaphysical discussion with which Shelley's letters to her are loaded demands more intelligence than many of their subsequent readers have suspected.

Never again in his relations with other individuals was Shelley to let himself go so utterly as in the letters to Elizabeth Hitchener. As the pressure of later events forced him more and more into a realization that complete companionship is possible only within one's own thoughts, the same ardor found expression in more generalized form in such poems as *Prometheus Unbound* and *Epipsychidion.*

Chapter VII

THE "STATE OF IRELAND" which Shelley so confidently hoped to amel-
iorate may be summarized in the Johnsonian phrase: "complicated
misery." A country of something less than five million inhabitants
was hopelessly divided in race, creed, and economic interests. The
Anglican Irish, scarcely more than a million, constituted the Protestant Ascendancy, owned nine tenths of the land, and completely
dominated all branches of the government. The Presbyterian Irish —
about half a million people in the north — were economically more
prosperous than the Catholic Irish, but were under similar civil disabilities. This should have been an incentive to unite with the Irish
Catholics, except that it was counterbalanced by a strong religious
antagonism. More than three million Irish Catholics lived miserably
under a system of absentee-landlordism and rack-rent middlemen,
their local and national affairs, their scant educational opportunities,
and their social and economic life completely dominated by the
Protestant Ascendancy.

Though the Irish had a Parliament of their own until 1800, it was
composed entirely of Protestants and was utterly servile to the English interests as expressed by the Lord Lieutenant, except when these
interests failed to coincide with the vested privileges of the Protestant Ascendancy. The considerable alleviation of conditions achieved
in the late eighteenth century had been largely wiped out in the
aftermath of the Rebellion of 1798. This rebellion, born of Ireland's
despair and the hopes held out by the French Revolution, had been
suppressed by a non-Catholic militia, with an ill-disciplined ferocity
that completely sickened such professional soldiers as Lord Corn-
wallis. It had been followed by torture and deportations, martial law,
and the suspension of the Habeas Corpus Act.

The Act of Union with England had been achieved by Pitt in 1800
at the cost of wholesale promises and bribery, including a promise
to lighten Catholic disabilities. In 1812, Irish Catholics were still
petitioning and waiting for this promise to be redeemed. Pitt had
made one or two efforts, perhaps not sufficiently determined, and
had been frustrated by the opposition of George III. When Catholics
began organizing committees all over Ireland, the authorities of
Dublin Castle revived the Convention Act of 1793, which declared un-

lawful all bodies appointed by delegation or having any representative character. Another persecution was begun, but the Catholic petitions continued, only to be decisively rejected by the English Parliament. On the 28th of February an aggregate meeting of the friends of Catholic emancipation was to be held in the historic old Fishamble Street Theatre, to be addressed by one of the principal veterans of their cause, Daniel O'Connell.

Shelley, Harriet, and Eliza Westbrook reached Dublin on the night of February 12, after a stormy passage involving considerable discomfort and delay. They took lodgings at 7 Sackville Street, near the beginning of the street at Carlisle Bridge, spanning the Liffey. A short distance across the bridge Shelley could see the walls and grounds of Trinity College. To the west of Trinity College stood the fine building that had housed the Parliament until Ireland ceased to have one; it was now the National Bank, which Shelley called a Temple of Mammon. Perhaps a half-mile to the east of this building rose the dirty red-brick walls of Dublin Castle, from which Ireland was governed by the Lord Lieutenant and the "Castle Junto" of place-men. At the western edge of the city were the extensive quarters of the military. Elsewhere and all around sprawled the ramshackle dwellings in which lived most of Dublin's population of nearly 200,000, often ten or twelve to the house.

Shelley's equipment for his new mission was not extraordinary. Catholic emancipation was an issue with which he had long been familiar in the conversation of his father and of the Duke of Norfolk, one of its leading protagonists in England. Doubtless he had read some of the discussion in such journals and reviews as the *Examiner,* the *Edinburgh Annual Register,* and the *Edinburgh Review.* He had only recently read the speeches of John Philpot Curran, who had brilliantly defended the Irish rebels of '98 and had more recently defended Peter Finnerty. Shelley brought with him from Godwin a letter of introduction to Curran, and the complete or nearly complete manuscript of his own *Address to the Irish People.*

If he lacked special knowledge, however, Shelley certainly did not lack zeal. The day after his arrival he sought to present his letter to Curran, but Curran was not at home. He immediately set about the publication of his *Address to the Irish People.* While this was going through the press, and afterwards, his optimistic hopes overflowed in letters to Elizabeth Hitchener. At the same time he conducted with Godwin a more reasoned, dispassionate correspondence, better suited to the philosophic calm of *Political Justice*. Harriet shared his enthusiasm completely. Even Eliza Westbrook caught the fever. Between completing a red cloak and acting as custodian of the family finances ("in some hole or corner of her dress") she found time for culling extracts from Tom Paine to be used in a later attack on religious intolerance. At the same time Shelley was thinking of another volume to be composed of moral and ethical extracts from the New Testament.

"My 'Address,'" he immediately informed Elizabeth, "will soon come out. It will be instantly followed by another, with downright proposals for instituting associations for bettering the condition of human-kind. I — even I, weak, young, poor, as I am — will attempt to organize them, the society of peace and love. Oh! that I [may] be a successful apostle of this only true religion, the religion of Philanthropy." "At all events," he added as a rather astonishing climax, "I *will* have a Debating Society, and see what will grow out of that."

Elizabeth Hitchener's letters furnished a whole-hearted, almost ecstatic support of Shelley's mission, Godwin's only an apprehensive skepticism. Since *Political Justice* in twenty years had done little to change England, the philosopher saw small hope of his young friend's changing Ireland in less than two months. He distrusted Shelley's youthful tendency to rush into print. The pervading principle of *Political Justice*, he reminded Shelley, was that little progress and much mischief were to be expected from reform "associations"; Shelley's course might easily encourage violence, in spite of his desire to avoid it. "Shelley," he warned,

> you are preparing a scene of blood! If your associations take
> effect to any extensive degree, tremendous consequences will
> follow, and hundreds, by their calamities and premature fate,
> will expiate your error. . . . Do not be restrained by a false
> shame from retracting your steps. . . .
> I wish to my heart you would come immediately to London.

Shelley's *Address to the Irish People* came from the press on February 24 and was duly advertised in the Dublin *Evening Post*. Copies were sent immediately to Mr. Timothy Shelley, to Godwin, and probably to the leading Irish patriots. Shelley's principal means of publication, however, was through his rather unprepossessing Irish servant, Daniel Hill (or Healey). Within two days he had distributed four hundred of his fifteen hundred copies, sixty of them to public houses. Every day his servant distributed them to "multitudes" of people, sometimes with the embarrassing misinformation that the author was only fifteen years old. Both Shelley and Harriet took a hand. Standing on the balcony of their Sackville Street lodgings, they would watch until someone came along who "looked likely" and throw him a pamphlet; or they would walk the streets and give copies to passers-by. It was deadly serious business to Percy, but Harriet's complete sympathy with the cause did not preclude some amusement at the means adopted for forwarding it: "For myself, I am ready to die of laughter when it is done, and Percy looks so grave, yesterday he put one into a woman's hood of a cloak. She knew nothing of it, and we passed her. I could hardly get on, my muscles were so irritated." By March 18 most of the copies had been distributed.

On March 2 appeared another address to the Irish, Shelley's eighteen-page octavo pamphlet entitled *Proposals for an Association of those Philanthropists, who Convinced of the Inadequacy of the Moral and Political State of Ireland to Produce Benefits which are Nevertheless Attainable are Willing to Unite to Accomplish its Regeneration.* Though intended for a better class of readers, the *Proposals* merely repeat the substance of the *Address,* with a more detailed account of the proposed association and with less of the repetition that marks the more popular document.

Both pamphlets fully justify Shelley's claims in his letters to Miss Hitchener and Godwin that the government could find nothing in them on which to base a prosecution. While making it clear that he considered Ireland deeply wronged by the Act of Union and the withholding of Catholic emancipation, Shelley repeatedly asserted that violence on the part of the Irish would only ruin their cause. Mobs and secret societies, he insisted, led directly to the methods of the oppressor and tended to justify them. The only remedy was virtue, to be attained through sobriety, moderation, and wisdom. To the force of virtue, and to that only, all government must succumb as soon as virtue prevailed among the governed, for the absence of virtue was government's only excuse for existence. He assured his readers that Catholic emancipation was sure of achievement within the near future, and that the abolition of the Union, which was even more to be desired, would certainly be achieved eventually.

He warned Irish patriots that when they achieved their aims they would probably be disappointed. Poverty, vice, and oppression would not thereby be abolished any more than they were in England already. Ireland should be regarded as the starting-point of a movement that should *truly* emancipate the human spirit, not only in Ireland, but elsewhere — a movement that could be grounded only in wisdom and virtue and that would take longer than one generation to reach its goal.

As a means of hastening the desired conclusion, Shelley proposed associations of philanthropists who by constant activity and discussion should ascertain and forward the ends of true virtue. Such associations, if they forswore secrecy and violence, could accomplish much, for was not discussion the main avenue to truth? Of course the associations would be opposed by the priesthood, the aristocracy, and the government. Though they would not be contrary to the English Constitution, that fact would not necessarily ensure them against danger from the government. No one, therefore, should join who was not willing to undergo persecution, if necessary, for the sake of humanity.

Incidental to his argument for the usefulness of such associations as he proposed, Shelley boldly faced the two greatest discouragements that liberals and radicals had to meet — the comparative failure of the French Revolution, and the inferences commonly drawn from the new Malthusian theory of population. He asserted that if the French Revolution had conduced to war, vice, and misery it was only because the doctrines of philanthropy and freedom were but shallowly understood. Voltaire had been a flatterer of kings, Rousseau an encourager of dangerous passions. Helvetius and Condorcet had drawn unsystematic conclusions which were not well understood by a people driven to revolution before they were morally and spiritually fitted for it. A philosopher like Godwin, and associations for the non-violent opposition of tyranny, such as those now proposed, might well have turned the French Revolution into a complete success. Eight years later, in his *Philosophical View of Reform,* Shelley's criticism of the French Revolution was essentially the same.

The Malthusian theory of the pressure of population, which was everywhere being used by the privileged classes to justify a complacent attitude of *laissez faire,* seemed to Shelley no argument against an attempt to achieve a greater measure of happiness: "War, vice, and misery are undeniably bad, they embrace all that we can conceive of temporal and eternal evil. Are we to be told that these are remedyless, because the earth would, in case of their remedy, be overstocked?" Scorning such moral cowardice, he presented the same analogy which was to be used so brilliantly seven years later in his "Ode to the West Wind":

What opinion should we form of that man who, when he walked in the freshness of the spring, beheld the fields enamelled with flowers, and the foliage bursting from the buds, should find fault with this beautiful order, and murmur his contemptible discontents because winter must come, and the landscape be robbed of its beauty for a while again? Yet this man is Mr. Malthus. Do we not see that the laws of nature perpetually act by disorganization and reproduction, each alternately becoming cause and effect?

Considered together, the two pamphlets show a great deal of penetrating political philosophy combined with a naïve ignorance of political tactics. Shelley was right in predicting the inevitability of Catholic emancipation and the abolition of the Union; he was right (at least for a hundred years to come) in sensing the temper of the age as progressively liberal. In insisting upon the ultimate obedience of government to opinion, and the inevitable dependence of all true emancipation on a denial of violence and special privilege and a cultivation of wisdom through patience, tolerance, temperance, and free discussion, he was announcing a creed from which he varied little to the end of his life, a creed that today is considered rather more liberal than radical. Later he gave this same creed undying expression in the last lines of *Prometheus Unbound*.

And yet Godwin was probably justified in fearing that Shelley's associations, if formed, would lead to bloodshed. Shelley was assuming a membership of Godwins and Shelleys, rather than Irishmen. Irishmen had already advocated assassination as the only remedy and were to advocate it again in later years. Moreover, Irishmen were faced with an immediate emergency; they had little patience with Shelley's assertion that this was trifling in comparison with the intellectual emancipation of their descendants. To Catholics and Protestants alike he insisted on the cruelty and intolerance of their creeds in the past, and practically admitted that he was a deist. He preached temperance to a people to whom drink was almost the only refuge from reality, and the cultivation of knowledge to a people who were tragically without the means of cultivating it. The great majority of them were unable even to read his exhortation.

The long-advertised great meeting of the friends of Catholic emancipation took place at the historic old Fishamble Street Theatre on February 28, four days after the appearance of Shelley's *Address*

98

and two days before that of his *Proposals*. Lord Fingal presided, and the principal address was made by Daniel O'Connell, one of the most distinguished patriotic orators of the day. When a resolution was proposed thanking the Protestant friends of Irish emancipation, young Shelley rose, introduced himself as a sympathetic Englishman devoted to the Irish cause, and addressed the audience for more than an hour. Earnestly, but in a style somewhat odd and jerky, he condemned English misgovernment, endorsed Catholic emancipation and repeal of the Union, and deprecated political and religious intolerance.

The reception of these unexpected remarks was mixed. The Irish Catholic nobility and gentry who controlled the meeting were no dispassionate rationalistic philosophers. They greeted with hisses Shelley's guarded remarks on religious intolerance. But they applauded his partisanship, and they were appreciatively curious. Shelley was disappointed with the "intolerance" of the Catholic aristocracy which caused his speech to be "misinterpreted." Two government spies, sent out to observe the meeting, evidently thought his speech harmless, and did not consider it worth mentioning in their secret reports to the Castle.

Six newspapers mentioned Shelley's speech in reporting the meeting. The earlier reports were brief and somewhat guarded, though they were kind enough or cautious enough not to mention the hisses. But there was a natural and growing curiosity. Who was this very youthful-looking, very confident young man who sowed all the taverns with his pamphlets, who was so sympathetic and yet so obviously different? What were his views and objects? The Dublin *Weekly Messenger* of March 7, in a highly laudatory article entitled "Pierce Byshe Shelly, Esq.," undertook to furnish a proper introduction.

Shelley was presented at some length as the son of a member of Parliament, "the *immediate* heir of one of the *first* fortunes in England," and a bold, energetic advocate of the highest principles of political and religious toleration, to whom the Irish Catholics should listen with respect as an example of the fact that there were still enlightened, liberty-loving Englishmen despite England's six hundred years' tyranny over Ireland. His two pamphlets were appreciatively described, and the *Proposals* was copiously quoted. This was too much for the Dublin *Journal*, a government organ, which published two letters, one signed "An Englishman," the other "A Dissenter." The former, characterizing Shelley as "a renegade Englishman," sarcastically congratulated the Irish on "so *patriotic* and *enlightened* an advocate"; the latter, deploring notoriety-seeking young "literary nondescripts and political adventurers," proceeded to criticize Shelley's pamphlets in a way best designed — without seeming to do so — to expose their latent antagonism to the Catholic Church.

In a brief moment of elation Shelley sent copies of the *Weekly Messenger* eulogy to his father, to Godwin, and to Elizabeth Hitchener, whom he charged to insert it in the Sussex papers. But he was already well on his way to disappointment and disillusion. "I do not like Lord Fingal or *any* of the Catholic aristocracy," he had written Elizabeth Hitchener immediately after the meeting at the Fishamble Street Theatre. Hamilton Rowan, a patriot of earlier days, ignored him after receiving a copy of the *Address*. Nor had any significant notice been taken of his two pamphlets; the government, from which he anticipated at least some annoyance, did not even bother to tamper with his mail. John Philpot Curran was still absent to his repeated calls, and when, after a month, Curran finally called and established hospitable relationships Shelley had already judged him very much as he judged Southey.

Meanwhile Shelley had been learning a good deal about another level of society. The thronging poor of Dublin, "the meanest and most miserable of all," "one mass of animated filth," filled him, as he confessed to Godwin, with both eagerness and despair. He came across particular instances of tyranny that made him boil with indignation. An Irishman living in Portugal had been torn from wife and family by Lord Beresford and compelled to serve in the Portuguese army; and Shelley wrote to Sir Francis Burdett on the subject and contemplated what action he himself could take. A desperately poor lad whom Shelley had befriended and was about to teach to read was falsely convicted of some misdemeanor and given the choice of military or penal servitude. The mother of three small children was arrested for stealing a penny loaf, but Shelley pleaded so powerfully with the constable that he relented, remarking at the same time that he sometimes executed twenty such arrests in one night. Yet Shelley could take no comfort in this minor success; he knew that the woman was a drunkard, destined to ultimate starvation and ruin.

Shelley's recital of these experiences in a letter to Elizabeth Hitchener concludes: "I am sick of this city, and long to be with you and peace. The rich *grind* the poor into abjectness, and then complain that they are abject. They goad them to famine, and hang them if they steal a loaf."

As he realized the comparative futility of his efforts, he sickened more and more of Dublin's hopeless misery. In the letter quoted above he confessed that the Association moved slowly, that he found himself more hated as a freethinker than loved as a friend of freedom. Though he had "set some men's minds afloat," he doubted if his Association could be set up in Dublin, or even in Wales, where he intended going from Dublin. He still thought that in Sussex, with Elizabeth's strong help (she was projecting a radical book club), it would be feasible.

Shelley's *Address* and the *Weekly Messenger* article had made it clear that he had money and would spend liberally for the cause. He now noted that his company was somewhat more sought after. But none of his callers, he saw, would quite do; everybody talked detestable cant about expediency.

There was one associate, however, from whom he received active collaboration. This was John Lawless, a republican patriot who was later editor of the *Weekly Messenger* and who was almost certainly the author of the article on "Pierce Byshe Shelly." Somewhat less disinterestedly than Goldsmith's village pastor, he "led the way." Shelley met him early in March and was soon planning to "have the command of a Newspaper" with him. Lawless was writing a history of Ireland, for which Shelley wrote a number of chapters. Shelley also attempted to borrow £250 to help publish the volume, but neither the loan nor the publication was ever achieved. "Honest Jack," as Lawless was called, seems to have been more honest politically than financially, for he was later charged, both by a fellow journalist and by Harriet, with having swindled Shelley.

A more unselfish friendship resulted when an elderly, hardworking Dublin seamstress, Miss Catherine Nugent, looked up the author of the *Address* soon after its publication. The Shelleys were immediately taken by her straightforward honesty and patriotism. She dined with them and spent the evening with the ladies when Shelley's affairs called him away from home. Harriet carried on an intermittent correspondence with her until January 1815. Miss Nugent obviously admired Shelley and regarded the young couple as "very much attached" to each other. Harriet she remembered as "an amiable and unaffected person — very young and very pleasing."

Miss Nugent was a witness, though not a victim, of a rather important change in the Shelleys' mode of living. Both Shelley and

Harriet had become vegetarians, but though they did not eat animal food themselves, they tolerated others' doing so; hence Miss Nugent could be invited to dine on "a murdered chicken." A letter of Harriet's to Elizabeth Hitchener shows that the new regimen had begun about March 1 and that after two weeks' trial they were both delighted with it.

For some weeks Shelley fought against his own growing conviction that the state of affairs in Dublin was so bad that he could not possibly improve it. Every letter from Godwin urged that his course was dangerous and might prove catastrophic. But with characteristic stubbornness, so quiet and courteous as almost to appear acquiescence, Shelley met Godwin's arguments until convinced by his own experience. By March 18, however, he freely admitted to Godwin that his scheme for an association was ill-timed, and that he was preparing to leave Dublin. That very day Shelley addressed to Miss Hitchener a box containing the remaining copies of *An Address to the Irish People* and a number of copies of his broadside, *A Declaration of Rights,* which he had printed, but not circulated, in Ireland. There is no evidence that the departure from Ireland was hurried, least of all by police interference. A plan to spend the summer in Wales had been formed before they came to Ireland and had been kept alive in the letters to Elizabeth Hitchener. Both Shelley and Harriet in their letters of March 18 had stated that they intended leaving Ireland about April 7. They actually left Dublin on April 4 and reached Holyhead thirty-six hours later, after a tedious and uncomfortable voyage.

In his first letter to Elizabeth Hitchener after returning to England Shelley thus dismissed the Irish sojourn: "We left Dublin because I had done all that I could do; if its effects were beneficial, they were not greatly so. I am dissatisfied with my success, but not with the attempt." The effect on Shelley, however, was far greater than that on Ireland. He had opened an active campaign of human amelioration toward which he considered his whole life should be dedicated. He had learned, or partly learned, that patriots may be almost as ignorant, intolerant, selfish, and grasping as tyrants; that between a clear abstraction of justice in a benevolent, philosophic mind and its effective application to conditions in a wretched community, even the professed friends of justice interposed almost insuperable obstacles. His devotion to reform and his confidence in its ultimate achievement remained unshaken, but the same surprising philo-

sophic maturity that marked his *Address to the Irish People* had
taught him that genuine and lasting enlightenment was far more
a matter of the distant future than he had previously supposed. At
close hand he had seen at its worst all the effects of tyranny against
which *Queen Mab* was soon to be written.

Even as they landed at Holyhead the Shelleys were under suspicion there as dangerous radicals. They did not know it and perhaps
never heard of it afterwards. Already the box sent from Dublin to
Elizabeth Hitchener on March 18 had been opened by the surveyor
of customs at Holyhead to see if its contents were dutiable. He had
found its contents, including a letter from Harriet to Miss Hitchener,
all very alarming. He had consulted the local postmaster and they
had reported the suspicious letter and the "inflammatory" Irish papers to Lord Sidmouth, Secretary of State for the Home Office, and
to the Secretary to the General Post Office, London. The Home Office seems to have taken no action beyond referring the matter to the
Secretary for Ireland, in Dublin, who returned the papers without
comment. Sir Francis Freeling, Secretary to the General Post Office,
sent his communication to the Postmaster General, Lord Chichester,
who answered from his seat at Stanmer Park, in Sussex, on April 5.
He knew something of Shelley and Miss Hitchener already, he informed the Secretary. Shelley was "a most extraordinary man," had
married "a Servant or some person of very low birth," and had addressed the Catholic Convention; Miss Hitchener, though of low
origin, he understood, was well spoken of. He undertook to have a
watch placed upon her actions.

Unconscious, therefore, of the petty-official excitement they had
created, and restored after the hardships of the voyage by vicious
but fortifying animal food, the party of three set out on Tuesday,
April 7. For a whole week they went from inn to inn in North Wales,
always hoping to find a place to settle and always disappointed.
Shelley had hoped to settle in Merionethshire, the home of young
Fleetwood in Godwin's *Fleetwood,* just as he had earlier settled in
Poland Street because of the association of the name. Failing to find
even temporary accommodation there, they came to rest on April 14
at Nantgwillt, Rhayader, Radnorshire, in South Wales.

Shelley was now on familiar ground, Rhayader being only five
miles from Cwm Elan, where he had spent most of the previous summer. His cousin Thomas Grove helped him with the initial arrange-

ments for leasing Nantgwillt, a house with two hundred acres, only a mile and a half from Cwm Elan. Living on the place while the negotiations for completing the lease were in progress, Shelley and Harriet fell deeply in love with it. It seemed ideal for the seminary of revolution they had been planning since the previous autumn at Keswick. Elizabeth (or Portia, as she was to be called, to avoid confusion with Harriet's sister, Eliza) was to live with them; her apartment was already picked out. Her father might accompany her and cultivate some of the arable land that went with the place. Some of the land could be sub-let, in order to reduce the rent. Godwin and his family might be induced to join them for the summer. The largest room was to be equipped, on credit, as a library, an extravagance which seemed justifiable to Shelley when he considered that this establishment was for the benefit of the human race. Later Miss Nugent was also invited to visit Nantgwillt.

But the owner of the house, a Mr. Hooper, required £500 cash for the furniture and stock and £98 a year rent. Shelley attempted to get financial aid for the venture from his father and from Mr. Thomas Medwin, but failed. Finally, after some six or seven weeks of fruitless negotiation, Mr. Hooper became angry at Shelley's inability to complete the bargain, and during the first week of June the Shelleys left to take up residence with the Grove family at Cwm Elan until they could find a new home. During the interim both Harriet and Bysshe suffered brief attacks of fever, which may well have been partly induced, in Shelley's case, by the strain and excitement of the situation.

A part of this strain and excitement had been occasioned by Elizabeth Hitchener. Though she was a loyal and enthusiastic coadjutor in the plan for a revolutionary seminary, it required much fervent argument from both Shelley and Harriet to win her consent to resigning her school and coming to live with them. No sooner had her consent been won than the local gossips in Sussex began to whisper. These whispers came back to Elizabeth through Shelley's aunt, Mrs. Pilfold. It was said that Elizabeth was to live with the Shelleys as Shelley's mistress, that she had refused to become Shelley's mistress before his marriage but had now consented under the impression that the relationship would be disguised by Harriet's presence. Shelley pronounced the talk absurd, and suspected that it had all originated in the fertile brain of Mrs. Pilfold, seeking to retain the services of a competent teacher for her children by manufacturing rumors and detailing them to Elizabeth as coming from general gossip: "*I*

unfaithful to my Harriet! *You* a female Hogg! Common sense should
laugh such an idea to scorn, if indignation would wait till it could
be looked upon!"

To Elizabeth, however, such rumors were not thus lightly to be
brushed aside. Captain Pilfold seemed to accept them and advised
against her joining the Shelleys. Her father, who had objected to the
plan from the first, now grew quite stubborn in opposing it. Elizabeth became ill with distress and begged Shelley to reconsider the
whole scheme.

Shelley was aroused. He wrote an indignant letter to Captain Pilfold and a polite remonstrance to Elizabeth's father. The Captain
disavowed any belief in "the 'Mistress' business," but asserted that
Shelley "certainly was very much attached" to Miss Hitchener, a
charge which Shelley admitted enthusiastically, while denying that
it was anything like what the Captain might suppose. When Mr.
Thomas Hitchener failed to yield to his remonstrance, Shelley accused him sternly of having agitated his daughter into illness by
asserting a non-existent right. "Neither the laws of Nature, nor of
England," he proclaimed, "have made children private property."

A threat to Shelley's most cherished plans always provoked his
fixed determination to succeed and sometimes elicited hectic outbursts of passion. The passion in this case, so far as indicated by
surviving evidence, vented itself on his aunt, "fertile in instant expedients, prepared to tell a thousand falsehoods," a mistress of
"ever-ready calumny." Neither she nor the "swinish multitude" who
made calumny effective should be allowed to destroy a long-estab-
lished plan for human betterment. "Are we," demanded Shelley, "or
are we not to sacrifice the immediate energizing of those reforms
which the thoughtless and the everyday beings cannot conceive of
as practicable or useful?" Such exhortations, loyally backed by Harriet and even Eliza, finally won Miss Hitchener's somewhat nervous
consent to go through with the original plans. By June 2 it was all
settled that Elizabeth was to join them in a fortnight.

These alarms and distresses doubtless limited the active prosecution of Shelley's campaign for enlightenment. He asked Elizabeth
to distribute his *Declaration of Rights* in Sussex, not knowing, apparently, that they were probably still under detention at Holyhead.
Through Elizabeth he also attempted, unsuccessfully, to secure publication in the Sussex papers of the oppression of Redfern, the
Irishman unjustly conscripted into the Portuguese army, in whom

he had become interested in Dublin. He wrote some verses "On
Robert Emmet's Tomb" and "To Ireland," and he read with enthusi-
asm — and later effect on his *Queen Mab* — Baron d'Holbach's *Le
Système de la nature.*

One poem of 154 lines, "The Retrospect: Cwm Elan, 1812," affords glowing evidence that Shelley was finding happiness in his
marriage to Harriet. Against a background of the natural beauty of
the environment, it describes his feelings when he visited the place
in 1811 and as he felt a year later. During the first visit, Shelley said,
he was desperately unhappy, living in a world totally out of sympathy with him. In the course of one year this had all been changed
to happiness, for which he paid glowing tribute to Harriet:

> Thou fair in form, and pure in mind,
> Whose ardent friendship rivets fast
> The flowery band our fates that bind,
> Which incorruptible shall last . . .
> The prospects of most doubtful hue
> That rise on Fancy's shuddering view,
> Are gilt by the reviving ray
> Which thou hast flung upon my day.

At the same time Shelley was becoming indignant over another
instance of tyranny of more immediate interest than the obscure oppressions of the Irishman Redfern. On May 15 Daniel Isaac Eaton, a
London radical bookseller, had been sentenced to exposure in the
pillory and to eighteen months' imprisonment for publication of the
Third Part of Thomas Paine's *The Age of Reason.* The case had attracted considerable attention since its inception in early March.
Eaton's first exposure in the pillory, on May 26, was the occasion for
a detailed and sympathetic article in the *Examiner* of May 31. Within
two weeks Shelley was at work on an address which he proposed to
publish on the subject, and which he asked Godwin to criticize.

As soon as Shelley's next quarterly allowance should become available the plan was to take a house at Ilfracombe, North Devon,
where Elizabeth would join them. After two changes of plan due to
Elizabeth's nervous worry and the general shortage of funds, Shelley's party started for Ilfracombe. On the way, however, they fell so
in love with the beautiful little village of Lynmouth that about
June 25 they settled there, intending to remain through the summer
months. Harriet wrote enthusiastically to Catherine Nugent:

It combines all the beauties of our late residence with the addition of a fine bold sea. We have taken the only cottage there was, which is most beautifully situated, commanding a fine view of the sea, with mountains at the side and behind us. . . . We have roses and myrtles creeping up the sides of the house, which is thatched at the top. It is such a little place that it seems more like a fairy scene than anything in reality.

Shelley was also delighted, both with the mild climate and with the picturesque Valley of Stones, leading steeply to the plateau above the beach.

It was perhaps just as well that their house was small and plainly furnished, for the Irish expedition and the expenses at Nantgwillt had made serious inroads on their funds, and economy was for a while necessary. Though Shelley could borrow money on his expectations, it was only at such an exorbitant rate that he declined to do so, as he had declined once before, when reduced to almost his last shilling in Keswick. He considered that he held his money and prospects in trust for the cause to which he had devoted his future. "The involvement of my patrimony would interfere with schemes on which it is my fondest delight to speculate."

Elizabeth Hitchener arrived about the middle of July, and was forthwith given the name of "Bessy," instead of "Portia." Harriet's naïve first impressions of her, in a letter to Catherine Nugent, would almost seem like unconscious ironic prophecy:

Our friend, Miss Hitchener, is come to us. She is very busy writing for the good of mankind. She is very dark in complexion, with a great quantity of long black hair. She talks a great deal. If you like great talkers she will suit you. She is taller than me or my sister, and as thin as it is possible to be. . . . I know you would love her did you know her. Her age is 30. She looks like as if she was only 24 and her spirits are excellent. She laughs and talks and writes all day.

A week later Harriet remarked: "She possesses too much feeling for her own happiness."

"Bessy's" presence was at first the great inspiration to Shelley that he had so constantly assured her it would be. There was walking, talking, arguing, and reading aloud such as the Shelleys had not experienced since the Edinburgh days with Hogg. Numerous plans for action were discussed. Since the Dublin printer, Stockdale, refused to complete printing the poems left in his hands unless he should receive part payment in advance, Shelley asked his friend John Lawless to get the manuscript back. He began to send out copies of his defense of Daniel Isaac Eaton, and opened relations with an English publisher, Thomas Hookham, of Old Bond Street, London, of whom he ordered a number of books. He went ahead with the plan for publishing the Irish history (which Harriet referred to as "Pieces of Irish History") by subscription. He wrote two poems, "The Voyage," a three-hundred-line fragment, and "A Retrospect of Times of Old." Much more important, he was definitely launched on the writing of *Queen Mab.* He had by no means given up the fight for Ireland, and was also active in other directions.

Through his new acquaintance with Thomas Hookham, Shelley became interested in one of Hookham's friends, Thomas Love Peacock, whom he was soon to meet; and also in the Chevalier Lawrence, whose *Empire of the Nairs; or, The Rights of Woman* (1811) caused Shelley to begin a correspondence with him, and influenced some of Shelley's later poetry. Hookham immediately fell into the role of literary confidant and adviser and metropolitan book agent.

Shelley was now resuming the voracious reading which his recent wanderings had somewhat diminished. Hookham and Clio Rickman, another London bookseller, received long lists of books to be bought — the works of Kant and Spinoza and various other ancient and modern philosophers, a wide selection of ancient and modern histories, scientific works, and a few modern poets such as Southey, Wordsworth, and Coleridge. In the single month of December Shelley ordered nearly seventy such works.

Elizabeth Hitchener's presence was an unclouded and ever present stimulus to discussion that partly compensated for Hogg's absence. The frequent discussions of ideas formerly found in his letters to her were now transferred to his correspondence with Godwin. They show that Shelley was still an admirer of materialistic philosophy and somewhat scornful of Berkeley's immaterialism, that he accepted Godwin's opinion that he needed to read a great deal more history, and presumed, modestly and tactfully, to suggest that Godwin overestimated the value of classical studies.

Two poems written at this time testify to the strength of Shelley's love for Harriet. Four lines of a birthday sonnet, presented to Harriet presumably on August 1, assert that Harriet's love will always be as ardent and her thoughts always as pure as at present. The

other poem is a seventy-two-line tribute in blank verse that very
definitely suggests Wordsworth's tribute to his sister in "Tintern
Abbey." From the point of view of Shelley's development as a poet
these verses afford some hints of the power of expressing passionate
personal devotion that was to become one of his distinctions. They
also show how deep and genuine his love for Harriet had become:

> Harriet! let death all mortal ties dissolve,
> But ours shall not be mortal! The cold hand
> Of Time may chill the love of earthly minds
> Half frozen now; the frigid intercourse
> Of common souls, lives but a summer's day;
> It dies, where it arose, upon the earth.
> But ours! oh, 'tis the stretch of fancy's hope
> To portray its continuance as now,
> Warm, tranquil, spirit-healing. . . .

Before the end of July Shelley had finished the protest against the
punishment of Daniel Isaac Eaton that he had begun in early June.
It consisted of a twenty-three-page open letter addressed to Lord
Ellenborough, who, with conspicuous unjudicial animus, had presided at Eaton's trial. Pausing only briefly to condemn the judge,
the pamphlet argues first the logical absurdity of punishing any man
for his beliefs: "Belief and disbelief are utterly distinct from and
unconnected with volition. . . . Volition is essential to merit or
demerit. . . . No man is accountable for his belief, because no man
is capable of directing it."

Shelley then proceeds to a bold defense of the reasonableness of
Eaton's beliefs, which seemed to him "more true and good than those
of his accuser." The very existence of numerous books and articles
demonstrating the truth of Christianity, he argued, was a proof that
its truth was subject to question. If Christianity were really true,
such questioning could only confirm it, but if Christianity after all
should be false, such men as Eaton would deserve thanks for destroying error:

> — Does not analogy favour the opinion, that as like other sys-
> tems it has arisen and augmented, so like them it will decay and
> perish; that as violence and falsehood, not reasoning and per-
> suasion, have procured its admission among mankind; so, when
> enthusiasm has subsided, and time, that infallible controverter
> of false opinions, has involved its pretended evidences in the

109

darkness of antiquity, it will become obsolete, and that men will then laugh as heartily at grace, faith, redemption, and original sin, as they now do at the metamorphoses of Jupiter, the miracles of Romish Saints, the efficacy of witchcraft, and the appearance of departed spirits?

The author was still under twenty years of age, but the argument and the style are anything but juvenile. The ideas are clearly conceived and are more firmly and sharply expressed than those of the Irish pamphlets. No reader not knowing the author would suppose him to be a youth whose practical judgment was as yet so far in arrears of his more abstract power of thought that he was seriously planning a seminary of world enlightenment based mainly on the assistance of a girl just escaped from boarding school and a radical-minded, intense spinster who had given up a school in the country in order to become a partner. Like many products of eighteenth-century rationalism, it is a very effective appeal to reason, in a matter in which reason has always been subservient to emotion.

Had the *Letter to Lord Ellenborough* been published, it might very well have brought a government prosecution upon the author. Shelley was quite aware of this and took considerable precautions. It was printed under his personal supervision, without the name of either author or printer, at the shop of a Mr. Syle, printer and bookseller of Barnstaple. A thousand copies were ordered. On July 29 Shelley sent twenty-five advance copies to Hookham, and on August 4 he sent copies to Catherine Nugent, Lord Stanhope, and Sir Francis Burdett. Miss Nugent was warned that the pamphlet must not be published, and Hookham was given permission to show them only to "any friends who *are not informers.*"

This caution was certainly not excessive in view of the bold nature of the pamphlet, nor, had Shelley but known it, in view of the suspicions arising in his own neighborhood. The villagers of Lynmouth observed strange deeds — deeds that in perilous times, shortly after the assassination of the Prime Minister, required patriotic attention. The slender, enthusiastic, shrill-voiced young man who had moved into the only vacant house in the village and who employed an Irish manservant and a foreign-looking "female servant" (probably Miss Hitchener) had been seen to mail many packages and as many as sixteen letters a day. Many of his packages and letters were directed to that well-known radical and enemy of the assassinated Perceval, Sir Francis Burdett. He was known to have with him large chests so heavy that three men could scarcely lift them. These were thought, correctly, to contain papers, since they were probably the boxes of publications Shelley had brought from Ireland. He had been seen to row out from shore a little distance and throw overboard a number of dark-green bottles, also to launch from the rocks curiously fitted little boxes, wrapped in bladder, rosined, waxed, and equipped with masts, sails, and lead ballast. When recovered and opened, the boxes proved to contain copies of *A Declaration of Rights,* and the bottles when broken gave up copies of a ballad entitled *The Devil's Walk.*

The launching of these messages was a symbolic pleasure which Shelley commemorated in sonnets written at the time. But a more practical means of propaganda was that of Tom Paine, which Shelley had decided to imitate even before he left Keswick. The blundering Irish servant, Dan Hill, who had hitherto been rather a useless dependent, was given a supply of the *Declaration of Rights* and *The Devil's Walk* and sent into Barnstaple with instructions to distribute them and to post them on buildings. Dan, however, had been insufficiently warned of the danger or he was too clumsy to avoid detection; he soon found himself in the local jail. He was charged, not with sedition, but with an offense that was too self-evident to be denied: circulating printed matter without the printer's name. He was fined twenty pounds on each of ten counts and was sent to jail for six months in default of his fine.

Under questioning, Dan clung loyally to the story with which he had probably been furnished. He had been accosted on his way to Barnstaple by a gentleman in black, totally unknown to him, who had given him five shillings to distribute some papers in the village. The authorities were not much impressed with this story. When they heard Dan repeat it to Shelley, they were more impressed by Shelley's strange omission to upbraid him for scattering sedition. Within a day they also knew that Dan's papers were the same as those launched by Shelley at Lynmouth. They refused, therefore, to yield to Shelley's arguments for Dan's release, but they allowed him to purchase certain liberties for his servant within the prison, at the cost of fifteen shillings weekly.

No doubt the local authorities preferred to take no action against the son of a member of Parliament unless they were assured of strong backing. Accordingly Henry Drake, the town clerk, wrote a letter placing all the circumstances before Lord Sidmouth, Secretary of State for the Home Office, and two days later (August 22) the local postmaster sent a similar account to Sir Francis Freeling, Secretary to the General Post Office, who, after consultation, referred the matter to the Home Office. The town clerk, meanwhile, had investigated at Lynmouth and furnished the Home Office with further suspicious details. Shelley's printer, Mr. Syle, getting wind of these matters, hastily destroyed all remaining copies of *A Letter to Lord Ellenborough* on hand and sought to recover and destroy all copies previously released, so that only one copy has survived to posterity. The Home Office, aware that this incident was connected with the earlier one at Holyhead, was still only mildly interested. It advised merely that Shelley's actions be watched.

The arrest of Daniel Hill destroyed Shelley's plans for a quiet, economical seminary of radicalism at Lynmouth as completely as his failure to secure Nantgwillt had uprooted his earlier plan. He not only lacked the £200 necessary to free Daniel Hill; there was not even money to pay his landlady and make a quick departure. The little rose- and myrtle-bowered cottage saw sudden activity and a quick need for funds. The friendly landlady, Mrs. Hooper, lent them twenty-five shillings and consented to wait for her rent. She even went forth and borrowed three pounds for them from one of her neighbors, and Shelley himself seems to have borrowed from another.

Thus when the town clerk of Barnstaple went to Lynmouth a day or two before September 8, he found that Shelley and his household had lately departed for Ilfracombe, evacuating Lynmouth about August 29, 1812, just as the Russians were evacuating Moscow. From Ilfracombe, when the sleuth arrived, they had already departed for Swansea. Here Reese Howell Gronow, one of Shelley's old Eton acquaintances, was surprised by a sudden call from Shelley "in a state of great distress and difficulty," probably desirous of a loan.

Meanwhile William Godwin, whom the Shelleys had so often pressed to visit them, had decided to spend part of his annual vacation in Devonshire and had written on September 13 to apprise the Shelleys of his coming. He reached Lynmouth on the 18th only to find that his disciple had fled. Tired, half-ill, and considerably disappointed as he was, it is to his credit that he expressed no irritation, but only a concern for the safety of the refugees. He solaced himself with the statement of the Shelleys' landlady that they expected to be in London in two weeks, and took a philosophic stroll through the picturesque Valley of Stones.

Chapter VIII

THE TOWN CLERK of Barnstaple could trace Shelley's party no further than Swansea, in South Wales. Apparently, judging from one of Harriet's letters, they intended going to Llangollen, but for some reason could not stop there. At any rate, about the middle of September they were settling down in Tremadoc, forty-five miles east of Llangollen.

Shelley would in any case have felt a strong desire to see what was being done in Tremadoc, for it would have seemed to him a conspicuous example of what intelligent, philanthropic science can do for a community. It was a village of from eighty to a hundred houses, with good shops, a handsome market-house, a bank, a good church, and public assembly rooms, all planned and built through the enterprise of one man, Mr. William Alexander Madocks, M.P. In 1807 he had been granted by Parliament title to such lands as he could reclaim from the sea by a dike across the estuary of Traeth Mawr, separating the counties of Carnarvon and Merioneth. Already two thousand acres of land had been recaptured from the sea, and a model village stood where previously there had been three feet of water at low tide. In 1812 the mile-long dike was complete, except for a gap of about a hundred yards in the center. Here the confined tides rushed through with such concentrated strength as to make completion of the work extremely difficult. Six months before the Shelleys' arrival the embankment had been greatly injured by an exceptionally high tide and wind.

The gap was still unclosed when the Shelleys came to Tremadoc, and in fact for some years afterwards. The unaided resources of Mr. Madocks were insufficient to complete the undertaking, and aid was being sought in the surrounding countryside. It was a perfect opportunity for a recently uprooted philanthropist who believed in a future made glorious by science.

Mr. Madocks was not then in the neighborhood, but Shelley immediately made the acquaintance of Mrs. Madocks and of Mr. John Williams, the local superintendent. He offered to rent Mr. Madocks's house for a year furnished, but the offer was declined because Shelley could not rent on a cash basis and could not obtain security. His interest and co-operation in the rebuilding of the embankment, however, were gratefully accepted.

For about a fortnight Shelley gave John Williams such assistance as he could, including a subscription of £100. Then, on September 28, a meeting of local gentry was called in Beaumaris, at the home of Lord Bulkeley, Lord Lieutenant of Wales, for the purpose of encouraging and aiding the rebuilding and completion of the embankment. Lord Bulkeley proposed handsome toasts to Mr. Madocks and to Mr. John Williams (the real hero of the enterprise). John Williams then rose and testified that it was through Mr. Shelley's providential intervention that he had been able to employ enough men to guarantee the safety of the embankment, provided "public encouragement" were secured. He then introduced Shelley, who made a modest speech, praising the fortitude and courage of Williams and the benevolence and patriotism of Madocks. "How can any one look on that work," he concluded, "and hesitate to join me, when I here publicly pledge myself to spend the last shilling of my fortune, and devote the last breath of my life to this great, this glorious cause?"

Shelley made to Mr. Madocks, through John Williams, some unknown definite proposals of assistance which Mr. Madocks characterized as "very handsome," but which he hesitated to accept from a stranger. Any considerable financial assistance from Shelley, however, could only be realized through loans based on his expectations, and no such loans were raised. But Shelley's probable offer to raise subscriptions in Sussex was not vetoed, for within two days of the Beaumaris meeting Shelley and his party left for London, whence Shelley soon visited Sussex and solicited subscriptions for the Tremadoc Embankment.

Shortly before leaving, however, and quite probably because he *was* leaving, the young philanthropist was arrested in Carnarvon for the relatively paltry debt of £70. The particulars are unknown, but it is probable that Shelley was not imprisoned, since John Williams and Mr. William Roberts, a rather distinguished citizen of Carnarvon, furnished bail. The account was settled within little more than a month by Shelley's London agent.

Even before the flight from Lynmouth the Shelleys had planned to be in London by October 3. They must have left Wales on the day after the Beaumaris meeting, for they dined with Godwin on October 4, two or three days after their arrival in London. Meanwhile Shelley had visited Sussex and had tried to raise money for the embankment. But his Sussex friends were not impressed by the emergency in Wales or by the opportunity of saving so distant a countryside from the sea. From their answers Shelley described them as "cold, selfish, and calculating animals, who seem to have no other aim or business, on earth, but to eat, drink, and sleep." The campaign for funds was continued from London, but with no recorded success. The Duke of Norfolk was given his opportunity to contribute, which he evaded with practiced politeness and ease.

Shelley's party remained in London for six weeks, until November 13. Most of this period was made glorious for Shelley by constant association with William Godwin, whom he had long admired as the greatest of living men. The Godwin of *Political Justice* (1793) was not, even to himself, the Godwin whom Shelley met nearly twenty years later, nor had he ever been quite the Godwin who existed in Shelley's mind, but the differences were not at first too evident to the young disciple. Objectively considered, the William Godwin of late 1812 was a short, thickset man of fifty-seven, with a fair complexion, a large bald forehead, and a head which Harriet compared to that of Socrates. In his plain, dark, old-fashioned clothes and with his reserved, didactic manner he somewhat suggested the dissenting minister he once had been. His indistinct articulation and a sort of sharp, dry catch in his voice occasionally made his conversation sound perhaps a little more unpleasant than he intended. He had been largely forgotten by the world he had once startled, and though he had not forgotten his former eminence, he had forgotten or slightly modified some of the doctrines and moral courage that had made it. Yet he was a hard worker, a scholar, and a systematic, comprehensive and logical thinker who merited on intellectual grounds much of the admiration that Shelley gave him.

Godwin was greatly taken with his young disciple; he was genial and obliging, and relaxed cheerfully in Shelley's favor the usually rigid time schedule of his daily work. For six weeks they talked together three or four times weekly, sometimes at family dinners in Godwin's Skinner Street lodgings, sometimes at dinners at the Shelleys' hotel, sometimes in walks together, and sometimes in calls upon each other.

The subjects discussed by the philosopher with his disciple, while Harriet looked on and thought of Socrates, are occasionally noted by Godwin in his highly abbreviated journal entries, such as "matter," "spirit," "atheism," "utility," "truth," "the clergy," "Church gov-

ernment," and the "characteristics of German thought and literature." Godwin mentions reading part of *Queen Mab,* from which it is
to be inferred that Shelley's first important poem was also a topic of
their conversation. On such subjects as these there could have been
little disagreement. But Godwin did not hesitate to urge his opinions
on more personal matters, and he expected an homage from his dis-
ciples that in time became a little irksome even to them. He thought
Shelley's style of living not plain enough; he probably urged Shelley
to make uncongenial concessions in order to become reconciled with
his family; and he pressed to the point of irritating at least Harriet
his idea that Shelley should enter Parliament as a regular Whig.
Within six weeks, without absolutely turning against him, the Shelleys gradually concluded that he was "changed" and tainted with
"prejudices."

During this time the Shelleys became well acquainted with most
of Godwin's household. Fanny Imlay, the daughter of Godwin's first
wife, Mary Wollstonecraft, and of Gilbert Imlay, was nearly nineteen
at this time. She was a plain-featured, modest, sweet-spirited girl
whom the Shelleys liked instantly. The second Mrs. Godwin, a rather
commonplace woman whom many people disliked, seemed quite
friendly, and also worthy of admiration for her business competence.
Her two children by a former marriage, Charles and Mary Jane Clairmont, were away at the time, as was also Godwin's fifteen-year-old
daughter, Mary, until three days before the Shelleys left London,
when she probably met them at dinner at Godwin's house on November 11. Godwin's only son, William, was a boy of nine with whom
Shelley enjoyed romping and exploding fireworks.

One of Godwin's friends was a John Frank Newton, author of an
essay, *The Return to Nature* (1810), in which he championed vegetable diet. Early in November, after one of the Godwin-Shelley family dinners, Shelley slipped away with young William Godwin, who
was going to set off fireworks with Mr. Newton's son. After the fireworks Shelley accompanied young Newton home and introduced
himself to the family. The Newtons were cultivated people of somewhat Bohemian tastes, who believed in nudism for children, as well
as in vegetarianism. They took to Shelley at once. Mr. Newton
thought that he had never before met "so young a man who had
acquired so much real knowledge of numerous authors."

Although it is not a matter of written record, the Shelleys undoubtedly developed their friendship with Thomas Hookham, the
young publisher of radical tendencies with whom Shelley had in

some way become acquainted before going to Lynmouth. It was at Hookham's rooms in New Bond Street, in all probability, that Shelley conversed two or three times with Thomas Love Peacock, shortly before returning to Wales.

The same crowded week that marked the foundation of the two new friendships also marked the re-establishment, on an altered basis, of an old one. Since parting from Shelley at York in 1811, Hogg had returned to London and entered as a student in the Middle Temple, in accordance with his original plans. He was also gaining practical experience in the office of a special pleader. He had inquired about Shelley of John Grove, but had met a significantly frosty profession of ignorance. When Hogg had about given up the search, Shelley, seeking for his old friend among the law offices, traced him to his lodgings through the special pleader for whom he worked.

One evening in early November Hogg was roused by a violent knocking at the street door and the sound of rapid feet upon the stairs. As he looked up, the door flew open and Bysshe rushed into the room, full of his old impetuosity and enthusiasm. Both friends seemed to regard the distressing circumstances of their separation as matters to be ignored, even while each knew that the old footing could never be completely restored. Hogg had become more of a conservative; he now rather scorned the current hero of British freedom, Sir Francis Burdett, as a foolish fellow who was much too noisy. Shelley, on his part, had learned a bitter lesson, and with the best will in the world could not wholly recapture the old unreserved confidence.

The Shelleys were even then packing their belongings to return to Wales, but Hogg dined with them the day after the reunion. Harriet was as cordial and radiant as ever, though she did not much relish the coldness with which he received her enthusiasm for the cause of Ireland. Eliza Westbrook was distantly polite, and both Eliza and Shelley were very enthusiastic about Wales.

Hogg called once more before the Shelleys left London, just in time to witness the downfall of Elizabeth Hitchener. Harriet's first description of Elizabeth, while she was still an admirer, had noted that she talked a great deal and was too intense. These qualities are much more agreeable in correspondence than in daily physical proximity, and it may be that no more specific reasons are needed to account for a revulsion of feeling toward their possessor. Hogg thought that Eliza Westbrook disliked Miss Hitchener personally and resented her influence over Shelley, and that she and Harriet rendered her odious to Shelley. Harriet said frankly that Elizabeth turned out in every way a pretender and a great disappointment, and that she even claimed Shelley was in love with her.

Shelley, however, was so far from "in love" with her that he referred to her as a "tormentor" and as "the Brown Demon." But realizing that she must go was a very different thing from getting rid of her. She contended that her reputation, her health, her peace of mind, and even her means of livelihood had been destroyed when the Shelleys uprooted her from her school. Shelley admitted at least that she had become poor and embarrassed partly through their "misjudging haste," and agreed to make some financial reparation. Finally she consented to leave and accept £100 a year. After four months in the same house she had changed from "the sister of my soul" to "an artful, superficial, ugly, hermaphroditical beast of a woman."

Elizabeth left about November 8, full of bitterness against the Shelleys. When she attempted to set up another school, she was unable to secure a single pupil. She proceeded to inform Captain Pilfold and his wife, and also John Williams of Tremadoc, exactly the sort of person she considered Shelley to be, but they were not impressed. When Shelley heard the threats she had uttered against him to Williams he characterized her as if she were a villainess in a Gothic novel: "a woman of desperate views and dreadful passions but of cool and undeviating revenge."

The departure of the Shelleys and Eliza Westbrook from London, on November 13, was fully as sudden as the earlier and more famous departure from York. In two letters written six days earlier Shelley had stated that he was leaving for Wales in a few days. Hogg had known it for about a week. Yet the Shelleys invited the Godwins and Fanny Imlay to dinner with them at their hotel on November 13 and left without warning or explanation before their guests arrived. This abrupt disappearance could hardly have been a second flight from Hogg, whose company had been sought and was to be sought again in Tremadoc and Ireland, nor can it be easily credited to financial pressure, because Shelley was representing himself to his mother at the time as in financial matters "to a certain degree independent." Neither could it have been a crisis in affairs at Tremadoc, for he had recently heard from Williams that the embankment was doing well.

Fanny Imlay wrote to Shelley expressing some sense of injury at this treatment. The Shelleys moved about, she complained, like characters in a modern novel. Shelley's reply admits the injury, but merely heightens the mystery as to its reason:

It must . . . have appeared an ill return for all the kind greetings we had received at your house, to leave it in haste and coldness, to pass over the enlightened and zealous benevolence of Godwin, ever inventive for good, and never deterred or discouraged in schemes for rectifying our perplexed affairs – to bid not one adieu to one of you. But had you . . . seen the opposite motives combating in our minds for mastery, had felt some tithe of the pain with which at the length we submitted to a galling yet unappealable necessity, you would have sympathized rather than condemned, have pitied rather than criminated, us unheard.

Shelley's life furnishes a number of sudden actions unexplainable to his friends, and even some that are best explained as prompted by novels. Perhaps this one was eventually explained, for the Godwins forgave it. Just possibly it may have been due to threats from Elizabeth Hitchener, or even to a desire to escape Godwin's "zealous benevolence" in their private affairs, about which Harriet expressed herself far less appreciatively in her next letter to Miss Nugent.

After two hundred and sixty miles of travel in a post chaise, the latter part of it through beautiful mountain scenery around Capel Curig and Snowdon, the Shelleys were back in Tremadoc by about the middle of November. Mr. Madocks's handsome new residence, Tanyrallt, a short distance outside the village, had been secured at a rental beyond their present means, with the privilege of deferring payment until Shelley reached his majority. The completion of the embankment was still highly doubtful. Shelley constantly traveled about the region with Mr. Williams, canvassing for subscriptions and urging that men and materials be sent for repairs. At other times he was in the office from morning till night helping write letters about embankment affairs.

Money was sometimes lacking to pay the laborers, who were forced to support their large families through moonlight cultivation of small spots of poor ground. There was considerable misery that winter in Tremadoc. Those who talked about it later agreed that Shelley devoted himself energetically to the relief of the distressed, supplying food, raiment, and fuel and in one case helping a poor widow with a five-pound note.

Shelley was probably much happier in these little offices of personal charity than he was in his dealings with persons of higher social rank or in his effort to save the embankment. The constant pressure of details foreign to his experience and taste was undoubtedly a trial. "I have been teased to death for the last fortnight," he wrote to Hogg. "Had you known the variety of the discomfitures I have undergone, you would attribute my silence to anything but unkindness or neglect. I allude to the embankment affairs."

Impatience with "embankment affairs" led easily to disillusion and suspicion about the embankment itself and its projectors. Harriet was surely echoing Shelley when she recanted all her former good opinions of Mr. Madocks. She had heard the local stories of his lively company brought down from London for theatrical entertainments, "insulting the spirit of nature's sublime scenery." "The harm that man has done through his extravagance is incalculable. Here he built the town of Tremadoc, and then almost ruined its shopkeepers by never paying their just debts. We have been the means of saving the bank from utter destruction, for which I am extremely glad, as that person who purchases it will reap very great benefit from it."

The Shelleys were far from being universally popular with their neighbors and the squires and professional men of the vicinity. In addition to the natural coldness with which provincial communities are apt to view self-appointed exhorters and collectors from the outside, Shelley provided a number of his neighbors with causes for more active antipathy by his frankly expressed views on politics and religion. One local gentleman, a Mr. Robert Leeson, had shown violent and open antagonism to him even during his first visit, as a result of Elizabeth Hitchener's boasting about his radical exploits in Ireland. Shelley must have felt some occasional sense of strain even between himself and John Williams, for Williams was a devout and active churchman. Wales had little use for atheism and republicanism, even if the latter was, as Shelley assured Hogg, far removed from pot-house democracy. And Shelley had even less use for the limitations of the ruling classes which made Wales, in his opinion, "the last stronghold of the most vulgar and commonplace prejudices of aristocracy."

In his own home at Tanyrallt, however, Shelley thought himself the "happiest of the happy" with Harriet. Harriet was a rather indifferent housekeeper, but she loved reading, had a warm heart and a pleasant, easy disposition, and had made remarkable progress in adopting and echoing Shelley's opinions on practically all matters that he considered important. More than one poem written at Tremadoc deals with Shelley's love for Harriet and his happiness at finding in her a spirit ardent as his own for truth and justice. In the matter of the Irish she was if anything more Irish than Shelley himself. She was now studying Latin under Shelley's tutelage and hoping soon to be able to write a Latin letter to that confirmed classicist Jefferson Hogg.

Both Shelley and Harriet desired children, and they knew now that Harriet was to have a baby in the spring. Shelley continued to rejoice in his vegetarianism, to which he gave principal credit for an improved state of health; Harriet occasionally ate meat and intended to continue this mild heresy until spring.

In this seclusion Shelley continued to follow his own private pattern of life, which not even expulsion from Oxford, estrangement from family and friends, financial difficulties, or marriage had ever seriously altered. The vexations of Tremadoc might retard but could not halt the continued progress of *Queen Mab.* Both Shelley and Hogg now realized that their views of religion and society had grown far apart. Hogg frankly wondered if this had not produced in Shelley a less cordial feeling toward his old friend, to which Shelley replied that since principles were involuntary he could not condemn Hogg for any belief that he sincerely held. He did not accuse Hogg of insincerity, and he did not think that he himself could be accused of bigotry or factionalism.

The relationship with Thomas Hookham was gradually expanding into something more than a mere business connection. Book orders and arrangements for publication were occasionally interspersed with more personal comments on such subjects as Peacock, Harriet's progress in Latin, and financial affairs. Since Hookham's leanings were radical, Shelley and Harriet sometimes interjected a remark or comment as from one radical to another. Thus it was, now that Hogg was no longer in complete sympathy, that Shelley and Harriet turned to Hookham for co-operation in giving aid and comfort to victims of tyranny in the larger world beyond Tanyrallt and Tremadoc.

For more than a year the north of England had been seething with industrial discontent from the Luddite troubles. Desperate weavers, driven out of employment by the new weaving-frames, were breaking frames and rioting. In November 1811 Shelley had been indignant when troops were sent to suppress the weavers in Nottingham. In March 1812 Parliament had passed the savage Frame-Breaking Bill, making the destruction of any manufacturing machinery a capital offense. Lord Byron, a pale, self-conscious newcomer making his maiden speech in the House of Lords, had attacked the bill in vain, asserting caustically that it would require "twelve butchers for a jury, and a Jeffreys for a judge." Eight Luddites had been hanged at Chester in May and eight more at Manchester in June. On January 9 and 16, 1813, before a large and very silent crowd at York, and under military guard, seventeen Luddites were hanged. The Shelleys were greatly concerned about the children whom, in Byron's scathing phrase, these victims had been "nefariously guilty of lawfully begetting." Harriet wrote to Thomas Hookham suggesting a subscription for the children and authorizing him to put down her name, Shelley's, and Eliza's for two guineas each.

Before Hookham could put this commission into effect he received a letter about another subscription that Shelley considered a more important matter. Leigh Hunt, with his brother John, had for the fourth time been indicted by the government, this time on a charge that could hardly fail to bring a conviction. In the pages of their *Examiner* they had opposed to the Tory flattery of the Prince Regent a scornful picture of "a corpulent gentleman of fifty" who was "a violator of his word, a libertine over head and ears in debt and disgrace, a despiser of domestic ties, the companion of gamblers and demireps, a man who has just closed half a century without one single claim on the gratitude of his country or the respect of posterity." Sentence was pronounced on February 4, 1812: the brothers were to pay a fine of £500 each, suffer imprisonment in separate prisons for two years, and give securities totaling £750 each for good behavior during five years.

It seemed to Shelley that such a sentence set the seal of abjectness and slavery upon England forever. Boiling with indignation at its "horrible injustice and tyranny,'" he wrote to Hookham to urge an immediate subscription to pay the fine of £1,000. Though "rather poor at present," he enclosed £20 and wished ardently that he might "wallow for one night in the Bank of England."

Shelley also wrote to Hunt. "It was this imprisonment," Hunt wrote in his autobiography, "that brought me acquainted with my friend of friends, Shelley. I had seen little of him before; but he wrote to me, making me a princely offer, which at the time I stood in no need of." Leigh Hunt explained in an editorial in the *Examiner* for Febru-

ary 21 that he and his brother must insist on assuming the responsibility for their own actions, and the fine was actually paid by the
Hunts themselves, who were financially handicapped for many years
afterwards by its crippling effects.

It was perhaps as well for Shelley that Leigh Hunt did not accept
his "princely offer," for he was short of ready money and he already
owed debts in Tremadoc amounting to almost £400, which was all
the regular income he and Harriet received in a year. Hogg advised
him to seek again the mediation of the Duke of Norfolk, which he
did, without result. A letter to his father brought an expression of
vague goodwill, but left matters otherwise just the same. Shelley was
neither surprised nor disturbed. "Do you know," he wrote to Hogg,
"I cannot prevail upon myself to care much about it. Harriet is very
happy as we are; and I am very happy. I question if intimacy with
my relations would add at all to our tranquillity. . . . I can say to
my conscience, 'I have done my best'; but I shall not be very unhappy if I fail."

Study, writing, and publication plans went on steadily. Shelley
asked Godwin to recommend a plan of reading and study, and on
December 10 Godwin sent him a long letter containing some excellent suggestions, some of which are reflected in the titles of the books
Shelley ordered within the next three weeks.

At this point, therefore, it might be well to pause and consider somewhat more in detail the books by which Shelley was surrounded as he
wrote his first important poem. Classified according to subject, these
titles show that Shelley was acting very seriously on Godwin's belief
that he needed to ground himself more thoroughly in the growth and
nature of the institutions on which modern society is based. "I am
determined to apply myself to a study that is hateful and disgusting
to my very soul," Shelley assured his principal agent, "but which is
above all studies necessary for him who would be listened to as a
mender of antiquated abuses. I mean that record of crimes and miseries — History." Accordingly, nearly a third of the books he ordered
were histories. This list covers the range of Greek and Roman history
with particular thoroughness, but Byzantine, Renaissance Italian,
Jewish, Scottish, English, American, Indian, Brazilian, and Peruvian
history are also included.

Almost as many more titles fall within the general range of philosophy, religion, and metaphysics, subjects in which Shelley's interest
had been steadily growing ever since he left Eton. Such writers as

Epicurus, Diderot, Condorcet, Paine, Hume, Godwin, Helvetius, Holbach, Volney, and Lucretius form the backbone of that logical, materialistic system of thought which brought everything to the bar of infallible Reason and there judged it by the evidence of infallible sense. It had dominated Shelley's view of human life and institutions and was at this moment reaching one of its most effective poetic expressions in *Queen Mab.*

Other volumes in the list bear evidence, as *Queen Mab* does also, that the side of his nature that could not content itself forever within the bounds of eighteenth-century rationalism was already vaguely beginning to assert itself. Berkeley, whom he had rejected almost with scorn a year earlier, he now ordered for himself; and he had recently ordered both Spinoza and Kant. His early interest in sensational novels seems to have been laid aside, but science was still a very active interest, as represented by books on medicine, physiology, astronomy, physical science, and language. The list of poetical and dramatic works is only slightly smaller than the philosophical and historical. The classical languages are well represented, but are outweighed in number by the English poets. In particular it is to be noted that, except for Milton, all the English poets who most notably affected the formation of Shelley's poetic style are on the list — Spenser, Shakespeare, Southey, Wordsworth, and Coleridge.

The completion of *Queen Mab* was now in sight. "I expect to have *Queen Mab* and the other Poems finished by March," Shelley informed Hookham, adding that *Queen Mab* would be equipped with long, philosophical notes, which seemed to him to be a safer way of expressing radical beliefs and to have the added merit of freeing the poem of an excess of didactic matter. Hogg had advised Shelley, among other things, to write the poem in rhyme. A part of Hogg's advice Shelley professed to have taken, but he rejected rhymed verse in favor of "blank heroic verse" and "blank lyrical measure," pointing to Milton's *Samson Agonistes,* the Greek choruses, and Southey's *Thalaba* as precedents. By February 19 the poem was finished and transcribed and Shelley was at work on the notes. It was not to reach Hookham, however, until about a month later.

The "other Poems" mentioned several times by Shelley were the shorter poems written from time to time since his return from Ireland, amounting to about 2,800 lines. Most of them are still unpublished, though extant in manuscript. Shelley contemplated publishing them as a volume of minor poems, but he was properly doubtful of their merit, beyond that of "breathing hatred to government and

religion, but . . . not too openly." There was also a volume of poems
which Shelley had intended publishing in Ireland and which he was
still unable to secure from the Dublin printer who held them. When
they were finally returned, probably through the efforts of Miss Nugent, Shelley had already outgrown his interest in them.

In spite of occasional nervous irritations over embankment affairs, and an accumulation of debts that seemed to be lightly regarded, Shelley and Harriet were quite happy at Tanyrallt in the
winter of 1812–13. Shelley was in good health and was making good
progress with his reading and writing; Harriet was coming along in
her Latin studies and was providing herself with some new songs –
Irish melodies, simple ballads, and old sentimental songs like "Robin
Adair" and "Kate of Kearney" – to add to the pleasure of long winter evenings in their isolated cottage. As matters stood thus, with
increasing domestic happiness balanced by growing irritations with
the local environment, the Shelleys suddenly found themselves uprooted by a mysterious occurrence rather strangely suggestive of the
assault made upon Shelley in Keswick only a year earlier.

On February 26 Daniel Hill found his way back to the Shelleys,
having just been released from the Barnstaple jail. The night of February 26 was a wild and stormy one, with the wind making a noise
like thunder and the rain falling in torrents. For some reason Shelley
was expecting trouble and had loaded a pair of pistols in anticipation. Half an hour after the family had retired to bed, Shelley thought
he heard a noise in one of the parlors. Armed with his pistols, he
went downstairs and heard steps retreating through the billiard
room. Following the sound through an adjoining small room, he
saw a man in the act of leaving through one of the windows. The
man fired at Shelley and missed; Shelley then attempted to fire, but
his pistol flashed in the pan. In the ensuing hand-to-hand struggle
Shelley was knocked down, but after some struggling on the floor
he managed to fire his second pistol. The marauder, apparently
wounded in the shoulder, sprang up shrieking: "By God, I will be
revenged! I will murder your wife. I will ravish your sister. By God.
I will be revenged!" – and disappeared through the window.

After this the whole household assembled in the parlor and remained there for two hours, but eventually retired to bed, leaving
Shelley and Daniel Hill on guard. Three hours later, at about four
o'clock, Shelley sent Dan to ascertain the time. While he was out of
the room a man thrust his hand through the window and fired at

Shelley, presumably with a pistol. The bullet went through the window curtain and through Shelley's flannel gown. Shelley's pistol again flashed in the pan, but he had armed himself with an old sword since the first affray, and he attacked the marauder with this. Dan Hill returned to the room just in time to cause the flight of the assailant, who had almost wrested the sword from Shelley's grasp. Harriet, rushing down the steps at the sound of the pistol shot, reached the room after the marauder had vanished.

Such are the details of a most harrowing experience, as related by Harriet two weeks later. Answering an agitated summons the next morning, John Williams found Shelley in a most distressing nervous condition and elicited an account of the affair somewhat at variance with Harriet's. According to this account, Shelley had seen a face against the window and had fired at it, shattering the glass. He had then rushed out upon the lawn, where he saw the devil leaning against a tree. As he told his story to Williams, Shelley seized pen and ink and sketched this vision upon a wooden screen and then attempted to burn the screen in order to destroy the apparition. The screen was saved with some difficulty, and a copy was subsequently made which testifies most eloquently that what Shelley thought he saw was not a man, but a veritable devil.

John Williams and other townsmen made a prompt examination of the premises. The grass on the lawn showed signs of some sort of disturbance, but they could discover only one set of tracks. Inside the house they found the mark of only one bullet, which must have been Shelley's, since it was fired from within the room, toward the window. The moon was in its fourth quarter and could not possibly have furnished sufficient illumination on a dark and stormy night — or on any night at the times clearly specified by Harriet — for Shelley to have seen what he claimed to have seen. His neighbors believed that he had been the victim of an imaginary attack, and his enemy Robert Leeson even sneered that the whole episode had been concocted by Shelley as an excuse for fleeing the country without paying his creditors. A few months later Thomas Love Peacock investigated the story on the scene and concluded that the attack was an imaginary one, a conclusion with which Hogg also agreed.

Fifty years after the episode, however, a Welshman named Robert Williams, but known as "Robin Pant Ifan," descended from his sheep farm on the plateau behind Tanyrallt to boast that he and several wild companions had gone to Tanyrallt on the night of

February 26 with the intent of frightening Shelley from the neighborhood, presumably because Shelley was said sometimes to have put sick sheep out of their misery by summarily shooting them. He told of firing a pistol to frighten Shelley and of grappling with him in the room, but not on the lawn. This boast, first published in 1905, has been carelessly taken as substantiating Shelley's story. It may now be dismissed forever with the information that Robin Pant Ifan's death certificate shows that he was only three years old at the time he "assaulted" Shelley.

It is of little actual importance that the assault upon Shelley almost certainly never happened. The essential reality was mental rather than physical. It was possibly a mental state that prompted loading the pistols in advance; it was certainly a mental state that made Shelley tell two stories of the events that differ so widely in essential details as partly to negate each other. The devil Shelley saw was certainly not real, but he was so real to Shelley that he sketched a picture of him and then sought to destroy him by destroying the picture. Throughout his whole life there were times when the reality of events existing only in his own mind far transcended the reality of ordinary physical occurrences. In 1815, in London, Shelley was so strongly convinced that the same assailant was following him with murderous intent that he refused to go out at night alone. Both these persecutors may owe something to suggestion from Godwin's *Caleb Williams,* for it is of record that Shelley ordered a copy of the book some six months before the first "assault" and again immediately before the episode of 1815.

The after effects were also much too real for anyone to suppose that Shelley deliberately fabricated the story, as an escape from creditors or for any other motive. In Mr. Williams's opinion he was actually out of his right mind immediately after the experience. The Shelleys at once quit Tanyrallt and took refuge in the house of a Mr. Nanney, the solicitor-general for the county, a friend of theirs who lived seven miles distant from Tanyrallt. Shelley suffered an illness of several days, brought on, as he said, "by watching, fatigue, and alarm." Either just before or immediately after this illness he wrote most urgently to Hookham: "I have just escaped an atrocious assassination. Oh send the £20 if you have it — you will perhaps hear of me no more." To this Harriet added an explanatory note, saying that Shelley was dreadfully nervous from having been up all night. It thus appears that the Shelleys expected and guarded against a repetition of the attack. Years afterwards, in fact, Shelley ascribed certain physical pains to the pressure of the Tanyrallt assailant's knee upon his body. He believed then and later that his assailant was Mr. Leeson.

The Shelleys did not wait to receive the supplicated remittance from Thomas Hookham. By March 6 they were at Bangor Ferry, on their way to Ireland. En route they were greatly cheered by receiving a remittance from Hookham, enough, Shelley assured him, to relieve them from all pecuniary difficulties. After a tedious, stormy passage, Shelley, Harriet, and Eliza arrived in Dublin on March 9 and put up at the home of "Jack" Lawless, or near by, whence Shelley wrote to Williams for a loan, describing his financial condition as quite desperate.

The little party lingered in or near Lawless's home at 35 Cuffe Street, Stephen's Green, for about a fortnight. Thence Shelley forwarded the manuscript of *Queen Mab* to Hookham, who was asked ("if you do not dread the arm of the law, or any exasperation of public opinion against yourself") to print 250 copies, on fine paper, "to catch the aristocrats: they will not read it, but their sons and daughters may." The "long, philosophical and Anti Christian" notes and the other poems would be sent later. Two or three letters to Hogg urged him to join them in Dublin and promised to return to London with him.

Having already planned to visit his friends in Wales during March, Hogg found it convenient to accept their altered invitation. After a journey of tremendous discomforts he arrived in Dublin only to find that the Shelleys had gone on to Killarney. He wrote to them and sat down to wait. For a week or ten days he lingered, seeing Dublin and its society under the genial tutelage of "Honest Jack" Lawless. Many of the people he met knew Shelley and spoke cordially of him. Still he heard nothing from Killarney. His money and his time being almost exhausted, he started back to London, leaving Dublin on March 30, only a day before Shelley and Harriet arrived to meet him, after two days and nights of hard traveling from Killarney.

When Shelley and Harriet reached Dublin they decided to follow Hogg to London as soon as they had rested from the recent long journey and could find money for the trip. Money having been found, they reached London on or shortly before April 5 and put up temporarily at the home of Mr. Westbrook, in Chapel Street. Eliza had been left to hold the fort — perhaps to hold off the landlord — on the banks of Lake Killarney. According to Hogg, Shelley was openly delighted to be rid of her company. "He made no secret of his satisfaction, but often gave vent to his feelings with his accustomed frankness and energy. The good Harriet smiled in silence. . . ."

Very soon, however, Eliza and Daniel Hill rejoined the Shelleys in London.

Chapter IX

WHEN SHELLEY reached London during the first week of April 1813, he had been married to Harriet over a year and a half. Though they had achieved real happiness in each other, yet in all those months they had never enjoyed peace and security. The flight from York, the apprehension and disappointment in Ireland, the flights from Lynmouth and from Wales, the domestic uproar caused by Elizabeth Hitchener — all constituted no very stable foundation for marital happiness. Yet happiness had been won, and was to continue for another year of sudden changes, flights, and almost constant financial desperation. That it succumbed in the end is perhaps less remarkable than that it endured so long.

The year which led imperceptibly toward a crisis is one of the most vaguely known periods of Shelley's life. After about a month with Harriet's parents the young couple moved to Cooke's Hotel near by, on Albemarle Street, whence they soon removed to lodgings in Half-Moon Street. In June they moved again to Pimlico. About two months later they were moving to Bracknell, where they remained quietly for nearly three months. Then a sudden flight to Edinburgh, and, after two months, London again. Then Windsor for three or four months, then Bracknell once more. These incessant moves were accompanied by a constantly increasing financial desperation, which was the principal cause for most of the moves and indeed formed the dominant current bearing Shelley and Harriet unconsciously toward disaster.

For over a month after reaching London Harriet reported herself as taken up completely with "the hurry and bustle of a city." Shelley was very busy with his *Queen Mab,* which was in press by May 21, and with a highly necessary attempt at reconciliation with his family. The Duke of Norfolk was again willing to help. John Grove, who had recently seen Mr. Timothy Shelley, urged Bysshe to write to his father, and Bysshe's mother and sister were anxious to see him home again. Shelley wrote to his father in a most concessive spirit, assuring him of changes "in some of the most unfavourable traits of my Character." Harriet expected to be at Field Place in a week or two.

But Mr. Shelley now required that his son inform the Oxford authorities that he had returned to Christianity; he refused to deal directly with him on any other basis. Shelley perceived that a genuine reconciliation was no longer possible. "I was prepared," he wrote to the Duke of Norfolk, "to make my father every reasonable concession, but I am not so degraded and miserable a slave as publicly to disavow an opinion which I believe to be true. Every man of common sense must plainly see that a sudden renunciation of sentiments seriously taken up is as unfortunate a test of intellectual uprightness as can possibly be devised."

Mr. Shelley's wife and daughters, although in general they supported the father against the son, evidently did not support his last position. They corresponded with Shelley and Harriet, furnished information as to Mr. Shelley's movements, and began planning a secret visit of Shelley to Field Place, in his father's absence.

Queen Mab left the press probably in May or June 1813, with a full understanding on the author's part that it was a dangerous venture. He took rather elaborate precautions; only 250 copies were printed, none of which were to be sold. Only seventy of them ever got into circulation during Shelley's life. Whenever Shelley presented anyone with a copy he generally removed the title page, the dedication, and the printer's imprint at the end of the volume. The dedicatory poem is a warm testimony of Shelley's love for Harriet, whose loving sympathy he calls his own purer mind and his inspiration.

The plan of *Queen Mab* is quite simple. The heroine, Ianthe, lies asleep while her disembodied soul is carried aloft by Queen Mab. From an immense distance she views the past, present, and future of the world, and is instructed by the fairy queen in the significance of what she sees. The voice of Queen Mab is that of Shelley at twenty and twenty-one, with overtones from most of the radical literature he had been reading since he left Eton, and especially during the preceding year. Lucretius, Tom Paine, Volney, Voltaire, Holbach, and J. F. Newton are known sources for various ideas, but the philosophical thought is so much the common property of eighteenth-century radical philosophy, and even sometimes of the ancient Epicureans, that it is futile to attempt to assign most of it to particular, exclusive sources. Shelley had read extensively and acutely and had assimilated his reading.

The ideas which the poem was written to express were mainly ideas that Shelley had held for several years already, and may be briefly summarized thus: The spirit of Nature and of life is Necessity, a passionless, impartial force knowing no limits or decay. It extends throughout the whole universe and governs every minute action of every atom of the natural world, and every whim of thought. Nothing acts but as it must act and was predestined to act, without the variation of a hair, from the first instant of time. Mankind is naturally virtuous and happy, but man has degenerated through the growth of certain evils. Eventually these evils must perish of their own corruption, restoring humanity to virtue and happiness. At present, however, "man's all-subduing will" tolerates his own evils, which depend upon selfishness, superstition, lust, and an animal diet that carries with it the seed of moral and physical evil. God (as in Volney and Voltaire) is a depraved creation of the human mind, a celestial tyrant on an earthly model. Human ignorance and selfishness, as best shown in priestcraft, kingcraft, and commerce, are the causes of tyranny and warfare. Marriage is an expression of selfishness and a violation of individual liberty. It becomes an intolerable tyranny as soon as either party grows tired of it.

The figure of Ahasuerus, the Wandering Jew, fiercely symbolizes the victim of Christianity, which to Shelley was the worst of all tyrannies. In nearly two hundred lines of impassioned diatribe he asserts the cruelty and injustice of God, ridicules the doctrine of atonement, presents Christ as a vengeful, hypocritical demagogue, and stands forth against celestial tyranny,

> Mocking my powerless tyrant's horrible curse
> With stubborn and unalterable will —

a clear prototype of Shelley's Prometheus.

The lyrical passages, in the unrhymed irregular verse of Southey's *Thalaba* and *The Curse of Kehama*, are certainly as good as their models; the regular blank verse, while far inferior in musical and imaginative quality to Shelley's later blank verse, is quite adequate to its purpose, which is more rhetorical than poetic. The poem is a spirited, clear, and well-planned culmination of Shelley's steady purpose to wage war on every form of oppression.

The circumstances under which it circulated naturally prevented *Queen Mab* from attracting attention at the time. Shelley was in the somewhat ridiculous position of having achieved a complete expression of his mission only to feel obliged to conceal it. It must have been his impatience at this circumstance that prompted him to follow *Queen Mab* with two pamphlets that could be published, dealing with two of its most important subjects, the evils of eating animal food, and the tyrannies of religion. The first of these was *A Vindica-tion of Natural Diet,* dated 1813 on the title page and priced at one shilling and sixpence. It repeats the *Queen Mab* note on vegetable diet, with slight alterations and additions. There was no reason why Shelley should have printed it anonymously except that it was presented as "one in a series of notes to Queen Mab, a Philosophical Poem."

The second, *A Refutation of Deism, in a Dialogue,* also anonymous, is dated 1814, and probably belongs to the early spring of that year. Here Shelley had the problem of repeating and elaborating the most dangerous ideas in *Queen Mab* without being prosecuted. He accomplished it by presenting his ideas as an argument between Theosophus, a deist, and Eusebes, a Christian. Superficially it might have been written by any well-read, fair-minded clergyman capable of such a clear and flexible prose style as Shelley had now attained. Shelley states his object in the Preface — to show that "Deism is untenable," that "there is no alternative between Atheism and Christianity," and that "the existence of a God can be argued only from Divine Revelation." During the long discussions Shelley presents more fully and subtly than in *Queen Mab* all his arguments against Christianity without once seeming to champion them. The irony throughout is certainly subtle enough to serve one of Shelley's purposes, safety; but it is altogether too subtle to have served effectively the other, an exposure of Christianity. Neither pamphlet, in fact, seems to have had much circulation. No contemporary comment has ever been recorded, and only eight copies of the former and five of the latter have since been discovered.

Financial negotiations with Mr. Timothy Shelley consumed many hours of time during the first two or three months in London, but by June, when the Shelleys moved to Pimlico, they had dissolved into nothing. For the last year Shelley's expectation of reaching a settlement upon attaining his majority had encouraged his tendency to spend beyond his means. It is almost incredible, yet true, that Shelley chose this moment to assume William Godwin's financial worries — and Godwin now owed £3,000.

Shelley now turned in real desperation to Mr. Thomas Charles Medwin, who had previously aided him with money and legal advice. Harriet's confinement was hourly expected, and he hoped that Mr. Medwin might see him through the attendant financial difficulties. After one or two unfruitful letters, on June 28 Shelley asked

Mr. Medwin for an early interview, informing him at the same time that Harriet had been safely delivered of a daughter and was rapidly recovering.

Mr. Medwin came to dinner on July 7, but the amount and precise nature of his aid is uncertain. Possibly he was the source of a belief expressed soon afterwards by Harriet that the Shelley family could and would deprive Shelley of his right to inherit – a belief which was kindly dissipated by Mr. Timothy Shelley himself, in an interview (probably the last) which Shelley somehow managed to obtain with him about the end of August.

There was a pressing danger that Shelley would be arrested for debt. Bailiffs actually did lock a door upon the shrinking figure of Mr. Thomas Jefferson Hogg, proclaiming that he was Mr. Percy Bysshe Shelley and under arrest for debt. Harriet was assured by Shelley's sister that Mr. Timothy Shelley was doing everything in his power to prevent Shelley's arrest. According to Hogg, many persons who were mere cranks or adventurers fastened themselves upon Shelley at this time, like limpets. Yet his desperate financial condition continued unabated and soon led to raising money on post-obits.

Despite financial difficulties, the Shelleys found life in London anything but dreary. Harriet was jolly and easy-going, Shelley too genuinely careless of mere creature comforts to be disturbed by circumstances that sorely grieved their most constant visitor. Even in retrospect Mr. Thomas Jefferson Hogg counted it a triumph of friendship to have endured their hospitality for the sake of their company. Ordering a dinner was a sacred rite to Hogg, but to Shelley it was an embarrassment and an impertinence, and to Harriet a matter of indifference. "Ask Harriet," Shelley would cry out in desperate self-defense. "Whatever you please," Harriet would say by way of ordering. Harriet had known nothing of housewifery when she married and had learned nothing since. The result was that Hogg was condemned to dinners for which he felt a profound disrespect. Tough mutton, watery gravy, poor cheese and potatoes, poor cooking – it was all pretty sad for Jefferson. He dropped cautious hints about a pudding, but puddings, Shelley announced with serene dogmatism, were a prejudice.

Had not Shelley and Harriet been practicing vegetarianism with renewed fervor (even though they did not require conformity in their guests), it might have been better for Hogg's comfort. Shelley did not really object to physical comforts, as Hogg shrewdly noticed; he accepted them casually when they came his way in the natural course of events; but he objected on principle to luxury and ostentation, and he thought quite simply of food as necessary if one were to continue long to learn and propagate the truth, but not in itself important. Thus he ate when he felt hungry and when it was convenient. He would dash into a shop, buy a loaf of bread, and break off and eat pieces from it as he walked along. In his pockets he generally carried raisins with which occasionally to supplement the dry bread. The spot where he sat reading or writing was often ringed about with crumbs. As he munched his bread, whether in a coffee-house, at home, or on the street, he sometimes practiced what seemed to Hogg totally unconscious marksmanship with bread pellets. He would roll a bread pellet between his fingers and flip it with his thumb unerringly toward its mark — a portrait, an image, or the nose of a pedestrian or fellow diner. He never missed, and he was never suspected by any of his victims because he was never himself actually conscious of being the offender.

Shelley objected, on theory, to muffins and crumpets with tea, because they were apt to be buttered, but when the buttered muffins were served him without comment he would eat them without noticing the defilement to which they had been subjected. Between Harriet's incompetence and their combined indifference they came to rely largely upon penny buns as an accessory to tea. Habits such as these might well be supposed to be injurious to health — as indeed Peacock did suppose a year or two later — but their early effects at least were not noticeably harmful. Harriet, according to Hogg, was as energetic as ever; Shelley bounded up and down steps and delivered his fine bravura knocks at his friends' doorways with undiminished vigor. He was reported by Harriet to be in perfect health.

The old walks with Hogg were resumed, even though they were less frequent and the discussions more reserved than in the days of more complete sympathy and confidence. Hogg would call for Shelley wherever he happened to be, or Shelley would call at Hogg's lodgings, and they would take long walks across the fields or through the streets, generally winding up at some coffee-house for tea. Sometimes, in lieu of the walk, Shelley and Hogg would sit up all night, discussing books and playing chess.

Hogg has little to say concerning the discussions that took place during his walks with Shelley, but he has left a rather vivid impression of the walks themselves. The two friends must have been a pair

135

well calculated to make the casual wayfarer turn for another look: the slender Shelley, with his delicate complexion and fine features, his slight, gentlemanly stoop, odd, quick voice and gestures, his careless dress, and his small bare head with its unruly hair, gliding along in earnest talk with the solid, heavy-featured Hogg, positive, laconic, and occasionally sarcastic, beginning already, no doubt, to cultivate the manner and appearance of the responsible barrister and future circuit judge.

Through many unknown London streets, said Hogg, "I always let him lead the way and followed his guidance: his course and choice of direction were erratic and uncommon, and he would dart across the road and quickly enter some unpromising, ill-omened street or passage, and hurry me along it: I have often wondered by what impulse he was thus borne along. His flight was to escape from, not to pursue; to get away from some object for which he had conceived a sudden dislike." It is just possible that on some of these occasions he was seeking to escape from Hogg's conversation, or possibly even a bailiff. Hogg annoyed Shelley by laughing at Godwin's *Political Justice*. "You laugh at everything!" Shelley once complained. "I am convinced that there can be no entire regeneration of mankind until laughter is put down!"

The Shelleys were now in a circle of friends both new and old. Thomas Hookham lived near Cooke's Hotel and the Half-Moon Street lodgings; Chester Street, where the Newtons lived, was within easy walking distance. At Hookham's house, probably at his shop while *Queen Mab* was going through the press, there must have been occasional talks with Thomas Love Peacock. Edward Graham and John Grove were seen occasionally, though Grove soon left London to enter the University of Edinburgh. A Mr. Ryan, whom the Shelleys had known in Dublin, saw them several times between early May and late June of 1813. Toward the end of June John Williams of Tremadoc was in London and in contact with the Shelleys.

For over two months there was little association with the Godwins, an odd circumstance that is partly explained by Harriet's resentment of Mrs. Godwin's "dreadfully disagreeable" disposition. After June 9, however, when Mrs. Godwin called on the Shelleys, relations became more friendly.

Among all of his London friends the Newtons seemed to Shelley the most delightful. Even the usually disdainful Hogg pronounced this family to be truly elegant and testified that Shelley derived great delight and advantage from their company. Some time before the middle of May Shelley took Hogg with him to dine at their home. Hogg was startled to see five healthy, happy, completely nude children rush to the door to greet Shelley. They fled incontinently to the nursery when they saw him accompanied by a stranger. Hogg was on this occasion so impressed with the Newtonian theory and practice of nudism, about which he had not been warned, that he actually failed to comment upon the food; but this oversight he later remedied by a general account of vegetarianism as practiced by the Shelleys and Newtons. Hence we know that on this as on later occasions he drank distilled water, tea, or coffee and ate bread-cakes with little or no butter, fruits, vegetables, and possibly honey. "Certainly," Hogg testified, "their vegetable dinners were delightful, elegant and excellent repasts."

Shelley reached the height of his vegetarianism in this environment. He argued that eating animal flesh was the basis not only of human disease, but of human vices as well. Man had only to confine himself to a harmless Newtonian diet in order to free himself from disease and from the various social and political evils to which he was addicted through his predatory, carnivorous habits. In practice Shelley was a strict vegetarian among the orthodox, but when alone or with non-vegetarians he sometimes lapsed. He could be as unconscious of his food as of any other physical circumstance, and it may be quite true, as Hogg reports, that in the Lake region a few months later he was seen settling down to a solitary meal of cold boiled beef.

The well-appointed house of the Newtons was almost a second home to Shelley while he was in London. Mr. Newton was a man of knowledge and refinement. He was Godwin's contemporary rather than Shelley's, being forty-six years of age in 1813, but he was an agreeable companion for the poet, and had a similar eagerness to improve humanity and to cultivate and advance his hobbies. Mrs. Newton, the daughter of a wealthy West Indian planter who had retired to England, was an attractive, sympathetic woman, the mother of five very healthy and well-trained young children. She expressed intelligent critical opinions of English literature and was an accomplished musician. Often while she was making music with some fellow artist, Shelley, whose musical tastes were simpler than those of the performers, retired to a corner of the room and told ghost stories to the children.

It was Mrs. Newton who successfully introduced Shelley to the gaieties of Vauxhall Gardens, with its multitude of twinkling lights, its fireworks, and it lively music. A mere mundane critic seeing the two there together, remarked Hogg, "might have declared that there was a most desperate flirtation between them; a more spiritualized observer . . . would discern in their union a strong and close sympathy, and would describe and designate it as such."

The Newtons' considerable acquaintance among people of culture and influence might have been of greater service to Shelley had he co-operated a little more fully with their well-intentioned efforts. The Chevalier Lawrence, with whom Shelley had previously opened a correspondence, was a visitor at their house and also at Shelley's. Most of the efforts to introduce Shelley to various people originated within the friendly, admiring group of which the Newtons were the center. But Shelley frequently disappointed both the Newtons and Hogg by failing to keep engagements they had made for him.

Through the Newtons the Shelleys became acquainted with Mrs. Boinville and her circle. Mrs. Boinville was an older sister of Mrs. Newton. Her husband, who had died only a few months before the Shelleys met her, had been a distinguished but penniless French émigré and a friend of Lafayette, who had returned to France under the Consulate and had rendered valuable service to Napoleon. When the Shelleys moved from Half-Moon Street to a quiet street in Pimlico, probably about the middle of June, it was in order to be near Mrs. Boinville and her eighteen-year-old married daughter, Cornelia Turner, only a few doors away. Shelley soon came to regard Mrs. Boinville as "the most admirable specimen of a human being" he had ever seen. "Nothing earthly ever appeared to be more perfect than her character and manners." He also admired Cornelia, whom he considered perhaps more sincere than her mother, though certainly less fascinating.

When the Boinville family moved to Bracknell, thirty miles from London, the Shelleys followed them about the middle of July and took a house in Bracknell known as High Elms House. Harriet described the move to Catherine Nugent as one "merely for convenience," which may refer equally well to avoiding association with the Middlesex bailiffs and preserving association with the Boinvilles.

The circle of people who forgathered in June and July 1813 at Mrs. Boinville's house in Pimlico and later at Bracknell overlapped somewhat with the Newton circle, but contained probably more French émigrés and more political and social radicals. Hogg, in spite of his conservative prejudices, approved of Shelley's friendship with the Newtons, but heartily disliked most of the company at Mrs. Boinville's. Mrs. Boinville herself he thought "an amiable and accomplished old lady, and tolerably agreeable, but too much of the French school to be quite so"; but "the greater part of her associates" were to him simply "odious," with "higgledy-piggledy ways" and half-baked sentiments that were doing Shelley no good.

With the ladies of both these circles Shelley was extraordinarily popular. His romantic personal beauty, his harmless eccentricity, gentle manners, and earnest enthusiasms made him, in Hogg's opinion, irresistibly attractive to them. They called him by affectionate names and thought elegant society his proper vocation. Mrs. Newton and Mrs. Boinville were both obviously very fond of him. Since his eloquence and enthusiasm commonly waxed brightest when other people should normally be ready for bed, it sometimes happened that he sat up all night enthralling two or three earnest young ladies with his talk of wisdom and virtue. It seems to have been well understood that Shelley's interest in these ladies depended primarily on their interest in the ideas that were all-important to him. "The whole soul of my ardent and imaginative young friend," says Hogg, "was inflamed at this period of his life by a glowing desire to witness and to promote the improvement and progress of civil society."

The reading of books went forward as steadily as ever. During the spring, while living in the Half-Moon Street lodgings, Shelley would sit long hours in a little projecting window looking so bright and happy that Mrs. Newton compared him to some young lady's lark, hanging outside for air and song. No matter how many books he may have left behind at various lodgings, Shelley never required more than a few days to assemble a respectable library at his next stop. In the little sitting-room on Half-Moon Street books were arranged in rows on the floor, they occupied the recesses on either side of the fireplace, were piled in disorder on tables and chairs, and were heaped up under the tables.

On occasion Shelley read aloud, usually some sublime passage from the *Iliad* or the *Odyssey*, both of which he had read through more than once. Hogg describes him as reading "with extreme rapidity, animation, and energy," raising his shrill voice as the excitement and pleasure of the reading increased. He often read Homer as he lay in front of the fire, striking the flame from the coals with shovel or fire-iron, gradually acquiring an eyestrain and a very ruddy color in the cheek next the fire. Similarly he pored over various moral and metaphysical writers, giving somewhat closer attention to the materialists than to the idealists.

In order that he might extend his reading even more widely, Shelley now took up the study of Italian with Hogg. Though Hogg applied himself industriously, he was soon far outdistanced by Shelley, whose quickness and insight made him a better linguist. Through Tasso's *Jerusalem Delivered* they proceeded at an even and equal pace, but when they came to Ariosto's *Orlando Furioso* Shelley was borne away on an enthusiastic flood of magic and marvels; parts of it he read again and again, sometimes aloud. He discoursed upon it "with wild rapture" during his walks with Hogg. Petrarch, says Hogg, was read under the tutelage of a lady [Cornelia Turner?] who considered herself a prey to pensive melancholy and admired Petrarch as the greatest of all poetic lovers, an attitude in which Bysshe, but not the flippant Hogg, fully concurred.

With his mental horizon thus steadily expanding, and with a number of pleasant associates, the year 1813 and the early months of 1814 were for Shelley and Harriet an "auspicious, beneficial, and happy period." Or so it seemed to Hogg, the closest observer. No one seemed much worried by the financial quicksands upon which the whole situation rested with an increasingly ominous insecurity.

The oddity that had characterized many of Shelley's earlier actions stands out rather prominently in the young man of twenty-one and twenty-two. Like Harriet, he talked a great deal about suicide. He was convinced that his health was precarious, and he actually did suffer occasionally from violent coughing and from pains in the side and chest; but both Hogg and Peacock were positive that his constitution and general health were good and that he suffered from nothing worse than imprudent dress and bad diet.

After having read somewhere an account of a rare disease called elephantiasis, characterized by an enormous swelling of the legs, Shelley observed that an old woman sitting opposite him in a crowded stagecoach possessed legs of an extraordinary thickness. He immediately imagined her to be a victim of this disease and feared that he had contracted it from her. Soon he discovered unmistakable symptoms in himself, nor could the ridicule or expostulations of his friends disabuse him of his conviction. One day while sitting in an armchair talking to Mr. and Mrs. Newton, he fell writhing upon the floor and informed his startled hosts that he had elephantiasis. He was persuaded to consult an eminent physician, who also failed to destroy the delusion. Convinced that he was doomed to an early and horrible death, he went about in great dejection examining his friends, even young ladies at a dance, for signs of the cracked and roughened skin that was supposed to be a symptom of the disease. He persisted in the delusion for several weeks and then gave way to some more cheerful exercise of the imagination.

Nothing about Shelley impressed Hogg more strongly than his extremely sympathetic and fanciful imagination. "He lived and moved and had his being under the absolute, despotical empire of a vivid, fervid fancy." This led him sometimes to identify himself completely with the subject of his thought or fancy. A few passing remarks about a fabulous shorthand writer alleged to have abbreviated his system to absolute zero led Shelley to the unconscious study of blank sheets of paper for invisible symbols. A consequent remark about the extreme fatigue probably endured by Tiro, the supposed inventor of shorthand, caused Shelley a few minutes later to exhibit the same fatigue that his fancy imputed to Tiro.

Shelley was often the creature of sudden impulse when there was no question of delusion. His friends were not surprised if he sometimes vanished for a while abruptly and without apparent cause. Hogg complained that "he had no perception, no notion of time." The impulse of the moment was often supreme and made him unconscious of times, persons, and seasons so that he easily ignored important engagements.

He was not entirely without a sense of humor, though a rather odd one. He liked occasionally to relate and listen to droll stories, and his laughter on such occasions seemed sometimes quite wild. His mirth could be quite unexpected and embarrassing, as once when he had dinner with Hogg at Lincoln's Inn and was suddenly so smitten with the weighty triviality of some remarks by the great Sir Thomas Plumer that he rushed from the room with wild shrieks of laughter. It was noticeable, however, that he would laugh at nothing that offended good feeling or tended to pervert moral judgment.

Shelley's general habits and behavior as a young man of twenty-one and twenty-two rested upon three principles evident in his character since boyhood: namely, an extreme sympathetic capacity to become the person with whom his imagination was busy, a tendency to act upon momentary impulse, and a simple, intense preoccupation with his own sense of mission which made it quite natural for him to ignore details of food, clothing, and conventional social obligations. He had a delusion of persecution which Hogg barely recognizes in a few chance phrases but which is clear from his earlier letters to Elizabeth Hitchener and Godwin and from his attitude toward his father and toward Robert Leeson of Tremadoc; Peacock clearly recognized it as important in the early summer of 1816. Here, if anywhere, was a young man whose imaginative childhood persisted side by side with a highly sensitive and sophisticated intellectual penetration. He pursued an absorbing purpose which his conduct never violated, and yet he was so impulsive that he seemed — superficially — quite erratic.

Here also was a young man not inconsistent with the rough and ready judgments of several people who observed and commented upon the youthful Shelley as not always entirely sane. He had written to Hogg (June 23, 1811): "I can find an excuse for madness, because I myself am often mad"; in letters to Elizabeth Hitchener he had referred semi-humorously to his reputation for madness; he had behaved at Field Place in October 1811 in a manner that convinced his father and apparently his mother and sisters of temporary madness; he had furiously accused his mother on the basis of an anonymous letter that he had shortly before pronounced ridiculous; and he was later to endow practically all of his autobiographical characters — Laon, Lionel, and the Maniac of *Julian and Maddalo* — with various degrees of occasional madness.

The conclusion seems inescapable. Tom Medwin saw and stated it quite clearly: "Insanity hung as by a hair suspended over the head of Shelley." A sudden alteration of health or an unusual mental shock might at any time result in conduct inconsistent with his basic character as a friendly, well-mannered young man of intellectual acuteness and great personal charm. But it would be a most stupid error indeed to substitute this possible Shelley of some particular moment for the much more apparent and stable character that was respected and loved by most people who knew him.

Harriet seemed always full of good health and good humor and as devoted as ever to reading aloud. The birth of Ianthe in June accounts for her absence from the various companies in which Hogg so frequently described Shelley. The Newtons sometimes saw her in her own home, and presumably in theirs, and it is to be supposed she exchanged neighborhood visits with the Boinvilles after she and Shelley moved to Pimlico to be near them. Eliza Westbrook, of course, was in constant attendance on her.

The Shelleys named their little daughter Eliza Ianthe, Ianthe for the heroine of *Queen Mab,* and Eliza for Harriet's sister, probably, rather than Shelley's. She was a beautiful, healthy child, but there was a slight defect in one of her eyes that Hogg thought may have been a source of some chagrin to the mother. Shelley was extremely fond of her and spent a great deal of time walking up and down the room with the child in his arms, singing a queer song of his own composition. The music consisted of three notes in a minor key; the words sounded like monotonous repetitions: "Yáhmani, Yáhmani, Yáhmani, Yáhmani." In September Shelley wrote a sonnet in which he expressed his love for Ianthe and her mother. Harriet made a rapid recovery after the birth of her child and was soon as lively and rosy as ever, "at times perhaps," says Hogg, with what may be intended as a significant pun, "rather too rosy."

As soon after Ianthe's birth as seemed practicable, probably about the middle of July 1813, the Shelleys had moved to Bracknell, where they planned to stay until the spring. While they were at High Elms, as their new home was called, they saw little of Hogg. He never visited Bracknell while the Shelleys were there, and though he saw Bysshe during various trips to the city, he was himself absent on his northern vacation from the beginning of August until the end of October. Peacock, who had previously been absent in Wales, returned during Hogg's absence and visited at High Elms. The Newtons, with their children, also made the Shelleys a visit, probably in late September or early October. After their return Mrs. Newton wrote to Hogg, who had not heard from the Shelleys since his departure in early August, that his friends were all well and happy, but had recently embarked upon a journey to the north, accompanied by Eliza Westbrook and Peacock.

Hogg was completely surprised at Shelley's undertaking a journey which he regarded as sudden, utterly causeless, and wildly extravagant. In this case, however, the motive was more substantial than the sudden impulse of a particular moment, or the "thick-coming fancies" which, in Peacock's phrase, "almost invariably preceded his change of place." Harriet had foreseen the probable necessity of such a move from their first arrival at Bracknell, and there can be little doubt that Mrs. Newton also understood. Shelley was in constant fear of the bailiffs and had already escaped arrest only by accident when Hogg had been arrested for Shelley's debt. The journey was occasioned, as Harriet said, by "necessity." Shelley owed bills at Tremadoc that fell due on his coming of age, and other creditors were doubtless awaiting that date with some eagerness.

But August 4 came and went without any financial settlement with Mr. Timothy Shelley. Attaining his majority only made it a little easier for Shelley to arrange post-obits at a perfectly ruinous rate. The fear of arrest continued, even after his return from the north. The best Shelley could do was to arrange an interview with his father for November. Meanwhile it was wise to vanish from his creditors. The Shelleys' departure from Bracknell was indeed secret, and involved further secrecy as to their destination, but it was not sudden.

A long journey with a wife, an infant, and two guests required some preparation. Shelley bought a coach, which was probably deemed necessary for the infant Ianthe, who could hardly be expected to risk the chances of having to ride "outside" in a public conveyance. Harriet's detractors later instanced this coach as a proof of her extravagance and love of show. Having bought the coach on credit, Shelley next sold to a moneylender named Starling a £2,000 post-obit bond for £500. On Monday, October 5, the Shelleys, Eliza Westbrook, and Peacock started for the Lakes.

In about a week they had completed their journey of more than three hundred miles and had reached their appointed inn on Lake Windermere, at Ambleside. This was no other than Lowood Inn, owning the same name and location as that inn from which Casimir Fleetwood, in Godwin's novel, introduced himself by letter to his philosophic friend somewhat as Shelley introduced himself to Godwin. Once before, when leaving Ireland for Wales, Shelley had planned to imitate Fleetwood by settling in Fleetwood's home county of Merionethshire, but had had to be content with settling on its border at Tremadoc. He now intended to take a furnished house and remain until spring, but no such house was available, and after a few days he moved on to Edinburgh, having seen the Calverts again, but not Southey.

By about the middle of October Shelley's party were in Edinburgh. Here, as at Bracknell and then at Ambleside, they intended at first to remain for the winter. Shelley expected to find in Edinburgh a more tolerant society and a higher regard for literature than in London. Harriet, at least, was very happy with the thriving little Ianthe, "so fair, with such blue eyes," and with the retrospect of the two "happiest and longest years of my life" to which she was inspired by being once more in the city and even the neighborhood in which she had been married. Shelley was zealously pushing forward his self-education, reading Tacitus, Cicero, Homer, and Hume, and beginning to fulfill a determination to master the physical sciences. Despite his opinion that Peacock was too lacking in generous enthusiasm, he found pleasure in Peacock's scholarly conversation and his easygoing, unbigoted, slightly cynical enlightenment.

Probably it was through John Grove, who was completing his medical education in Edinburgh, that Shelley met a young Brazilian medical student named Joachimo B. Pereira, a frank, warm-hearted, gentlemanly young man, forced to study medicine against his inclination. He shared earnestly in Shelley's enthusiasms, adopted the vegetable diet, and began a translation of *Queen Mab* into Portuguese. This translation was to be introduced by a sonnet beginning, "Sublime Shelley, cantor di verdade," and ending, "Surja *Queen Mab* a restaurar o mundo." The translation was probably never completed, on account of the attractive young Brazilian's early death, and the sonnet survives only in the two lines that Peacock recalled. It was the first of at least fifteen poems written to or about Shelley during his lifetime and within the year of his death.

Nevertheless, Shelley was very soon discontented with the idea of remaining in Edinburgh all winter. He wrote to Hogg on November 26 that he expected soon to return to London alone. The £500 raised on a post-obit early in October lasted apparently less than two months, and on November 28 Shelley was writing to an unidentified person earnestly requesting him not to decline accepting a draft of £30, "as the consequence would be, *our being driven out of our lodgings.*"

Shortly before the 10th of December Shelley was back in London, not alone, but with the rest of his party. During the next two or three weeks he saw Godwin, Hogg, and the Newtons frequently. Near the end of the year the Shelleys took a furnished house at Windsor, a neighborhood familiar to Shelley from his Eton days, and only eight or ten miles from the home of the Boinvilles at Bracknell. Here they lived for about two months, Shelley spending much of his time in town or with the Boinvilles, Harriet and Eliza probably spending considerable time in London at the Westbrook house.

It is very likely that some of the five hundred pounds Shelley had raised in October went to Godwin's needs, thus beginning what was to prove the greatest single drain on Shelley's finances for most of the remaining years of his life. Two undated notes, apparently written about the second week in December, were endorsed from 41

Skinner Street and show that Shelley was trying to raise more money. Before leaving London it had been his intention to raise only enough money on post-obits to pay his own debts. But Godwin's debts were an exception, having been assumed by Shelley before September 1813. Now, at a time when his own financial position was desperate, he seems even to have given them pre-eminence.

Chapter X

WHEN HOGG saw Harriet again, in December and January, he felt that she had changed considerably since the birth of Ianthe. She seemed as healthy, cheerful, and vigorous as ever, but she had given up all effort to share Shelley's intellectual interests. Her old habit of reading aloud and her former devotion to study were now completely abandoned. Shelley seemed to accept her mental complacency as a settled fact and no longer urged her to cultivate her mind. Instead of reading to Hogg when he called and Shelley was away, she now proposed a walk, during which her conversation dwelt largely on the bonnets and caps displayed in millinery shop windows. When Hogg called he often found either Shelley or Harriet at home alone. Whether from indifference to home or the hard necessity of avoiding bailiffs, Shelley now kept rooms both at Mrs. Boinville's at Bracknell and at the lodgings of his publisher in London, Thomas Hookham. Harriet still talked of suicide as cheerfully as ever.

While living at Windsor, Shelley spend much of his time with the Boinvilles, at Bracknell. Hogg made a brief visit there, unfortunately during Shelley's absence. He slept in Shelley's disordered, book-strewn bedroom, and reported on the society that Shelley kept. Mrs. Newton was then visiting her sister, Mrs. Boinville. The two sisters and Cornelia Turner were "never weary of the sweet courtesies of making tea"; hours were late, meals were, to Hogg's chagrin, rather irregular, sketchy affairs, but there was plenty of good bread and butter and sprightly conversation.

Wieland's long, weary romance of *Agathon,* in a French translation, was at that time the favorite reading of the group. Against Hogg's skepticism, the ladies championed it as a demonstration of the superior value of purely Platonic love, an estimate which Shelley heartily endorsed. Peacock, who was occasionally with the Boinville circle in the company of Shelley and Harriet, was regarded with disapproval by the more fervent theorists because he sometimes laughed at them. Harriet, formerly a faithful echo of Shelley's enthusiasms, now often laughed with Peacock.

More serious differences were appearing about Ianthe. Harriet declined to suckle the child herself and engaged a wet nurse whom

Shelley did not like. In a recent medical book he had read repeated statements of the dire effects of wet nursing. He was horrified at Harriet's "unnatural" conduct; after long, fruitless arguments with her he even tried in desperation — so Peacock testifies — to suckle the child himself. Eliza Westbrook's fondness for Ianthe made Shelley positively ill. His former distaste for Eliza had now become an overwhelming hatred. "I sometimes feel faint with the fatigue of checking the overflowings of my unbounded abhorrence for this miserable wretch," he wrote to Hogg on March 16.

Shelley did not conceal his domestic unhappiness from Hogg, and yet, less than a week after this letter, on March 22, he remarried Harriet for the express purpose of removing all possible doubt as to the legality of his first marriage. This hardly looks as if he considered his present unhappiness incurable.

The disheartening shadow which now threatened Shelley's home life was accompanied by an increasing financial desperation. Bailiffs might find it harder to catch him at Windsor or at one of his two lodgings, but they were sure to redouble their energies, now that his twenty-first birthday had passed without a settlement. Shelley had employed a Mr. Amory, a solicitor, for his financial negotiations with his father, who was now genuinely concerned. If, as Mr. Shelley thought, there was doubt of Shelley's ability to raise enough money for his creditors by post-obits, it was evident that he might be forced seriously to embarrass the Shelley estate and yet still be unable to rescue himself. Sir Bysshe talked of selling Castle Goring, but remained so stubbornly wedded to his old dream that his son feared to urge his own idea, which was to pay the debts, give Shelley an allowance, and put him under bond to stay within it.

On March 4 Shelley sold to Andrew John Nash and George Augustus Nash a post-obit of £8,000 for £2,593, 10s., half of which was for Godwin. But until July 12 he refrained from completing the transaction by signing the indenture, hoping still to complete arrangements with his father and grandfather. Soon afterwards (March 13) he wrote to his father expressing gratitude for his concern and saying that he could no longer delay raising a considerable amount on post-obits unless he received quick relief. He pointed out that such sales, at the usual ruinous rates (three or four to one) might completely frustrate his grandfather's desire to keep the estate intact, and he hoped his father might persuade Sir Bysshe to prevent such a disaster. This letter, Mr. Shelley remarked in turning it over to

Whitton, "would not at all suit his grandfather's notions." "And on my own part," he added, "I would rather he would first acknowledge his God, then I might be led to believe his assertions."

During these negotiations Shelley had been staying for about a month with the Boinvilles, completely dejected, and endeavoring to escape, as he phrased it, "from the dismaying solitude of myself." Harried by duns and bailiffs, despondent of financial succor, unhappy for the first time in his home, he was in a state bordering upon physical and nervous collapse. "Seriously," Mrs. Boinville wrote to Hogg, "I think his mind and body want rest." He described himself to Hogg as having "sunk into a premature old age of exhaustion . . . and a terrible susceptibility to objects of disgust or hatred." He was still interested in reading; he even resumed his Italian with Cornelia Turner as his helper — Cornelia, whom he no longer regarded as cold and reserved, but as inheriting "all the divinity of her mother." Except for pleasant moments that he owed to the ministering kindness of Mrs. Boinville and her daughter he now regarded life almost as a disgusting burden. He confessed to Cornelia that the reason for his lingering late in conversation with her was that he "dreaded the visions which pursued him when alone at night."

In March or April the Shelleys seem to have left Windsor and taken a house at Bracknell. Soon thereafter Harriet took Ianthe to London for a visit and Eliza went to Southampton to live, thus removing a very important cause of Shelley's unhappiness. Shelley reoccupied his room at the Boinvilles', still in a very low state of mind and body. In a poem written at Bracknell in April he pictured himself as returning unwillingly at midnight to his own "sad and silent home," driven by "duty and dereliction" (and possibly the "ungentle mood" of Mrs. Boinville) to remember in hopeless solitude "the music of two voices and the light of one sweet smile."

The one sweet smile was certainly Cornelia Turner's. For Shelley's nature complete sympathy was almost a vital necessity; his whole life and works are a record of his search for it. For two years he had thought himself enjoying it or on the road to enjoying it with Harriet, but that sympathy had been broken and appeared incapable of complete restoration. Mrs. Boinville and her daughter now seemed to understand him better than Harriet — Mrs. Boinville perhaps a little too well, because she evidently distrusted the drift of his emotions.

Cornelia Turner was young, accomplished, and physically attractive. She spoke the language of sentimental sympathy and Platonic love, feeling secure, perhaps, in her own marriage and Shelley's. In his letter of March 16 to Hogg, Shelley had enclosed the following lines:

> Thy dewy looks sink in my breast;
> Thy gentle words stir poison there;
> Thou hast disturbed the only rest
> That was the portion of despair!
> Subdued to Duty's hard control,
> I could have borne my wayward lot;
> The chains that bind this ruined soul
> Had cankered then — but crushed it not.

Quite probably he believed his assertion to Hogg at the time that these lines had no literal application to reality, but were "the vision of a delirious and distempered dream." Yet in the same letter he characterized Cornelia as a divine creature, "the reverse of everything bad." Two or three weeks afterwards, in the poem previously described, he was referring to her as his "lover."

To Mark Twain and to many others these circumstances could only mean that Shelley was frankly in love with Cornelia; but in a circle which believed that the only real love was sentimental or Platonic love, the word "lover" would hardly mean what it meant to Mark Twain. It is easier to see a Platonic than a carnal lover in one who confesses, as Shelley did to Cornelia, that he sought her company as a protection against terrifying visions when alone at night. Yet Shelley's own words prove that this "love" was in conflict with "duty," which should not be true of Platonic love.

Mrs. Boinville, with the happiness of two families at stake, obviously saw more in duty than Shelley did; she required him to go home, showing plainly that she regarded the situation as dangerous. Harriet said later that Shelley fell in love with Cornelia and paid her such marked attention that her husband carried her off to Devonshire; Jane Clairmont, who knew the Boinvilles, supported this with a statement that the Boinvilles indignantly broke off his acquaintance for a time, but not Harriet's. Whatever the real state of Shelley's mind toward Cornelia Turner, it seems plain that Cornelia's mother was alarmed and that Harriet felt she had a just grievance against Shelley.

Shelley seems to have reasoned with himself very much as Mrs.

Boinville must have reasoned with him. In a poem evidently addressed to himself he speaks of having

> . . . sought in starry eyes
> Beams that were never meant for thine,
> Another's wealth. . . .

He describes a state of spiritual loneliness in which his own soul, changed to a fiend, tempts him to a pursuit he knows would be disastrous. Any change, he concludes, would only be for the worse.

A change occurred, however, soon after Mrs. Boinville required Shelley to leave her house, and it was not necessarily for the worse. In May Shelley wrote a poem entitled "To Harriet" which shows that the Cornelia Turner infatuation was definitely over. In it he recognized Harriet's scorn or resentment and pleaded that "a slight endurance" on her part would give him lasting happiness and cure a deep misery of soul. He begged her to reject any "erring guide" counseling obduracy, and to yield to her own fine nature and pity him if she could not love:

> Thy look of love has power to calm
> The stormiest passion of my soul;
> Thy gentle words are drops of balm
> In life's too bitter bowl;
> No grief is mine, but that alone
> These choicest blessings I have known.

How Harriet received Shelley's appeal to her generosity is unknown, but may be inferred from the fact that she copied and preserved this poem. Both she and Shelley remained at home together at Bracknell (without Eliza) save for Shelley's necessary occasional absences in London on financial matters. No poems or letters of Shelley's are extant showing any of the desperate distress that he had felt since the middle of March. He and Harriet revived a plan formed during the previous September, to retire to Nantgwillt, in Wales, as soon as possible.

It was about this time, probably the first week in June, that Shelley visited Field Place — the last time he was ever allowed to cross its threshold. In Mr. Shelley's absence with the three youngest children, Shelley's mother invited him home for a short, secret visit. He was cordially welcomed, and everyone entered into a conspiracy of silence to keep his visit a secret. When he went walking it was as "Captain Jones," wearing a military uniform borrowed from Captain

Kennedy, a friendly young officer quartered at Horsham. Perhaps Mrs. Shelley had thought that a secret visit would lead to a solution of Shelley's difficulties, but if so, she was mistaken.

Since Sir Bysshe Shelley's obduracy blocked all other relief, it was necessary for Shelley to conclude the post-obit sale arranged with the Nashes on March 4. On June 18 Shelley went to London to complete the sale, leaving Harriet at Bracknell, expecting his early return. But unexpected legal complications arose. Godwin, whose desperate finances were also to be relieved by the proceeds, insisted on Shelley's remaining in London. Shelley remained from day to day until the transaction was finally completed on July 6. In order to escape arrest for debts he lodged in Fleet Street and ate his meals with the Godwins.

During the first week, apparently as long as Harriet remained in Bracknell, Shelley was impatient to return and prosecute his plans for removing to Nantgwillt, but Godwin stubbornly refused consent to his absence for even one night. Harriet was now nearly three months advanced in pregnancy, and it is probable that both she and Shelley thought it bad for her to be alone at Bracknell. Nevertheless she waited for Shelley in Bracknell as late as June 25 and then went to Bath, where she received frequent letters from him.

Had the money from the post-obit been secured at the time it was expected, or had Godwin been less stubborn, there is every reason for supposing that Shelley and Harriet would have retired with Ianthe to Nantgwillt, there to attempt to recapture some of their former happiness. Harriet was young enough, and sufficiently devoted and frightened, to return to her former habits of reading and study and become once more the disciple that Shelley craved. Limitations of mind and character, however, probably made it impossible for her to go much further along that road than she had already gone — and motherhood introduced interests that clashed with discipleship. Possibly Harriet lacked the imagination to perceive that Shelley was not an ordinary philanderer, but was physically and spiritually ill, from reasons that were not entirely domestic, and that Cornelia Turner was only the straw at which he grasped, rather blindly and deliriously. The pathological violence of his antipathy to Eliza Westbrook, and the complete dejection and exhaustion — mental, physical, and emotional — shown by Shelley's poems and letters of March, April, and May, all suggest that his coincident domestic unhappiness may have been more an effect than a cause.

With her abundant, cheerful health and her rather ordinary extroverted mind Harriet was ill equipped to recognize and cope with such a situation, even with the best will to do so. Some of its causes still remained, in spite of the superficial restoration of domestic happiness. Cornelia Turner had vanished, but what if the next straw should prove more substantial, and even exhibit a reciprocal power of grasping? It was this that Harriet had to fear, more than the absurd shortcomings attributed to her by some of Shelley's biographers.

Even before Shelley went up to London on June 18 to complete his financial arrangements with the Nash brothers, he had begun the friendship which was to wreck his marriage with Harriet. On June 8 Hogg had accidentally encountered Shelley in Cheapside and had accompanied him to Godwin's house in Skinner Street. While they were waiting for Godwin the door opened softly a little and a thrilling voice called: "Shelley!" Hogg caught a glimpse of the speaker as Shelley darted through the door to speak with her; she was a young girl, fair-haired and fair-skinned to the point of paleness, with a piercing look. She was dressed, rather oddly for London, in tartan.

Shelley returned in a moment with the announcement that there was no use waiting for Godwin. "Who was that?" Hogg asked as they resumed their walk. Shelley replied: "The daughter of Godwin and Mary." It was about this time that Mary Godwin wrote in the book she was using for her Latin exercises: "Shall I write a poem on receiving a cordial shake of the hand from an esteemed and excellent person ah I cannot write poetry."

In the year and a half that had elapsed since their first meeting Mary Godwin had ceased to be a child. Ten months of open air and sea bathing, reading and day dreaming in Scotland had restored and fortified her health and improved her mind. She was now an agreeable, vivacious, and sparkling young woman. She admired the character and principles of her mother, perhaps the more by contrast with the acerbities of the present Mrs. Godwin, who sometimes nagged her for reading too much. At such times it was her custom to slip away to Saint Pancras churchyard and read her book under the willow tree that shaded her mother's grave.

When Hogg first saw Mary Godwin, Shelley had been in and out of the Godwin household rather constantly for five or six weeks. Beginning on June 18 and continuing until July 7, he took practically all his meals with the Godwins. Mrs. Godwin was even then not unaware that the developing friendship might contain some seeds of danger. Having suspected a little earlier that Mary's half sister, Fanny Imlay, was beginning to fall in love with their ardent, erratic young guest (though without his knowledge), she had prudently sent Fanny on a visit to Wales. Thus when Godwin spoke to Shelley about his attentions to Mary and received the answer that it was only his manner with all women, there was no reason why anyone should doubt his explanation. At the time, with Shelley begging hard for permission to return to Bracknell, it was undoubtedly true.

A part of Mary's attraction for Shelley (and, according to Harriet's later opinion, a really decisive part) was Shelley's adoration of Mary's mother, Mary Wollstonecraft, whose fine portrait by John Opie presided over Godwin's octagon-shaped, book-lined sitting-room. Shelley began accompanying Mary on her frequent visits to her mother's grave in Saint Pancras churchyard. Very soon, according to his own statement, he was deeply in love with her, though he succeeded for a while in deceiving even himself as to the true nature of his feelings.

It was Mary, in fact, and not Shelley, who first clarified the situation between them. While Shelley floundered hopelessly and silently, confused between duty and virtue, Mary exploded every doubt by simply and frankly declaring her love for him. "No expressions," Shelley later wrote to Hogg, "can convey the remotest conception of the *manner* in which she dispelled my delusions. The sublime and rapturous moment when she confessed herself mine, who had so long been hers in secret, cannot be painted to mortal imagination. . . ."

The very time and place of this momentous scene are fixed by the later testimony of Shelley and Mary to William Godwin. On Sunday, June 26, 1814, Shelley accompanied Mary and Jane Clairmont to the grave of Mary Wollstonecraft, in Saint Pancras churchyard. Jane, as on later occasions, soon absented herself. The scene is described in Shelley's own words, in a poem addressed to Mary within four days after the event. Describing first his embarrassed distress (because he was resolved to conceal his love and was ignorant of her real feelings), then his general state of misery, followed by overwhelming joy at Mary's disclosure, the poem continues:

> Upon my heart your accents sweet
> Of peace and pity fell like dew
> On flowers half dead; — thy lips did meet
> Mine tremblingly; thy dark eyes threw

Their soft persuasion on my brain,
Turning to bliss its wayward pain,
Charming away its dream of ——.

We are not happy, sweet! our state
    Is strange and full of doubt and fear;
More need of words that ills abate; —
    Reserve or censure come not near
Our sacred friendship, lest there be
No solace left for you and me.

Gentle and good and mild thou art,
    Nor can I live if thou appear
Aught but thyself, or turn thine heart
    Away from me, or stoop to wear
The mask of scorn, although it be
To hide the love thou feel'st for me.

It was almost precisely at this moment that Harriet, in Bath, began to grow uneasy at the sudden stoppage of Shelley's letters to her.
At first, apparently, the lovers were too full of doubt and fear to have
any plans or to know if any were possible. When they did settle on
a plan, it still seemed necessary to keep everything secret until Godwin had been freed from his financial dependence on Shelley. But on
Wednesday, July 6, the long-delayed post-obit sale was completed
and Godwin received his half of the proceeds — about £1,200. That
very evening, in Godwin's phrase, Shelley "had the madness to dis-
close his plans to me and to ask my consent." To the young lovers,
acting on the principles of *Political Justice*, such a judgment probably appeared harsh, but Godwin was thinking (with a touch of true
prophecy) of what people would say about him. And so Shelley's
idea was "impious," and Shelley a "traitor" and a "seducer."

Godwin immediately required Shelley to discontinue all visits to
Skinner Street. But Shelley sent Mary a copy of *Queen Mab* containing a cryptic inscription, under the dedicatory poem to Harriet,
which seemed to accuse Harriet of abandoning him to misery. To
this Mary added a much longer inscription of her own. It was impassioned, a little incoherent, and contained two stanzas of poetry.
The gift, she asserted, was sacred to her, and since no other person
would see it, she would write in it what she pleased — namely, that
she loved the author beyond expression and could never be an-

155

other's: "I have pledged myself to thee, and sacred is the gift. I remember your words: 'You are now, Mary, going to mix with many, and for a moment I shall depart, but in the solitude of your chamber I shall be with you.' Yes, you are ever with me, sacred vision."

Meanwhile Harriet had gone four days without hearing from Shelley and had become so alarmed that she wrote to Thomas Hookham expressing her fears and enclosing a letter to be delivered to Shelley. Shelley then wrote to Harriet begging her to come at once to London. She arrived promptly, on July 14. He told her that he was desperately in love with Mary, that both he and Mary had thought of committing suicide, and that only her generosity could save them. The version of the crisis which he then gave Harriet was later repeated by her, with her own coloring, in a letter to Catherine Nugent:

Mary was determined to seduce him. She is to blame. She heated his imagination by talking of her mother, and going to her grave with him every day, till at last she told him she was dying in love for him, accompanied with the most violent gestures and vehement expostulations. He thought of me and my sufferings, and begged her to get the better of a passion as degrading to him as herself. She then told him that she would die — he had rejected her, and what appeared to her as the sublimest virtue was to him a crime. Why could we not all live together? I as his sister, she as his wife?

Shelley's proposal of a *ménage à trois* may be another instance of the peculiar suggestive power of books to which he was subject. At Bracknell he had been greatly impressed by Wieland's *Agathon*, the emotional situation of whose philanthropic and philosophical-sentimental hero much resembled his own. Agathon also had veered between two loves, a spiritual and a sensual. He had abandoned one for the other, and had ultimately found happiness by living with them both on a Platonic basis, having meanwhile discovered that the first one was really his sister.

To Harriet, Shelley's proposal appeared monstrous, but she behaved with considerable self-control and presence of mind. Alarmed more by Shelley's present desperate mood than by any fear that she had lost his love permanently, she allowed him to believe that if his present feelings were not a passing fever she would not continue to oppose them. The wild surge of hope and relief with which Shelley viewed Harriet's attitude is seen in the following letter, written within a few hours of the interview:

My Dearest Friend,

Exhausted as I am with our interview, and secure of seeing you tomorrow at 12, I cannot yet refrain from writing to you.

I am made calmer and happier by your assurances. It is true that my confidence in the integrity and disinterestedness of your conduct has ever remained firm; but I dreaded lest the shock might inflict on you some incurable unhappiness; lest you should doubt the continuance of my affection for you, lest you should see, what I so deeply felt, nothing but misery and despair.

My spirit turned to you for consolation, and it found it; all that vulgar minds regard as so important was considered by you with consistent and becoming contempt. Feeling still persuaded that my affection for you was undim[in]ished, you offered to my view, and anticipated for yourself that pure and lasting happiness which is the portion only of the great and good.

For this, dearest Harriet, from my inmost Soul, I thank you. This is perhaps the greatest among the many blessing which I have received, and still am destined to receive at your hands. I loathed the very light of day, and looked upon my own being with deep and unutterable abhorrence. I lived — Mary too consented to survive — I lived in the hope of consolation and happiness from you, and I have not been deceived. . . .

After three paragraphs assuring Harriet that "friendship and not passion" had been the bond of their attachment and reminding her that Mrs. Boinville had prophesied the present outcome, Shelley continued:

Can your feelings for me differ in their nature from those which I cherish towards you? Are you my lover whilst I am only your friend, the brother of your heart? If they do not, the purest and most perfect happiness is ours. I wish that you could see Mary; to the most indifferent eyes she would be interesting only for her sufferings, and the tyranny which is exercised upon her. I murmur not if you feel incapable of compassion and love for the object and sharer of my passion.

If you want to draw on the Bankers before I see you, Hookham will give you the checks.

Adieu. Bring my sweet babe. I must ever love her for your sake.

Ever most affectionately yours

P. B. SHELLEY

On the next day, Friday, July 15, Harriet and Shelley called on Godwin together, and Godwin called on Harriet in Shelley's absence; on Saturday Godwin visited the two together and went out in a coach with Shelley alone. According to one of Mrs. Godwin's letters, Harriet also came to the Godwins' alone:

> She was very much agitated, and wept, poor dear young lady, a great deal. . . . She implored us to forbid him our house and prevent his seeing Mary. . . . We sympathized with her, and she went away contented, feeling, as she said, quite sure that, not seeing Mary, he would forget her. We then spoke to Mary on the subject, and she behaved as well as possible — approved our renouncing his acquaintance, and wrote a few lines to Harriet to pray her not to be unhappy, as she would not see Mr. S — again.

Jane Clairmont, who copied this letter, added on her own authority that she accompanied Mary to Chapel Street and heard Mary assure Harriet that she would discourage Shelley's love for her.

So Harriet still loved Shelley and still believed in his love for her. She was becoming frightened, but she still regarded the affair with Mary as an infatuation from which Shelley would suddenly recover, like the affair with Cornelia Turner, which she mentioned during the same interview. But the reassurance she received from Mary was not sufficient; she distrusted Mary. Her instinct and observation told her that this was far more serious than the former affair. She was expecting to become a mother again in December, and the shock was too great for her. Something of the agony of the next two weeks, both for herself and for Shelley, may be gathered from Harriet's brief account to Catherine Nugent:

> You may suppose how I felt at the disclosure. I was laid up for a fortnight after. I could do nothing for myself. He begged me to live. The doctors gave me over. They said 'twas impossible. I saw his despair, the agony of my beloved sister; and owing to the great strength of my constitution I lived; and here I am, my dear friend, waiting to bring another infant into this woful world.

If Mary had earlier resolved to make Shelley love her, she now appears to have formed an honest intention of discouraging his love. She concurred in her father's decision to forbid Shelley the house. For a short while thereafter tranquillity seemed to be restored. During this time Godwin continued to visit Shelley and to discuss philosophy, logic, and history with him, still confident, seemingly, of the power of calm philosophy over passion.

Then one day a wild and disheveled Shelley entered the Skinner Street shop in Godwin's absence and rushed upstairs. Gone now was all the Spartan self-control he had urged upon Hogg when the latter was similarly possessed. He had tried that, and it was no good. How could he ever have written so ignorantly, less than three years ago: "Love is not a whirlwind, that it is unvanquishable"? He pushed Mrs. Godwin violently aside and walked straight up to Mary. "They wish to separate us, my beloved, but Death shall unite us." He offered her a bottle of laudanum. "By this you can escape from tyranny."

"This," he said, taking a small pistol from his pocket, "shall reunite me to you." Mary turned pale as a ghost; Jane Clairmont, who was in the room, shrieked again and again. Mrs. Godwin rushed out for aid and returned with Mr. Marshall, a friend who was waiting downstairs to have dinner with the family. Between them they persuaded Shelley to go home. Mary wept and was so distressed that she hardly knew what she said. As well as she could remember, she had said to him: "I won't take this laudanum; but if you will only be reasonable and calm, I will promise to be ever faithful to you."

There was another brief period of quiet. Mary seemed to be still adhering to her resolution. Shelley was in a dreadful state of mind, pulled first one way by a violent, uncontrollable passion, then the other way by deep affection for Harriet and sympathy with her sufferings. More than two years of love and loyal sympathy from Harriet could not be canceled overnight. Either Hogg was absent on his northern vacation, or else Shelley feared he would not sympathize; at any rate, Shelley ignored him. Instead he sent Peacock an urgent summons to come up from Marlow.

Peacock came and was deeply surprised and shocked. He found Shelley in a state of wild mental storm surpassing anything he had ever seen or imagined — violent and incoherent in speech and gesture, with bloodshot eyes and disordered hair and dress, pacing wildly up and down, and flourishing a bottle of laudanum which he said he always kept at hand. It was in fact precisely what Shelley himself had once described as the worst possible state for such a person as himself: "For what conflict of a frank mind," he had once philosophized to Elizabeth Hitchener, "is more terrible than the balance between two opposing importances of morality . . . this is

surely the only wretchedness which a mind who only acknowledges
virtue its master can feel."

Peacock was not the man to become the stern, unyielding champion of duty, even though he was himself fond of Harriet. He did
remark: "It always appeared to me that you were very fond of Harriet," and Shelley brushed this aside with: "But you did not know
how I hated her sister." Perhaps Peacock reminded him (as he later
reminded Harriet's detractors) that Harriet had beauty, good taste,
a frank, spontaneous manner, and a good humor and sympathy by
which she accommodated herself to his ideas and his restless changes
of environment. Shelley clearly realized all this. But "Every one who
knows me," he said, "must know that the partner of my life should
be one who can feel poetry and understand philosophy. Harriet is a
noble animal, but she can do neither."

For Shelley the force of this undeniable fact must have been overwhelming. Long ago he had set himself with almost deadly tenacity
to the mission of making mankind listen to a better notion of right
and wrong. It is probable that his depression of the previous spring
was caused partly by a subconscious apprehension of Harriet as no
longer a partner in this purpose. In the beginning he had calmly set
out to "form" Harriet's mind, but Mary's mind he considered superior to his own.

One midnight the Godwins' doorbell rang violently; the master of
the house in which Shelley lodged had come to say that Shelley was
at death's door from an overdose of laudanum. When Mr. and Mrs.
Godwin hastened to him they found Shelley already in the hands of a
doctor, who was forcing him to walk up and down the room. For the
next day, while Mrs. Godwin nursed him, he could say nothing beyond "Yes" and "No" — which was, in fact, about all he would ever
have desired to say to Mrs. Godwin. Mrs. Boinville then came and
stayed with Shelley a week until he had recovered.

Shelley's recovery was hastened, Mrs. Godwin suspected, by secret
notes from Mary. His spirits rose and he promised not to attempt
suicide again. Mrs. Godwin was right; Shelley had bribed the shop
porter at Skinner Street to convey notes between him and Mary.

There was no further hesitation, at least on his part, as to what was
to be done. Mary still needed persuasion, but that can hardly have
been difficult when Shelley was so determined and when her own
emotions argued so strongly on his side. Mary and Jane used to
take a walk every day in the neighborhood of the Charterhouse.

Here Shelley would join them, and Jane would walk up and down
at a distance, while Shelley and Mary sat and talked in one of the
arbors. It was here that Shelley overcame Mary's reluctance to elope
by assuring her that Harriet no longer loved him and was in fact
an adulteress. He even named her lover as a Major Ryan, a man whom
they had met in Dublin and had seen since, occasionally, in London.

Mary accepted this as a fact and considered that it justified Shelley's behavior. Yet it had not been a fortnight since Shelley himself
had testified eloquently to Harriet's nobility and fidelity. In all subsequent references to Harriet's two children he plainly assumed pa-
ternity. Charles Clairmont, who drew his information from Shelley,
later expressly exonerated Harriet from this charge while condemning her on other grounds. Either Shelley knew at the time that his
argument was false, or else its truth was so utterly necessary to him
that he believed it himself because he so intensely longed to do so.

Shelley had already informed Harriet that she could draw money
through Hookham. In the hands of a lawyer named Tahourdin he
had placed deeds and settlement papers providing for a separation
and separate maintenance for Harriet. There was money at his
bankers'.

By the night of July 27 Shelley and Mary could delay no longer.
Shelley ordered a chaise to be ready at four o'clock in the morning,
and "watched until the lightning and the stars became pale." At four
o'clock Shelley was waiting. Mary joined him, then left him again
for a short time — possibly to leave the note that Godwin found on
his dressing-table an hour later. "How dreadful," Shelley wrote in his
journal, "did this time appear; it seemed that we trifled with life and
hope; a few minutes passed, she was in my arms — we were safe; we
were on our road to Dover."

Jane Clairmont was with them; she would be useful as an inter-
preter, since neither Shelley nor Mary possessed her fluency in
French. Doubtless she, too, needed liberation from "tyranny." As
the sun rose higher, the heat became excessive; it was one of the hottest days for many years. Mary was ill and faint with the heat and
the strain and leaned her head listlessly against the side of the
chaise. Shelley sat in the middle, whispering consolation to her,
while Jane, very much alone, sat on the other side, watching the
landscape whirl past, and feeling as if the end of the world had
come.

It was necessary for Mary to rest at every stage, and it was extremely necessary to keep ahead of the pursuit. They knew Godwin's

161

early-rising habits; they probably guessed pretty accurately what had been happening in Skinner Street — Godwin's finding Mary's letter at five o'clock, the prompt inquiries among neighboring livery stables, Mrs. Godwin's departure to overtake them.

Shelley hurried the flight by every possible means, imagining pursuers at his heels. At Dartford they took four horses instead of two. Reaching Dover at four o'clock, they found that the packet would not sail until next day. Had they waited for it Mrs. Godwin would have caught them in England. Taking time only for Mary to refresh herself with a sea-bath and for Shelley to interview the customs officers and engage a small boat, they set sail ahead of the packet, at six in the evening.

For the first time the fugitives felt safe. The cliffs of Dover slowly receded, the sails flapped in a flagging breeze, and the moon came up over a slow, heavy Channel swell. Soon, however, the breeze freshened into a gale, Mary became so ill that she could scarcely move, and Shelley himself was almost too exhausted to support the weight of her head against him. As the winds grew more violent and contrary, what had been promised as a passage of two hours lengthened into a whole night. A thunder-squall caused the small boat to ship water in a manner that alarmed even the sailors. For a few moments Shelley thought himself facing death with his beloved:

> Mary did not know our danger; she was resting between my knees, that were unable to support her; she did not speak or look, but I felt that she was there. I had time in that moment to reflect, and even to reason upon death; it was rather a thing of discomfort . . . than horror to me. We should never be separated, but in death we might not know and feel our union as now.

The wind changed once more and drove them on toward Calais. They landed in the early dawn, on Friday, July 29. "Mary, look!" Shelley exclaimed, "the sun rises over France." Completely worn out, they engaged a room at Dessein's Hotel and rested until evening.

Before the evening was over, Mrs. Godwin reached Calais on the packet Shelley had refused to wait for. Godwin, who knew how Shelley hated her, had made her promise not to see him, lest he do her some personal violence. In the evening a Captain Davison came to Shelley with the information that a fat lady had arrived who claimed that he had run away with her daughter. Jane spent the night with her mother and promised to return to London with her,

but next day she thought better — or worse — of her promise and decided to remain with the culprits. Mrs. Godwin had expended all
her feelings and persuasions on the previous argument; she now left
without a word, and Shelley passed her on the street as she made her
way back to the dock.

Chapter XI

SCARCELY HAD Mrs. Godwin taken her dejected way to the Dover packet before Shelley's party were again on the road, fugitives no longer, traveling across France in a two-wheeled, un-English-looking vehicle called a cabriolet. That same evening they left Calais for Boulogne, where they spent the night. Next morning the stiff-peruked postilion resumed his interminable cracking of the whip. Traveling two days and a night, they reached Paris about two o'clock in the afternoon of August 2 and engaged lodgings at the Hôtel de Vienne. The excessive heat continued, and Mary continued to suffer from it. Their funds were already beginning to run low.

They remained in Paris for six days, from August 2 until the evening of August 8. Shelley's first action was to look over with Mary the contents of a box containing some of her youthful compositions, together with letters she had received from her father and friends, including Shelley. Characteristically, he was interested in the "productions of her mind." They visited the Tuileries, the Louvre, and Notre Dame, but found nothing remarkable except a "terribly impressive" painting of the Deluge. For the first day or two Mary was still ill. The specter of financial difficulties had already reappeared, but they were too happy in each other to be dejected by it.

They were now keeping a joint journal, dating from their elopement. "The morning [August 7] passes in delightful converse. We almost forget that we are prisoners in Paris; Mary especially seems insensible to all future evil. She feels as if our love would alone suffice to resist the invasions of calamity." Even two dour, unsympathetic letters from Thomas Hookham, showing plainly enough what would have to be faced from old friends in London, failed to dishearten them.

The financial situation was in fact quite embarrassing. They had reached Paris almost penniless. On his birthday Shelley sold his watch and chain for eight napoleons, five francs. A French man of business through whom he hoped to raise funds proved dilatory or unwilling; Shelley called him "an idiot." An obscure French author named R. de Sair, with whom they once or twice dined and breakfasted, took them to a banker, who refused to advance them anything. Fortunately they received a remittance of £60 on August 7 and were enabled to pay their bills in Paris and proceed with their plans.

With money in hand they now prepared to resume their journey. They were headed for Switzerland — more precisely for Uri, a district made sacred to Shelley by Godwin's novel *Fleetwood*. In vain their landlady urged the danger and discomfort of such an undertaking. Jane and Shelley went to market and bought an ass, which turned out to be too weak to carry a burden and accompanied them to Charenton merely as a companion. Next morning at Charenton they sold the ass and bought a mule, losing heavily on the transaction. Hence to Guignes, nine leagues distant. Shelley led the mule and Mary rode it, with the exception of eight miles during which Jane rode and Mary walked.

The journey had been planned as a pedestrian one, the ass to carry the light luggage and one of the ladies occasionally. With the incompetent ass replaced by a mule, this plan worked for three days. Mary and Jane, clad in black silk gowns, rode by turns, Shelley leading the mule and carrying a light basket of fruit and bread. Their heavy luggage was to follow. Mary, who was still ill from time to time, did most of the riding. At Trois Maisons, however, Shelley strained his leg so badly that it was impossible for him to walk, so Mary surrendered the mule and Shelley rode for the rest of the day. Six days later Jane also was "very unable to walk." At Troyes they engaged a voiture and sold the mule, having lost, from ass to voiture, fifteen napoleons on their ownership of livestock. Thereafter all rode, even though the driver engaged at Troyes proved surly and obstinate and finally left them when they came to mountainous country. The mule of the next driver went lame shortly after they crossed the Swiss frontier. At Neuchâtel, just as the money they had secured in Paris was running low, Shelley visited a banker and returned with a large canvas bag full of silver, the equivalent of about thirty-eight pounds.

Most of the country over which they passed between Paris and the Swiss frontier had been laid desolate by war within the previous six months. It was here that Napoleon had fought his last desperate, brilliant campaign in the winter and spring of 1814 to keep the invaders from Paris. At Guignes they slept at the same inn and in the same beds that Napoleon and his staff had occupied only shortly before. Nogent had been completely desolated by the Cossacks; its bridge was broken and its houses were in ashes. Most of the little villages had been burned, the cows had been killed or driven away, the fields were no longer cultivated. Echemine, Pavillon, and practically every village they saw before reaching Troyes had been completely ruined. Similar devastation reigned in the outskirts of Troyes and beyond toward the Swiss frontier. On the road to Troyes they met an old man who said his children had been murdered by the Cossacks. For the first time Shelley beheld the actual physical effects of warfare, for which he had long entertained an abstract horror. The experience impressed him more than the somewhat matter-of-fact contemporary chronicle reveals, and is echoed three years later in the preface to *Laon and Cythna*.

Inns and beds everywhere were almost incredibly filthy. The countryfolk were so surly and inhospitable that the travelers "could hardly pity them." What with Mary's illness (on August 8 she recorded "one horrible spasm"), the lameness in turn of Shelley, Jane, and the mule, the continued dirt and discomfort, and the uncertainty of additional funds, one might naturally conclude that this unusual honeymoon tour was a very dismal one. But such was not the case. The high spirits of the wayfarers that had been proof against the pessimism of their Paris landlady and Hookham's disappointing letters remained high; neither their joint journal nor Jane's contains a single note of apprehension.

Jane was a natural enthusiast who, beginning with Charenton, thought various places "wonderful"; Shelley and Mary were too much in love to regard physical discomforts. All three were lovers of romantic scenes, whether mountains and streams and pine forests or quaint old towns like Provins and Besançon. "The approach to Provins is most beautiful," wrote Shelley (August 10); "a ruined citadel, with extensive walls and towers, stood above the town; the cathedral was beyond; it formed one scene. We slept at a little old woman's, whose beds were infinitely detestable." To all three travelers the first view of the Alps was plainly a much more significant matter than all the difficulties of the journey.

At Troyes, where they had waited a day, Shelley had written to Harriet, "to shew you that I do not forget you." He assured her that he was her best friend and adviser and urged her to join him in Switzerland, bringing with her the deeds then in his lawyer's hands that had been prepared to legalize the separation and provide a settlement for her.

At Brunen, where Fleetwood had visited Russigny in Godwin's *Fleetwood*, they had planned to stop for the winter. But Mary could not endure the filth of their first apartment, and it proved impossible to procure a house. They rented a two-room apartment for six months, moved in, and received with somewhat scant politeness a visit from the old abbé and the local doctor. It was on the 25th that they took possession. Shelley immediately set to work on a new romance, *The Assassins*, which Mary wrote down at his dictation. This fragmentary novel, never finished, seems to have been imagined somewhat after the general plan of Johnson's *Rasselas*. The Assassins (whose real nature was then unknown) were depicted as an isolated sect practicing a purer form of religion than the rest of the world could understand or accept. Next day Shelley worked on his romance until three o'clock, after which they suddenly decided to return to England as soon as the laundress appeared with the clean linen. Only the circumstance of the linen's being too damp to pack postponed their departure until the following day.

Of the money received at Neuchâtel, only twenty-eight pounds remained. No more was procurable except by Shelley's presence in London. It was necessary not only to return, but to return by the cheapest route possible. Accordingly they decided to make the return almost entirely by water by descending the Rhine.

From Brunen, which they left on August 27, to Rotterdam, where they arrived on September 8, their mode of conveyance varied considerably. They floated in moderately comfortable little passenger boats known as water-diligences, in a freight boat, and once in a long, narrow, flat-bottomed boat of unpainted deal, so crazily knocked together that it leaked at every seam. Their first land conveyance was a cabriolet that broke down and left them to continue on foot. From Bonn to Cologne they traveled by slow post coaches that seldom exceeded a mile and a half an hour; thereafter they journeyed to Clèves by diligence and cabriolet, which they found if anything slower. Finally, in Holland they traveled by post chaise about as rapidly as in England.

Their fellow passengers were mostly Germans compelled, like themselves, to travel by the very cheapest method. On the second day (August 28) Mary's journal speaks with loathing of "the horrid and slimy faces of our companions in voyage." "Never did I see such a set as were in the boat with us," wrote Jane on the same day. On September 4 (having met a few more tolerable passengers meanwhile) Jane wrote: "Nothing could surpass the [word crossed out] Manners that prevailed in the Cabin below — Drinking, smoking, singing, and cracking jokes of a disagreeable nature — We sat upon the deck the whole day with one or two tolerable men who smoked it is true but were brought to own it was wrong." Shelley's party were republicans, but they were also English travelers of the early nineteenth century. These people were "canaille" (Jane's word). When one of them who spoke a little English sought to talk with the travelers they frightened him off by talking dangerously of cutting off the heads of kings.

In spite of everything they enjoyed the journey. The swift green waters of the Reuss, the foaming rapids of the upper Rhine, thrilled them with admiration and a mild sense of danger. Their journals show full appreciation of the romantic scenery, such as the "ruined tower, with its desolate windows," described by Mary, which crowned a hill jutting into the river, while "the sunset was illumining the mountains and the clouds, and casting the reflection of its hues on the agitated river."

In Holland they traveled at good speed over well-kept roads squeezed so tightly between canals at times that carriages could not pass one another. They reached Rotterdam on the evening of September 8, with only twenty écus left in the exchequer. A captain was found who would take them to England for three guineas each, to be paid on arrival. On the next day they embarked, and after being held up for two days by contrary winds, they reached Gravesend on September 13. Here they were able to persuade the captain, though "with great difficulty," to trust them for their passage money.

For forty-two days Shelley, Mary, and Jane had been constantly on the move, never stopping more than two days except for six days at Paris. Not even during this exciting period did Shelley forget his character as an apostle and devotee of freedom. At Paris his first interest was to make himself further acquainted with the possibilities of Mary's mind. Here was a new companion-in-arms rather than a mere disciple, as his sister Elizabeth and Harriet had been. On the way to Switzerland and back again, whenever there was a good opportunity, Shelley and Mary read together, from Mary Wollstonecraft, the Abbé Barruel, Tacitus, and Shakespeare. Under Shelley's stimulus both Mary and Jane began writing stories. Jane was also doing considerable reading. Shelley, true to his self-dedication to freedom, was beginning *The Assassins.* Likewise the tour had stimulated Shelley's sense of natural grandeur and beauty, or, as he himself stated it, "the inconstant summer of delight and beauty which invests this visible world."

They had reached home without a penny and apparently without a care. The whole of their extraordinary excursion of six weeks had been care-free, almost high-spirited. Nowhere in either of their two journals is there any note of dejection or any feeling that they had plunged themselves into a complicated and difficult situation, except that Mary once permitted herself a moment of sadness at the thought of Godwin deserted and almost alone.

Shelley's first day in London – Tuesday, September 13 – brought him face to face with the fact that ignoring a desperate situation does not necessarily abolish it. His small balance at his bankers' had been exhausted. Edward Hookham (brother of Shelley's publisher, Thomas) and Mrs. Voisey, a friend of Mary's, both showed resentment over the elopement. Harriet, whom Shelley saw on both the 13th and the 14th, was unwilling to accept the new situation – Mary noted in her journal that she was "a very odd creature." On the night of September 14 Shelley's party moved into lodgings at No. 56 Margaret Street, Cavendish Square. Shelley wrote some letters, obtained some clothes he had left with Thomas Hookham, and settled down for the rest of the evening to read Wordsworth's *Excursion* with Mary. But Wordsworth, too, seemed to have turned against them. "Much disappointed," Mary wrote of the *Excursion;* "he is a slave."

So began a long, dreary period characterized by fruitless efforts to raise money and to reach an understanding with Harriet, and by a more successful effort to dodge bailiffs. The £1,200 Shelley had reserved from Godwin in July only incited his creditors if, indeed, they received it, for there is no record at all of what happened to it.

Hookham called rather frequently, but was still somewhat cool and was suspected of siding with Harriet. The Godwins would have no dealings with them; when Shelley saw Mrs. Godwin and Fanny pass by the window and ran out to them they would not speak. Shelley made frequent calls on moneylenders. He also began teaching Greek to both Jane and Mary. All three read much in the evenings, and Shelley often read aloud from "The Ancient Mariner," the *Excursion, Caleb Williams,* and *The Curse of Kehama.*

Shelley sought a better understanding with Harriet, based upon her acceptance of his love for Mary as something not to be tampered with or reviled. "My attachment to Mary," he uncompromisingly asserted, "neither could nor ought to have been overcome." He still professed a strong friendship for Harriet and deprecated her tendency to confide her troubles to others whose influence he distrusted. "I deem myself," he protested, "far worthier and better than any of your nominal friends." Shelley hoped at first that Harriet might still consent to accept his view of the situation and come to live with him and Mary on these terms. He thought it "not well" that Harriet should wound him with reproach and blame when he was still perpetually concerned about furthering her best interests.

When Harriet remained obdurate, Shelley warned her that their friendship must fall to a lower level unless she could respect the confidence he reposed in her. Indiscretions such as her recent one of divulging his address to an attorney might lead to his arrest by the bailiffs. He desired to make a settlement upon her without delay, and he wished her to determine at once the future nature of their friendship. These letters did not change Harriet's point of view. She did nothing to further the execution of Shelley's deed of settlement because it would have set the seal of finality on what she still hoped was only a temporary aberration.

Shelley and his party remained in their Cavendish Square lodgings less than a fortnight. On September 26, fearing arrest by creditors, they moved to new lodgings on Church Street, Pancras, kept by a Mrs. Page. Here, for nearly a month, their lives followed the same harried, constricted pattern as before. Nearly every day Shelley went about his unsuccessful efforts to raise money, accompanied sometimes by Hookham or Peacock. Sensing his desperation, perhaps, the moneylenders raised their rates to six to one, but even at this rate Shelley could sell no more post-obits. One creditor found him at home and forced him to sign a bill at one month, with no prospect of paying it. Harriet was pressing him for money which he no longer had to send. His regular allowance was mortgaged to Hookham, who doled out small sums to him from time to time as maintenance money.

The friends of earlier days were mostly alienated. The Godwins, the Boinvilles, and the Newtons held aloof. Godwin was trying unsuccessfully to induce Jane to leave Shelley, at the same time that he was refusing to speak to Shelley or even to speak about him, except to an attorney.

Hogg had been out of town, on his regular northern vacation, ever since the elopement or shortly after. On October 4 Shelley wrote to him. It was apparently the first communication between the two friends since the elopement. Shelley expressed his anxiety for Hogg's return so that he could perceive and share in his friend's new-found happiness. He assured Hogg that he was in fact a new and different person, contented for the first time in his life, free of the old feeling of civil war within himself, far more capable of genuine friendship and more useful to society than he had ever been before. And all this he owed to Mary. Hogg was not greatly impressed and answered — at leisure — so coldly that Mary wrote in her journal: "Few friendly spirits in the world."

"We still hear nothing from any friend of Mr. Shelley's," Jane wrote in her journal on October 20. Even Shelley's mother no longer wished to see him. There was no welcome for Shelley and Mary in the home of either the Shelleys or the Godwins; instead, they sometimes repaired to the grave of Mary Wollstonecraft, there to recollect their first falling in love or to read Godwin's *Essay on Sepulchres*. It was the most friendless period of Shelley's life.

Hookham, though not fully trusted, still maintained friendly rela- tions, and Peacock was often on hand, for dinner or breakfast or to accompany Shelley on his financial rounds. Sometimes he accom- panied the whole party on walks in the fields, or to a pond beyond Primrose Hill where Shelley liked to launch paper boats. Once he functioned as an unsuccessful ambassador from Shelley to Godwin. Shelley admired and enjoyed his conversation, but believed him at the same time to be somewhat cold and selfish. Jane and Mary were not particularly fond of him and found his visits often too frequent and too long.

This particular time was scarcely a favorable one for the formation of quixotic schemes of liberation. Yet in the first week of October, in the midst of their other difficulties, Shelley, Mary, and Jane devoted many hours to discussion of a plan for "converting and liberating two heiresses" from boarding school, fleeing with them to the west of Ireland, and there, with Peacock and his fiancée, Marianne de St. Croix, founding a little seminary of radical opinion such as Shelley and Elizabeth Hitchener had once planned in Wales. The two girls, who are called "poor Eliza and Helen" in Jane's journal, were prob- ably Shelley's sisters, or else (considering that Elizabeth was already "lost" and was probably not in school) his sister Hellen and a ro- mantic schoolmate. After much discussion and a visit to the school to see the schoolgirls, the plan inevitably disintegrated. That the sup- posedly cold, skeptical Peacock entered briskly into such a scheme is more intelligible from the fact that it included providing money for his marriage — assuming, of course, that money would be provided for the scheme as a whole.

Within a week another incident occurred showing how Shelley's mind could be temporarily dominated by the atmosphere of his earlier Gothic novel reading and could even draw others into the same mood. On the night of October 7 Mary went rather early to bed. Shelley and Jane sat up over the fire, talking late into the night. For some time the talk was of oppression and reform, of an association of philosophical people, the cruel punishments suffered by soldiers, Shelley's two favorite sisters, of Hogg, Harriet, and Elizabeth Hitchener. At one o'clock Shelley observed that it was the witching hour of night. Was it not horrible, he asked, to feel the silence of night tingling in one's ears? The conversation turned upon "unaccountable and mysterious feelings about supernatural things"; and Jane thought Shelley's expression indescribably melancholy and awe-inspiring. By two o'clock they were both so stricken with awe that they scarcely dared breathe.

When they went to their rooms Shelley was too disturbed to sleep. He was preparing to read for the rest of the night when Jane rushed down the stairs in a state of complete terror — her cheeks and even her lips deathly white, eyes wide and staring, hair stiff and erect, skin drawn into innumerable wrinkles. Shelley calmed her with some difficulty, and learned that a pillow, which she had just been staring at in the middle of her bed, had been moved instantly to a chair, through no discoverable human agency. For the rest of the night they sat by the fire, fearing that their candle would not last till daylight, and engaging at intervals in awful conversation "relative to the nature of these mysteries." As daylight was returning, Jane was again overwhelmed by Shelley's terrible expression, which she later described to him as "a mixture of deep sadness and conscious power over her." Shelley was unable to calm her; she fell into convulsions, shrieked, and writhed on the floor. (This is Shelley's phraseology; Jane says simply: "I was ill.") The next day Jane was ill and melancholy most of the day.

Peacock laughed at this story, and even Shelley betrayed a touch of humorous skepticism when similar mysteries occurred a week later. Mary's comment on October 18 leaves little doubt as to what she thought of these midnight sessions of terrifying conversation. "I go to bed soon; but Shelley and Jane sit up ["till two," in Jane's account], and, for a wonder, do not frighten themselves."

Even Mary, whose imagination was under better nervous control, was not proof against the fears that were to some extent justified by their precarious situation. On October 12 she received a letter which she apparently feared to open. After deliberating for some time she burned it. The next day she announced what she had done. Immediately there was "much dispute and discussion concerning its probable contents." "Alarm," continues Mary's account. "Determine to quit London." They sent to Hookham for five pounds in order to meet the emergency. Then they changed their minds and all three went to Drury Lane to occupy box seats for Kean's performance of Hamlet — which they found so disappointing that they left in disgust at the end of the second act. When they returned to their lodgings they were again smitten with alarm. Calling a coach, they drove to the Stratford Hotel and spent the night there.

Mainly unreal as all these excursions and alarms must have been, Harriet at least was a difficulty not likely to vanish with the clear morning sunlight. Letters continued to pass between Harriet and Shelley, but with no appreciable advantage to either. Shelley's position throughout was firm and consistent. Harriet, although stubbornly resolved not to give up the fight, was from the first unfortunate and inconsistent in her manner of waging it. She hoped to win Shelley back, yet she could not abstain from wounding him by making violent attacks on the woman with whom, according to her theory, he was infatuated. She reproached him for doing her a great injury, while at the same time Shelley reproached her for acting basely and ignobly by refusing to accept the inevitable. She who had always taken her opinions from him now took the advice of people he despised; she even consulted a lawyer. Although Harriet explained that she did not intend bringing legal action, Shelley continued to resent this as an imputation on the generosity of his intentions toward her.

Harriet's nervousness over her approaching confinement may have made her occasionally vindictive. She took the story of her misfortunes to Shelley's solicitor, Amory, who sympathized with her and declined for a while to continue as Shelley's representative. Shelley interpreted this as an act of deliberate malice on Harriet's part. Shelley and Mary also believed that she was spreading the story that Godwin had encouraged their love affair, and Harriet appears to have admitted and defended doing so. If she really believed this, in the face of what she had seen, she had reached the point of those who seek solutions for their difficulties by believing only what they wish to believe, for in her calmer moments she charged only that Shelley had been perverted by the doctrines of *Political Justice*.

Shelley was now convinced that the highest type of friendship was no longer possible between him and Harriet. Occasionally he would express sharp denunciation: "In your heart it seems you were always enslaved to the vilest superstitions, or ready to accept their support for your own narrow and worldly views." More calmly he would write: "Do not mistake me. I am and will be your friend in every sense of the word but that most delicate and exalted one. I solemnly protest to you that not the slightest unkindness or enmity toward you has ever entered my heart." Since the confidence that Shelley demanded as a prerequisite for the highest friendship involved Harriet's desertion of the "selfish and worldly wretches" who were her advisers, and her complete acceptance of Shelley's point of view, Harriet could not hope to be "ranked among the wise and good" without abandoning her own case completely. Naturally the difficulty remained unsettled.

Shelley and Mary had recently been convinced, through information secretly furnished by Fanny Imlay and Charles Clairmont, that Thomas Hookham was preparing to betray Shelley to the bailiffs. Probably they were mistaken, for by October 27 Hookham had promised to furnish bail if Shelley was arrested. Perhaps because he had some definite financial expectations, Shelley expected the danger of arrest to be past by November 6, but meanwhile he felt it necessary to take cover.

At nine o'clock on the night of Sunday, October 23, Shelley left his lodgings to take up a furtive existence until the bailiffs could be faced. He went into hiding none too soon, for the very next day suspicious callers arrived whom Mary and Jane took to be bailiffs. Thereafter until November 9 there were only two nights (those of October 29 and November 5) that Shelley spent at home. These were Saturday nights when at midnight debtors were immune from arrest for twenty-four hours. During this period he had to meet Mary by stealth, taking whatever precautions he could against her being followed. Mary's journal for the sixteen days shows only two days in which it is not clear that they met, most commonly for two hours at a time. On some days they met more than once, and on most days they wrote to each other — desperate, impassioned little notes, generally, that show why the absolute nadir of Shelley's physical fortunes was not, after all, the most depressed period of his life.

Peacock's lodgings in Southampton Buildings had already been agreed upon as a point of contact. On the first day Mary sought for him vainly at Peacock's, then up and down Fleet Street, until she finally found him in a coffee-house, and returned home in a cab "tired to death." Thereafter they met at Peacock's, in Holborn, at St. Paul's, at Gray's Inn Gardens, and at unnamed hotels and coffee-houses, shifting the meeting-places constantly in order to foil the bailiffs. Meanwhile these minions called once or twice, in their un-imaginative way, at the Pancras lodgings, departing empty-handed and angry.

Shelley also saw Peacock and Jane occasionally, and corresponded with Jane. At Peacock's (on November 7) he met Hogg, but the meeting did nothing to encourage him. Hogg was very witty but very cold, and asked Shelley about his "two wives." Hogg's coldness to Shelley was matched by Mary's loss of her best friend, Isabel Baxter, in whose home she had been visiting shortly before her elopement. "So all my hopes are over there," Mary wrote in her journal. "Ah! Isabel; I did not think you would act thus."

Mary was also distressed about her father. The Godwins were in an almost hopeless plight financially, and were repulsing with cold reproach Mary's efforts at reconciliation. They even threatened and punished Fanny Imlay for seeing Mary. Knowing that Mrs. Godwin disliked her, Mary detested her in turn and held her responsible for Godwin's intransigence. Concerning Godwin she could only record in her journal the somewhat mournful comment: "Oh! philosophy." Under these circumstances, with Shelley a fugitive, Mary learned that in early spring she was to have a baby. Jane's flightiness of character had already become a mild source of worry to Shelley; she was occasionally captious to both Shelley and Mary, was thinking of returning to the Godwins, and actually did return for a day or two.

Shelley learned all the discouraging news in his furtive interviews and certainly felt it as an added burden upon his spirits. He con-sidered himself still responsible for Godwin's debts as well as his own. On November 5, before he had attained security from his own creditors, he eased matters somewhat for the Skinner Street house-hold by "settling" Lambert, one of Godwin's creditors.

Though he expected relief early in November, the plight of Shelley and Mary was now becoming for a while quite desperate. With Mary and Jane he had been living on four pounds a week, doled out by Hookham, to whom the rest of his allowance was mortgaged, but even this was slightly more than his allowance. He was now faced with actual hunger. Before going into hiding he wrote a letter to

Harriet begging her to send money to prevent his arrest, which she answered on October 23, promising help. On the same day, as we have seen, Shelley left his lodgings.

The next day he pawned or sold his microscope for five pounds and wrote Harriet a most urgent plea for immediate help, saying that she alone now stood between him and prison, and that although all their valuables had been sold to buy food, Mary and Jane had "very near perished with hunger." This statement was an exaggeration, but within a week Mrs. Page, their landlady, was pressing for money, an innkeeper refused to send up a meal without advance payment, and the day was saved only by securing some cakes from Peacock and a small advance of money from Hookham. On November 4 Jane wrote in her journal: "This is the Morning when S will receive money – If he does not I know not what we shall do."

Frequent, dangerous meetings were not enough for Shelley and Mary during Shelley's sixteen days of exile from home; they constantly sent each other little notes tense with emotion. On October 24 Shelley wrote:

> My imagination is confounded by the uniform prospect of the perfidy and wickedness and hardheartedness of mankind. Mary most amply redeems their blackest crimes. But I confess to you that I have been shocked and staggered by Godwin's cold injustice. The places where I have seen that mans fine countenance bring bitterness home to my heart to think of his cutting cruelty.

"Oh, my love," Mary answered next day, "you have no friends; why then should you be torn from the only one who has affection for you?" Three days later (October 28) she wrote:

> . . . Oh we must meet soon, for this is a dreary life I am weary of it – a poor widowed deserted thing no one cares for her – but ah – love is not that enough – indeed I have a very sincere affection for my own Shelley.
> But Good night I am woefully tired and so sleepy. I shall dream of you, ten to one, when you, naughty one, have quite forgotten me.
> Take me – one kiss – well, that is enough. to-morrow!

Shelley's letters to Mary, in spite of occasional depression, were hopeful. They abound in such expressions as "this will not last," "we shall soon be restored to each other," "but this will soon pass," "I am full of business and hopes," "a few days, perhaps a few hours will

terminate our difficulties." His greatest privation was his separation
from Mary, his greatest inspiration the hope of being reunited with
her in security. "How hard and stubborn," he wrote on October 27th,

> must be the spirit that does not confess you to be the subtlest
> and most exquisitely fashioned intelligence; that among women
> there is no equal mind to yours! And I possess this treasure!
> How beyond all estimate is my felicity! Yes; I am encouraged —
> I care not what happens; I am most happy.

On October 28 he wrote:

> Your thoughts alone can waken mine to energy; [my mind]
> without yours is dead and cold as the dark midnight river when
> the moon is down. It seems as if you alone could shield me from
> impurity and vice. If I were absent from you long I should
> shudder with horror at myself. My understanding becomes un-
> disciplined without you. I believe I must become in Mary's hands
> what Harriet was in mine.

Shelley and Mary were looking forward to a retreat from the world
just as Shelley and Harriet had done a month before the elopement
with Mary. While hiding from the bailiffs Shelley was also corresponding with Mr. Hooper, owner of Nantgwillt, trying to arrange
a lease or purchase. But for unknown reasons nothing ever came of
the matter.

For about two months after Shelley returned to the Pancras lodgings his daily existence, as shown by Mary's journal, was quite similar
to that of the five and a half weeks preceding his flight — a rather
monotonous round of reading, studying, talking, walking, and interviewing moneylenders and lawyers. As before, he was still subject
to wild imaginings. When he went out walking at night he would
not walk alone, because he feared that Mr. Leeson, his fancied assailant at Tanyrallt, was following him with a dagger. Perhaps this
fear was revived by the similar circumstances in Godwin's *Caleb
Williams*, which he had just been re-reading. A more real danger was
that there were still plenty of unpaid debts for which he might be
arrested; he had avoided only the most immediate danger. Two or
three times at least, between November 9 and January 7, Shelley's
party moved to new lodgings.

Jane, who now insisted on being called Claire, was becoming more
and more a household problem. She quarreled occasionally with both

Shelley and Mary. For two days after Shelley's return home she was gloomy and sullen. Against his advice she returned to her mother, only to be back two days later. In late November she became quite ill with an inflammation of the liver and had to be bled. The next day she was again in ill humor, and again Shelley sat up with her that night and "talked her into reason" (Shelley's phrase). On December 19 Shelley wrote in the journal: "Clara imagines that I treat her unkindly. Mary consoles her with her all-powerful benevolence. I rise (having already gone to bed), and speak with Clara; she was very unhappy; I leave her tranquil."

Both Claire and Godwin were destined to remain problems during the rest of Shelley's life. Godwin's proceeds from Shelley's post-obit sale shortly before the elopement with Mary had been insufficient to meet all of his obligations at the time, and his financial situation had meanwhile grown steadily worse. Shelley had expected from the first to meet an obligation of Godwin's for two hundred pounds falling due on December 1. Early in November Godwin received a letter from Longdill, Shelley's solicitor, saying that Shelley had requested him to pay this bill. Godwin was still so resentful of Shelley's treatment of him and of the consequent rumor crediting him with having sold Mary and Claire to Shelley that he wished to refuse Shelley's aid. He agreed to accept the money only under the combined persuasions of Mr. Marshall, Mrs. Boinville, and Cornelia Turner.

Still refusing to thank Shelley, he consented grudgingly to Mrs. Godwin's doing so, through Longdill. In addition, probably more by promises than by cash, Shelley "settled" — at least temporarily — two of Godwin's most pressing creditors. But on December 7 Skinner Street affairs reached another crisis — there was no money to pay the rent, which was likely to be demanded at any time. One hundred pounds was needed, ninety of which Shelley secured next day from Hookham. For a short time after this Godwin's difficulties seemed quiescent, although certain to recur sooner or later.

Godwin's debts which Shelley had guaranteed stood in December at £1,200, and Shelley's own most immediate needs required £300. Shelley tried in vain to get his father to increase his allowance of £200 a year. He then tried to secure £1,500 from his family instead of going to the moneylenders with another post-obit. This could not be done, however, even though Mr. Timothy Shelley desired it, because Sir Bysshe's consent was necessary and he was too old and feeble to be consulted. On December 21, therefore, Shelley entered into another post-obit agreement by which he was to receive £3,000 for £10,000.

In November Hogg returned to the fold, gradually, with caution on both sides. Since he had treated Shelley's earlier advances coldly, almost sarcastically, Shelley received his first visit, on November 14, with some misgivings. If Hogg liked Mary, Shelley decided, they might still be friends, in spite of radical differences in their sympathies. Hogg did like Mary, and Mary was sufficiently pleased with his conversation "on many interesting subjects" to forget for the moment that she was ill. Thereafter Hogg was a frequent caller, whom Mary found increasingly interesting. He generally stayed until midnight and talked or argued on such subjects as virtue, love of wisdom, free will, necessity, the law, the sexes, and sport.

But though Mary found him interesting from the first, she was very cautious in deciding that she really liked this friend of Harriet's who was so often on the wrong side of an argument. In her opinion he bungled his arguments on virtue, was "quite wrong, but quite puzzled" on some other points, and was in general "sadly perverted" in his notions. Through December her liking steadily increased. Thereafter, if any doubt remained, it must have been dispelled by the receipt, on New Year's Day, of a gallant little note and a present. For the next few months, as long as Shelley and Mary remained in London, Hogg was an intimate of their household. He came to be referred to occasionally as Jefferson or as Alexy, from his novel *Prince Alexy Haimatoff*, which they had all read and Shelley had reviewed on November 16.

Shelley's earlier efforts to come to an agreement with Harriet had ended in her forbidding him to call on her and in a threat from Shelley to cease writing to her unless she changed her manner. For a few weeks, apparently, they neither saw nor heard of each other. Harriet was expecting the birth of her child about the end of December, but it was born a month prematurely, on November 30. It was a boy, very healthy for an eight months' child, and very like its father. Harriet named him Charles. Shelley first heard of it on December 6, in successive letters from Hookham and Harriet — the latter signing herself, as Mary noted with two exclamation points: *"a deserted wife!!"* When Shelley immediately began writing announcement circulars, Mary could not help thinking of the child she was expecting. She commented bitterly that Charles's birth should be announced with ringing of bells, "for it is the son of his *wife*."

Harriet, too, had her bitterness, having possibly hoped that Charles's birth might detach Shelley from Mary. "Oh, my dear friend," she wrote to Catherine Nugent, "what a dreadful trial it is to bring children into the world so utterly helpless as he is, with no kind father's care to heal the wounded frame. . . . I have seen his father; he came to me as soon as he knew of the event; but as to his tenderness to me, none remains. He said he was glad it was a boy, because he would make money cheaper. You see how the noble soul is debased. Money now, not philosophy, is the grand spring of his actions." This interview was painful to Shelley as well, as reflected in Mary's brief account of it on December 7: "Shelley calls on the lawyers and on Harriet, who treats him with insulting selfishness."

After this Harriet gave up all hope of Shelley. On December 20 she wrote him a letter threatening him with her lawyer. A month later she wrote again to Catherine Nugent: "I am truly miserable, my dear friend. I really see no termination to my sorrows. As to Mr. Shelley I know nothing of him. He neither sends nor comes to see me. I am still at my father's, which is very wretched. When I shall quit this house I know not. Everything goes against me. I am weary of my life. I am so restrained here that life is scarcely worth living. . . . I live for others. At nineteen I could descend a willing victim to the tomb. . . . Mr. Shelley has much to answer for. He has been the cause of great misery to me and mine. I shall never live with him again. 'Tis impossible. I have been so deceived, so cruelly treated, that I can never forget it. . . . Is it wrong, do you think, to put an end to one's sorrow? I often think of it — all is so gloomy and desolate."

Just as Harriet was giving up Shelley for lost, an incredibly strange situation was developing between Shelley, Mary, and Hogg. The gallant little note accompanying Hogg's New Year's present to Mary was swiftly followed by a declaration of his love. Mary was by this time genuinely fond of Hogg. Unlike Harriet she did not consider matrimony necessarily exclusive, and she knew (as her subsequent letters plainly establish) that Shelley approved of Hogg's proposals.

Theoretically, Mary yielded at once — openly, affectionately, and in full confidence that by so doing she was adding to Shelley's happiness. She informed her "Dearest Hogg" that he was so generous and disinterested that one could not help loving him. Even though she had not previously realized it, she now knew that she regarded him with a deep affection which in time would turn into the passionate love he so richly deserved. A few notes were exchanged during the first week in January 1815 in which Mary assured him of her growing affection and of her desire to make him completely happy — in time. She reminded him that there were physical causes which made it necessary to wait, causes to which Shelley as well as Hogg must be subject. Meanwhile they could hope.

Whatever letters may have been written to Hogg during the next sixteen days have been lost. But a letter of January 23 shows clearly why Mary was willing to look forward to a passion which she had honestly stated she could not feel at present. Addressing Hogg as "My own Alexy" she promised the fulfillment of their love after the birth of her baby. Hogg would teach her Italian and they would read many books together. Their greatest happiness would be in Shelley, and everything they did would make him happy. This prospect is followed by a really passionate assertion of her utter devotion, not to Hogg, but to Shelley. It was obviously Shelley's pleasure in her union with Hogg that constituted the chief attraction of the idea for Mary!

During January and February Hogg was regarded as practically a member of the family. He introduced chess as an amusement, constituted himself Mary's Latin teacher, went walking, and read — sometimes aloud, like Harriet. When Shelley and Mary were both ill on February 14 Hogg remained for the night.

On February 22, probably, Mary's baby was born, more than two months before its time. The doctor (who arrived five minutes too late) had small hopes that the child would live. Shelley was too agitated and exhausted to be of much help; on the contrary he was ill for several days and on February 26 had a spasm. Both Mary and the child improved, however, and by March 2 were ready to move to new lodgings. During this time Hogg was with them every evening until eleven, and when the child was born he spent the night in the house. Even Mrs. Godwin softened her animosity to the extent of sending some linen by Charles Clairmont. Then, on March 6, Mary woke up in the night to find that her child was dead. Hogg was immediately summoned and again spent the night.

Mary was in wretched health and spirits. Shelley, having consulted Dr. Pemberton on February 28, was told that abscesses were forming on his lungs and that he was dying rapidly of consumption. Claire was a domestic problem; Godwin's difficulties still hung over the whole family like a heavy pall. Hogg, whose vacation began on

181

March 10, decided to forgo his usual trip north and remain with his friends. Thereafter, until April 17, he lived in the same lodgings with the Shelleys.

In the very week in which Hogg declared his love for Mary, Shelley received news that radically changed his prospects for the rest of his life. On January 7 Shelley wrote in the journal: "See the death of Sir Bysshe in the papers. Hookham calls, and is very gracious." Sir Bysshe died on January 5, at the age of eighty-three.

Shelley went to Sussex in spite of a message from Mr. Whitton, the family attorney, that his presence would be "most painful to Mrs. S." He appeared at his father's door on January 12 and was refused admission by order of his father, now Sir Timothy. While the will was being read, Shelley sat before the door reading *Comus* in Mary's pocket edition of Milton. Dr. Blocksome emerged and informed Shelley (somewhat superfluously) that his father was very angry with him.

Mr. John Shelley-Sidney, Shelley's half-uncle, who had always been rather friendly to Shelley, emerged next and remarked that it was a most remarkable will. For an explanation of its meaning Shelley was referred to Whitton. Whitton informed him that night that he was now the next heir to the income on a hundred thousand pounds provided he would entail the estate. He gave Shelley a general notion of the will and its codicils and promised a more detailed explanation after the funeral. The funeral took place next day, but Shelley did not attend. His feelings about his grandfather had not changed from those he had formerly expressed to Elizabeth Hitchener: "He is a bad man. I never had respect for him: I always regarded him as a curse on society. I shall not grieve at his death. I will not wear mourning: I will not attend his funeral."

On January 20 Shelley received from Whitton a copy of the will and its various codicils, together with an assurance of Sir Timothy's willingness to concur with him in executing its provisions. The estate consisted of a residuary personal estate of £143,675, 12s., 5d., and of certain entailed real properties that had been added under different settlements. Sir Bysshe's will provided that the Mitchell and Edward Shelley estates be held for life by Timothy Shelley and after him by Percy Bysshe Shelley, and thereafter by sons of Percy Bysshe in order of seniority. These estates were to be increased by the trustees (William Whitton and a Mr. Du Cane) through the investment of one half the residuary personal property in real estate to be subject to the same regulations. No one could inherit either of these estates without agreeing to resettle it according to the terms of Sir Bysshe's will. There was one portion of his estate, however, his inheritance under the will of his brother, John Shelley of Field Place, worth £800 a year, to which Percy Bysshe was heir in tail male after his father, for the resettling of which Sir Bysshe's will made no provision. The total value of the estate, personal and real, was estimated at about £200,000.

Thus, even after his death, Sir Bysshe sought to make his dream of family grandeur binding upon his descendants. When Shelley eloped with Harriet Sir Bysshe had tightened his will by a codicil evidently intended to draw all of his estates into the entail, but through Whitton's carelessness the John Shelley estate had not been tied in with the others. Percy Bysshe could inherit it without entailing it. Moreover, after his father's death there was a legal method of becoming owner in fee simple of other estates to the value of £80,000. Sir Bysshe, by providing for augmenting the entailed estates, evidently hoped to induce Shelley to accept them and prolong the entail.

Percy Bysshe had a year in which to decide whether or not to agree to prolong the entail, but he decided instantly. He had always objected to entailing estates, on the ground that it might place great economic power in unworthy hands. He could obtain an adequate income for himself by selling his father the reversion of the unencumbered John Shelley estate, for which he could expect about £18,000. This suited Sir Timothy's wishes exactly, as it would enable Bysshe to pay off his present debts and would be a partial protection against Shelley's ruining the inalienable remainder of his inheritance by post-obits.

On March 8, 1815 Shelley executed a deed poll by which he renounced for himself and his heirs forever all benefits conditioned upon his resettling his eventual inheritance in accord with his grandfather's wishes. Godwin, contrary to his own principles, on which Shelley was acting, disapproved. Shelley's own solicitor, Longdill, also advised against this procedure. He was purchasing freedom in the use of his eventual inheritance of about £80,000 by depriving himself and his son of a much larger expectation. Being thus freed from entailing the remainder of his expectations, on May 13 Shelley entered into an indenture with his father by which he sold him the reversion of the estates devised by the will of John Shelley for the sum of £7,400 and an annuity of £1,000, to be paid quarterly. He received his first quarterly payment on June 24, 1815.

Between the death of Sir Bysshe and the signing of this agreement with Sir Timothy some five months elapsed during which, in
spite of Shelley's definite immediate expectations, the bailiffs remained stolidly unimpressed. They were still hunting for him, at
least occasionally, and frequent changes of lodgings still seemed
necessary. By the last week in April no place in London seemed safe.
Apparently leaving Claire in London, Shelley and Mary took lodgings at the Windmill Inn, Salt Hill, whence Mary wrote coquettish
letters seeking to persuade the prudent Hogg to join them. From
this rural retreat Shelley still made the necessary but perilous calls
upon his London solicitor, Longdill. How long they remained here is
uncertain, but on May 5 they were again living in London.

While the Shelleys were at Salt Hill, Mary wrote to Hogg on April
25 and 26 three letters that constitute the last documents in their
love affair. The three troubled months that had elapsed since her
letters of early January had given added proofs of Hogg's kindness
and had placed him in possession of the pet names (the Maie and the
Dormouse) which Shelley sometimes used with Mary. But either
the personal contacts of several weeks' living in the same lodgings or
the shock of her own grief and despondency during that time would
seem from these letters to have altered Mary's feelings and possibly
Hogg's. The later letters deal with other circumstances besides
Hogg's love, which is mentioned but once, and their emotion is
limited to affectionate, coquettish admonitions and entreaties. There
is no further mention of passionate love in the future. Indeed, it
seems probable from a variety of later details that Mary's pseudo-
infatuation with Hogg was already ended.

From the first week of November until the new year Shelley and
Mary saw almost nothing of Peacock. At the beginning of January
he had abandoned his fiancée and was living with a supposedly rich
widow, whom he expected to marry, but who landed him in prison
for a £40 debt after he had spent his money. After his enlargement
he appears again in the Shelley journals as dropping in occasionally
for a meal or a walk culminating in the sailing of paper boats.

Until Shelley procured his money in May, Godwin's affairs remained as gloomy as ever. "I am afraid nothing can be done to save
them," Mary wrote in her journal on March 19. In April one of Godwin's creditors was threatening an arrest. In addition, Godwin was
ill. But he still refused to see Mary and would consent to correspond
with Shelley on financial matters only — which he did "in a style of
freezing coldness."

Claire Clairmont was becoming a more constant source of irritation than formerly. Mary's "powerful benevolence" that had previously soothed Claire in one of her moods had worn thinner under stress of Mary's own sufferings. Perhaps Mary was jealous of the attention Shelley paid to Claire. "Very unwell," Mary wrote in her journal for March 11. ". . . Talk about Clara's going away; nothing settled; I fear it is hopeless. She will not go to Skinner Street; then our house is the only remaining place, I see plainly. What is to be done?" The next day's entry contains the decidedly edged remark: "Very quiet in the morning, and happy, for Clara does not get up till 4." Two days later there was another conference between Shelley and Mary over Claire which left Mary feeling that the prospect was "more dismal than ever; not the least hope" — a conclusion she pro nounced "indeed hard to bear."

One reason why Claire could not return to Skinner Street was that Mrs. Bishop, Fanny Imlay's aunt, objected. Mrs. Bishop was planning to take Fanny into the girls' school that she conducted in Dublin with her sister, and she felt that Fanny's association with Claire would cause unfavorable gossip. Mrs. Godwin sent Mrs. Bishop's letter to Shelley, to show him that he had deprived Claire of a home. Shelley replied that he would never regret having saved a victim of prejudice and promised to provide for Claire in his will. The Shelleys appear to have advertised for a position for Claire, probably as governess or companion. In the end, on May 13, Claire went to stay with a Mrs. Bicknell, a widow, at Lynmouth. Thence she soon wrote to Fanny Imlay, giving a cheerful picture of her environment and state of mind. Mary, on her part, was so pleased that she wrote in her journal, "I begin a new Journal with our regeneration."

"Regeneration" was not too strong a word to apply to the situation of Shelley and Mary on May 13, 1815. A source of domestic friction had just been removed from their home. On the same day Shelley concluded his financial agreement with Sir Timothy, which enabled him to send Godwin £1,000 and to give Harriet £200 for her debts, in addition to an annuity of £200. The agreement with his father provided that out of Shelley's cash proceeds all outstanding post-obits should be redeemed and all debts paid. This was done by Sir Timothy himself, with the exception of a few minor debts and of the post-obit sold for £2,600 in the previous May, whose owner refused to sell. These settlements took all or most of Shelley's cash proceeds, but left him an income of £800 a year, after deducting

Harriet's annuity. It also freed him of the danger of arrest, and it rendered Godwin temporarily secure — though bitter, because he insisted that Shelley had promised him £1,200. Shelley explained repeatedly that, although he had entered £1,200 in the settlement as a debt to Godwin, it had nevertheless been made plain to Godwin that £200 of this was for Shelley's own purposes.

For more than nine months the Shelleys had been to only one or two operas or plays. Their amusement away from home had been limited to walks, paper-boat sailing, one or two lectures, and two or three visits to the British Museum and the Zoological Gardens. These, however, were trifling privations for Shelley. Far greater were the mental stress of the vain effort to settle matters with Harriet, the continual dodging of bailiffs and trying to arrange financial expedients with grasping moneylenders, Mary's danger when her child was born, the domestic friction between Mary and Claire (and possibly even with Mary about Claire), the falling-off of old friends, and particularly the animosity and distress of Godwin. Shelley had rather expected and would always expect misunderstanding and persecution, but to be misunderstood and scorned by one whom he still reverenced as the author of *Political Justice* was peculiarly hard to bear.

The effect of such continuous mental stress upon Shelley's literary production was devastating. He had vowed to devote his life to the abolition of tyranny, and in nine months he had written for part of one day (September 19) on *The Assassins* and part of one evening (November 16) on a review of Hogg's novel, *Memoirs of Prince Alexy Haimatoff*. The immense difference in poetic quality between *Alastor*, written in the autumn of 1815, and the earlier *Queen Mab* indicates that Shelley must have written considerable practice verse between writing these two poems, but there is no record of it except an unfinished poem in the back of one Claire Clairmont's journals. One day Shelley suddenly asked Peacock: "Do you think Wordsworth could have written such poetry, if he had ever had dealings with money lenders?" In August, when both his health and his spirits had greatly improved, Shelley wrote to Hogg: "My health has been considerably improved under Lawrence's care, and I am so much more free from the continual irritation under which I lived as to devote myself with more effect and consistency to study."

The "continual irritation" was more mental than physical. The actual daily record seems to show that Shelley was rarely ill during this period, and only once (during the great nervous strain after the

birth of Mary's baby) for more than one day. Hogg and Peacock always thought he exaggerated his ill health. His extraordinarily sensitive nerves and highly susceptible imagination often convinced him,
and apparently Mary and Claire, that his health was desperate, but
it was really more his nervous than his physical health. The "consumption" of which Dr. Pemberton thought him rapidly dying in late
February was plainly another diagnostic chimera.

Neither health nor nerves were allowed seriously to interfere with
the important business of reading and study. For Claire and Mary,
as well as for Shelley, this was both a duty and a recreation. Shelley
regarded them as of the elect, who were to be fitted by reading and
study for a war against tyranny and injustice. This was why he objected to Claire's return to her mother, "a vulgar, commonplace
woman, without an idea of philosophy . . . not . . . a proper person to form the mind of a young girl." Having failed in his attempts
to "form the mind" of Harriet, he was now presented with another
opportunity. He set lessons for Claire in French, Latin, Italian, Greek,
and history, and for Mary in Greek. Both girls were willing, intelligent students, whose journals show a great amount of reading and
study and a desire not to disappoint Shelley's rather strict expectations.

Except possibly for the sixteen days when he was a semi-fugitive,
hardly a day went by in which Shelley and Mary did not read. Daily
records like that of February 6, 1815 may be taken as almost a pattern: "Read Gibbon all morning. Shelley reads Livy. Shelley writes
and sends letters. After dinner read Gibbon (finish vol. 2) Hogg
comes at nine. Work. He goes at half-past 11. Talk a little, and then
go to bed." At the end of 1814 Mary listed sixty volumes read by
Shelley and sixty-two by herself. All but three or four of these were
read after the second week in September, averaging for Shelley about
twenty volumes a month. In the first four months of 1815 Shelley's
pace slowed perceptibly, but he nevertheless read considerably.
Twelve hundred pages in seventeen days Shelley characterized
(February 13) as "desultory," even though a large part of it consisted
of Latin and Greek in the original. Almost all the rest of the books
read had a direct application to Shelley's interest in poetry and
revolutionary reform.

For over fourteen months after the "regeneration" the new journal
which Mary had begun is lost, and other surviving records are so
scanty that it is the most obscure period in Shelley's life. In June

1815 Shelley and Mary were touring the southern coast of Devonshire, intending soon to secure a house and settle down. Shelley still wished to rent or purchase a house in Merionethshire, but for some reason this scheme was again abandoned, and Shelley returned to London to look for a house, while Mary remained at Clifton. Early in August, probably on August 3, they moved into a house at Bishopsgate, near London.

Meanwhile, between March and September, the anonymous author of *Queen Mab* had been receiving a great deal of praise at the hands of a mysterious new magazine in London, the *Theological Inquirer, or Polemical Magazine,* an organ of philosophic religious radicalism. It reprinted the *Refutation of Deism* with corrections from the previous edition that were very probably furnished by the author. It published also a copious, extremely laudatory review of *Queen Mab* in four installments, also several letters from obviously pseudonymous contributors further enlarging the discussion of *Queen Mab.* In the July number appeared an "Ode to the Author of *Queen Mab*," the first poem ever published about Shelley.

Practically nothing is known about the *Theological Inquirer* or its mysterious editor, Erasmus Perkins. Since *Queen Mab* and its anonymous author received more attention than any other subject, one assumes that the editor probably had a special interest in Shelley. Remembering Shelley's notion of founding a periodical in Ireland and his part later in founding the *Liberal* in Italy, it is difficult to resist the suspicion that he had a considerably more important connection with this periodical than surviving evidence substantiates. One wonders, without evidence, if the £1,200 which Shelley had in hand in July 1814, and which seems to have vanished at once without record, could be connected with the appearance in the following March of a periodical that could hardly have been founded without a subsidy.

Whatever his connection with this magazine, its appearance must have been a great encouragement to Shelley during his apparent literary inactivity in the spring of 1815. It was no small pleasure to feel that his missionary purposes were being carried forward by a well-written periodical, and that he had been hailed in a published poem, as well as in a long review, as a bold and inspired prophet of freedom, at present unknown, but destined for future greatness:

These truths the voice of nations shall proclaim
In coming times, and know, and bless thy name: —
Hail then, immortal bard! hail to thy future fame!

Chapter XII

THE LOW-ROOFED furnished cottage that Shelley took at Bishopsgate was situated down a secluded lane close to the Rhododendron Walk, Windsor Park. It faced Bishopsgate Heath; to the west was Chapel Wood and Virginia Water. Standing on the edge of the more ancient part of the forest, it was shaded by gnarled and decayed oaks of great antiquity struggling for supremacy with an energetic growth of younger trees. A garden, enclosed with a light railing, provided flowers. Here Shelley and Mary could find more privacy and security than they had previously enjoyed in the harried months following their return from the Continent.

Political events and the manifold ills of this world no longer excited Shelley to a feverish determination to rectify matters single-handed and at once. Napoleon's escape from Elba in March, his quick mastery of France, the Battle of Waterloo, his banishment to St. Helena, and the reactionary plans of the Allies moved him much less deeply than one would expect. The only echo of these events in the journal is a bare mention, on March 23, of Napoleon's entry into Paris. Shelley had concluded that the time for action was not yet, and could only be prepared for, rather than precipitated, by writing. It was not always easy to feel so. Napoleon's downfall interested him to the extent of evoking a sonnet, "Feelings of a Republican on the Fall of Bonaparte," regretting the event only as the victory of a worse tyranny even than Napoleon's.

Hogg was in the north on his annual vacation, but Peacock was near by, at Marlow, and was a frequent caller. Charles Clairmont was on hand with a scheme for which he needed Shelley's financial assistance. Though Charles was a financial leech, his letters indicate that he was by no means stupid company. He was waiting until Shelley could find money to pay his expenses to Ireland to investigate buying a distillery business at Enniscorthy. Claire, who was already restless at Lynmouth, was to accompany him.

While the money for Charles was still to be sought, the whole party — Shelley, Mary, Charles, and Peacock — embarked about the end of August upon a ten-day boat excursion up the Thames. Between flat green banks, past many little villages and the large town of Reading, they followed the river's leisurely windings to Oxford, where they stopped briefly while Shelley showed his companions the Bodleian Library, the Clarendon Press, various college quadrangles, and "the very rooms" — as Charles Clairmont related it — "where the two noted infidels, Shelley and Hogg . . . pored . . . over the . . . boundaries of human knowledge." A threatened or imagined illness of Shelley's was overcome by Peacock's prescription of "three mutton-chops, well peppered," after which Shelley "rowed vigorously, was cheerful, merry, overflowing with animal spirits, and had certainly one week of thorough enjoyment of life."

In a day or two they had reached Lechlade, about fourteen miles from the source of the Thames. Three miles above the town, however, they were halted by shallow water and by water weeds too thick and high to be overcome. So, turning back to Lechlade, they started next morning on the homeward voyage. In four days they were back at Windsor. All of his fellow travelers commented on the remarkable improvement in Shelley's health and spirits. "He has now the ruddy, healthy complexion of the autumn upon his countenance," Charles Clairmont wrote after their return, "and he is twice as fat as he used to be."

An unmistakable mark of Shelley's growing poetic power is seen in the poem written on one of the two days spent in the inn at Lechlade. The opening descriptive stanzas of "A Summer-Evening Churchyard, Lechlade, Gloucestershire," show only slight touches of influence from eighteenth-century churchyard verse, even though Shelley had often walked in the churchyard at Stoke Poges while thinking of Gray's "Elegy." The elegiac note of the concluding stanza is the characteristically Shelleyan one that occurs with increased power many times in his later poetry:

> Thus solemnized and softened, death is mild
> And terrorless as this serenest night:
> Here could I hope, like some enquiring child
> Sporting on graves, that death did hide from human sight
> Sweet secrets, or beside its breathless sleep
> That loveliest dreams perpetual watch did keep.

A week after his return to Bishopsgate, Shelley wrote to Hogg in a very cheerful tone: "The exercise and dissipation of mind attached to such an expedition have produced so favourable an effect on my health that my habitual dejection and irritability have almost deserted me, and I can devote six hours in the day to study without difficulty. I have been engaged lately in the commencement of several literary plans which, if my present temper of mind endures, I shall probably complete in the winter."

Since April, apparently, there had been no contact between Shelley and Harriet. About November, however, Harriet demanded an additional allowance for the support of the two children. This Shelley refused. He offered to take Ianthe into his own home and urged a deed of separation. Harriet, on the advice of friends, would consent to neither, whereupon Shelley threatened to withdraw Harriet's present allowance of two hundred pounds. Harriet's father and her attorney, Mr. Desse, then called upon Mr. William Whitton to see if Sir Timothy would provide for one of the children on condition that Mr. Westbrook provide for the other. If not, they proposed to bring proceedings against Shelley in the Ecclesiastical Court for alimony and in the Court of Chancery for separate maintenance for the children, alleging Shelley's religious opinions as grounds for refusing to yield him custody of the children. Sir Timothy declined to take any action, however, and Mr. Westbrook forbore to execute his really dangerous threat. Shelley, on his part, continued his allowance to Harriet.

Improving his new freedom from ill health and worry, Shelley settled himself with his old determination to studying and writing. Once more he could — and did — buy books as he liked. The autumn months were warm and dry; the cool oak shades of Windsor Great Forest and the grassy borders of the Thames offered ideal seclusion for the study and thought that were going into *Alastor.* The new poem was one that could hardly have been credited to the author of such a vigorous, objective call to arms as *Queen Mab.* Physical sufferings, ill health, and the loss of friends had, as Mrs. Shelley wrote, "brought home to him the sad realities of life . . . inclining him rather to brood over the thoughts and emotions of his own soul than to glance abroad." He still indulged his earlier hopes of human regeneration, but he had realized more keenly the difficulty of their fulfillment.

The theme of *Alastor,* according to Shelley's Preface, is that concentration upon high and lofty ideals may bring with it an avenging fury, which makes the actual world seem dark and dead to those who have pursued perfection too far. Even an idealist cannot subsist without human sympathy. Such a ruin, however, is glorious, Shelley hastens to add, compared with the slow and poisonous decay of those selfish beings who are "deluded by no generous error, instigated by no sacred thirst of doubtful knowledge." Unfortunately, Shelley's criticism of himself — for the over-idealistic poet as described in both the Preface and the poem is undoubtedly Shelley — goes too much against the grain to be perfectly clear and consistent. The young poet's progress to an untimely death is presented with such sympathy that no one who had not read the Preface would suppose that the author intended the poem as a criticism of him.

Like Shelley, the young poet of *Alastor* was nurtured "By solemn vision and bright silver dream," sought "The fountains of divine philosophy," and left an "alienated home" as a mere youth to pursue knowledge to its utmost bounds. Like Shelley, too, he was a vegetarian. His wanderings in his search were more those of Shelley's reading than of Shelley's actual footsteps, but the beauty of the scenery derives from Shelley's own impressions of the Alps, the Rhine, the Thames, and Windsor Forest. Like Volney, a favorite author with Shelley, the young poet visited the ruins of ancient empire, and like Shelley's friend Newton he was enthralled by "the Zodiac's brazen mystery" in ancient temples. His ruin started when in a dream he beheld a vision of a veiled maid whose "voice was like the voice of his own soul." In his sleep he sought to clasp this vision and succeeded. More and more wasted by his own intensity, he pursued it beyond the bounds of sleep, until after many wanderings that are not always easy to follow he expired in a green recess by a lonely mountain stream.

The blank verse of *Alastor* is quite different from that of *Queen Mab* and greatly superior. In little more than two years Shelley had progressed from an undistinguished matter-of-fact blank verse to an imaginative, subtly modulated style that is practically on a par with his high models without being in the slightest sense subservient to them. The hero of the poem might be a little pathetic and the detail a trifle confusing, but the solid intellectual background, the descriptive power, and the mature technique told anyone who cared to listen that here was a poet capable of great poetry. At twenty-three Shelley was entitled to rank with the really important poets of his age.

The *Alastor* volume was published during the last two weeks of February 1816, by Carpenter and Son as co-publishers with Baldwin, Craddock, and Joy. Shelley sent a copy to Southey, with a graceful little note of gratitude for his friendship and an apology for not having written to him since going to Ireland. He referred to their wide differences in moral and political opinions as something to be charitably overlooked on both sides, and made no mention of Harriet or Mary.

The reviews of *Alastor* were far from encouraging. All three of the reviewers who deigned to notice the volume in 1816 agreed in vigorous condemnation of its obscurity. The *Monthly Review* scornfully professed inability to obtain a clue to Shelley's "sublime obscurity" — "till an address to Mr. Wordsworth explained in what school the author had formed his taste." Shelley was advised in his next publication to benefit his readers ("if he has any") by "an *ordo*, a glossary, and copious notes . . . explanatory of his meaning." The *British Critic*, acknowledging considerable experience with "profound and prosing stupidity," professed itself "not a little delighted with the nonsense [of *Alastor*] which mounts, which rises, which spurns the earth and all its dull realities," and offered a merrily sarcastic illustration of some of the offending passages. The *Eclectic Review* was a little more just and dignified. It quoted a passage to show Shelley's "very considerable talent for descriptive poetry," and gave Shelley's own explanation of the poem's meaning, but found the explanation inadequate. "All is wild and specious, untangible and incoherent as a dream. We should be utterly at a loss to convey any distinct idea of the plan or purpose of the poem." It comments suspiciously "that every indication of the Author's belief in a future state of existence, and in the moral government of God, is carefully avoided" except one profane reference to a God "'profuse of poisons.'" So well justified were these suspicions by Shelley's later career that the *Eclectic* never reviewed another work of Shelley's during his lifetime.

If Shelley had hoped that his new moderation would procure a fair critical reception for *Alastor*, he was deceived. One out of three critics still caught a faint whiff of brimstone. It is not necessary to suppose that the critic knew something of Shelley's private history or even that the volume would have been favorably received had it been pious and conservative. In spite of new subjects and trends in poetic technique introduced by Cowper, Burns, Blake, and Wordsworth, there was not in England in 1816 a single review that did not respect the views expressed in Dr. Johnson's *Rasselas* on the dangers of imagination far more than Wordsworth's still-derided Preface to *Lyrical Ballads*. *Alastor* was in fact contrary to the prevailing idea of poetic excellence.

At Bishopsgate Shelley was also writing some of the fragmentary essays which have been too little considered in the effort to understand his thought and his intellectual development. In his essay "On Love" occurs his first definition of love as complete human sympathy merging into universal sympathy. Passages in several other fragments show that at the age of twenty-three Shelley had attained the intellectual depth and subtlety and the just estimate of imagination and human sympathies that are also necessary for great poetry. Man, he asserted, was not merely a moral and intellectual being, "but also, and pre-eminently, an imaginative being." He believed that words often obscure rather than elucidate the real significance of life, because they are instruments of logic that are ill adapted to intuitive perceptions and are encrusted with all the trite associations of long and hackneyed use. The human mind, in fact, like the infinite variety of life itself, is much too intricate for exploration through the medium of words. "But thought can with difficulty visit the intricate and winding chambers which it inhabits. It is like a river whose rapid and perpetual stream flows outwards; like one in dread who speeds through the recesses of some haunted pile, and dares not look behind. The caverns of the mind are obscure, and shadowy; or pervaded with a lustre, beautifully bright indeed, but shining not beyond their portals."

Here we have, if not the source of Shelley's significant use of images in his poetry, at least their intellectual justification. Words in their logical meaning being by nature often inadequate to the uses of great poetry, images and symbols may sometimes be employed to speak more directly to the imagination and intuition. The passage itself is built of images all of which occur in *Alastor*. Clouds, caves, and serpents, probably, had already acquired some symbolic significance to Shelley; but after 1816 we find them used increasingly, along with eagles, boats, streams, veils, in an attempt to make poetry express more justly the extreme subtlety of the matter with which it must deal in order to widen the scope of human understanding.

At the same time Shelley was laying a philosophical foundation for the optimistic view of human nature that is so characteristic of his poetry. In the fragmentary "Speculations on Morals" he admits that there are human impulses to inflict pain, seize power, and exhibit revenge, pride, and selfishness — impulses that cannot be abolished by the anticipation of reward or punishment in a future existence. But the behavior of children, he argues, demonstrates that there is also a powerful, fundamental benevolence in human nature. A very young child is sensitive to its own pain but insensitive to its mother's pain. This is because it has not yet learned to associate pain with its signs and indications; but as soon as this lesson is learned, the child is distressed by the signs of pain in those most dear to it. We are selfish in direct ratio to our limitations of experience and knowledge:

> Thus an infant, a savage, and a solitary beast, is selfish, because its mind is incapable [of] receiving an accurate intimation of the nature of pain as existing in beings resembling itself. The inhabitant of a highly civilized community will more acutely sympathize with the sufferings and enjoyments of others, than the inhabitant of a society of a less degree of civilization. He who shall have cultivated his intellectual powers by familiarity with the finest specimens of poetry and philosophy will usually [sympathize more] than one engaged in the less refined functions of manual labour. . . . The only distinction between the selfish man, and the virtuous man, is that the imagination of the former is confined within a narrow limit, whilst that of the latter embraces a comprehensive circumference.

In this passage Shelley anticipates his profound defense of poetry as the language of the one power — Imagination — by which men's natures are ennobled.

The winter of 1815–16 passed agreeably and quietly. Hogg had returned from his northern vacation and was a frequent visitor. He might be on the wrong side of a moral or metaphysical argument, but he told amusing stories, and he knew and loved learning. Despite certain Toryish trends since leaving Oxford, he still hated tyranny and priestcraft. Peacock, like Hogg a lover of the classics, was constantly dropping in from Marlow. The winter, as Hogg said, was a mere Atticism. Of course there were arguments and high discussions, during which Peacock stored up a few points for the character of Scythrop, in which (in *Nightmare Abbey*) he was to make mild fun of Shelley the next year. These arguments were always amiable, however; even when Peacock argued against his "delusions," Shelley maintained his position with a sweet, inflexible courtesy.

Mary's second child was born on January 24, a healthy, amiable boy with smooth rosy cheeks and auburn hair. On January 25 Shelley concluded one of his patient, impersonal business letters to Mary's estranged father: "Fanny and Mrs. Godwin will probably be glad to hear that Mary has safely recovered from a very favourable confinement, and that her child is well." Godwin's continued refusal to see either Shelley or Mary did not prevent their naming the child William.

When the weather permitted, Shelley spent considerable time on the water or among the oaks of Windsor Great Park. There were many country rambles. Bracknell, where some of Shelley's friends of 1813 still resided, was not far away. On the heath just above Bracknell was a pool of clear water, with firm, clean banks, that was the best place Shelley ever found for launching paper boats. He could seldom pass a pool of water without launching a flotilla. If no other paper was handy, he made his boats from whatever letters happened to be in his pockets at the time. Peacock, who had known the sport before Shelley, encouraged him. Hogg, on the other hand, cordially abominated the practice, particularly if it interrupted a brisk walk on a cold winter day.

Visitors other than Hogg or Peacock were discouraged. On one occasion, while walking on Egham Hill, Shelley spied a particularly insistent bore whom he supposed to be heading for his cottage. Promptly he jumped through a hedge, ran across a field, and hid in a dry ditch. Here he was nearly betrayed by some mowers who ran up to see what was the matter, but who vanished promptly when Shelley claimed to be dodging a bailiff.

When Shelley gave Godwin £1,000 in May 1815, he expected to give him another sum, probably £1,200, in November. This was to have come from an additional settlement with his father which was held up by court decisions. Meanwhile Shelley could not raise money by post-obits without jeopardizing his whole arrangement with his father. But by January 1816 Godwin was desperate and insisted on Shelley's raising the money for his relief by whatever means. Shelley still refused to sell post-obits, but offered various expedients, such as signing bonds, selling an annuity, or attempting to borrow. The best he could do was to satisfy Godwin's most pressing creditor with some sort of deed guaranteeing a debt of between £200 and £300. This was in February. Some time later, following a supplementary settlement with his father, he found £300 more for Godwin, and he hoped to obtain another £300 for him through some sort of negotiation being carried on by Godwin's attorney, Hayward.

This partial relief of Godwin did not seriously imperil Shelley's financial security, but it was a heavy strain on his temper. Godwin was often harsh and insulting. Shelley was uniformly patient and courteous in everything that involved carrying out his obligation; he even informed Godwin that he *would* carry it out, regardless of Godwin's treatment of Mary and himself. Because he still valued Godwin's good opinion above that of anyone else he was the more deeply hurt by Godwin's repudiation of him. This he was forced to bear, but to bear Godwin's haughty tone of moral superiority and his talk of forgiveness was beyond even Shelleyan patience. "Perhaps," he warned Godwin early in the correspondence, "it is well that you should be informed that I consider your last letter to be written in a certain style of haughtiness and encroachment which neither awes nor imposes on me."

Shelley was so bitterly depressed by the realization that his character was scornfully regarded where it should have been best known that the thought sometimes made him physically ill. Some of his disappointment was for Godwin. He had discovered, like Godwin's earlier friend Francis Place, that in some matters his idol was unjust and unscrupulous — Godwin was no longer the great Godwin. This perception Shelley's natural delicacy inclined him to suppress, but continued provocation finally forced him to express it. "I lamented also over my ruined hopes, hopes of all that your genius once taught me to expect from your virtue, when I found that for yourself, your family, and your creditors, you would submit to that communication with me which you once rejected and abhorred, and which no pity for my poverty or sufferings, assumed willingly for you, could avail to extort. Do not talk of *forgiveness* again to me," he continued with rising indignation, "for my blood boils in my veins, and my gall rises against all that bears the human form, when I think of what I, their benefactor and ardent lover, have endured of enmity and contempt . . . from all mankind."

In other letters Shelley apologized for these outbursts and begged Godwin to burn them. His stubborn idealism would permit him in calmer moments to recognize only those faults in Godwin that it was impossible to ignore. "I respect you," he confessed with obvious truth, "I think well of you, better perhaps than of any other person whom England contains; you were the philosopher who first awakened, and who still as a philosopher to a very great degree regulate my understanding. It is unfortunate for me that the part of your character which is least excellent should have been met by my convictions of what was right to do. But I have been too indignant, I have been unjust to you. — Forgive me. — Burn those letters which contain the records of my violence, and believe that however what you erroneously call fame and honour separate us, I shall always feel towards you as the most affectionate of friends."

Godwin was not the only cause of Shelley's growing feeling of dejection. In April the scornful reviews of *Alastor* were beginning to appear. Shelley had seen the anonymous *Queen Mab* warmly and continuously praised in the *Theological Inquirer;* he now saw a superior poem, in which he had gone out of his way to avoid offending popular prejudices, treated with a careless contempt utterly ruinous to the hopes of fame that were probably built on it. Before this, chiefly because of Godwin, Shelley had resolved either to desert England or to retire into some solitary region of the country, "hiding myself and Mary from that contempt which we so unjustly endure." Italy would be his ultimate destination, he thought, but he expected to spend a few years first in Cumberland or Scotland.

Peacock thought that Shelley was growing very restless and that he was firmly convinced that his father and his uncle had designs against his liberty. No reasons for such designs are discoverable, and it is far more likely that Shelley's nervous depression was conjuring up unreal visions as it had done before. An incident which happened at about this time lends strong support to this probability. One day Shelley told Peacock that he was just back from a walk to Egham with John Williams, who had come up from Tremadoc to warn him. "He came to tell me of a plot laid by my father and uncle, to entrap me and lock me up." "What hat did you wear?" asked Peacock, who had noticed his own hat in Shelley's hands. "This, to be sure," said Shelley, indicating Peacock's hat. When Peacock showed him that the hat came down over his face and that he couldn't have worn it to Egham, he answered that he must have carried it — and that it was very hard on a man who had devoted his life to truth to be treated with skepticism. He undertook to take Peacock to the London coffee-house where Williams was stopping, but when Peacock set out with him he said he thought Williams had left London a day early, and gave up the demonstration. Later he told Peacock that Williams had sent him a letter enclosing a diamond necklace, but he failed in the end to exhibit either.

Claire Clairmont's movements after returning from her Irish journey with her brother Charles are for some time uncertain. For short periods she seems to have been with Shelley and Mary, and again with the Godwins. Several checks drawn by Shelley in her favor in March 1816 seem to suggest that she was then living in London on Shelley's bounty. It goes almost without saying that she was discontented and restless. She was fully ready, in fact, for the great adventure that was to wreck her life and deeply complicate the lives of Shelley and Mary.

Lord Byron was at this time approaching the end of his glittering career as the liberal-minded, attractively cynical and wicked author-about-town. The restless and impulsive Claire, at loose ends in London, ambitiously "fell in love" with him at a distance like many another. Claire, however, possessed boldness and initiative; she believed thoroughly in the creed of Godwin and Shelley and thus had no terrifying social and moral inhibitions. Under the name of E. Trefusis she wrote Byron that though an utter stranger she had loved him many years, that her happiness was in his hands — that she placed a reputation as yet unstained and an infinite capacity for affection and devotion entirely at his mercy.

Byron could not be bothered. Under the signature "G. C. B.," Claire asked for an appointment "on business of peculiar importance," which Byron granted in a most forbidding manner and twice failed to keep. Claire then under her own name wrote again, having previously either seen Byron or told her story in a letter. She now wished his advice, as one of the subcommittee of the Drury Lane Theatre, about her desire to become an actress. Byron referred her to his friend Douglas Kinnaird. Omitting to see Kinnaird, she then asked Byron's help in deciding between a literary or a dramatic career, submitting a manuscript and talking also about the works and opinions of her one friend, Shelley. Byron was still decidedly bored. He bade her write briefly when she wrote and called her "a little fiend," which caused Claire to quote Shelley's candid but somewhat more favorable view of her character.

Byron probably cared no more at this time for Shelley's opinion than for Claire. Lady Byron, however, had just left him; he was irritable and harassed, and the persistent Claire, though her cleverness and independence were obvious, was doing her best to exhibit the submissive qualities that he most admired. Claire had already proposed that they spend the night together at some quiet place ten or twelve miles out of London. He made counter suggestions and changed the date, but some time before Byron left England (April 25) Claire was established as his mistress. Mary, and possibly Shelley, had recently learned of Claire's acquaintance with Byron, but both were ignorant as yet that she was his mistress.

It was probably immediately after Byron's departure that Claire

revealed her secret to Shelley and Mary in order to persuade them
to go to Geneva instead of Italy, upon which they had just agreed.
Hogg had supposed to the last minute that he was to accompany
them, nor was he undeceived until the party was actually on its way
to Switzerland. "Mauvaise honte or awkwardness" and "circumstances [which] have occurred since I last saw you" and which were
"more fit to be made the subject of conversation than of a letter"
were the only explanations Shelley somewhat vaguely assigned Hogg
for his unannounced departure. This situation was probably created
by Claire's revelation. As soon as they reached Paris, Claire wrote to
inform Byron that Shelley had yielded to her "pressing solicitations"
and that she would soon join him at Geneva, under the name of
Madame Clairville.

On May 3, as soon as the final settlement with his father made it
possible to leave, Shelley was on his way to the Continent. "The
motives which determined me to leave England and which I stated
to you in a former letter," he wrote Godwin before sailing, "have
continued since that period to press on me with accumulated force.
Continually detained in a situation where what I esteem a prejudice
does not permit me to live on equal terms with my fellow-beings I
resolved to commit myself to a decided step. I therefore take Mary
to Geneva, where I shall devise some plan of settlement and only
leave her to return to London and exclusively devote myself to business." Concerning Claire he said nothing, and it was in fact four years
before Godwin learned of Claire's liaison with Byron.

By May 8, 1816, Shelley, Mary, and Claire were in Paris, where
they observed with some disgust the conduct of the foreign troops
still quartered in Paris to support the Bourbon restoration. From
Paris to Troyes they repeated their travels of 1814. Passing through
Dijon and Dôle, they reached the Jura Mountains at Poligny. Over
a steep, narrow road by moonlight, with a dark ravine on one side
and an overhanging precipice on the other, they came to Cham-
pagnolles at midnight, in the midst of a driving rainstorm. The rain
changed to snow; over the edge of the road they could see in the valleys below them impenetrable forests of huge pines almost buried
in the deep drifts. At the village of Les Rousses a little bribery enabled them to proceed by a shorter and less dangerous route than
their passport specified. Even so they completed the last stage of the
journey only with the aid of four horses and ten men to support the
carriage.

After this white wilderness of incessant snowstorms and penetrating cold the warm sunshine of Geneva and the hum of sun-loving insects was very pleasant. In the suburb of Sécheron, from their windows at Dejean's Hôtel d'Angleterre they looked over a sparkling blue lake to a sloping shore dotted with vineyards and country houses, with mountains rising in the background, ridge after ridge, until they reached their limit of imposing grandeur in Mont Blanc. "You know," Mary wrote to a friend, "that we have just escaped from the gloom of winter and of London; and coming to this delightful spot during this divine weather, I feel as happy as a new-fledged bird. . . ."

Shelley shared these feelings, but with him they mingled with a newly realized love for England, now that it seemed possible that he might see England again only on brief visits. A man never fully realizes his love for England, he wrote to Peacock, until he has learned by foreign travel, as Wordsworth did, to put a just value upon his native land. England, he asserted, was of all countries the most free and refined. "Our poets and our philosophers, our mountains and our lakes, the rural lanes and fields which are ours so especially, are ties which, until I become utterly senseless, can never be broken asunder."

Byron, with his youthful physician, Dr. John William Polidori, had left England ten days before the Shelleys, but his route was the longer one through Belgium and the Rhine country. Traveling more slowly and pausing more often, he reached Geneva some ten days after the arrival of Shelley's party. When he lounged into Shelley's hotel on May 25, with the slight mortifying limp that could never be quite fully concealed, Claire Clairmont had brought about a junction of literary influences that was to have an important effect upon both men and upon English public opinion. Byron probably realized little more importance in the meeting at the time than the curious observers. He had read Shelley's *Queen Mab* with some admiration without even knowing the author's name; he had heard Shelley's character praised by Claire; and he had read the *Alastor* volume very probably with some impatience, if one may generalize from his own taste and practice in poetry at the time.

As soon as Shelley's party reached Geneva they settled down into the quiet way of living always observed by Shelley whenever there was opportunity. Seeking only their own society, they spent the heat of the day in reading Latin and Italian, and the early afternoon walk-

201

ing in the hotel garden. They hired a boat in which they sailed on the lake every evening from about six o'clock until ten. After Byron's arrival he and Polidori joined the nightly sailing parties. Mary, who could never enjoy a sea voyage, was almost hilariously delighted with their evening sails. As they glided home to their dock they never failed to take pleasure in the scent of flowers and new-mown grass, the chirp of the grasshoppers, and the song of the evening birds. Soon Byron was to record his delight in the same phenomena:

> . . . and drawing near,
> There breathes a living fragrance from the shore,
> Of flowers yet fresh with childhood; on the ear
> Drops the light drip of the suspended oar,
> Or chirps the grasshopper one goodnight carol more.

Until about June 1 both groups continued to live in Sécheron, at Dejean's Hôtel d'Angleterre. Shelley's family then moved to a little cottage called Mont Alègre, on the opposite side of the lake, exchanging a view of Mont Blanc for "dark, frowning Jura." Their boat was still a prime source of pleasure, though constant rains now kept them more often indoors. Frequent thunderstorms seemed often to them, as to Byron, magnificently beautiful. "One night," Mary wrote, "we *enjoyed* a finer storm than I had ever before beheld. The lake was lit up — the pines on Jura made visible, and all the scene illuminated for an instant, when a pitchy blackness succeeded, and the thunder came in frightful bursts over our heads amid the darkness."

In sunnier weather, on still afternoons, they listened to the monotonous simple ballads of the peasant women who worked as vinedressers in the vineyard separating Mont Alègre from the Villa Diodati. Sometimes at night they heard a more distinguished voice floating back from the darkness of the lake. Byron, returning to his hotel with Dr. Polidori after one of his evening visits to Mont Alègre, was chanting to the elements Moore's "Tyrolese Song of Liberty."

On June 10 Byron left his hotel and came to live at the Villa Diodati, only seven or eight minutes' walk from Mont Alègre through an intervening vineyard. Here he hoped (but vainly) that he could be free from the telescopes of vulgar tourists. His unofficial observers had already been talking and writing. Back to England were drifting stories that Byron, Claire, Shelley, and Mary were living together in a state of general promiscuity.

Byron and Shelley were now much more often in each other's company. Dr. Polidori was also generally with them, as were Claire and Mary. Every morning Byron called at Shelley's cottage, after which the party usually sailed on the lake. Every evening, when the weather was fine, there was another sailing expedition. On one such evening Byron burst into a strange wild howl of music that he assured them was an Albanian song. At times they would vary their boating with a stroll along the shores, Byron always bringing up the rear, musing and trailing his sword-stick as he walked. Sometimes there were evening gatherings, generally at the Villa Diodati. The conversation often lasted until early morning.

In such company the self-conscious Polidori was more than apt to make himself ridiculous. Byron said of him, not uncharitably, that he was "young and hot-headed" and "had no kind of conduct," but was "not a bad fellow." Though he was unable to restrain his pique at the growing friendship of Shelley and Byron, Mary Godwin liked him well enough at times to call him her younger brother.

It was the usually silent Mary who produced the most tangible result of the nightly séances around Byron's fireside. Her novel *Frankenstein* has for its immediate background another of those curious incidents that illustrate Shelley's extreme susceptibility to suggestion. About the middle of June the group was amusing itself during a spell of rainy weather by reading a collection of ghost stories. On the night of June 16 there was much talk of these horrors around the fire at Diodati. Two nights later there was similar talk. Byron adduced Coleridge's recently published "Christabel," which he had seen in manuscript and partly memorized, as an admirable example of the poetic use of such materials. He quoted the lines describing the horrible secret of Geraldine's deformity. For a moment there was silence; then Shelley, who had been staring at Mary, uttered a sudden shriek, pressed his hands over his head, seized a candle, and fled from the room. It required Polidori's professional services with cold water and ether to restore him to anything like normality. As he looked at Mary he had been shocked into uncontrollable horror by seeing a vision of a woman he had once heard of who had eyes for nipples.

On the conclusion of the first of these ghostly séances Byron proposed that each one present should write a ghost story. "You and I," he gallantly promised Mary, "will publish ours together." Shelley began and abandoned a story based on his own life. By the next evening all but Mary and Polidori had begun stories. Polidori, after beginning and dropping a story of his own, eventually finished one begun by Byron. As *The Vampire*, published in 1819, it became quite popular under the supposition that it was Byron's.

But Mary could not at first get started. Every morning Shelley asked: "Have you thought of a story?" Eventually the idea was suggested by a conversation between Byron and Shelley on the vital principle. Gradually she formulated her idea of a mechanical monster endowed with life by a student of magic and driven to criminal behavior by the absence of human sympathy. Published the next year as *Frankenstein* with a preface by Shelley, it achieved many more readers than any work of Shelley's during his lifetime.

On the afternoon of June 23 Shelley and Byron, leaving the rest of the two parties, began an eight days' excursion of the lake in a boat which they jointly owned. Once they were almost capsized when a sudden heavy squall broke the rudder and rendered the boat unmanageable. Byron, an excellent swimmer, took off his coat and waited; Shelley, unable to swim and knowing that Byron would attempt to save him, caught hold of a locker and declared his determination to sink with it rather than endanger another life by accepting Byron's aid.

At Meillerie and Clarens both travelers were immensely impressed by the associations with Rousseau and his *Julie*. Byron wrote at once his famous stanzas beginning: "Clarens, sweet Clarens, birthplace of deep Love!" As for Shelley, "I read 'Julie' all day," he wrote; "an overflowing, as it now seems, surrounded by the scenes which it has so wonderfully peopled, of sublimest genius, and more than human sensibility. . . . They were created indeed by one mind, but a mind so powerfully bright as to cast a shade of falsehood on the records that are called reality."

Some days later, when they were at Lausanne, standing among the old acacias through which Gibbon had taken his memorable stroll after regretfully ending the last page of his *Decline and Fall of the Roman Empire*, the harder-minded Byron had recovered sufficiently from the emotional intoxication of Rousseau to write some fine lines about the "lord of irony" who studied here so long and deeply. Being rather a souvenir-hunter, he gathered some acacia leaves to send to his friend and publisher, John Murray. But Shelley was still so much under the influence of Rousseau's passion that he would pluck no memento of Gibbon for fear of outraging "the greater and more sacred name of Rousseau," compared with whom Gibbon was so "cold and unimpassioned."

The castle of Chillon was to both poets a terribly significant monument, inspiring Shelley to a long prose passage and Byron to two famous poems written under its immediate stimulation. Here, however, Byron was the optimist and Shelley the pessimist. To Byron it typified, through Bonnivard, the "eternal spirit of the chainless mind." Shelley wrote to Peacock: "I never saw a monument more terrible of that cold and inhuman tyranny which it had been the delight of man to exercise over man. It was indeed one of those many tremendous fulfilments which render the 'pernicies humani generis' of the great Tacitus so solemn and irrefragable a prophecy."

Before the journey was over, Shelley had composed a poem in which he sought to give a spiritual meaning to the unutterable beauty by which he felt himself surrounded. In *Alastor* he had already found his old doctrine of a dispassionate Necessity too cold and rigid for his expansive sympathies. He had referred in the Preface to a "Power" whose exquisite influences it was dangerous to perceive too suddenly, and fatal to ignore. To this power in his "Hymn to Intellectual Beauty," he now gave a definite name and definite functions. It was "Intellectual Beauty," or beauty which can only be conceived as an idea, rather than experienced in its fullness. Even its shadow, Shelley asserts, is unseen, and visits the world infrequently, but is nevertheless the secret of all that is true and beautiful both in the natural world and in humanity. Poets, sages, and prophets have tried vainly to understand it and to give it a name. If it could only be understood and brought to keep firm state in the human heart, "Man were immortal and omnipotent." As he formulated for the first time his conception of a beneficent principle that was to play so important a part in his later poetry, Shelley perceived and recorded that it had been the object of his study and allegiance ever since the hour when, as an indignant schoolboy, he had sworn undying hatred of tyranny.

Already Shelley knew that he must soon return to England. Godwin was again in financial difficulties in which only Shelley could save him. Though Godwin and his attorney could handle some of the preliminary arrangements, eventually Shelley would have to appear and sign papers. Shelley requested an increase of his annuity from £2,000 to £2,500. Sir Timothy, who had been offended at Shelley's sudden, unannounced departure from England, not only refused this request, but declined to complete a loan previously agreed upon, or to enter upon any other financial arrangements, unless Shelley returned to England.

Though he was already making great plans for tremendous boat trips on the great rivers of Europe, Shelley was not really sorry to face an early return to "the best of nations." Having had to resign his house at Bishopsgate, he wrote to Peacock to look for a new home for him and to take care of his furniture. "You must shelter my roofless Penates, dedicate some new temple to them, and perform the functions of a priest in my absence. They are innocent deities, and their worship neither sanguinary nor absurd. Leave Mammon and Jehovah to those who delight in wickedness and slavery — their altars are stained with blood or polluted with gold, the price of blood. But the shrines of the Penates are good wood fires, or window frames intertwined with creeping plants; their hymns are the purring of kittens, the hissing of kettles; the long talks over the past and dead, the laugh of children, the warm wind of summer filling the quiet house, and the pelting storm of winter struggling in vain for entrance." This surprising tribute to domesticity Shelley knew might seem amusing to Peacock, for he added: "In talking of the Penates, will you not liken me to Julius Caesar dedicating a temple to Liberty?"

For three weeks more there was constant visiting back and forth between Mont Alègre and Villa Diodati. Day after day glided by in the old unhurried daily and nightly routine of sailing, walking, and discussing.

Shelley read less than usual while in Switzerland and as yet had written only one poem. Byron, on the other hand, had written "The Prisoner of Chillon" and most of the third canto of *Childe Harold's Pilgrimage* since his meeting with Shelley. Possibly Byron's genius, as Mrs. Shelley later suggested, inhibited Shelley's. Shelley was too genuinely modest, perhaps, to think of competition with a man whom most people were coming to regard as the greatest poetic genius of the age. On the other hand, he was far too deeply grounded in learning and good taste not to realize that on these grounds he was independent of Byron and possibly his superior. "Lord Byron," he wrote to Peacock, passing his judgment with calm equality, "is an exceedingly interesting person, and as such is it not to be regretted that he is a slave to the vilest and most vulgar prejudices, and as mad as the winds?"

Frequent daily discussions between two such lively minds as Byron's and Shelley's must have been of great benefit to both. For Shelley the advantage consisted mainly in an intellectual stimulation derived from Byron's strong vitality and sharp, incisive comments. Byron, who partly agreed with Shelley's political views and mainly disagreed with his social and religious ideas, respected his knowledge and was probably at times almost awed by his moral earnestness. Shelley saw in Byron a great potential force for truth and righteousness and sought tactfully to inspire him with a high moral purpose such as he himself had expressed in the "Hymn to Intellectual Beauty." Perhaps it was Shelley's talk on this subject that inspired Byron at the same time to his fine stanzas on love in the third canto of *Childe Harold's Pilgrimage,* just as the Wordsworthian tone of many passages in that poem are due to Shelley's insistence on "dosing" him, as Byron phrased it, with Wordsworth.

Mary was usually a silent listener during these conversations. Yet they impressed themselves so deeply on her memory that never after Shelley's death could she hear Byron talk without unconsciously waiting for Shelley's eager answer. It was, she recorded, "like thunder without rain," or like "any familiar object . . . shorn of its best attributes," to hear Byron's voice without Shelley's; it afflicted her with "unspeakable melancholy."

At half past eight on the morning of July 21, Shelley, Mary, and Claire began their previously planned expedition to Chamouni. William was left behind in the care of Elise, his Swiss nurse. Byron was expecting visitors from England and remained at Diodati. Four hours' travel through steamy hot lowlands brought the party to Bonneville, where the Alps began to close in on them. Between Bonneville and Cluses they passed two waterfalls, one of them about three hundred feet high. Next morning, on muleback, they passed another waterfall — two hundred and fifty feet of wavering, fluctuating spray that filled the valley with a wind-swept mist. As they climbed still higher, they could see gleaming glaciers and mighty pines above them, while far below was the rushing, foaming Arve, bordered by pines and fretted by boulders. They entered the vale of Chamouni, where the mountains spread apart sufficiently to permit cultivated fields, cottages, and little villages. The glacier of Boisson, dotted with conical and pyramidal towers and seamed with precipices, was now very close; the way became more dangerous. Behind them they heard a thunderous noise and turned to see an avalanche plunge down a ravine and turn from its course a stream they had crossed earlier in the day. Very much fatigued, they reached the inn at Chamouni at seven o'clock.

After breakfast the next day, July 23, the party mounted mules for the difficult ascent to the source of the Arveyron. The last mile had to be negotiated on foot among treacherous boulders. Seated on a rock beside one of the streams of the Arveyron, they could see the river rolling impetuously from its cavern of ice. On the opposite glacier of Montanvert they could see masses of ice detach themselves and fall with such thunderous force that they were converted into powder. That evening Shelley went with the guide to visit another glacier, that of Boisson. The inexorable, devastating encroachments of these glaciers offered a grand and gloomy stimulation. The scientific side of his mind saw in them the gradual extinction of all life in the valleys in a smother of "avalanches, torrents, rocks and thunders." To his poetic mind they were a symbol of unutterable and incomprehensible power. Such thoughts, he wrote Peacock, were best reserved for later conversations.

That evening, however, he transmitted some of these feelings into poetry. "Mont Blanc — Lines Written in the Vale of Chamouni" blends the river Arve and its parent mountain into one impressive symbol of Power. Through a scene of beauty and wild desolation rivers and glaciers roll their "flood of ruin" down the heights, obliterating all obstacles and uniting finally in "one majestic River." For both the Arve and the glaciers the sources of power are the secret and inaccessible fastnesses of Mont Blanc, where "Power dwells apart in its tranquillity."

On July 24 the party set out to climb the glacier of Montanvert, but soon returned, wet to the skin. Next day they accomplished the climb. The mountainside appeared, as Shelley wrote to Peacock, "as if frost had suddenly bound up the waves and whirlpools of a mighty torrent. . . . The waves are elevated about twelve or fifteen feet from the surface of the mass, which is intersected with long gaps of unfathomable depth, the ice of whose sides is more beautifully azure than the sky."

They dined at a little inn on Montanvert. Here occurred an incident destined for several years thereafter to be told around England to the detriment of Shelley's reputation. The generosity of a former tourist had provided an album in which a succession of visitors had inscribed their names, often with trite pious comments on the scene as a striking testimony to the glory of God. What Shelley felt as he read these inscriptions only Shelley could say; we only know that in his own way, inspired by the same sights, he had just finished an impassioned tribute to *his* notion of a supreme Power. Perhaps his predecessors seemed intolerably smug. Perhaps the excitement "not unallied to madness" with which he was filled prompted him to a last outburst of youthful exhibitionism. At any rate he inscribed his name, and after it four words in Greek characterizing himself as "democrat, philanthropist, and atheist."

Shelley had already written a similar inscription in the album of the Hôtel de Londres at Chamouni, and very probably a still earlier one at the inn at Sallanches where the party had spent the first night after leaving Geneva. One of these inscriptions, but certainly not the one at Montanvert, was noticed and considerately scratched out by Byron a month later, when he visited the same region with John Cam Hobhouse, Scrope Davies, and Polidori. About a year after Shelley wrote the inscription at Montanvert, Robert Southey visited the same little inn, copied Shelley's inscription, and carried it back to England, where it was quoted in print to Shelley's disadvantage.

On the evening of July 27 the party was back again at Mont Alègre. The month of August passed quietly in a regular routine of boating, reading, walking, and talking. Mary was writing her novel, reading almost every day, and keeping up her Latin studies. Shelley was reading also, mainly Lucretius and Pliny, but not so much as usual. Shelley's twenty-fourth birthday, August 4, was duly observed. Mary presented him with a telescope and made a fire-balloon for him to send up from the lake; also she read to him aloud Book IV of the *Æneid*. Almost every evening during the first part of the month they went up to Diodati. Two or three letters arrived from Fanny Imlay and Charles Clairmont. Fanny reported that Godwin was sleepless and miserable over financial worries, and that she was herself terribly depressed, but hoped soon to obtain a position as teacher in a school conducted in Dublin by her two aunts. Charles wrote reams of delighted description about his travels and observations in the Hautes-Pyrénées — and hoped that Shelley would finance him for six months while he studied French and Spanish.

Claire Clairmont's liaison with Byron was now ended. Byron had been virtually kidnapped into it and had probably never really loved Claire. She remained in love with him long after his position had been made perfectly clear, and was doubtless precariously happy copying his poems for him at Villa Diodati. But Claire's moody variability and even her independence and sprightly intelligence were not the qualities that attracted Byron in women. Moreover he was trying to live respectably and avoid gossip. He seems to have stated the case truly, though brutally, when he wrote to reassure his half sister, Augusta, on September 8: "Now, dearest, I do most truly tell thee, that I could not help this, that I did all I could to prevent it, and have at last put an end to it. I was not in love, nor have any love left for any; but I could not exactly play the Stoic with a woman, who had scrambled eight hundred miles to unphilosophize me."

In any event, Claire would have had to leave soon, for she now knew she was to bear Byron a child, and it would never do to allow her pregnancy to become associated with the local gossip already current. There was some disagreement about Byron's provisions for the child. Byron proposed to place the child shortly after its birth in the care of his half sister, but Claire objected. Byron finally agreed, according to Claire's statement, to leave her in charge of the child, as its "aunt," until it was seven years old.

The necessity for Claire's return to England coincided with Shelley's own necessities due largely to his father's attitude. Longdill, Shelley's attorney, insisted that his early return was necessary. Shelley spent some of the last evenings in August in agreeable conversation with Byron and his recent guests, "Monk" Lewis, John Cam Hobhouse, and Scrope Davies. On the 28th Byron came down from Villa Diodati to say good-by; and on the 29th Shelley's party began their return journey, taking with them little William's Swiss nurse, Elise, two kittens, some Swiss flower seeds, and some of Byron's manuscripts.

The return journey occupied nine days, with no particular incident except a visit to Versailles which confirmed Shelley's impressions of the extravagance of tyranny and helped him to realize more clearly how an impoverished people could be goaded into fury and horrible excess. After landing at Portsmouth Shelley set off for London to attend to business affairs and to complete arrangements for a house at Marlow, not far from Bishopsgate. The others went to Bath, to remain there until the house could be occupied, and also, very probably, to conceal Claire's pregnancy from the Godwins.

The sojourn in Switzerland had been of wonderful benefit to Shelley. On his arrival Dr. Polidori had described him as consumptive, bashful, and shy. Many hours of mountain-climbing and of boating in the wind and sunshine had produced a physical improvement. The association with Byron had strengthened his confidence in himself. Even as Fanny Imlay's letters were chiding him for not writing more he was firmly announcing in the "Hymn to Intellectual Beauty" that he had kept and would keep his early vow to "free this world from its dark slavery." Above all, he had acquired a much more elevated sense of the grandeur and mystery of "this unfathomable world." "Before we return," Shelley had assured Peacock, "we shall have seen, and felt, and heard, a multiplicity of things which will haunt our talk and make us a little better worth knowing than we were before our departure."

That these things at least haunted their thoughts is shown by a later entry in Mary's journal: "I am melancholy with reading the 3rd canto of *Childe Harold*. Do you not remember, Shelley, when you first read it to me? One evening after returning from Diodati. It was in our little room at Chapuis. The lake was before us, and the mighty Jura. That time is past, and this will also pass, when I may weep to read these words, and again moralize on the flight of time. Dear Lake! I shall ever love thee. . . . I think of our excursions on the lake. How we saw him [Byron] when he came down to us, or welcomed our arrival, with a good-humoured smile. How vividly does each verse of his poem recall some scene of this kind to my memory!"

Chapter XIII

WHEN SHELLEY arrived in London on September 9 he found that Longdill, his solicitor, was out of town. He delivered to John Murray, Byron's publisher, Canto iii of *Childe Harold's Pilgrimage,* had a somewhat encouraging talk with Fanny Imlay about Godwin's finances, and by September 14 was Peacock's guest at Marlow. Here Mary joined him five days later, and for several days the party spent most of their time in conversation and in country walks.

On the 24th Shelley returned to London to complete the financial settlement agreed upon with his father before he went to Switzerland. Sir Timothy, who was generally pretty well informed about his son's affairs, knew that Shelley still had a number of debts outstanding. He may even have known, through Longdill or Whitton, of Shelley's efforts to relieve Godwin, of which he would certainly have disapproved. Nothing could be more evident than his fear of future embarrassments to the estate and his complete lack of confidence in his son's ability to handle money. This fear was justified by the fact that in spite of the debts paid in 1815 and the income of £800, Shelley was now over £1,400 in debt. Sir Timothy made it an indispensable condition of completing his agreement that Shelley should pay all of his past debts out of the money provided. Shelley had expected to have £500 or £600 left, out of which he would furnish the £300 that Godwin so desperately awaited. Instead, he had only £248 remaining. Most of this he now sent to Godwin with the bitter confession that he did not know how to provide the remainder. Shelley's letter to Godwin, as Fanny Imlay noted after watching its reception, "came like a thunderclap." But before the year's end he completed some sort of sale or loan that effected Godwin's relief, at least temporarily.

Though Shelley had very little actual money to disburse after his creditors were paid, he still had a considerable fortune in prospect. On the same day (September 24) that he completed his agreement with his father he also made his first will. To Harriet he left £6,000, to Ianthe and Charles £5,000 each, to Mary Jane Clairmont £6,000 to be invested in an annuity, and to Thomas Love Peacock £2,000 to be invested in an annuity. All these sums were placed in trust with Byron and Peacock as trustees. In addition, Claire was to receive

£6,000 outright, Hogg and Byron £2,000 each, Peacock £500. The residue of his estate he bequeathed to Mary Wollstonecraft Godwin. It is natural that Shelley made no provision for Godwin, Fanny Imlay, or William Shelley. Godwin would have felt insulted by being mentioned, and a mention of Fanny or little William might call attention to their illegitimacy. It would be better to trust their fortunes to Mary, whose inheritance would comprise the bulk of Shelley's estate.

From September 25 to October 9 Shelley, Mary, and Claire led a placid, featureless existence at Bath, unconscious of impending tragedy. Shelley wrote Byron a friendly letter reassuring him about his affairs in England and encouraging him to fulfill his destiny as a great poet. He took frequent walks, and read a variety of books — Lucian, Peter Pindar, the life of Holcroft, *History of the French Revolution*, Tasso, *Don Quixote* — some of them aloud to Mary. Mary kept up her Latin, read even more than Shelley, took drawing lessons, walked, and looked after her child. Claire interested herself in her music and the baby and awaited her own confinement in January.

Into this quiet, somewhat monotonous routine dropped the shattering bombshell of Fanny Imlay's suicide. Fanny had been despondent for some time; very probably she had a touch of the melancholia that had once led her mother, Mary Wollstonecraft, to attempt suicide. Claire had noticed it and remonstrated as early as May 28, 1815: "For heaven's sake be cheerful; so young in life, and so melancholy." It had appeared in the letters Fanny wrote to Shelley's little party in Switzerland: "I have determined never to live to be a disgrace to such a Mother." She wrote of "the dreadful state of mind I generally labour under, and which I in vain try to get rid of." Recently she had been more cheerful; her two aunts from Dublin had been in London during the latter part of September and might offer her a position as a teacher in their school.

Whether or not the offer was made is uncertain, but early in October Fanny suddenly left Godwin's house, ostensibly to visit her aunts in Dublin, but actually without enough money to get there. She passed through Bath to Bristol and Swansea without calling at Shelley's lodgings. From Bristol she wrote to Godwin: "I depart immediately to the spot from which I hope never to remove." A similarly desperate note was received by Shelley and Mary on October 9, and Shelley hurried immediately to Bristol, but returned without news. Next day he returned to Bristol and traced Fanny to Swansea. Here he learned that on the night of October 9 she had taken a room at the Mackworth Arms, had dismissed the chambermaid, and had been found dead next morning, with a bottle of laudanum on the table near by.

A note on the same table read: "I have long determined that the best thing I could do was to put an end to the existence of a being whose birth was unfortunate, and whose life has only been a series of pain to those persons who have hurt their health in endeavouring to promote her welfare. Perhaps to hear of my death will give you pain, but you will soon have the blessing of forgetting that such a creature ever existed as . . ." Apparently the signature had been torn off and burned. If the local authorities ever penetrated her decent, pathetic anonymity, the fact was never published. By reporting her simply as "found dead" the coroner's jury saved her from the disgraceful burial that English law still prescribed for suicides.

No doubt in the miserable evenings that followed Shelley's return to Bath all three of his household saw only too clearly how the tragedy had been prepared. Fanny's unfortunate position in the Godwin household made her the scapegoat for the two others who had escaped Mrs. Godwin's uncertain moods. Her sensitive, sympathetic, rather brooding nature was especially susceptible to Godwin's miseries and her own feeling of penniless dependence. Did Shelley's disappointment of Godwin's financial hopes, which fell at this moment, convince Fanny that she could never be more than a hopeless burden on others? She had only recently learned that she was not Godwin's child, but an illegitimate daughter born to her mother before she knew Godwin — was this the additional straw that brought about her decision? Or had she learned that Claire was soon to give birth to an illegitimate child, thus ruining once more her hopes of a teaching position in Ireland? Miss Mary Hutton, an acquaintance of Fanny's aunts, felt sure that Aunt Everina had caused Fanny's suicide by declining to receive her in Dublin. If Shelley's little circle knew, they kept silence. They could hardly help realizing that nearly all possible clues led, one way or another, to the elopement of Shelley and Mary. And being intensely certain that their action was not blameworthy, they could only feel a dumb misery.

Mary felt later that if Fanny had only waited until her marriage with Shelley she could have had a happy home at Marlow. This indicates that Mary at least, who would have been a competent judge in such matters, took no stock in a belief stated later by Godwin that Fanny's death was due to a hopeless love for Shelley. Shelley said nothing, except for two veiled references in a letter to Byron to a very severe anguish. But he wrote the following lines, which very probably refer to his last talk with Fanny, on September 24:

> Her voice did quiver as we parted,
>   Yet knew I not that heart was broken
> From which it came, and I departed
>   Heeding not the word then spoken.
>   Misery — O Misery,
>   This world is all too wide for thee.

Godwin, now that the last and most devoted of his "daughters" had gone, admitted that he was not surprised. It was a heavy blow, which he accepted with stoical, dignified resignation. All that remained was to shield Fanny's name. "Go not to Swansea," he wrote to Mary, "disturb not the silent dead; do nothing to destroy the obscurity she so much desired that now rests upon the event. . . . We have so conducted ourselves that not one person in our home has the smallest apprehension of the truth." These wishes were rigorously observed. Neither Claire nor Shelley in writing to Byron disclosed the fact that Fanny was a suicide; even Charles Clairmont was kept ignorant, not only of the nature, but even of the fact of Fanny's death.

Claire wrote to Byron: "We have spent a most dismal time. Fanny (the daughter of Mary Wollstonecraft and Imlay) has died, and her death was attended by such melancholy consequences as (at least for me) can never be forgotten. Poor Shelley's health is broken up, and I never passed such wretched hours. Everything is so miserable that I often wish myself quite dead."

Mary bought mourning, and went steadily ahead with her *Frankenstein*, her Latin, her drawing, and her general reading. She began the study of chemistry with Shelley on October 28. Shelley wrote a little and continued his reading, finding particular pleasure in Montaigne's *Essays*. Both Shelley and Mary went frequently for walks; Shelley even set out for Oxford, but was stopped by some mysterious "men dressed in black" and decided to return to Bath. There is no mention in the journal of Shelley's illness, and the fullness and regularity of his daily occupations seem inconsistent with the state of broken health that Claire ascribed to him.

Shelley was now about to take upon himself another pensioner, albeit one whose friendship was to be one of his principal pleasures during the rest of his life. He was already acquainted with Leigh

Hunt, but the acquaintance had hardly been more than casual and had been interrupted by Hunt's imprisonment and by Shelley's vicissitudes of the last two years. In October Shelley had sent to Hunt's *Examiner* his "Hymn to Intellectual Beauty," signed with one of Mary's pet names, "Elfin Knight." On December 1 Hunt's *Examiner* contained a little article entitled "Young Poets." Briefly, before announcing more fully that John Keats and John Hamilton Reynolds were young poets of great promise, the reviewer (Leigh Hunt) encouraged "Percy Bysshe Shelley, author of *Alastor, or the Spirit of Solitude.*" As yet he had seen little of Shelley's work, "but if the rest answer to what we have seen, we shall have no hesitation in announcing him for a very striking and original thinker."

Despite the bold conclusion this was decidedly cautious praise. It filled less than half a dozen lines and was not to be compared with the full glowing tributes paids to the anonymous author of *Queen Mab* in the pages of that mysterious journal the *Theological Inquirer*. Here, however, Shelley's name was printed in bold capitals, the writer was a man whose good opinion Shelley particularly esteemed, and his conditional encomium could not have been better phrased to please the young poet. Coming at a time of great discouragement, it lifted Shelley's spirits enormously. He immediately sent Hunt a present of a sum of money.

Two letters from Hunt to Shelley soon reached him at Marlow, where he had gone from Bath on December 5 to resume his search for a house. The eagerness with which he welcomed Leigh Hunt's friendship is expressed in Shelley's prompt and deeply felt reply:

. . . I have not in all my intercourse with mankind experienced sympathy and kindness with which I have been so affected or which my whole being has so sprung forward to meet and to return. . . . I am undeceived in the belief that I have powers deeply to interest, or substantially to improve, mankind. How far my conduct and my opinions have rendered the zeal and ardour with which I have engaged in the attempt ineffectual, I know not. Self love prompts me to assign much weight to a cause which perhaps has none. But thus much I do not seek to conceal from myself, that I am an outcast from human society; my name is execrated by all who understand its entire import — by those very beings whose happiness I ardently desire. I am an object of compassion to a few more benevolent than the rest, all else abhor

216

and avoid me. With you, and perhaps some others (though in a less degree I fear) my gentleness and sincerity find favour, because they are themselves gentle and sincere: they believe in self devotion and generosity, because they are themselves generous and self devoted. Perhaps I should have shrunk from persisting in the task which I had undertaken in early life, of opposing myself in these evil times and among these evil tongues, to what I esteem misery and vice. If I must have lived in the solitude of the heart, fortunately my domestic circle incloses that within it which compensates for the loss. But these are subjects for conversation, and I find that in using the privilege which you have permitted me of friendship, I have indulged in that garrulity of self-love which only friendship can excuse or endure. . . .

Mary was writing Shelley news of little William and urging him to be prompt and sensible about choosing "our little mouse hole to retire to. . . . Give me a garden and *absentia Clara,* and I will thank my love for many favours." Shelley remained at Marlow only a week and then, having leased a house and grounds and commissioned Peacock to oversee the conditioning of them, he proceeded to visit Leigh Hunt.

Since shortly after his liberation from prison, Hunt had been living in a little cottage in the Vale of Health, Hampstead. Here, amid rural surroundings that have long since vanished, he maintained a cheerful, lively rendezvous for all of his friends and admirers who cared to walk or ride out from the city for an evening of literary or political comradeship. The accommodations were limited, and a bit haphazard; the guest might have to sleep on the sofa in Hunt's study, but the welcome was warm. Even in his essays Hunt is unusually companionable, but in his personal relations he was one of the most friendly and amiable men alive. A few months before Shelley's visit John Keats had already begun to drink deep of the somewhat imperfect poetic inspiration to be found in Hunt's cottage — long evenings of political liberalism, rather sentimental dilettantish enthusiasms for "nature" and "art," and a demand for a radically new poetry that based itself too much on an uncomprehending scorn of Pope and Gray. At about the time Shelley visited Hunt, Keats was writing a sonnet in which he expressed himself as

brimful of the friendliness
That in a little cottage I have found,

and was packing somewhat loosely into his "Sleep and Poetry" most of the Huntian enthusiasms and excesses that he was soon to outgrow.

Other frequent visitors at the time were Charles Lamb, William Hazlitt, John Hamilton Reynolds, Charles Cowden Clarke, B. R. Haydon, and James and Horatio Smith. Sooner or later, in the frequent visits to Hampstead that were to follow, Shelley became acquainted with nearly all of them. Shelley's first visit with Hunt lasted only two or three days; long enough, however, for him to feel distinctly pleased with his new friend and to make the acquaintance of Horace Smith and John Keats.

Horace Smith, already a successful banker and writer of light verse, had recently read some of Shelley's poems and was looking forward to meeting him. His instantaneous impression, in spite of certain oddities of appearance, was that here was a *gentleman*. A few moments later, observing Shelley's quiet detachment from the bantering, facetious sallies of Hunt, Smith realized that here was a mind so deeply impressed with its own wrongs and those of the world that it was naturally more disposed to seriousness than to levity. When the whole party (which included Keats) sallied forth for a walk upon the heath, Smith attached himself to Shelley and listened with astonished sympathy while Shelley poured forth his ideals and aspirations in complete defiance of the conventional reticences. Like John Frank Newton before him, he was amazed at the extensive reading so young a person had at his command.

Never did Shelley form friendships more in the nick of time. Already another calamity had befallen him, though he was not yet aware of it. He had been back in Bath only a day when, on December 15, he received a letter from Hookham conveying devastating news of Harriet.

Shelley had apparently heard nothing of Harriet's actions since June, when she had made an unsuccessful effort, through Peacock, to obtain an increased allowance. There is no mention of Harriet in the journal of Shelley and Mary between its resumption on July 21, 1816 and Harriet's death. So far as Shelley's personal interest was concerned, she was by this time practically out of his life; he said he would have supposed that such an event as her death would be a matter of complete indifference to him. That there were other obligations, however, which he had no thought of denying, is shown by his provision for Harriet and her children in his will of September 24.

A few weeks after making this will, perhaps as a result of it, he had written to Thomas Hookham to ascertain Harriet's address.

But Harriet had recently vanished from Hookham's ken also, and while he was still inquiring for her address, he received the news that she had destroyed herself. "This shocking communication," Hookham informed Shelley, "must stand single and alone in the letter which I now address to you: I have no inclination to fill it with subjects comparatively trifling: you will judge of my feelings and excuse the brevity of this communication."

About September 9, the day after Shelley's return to England, Harriet had left her father's house at 23 Chapel Street. There is no evidence other than Shelley's word that she was driven forth by the greed and jealousy of her sister Eliza; she had left her father's house twice before for brief visits or residences elsewhere. She had rented the second floor of a house at 7 Elizabeth Street, Hans Place. What name she gave is unknown, but she stated truly that she was married and that her husband was abroad. Both the landlady and her servant noticed that she appeared very gloomy and despondent, and the former testified at the inquest that she appeared to be pregnant. Her behavior was quiet and entirely respectable; she talked little, and spent much of her time in bed. On Saturday, November 9, she asked for an early dinner, which was served to her at four o'clock and which she scarcely touched. Before five o'clock she had left the house, never to return. No one saw or heard more of her until December 10.

A week after her disappearance her family became uneasy and employed William Alder, who had accompanied her to the door when she engaged her Hans Place lodgings, to drag the Serpentine and the neighboring ponds in a search for her. This indicates that Harriet's family knew of her residence at Hans Place and were aware of the same lowness of spirits that had been remarked by all who knew her in her last days. They knew Harriet's curious pleasure in talking of suicide even in her happier days. For this reason it is very probable that they were not seriously alarmed by a farewell letter from Harriet dated "Sat. eve," until they found that she had actually disappeared. Harriet disappeared on a Saturday evening, November 9, presumably the same "Sat. eve" on which the following farewell letter was written:

My Dearest and much Beloved Sister, — When you read this letter, I shall be no more an inhabitant of this miserable world.

Do not regret the loss of one who could never be anything but a source of vexation and misery to you all belonging to me. Too wretched to exert myself, lowered in the opinion of everyone, why should I drag on a miserable existence? embittered by past recollections and not one ray of hope to rest on for the future. The remembrance of all your kindness which I have so unworthily repaid has often made my heart ache. I know that you will forgive me — because it is not in your nature to be unkind or severe to any. Dear amiable woman that I had never left you, oh! that I had always taken your advice. I might have lived long and happy, but weak and unsteady have rushed on to my destruction. I have not written to Bysshe. Oh, no, what would it avail, my wishes or my prayers would not be attended to by him, and yet should he rec. this, perhaps he might grant my request to let Ianthe remain with you always. Dear lovely child, with you she will enjoy much happiness, with him none. My dear Bysshe, let me conjure you by the remembrance of our days of happiness to grant my last wish. Do not take your innocent child from Eliza who has been more than I have, who has watched over her with such unceasing care. Do not refuse my last request, I never could refuse you and if you had never left me I might have lived, but as it is I freely forgive you and may you enjoy that happiness which you have deprived me of. There is your beautiful boy, oh! be careful of him, and his love may prove one day a rich reward. As you form his infant mind so will you reap the fruits hereafter. Now comes the sad task of saying farewell. Oh! I must be quick. God bless and watch over you all. You dear Bysshe and you dear Eliza. May all happiness attend ye both is the last wish of her who loved ye more than all others. My children — I dare not trust myself there, they are too young to regret me and ye will be kind to them for their own sakes more than mine. My parents — do not regret me, I was unworthy of your love and care. Be happy all of ye, so shall my spirit find rest and forgiveness. God bless you is the last prayer of the unfortunate

HARRIET S.

To you my dear Sister I leave all my things; as they more properly belong to you than anyone and you will preserve them for Ianthe. God bless you both.

William Alder's search was unsuccessful, but a month later, on the morning of December 10, a body was noticed floating in the Serpentine River. It was brought ashore and carried to the Fox public house, near by. There it was recognized by the landlord's daughter, who knew Harriet, and William Alder, who happened to live there. At the inquest it was also identified by the landlady and her servant. None of them, not even William Alder, identified it as the body of Harriet Shelley, however. The body bore no marks of violence and a valuable ring was found on one of Harriet's fingers. This precluded a verdict indicating robbery and murder. Though three witnesses had testified to Harriet's extreme depression, the verdict was not suicide, but simply: "Found dead in the Serpentine River." Some of the jurors, like the landlord's daughter and William Alder, may have known Harriet or her family. Had they brought in a verdict of suicide, Harriet must have been buried at the cross-roads, according to the English law on suicide.

The coroner's verdict was delivered on December 11, and the *Times* for the next day carried a brief notice of the death of "a respectable female far advanced in pregnancy." When and where Harriet was buried is unknown; the burial would have to be prompt and would be likely to be very quiet, so it probably occurred before Shelley reached London. In the parish register of Paddington, the late Mr. Roger Ingpen discovered that on December 13, 1816 Harriett Smith, of Mount Street, St. George's, Hanover Square, aged twenty-one, had been buried in that parish. Very probably this refers to Harriet Shelley, who sometimes spelled her name Harriett, who was twenty-one at the time of her death, and who would most probably have been buried on the 13th. The address is quite near that of Harriet's father and also of the Mount Coffee House, which he had conducted.

Harriet had entered Shelley's life with a threat of suicide if he did not return her love; she had left it with the execution of her threat. The charges made by Shelley, Mary, the Clairmonts and Godwins that she subjected Shelley to some petty persecutions after he left her are at least partly true, though exaggerated. But even if they were entirely true they could hardly counterbalance the evidence of her last letter that she loved Shelley until she died.

It is very unlikely that Shelley ever saw Harriet's last letter. On December 15, when he received Hookham's letter announcing Harriet's death, he took a walk with Mary to discuss the situation and immediately set off for London. His main concern was the children; Harriet was already in her grave. The next day he wrote to Mary:

> I have spent a day, my beloved, of somewhat agonising sensations; such as the contemplation of vice and folly and hard heartedness exceeding all conception must produce. Leigh Hunt has been with me all day and his delicate and tender attentions to me, his kind speeches of you, have sustained me against the weight of the horror of this event.

After some remarks about his hopes of soon acquiring possession of Harriet's children, Shelley continued with the following remarks on Harriet's suicide:

> It seems that this poor woman — the most innocent of her abhorred and unnatural family — was driven from her father's house, and descended the steps of prostitution until she lived with a groom of the name of Smith, who deserting her, she killed herself. — There can be no question that the beastly viper her sister, unable to gain profit from her connexion with me — has secured to herself the fortune of the old man — who is now dying — by the murder of this poor creature. Every thing tends to prove, however, that beyond the mere shock of so hideous a catastrophe having fallen on a human being once so nearly connected with me, there would, in any case, have been little to regret. Hookham, Longdill — every one, does *me* full justice; — bears testimony to the upright spirit and liberality of my conduct to her: — there is but one voice in condemnation of the detestable Westbrooks. If they should dare to bring it before Chancery, a scene of such fearful horror would be unfolded as would cover them with scorn and shame. . . .

The sworn testimony of the coroner's inquest disproves Shelley's statement that Harriet "descended the steps of prostitution until she lived with a groom of the name of Smith." The name Smith would seem to have been borrowed from a neighbor after Harriet's death. Shelley may have deduced his story from a garbled and second-hand account of the inquest, but Harriet was accompanied to the door of her last lodgings by one who had known her for five years as Harriet Shelley, and she lived there respectably alone until she drowned herself. There is not even any medical testimony to support the newspaper statement that Harriet was in "an advanced state of pregnancy." This may indeed be true, but seems to have been founded only on the landlady's impression that Harriet seemed "in a family way" – an impression made plausible later perhaps by the appearance of a body that had been long under water.

Shelley never told his friends anything to convince them of Harriet's guilt, nor did he show until several weeks afterwards that he was deeply disturbed by her tragic end. He was never more calm and self-possessed, Peacock observed, than in the early days of January. Soon, however, Peacock observed that Harriet's fate caused Shelley "deep agony of mind," which he usually managed to conceal. One evening in 1817, as the two were walking and talking in Bisham Wood, Shelley fell into a gloomy reverie from which Peacock's sallies were powerless to rouse him. "There is one thing," Shelley remarked gloomily, "to which I have decidedly made up my mind. I will take a great glass of ale every night." "A very good resolution," said Peacock laughingly, "as the result of a melancholy musing." "Yes," said Shelley, "but you do not know why I take it. I shall do it to deaden my feelings, for I see that those who drink ale have none." The next day he reverted to his remark and explained its apparent oddity. "I will tell you what I would not tell anyone else. I was thinking of Harriet."

Mary met the crisis with an immediate affection and loyalty that inspire admiration. "Ah, my best love, to you do I owe every joy, every perfection that I may enjoy or boast of. Love me, sweet, for ever. I hardly know what I mean, I am so agitated." She sympathized in his indignation against the Westbrooks, and in his desire to obtain immediate possession of his children. "How very happy I shall be to possess those darling treasures that are yours. . . . Now I long more than ever that our house should be quickly ready for the reception of those dear Children, whom I love so tenderly. Then there will be a sweet Brother and Sister for my William, who will lose his pre-eminence as eldest and be helped third at table, as Claire is continually reminding him. . . . Come back to reassure me, my Shelley, and bring with you your darling Ianthe and Charles."

But Ianthe and Charles were at Warwick, where some time previous to Harriet's death they had been placed in the care of the Reverend Mr. John Kendall. The Westbrooks had no intention of surrendering them. Shelley called twice on Eliza without being able to see her. He then sent Mrs. Boinville, but without result. On December 18 he wrote Eliza a letter. He began by assuring her that he bore her no ill will and that he did not credit the imputations cast upon her conduct and her father's toward Harriet. Only two days earlier, as we have seen, he had denounced the Westbrooks to Mary as the chief cause of Harriet's ruin, and he soon afterwards expressed the same opinion in a letter to Byron. But if he was less than frank in his approach to the problem, he was frankness itself on the main point. He told Eliza politely but firmly that he could not leave Ianthe with her (as he possibly knew Harriet had requested) because of Eliza's natural prejudice against Mary, and also because Eliza would probably not "refrain from inculcating prepossessions . . . the most adverse to my views." Since nothing could alter his determination, he urged Eliza to surrender the children at once to Leigh Hunt, who would attend her at any time. To all this Eliza opposed a grim silence, and held on to the children.

One of Shelley's first thoughts on hearing of Harriet's death was that the way was now open to legalize his connection with Mary by marriage. He mentioned it in his first letter to Mary from London, and Mary in her reply stipulated only that it should take place in London. Shelley returned to Bath and brought Mary up to London, where they spent some days with the Hunts. On December 28 Shelley and Godwin visited the office of the Vicar General and obtained a marriage license. On the morning of the 29th, with Mr. and Mrs. Godwin as witnesses, a quiet marriage was performed at St. Mildred's Church, Bread Street. In writing to Claire that evening Shelley gave an account of the ceremony, "so magical in its effects." Godwin, he wrote, was already treating him with almost distinguished courtesy, which he could not resist; but he could still scarcely endure Mrs. Godwin, or the unhappy associations of Skinner Street.

Two days later the Shelleys returned to Bath, but on January 6 Shelley set out again for London. Far from surrendering his children, the Westbrooks now took the offensive. John Westbrook filed a bill in Chancery praying the court to appoint as guardians for the children John and Eliza Westbrook or some other proper persons, and to restrain their father from taking custody of them. This bill recited the history of Shelley's connection with Harriet and Mary and was supported by documentary evidence in the shape of a copy of *Queen Mab*, the *Letter to Lord Ellenborough*, and nine of Shelley's letters.

Shelley was given five days in which to prepare an answer. He had come to London to claim his children through habeas corpus proceedings, but the case now seemed likely to be settled in the Court of Chancery before habeas corpus proceedings could become effective. Moreover, if he admitted the charges brought against him, principally on the basis of *Queen Mab*, or if the court sustained these charges, he was open to conviction in a criminal court on the charge of blasphemous libel.

He now believed that the Westbrooks intended to hound him into jail. Everything, he wrote to Mary, except the happiness that was dependent on her alone, hung on the issue of this trial. To Byron Shelley wrote:

> The sister has now instituted a Chancery process against me, the intended effect of which is to deprive me of my unfortunate children, now more than ever dear to me; of my inheritance, and to throw me into prison, and expose me in the pillory, on the ground of my being a REVOLUTIONIST, and an *Atheist*. It seems whilst she lived in my house she possessed herself of such papers as go to establish these allegations. The opinion of Counsel is, that she will certainly succeed to a considerable extent, but that I may probably escape entire ruin, in the worldly sense of it. So I am here, dragged before the tribunals of tyranny and superstition, to answer with my children, my property, my liberty, and my fame, for having exposed their frauds, and scorned the insolence of their power. Yet I will not fail; though I have been given to understand that I could purchase victory by recantation.

The plain truth seems to be that the Westbrooks cared nothing about Shelley's opinions except to use them as a means of retaining Harriet's children. Otherwise they would certainly have brought a criminal action such as both Whitton and Shelley's advisers thought bound to succeed. The situation was a purely domestic one. The Westbrooks, rather than church and state, were the complainants; Shelley's treatment of Harriet, rather than his assault upon recognized institutions, was the cause of their action. Except for letters to herself and Harriet, Eliza did not introduce as evidence any papers that Shelley had not printed. But Shelley was thoroughly convinced, in spite of the facts, that this was simply a case of tyrannous society seeking to crucify a philanthropist for his philanthropy.

Shelley filed his answer to the bill of complaint on January 18, 1817. He flatly denied that he had deserted Harriet — "this Defendant and his said late wife agreed, in consequence of certain differences between them, to live separate and apart from each other." He asserted that he had left the children in Harriet's care only on her solicitation and on account of their tender age, that he had contributed regularly to their support, that he now wished to educate them to their proper station in life, and that as their father he was entitled to do so.

Both sides had engaged distinguished counsel. Sir Samuel Romilly, who represented the Westbrooks, was probably the most distinguished lawyer of the age. It is probable that Shelley had already heard bitter words about him, for he was the first lawyer consulted by Lady Byron's family at the time of the Byron separation. Shelley had Charles Wetherell, Basil Montagu, and a Mr. Bell. A year later Wetherell was to be better known as the defender of the radicals Thistlewood and Watson. Godwin's friend Basil Montagu was a really wise and learned lawyer, but a better consultant than pleader; Bell, less polished and learned than Basil Montagu, was possibly his superior as a practical pleader.

Lord Chancellor Eldon, who now held Shelley's fate in his hands, has been vividly sketched by William Hazlitt as a good-natured, able judge, proverbially careful, impartial and conscientious in all matters not affecting his personal or political interests, but a man who never deviated an instant from a calm, placid support of the most out-and-out Toryism. "The Lord Chancellor's impartiality and conscientious exactness are proverbial. . . . He delights to balance a straw, to see a feather turn the scale or make it even again; and divides or subdivides a scruple to the smallest fraction. He unravels the web of argument and pieces it together again; folds it up and lays it aside, that he may examine it more at leisure. He hugs indecision to his breast, and takes home a modest doubt or a nice point to solace himself with it in protracted, luxurious dalliance. Delay seems, in his mind, to be of the very essence of justice."

Shelley's case was heard on Friday, January 24, 1817. Sir Samuel Romilly argued that *Queen Mab* proved clearly that Shelley's opinions on religion rendered him unfit to be the guardian of his children. Basil Montagu answered that *Queen Mab* was a youthful work that had never been published and that a man might write many things he did not intend his children to see. He therefore prayed Lord Eldon to dismiss the complaint, with costs. It was further argued in Wetherell's brief for the defense that not twenty copies of *Queen Mab* had ever got abroad, that only a few copies of the *Letter to Lord Ellenborough* had been printed, that the author himself could not find a copy of it, that Shelley's youthful diatribes against marriage could not be taken seriously in the light of the fact that he had married twice before he was twenty-five, that there was no precedent for depriving a parent of his children on the grounds of religious opinions alone, and that the worldly interests of the children would suffer by their being taken from a father of prospective rank and fortune and given to a former coffee-house keeper and an illiterate, vulgar woman whose matrimonial scheming had produced the present situation.

Lord Eldon listened with his usual air of careful impartiality and pronounced that he should have to consider the case further and would announce his decision at a future date. Any further hearings would be in the Lord Chancellor's private room. This was in effect an initial victory for the Westbrooks. The Lord Chancellor had not dismissed their complaint. Shelley was still deprived of his children, and a definite possibility was established that a criminal action might be based upon the Chancery evidence as soon as the case was concluded.

The Lord Chancellor took slightly over two months to consider. The complainants shifted their emphasis from Shelley's attacks on religion to his attacks on matrimony. Shelley was hard at work on a written Declaration setting forth his defense. With some assistance from Godwin, and probably Hunt, the document was finished by February 2. "If I have attacked religion," Shelley wrote, ". . . I am punishable, but not by the loss of my children; if I have imagined a system of social life inconsistent with the constitution of England, I am punishable, but not by the loss of my children." Since the argument on religious grounds had been abandoned, Shelley went on to observe that the point on which the Chancellor had to decide the case seemed to be "not whether I shall teach my children religious infidelity, not whether I shall teach them political heterodoxy, but whether I shall educate them in immodest and loose sentiments of sexual connection." On this issue he stated boldly that he considered marriage, as it existed in England, "a mischievous and tyrannical institution" and would continue publicly to state his reason for so thinking. If this, however, disqualified him as a guardian, then no man in England could ever protest against prevailing opinions without the fear of having the courts converted into instruments of private vengeance against him. In practice he sought to conform to the institution which in theory he condemned. Estranged from his former wife by "incurable dissensions," it had been a great grief to him that he could not at once marry the woman to whom he felt himself genuinely united, but he had done this as soon as possible.

Having considered all these matters, Lord Eldon gave his judgment on March 27. He was still cautiously unwilling to commit himself to a sweeping decision. It was clear to him only that the children should not be placed in the exclusive care of their father, but it was not clear that they should be given to the Westbrooks. They should be brought up under a proper plan for their maintenance and education, and both sides were authorized to submit plans and nominate guardians. The Lord Chancellor's judgment, he was careful to state, was based not upon Shelley's opinions either religious or moral, nor upon his entering into an irregular union with Mary Godwin, but upon the fact that in his case immoral opinions had led to conduct that the court was bound to consider immoral. Furthermore he was convinced by the evidence adduced that Shelley would certainly inculcate similar opinions and conduct in his children if given sole custody of them. Shelley was restrained from intermeddling with the children until further order of the court, and one of the Masters in Chancery, Mr. William Alexander, was directed to decide on a proper plan for the children's education and maintenance. Lord Eldon's judgment, he remarked, was not final. He also observed, rather ominously, that any attempt to publish an account of the case would be treated as contempt of court. Perhaps he had read Leigh Hunt's guarded comment in the *Examiner* or suspected that Shelley might print his Declaration.

Chapter XIV

SHELLEY REMAINED in London, very busy with lawyers and consult-
ants, until after the Lord Chancellor's first decision, on January 24.
Mary continued awhile at Bath, but became so uneasy at the accounts she received of the legal proceedings that on January 26 she
went up to London to join her husband.

It is typical of Mary's circumspection as a diarist that she made no
mention in the journal of the birth of Claire's child, on January 12.
Until February 18 Claire remained at Bath under the assumed title
of Mrs. Clairmont. The child, a healthy, beautiful girl, was temporarily named Alba ("Dawn") until the wishes of Byron ("Albè")
could be consulted.

While in town, Shelley and Mary stayed with the Hunts, dining
and sleeping occasionally in Skinner Street, as convenience dictated.
Shelley was busy writing out his second Chancery statement (copied
by Mary on February 2) and interviewing counsel and advisers.

Undoubtedly there were moments of great suffering and anxiety.
Leigh Hunt's precocious young son, Thornton, not only noticed and
described Shelley's agitation over the Chancery trial, but in almost
the same breath described one of Shelley's physical seizures, whose
occurrences are generally to be noted at such times:

> The emotions that he underwent were but too manifest in the
> unconcealed anxiety and the eager recital of newly awakened
> hopes, with intervals of the deepest depression. He suffered also
> from physical causes. . . . I can remember one day at Hamp-
> stead: it was soon after breakfast, and Shelley sat reading, when
> he suddenly threw up his book and hands, and fell back, the
> chair sliding sharply from under him, and he poured forth shrieks,
> loud and continuous, stamping his feet madly on the ground.
> My father rushed to him, and, while the women looked out for
> the usual remedies of cold water and hand-rubbing, applied a
> strong pressure to his side, kneading it with his hands; and the
> patient seemed gradually to be relieved by that process.

There was ample time between Chancery engagements to become
better acquainted with the circles that revolved around Leigh Hunt
and Godwin. In the month following Mary's arrival in town on Janu-

ary 26, her journal mentions dinners or other social engagments with Godwin, Basil Montagu, Brougham, Keats, John Hamilton Reynolds, Horace Smith, the Lambs, and the Hazlitts. Mary went several times to plays or operas, usually while Shelley was elsewhere. At Godwin's the talk was apt to be serious, punctuated occasionally by a pun from Lamb or by Godwin's abrupt, flat bark of a laugh or his rather snarling, cutting manner of insisting upon logic and accuracy. At Leigh Hunt's there were often music — commonly Hunt's "sweet, small baritone" in an Irish or Italian song — frequent puns and witticisms, an open forum for talk of all sorts. Whether strolling on the heath or holding forth informally after breakfast in his flowered dressing-gown, Hunt was a good raconteur and a sympathetic, discerning listener.

Rapidly the Shelleys became friendly with other members of Leigh Hunt's circle. One of these was Walter Coulson, then editor of the *Globe* newspaper, a man whose extensive miscellaneous information filled the others with awe-stricken wonder. Another was Vincent Novello, the musician, later a friend of Mendelssohn's. Novello's home, with its admirable hostess, its music, and its attractive bevy of children, was the scene of more than one dinner where Hunt, Keats, Shelley, Charles Cowden Clarke, and the Lambs dined by mutual agreement on bread and cheese, celery, and Lamb's "Lutheran beer." Mary Novello, later Mrs. Charles Cowden Clarke, at that time still in the nursery play-room, remembered standing on a chair in order to look out of the play-room window and catch a glimpse of the young poet of whom she had heard her parents talk.

In Leigh Hunt and Horace Smith, Shelley found two of his firmest and most valuable friends. To the end of his life Hunt thought Shelley the finest character he had ever met — so fine, in fact, that he sometimes half doubted if Shelley were mortal in the same sense as other people. In the early days of their friendship Hunt began by laughing at Shelley's naïve supposition that the editor wrote every word that appeared in the *Examiner;* soon, although older and more experienced, he was going to Shelley for advice in a spirit of humility that to Shelley seemed almost ridiculous.

Shelley characterized Hunt in his "Letter to Maria Gisborne" (1820) as "one of those happy souls which are the salt of the earth." In the dedicatory letter to *The Cenci* he wrote "One more gentle, honourable, innocent and brave; one of more exalted toleration for all who do and think evil, and yet himself more free from evil;

one who knows better how to receive, and how to confer a benefit, though he must ever confer far more than he can receive; one of simpler, and, in the highest sense of the word, of purer life and manners I never knew." Except for Hogg during a brief year of youth, Leigh Hunt was the best and fittest friend that Shelley ever knew.

Of Horace Smith, Shelley wrote to Maria Gisborne that his character combined enough "wit and sense, Virtue and human knowledge" to "Make this dull world a business of delight." Smith did not agree with Shelley on all points, and at times thought him rather an odd fellow, but odd mainly in the sense that he was "so utterly self-denying and unworldly." After one long intimate conversation with Shelley, Smith came away with a mingled reverence and admiration for something he felt to be uncarthly in his friend. Without a doubt, Shelley would have made any sacrifice for either Hunt or Smith, nor did he doubt their willingness to do the same for him. Shelley was Hunt's banker on all possible occasions after 1816, and Horace Smith, to a less extent, acted in the same capacity for Shelley.

The Novellos, as their daughter afterwards recalled, spoke of Shelley with admiration, as did both the Clarkes in retrospect. But Godwin, for all his new courtesy, regarded his son-in-law as a person far from perfect. He was quite aware, he said, that Shelley's temper was "occasionally fiery, resentful, and indignant." After three years' further knowledge of Shelley he accused him of immorality and deceit and of being a lover of falsehood for its own sake. Lamb knew Shelley only slightly and did not desire to know him better. Shelley thought well of Lamb and was disappointed that "the calumny of an enemy" had caused Lamb to avoid him. Hazlitt, though he would argue with Shelley against Hunt and Coulson on the subject of a monarchy versus a republic, was very far from any real sympathy with him. He regarded Shelley's enthusiasm as too extreme to be of practical service to the radical cause. To him Shelley had "a fire in his eye, a fever in his blood, a maggot in his brain, a hectic flutter in his speech, which mark out the philosophic fanatic." Henry Crabb Robinson, who seems to have met Shelley but once, was also rather unfavorably impressed, possibly because Shelley spoke with great bitterness of Southey as a renegade and made insinuations against Wordsworth. Much of his talk seemed to Robinson "vehement and arrogant and intolerant."

Keats might well have been expected to take a great liking to Shelley, who was eager to befriend him. Nevertheless, Keats showed a definite reserve and restraint. This seemed to Leigh Hunt to be due largely to his excessive consciousness of their different social stations and to the great difference in their poetic styles and interests. His intellectual interests were far less extensive and subtle than Shelley's, some of which he probably regarded without sympathy. It is a dangerous matter to advise an aspiring young poet not to publish, as Shelley advised Keats in 1817 — nor did Keats forget it, even though Shelley helped him print his volume after advising against it. When Shelley invited him to Marlow he declined, explaining to Benjamin Bailey that he wished to keep his "own unfettered scope." This looks as if Keats distrusted his own powers in close contact with Shelley very much as Shelley distrusted himself in contact with Byron at Geneva. There was ample ground for such a feeling in a self-conscious, independent young poet who may have noticed that some of his lines already seemed to be tinged with echoes from *Queen Mab* and *Alastor*.

Since the battle of Waterloo the internal condition of England had grown progressively worse and worse. As the evils of unemployment, high taxes, high prices, and government repression had mounted steadily throughout the year 1816, as foreign markets had languished and incendiary fires, mendicancy, local riots and hunger marches of colliers and iron-workers increased, Hampden Clubs and clubs of Spencean Philanthropists had sprung up all over England and Scotland. The former, led by the moderate Major Cartwright and the veteran champion of Parliamentary reform Sir Francis Burdett, were quite reasonable champions of governmental reform; the latter, more visionary, championed community of land and the abolition of machinery. Both societies were soon sown with government spies and *agents provocateurs*. A secret committee of the House of Commons reported in 1817 that "nothing short of a revolution" was the real object of the Hampden Clubs. The mob spirit was very much alive all over England.

William Cobbett, suddenly reducing the price of Cobbett's *Political Register* in November 1816 from one shilling halfpenny to twopence, had become overnight one of the most powerful leaders of popular opinion. On December 2, 1816 a mass meeting at Spafields had been exhorted to begin at once to take what was wanted, and had proceeded to a considerable orgy of looting. This was the occasion for the famous trial of Watson and others for treason, a trial in which Shelley's Chancery counsel, Wetherell, ably secured an acquittal. While the House of Lords was being told by a secret committee that a traitorous conspiracy existed for overthrowing the government by general insurrection, the Corporation of London petitioned the King to remove a number of specified grievances and urged Parliamentary reform.

In this state of alarm the right of habeas corpus was suspended in 1817. Cobbett and other radicals who had been inaccessible to prosecution as long as they avoided libel, blasphemy, and incitement to violence took flight to America; Leigh Hunt remained, kept up the fight, and became increasingly a target for Tory abuse. "I like the freedom of the press and quill," Byron jeered from Italy; "I like the Habeas Corpus (when we've got it)."

Shelley had watched all this with close interest, but without the feverish thirst for action with which he might have viewed it two or three years earlier. "The whole fabric of society presents a most threatening aspect," he had written to Byron on November 20, 1816. "What is most ominous of an approaching change is the strength which the popular party have suddenly acquired, and the importance which the violence of demagogues has assumed. But the people appear calm, and steady even under situations of great excitement; and reform may come without revolution." In a moment of dejection in December 1816 he had confessed to Hunt: "I am undeceived in the belief that I have powers deeply to interest or substantially to improve, mankind." Looking back at this same period, Mary wrote later that "his life was spent more in thought than action — he had lost the eager spirit which believed it could achieve what it projected for the benefit of mankind."

But Shelley's interests were really unchanged. He still followed eagerly the *Examiner's* gallant weekly assaults upon injustice and maladministration. He was still an ardent crusader, and could not be otherwise, but his efforts were directed almost entirely to preparing men's minds so that they would be ready when "that sure slow Angel" "watching the beck of Mutability" summoned them to a new order.

Nevertheless Shelley never completely deserted the practical and immediate aspects of human improvement. Before he left London to take up his residence in Great Marlow, he had finished a thirteen-page pamphlet entitled *A Proposal for Putting Reform to the Vote throughout the Kingdom.* It was the first work of Shelley's to be published by Charles and James Ollier, two enterprising young liberal publishers whom Shelley had met in Hunt's circle. The pamphlet appeared within a day or two of either March 2 or March 20, as by

"The Hermit of Marlow." It passed almost unnoticed except that Hunt commented on it briefly in the *Examiner* of March 2 and commended it in an editorial on the 29th. So little comment must have been disappointing to Shelley, who had urged Ollier to advertise generously and had made personal arrangements for the disposal of forty or fifty copies, besides sending Ollier a mailing list of thirty-eight persons and institutions.

Shelley's pamphlet proposed to call a meeting at the Crown and Anchor Tavern, in London, where a great meeting of delegates had already been held earlier in the year, to plan a house-to-house canvass of the United Kingdom on the one subject of whether or not the nation desired a Parliamentary reform that would make the Commons actually representative. Avoiding all questions likely to cause internal dissensions, this meeting should sit until it had completed practical details of the canvass and arranged to finance it by subscription. Shelley himself pledged a hundred pounds, one tenth of his income, toward the expenses. No man, Shelley urged, should be taxed without consent. Parliament should meet annually. Rather surprisingly he stated his opinion that the country was not yet ready for the universal male suffrage that public meetings and reform clubs were demanding, or for the abolition of kings and aristocracy. Such sudden action, he stated, would place the country in the hands of demagogues and mobs, "men who have been rendered brutal and torpid and ferocious by ages of slavery." Only by "many gradations of improvement" could the nation arrive at the best social and political system, a pure and stable republic. These are the words, not of a political radical, but of a moderate liberal with a fully developed sense of political responsibility.

At about the time he was writing his temperate *Proposal*, Shelley had a personal experience which provoked him to more passionate expression. A poor woman whose son was on trial before one of the London courts was returning home one night with her son, walking through Hampstead. It was a bitterly cold night in midwinter. Not far from Leigh Hunt's house the woman was overcome and sank to the ground in convulsions. Shelley came along as her son was trying to assist her and immediately applied for aid at the nearest houses. The occupants would not take the woman in or even allow her to be placed in an outhouse while Shelley went for a doctor. As Shelley was vainly arguing, a carriage drove up to a house near by, and an elderly gentleman and his family began to alight. Again the poet told his story, more hopefully, but the gentleman would hear nothing of it. Like the rest, he considered the woman an impostor — "Sir, your conduct is extraordinary!" "Sir!" cried Shelley, with sudden sternness, "I am sorry to say that *your* conduct is *not* extraordinary. . . . It is such men as you who madden the spirits and the patience of the poor and wretched; and if ever a convulsion comes in this country (which is very probable), recollect what I tell you: you will have your house, that you refuse to put this miserable woman into, burnt over your head." Shelley and the woman's son then managed to convey her to Leigh Hunt's house, where Hunt, arriving about that time from the opera, found them holding her until the arrival of a doctor. Next day she was sufficiently recovered to be sent on to her home at Hendon.

By the 18th of March the house at Marlow had been put in condition and the Shelleys were living in it. Albion House, as it was called, was a fairly large, rambling, two-story structure with a gabled roof and dormer windows, standing some distance back from the Thames, on the edge of open country. One of its rooms, large enough for a ballroom, Shelley fitted up as a study, with life-size casts of Venus and Apollo. In the rear was a garden with a lawn, enclosed by high hedges. Here the view was partly obscured by a mound, behind which was a kitchen garden and a flower garden. Firs, cypresses, and apple trees made rather more shade than was desirable. Shelley had taken the house on a twenty-one-year lease before Harriet's suicide, hoping to settle there for many years, but it soon became evident that it was both too dark and too damp for comfort.

To the Swiss cats were added a dog which turned out to be too vicious to keep. Shelley wrote at once to London for Mawe's *Gardening Calendar*. A manservant and a cook were employed, in addition to Elise, the Swiss nurse. Later (April 29), with the aid of Vincent Novello's expert advice, a piano was selected in London and sent down for Claire's benefit. Claire, incidentally, had no ostensible connection with her infant, who was given out to be the child of a friend, sent down from London for its health.

The Shelleys were hardly settled in their new home before they began inviting guests. Godwin was the first. He arrived on April 2, and for four days shared the pleasures of excursions by land and water to Maidenhead, Medmenham Abbey, and Bisham Wood. On the evening of Godwin's departure the Hunts arrived with their four children. The weather was cold and disagreeable, but the society was good. The Hunts remained for about a month. During a part of this month Mrs. Hunt's sister, Elizabeth Kent, was also at Albion House, a considerable help with the children, since Mrs. Hunt was ill much of the time. Before the Hunts had left, Byron was given a pressing invitation, should he return to England, and Hogg was urged by Shelley to hasten his promised visit to Peacock.

"Ought we not to be happy?" Mary demanded on first coming to Marlow; "and so indeed we are, in spite of the Lord Chancellor and the Suspension Act." Shelley's health, she added, had been very good. The presence of visitors did not hinder Mary's working steadily on the correction and copying of *Frankenstein,* nor Shelley in his reading. Shelley was reading mainly Latin and Greek authors, the history of the French Revolution, and Spenser, from whom he often read aloud in the evening. Mary, in addition to her work on *Frankenstein,* was keeping up her Latin studies and was reading apparently more books than Shelley. Shelley had been at work on *Laon and Cythna* since the latter part of April.

Occasionally Mary, like Shelley, gave some slight indication that the ordeal through which she had come had left its mark upon her. Remarkably self-controlled as she was, she was then only a girl of twenty. Her calm classic beauty and repose, so admired by Mary Cowden Clarke a few years later, were not yet evident; she seemed to the observant little Thornton Hunt in 1817 to be a rather harassed, sharp-tongued, carelessly dressed young woman who was not in the best of health. Since Harriet's death she expressed herself to Shelley and the Hunts with increased scorn of Peacock and with a reversion to her original scorn of Hogg. In her journal she pointedly ignored them both, as far as possible.

With constant rowing, sailing, and walking trips with various friends, life at Marlow was much more social than it had been at Bishopsgate. The new grand piano — still unpaid for — was often called into service to duplicate the musical evenings the Shelleys had enjoyed when visiting the Hunts. Hunt had been enjoined by Mary to learn the *Ranz des Vaches* and the *Marseillaise* in French and was assured that the piano would be in tune for him. Claire's voice, according to her instructor, was like a string of pearls.

What all this meant to the poet is indicated by no less than four unfinished poems, all begun at Marlow under the influence of music. The finest of these, "To Constantia Singing," which he all but finished, shows how Claire's voice could cause Shelley to idealize a girl with whose weaknesses he had been painfully familiar for several years. "To Constantia Singing" and "To Constantia" contains a note of reproach that may well be Shelley's grief over Claire's desertion to Byron in 1816.

But Shelley's sociability was limited to kindred spirits. For mere casual, time-killing acquaintances he felt a very distinct aversion. Before going to Marlow he notified the neighbors through his upholsterer that his family "would associate with no one in the village, would never go to church, and would [do] as they chose in defiance of public opinion." The poor knew him through his charities, and two or three local residents knew him through common interests. Among these were the brothers Tyler, who happened to be cultivated men, though linen-drapers' assistants, a Mr. Pilcher, and a Mr. Brooks, admirer of Robert Owen. With Mr. Madocks, his local man of business, Shelley used to engage in long conversations on all manner of subjects.

Usually the villagers saw Shelley only at a distance, going or coming from his island retreat near Medmenham Abbey, dashing along through the streets or groves, regardless of all he met, sailing his paper boats on the river, or returning alone late at night from Bisham Wood. At such times there was not wanting an occasional touch of his earlier love for the fantastic; his head might be crowned with wild flowers, or he might assert that he had been engaged in raising the devil, and repeat the incantation he had used. Some of these occasions were probably enhanced by Shelley's love of reciting aloud — "with wild energy," as Mary noted — "The Ancient Mariner" or Southey's "Old Woman of Berkeley."

Dr. Furnivall, whose son later founded the Shelley Society, lived not far away at Egham and continued to attend Shelley's family as in the Bishopsgate days. He recalled many a "dish of tea" with Shelley, accompanied by typical Shelleyan conversation. Once he arrived at Albion House just as Shelley, Peacock, and Hunt were concluding an animated conversation on suicide. It was a queer subject, if one remembers Harriet. Dr. Furnivall heard them all subscribe to Peacock's view that suicide was desirable, and suspecting the reality of such sentiments, he did not scruple to offer the means of exit to anyone present who really desired them. All three survived this opportunity for extinction.

One day the servant announced the arrival of a man who was being engaged as Claire's music master. His name happened to resemble that of a local resident whom Shelley had learned to dread as a prince of bores. Confusing the two names, Shelley sprang up from his chair in quick alarm. "I would just as soon see the devil!"

he exclaimed, and straightway jumped through the window and vanished rapidly over the garden fence. Following a back path he arrived at Peacock's still much excited, and rushed in upon the surprised novelist with the exclamation: "Barricade the doors; give orders that you are not at home. Here is —— in the town."

The humor of such incidents was not lost upon Shelley himself. When the purely ludicrous presented itself uncontaminated by a suggestion of social or moral wrong, he laughed heartily, as Peacock says he often laughed in recalling his flight from the bore. "He was playful," Mary Shelley observed, "and indulged in the wild spirit that mocked itself and others — not in bitterness, but in sport." Once, within a few months of the former incident, Leigh Hunt and Shelley were riding to London together on the Hampstead stage when Shelley, moved by some impulsive dislike of an old lady who was a fellow passenger, yielded to one of his sudden impulses to astonish. Being at that time rather fond of quoting the passage in Shakespeare's *King Richard II* in which the King indulges his misery, he startled the old lady into a state of alarm by suddenly breaking forth most earnestly: "Hunt!

> For God's sake, let us sit upon the ground
> And tell sad stories of the death of kings."

In his play with children Shelley could give free vent to his boyish penchant for semi-frightful humor. His own son was just cutting his teeth and learning to walk, and was as yet too young for such entertainment. So also was Claire's child, the delicately beautiful, blue-eyed, black-haired little Alba. Hunt's four children were older, Thornton, the eldest, being seven in 1817 and John five. These children, whether at Hampstead or Albion House, treated Shelley as a member of their own family. Thornton Hunt, looking backward over forty-six years, remembered obeying Shelley as he would his own father, listening to Shelley's wildly imaginative tales very much as the Newton children had done three years earlier, romping with him almost as a fellow child, and taking long, talkative tramps with him which sometimes ended in his being carried home by his older companion.

Sometimes, like an older playmate, Shelley teased Thornton into exasperation. But what Thornton remembered most vividly, and what his father also recalled, was Shelley's pleasure in assuming a frightful, threatening aspect which the Hunt children found de-

liciously dangerous. This was known as "doing the horn," and consisted in screwing up his long hair into a semblance of a horn, assuming a ferocious facial expression, and advancing "with rampant
paws and frightful gestures." The children were horribly impressed.
They did not suspect that the mature, metaphysical Shelley was
finding a psychological interest in the childish reaction to "grim
impressions" in addition to the purely naïve pleasure he found in
producing thrills.

At Marlow, Shelley had another small friend who remembered
him vividly in later years. One day in early summer a little girl named
Polly Rose, who lived in the neighborhood, was somewhat startled
to see a strange-looking, bright-eyed, bareheaded young gentleman
emerge from the woods, with wreaths of wild clematis wound about
him. He glanced at her observingly and hastened on, but in a short
while returned with a young lady. They questioned her and then
went to her mother with a request that they be allowed to take her
into their home and educate her. Thus Shelley partly achieved for
a few months his long-standing, persistent desire to adopt and educate a young girl. From that time Polly spent a part of almost every
day at Albion House, took many of her meals there, and often slept
there. The education appears to have consisted mainly in bedtime
discussions between Polly and Mary of the questions previously discussed between Mary and Shelley. With Polly, as with the Hunt children, Shelley easily reverted to his own childhood. Often he would
place Polly on a table and tilt it up until she slid to the bottom. Or
he would place Polly and Claire (another child for the moment) on a
table and run it rapidly from one end of the room to the other.

His pleasure with the children of others probably made Shelley
feel more keenly the loss of his own children by Harriet. The Chancery proceedings regarding these children were still dragging on.
Meanwhile he was prevented from seeing them or even knowing
where they were.

Lord Eldon's decision denying Shelley sole guardianship of the
children had suggested that fit guardians of his choice might be approved. On June 21 Mr. William Alexander, the Master in Chancery
to whom Lord Eldon had referred the final details, received from
Mr. P. W. Longdill, Shelley's nominee for guardian, a pious, stuffy
scheme for the children's education that must have cost Shelley pain
even to read. On July 1 the Westbrooks had made counter-proposals,
and a month later Mr. Alexander accepted the Westbrook scheme
with one slight alteration. This was too much even for Lord Eldon,

who, on appeal, on November 10 directed a reconsideration which eventually resulted in the selection as guardian of Shelley's second nominee, Dr. Thomas Hume, a reputable medical doctor who was a friend and neighbor of Mr. Longdill. Under this final settlement Shelley was allowed to see his children once a month, in the presence of their guardian. By now, however (Lord Eldon's confirmation was dated July 25, 1818), the proceedings had been drawn out over eighteen months, and the Shelleys had already left England never to return. Shelley never saw either of Harriet's children again.

While the Chancery proceedings were thus slowly and excruciatingly dragging along, Shelley was subject to strong attacks of both apprehension and rage. He believed that the Lord Chancellor might seek to deprive him of little William also, and of a second child whose birth was expected in August or September. He wrote a poem "To William Shelley," full of his sense of injustice, inviting his infant son to flee the country with him:

> . . . we must not stay
> Or the slaves of the law may rend thee away.

Sixteen stanzas of strong, bitter invective were entitled "To the Lord Chancellor," concluding:

> I curse thee, though I hate thee not; O slave!
> If thou couldst quench the earth-consuming hell
> Of which thou art a daemon, on thy grave
> This curse should prove a blessing. Fare thee well!

This would-be hateless hate Shelley carried with him through the rest of his life. On November 8, 1820 Claire Clairmont noted in her journal: "Shelley's three aversions, God Almighty, Lord Chancellor and didactic poetry."

At Marlow Shelley continued his personal interest in the poor. Many of the inhabitants were lace-makers, whose trade suffered the usual fate of luxury trades at a time when many people were able to purchase only the barest necessities. These ill-paid, starving workers came to know Shelley well. He visited them in their cottages and attended their illnesses, for which he would prescribe and provide broth or pea soup. Once, being without money or writing materials at the moment, he gave the shoes off his feet to a poor woman whom he found limping barefoot over the stones. Once "a portion of the warmest of Mrs. Shelley's wardrobe" was discovered to be missing; Shelley had impulsively given it to someone more needy. Shelley carried little money on his person, but he generally carried pencil and paper or a book. Many times Mr. Madocks, a neighbor who sometimes acted as Shelley's deputy and petty banker, received notes scribbled on notebook leaves or leaves torn from books, directing that the bearer be paid a specified small sum.

On Saturday evenings Shelley held audiences with the poor of Albion House, a bag of coins at his elbow. When he was absent — and he was probably as unreliable in his engagements with the poor as with Godwin and Hogg — the coins and the authority were delegated to Mrs. Madocks. In the winter of 1817, as distress and cold weather increased together according to their immemorial association, Shelley bought some sheeting and twenty blankets, such as army officers were furnished with, for distribution among the needy. During this winter Shelley contracted ophthalmia, as a result, Mary thought, of his visits to the poor.

Practical as it was, Shelley's benevolence at Marlow had also a tinge of his doctrine of universal love and brotherhood which he expressed more clearly in his later poetry. *Alastor* had stressed the sympathy existing between the poet and wild creatures, and the Lady of the Garden in "The Sensitive Plant" (1820) carefully preserved the lives even of "all killing insects and gnawing worms." At Marlow Shelley dissuaded small boys from persecuting squirrels with stones and commissioned his gardener to buy living crayfish as they were hawked through the streets and return them to the Thames.

Daily life at Albion House was a matter of very simple routine. Leigh Hunt, an early visitor who spent all together nearly three months there, indignantly answered the current slanders on Shelley's private life by printing what he had seen:

> This was the round of his daily life: — He was up early; breakfasted sparingly; wrote . . . all the morning; went out in his boat or into the woods with some Greek author or the Bible in his hands; came home to a dinner of vegetables (for he took neither meat nor wine); visited, if necessary, "the sick and the fatherless," whom others gave Bibles to and no help; wrote or studied again, or read to his wife and friends the whole evening; took a crust of bread or a glass of whey for his supper; and went early to bed. This is literally the whole of the life he led.

241

When Shelley was writing he sometimes spent most of the day in his boat, or on a hill in Bisham Wood. A Marlow gentleman told Medwin that Shelley sometimes spent whole nights in his boat, taking up an occasional abode at a small inn down the river. Numerous and sometimes long were the walks he took with Hunt, Hogg, or Peacock. "We took many walks in all directions from Marlow," says Peacock, "and saw everything worth seeing within a radius of sixteen miles." . . . "We often walked to London, frequently in company with Mr. Hogg. It was our usual way of going there, when not pressed for time. . . . The total distance was thirty-two miles to Tyburn turnpike. We usually stayed two nights and walked back on the third day. I never saw Shelley tired with these walks. Delicate and fragile as he appeared, he had great muscular strength."

In the numerous rowing and sailing excursions on the Thames, Shelley often preferred steering to taking an oar, but when he rowed he "could stick to his seat for any time against any force of current or of wind, not only without complaining, but without being compelled to give in until the set task was accomplished, though it should involve some miles of hard pulling." He did not shrink from towing his boat back to its moorings after a row or sail of considerable length.

During his residence at Marlow, Shelley was frequently in London for short periods, whether on business or pleasure. On these visits Leigh Hunt's cottage in the Vale of Health, Hampstead, was his second home, though he spent some evenings also at Godwin's. One such occasion arrived when Mary finished *Frankenstein* and a publisher must be sought. On May 22 Mary and Shelley left their guests at Albion House and went down to London for a few days, descending the river in their boat. Mary remained until the end of the month, Mrs. Godwin being mercifully absent in France. Shelley stayed only four days (May 22–6) during which he attended the opera (*Don Giovanni*) and an exhibition of sculpture and painting, dined with Hogg at Godwin's, and passed an evening with Hazlitt there.

On his visits to Hampstead, which sometimes lasted several days, Shelley delighted in walking over rough broken ground. The fresh northwest wind, as Hunt observed, gave him "an intoxication of animal spirits." The city streets were apt to cause a sudden, characteristic mood of depression. "Look at all these worn and miserable faces that pass us," he burst out one day as he and Hunt were walking in the Strand, "and tell me what is to be thought of the world they appear in."

In these visits to town Shelley became an appreciative frequenter of the Italian opera. Seated in the old Italian Theatre, with its comparatively quiet, decorous audiences, he would remark to Peacock that it was "delightful to see human beings so civilized." Mademoiselle Mélanie, the principal danseuse there in 1817, enchanted him; he had never imagined before, he said, such grace of motion. The music of Mozart, especially in *The Marriage of Figaro*, delighted him.

He regarded the regular stage, however, as a corrupter of principles that were much dearer to him than the entertainment of an hour. Miss O'Neill in Milman's *Fazio* compelled his admiration to the extent that two years later he hoped to secure her for the part of Beatrice in *The Cenci*, but this was the only play Peacock ever saw Shelley enjoy. In fact, Peacock, a confirmed theater-goer himself, never enticed Shelley to attend any other play except Sheridan's *School for Scandal*. Here, in the fourth act, Shelley could hardly be persuaded to remain in the theater. "I see the purpose of this comedy," he protested. "It is to associate virtue with bottles and glasses, and villainy with books." He often talked of "the withering and perverting spirit of comedy," and maintained that it fortified oppression by ridiculing infirmities that were more properly subjects for pity and sympathy.

Chapter XV

BY THE END of June several clouds were beginning to threaten the serenity of Albion House. Godwin was again in financial difficulties and Byron was showing a complete lack of interest in providing for his infant daughter, on whose account the Shelleys were already suffering some inconvenience and embarrassment. Shelley was for several days quite unwell. On June 29 he wrote to Leigh Hunt: "I have so constant a pain in my side, and such a depression of strength and spirits, as to make my holding the pen whilst I write to you an almost intolerable exertion. This, you know, with me is transitory." For the next six months the Shelleys continued the same regular round of reading and study which was now second nature to both Shelley and Mary; but there was gradual, uneven acceleration of the disquieting forces, until in the end a flight to Italy seemed the only answer to all problems at once.

It was a long time before the first faint warnings terminated in a departure from Marlow and England. While the present situation was gradually becoming more untenable Shelley was obliviously and whole-heartedly committing himself to poetry. If under adverse circumstances he had clung to his reading with inflexible stubbornness, he had not forgotten that his studies were part of a still greater purpose to become a poet who could compel the world to listen to the truth as he saw it.

While at Marlow, Shelley not only wrote a great deal, but, as before, stimulated both Mary and Claire to activity. *The Revolt of Islam*, considerably the longest poem Shelley ever wrote, "Prince Athanase," a fragmentary poem of over three hundred lines, a good part of *Rosalind and Helen*, and twenty-six shorter poems and fragments — a total of about six thousand lines — constitute Shelley's poetic production within a little less than a year. In addition he wrote the prefaces to *Frankenstein* and *History of a Six Weeks' Tour*, and his pamphlet on the death of the Princess Charlotte. He began his translation of the Homeric Hymns, dictated a translation from Spinoza, marketed three volumes, and saw them through the press. These poems not only show (in Mary's phrase) "how full of passion and reflection were his solitary hours," they *were* his solitary hours. Much more than the journal in which they are so briefly and seldom

244

mentioned, they constitute the picture of Shelley in 1817. "He never wandered," said Mary, as she wrote of Shelley's life at Marlow, "without a book, and without implements of writing."

Of the longer poems and fragments, *Laon and Cythna*, or *The Revolt of Islam*, as it was renamed, was apparently the first undertaken. It was begun probably about the middle of March and was finished on September 23. Ever since he had visited Versailles it had been in Shelley's mind that someone should write a poem on the French Revolution that would show the real basis of revolutionary change and, by presenting the *beau idéal* of a revolution in contrast with the errors into which the French Revolution had fallen, show that the gloom and depression felt by so many liberals on account of its failure were really unjustified. He had at first suggested the subject to Byron, but in vain. "Our faithless Albè," as Mary now called him, was in too indolent a mood to pay serious attention even to Shelley's urgent letters about Claire and her child.

As soon as the Chancery business would allow, Shelley himself took up the design he had urged upon Byron. Day after day he sought his "high prominence in Bisham Wood," retreated to Medmenham Abbey, or moored his boat under an island or a chalky cliff. Alone in any of these spots with his "unbounded and sustained enthusiasm," Shelley went through the " 'agony and bloody sweat' of intellectual travail." These expressions of Shelley after Godwin had disappointed him by failing utterly to appreciate the poem at its proper worth may be a little intensified by the circumstances, but they are amply supported in the main by the poem itself and its Preface. "I felt the precariousness of my life," Shelley told Godwin, "and I engaged in this task resolved to leave some records of myself. Much of what the volume contains was written with the same feeling, as real, though not so prophetic, as the communications of a dying man."

In the Preface Shelley informed his readers that the poem was intended not only to test the public desire for a better state of things, but also to test whether or not he possessed the one most important requisite of a poet, the power of communicating his sensations and enthusiasms to others. He said he had written fearlessly, in the belief that contemporary criticism was a matter of only trifling moment; but since his poem was narrative, and not didactic, he hoped the reader would not impute to the author opinions belonging more properly to his dramatic characters. Whatever certain characters said in their own persons, the author intended no attack upon the Supreme Being, but only upon the erroneous and degraded idea of Him. Just as later in his preface to *Prometheus Unbound* and in his *Defence of Poetry*, Shelley disclaimed any didactic purpose of recommending his principles "by methodical and systematic argument. Instead, he hoped "to awaken the feelings, so that the reader should see the beauty of true virtue" and so find his own way to true principles. He then summarized, or rather described, the action of the poem as follows:

It is a succession of pictures illustrating the growth and progress of individual mind aspiring after excellence, and devoted to the love of mankind; its influence in refining and making pure the most daring and uncommon impulses of the imagination, the understanding, and the senses; its impatience at "all the oppressions which are done under the sun;" its tendency to awaken public hope, and to enlighten and improve mankind; the rapid effects of the application of that tendency; the awakening of an immense nation from their slavery and degradation to a true sense of moral dignity and freedom; the bloodless dethronement of their oppressors, and the unveiling of the religious frauds by which they had been deluded into submission; the tranquillity of successful patriotism, and the universal toleration and benevolence of true philanthropy; the treachery and barbarity of hired soldiers; vice not the object of punishment and hatred, but kindness and pity; the faithlessness of tyrants; the confederacy of the Rulers of the World, and the restoration of the expelled Dynasty by foreign arms; the massacre and extermination of the Patriots, and the victory of established power; the consequences of legitimate despotism, civil war, famine, plague, superstition, and an utter extinction of the domestic affections; the judicial murder of the advocates of Liberty; the temporary triumph of oppression, that secure earnest of its final and inevitable fall; the transient nature of ignorance and error, and the eternity of genius and virtue. Such is the series of delineations of which the Poem consists.

Even to modern readers, more familiar than Shelley's contemporaries with the new style of poetry, *The Revolt of Islam* is more difficult reading than Shelley could have anticipated. If he had any special fitness as a poet, Shelley informed Godwin, it was "to apprehend minute and remote distinctions of feeling, whether relative to

external nature, or the living beings which surround us." He had decided some time before that language itself might sometimes be inadequate to convey ideas, and he had already begun to develop a
symbolism which by appealing directly to the imagination and sympathies might heighten the effect of literal language. In *The Revolt
of Islam* this use of symbols, while by no means necessary to the
general meaning, undoubtedly puzzles the reader at times. This is
particularly true when Shelley deliberately goes contrary to conventional notions and makes the serpent symbolize the good, in the
eternal warfare between good and evil. The poem is rather over-
weighted with description, much of which is excellent poetry, but
repetitious. Even Leigh Hunt complained mildly of the numerous
similar descriptions of water scenes, and Byron said that its few
readers could not understand it, "I for one."

But the principal weakness of the poem is structural. The first
canto, including a kind of survey of the French Revolution and a
partly symbolical explanation of Shelley's philosophy of good and
evil, is far too elaborate as an introduction to a story. Having reached
his story in the second canto, Shelley does not proceed directly, but
allows his two protagonists to tell their stories individually, with a
consequent effect of overlapping, stopping and starting again. Even
with Shelley's clear outline in the Preface it is hard to follow and
understand.

Both the merits and the defects of the poem were fairly stated in
one of the best criticisms it has ever received, Leigh Hunt's review
in the *Examiner:*

> The beauties of the poem consist in depth of sentiment, in
> grandeur of imagery, and a versification remarkably sweet, vari-
> ous, and noble, like the placid playing of a great organ. If the
> author's genius reminds us of any other poets, it is of two very
> opposite ones, Lucretius and Dante. . . . Mr. Shelley's defects
> as a poet are obscurity, inartificial and yet not natural economy,
> violation of costume, and too great a sameness and gratuitous-
> ness of image and metaphor, and of image and metaphor too
> drawn from the elements, particularly the sea. The book is full
> of humanity; and yet it certainly does not go the best way to
> work of appealing to it, because it does not appeal to it through
> the medium of its common knowledges. It is for this reason that
> we must say something, which we would willingly leave unsaid,
> both from admiration of Mr. Shelley's genius and love of his

benevolence; and this is, that the work cannot possibly become popular.

The core of Shelley's optimism was that it was natural for men to behave like brutes when suddenly liberated from a long brutalizing tyranny. Pessimism because they do so was unreasonable. Nations became liberal-minded only as the result of "resolute perseverance and indefatigable hope, and long-suffering and long-believing courage, and the systematic efforts of generations of men of intellect and virtue." In the first canto the splendid conflict between the eagle of oppression and the serpent of righteousness symbolizes Shelley's belief that the contest between good and evil principles is everlasting — the serpent, though often defeated, is never slain, and always returns to the conflict. The disappointments of the French Revolution, therefore, were a mere incident. The ideal revolution described in the poem is crushed, but this is no reason for gloom — the serpent is merely recruiting his strength for another fight. In the operation of a vague principle of mutability another opportunity would surely be presented, and if men only learned meanwhile to overcome revenge, envy, and prejudice and to depend solely on love, or universal sympathy, the final outcome could not be doubtful. Already Shelley, as he said in the Preface, felt aware of a "slow, gradual, silent change." Had not Malthus, he exulted, the very high priest of hopelessness, recently altered his *Essay on Population* so that it was now merely a commentary on the unanswerableness of *Political Justice*?

This long-range optimism contains more inspiration for the philosophic than for the practical radical, who will always be much more sympathetic with the vigorous, clear directness of *Queen Mab*. Nothing could be more sanely tempered than the view of revolutionary change set forth in the Preface and first canto of *The Revolt of Islam*. And yet in its subsequent attacks upon kings, priests, outworn custom, and perverted religion the poem is quite as vigorous as *Queen Mab*. Shelley was still far too ardent and impetuous to submit his feelings consistently to the disciplined patience that his experience and his fine intellectual insight taught him were necessary. His revolution is brought about largely by the fact that both Laon and Cythna are freed by the tyrants to preach revolution. They go free through no compulsion except the power of persuasion — a piece of good fortune which escaped Bonnivard and which a practical revolutionist no doubt would consider almost as miraculous as the liberation of Daniel or Saint Paul.

Rosalind and Helen was begun at some time during the composition of *The Revolt of Islam,* or even shortly before, and was thrown aside for a while unfinished late in September of 1817 when Shelley's doctor forbade further creative writing. It appears to have been finished in an earlier form by February 18 of the following year, but in the form in which it was published it was not completed until the summer of 1818. "My pretty eclogue," as Mary called it, tells the story of two contrasted pairs of lovers in a manner apparently designed to justify the love of Shelley and Mary.

The longest of the eight fragments of "Prince Athanase" was written in December 1817; the others either then or earlier. Its writing is undoubtedly connected with Shelley's reading of Plato's *Symposium* about the middle of September; Shelley's first name for it, "Pandemos and Urania," shows that it was intended to present the two types of love, earthly and spiritual (Pandemian and Uranian), which Plato so nobly discusses. It also furnishes the earliest of Shelley's fine descriptions of spiritual love:

> Thou art the radiance which where ocean rolls
>
> Investeth it; and when the heavens are blue
> Thou fillest them; and when the earth is fair
> The shadow of thy moving wings imbue
>
> Its deserts and its mountains, till they wear
> Beauty [like some] light robe; — thou ever soarest
> Among the towers of men, and as soft air
>
> In Spring, which moves the unawakened forest,
> Clothing with leaves its branches bare and bleak,
> Thou floatest among men. . . .

Shelley's purpose in the poems of the Marlow period was, as he said himself, to fulfill his compelling sense of mission as well as possible while it was still possible. No one can read *The Revolt of Islam,* with its earnest enthusiasm for the improvement of humanity, and still doubt Shelley's statement. But it was also a necessity of Shelley's nature to feel justified; he could scarcely maintain confidence in his mission otherwise. There was never a time in his life when his sense of rectitude was more necessary to him than in the year following Harriet's suicide and the beginning of the Chancery proceedings involving his children. Under the surface of his greater concern for the world may be clearly seen his keen feeling for his personal situation. Prince Athanase with his false and true loves offers a close parallel to Shelley's conception of his own history. *The Revolt of Islam* and *Rosalind and Helen* both show parents whose children have been torn from them by an exercise of tyranny, and both offer impressive examples of true love without marriage. *Rosalind and Helen,* in fact, is primarily the study of two unions, the fine love of Helen and Lionel without marriage, and the legalized union of Rosalind and her husband, without love, which is apparently based upon Mary's impression that her friend Isabel Baxter's marriage was turning out badly. Occasional passages in Shelley's letters show how closely his view of his own character tallies with those he assigns his three heroes. Three shorter poems written during the same year — "Lines to the Lord Chancellor," "To William Shelley," and "Dedication: To Mary" — speak openly and intensely on the same themes.

The relapse in Shelley's health in late June and early July mentioned in his letters to the Hunts and Byron was only temporarily alarming. July turned to August without any further alarm. Shelley's twenty-fifth birthday passed happily. Mary was expecting soon to be confined and asked Mrs. Hunt to provide her with a nurse from London by August 20. The child, Clara Everina, was born on September 2.

The autumn brought several visitors to Marlow, among them, in September, Mr. William Baxter, the father of Mary's estranged girlhood friend, Isabel Baxter. He was delighted with Shelley and Mary, perhaps the more readily because he was himself a man of liberal sentiments. "He has taken a prodigious fancy to us," wrote Mary to Shelley during Shelley's absence in London, "and is continually talking of and praising 'Queen Mab,' which he vows is the best poem of modern days." He had expected to find in Shelley "an ignorant, silly, half-witted enthusiast" with "morals that fitted him only for a brothel." Instead he had been astonished and delighted to find him "a being of rare genius and talent, of truly republican frugality and plainness of manners, and of a soundness of principle and delicacy of moral tact that might put to shame (if shame they had) many of his detractors; and, with all this so amiable that you have only to be half an hour in his company to convince you that there is not an atom of malevolence in his whole composition." In his opinion his daughter's failure to answer Mary's letters was due entirely to the opposi-

tion of her husband, Mr. Booth, whose ill temper and jealousy bade
fair to make Isabel "another victim of that ceremony."

The Hunts arrived for a week's visit on September 19. It was at
this time, just as he was finishing *The Revolt of Islam,* that Shelley's
health became really alarming. On September 24 he wrote to Byron:
"My health is in a miserable state, so that some care will be required
to prevent it speedily terminating in death. . . . They recommend
Italy as a certain remedy for my disease." At the same time Mary
was writing to Shelley: "Ah! my love you cannot guess how wretched
it was to see your languor and increasing illness. I now say to myself, perhaps he is better; but then I watched you every moment, and
every moment was full of pain both to you and to me."

During October and November Shelley's health mended only from
time to time; basically it remained the same. Mary was becoming
more and more distressed. "When I see you, drooping and languid,
in pain, and unable to enjoy life," Mary wrote, "then on your account
I ardently wish for bright skies and Italian sun." As the weather grew
colder and the hours of sunlight shorter, the dampness and darkness
of Albion House became more and more apparent; both felt that they
could not remain there much longer.

In writing to Godwin on December 7 Shelley gave a particular description of his ailment:

> My health has been materially worse. My feelings at intervals
> are of a deadly and torpid kind, or awakened to a state of such
> unnatural and keen excitement that only to instance the organ
> of sight, I find the very blades of grass and the boughs of distant
> trees present themselves to me with microscopical distinctness.
> Towards evening I sink into a state of lethargy and inanimation,
> and often remain for hours on the sofa between sleep and waking
> a prey to the most painful irritability of thought. Such with little
> intermission is my condition.

Hours for work, Shelley continued, had to be selected with care
and caution. He had recently experienced "a decisive pulmonary attack," and it might be necessary to go to Italy to avoid a lingering
death from consumption. Incidentally, he had tried the effect of
adopting a meat diet, but found himself unable to continue it.

Long before this Shelley had consulted physicians who ordered
him to discontinue writing and recommended a warmer climate. Italy
had already been practically decided upon, but Godwin was still
kept ignorant of the decision, because he was almost certain to ob-

ject. This threw an added burden upon Mary, who expected Godwin to come to Marlow for a visit. Dreading his certain opposition to their leaving England, and dreading even more the ordeal of lying to him about their plans, she begged Shelley to inform Godwin and have it over.

Between September 23, when he finished *The Revolt of Islam,* and November 19 Shelley was in London most of the time, consulting moneylenders, lawyers, and doctors, returning to Marlow only three times during the first month. It was during the first ten days of this period that affairs came to a decision. Mary, with a constitutional tendency to despair, was also in a weak state of health from recent childbirth. Peacock annoyed her by coming uninvited every day to dine and to "drink his bottle." Claire, who had accompanied Shelley to London, returned to irritate her with ill humor, restlessness, and disturbing reports of the affairs Shelley was trying to settle in London. Godwin had recently taken umbrage at some real or imagined slight to his wife, whom he well knew both the Shelleys disliked. Even Hunt, usually a most welcome visitor, thoughtlessly neglected to accompany her when he knew she was too weak to walk alone.

The house was incredibly dark and clammy. Mary's letters to Shelley became more and more urgent. They *must* quit the house and go either to Italy or to the Kentish coast. She slightly preferred the latter, but would abide by Shelley's decision. Whether or not they went to Italy, Alba must go there, and soon. It would be unjust as well as impossible to keep her much longer, and ridiculous to rely upon any promises Byron might make in the matter — "We must decide to go ourselves, or send her, within a month." "You do not seem enough to feel the absolute necessity there is that she should join her Father with every possible speed." "Indeed, my love, her departure must not be delayed. . . . After all, dear Shelley, indecision will be our bane." Shelley agreed that Alba must join her father and on October 6 decided: "We must go to Italy, on every ground."

There could be no migration to Italy, however, without another financial house-cleaning. Not to mention Godwin's continuing needs, Shelley's own expenses had for some time been getting more and more out of hand and may indeed have contributed, with other worries, to his recent ill health. The long-term lease on Albion House had cost about twelve hundred pounds, and a good deal of money had been spent on furniture. What Shelley's numerous petty local charities cost is unknown and was probably never known to Shelley himself — he was always careless about small sums and wrote out his money orders for Mr. Madocks, dispensed his coins on Saturday evenings, provided his soup, blankets, and sheets, with a very hazy notion of the aggregate cost. If Mary missed a pound note from her bureau her natural supposition was that Shelley had taken it to London with him without mentioning the fact.

Likewise he had no clear notion of the total amount of his debts to local tradesmen. Mary, with more exact ideas on such matters, became worried. "Do get the state of your accounts from your Banker," she insisted. Shelley borrowed £250 from Horace Smith under the impression that it would be sufficient, but Mary wrote: "Your account of our expences is by very much too favourable. . . . Our debts at Marlow are greater than you are aware of, besides living in the mean time and articles of dress that I must buy." For the first time, apparently, they now discovered that a large amount of Harriet's debts were still unpaid, and that Longdill had undertaken their payment — as indeed he was legally obliged to do. Longdill had a considerable bill of his own to submit, and there were the other expenses of the recent Chancery trial which Shelley now informed Mary "*must* be paid."

Over and above all this were Shelley's regular pensioners. Claire was still dependent on him, and so was her brother Charles. Leigh Hunt had ceased to assert his financial independence and was now a regular pensioner. So was Peacock, to whom Shelley made an allowance of a hundred pounds, though the regularity of payment is very doubtful. Godwin, of course, was exigent as ever. His *Mandeville*, the proceeds of which were to relieve his distresses, was now published, but the distress still needed relief. Even the neighbors noticed how Hunt and Godwin had come to depend on Shelley. Leigh Hunt has testified that on one occasion alone (undated) Shelley gave him £1,400, and Horace Smith asserted that to his knowledge Shelley gave Godwin and other literary men upwards of £5,000 in all. Some of these undated gifts certainly occurred in 1817. In an unsuccessful effort to borrow money for Hunt, Shelley introduced himself to the banker poet Samuel Rogers in early July. He did borrow money in small amounts from others besides Horace Smith.

It was no wonder, then, that Shelley turned once more to the post-obit brokers. His debts in October amounted to more than £1,500. Some of his creditors were becoming impatient. He had been in town only a short while when he was arrested for debt and held for two days, at the instance of no less a person than his uncle, the gal-

lant Captain Pilfold, who had formerly been his champion. Just
when Shelley was arrested and how released does not appear, but on
October 16 Mary wrote: "You say nothing of the late arrest, and
what may be the consequences." Shelley hoped that Sir Timothy
could now be prevailed upon to advance money in order to prevent
the necessity of selling certain property rights, but Sir Timothy was
advised by Whitton that Shelley would soon sell them in any case. At
the same time Mary feared to urge Shelley to return to Marlow lest
he be arrested there.

Thus Mary's fears that their affairs might be drifting toward an
insuperable fiasco were not at all surprising. "Nothing is done . . ."
she complained, "and indeed I do not expect anything to be done
these many months." The necessity of a post-obit transaction meant
further delay. "I wish to hear extremely the account of your money at
the bankers." "You tell me that the Italian sun will be the best physician — be it so — but money, money." And still, whatever happened,
"Godwin must not be left unprovided." Just when Shelley solved his
financial difficulties is uncertain. It seems probable that an agreement was reached by the middle of December and that the actual
cash was not secured until the end of January.

It was also about the middle of December that the alarm over
Shelley's health subsided. Four days after describing his illness to
Godwin, Shelley wrote: "This dry and frosty weather fills me with
health and spirits; I wish I could believe that it would last." It may
be significant that Shelley's worst state of health again coincided
almost exactly with a state of nervous worry over other matters.
After Italy had been decided upon and the other worries abated,
we hear no more of Shelley's poor health.

Very little of these worries was apparent to Shelley's visitors or
associates. Life at Albion House continued as usual, except that
Shelley was often absent in London. If the Hunts knew that the
Shelleys were in serious difficulties during October, they left no
mention of the fact, though they were visitors at Marlow when Shelley went up to London on September 23 and for a little while afterwards. Peacock, who to Mary's disgust often dined, took tea, or spent
the evening at Albion House, remembered only that "This was an
agreeable year to all of us," and supposed the departure from Marlow to be caused entirely by Shelley's restlessness.

Meanwhile, on November 8 Mary had joined Shelley in London,
where they remained together till the 19th, calling on the Godwins,

the Hunts, and Ollier and receiving calls from them and from Keats, Coulson, Mr. Baxter, and Mr. Booth.

When Charles Ollier and Godwin called on the Shelleys on November 10 and 11, the conversation turned to a subject about which all liberals and radicals were suddenly concerned. The Princess Charlotte, daughter of the Prince Regent, had died in childbirth on November 6. The English people had long since lost faith in the disreputable sons of George III. Now they were disappointed in their hope that the throne might soon pass to the one really popular and respected member of the royal family. The whole nation was griefstricken, and the cause of reform looked gloomier than ever. Shelley immediately set to work on a pamphlet suggested by his conversations with Ollier and Godwin, and sent it complete to Ollier next day, to be printed "without an hour's delay."

An Address to the People on the Death of the Princess Charlotte began by remarking that the death of the beautiful young Princess was indeed a public calamity, but that an even greater public calamity had happened almost simultaneously and was being neglected. Three ignorant laborers, Brandreth, Turner, and Ludlam, had just been executed on the testimony of spies for taking part in the so-called Derby insurrection, which had actually been instigated by one of the spy witnesses. England's greater grief should be that its rulers trampled upon human rights, imprisoned its critics at will, piled up a public debt which ensured a general calamity in the future, created a choice between anarchy and oppression, and conspired through spies and bloodshed to frighten the people into choosing the latter. Let England mourn, then, for a Princess who, like Liberty, was young, innocent, and lovely. But Liberty also was dead, and whereas the Princess had perished through natural causes, Liberty had been murdered. It was an eloquent and dignified criticism of the state of England, anticipating the temperate reformism of his *Philosophical View of Reform.* But for unknown reasons it was not published with the hot haste that Shelley desired. No copy of an original edition is known, though an alleged facsimile edition was published in or about 1843.

The day after this pamphlet was dispatched, the Shelleys received an evening call from Mr. Baxter and his son-in-law, Mr. Booth. Though perhaps not so enjoyable as the dinner next day at Hunt's with music afterwards, this must have been one of the most interesting evenings during their visit. The Shelleys still hoped that Isabel Baxter Booth would be allowed to accompany them to Italy. Mr.

Baxter greatly liked and admired the Shelleys and had even become a temporary convert to vegetarianism; but Mr. Booth had heard talk of Shelley and his opinions that made him deeply dubious. A self-educated, strong-minded little man of dynamic personality and odd appearance, Booth was radical in his political beliefs, but conservative and suspicious on social and moral questions. It must have required considerable persuasion on Baxter's part to bring him to the interview.

The argument was keen and well sustained on both sides. "I never met a man," Shelley testified, "by whom, in the short time we exchanged ideas, I felt myself excited to so much severe and sustained mental competition, or from whom I derived so much amusement and instruction." But if Booth felt himself similarly extended it only increased his conviction that Shelley was a dangerous character. Not only was he not converted through Baxter's good offices, but within a short while he converted or overawed Baxter. So ended Mary's hope of renewing her dearest friendship.

Within a fortnight after Shelley and Mary returned to Marlow trouble developed over the publication of *The Revolt of Islam*. Shelley realized that the poem, repeating as it did the doctrines of *Queen Mab*, might be a dangerous publication. But, as he wrote to Byron, it was to be published in spite of the risk. "As to me," he continued almost as if mounting the scaffold at the moment, and enjoying it, "I can but die; I can but be torn to pieces, or devoted to infamy most undeserved; and whether this is inflicted by the necessity of nature, and circumstances, or through a principle, pregnant, as I believe, with important benefit to mankind, is an alternative to which I cannot be indifferent."

He argued somewhat differently soon afterwards, however, when his publishers, Charles and James Ollier, suddenly became recalcitrant. Some copies of the book, postdated 1818, had already gone forth in early December, when the Olliers became convinced that publication of the book would convict them of condoning incest, as well as the other more ordinary attacks on social and religious conventions. Shelley had indeed presented a hero and a heroine who were brother and sister and also lovers without benefit of clergy, but he had explained in his Preface that he did not present this as a situation which he endorsed, but only as a calculated shock, "merely to accustom men to that charity and toleration which . . . a practice widely differing from their own has a tendency to promote." Nevertheless the Olliers had become frightened and they flatly refused to publish the book without certain alterations.

Shelley was now in an extremely trying situation. For months he had devoted most of his time and enthusiasm to the poem and was passionately committed to publishing it. The printing had been at his own expense; he could hardly afford to reprint the whole book. Even if he did, it would be damned in advance by the whisper that a fairly courageous publisher of known liberal tendencies had already washed his hands of it. Under circumstances that would have infuriated even a phlegmatic author he wrote Charles Ollier one of the most eloquent letters he ever penned. He pointed out that Ollier's fears were based on no circumstances that were not already to be foreseen when the book was accepted and that its withdrawal after having been actually published placed the author under a false and unjust imputation of deceit which would damage the work irretrievably. He appealed to Ollier's courage and liberal principles; he argued very acutely that the government would scarcely prosecute a book so obviously "remote from the conceptions of the vulgar," if it were only published quietly and naturally, but that failure to go through with the publication now would by its very timidity stimulate the government to prosecute such books thereafter.

It soon appeared, however, that Ollier's demands could all be met by canceling the title page and twenty-six pages of text and substituting new pages. "The contents of your letter this morning certainly alters the question," Shelley wrote Ollier two days later, probably referring to some such suggestion. He urged Ollier to see him at the first opportunity. Next day Ollier appeared at Albion House; he remained for two days and returned to London with the revised text ready to print. The bulk of the revisions had to do with changing the relationship of Laon and Cythna from brother and sister to cousins. The title was changed from *Laon and Cythna* to *The Revolt of Islam*, and in order to protect the change every effort was to be made to call in the few copies that had been prematurely issued under the original title.

Peacock has left a vivid description of Shelley contesting every change point by point, protesting that his poem was ruined, refusing for a long time to alter a single line, yielding only on the united advice of his friends. But there was nothing he could do except make the best of it. Not only did he do this as soon as the device of substituting cancel-leaves was suggested, but he did it — or at least described doing it — with a good grace. Writing shortly afterwards to

Thomas Moore, who had seen the original version, he explained the changes to be made and stated that he was quite willing to make them after being convinced that the original passages would unnecessarily offend some readers who might otherwise sympathize with his general views.

Throughout the month of December there were few days in which Shelley did not read Hume or Berkeley (two contrasting philosophers who well illustrate the difference between Shelley's youth and maturity), Gibbon, Lady Morgan's *France,* Shakespeare, or *Paradise Lost.* He was not too absorbed in his own difficulties to take an interest in the third trial of William Hone for treason, or to send two checks to the fund raised for Hone's benefit following his acquittal.

Christmas passed pleasantly and peacefully in reading and walking. On Christmas Eve Shelley indulged his bent for telling children tales of horror; his temporarily adopted ward Polly Rose listened with mingled terror and delight to the tale of Bürger's *Lenore,* told shudderingly. Horace Smith arrived the day after Christmas on his last visit to the Shelleys at Marlow. He arranged to act as Shelley's London financial agent, so that while Shelley was abroad he might be saved brokerage and agency fees in receiving his income.

Only a few more weeks now remained to be spent in Marlow. Shelley and Mary read steadily, as usual. Claire began the study of Italian. On January 3 Hogg arrived for a short visit. Shelley was ill again for two or three days, but his illness did not prevent the increase in the amount of Latin reading that generally occurred when Hogg was present. Godwin came with his young son William, now a schoolboy; he arrived at a new financial misunderstanding with Shelley, and departed. Shelley set about translating the Homeric Hymns, but was interrupted by a return of the ophthalmia probably contracted in visiting the poor. For a while thereafter he seems to have discontinued his reading, but Mary read to him occasionally and engaged him in chess.

On January 29 Shelley, Claire, and Peacock drove up to London in the family carriage. The primary object was to conclude Shelley's financial arrangements with Mr. William Willats, a dealer in post-obits, with whom Shelley signed the final papers on January 31. Shelley at once dispatched a sum of money to Godwin. By this time he had probably reached the conclusion that Francis Place had arrived at long before: namely, that no matter how large the sums turned over to Godwin, it was hopeless to look for an end to his demands. He sent Godwin only a part of the sum apparently agreed upon, stating frankly that he was resolved to keep in his own hands "the power conferred by the difference of the two sums." Godwin's reply was so prompt that it was dated on the same day on which Shelley concluded his loan. "I acknowledge the receipt of the sum mentioned in your letter. I acknowledge with equal explicitness my complete disappointment." After challenging Shelley to place the difference between the two sums in the hands of a banker, subject only to their joint signatures, he continued with bitter Godwinian dignity to protest his shame at ever having appealed to Shelley on other than philosophic grounds and his desire to state the case finally on those grounds, without passion and without a witness. "If you have the courage to hear me, come; if you have not, be it so."

Whether or not Shelley accepted Godwin's challenge is unknown. We only know that with money in hand he returned to Marlow on February 5, having spent an agreeable evening at the opera with Claire, Hogg, Peacock, and the Hunts, and having passed at least part of one evening in a sonnet-writing contest with Hunt and Keats, the product of which was three rather undistinguished sonnets on the Nile.

On February 11, having completed all their packing at Marlow, Shelley's whole party settled in lodgings at 119 Great Russell Street, for a final month of London.

With their affairs practically settled, Shelley and Mary now devoted themselves almost entirely to a round of social pleasures quite rare in their experience. Reading seems for once to have been neglected; the fact that Shelley is mentioned once (February 25) as "not well" seems to have made no difference. They visited the Indian Library, Apollonicon, the "Panorama of Rome," and the British Museum, where they saw the Elgin Marbles and the "casts from Phidias." Twice they went to the theater, to see Milman's *Fazio* and Byron's *Bride of Abydos.* Five times they went to the opera. Hogg and Peacock came to dinner eight times together, once with the Hunts, and once or twice separately. Four times the Shelleys spent the day or evening with the Hunts; once they dined with Horace Smith. All this in the last seventeen days of February.

One of their last actions before leaving London was the christening of all three of the children, a performance rather inconsistent with the views of the three parents, but a practical convenience for travelers. At this time Claire's child received the new name of Allegra. On March 10 Leigh and Marianne Hunt spent the day with the Shelleys, Mary Lamb called, and Godwin came in the evening to say good-by. On the next morning Shelley's party took coach for Dover, and on the morning of March 12 they embarked once more for the Continent.

Shelley was now a young man midway between twenty-five and twenty-six years of age, round-shouldered, narrow-chested, slender, and of somewhat better than average height when he straightened up from his habitual stoop. He walked with a lounging or weaving gait that contributed to a general suggestion of youthful immaturity. He dressed well, but carelessly, usually exposing to view a throat that appeared curiously small and undeveloped, and a thick, somewhat unruly thatch of wavy, golden-brown hair. His face was round and rather flat, with small features, receding chin, and nose slightly retroussé. Under the influence of dejection or ill health his fair, freckled face seemed rather pasty, but excitement or exercise easily brought the color to his cheeks. Intensely blue eyes and a well-shaped mouth were his finest, most expressive features. In repose these features conveyed an impression of thoughtful, courteous attention, alert and gravely comprehending. Under stress of argument or excitement they reflected instantly Shelley's characteristic lively changes of mood. A vehement mood was emphasized by somewhat awkward gestures and by the conversion of a voice ordinarily low, clear, and distinct into a shrill, dissonant vehemence that sometimes made him seem to strangers more antagonizing than he intended to be. His manners were gentle and sympathetic, with a simple native dignity born of his sincerity. Intimates like Hogg, Peacock, and Hunt soon learned that occasional unconventionalities were generally the unconscious expression either of abstraction or of sudden impulse.

Shelley had learned by bitter personal experience that strong conviction and utter sincerity of purpose, even when reinforced by extensive reading and study, are no guarantees against misunderstanding and partial frustration. The shock of this surprising discovery — the knowledge that even his particular idol, the author of *Political Justice,* could not do him personal justice — depressed and sobered him. Without yielding anything of his fundamental beliefs and purposes, Shelley had come to realize that Godwin's first advice was sound, that he could accomplish little or nothing by premature direct action, that he must inform himself further about the origin and growth of the customs and prejudices he hoped to help overthrow. In moments of extreme depression he now doubted his ability to contribute significantly to this result even at long range, though he would never cease trying.

Superficially at least, he had attained a juster notion of the power and value of money. But Sir Timothy and his attorney were both convinced, upon good evidence, of his financial irresponsibility. Godwin and his friend Turner felt likewise, and so, undoubtedly, did Mr. Madocks and a number of small creditors whose accounts Shelley left unsettled. There were people in Marlow who knew him mainly by sight and local rumor and thought him a little crazy; and there were people in the same town, who knew him perhaps better, who thought him a kindly, sympathetic, and even practical-minded benefactor of the poor. Few if any of the people who had thought the youthful Shelley mad would say so now. He had achieved a kind of perspective on his own peculiar mental complexion and even wrote calmly of two of his autobiographical characters, Laon and Lionel, as having been mad for a time. Soon, in "Julian and Maddalo," he was to add a third, who also possessed the very Shelleyan quality of mistaking illusion for reality.

Philosophically he had come a long way from his early materialistic bias. As a convert to Berkeley's idealistic philosophy, he was about ready to suggest that reality, so called, was actually illusion. His early ideas of love had become much more definite and important to him, largely on account of his reading in Plato. The old doctrine of Necessity had made way for the doctrine of Intellectual Beauty, which was already in process of being merged in his conception of the supreme importance of Love, or universal sympathy.

As Shelley left England the sound of Leigh Hunt's favorable review of *The Revolt of Islam* was yet pleasant in his ears. He had in his luggage a copy of Hunt's *Foliage*, published late in 1817, containing two sonnets, one entitled "To Percy Bysshe Shelley, on the Degrading Notions of Deity," and the second simply "To the Same." That men should "defame the kindly and the wise" was no wonder, Hunt asserted in the first sonnet, because such men held an idea of Deity that converted beauty into ugliness and hatred. The truly wise, he continued in the second, should never be thwarted by such misunderstanding. The same theme of admiration and encouragement echoed from a more recent sonnet by Horace Smith, published in the *Examiner* for February 8 under the title "Sonnet: To the Author of *The Revolt of Islam*." As yet the *Quarterly*, which could alone almost make or break an author, had not spoken, but its words would be none the softer for Leigh Hunt's praise.

Chapter XVI

THERE WERE EIGHT in the little party of emigrants – Shelley and Mary and their two children, Claire and Allegra, the Swiss nurse Elise, and Amelia ("Milly") Shields, who had been engaged as a second nurse some months earlier at Marlow. They landed at Calais on Thursday, March 12, 1818, and spent the night at the Grand Cerf Hotel. The next day they bought a carriage, loaded their belongings, and set out in the afternoon for Saint-Omer. Here they found the city gates already closed for the night, but after an hour's delay they were admitted upon a promise of "remembering the guard." Thence to Lyon required seven days of rough, uncomfortable travel. At times the road was so bad that the carriage was in constant danger of overturning. Once they were delayed three hours by the breaking of a carriage spring. Shelley sought to beguile the tedium by reading Schlegel aloud.

Having arrived at Lyon, the party put up at the Hôtel de l'Europe and allowed themselves four days of rest and recreation. "Lyons," Claire wrote in her journal, "is a most Beautiful City, but its best parts are all the work of Napoleon." After the weeks of strain and discomfort Shelley's spirits were again rising. From Lyon he wrote to Leigh Hunt:

We have journeyed towards the spring, that has been hastening to meet us from the south; and though our weather was at first abominable, we have now warm sunny days, and soft winds, and a sky of deep azure, the most serene I ever saw. The heat in this city to-day is like that of London in the midst of summer. My spirits and health sympathize in the change. Indeed, before I left London, my spirits were as feeble as my health, and I had demands upon them which I found difficult to supply.

A letter was dispatched to the indifferent Lord Byron informing him of Allegra's coming arrival at Milan, and the journey was resumed. They were now passing through wooded valleys dotted with white châteaux and scattered cottages. Everywhere they saw grapevines trellised upon huge stakes, and orchards of apple and pear trees. Early the first day (March 26) they reached the boundaries of Savoy at Pont Bonvoisin. Here, in the middle of a bridge guarded

at one end by the soldiers of France and at the other by those of
Savoy, they submitted with some misgivings to the customs examination. Shelley's luggage contained books by Rousseau and Voltaire, both proscribed authors in Savoyard territory. After some discussion the books were sent to Chambéry to be examined by the
censor — a priest, as Shelley noted.

They were now in the midst of such magnificent mountain scenery
as had never failed to stimulate Shelley's imagination. They had
crossed the Echelles to Chambéry over the high, winding road cut
through the perpendicular rocks by Charles Emmanuel, Duke of
Savoy, in 1582. "The rocks," as Shelley wrote of this passage,

> which cannot be less than a thousand feet in perpendicular
> height, sometimes overhang the road on each side, and almost
> shut out the sky. The scene is like that described in the Prome-
> theus of Aeschylus. Vast rifts and caverns in the granite preci-
> pices, wintry mountains with ice and snow above; the loud
> sounds of unseen waters within the caverns, and walls of top-
> pling rocks, only to be scaled as he described, by the winged
> chariot of the ocean nymphs.

In these words we have the definite germ of Shelley's greatest poem,
which was to be begun five months later. Passing the same spot five
years later, Mary Shelley wrote that "the dark high precipices tower-
ing above gave Shelley the idea of his Prometheus."

Leaving Chambéry, they could see the sunlight flashing from the
highest Alps. Soon they were enclosed by valleys as they followed
the windings of a river higher and higher. At Saint-Jean-de-Mau-
rienne, where they slept the first night, the town was deep in snow.
As they ascended Mont Cenis next morning, the snow on the edges of
the road was as high as their carriage. On March 30, two days after
leaving Chambéry, they crossed Mont Cenis, blessing Napoleon for
having improved the road, and stopped at Susa, the first town in
cisalpine Italy.

To Mary, though she enjoyed the mountain scenery, there was
"something dreadful" in traveling on the edge of an overhanging
precipice that was "armoured from top to bottom with a cascade of
ice." Shelley felt the cold of the higher altitudes as a discomfort, but
he was elated. Marlow with its dampness and debts, Godwin with
his incessant demands and ungracious lack of friendship, were far
behind; over the Alps, as Napoleon had said, lay Italy. Like Cæsar's
veterans singing their *Ecce Cæsar nunc triumphat* through the

streets of Rome, Shelley sang all the way as they climbed the last
heights of the pass over Mont Cenis:

> Now Heaven neglected is by Men
> And Gods are hung upon every tree
> But not the more for [loss] of them
> Shall this fair world unhappy be.

The mountains, he asserted, were God's corps de ballet.

The snow and ice of Mont Cenis were now behind them; ahead
and below them were green, sunny slopes and wooded glades. Prim-
roses were blooming everywhere. The air was full of the fragrance of
fruit trees in full bloom — "A sky without one cloud — everything
bright and serene — the cloudless sky of Italy — the bright and the
beautiful."

A day's journey from Susa brought the party to Turin (March 31),
where they attended a rather indifferent opera. Thence it was three
days of leisurely travel to Milan, their first pause of more than one
day since leaving Lyon on March 25. The countryside was now less
picturesque, but they were still delighted with Italy.

At Milan, which they reached on the evening of April 4, the party
lodged at the Hôtel Reale. The next day they visited the cathedral,
which they all admired extremely. The same evening (April 5) they
were delighted with the ballet of the Milan opera. Even though they
missed their favorite Mademoiselle Mélanie of the London opera,
Shelley thought the performance "the most splendid spectacle I ever
saw," and Mary called it "infinitely magnificent." "I like this town,"
Mary added. "We think, however, of spending the summer on the
banks of the lake of Como, which is only twenty miles from here.
Shelley's health is infinitely improved and the rest of the chicks are
quite well." Already Shelley's head was full of literary schemes to be
put into practice as soon as they were settled. The first of these was
a dramatic poem on the life of Tasso. On April 6 Shelley and Mary
began reading Tasso's *Aminta* together, and Shelley began reading
a life of Tasso.

After writing letters to the Hunts and Peacock, Shelley and Mary
left Claire and the rest of the party at Milan and set out for Lake
Como to find a house for the summer. "This lake," wrote Shelley
after his return, "exceeds anything I ever beheld in beauty with the
exception of the arbutus islands of Killarney." They examined three
houses, one of which was too small and one of which was out of repair, with a beautiful garden "full of serpents." The third, Villa

Pliniana, they hoped to secure for the summer. Shelley sent Peacock an enthusiastic description of it in his next letter.

While at Como Shelley was politely arrested for carrying firearms contrary to law. In spite of his expostulations he was taken before the local prefect, who suavely released him from arrest but would not return the pistol until Madame Shelley came before him and certified that her husband had no intention of shooting himself with it.

By April 12 they were back in Milan, with trouble already in the offing. Byron had not yet answered the letter written from Lyon asking his wishes with regard to Allegra. Shelley wrote him again on April 13:

> Will you spend a few weeks with us this summer? Our mode of life is uniform, and such as you remember it at Geneva, and the situation which I imagine we have chosen (the Villa Pliniana) is solitary, and surrounded by scenery of astonishing grandeur, with the lake at our feet. If you would visit us — and I don't know where you could find a heartier welcome — little Allegra might return with you.

But Byron was resolved to have nothing more to do with Claire, and he was somewhat suspicious of Shelley's efforts. Byron's letter to Shelley arrived on April 21, on which day Claire wrote in her journal: "Letter from Albè. Nothing but Discomfort." He offered to take Allegra and provide for her, but only on condition that Claire should resign her completely and absolutely to his care.

Shelley knew himself to be half suspected by Byron; he regarded Allegra almost as one of his own children; and he was torn and agonized by Claire's distress. Under these circumstances the tact and humanity of his answering letter does him infinite credit:

> *Milan*
> *April 22, 1818.*
>
> My dear Lord Byron,
>
> Clare will write to you herself a detail of her motives and feelings relating to Allegra's being absent as you desire. Her interference as the mother of course supersedes *mine,* which was never undertaken but from the deep interest I have ever felt for all the parties concerned. Here my letter might well close, but that I would not the affair should finish so.
>
> You write as if from the instant of its departure all future inter-

course were to cease between Clare and her child. This I cannot think you ought to have expected, or even to have desired. Let us estimate our own sensations, and consider, if those of a father be acute, what must be those of a mother? What should we think of a woman who should resign her infant child with no prospect of ever seeing it again, even to a father in whose tenderness she entirely confided? If she forces herself to such a sacrifice for the sake of her child's welfare, there is something heroically great in thus trampling upon the strongest affections, and even the most unappeasable instincts of our nature. But the world will not judge so; she would be despised as an unnatural mother, even by those who might see little to condemn in her becoming a mother without the formalities of marriage. She would thus resign her only good, and take to herself, in its stead, contempt on every hand. Besides, she might say, "What assurance have I of the tenderness of the father for his child, if he treats the feelings of the mother with so little consideration?" . . . I assure you, my dear Lord Byron, I speak earnestly, and sincerely. It is not that I wish to make out a case for Clare; my *interest*, as you must be aware, is entirely on the opposite side. Nor have I in any manner influenced her. I have esteemed it a duty to leave her to the impulse of her own feelings in a case where, if she has no feeling, she has no claim. But in truth, if she is to be brought to part with her child, she requires reassurance and tenderness. A tie so near the heart should not be rudely snapt. It was in this persuasion that I hoped (I had a thousand other reasons for wishing to see you) that you would have accepted our invitation to the Pliniana. Clare's pain would then have been mitigated by the prospect of seeing her child with you, and she would have been reassured of the fears which your letter has just confirmed, by the idea of a repetition of the visit. Your conduct must at present wear the aspect of great cruelty, however you justify it to yourself. Surely, it is better if we err, to err on the side of kindness, than of rigour. You can stop when you please; and you are not so infirm of purpose that soothing words, and gentle conduct need betray you in essential matters further than you mean to go.

I am a third person in this painful controversy, who, in the invidious office of mediator, can have no interest, but in the interests of those concerned. I am now deprived of the power to act; but I would willingly persuade. . . .

Even this letter did not entirely remove Byron's distrust and irritation. Perhaps it would have done so but for the wild letters that Claire was now writing him. Very likely these letters accused Byron of violating his promise at Diodati to leave the child in her possession until it was seven years old. Nevertheless Claire decided to accept Byron's terms. On April 30 Shelley wrote to Byron with a firmness that compelled respect:

> Allow me also to *repeat* my assertion that Clare's late conduct with respect to the child was wholly unconnected with, and uninfluenced by me. The correspondence from which these misinterpretations have arisen was undertaken on my part solely because you refused to correspond with Clare. My conduct in the affair has been simple, and intelligible. I am sorry that I misunderstood your letter; and I hope that on both sides there is here an end of misunderstandings. . . .
>
> Clare, as you may imagine, is dreadfully unhappy. As you have not written to her, it has been a kind of custom that she should see your letters; and I daresay you know that you have sometimes said things which I do not think you would have addressed to her. It could not in any way compromise you to be cautious in this respect, as, unless you write to her, I cannot well refuse to let her see your letters. I have not seen any of those which she has written to you; nor even have I often known when they were sent.

In the same letter Shelley informed Byron that he had been unable to take the Villa Pliniana and that his party would leave next day for Pisa. Claire was wretchedly disconsolate, and the use of some letters of introduction at Pisa might serve to divert her melancholy. Her melancholy, and perhaps also something of the final outcome, had been foreseen by Shelley, who was further alarmed by an unfavorable account of Byron's life in Venice that he received from a Venetian with whom he fell into conversation at the post office. He had urged Claire not to part with Allegra on Byron's terms. But Claire pinned her hopes on a future softening of Byron's attitude, and Allegra departed with Elise on April 28.

Shelley's state of health almost invariably reflected his emotional crises. Mary now wrote in her journal for April 22: "Shelley unwell; he reads the 'Paradiso;' writes to Albè." Other than this there is no indication in the reticent, impersonal journals of either Mary or Claire that the whole household was in a state of emotional strain.

They rode in the Corso, walked in the public gardens with the children, visited the cathedral, enjoyed the opera, played chess, wrote and received letters, wrote Italian exercises, and read Dante and *Clarissa Harlowe* in Italian and Wieland's *Aristippus* in a French translation.

The journey from Milan to Pisa occupied seven days, May 1–7. On May 4 they dined at Bologna and slept at a solitary inn high up in the Apennines, having passed the three previous nights at Piacenza, Parma, and Modena. Throughout the next day they traveled across chestnut-wooded ridges very different from the rugged Alps, and slept at the village of Barberino. On May 6 they began descending the valley of the Arno toward Pisa. That night they slept at La Scala, and next day they arrived at Pisa and put up at the Tre Donzelle. During their journey the sky had been regularly high and cloudless, in spite of constant winds. Claire, the most dejected member of the party, felt some hope that "the long strait road I see before me will take me to some place where I shall be happier."

Pisa did not at first seem to be such a place. Wherever they went, Shelley, Mary, and Claire were always sensitive to any contrast between the beauty of nature and art and the degradation of man. It had been so in Switzerland and when they crossed Savoy. It could hardly be less so in Italy, a country, or rather ten countries, that had experienced the enlightened tyranny of Napoleon only to be returned by the Congress of Vienna to the reactionary domination of Austria, the Pope, and some five or six hereditary Habsburgs and Bourbons to whom the French Revolution was an unforgettable nightmare.

In Milan Shelley had already begun to feel this contrast. "The people here," he had written to Peacock, "though inoffensive enough, seem both in body and soul a miserable race. The men are hardly men; they look like a tribe of stupid and shrivelled slaves, and I do not think that I have seen a gleam of intelligence in the countenance of man since I passed the Alps." Though they admired the cathedral and the leaning tower of Pisa, they were far more impressed by a general air of poverty and wretchedness in the town. The streets were cleaned by a numerous gang of convicts, clad in red and chained together two-and-two. "All the day long one hears the slow clanking of their chains, and the rumbling of the cart they drag as if they were so many Beasts of Burden and if one goes to the window one is sure to see their yellow faces and emaciated forms."

After a few days' pause at Pisa, Shelley's party arrived at Leghorn

(Livorno) on May 9, where they put up for a few days at the Aquila Nera and then took apartments.

For nearly two months Shelley's party had been almost constantly on the move, meeting no one they knew, forming no new acquaintances except a very few which were immediately severed. Apparently they had received only one English letter, from Peacock. At Leghorn, though they did not originally intend it, they settled down for a month. Leghorn was a noisy trading city, a seaport containing a number of English business houses. The Shelleys were none too delighted with this "Wapping of Italy." Mary's journal on the day of their arrival labeled it "a stupid town," and Shelley described it to Peacock as "the most unattractive of cities."

Here the Shelleys were to present a letter of introduction from Godwin to Mrs. John Gisborne, better known as Maria Gisborne. Long ago in London Mrs. Gisborne, then Mrs. Reveley, a beautiful young matron of unusual musical and artistic abilities, had been an admiring friend of both Godwin and Mary Wollstonecraft. When Mary Wollstonecraft died after childbirth and left a helpless, bookish widower in charge of the infant Fanny Imlay and the newly-born Mary Godwin, Mrs. Reveley had taken Mary into her own home. After her husband's death two years later she declined Godwin's almost immediate proposal of marriage. On the first evening that the Shelleys spent in Leghorn she called with her second husband on the young woman to whom she had been practically a godmother twenty years before. "She is reserved," Mary wrote in her journal that night (May 9), "yet with easy manners." The next day they had a long talk about Mary's parents, and thereafter the Shelleys and Gisbornes were constantly calling upon each other or taking long walks together. It was principally on her account that the Shelleys remained over a month in Leghorn.

Mrs. Gisborne, a woman of forty-eight, was not handsome, but her features were good; there was a pleasant expression about her mouth and eyes that marked her immediately as sensitive and intelligent. She had the calm, slightly reserved manner that can sympathize with enthusiasm without catching fire from it, and when she spoke, which was not too often, she dropped her words, as Leigh Hunt said, "deliciously."

Mr. Gisborne was an unsuccessful merchant who had retired on the remainder of his property and had devoted himself for some years mainly to his books and the education of his stepson. He was a prosy, thin-lipped, placid man with a receding forehead and a most prodigious nose, which Shelley could never forget nor completely forgive. Both the Shelleys thought him quite a bore at first, but he improved upon further acquaintance.

Mrs. Gisborne's son by her first marriage, Henry Reveley, was a young man of about thirty, "an excellent fellow," as Shelley thought, "but not very communicative." Henry was an engineer who had received the best training Italy could offer. In 1818 he was busily at work on the construction of a steamboat that he hoped would revolutionize maritime traffic in the Mediterranean. His room was a jumble of nautical instruments, books on mathematics, engine models, screws, wheels, and blocks. On May 28 the Shelleys went with him and the Gisbornes to see his engine. Henry was full of high hopes, and Shelley, listening, lived again in his old dream of science regenerating the world.

As usual, the Shelleys spent much of their time in reading. Shelley read the *Hippolytus* of Euripides, and the *Electra, Philoctetes*, and *Ajax* of Sophocles, Ariosto's sixth canto with Mary, and Manso's life of Tasso. Mary was reading even more extensively, in Italian, French, and Latin. Nevertheless she found time to copy, late in May, the manuscript history of Beatrice Cenci which was to furnish the materials a year later for Shelley's tragedy of *The Cenci*.

Summer was now approaching, when all who could left the hot lowland cities and sought a retreat in the mountains. The Shelleys did not find Leghorn uncomfortably hot, but they did object to its noise and bustle. On June 11 Shelley's party settled themselves for the summer at Bagni di Lucca, in the Apennines, about sixty miles north of Leghorn.

The nine weeks during which they remained at Bagni di Lucca were among the most comfortable weeks spent in Italy. They had a small house (Casa Bertini), clean, freshly painted and furnished, with a small garden at the end of which was a thick laurel grove. After the grating noise of Leghorn it was soothing to hear only the sound of the river rushing through its valley below their little villa. The hills were picturesque and were covered with chestnut woods through which numerous paths offered opportunities for long quiet walks.

As yet the Baths were not crowded. The Casino, which usually offered every kind of amusement, particularly dancing, was still closed. Their only caller at first was a Signor Chiappa, probably their landlord. He was dull enough, but he was at least useful in providing them with servants — a cleaning-woman at one paul a day, and a cook and general factotum named Paolo Foggi, at three pauls daily. Paolo was a great treasure. He cooked acceptably and managed all the little details of domestic economy so neatly and cleanly, without bothersome consultations, that he was able to cheat his employers from the first in comparative security. They knew his dishonesty, but ignored it, not realizing what a bitter price it was to cost them in the end.

All that was needed was the sympathetic company of the Gisbornes, whom they immediately tried to induce to join them. But the Gisbornes were now involved in exasperating complications of a legal or financial nature over Henry's steam engine and felt compelled to stay in Leghorn, where they amused themselves with a kaleidoscope built by Henry according to a description Shelley had received from Hogg.

Throughout June, Shelley and Mary settled into their beloved quiet routine of reading and walking. Signor Chiappa appears to have troubled them only once or twice with his tiresome calls, and they saw no one else. Shelley continued to read mainly in the Greek classics, Xenophon's *Memorabilia*, Aristophanes' *Clouds*, *Plutus*, and *Lysistrata*, and Barthélemy's *Anacharsis*. He continued reading Ariosto with Mary. He also read aloud part of Spenser's *Shepherd's Calendar* and Hume's *History of England*. Mary read mainly Ariosto and the Latin classics, Gibbon, and Ben Jonson's *Every Man in His Humour* and *Volpone*.

Late June and early July brought to the Baths a considerable number of new people, particularly English people. "We see none but English," Mary complained to Mrs. Gisborne. Yet Shelley's letter to the Gisbornes a week or two later shows how little the increase of population and social activity at the Baths impinged upon their chosen manner of living:

We have spent a month here already in our accustomed solitude, (with the exception of one night at the Casino) and the choice society of all ages, which I took care to pack up in a large trunk before we left England, have revisited us here. I am employed just now, having little better to do, in translating into my fainting and inefficient periods the divine eloquence of Plato's Symposium; only as an exercise or perhaps to give Mary some idea of the manners and feelings of the Athenians — so different on many subjects from that of any other community that ever existed. . . .

I take great delight in watching the changes of the atmosphere

here, and the growth of the thunder showers with which the moon is often over shadowed, and which break and fade away towards evening into flocks of delicate clouds. Our fire flies are fading away fast; but there is the planet Jupiter, who rises majestically over the rift in the forest-covered mountains to the south, and the pale summer lightning which is spread out every night, at intervals, over the sky. No doubt Providence has contrived these things, that, when the fire flies go out, the low-flying owl may see her way home.

Through July and the middle of August the same calm, happy serenity continued. Shelley read *Anacharsis*, Aristophanes, Herodotus, *The Persians* of Æschylus, Theocritus, Virgil's *Georgics*, Hume, *The Maid's Tragedy*, *Philaster*, *Wife for a Month*, *Richard III*, *Henry VIII*, and Eustace's *Travels*. In the evening he frequently read aloud from Hume or Shakespeare. The days succeeded one another with very few distinguishing incidents. They still knew practically none of the people who thronged the Baths. Three times (July 5, 12, and August 2) they visited the Casino, and once (July 27) they attended a *festa di ballo* in the evening. They took up horseback riding, a favorite amusement with the other summer residents, and Shelley rode over to see the adjacent city of Lucca. Claire fell off her horse twice, and injured her knee, but was able to ride with Shelley on their two visits to Lucca, July 17 and 18.

All this was in the mornings and evenings. As for midday, Shelley wrote:

In the middle of the day, I bathe in a pool or fountain, formed in the middle of the forests by a torrent. It is surrounded on all sides by precipitous rocks, and the waterfall of the stream which forms it falls into it on one side with perpetual dashing. Close to it, on the top of the rocks, are alders, and above the great chestnut trees, whose long and pointed leaves pierce the deep blue sky in strong relief. The water of this pool, which, to venture an unrhythmical paraphrase, is "sixteen feet long and ten feet wide," is as transparent as the air, so that the stones and sand at the bottom seem, as it were, trembling in the light of noonday. It is exceedingly cold also. My custom [is] to undress, and sit on the rocks, reading Herodotus, until the perspiration has subsided, and then to leap from the edge of the rock into this fountain — a practice in the hot weather excessively refreshing. This torrent is composed, as it were, of a succession of pools and waterfalls, up which I sometimes amuse myself by climbing when I bathe, and receiving the spray over all my body, whilst I clamber up the moist crags with difficulty.

Shelley was full of ideas for writing. His plan of a drama on Tasso's madness was still in mind. Very likely he was already thinking of *Prometheus Unbound* and *The Cenci* and of a tragedy based on the Book of Job. As yet, however, he was doing little writing. *Rosalind and Helen* was finished. Mary's journal shows that she was copying it on August 14 and 16, but she laid it aside until December 18.

Shelley's only complete literary production at Bagni di Lucca was his translation of Plato's *Symposium*. From the very beginning of this dialogue Mary must have wondered at the instinct that led Shelley to so sympathetic a subject. The praise of the higher or Uranian love as the chief inspirer to an excellent life, the analysis of love as a mystic, universal force subsisting in all natures both animate and inanimate, were a prophecy of Shelley's own triumphant description of a similar "Light whose smile kindles the universe." Aristophanes' fable of man's double, androgynous nature, cleft asunder by the gods and seeking always to reunite "in the pursuit of integrity and union . . . which we call love," might have reminded Mary of *Alastor*. She could easily recognize the Shelleyan quality of Agathon's tribute to love as the power that "divests us of all alienation from each other and fills our vacant hearts with overflowing sympathy." In the end, when Diotima expounded to Socrates the highest state of love, the words might almost have been Shelley's own:

> It is eternal, unproduced, indestructible; neither subject to increase nor decay: not, like other things, partly beautiful and partly deformed; not at one time beautiful and at another time not; not beautiful in relation to one thing and deformed in relation to another; not here beautiful and there deformed; not beautiful in the estimation of one person and deformed in that of another; nor can this supreme beauty be figured to the imagination like a beautiful face, or beautiful hands, or any portion of the body, nor like any discourse, nor any science. Nor does it subsist in any other that lives or is, either in earth, or in heaven, or in any other place; but it is eternally uniform and consistent, and monoeidic with itself. All other things are beautiful through a participation of it, with this condition, that although they are

subject to production and decay, it never becomes more or less, or endures any change.

Shelley's own definition of love, evolved under the influence of this reading, is stated in a fragment written almost immediately afterwards:

. . . that profound and complicated sentiment, which we call love, which is rather the universal thirst for a communion not merely of the senses, but of our whole nature, intellectual, imaginative and sensitive; and which, when individualised, becomes an imperious necessity, only to be satisfied by the complete or partial, actual or supposed, fulfilment of its claims.

Because the *Symposium* contains an episode in which Alcibiades speaks of his homosexual love-making to Socrates, Shelley had no present intention of publishing his translation. It was one of the most striking of several circumstances in which the ancient and modern views of love differed, and it interested Shelley in this respect very much as he was interested in the subject of incest. He immediately wrote an essay, "A Discourse on the Manners of the Ancients Relative to the Subject of Love," designed to soften or remove the antipathies which he felt would otherwise prevent a fair appreciation of the *Symposium* on account of its homosexual episode. This essay, though apparently complete, and recently printed (1931) in a limited private edition, appears in Shelley's collected works only as a brief fragment. Its main content, Shelley's finely tactful and sensitive discussion of homosexual love among the ancients, was considered unpublishable, and the essay is generally known only for the opening paragraphs, which contain the best expressions of Shelley's admiration for ancient Greece.

The period from the birth of Pericles to the death of Aristotle (490–322 B.C.) Shelley called "the most memorable in the history of the world" — an influence and inspiration to all posterity. Subsequent ages had improved upon it in only two important particulars, the abolition of slavery and a more elevated conception of love between the sexes. For these improvements, as in his later "Defence of Poetry," he gave the credit to Christianity and chivalry. Thus, while he was reading everything he could find that might conduce toward a fuller knowledge of Greek life, he was also making unexpected concessions to what he considered its destroyer. The explanation lies partly in the fact that the finest Greek ideals, as expressed by Plato, were occupying his mind at the same time that he was reading the best products of Christianity and chivalry in Italian literature — Dante, Petrarch, Tasso, and Ariosto. He could not escape their influence toward a greater sympathy and tolerance. Toward institutional Christianity his attitude continued unchanged, but he was now far better qualified to see the nobility of certain Christian ideals.

Letters from Godwin, Peacock, and the Hunts, reinforced probably by Cobbett's *Political Register,* Hunt's *Examiner,* and some of the reviews, now brought the Shelleys up to date on recent political events in England. An election had just been called, and the government, out of ten members to be elected for London, Westminster, and Southwark, had failed to return a single supporter. This was cheering news for Shelley, convinced as he was that the policies of the Castlereagh administration were hurrying England toward a catastrophe. The *Quarterly,* he learned, was proclaiming that no country was ever in a more combustible state than England at that moment; the *Courier* was calling loudly for a censorship of the weekly press. In the recent Westmorland election Brougham had been defeated by the Tories, aided by Wordsworth and Southey. Wordsworth had even published two addresses *To the Freeholders of Westmoreland* arguing (in Peacock's interpretation) that Brougham's lack of wealth would make him an inferior representative and that the Commons should be chosen by the Peers — a pretty example, Peacock thought, of the moral degradation of which "self-sellers" were capable.

All this provoked Shelley's deep interest and indignation. "I wish that I had health or spirits that would enable me to enter into public affairs," he wrote Godwin. "If the Ministers do not find some means, totally inconceivable to me, of plunging the nation in war, do you imagine that they can subsist?" To Peacock, apropos of the Westmorland election, he burst out: "I wish you had sent me some of the overflowing villainy of those apostates. What a beastly and pitiful wretch that Wordsworth! That such a man should be such a poet! I can compare him with no one but Simonides, that flatterer of the Sicilian tyrants, and at the same time the most natural and tender of lyric poets."

Peacock's picture of a warm, sunny summer in Buckinghamshire made Shelley homesick for the old cool, shady strolls through the woods near Marlow and solitary moonlit evenings on the river. "What pleasure it would have given me," he answered, "if the wings of imagination could have divided the space which divides us, and I could have been of your party. I have seen nothing so beautiful as

Virginia Water — in its kind. And my thoughts forever cling to Windsor Forest, and the copses of Marlow. . . ."

Godwin wrote in a mood that might well have made Shelley feel more warmly even toward such an iceberg as his father-in-law. He was cheerfully finishing his *Reply to Malthus,* which Shelley believed would restore to society some of the hopes Malthus had almost ruined. He no longer nagged for money, though fully confident that "a tempest was brewing" for him "in the distance." "Write as to your equal," he urged with a complacence not unnatural toward a professed disciple, "and, if that word is not discordant to your feelings, your friend. It would be strange indeed if we could not find topics of communication that may be gratifying to both. Let each of us dwell on those qualities in the other which may contribute most to the increase of mutual kindness." Shelley's reply ignored this rather gnarled olive branch and maintained the same courteous, controlled, half-impersonal tone that he reserved for correspondents of antipathetic personality.

Both Godwin and Peacock sent the good news that Mary's *Frankenstein* was now receiving favorable notice. Even the most unfavorable review, the *Quarterly's,* granted the book considerable merit. This was much, considering that the reviewer believed Shelley to be the author and took this occasion to condemn the way in which he usually employed his talents.

A much clearer warning of what Shelley was to expect from the *Quarterly* appeared in its review of Leigh Hunt's *Foliage,* which appeared in the same number. A footnote referred to the production of one of Leigh Hunt's friends then before the reviewer, who doubted whether it "would be morally right" to "lend notoriety" to it by a review. He then gave an unfavorable picture of the author, still not mentioning Shelley's name, as the writer (John Taylor Coleridge) had known him at Eton. Reviewing the same book, the *British Critic* for July also digressed briefly to characterize Mr. Percy Bysshe Shelley as a subject too vile, too dangerous to the public morals, to be discussed. Shelley now knew what to expect when the conservative reviewers got to *The Revolt of Islam.* "Their notice of me," he said of the *Quarterly,* "and their exposure of the true motives for not noticing my book, shews how well understood an hostility must subsist between me and them."

Shelley still thought his health and spirits not quite equal to the task of original writing, though it is a little difficult to see why. Both

276

he and Mary had reported his health as wonderfully improved since entering Italy. He had been ill once at Milan under the strain of Claire's difficulties over Allegra, and again for one day, the day after arriving at Bagni di Lucca. Otherwise he seemed to be enjoying and profiting by the kind of life he loved best. Again it was Claire's troubles that set events in motion toward a calamity.

Claire was uneasy about Allegra. There seems to have been no special reason for this other than a mother's desire to see her child. Byron was already quite fond of the curly-haired, blue-eyed, high-spirited child of fifteen months, to whom he had referred so bluntly as "my bastard." He was proud of the way in which she accepted the admiration of Venetians, from the Governor's wife down, wherever she was shown. Obviously she was being spoiled by too much attention, and still more obviously Byron's disorderly household of caged wild animals and uncaged mistresses was hardly a fit place for her. Byron realized this himself and placed her in the home of his friends, Mr. and Mrs. R. B. Hoppner.

Mr. Hoppner was the British consul at Naples, a son of the well-known portrait painter, himself an amateur artist. Mrs. Hoppner, a Swiss, had a young child of her own and felt keenly the unfitness of Allegra's surroundings in Byron's household.

Claire received letters from Elise on August 14 and 16. Either Allegra had some soon-forgotten childish ailment, or else her situation outside of Byron's household overcame Claire with a desire to visit her. Whichever it was, Claire evidently made a scene. The same entry in Mary's journal that chronicles Elise's second letter records also the common result of unusual emotional strain: "Shelley is not well." Claire was determined to visit her child surreptitiously. Shelley was sure such a plan would fail and would irritate Byron into reprisals, but there was no arguing with Claire. On the next day, August 17, Shelley and Claire departed for Venice, accompanied as far as Florence by Paolo. En route Shelley seems to have persuaded her not to attempt a secret visit, but to wait in some near-by city while he entered Venice and tried to win Byron's permission for the meeting.

Mary remained at Bagni di Lucca with the two children and the servants. She had probably opposed the wild journey and given signs of one of her occasional characteristic fits of despondency. En route Shelley seized the first opportunity to improve her spirits: "Well my dearest Mary, are you very lonely? Tell me truth, my sweetest, do you ever cry? I shall hear from you once at Venice and once on my return here [Florence]. If you love me you will keep up your spirits

— and at all events tell me truth about it; for I assure you I am not of a disposition to be flattered by your sorrow, though I should be by your cheerfulness. . . ."

Before this letter reached Mary (August 23) she had already been disturbed by the illness of little Clara (August 21) and by her own illness the next two days. On the day of Shelley's departure she had written to urge the Gisbornes, once more, to visit the Baths. This time they accepted the invitation, arriving on August 25. They had been present only three days, however, when a letter was received from Shelley that completely altered all previous plans and required Mary's immediate departure with her household.

Chapter XVII

SHELLEY AND CLAIRE reached Florence on August 20 after a slow and somewhat rough and uncomfortable journey. Since the Congress of Vienna, Venice was again Austrian territory; hence it was necessary to obtain a passport from the Austrian ambassador at Florence. This occasioned a delay of four hours or more, during which arrangements were made for continuing the journey to Padua. From Florence to Padua there were no particular episodes. Partly because the inns were bad, Claire again changed her plans and determined to accompany Shelley all the way into Venice.

From Padua to Venice the journey was completed by gondola, in nine hours of luxurious travel. These gondolas, upholstered, finely carpeted, and well appointed throughout, won Shelley's admiration as "the most beautiful and convenient boats in the world." The gondolier, not knowing that his passengers had any particular interest in Lord Byron, of his own initiative began talking about the wild young English milord whom he claimed to have carried in his gondola. Shelley and Claire learned that Byron had a *nome stravagante* and had recently brought over from England two daughters, one of them almost as old as the gondolier himself. They had no sooner reached their inn in Venice than the waiter also began gossiping about Byron.

Without waiting to see any of the sights of Venice, Shelley and Claire took a gondola immediately after breakfast and visited Mr. and Mrs. Hoppner, with whom Elise and Allegra were now domiciled. They were by no means sure of a cordial reception, for they came as unannounced strangers to friends of Byron who might be expected to be biased by his opinion of Claire. But they were received with a politeness that soon turned to active friendliness. Elise and Allegra were sent for immediately, and the Hoppners entered quite sympathetically into a discussion of the best way of approaching Byron. They were convinced that Claire's arrival, if known, would result in his immediate departure from Venice. It was therefore decided that Shelley should see Byron alone and that Claire's presence should be concealed.

Byron received Shelley with real cordiality on his own account and with unexpected good humor and reasonableness on Claire's. Sup-

posing Claire and Mary to be then at Padua, he offered to allow
Allegra to go there for a week. "In fact," he concluded, "after all, I
have no right over the child. If Claire likes to take it, let her take it.
I do not say what most people would in that situation, that I will
refuse to provide for it, or abandon it, if she does this; but she must
surely be aware herself how very imprudent such a measure would
be!" Byron then proposed a horseback ride along the sands of the
Lido.

Byron's gondola bore them through the canals and across the lagoon to the long sandy island known as the Lido, where horses were
waiting for them. It was a lonely spot, bare except for wrecks, a
dwarfish tree or two, and the drying nets of a solitary fisherman.
Here, over a thin strip of beach made firm and level by the tide,
Byron and Shelley rode and talked until nearly sundown. It was their
first meeting since the old familiar association at Geneva two years
before, and there was much to tell. Byron was full of his wounded
feelings and of the fourth canto of *Childe Harold's Pilgrimage*, which
he was then writing. Shelley told the story of his wrongs at the hands
of the Lord Chancellor. Byron exclaimed warmly that had he been
in England at the time he would have moved heaven and earth to
prevent such an unjust decision.

There were lighter memories of the old days at Geneva to be renewed. Byron had considerable fun, perhaps a little to Shelley's
embarrassment, quizzing Leigh Hunt's *Foliage*. Both poets felt that
it was a fine, genial reunion. As they recrossed the lagoon to Venice
in the sunset the Euganean hills in the distance were islands in a sea
of fire, and the domes and turrets of the city rose from the floor of the
ocean as if by some enchantment.

The talk, which had turned to raillery, now grew serious. Old arguments that had beguiled long summer evenings at Villa Diodati came
up again and found both disputants still standing on familiar ground.
Shelley argued, as always, against despondency and pride, the more
earnestly because he thought they prevented Byron's great genius
from exercising its full power. No one really knew, he maintained,
the actual strength of the chains supposed to bind the human spirit;
there was a vast, unknown power in the human will to suffer and to
conquer; evil existed mainly because the human will consented to it.

Such conversation continued at Byron's palace long into the night.
Byron, now "changed into the liveliest and happiest looking man I
ever met," was so different from what everything had led Shelley to

anticipate that he may have lingered longer than suited Claire, waiting impatiently since three o'clock in the afternoon. His letter describing the meeting is dated "five o'clock in the morn" of the next day, August 24.

At some time during the evening Byron had placed at Shelley's disposal I Capuccini, his villa at Este, and Shelley had accepted it. Since Byron supposed Claire and Mary to be near by at Padua it was necessary to get them both to Este as soon as possible. Not knowing that little Clara had been ill since his departure, Shelley sent careful instructions to Mary for proceeding instantly to Este. "I have been obliged to decide on all these things without you," he explained, "— I have done for the best and, my own beloved Mary, you must soon come and scold me if I have done wrong, and kiss me if I have done right — for, I am sure, I do not know which — and it is only the event that can show."

Mary's receipt of this letter on August 28 occasioned an immediate consultation with the Gisbornes. The next day Mary's journal laconically records: "Bustle," and the next (August 30, Mary's birthday): "Packing." Mrs. Gisborne accompanied Mary and the children to Lucca, whence they proceeded under Paolo's care to Este, arriving on Saturday, September 5. The weather had been hot, and there had been various delays, including one whole day at Florence waiting for passports.

Clara's illness, which was merely a teething ailment at Bagni di Lucca, was converted by the heat and fatigue of the journey into a serious attack of dysentery. Shortly after the arrival at Este her condition was quite alarming. The local physician seemed to Mary to be a stupid fellow, but after a more competent doctor was engaged to come from Padua, Clara's condition, though still serious, seemed to be somewhat improved. When Mary arrived, Shelley was also quite unwell, "from taking poison in Italian cakes," and Claire was finding it necessary to visit a physician in Padua. Nevertheless, both Shelley and Mary set immediately to work, the former on the first act of *Prometheus Unbound,* the latter on a translation of Monti's *A Cajo Graccho,* which was apparently abandoned and is now lost.

I Capuccini, as their dwelling was called from the Capuchin convent that had formerly stood on its site, was a comfortable-looking villa crowning a low hill. A vine-trellised walk led to a summer house which Shelley converted into a study. Across a sunken road, on a neighboring hill stood the ruined ancient castle of Este; to the west, across the plains of Lombardy, rose the Apennines; to the east was unbroken distance.

Shelley was soon writing steadily on the first act of *Prometheus Unbound* and probably on "Julian and Maddalo." The regular program of reading continued. Mary had begun or planned to begin her projected drama on Charles I and a translation of Alfieri's *Myrrha*. A few letters arrived from England. Either from letters or travelers' gossip they heard that Sir Timothy Shelley was ill and likely to die. But the rumor was false, and Shelley was spared the long journey home, which he dreaded.

Leigh Hunt sent as a birthday present a life-size portrait of his own head, done in chalk by young Thornton's drawing-master. In his old sympathetic, easy way he chatted with occasional touches of humor about personal matters — their friends in England, his literary plans and Shelley's, and the Italian literature that Shelley was reading or ought to read. Describing the veiled attack on Shelley that had appeared in the *Quarterly's* review of *Frankenstein*, he offered a more than sufficient antidote:

> I can tell him that his name gets more known and respected every day, in *spite* of the *Quarterly Reviewers*, who have attacked him, and me, and Hazlitt (though not Shelley by name), in their old false, furious, and recoiling way. The candid part of their friends are, I believe, really ashamed of them, — one or two I know, are.

By September 22 little Clara seemed well enough for Shelley to carry out his long-deferred return to Venice. Leaving Claire to look after William and Allegra (who was being allowed by Byron to visit her mother), Shelley and Mary set out for Venice with Clara. On the way the child grew rapidly worse. As her weakness increased and convulsive motions set in about the mouth and eyes, Shelley and Mary made all possible haste toward Venice in order to see a physician. They reached Fusina, across the lagoon from Venice, and the soldiers on duty demanded their passports. A desperate, frenzied search revealed that the passports had been forgotten. How Shelley, with his uncertain Italian, overcame the objections of the soldiers and induced them to violate regulations probably neither he nor Mary ever clearly remembered. Mary simply recorded that "they could not resist Shelley's impetuosity at such a moment."

As they crossed the lagoon Clara's condition became steadily worse. Mary hastened with the child to the inn where Shelley had reserved quarters, while Shelley rushed off from the dock to find Dr. Aglietti. When he returned, Mary was waiting for him in the inn hall in a state of dreadful distress. Another doctor was already with Clara, but the case was hopeless. In an hour the child was dead. The brief, restrained account of this tragedy which Shelley sent next day (September 25) to Claire concludes very characteristically: "All this is miserable enough — is it not? but must be borne [Here a line is erased in the original manuscript.] — And above all, my dear girl, take care of yourself."

The Hoppners came instantly and took Shelley and Mary to their home. In Mary's state of complete despair Shelley was glad to accept so kindly an offer from comparative strangers.

For five days (September 24–9) the Hoppners, with some assistance from Byron, did what they could to keep their guests from dwelling on the recent tragedy. Visits to the Lido, to Byron's palace, the Bridge of Sighs, the Doge's Palace, the library, and the shops, and Shelley's reading aloud the fourth canto of *Childe Harold* are duly noted in Mary's journal as if nothing else had happened. For the day of Clara's death (September 24) she had written: "This is the Journal of misfortunes. . . . We go to Venice with my poor Clara, who dies the moment we get there. Mr. Hoppner comes, and takes us away from the inn to his house." No more than this at the time of her sorrow, and nothing afterwards.

Godwin wrote in due time (October 27) to condole somewhat aloofly on "the first severe trial of your constancy and the firmness of your temper," and to remind Mary that "we seldom indulge long in depression and mourning, except when we think secretly that there is something very refined in it." On the surface both Shelley and Mary were stoically silent. But beneath the surface was a deep feeling of misery that was to have a far more important effect upon the events of the next few months than the trivial details that Mary so mechanically set down in her journal or the sightseeing that Shelley recorded so calmly in his letters to Peacock.

They returned to Este on September 29 and remained there for twelve days, occupied as usual. Mary had brought from Venice the manuscripts of Byron's *Mazeppa* and "Ode to Venice," which she copied for him. She read Livy and Virgil, Shakespeare, and the life and tragedies of Alfieri. Shelley read Shakespeare's *Cymbeline* and *The Winter's Tale* aloud. Reading by himself Malthus's *Essay on*

Population, he felt constrained, in spite of his abhorrence of the popular interpretation, to pronounce Malthus "a very clever man."

Shelley was now writing again. "Lines Written among the Euganean Hills" and "Julian and Maddalo," as well as the first act of *Prometheus Unbound,* were all written at Este in 1818. If we include "Julian and Maddalo," which cannot be exactly dated, Shelley completed seven poems in 1818 after Clara Shelley's death, and every single one of them is tinged with the same melancholy and despondence.

"Lines Written among the Euganean Hills" represents a faintly successful struggle against utter despair. There must be green isles in the deep wide sea of Misery, it argues, or humanity would not continue to struggle. Shelley's present despair seems to proceed from the thought of a dead body by a "northern sea," which he speaks of as "unburied" and unlamented. This must be the body of Clara, which was buried on the Lido, by the northern Adriatic. But the only death that Shelley commonly spoke of as "unlamented" was his own; hence the lines may suggest Shelley's feeling that he himself died at the same time with Clara. "Unburied," as will later be made apparent, suggests that Mary was in a state of mind which kept Clara's grave constantly open.

From this despair, the poet seeks "flowering islands" in the beauties of sunrise over the plains of Lombardy, in a view of Padua under the noontide sun, and of. the gradually waning afternoon and evening as seen from his point of vantage among the hills. Both Venice and Padua are somewhat somberly represented as trampled by tyranny, but Shelley thought that the tyranny would be eventually overthrown — and this, together with the beauty of the day, constituted "green isles" that enabled him to close with a faintly hopeful feeling that

Other flowering isles must be
In the sea of life and agony.

"Julian and Maddalo" would seem to have been begun at Este during the period (September 5–22) when Clara's health was improving. The first third of the poem gives an agreeable and unimpassioned account of the reunion of Byron and Shelley — their ride along the Lido, their return across the lagoons, and their conversation. Then Byron (Maddalo), to illustrate one of his arguments, proposes to visit a Maniac in whose story he is sure Shelley (Julian) will be interested. From this point, the Maniac dominates the poem, and its former tone and plan are never resumed. His story is told brokenly and obscurely in a series of highly impassioned outbursts which are ostensibly the ravings of a lover whose lady has reviled and deserted him.

To think, as practically all critics have thought for over a century, that "Julian and Maddalo" is a rambling poem that unconsciously lost its way is to ignore the overwhelming evidence of the poem itself, as well as the external evidence. Shelley obviously began to write a quiet poetic dialogue, which suddenly converted itself into the most impassioned poem he had yet written. But he was aware of the change and accepted it, as shown by his taking from Virgil as a motto for the whole poem a passage that applies only to the story of the Maniac. The only conceivable reason for this conversion was the death of Clara while the poem was being written, and the consequent effect on Shelley's private life.

When both Mary and Shelley were desolated by Clara's death, Mary withdrew into such a bitter closed atmosphere of self-pity and willful despair that her father remonstrated strongly. Twenty years later, in commenting on the series of despondent poems which includes "Julian and Maddalo" Mary called them "morbid, but too natural bursts of discontent and sadness" which Shelley hid from her. (This concealment is avowed in "Julian and Maddalo" and is borne out by the fact that Mary's contemporary journal shows no knowledge of these poems.) "One looks back," Mary added, "with unspeakable regret and gnawing remorse to such periods." Shortly after Shelley's death she expressed this remorse more plainly in a poem called "The Choice," addressed to Shelley and referring to some of his poems as telling of his despair, his "unrequitted love," and of

> cold neglect, averted eyes,
> That blindly crushed the soul's fond sacrifice.

For this she felt "fierce remorse." Her former aversion, she explained, "was not anger," but an "impenetrable shell" in which her heart was enclosed, even while it remained all Shelley's own.

That a feeling of intense strain existed between Shelley and Mary in the autumn of 1818 is thus clear from Mary's testimony alone, even though there is no evidence of it in any strictly contemporary record except the poems whose real nature is now to be explained. Shelley and Mary both suffered an emotional crisis at the time these poems were written. The cause was the death of Clara and its after effects; no other cause is possible. To assume a cause in a supposed guilty affair between Shelley and Claire is to assume something for which there is no support except conjecture, to ignore the known effects of Clara's death, and to make Mary Shelley's remorse and self-accusation absurd. If Mary knew of such an affair she could not have felt "fierce remorse" for resenting it, and if she did not know, she could not have resented it at all.

Shelley's letters furnish several clear hints that the Maniac's story is autobiographical. A year later he expected it to be published anonymously with some "accompanying poems" written at about the same time. He then referred to the group as "all my saddest poems raked up into one heap." In other letters he referred once to the poem as being based upon a "dreadful reality" and once to the Maniac as a real person. The poem was not published during Shelley's life, and when it was published later in *Posthumous Poems* by Mary Shelley the most suggestive of the "accompanying poems," which might have made its meaning clear, was omitted, and the others were carefully spaced so that they would not be read as a related group.

It is highly significant in this respect that "Julian and Maddalo" and *Epipsychidion* are the only longer poems for which Mary did not later offer explanatory notes. On both these poems she kept silent because no explanations could be offered without making revelations that she was incapable of offering except in safely general terms.

Twice before, in autobiographical passages in *The Revolt of Islam* and *Rosalind and Helen,* Shelley had spoken of himself as passing through a period of madness. In "Julian and Maddalo" he presents himself in the very frenzy of this state, with the probable feeling as he wrote that the madness might be partly real. The Maniac is described by Maddalo (Byron) as the mental wreck of a person once like Julian (Shelley). He had come from France to Venice accompanied by a lady whom he loved, and by whom he was spurned and deserted. It was her love that had first awakened his, but her love had turned to scorn and insult; she had rejected his embraces with physical loathing, and had left him. So far the Maniac reveals an autobiography remarkably true to Shelley's crisis with Mary except that there is no proof of the rejected embraces, and Mary had not actually left Shelley. But there are other poems written at the time — not to mention Mary's confession later — showing that Mary had deserted Shelley spiritually. These same poems, written within less than three months after "Julian and Maddalo," reveal Mary's complete physical coldness and apathy, without the scorn and insult imputed earlier.

Under the Lady's unwarranted scorn and insult the Maniac compares himself to a trodden worm which cannot die, but endures an apparent immortality of agony. He writhes under pain and injustice with an intense sensitiveness, but protests like Shelley that he has no idea of revenge (he is in fact still in love) and that he will not allow his agony to silence his opposition to tyranny.

He thinks of suicide, as Shelley almost certainly did at the time, and as he told Trelawny he did two months later at Naples. Exactly like Shelley, the Maniac is extremely sensitive, determined to forgive injury, determined to keep the secret of his grief even from the Lady, and self-dedicated from his youth to love and justice. He describes himself in the same tones later in his "Ode to the West Wind" and *Adonais,* as one

> Who loved and pitied all things, and could moan
> For woes which others hear not, and could see
> The absent with a glance of phantasy . . .
> *Me* — who am as a nerve o'er which do creep
> The else unfelt oppressions of this earth.

Addressing the absent Lady as though present, he exclaims:

> Do I not live
> That thou mayst have less bitter cause to grieve?
> I give thee tears for scorn and love for hate;
> And that thy lot may be less desolate
> Than his on whom thou tramplest, I refrain
> From that sweet sleep that medicines all pain.

There is another lady, however, "compassionate and wise" as the first is bitter and scornful, from whom the Maniac would receive sympathy if only she could know his condition. He addresses her as "my spirit's mate," but he is now only a "lost friend" and must never communicate his woe to her. The description is so like that of Mary in Shelley's earlier poems, and the concealment of his poem from her so exactly paralleled by Shelley's similar concealment from Mary, that this lady, too, must be Mary Shelley — or rather the Mary-that-was, before bitterness had abolished her former personality. The idea of two personalities for the same person was not a strange one to Shelley; he had employed it before and would do so again, and was in fact presenting himself as both Julian and the Maniac in this very poem.

The all too probable cause of the Lady's antagonism is that Mary must have blamed Shelley for Clara's death. He had left Mary with the children at Bagni di Lucca in order to make a long overland journey with Claire for reasons that turned out in the end to be quite frivolous. But the result was that Mary was summoned to take the same journey with her own children, one of whom was really ill and died shortly afterwards. The long, hard journey would then seem — and probably was — the cause of Clara's death, and Shelley's fondness for Claire was the cause of the journey. This fondness was an old cause of occasional friction and was to continue to be one.

Mary may not have expressed quite the same degree of loathing as the Maniac's Lady, and Shelley may not have expressed quite the Maniac's wild resentment — though earlier outbursts to his father and mother show that the Maniac's frenzy was quite possible for Shelley under severe mental and physical strain. Otherwise the picture is literal autobiography.

One of the most excruciating agonies for both Shelley and the Maniac was the necessity of dissembling a state of mind so genuinely volcanic. To both Shelley and the Maniac such repression was "a blot of falsehood" intolerable to a mind naturally devoted to truth, for truth was, as the Maniac asserted, the only road to peace. Neither could bring himself openly to declare the truth, and yet not to declare it was agony. Says the Maniac:

> O, not to dare
> To give a human voice to my despair
> But live and move, and wretched thing! smile on
> As if I never went aside to groan,
> And wear this mask of falsehood even to those
> Who are most dear. . . .

He partly reconciles himself by reflecting that to speak would produce more estrangement and mistrust from others. The "more" is significant and shows that at this instant the Maniac is even more Shelley than Maniac, for it is true of Shelley and not of the Maniac that he regarded himself as a victim of persecution and estrangement before the Lady's desertion.

The Maniac, however, could not wholly keep his resolve. He announced that he must yield to the pressure, and that he had done so:

> I must remove
> A veil from my pent mind. 'Tis torn aside!

And torn aside it was for the Maniac, and for Shelley's purposes of emotional relief, but not otherwise. Shelley's obvious desire and expectation that this emotionally necessary but highly dangerous discharge should serve only his private purposes is curiously similar to a mysterious passage in *Epipsychidion*, to be discussed later. Yet for a hundred and twenty years Shelley's readers remained as ignorant of the real meaning of the poem as he intended them to be.

From Este in late September to Naples in late December the tone of Shelley's poems moderated somewhat, but remained consistently despondent. These were the "accompanying poems" sent with "Julian and Maddalo" to Leigh Hunt in August 1819. They were never published in Shelley's lifetime, and never, even afterwards, as the group that Shelley intended. There may have been poems in this group that have been lost, but if not, then Shelley's only known poems that could have been the "accompanying poems" with "Julian and Maddalo" are "The Past," "On a Faded Violet," "Invocation to Misery," "Stanzas Written in Dejection, near Naples," and "Sonnet: Lift Not the Painted Veil." "The Question" and "Death" could also be included if written by August 1819 instead of in 1820, as dated later by Mary Shelley. These were also the only poems in addition to "Julian and Maddalo" to which Mary Shelley could have referred as having been concealed from her for fear of wounding her feelings.

Four of these poems were published by Mary Shelley, though not together, in *Posthumous Poems* (1824), but the most significant one, "Invocation to Misery," was omitted. "The Past" is a brief, clear protest against forgetting a love that has been happy, and a warning that such a course brings only added sorrow. The sonnet "Lift not the Painted Veil" warns the reader against seeking behind "the painted veil" called Life the deeper realities which may not be found there, and instances one sensitive soul who lifted the veil in vain, seeking things to love. "Stanzas Written in Dejection, near Naples," draws a frank open contrast between the beauty by which Shelley is surrounded and the despair in which he lives. He describes himself as without spiritual sympathy, hope, health, fame, power, peace, calm — or love.

"On a Faded Violet" is not a pretty sentimental poem about a withered flower, as it has always been considered, but is a deeply felt lament for a withered form, a deadened spirit, and a lifeless love:

> The colour from the flower is gone,
> Which like thy sweet eyes smiled on me;

> The odour from the flower is flown,
> Which breathed of thee and only thee!
>
> A withered, lifeless, vacant form,
> It lies on my abandoned breast,
> And mocks the heart which yet is warm
> With cold and silent rest.
>
> I weep — my tears revive it not.
> I sigh — it breathes no more on me;
> Its mute and uncomplaining lot
> Is such as mine should be.

The last poem of this group, "Invocation to Misery," which apparently Mary Shelley dared not print in *Posthumous Poems*, is the clearest of all. Misery is one with Mary Shelley; it is Mary who is being invoked to return to life and love:

> Come, be happy! sit near me,
> Shadow-vested misery!
> Coy, unwilling, silent bride,
> Mourning in thy robe of pride,
> Desolation deified! —
>
> Come, be happy! sit near me:
> Sad as I may seem to thee,
> I am happier far than thou,
> Lady, whose imperial brow
> Is endiademed with woe.

In succeeding stanzas it is suggested that though her lips are cold and her arms around his neck are chill and dead, she may yet love him with a love that is too frozen for utterance. This is pretty close to the explanation actually offered by Mary in "The Choice," previously quoted. Life, after all, is but an illusion of puppets, Shelley concludes, to be laughed at in the light of such experience as his and Misery's. In two stanzas just before the end Misery is invited by the poet to be his bride on the bridal bed of death. This passage is a very obvious paraphrase of lines 384–96 in "Julian and Maddalo," where the Maniac similarly addresses his Lady. It is one more key to the fact that the Maniac is literally Shelley and his Lady literally Mary.

Tom Medwin, who saw this poem in 1821 or 1822, was more percipient than Shelley's later biographers and critics in suspecting that it had a definite personal meaning. He evidently pressed Shelley about it, for Shelley told him a wild story, demonstrably impossible, of how a lady had followed him years before from England to the Continent, how he had seen her again in Italy, and how she had died in Naples while he was there. With Venice for Naples, this is somewhat similar to the Maniac's story, and it was later advanced by Medwin as a possible reason for Shelley's "Lines Written in Dejection, near Naples." This little episode is worth remembering when we consider the strange circumstances of the Shelleys' stay in Naples, for it indicates that in Shelley's mind the mystery of Naples and the mystery of "Julian and Maddalo" were closely related.

These "accompanying poems," by the indirect testimony of both Shelley and Mary, are autobiographical and are connected with "Julian and Maddalo." When the attendant circumstances are considered, they could not possibly apply to anything except the relations of Shelley and Mary in the autumn and winter of 1818. They exclude, definitely and completely, both Claire Clairmont and the absurd mysterious lady whom Medwin presented as the key to the mystery of Shelley's dejection. They show that Mary probably abandoned the inimical attitude reflected in "Julian and Maddalo" and sank into an apathy of grief, which desolated Shelley, but which he soon came to regard with mournful sympathy rather than with wild resentment, as at first.

Thus it is that for three vitally important months of Shelley's life the most significant circumstances have been concealed by highly subjective confession poems that were never intended as full confessions, but were deliberately obscured by both Shelley and Mary. Neither Mary's journal nor Shelley's letters give any hint of the abnormal emotional situation which both concealed from their friends, but which nevertheless dominated most of Shelley's poetry at the time.

Though there is plenty of evidence of the mutual continued love and respect of Shelley and Mary thereafter, it was never the same as it had been before. There were later minor domestic crises. Neither Shelley nor Mary ever quite retraced all the steps by which they had withdrawn from their early rapturous union. At different times afterwards, in a number of poems that have commonly been supposed to have no particular personal significance, Shelley returned to the mood of mournful disappointment that followed upon the agonized resentment of his Maniac.

For four months after the death of Clara less than a dozen letters of Shelley's are extant, two of which are short business notes. Beyond a record of movements and a few personal opinions these letters give practically no hint of Shelley's misery while he was writing, far less of its cause. They do, however, mention a much worse state of health — and Shelley's health of body and mind usually kept fairly parallel. Otherwise the letters are remarkably impersonal; one recalls the Maniac's resolve to keep the life of the understanding free from that of the emotions and wonders at Shelley's success in doing so. His fine, impersonal descriptions of Venice, Rome, and Naples are generally admitted to be among the best letters of the sort that English literature affords. Like the Lady in the poem and like some of the characters in *Prometheus Unbound*, Shelley had divided his personality. During these four months the intellectual, more impersonal side of his nature was producing an almost matchless series of travel-letters, and at the same time the Maniac was giving utterance to his veiled sorrow in practically every poem Shelley wrote.

Before the ill-fated journey from Bagni di Lucca to Venice it had already been decided to go to Naples for the winter. This plan was now resumed. On October 11 Shelley and Mary set out for a last visit to Venice before their departure south, leaving William and Allegra en route at Padua, presumably with Claire. For ten days they dined with the Hoppners almost every day and spent most of the evenings with them, except for three evenings (October 13, 21, 22) that Shelley spent with Byron. It is of some possible significance in view of what happened soon afterwards at Naples to know that the principal object of his evenings with Byron was to secure Byron's consent to prolonging Allegra's visit. He argued and begged, but in vain. Byron, with whom he had at first been so delighted, was now a great disappointment to him — a man dominated by obstinate, self-willed folly, degrading himself with the lowest associations and debaucheries, whose candor to his friends was not to be fully trusted — and yet a great poet still.

On October 24 Shelley went to Este to fetch Allegra, who must now be returned to Byron, and on the 31st, the day after Shelley's return with Allegra, Shelley and Mary took leave of the Hoppners and set out for Este. November 5 saw the party started on the long overland trip to Rome and thence to Naples, using Paolo as coachman.

From Ferrara on November 6 Shelley sent Peacock a long and interesting account of the prosperous farms between Este and Ferrara and of the sights of Ferrara, rich in relics of Ariosto and Tasso. The fresh beauty of old illuminated manuscripts in the large public library, the armchair, the inkstand, and the handwriting of Ariosto are all thoughtfully described. The dungeon in which Tasso had been for so many years imprisoned seemed to Shelley "a horrible abode for the coarsest and the meanest thing that ever wore the shape of man, much more for one of delicate sensibilities and elevated fancies." His pity was particularly aroused by a sight of some of the manuscripts in which Tasso flattered his persecutor: "There is something irresistibly pathetic to me in the sight of Tasso's own handwriting moulding expressions of adulation and entreaty to a deaf and stupid tyrant. . . ."

At Bologna the Shelleys and Claire spent the better part of two days in churches and palaces and in the Accademia di Belle Arti looking at paintings. A long letter to Peacock is devoted almost entirely to an account of these paintings. Shelley was especially impressed with Guido's *Rape of Proserpine*. Guercino's painting of Saint Bruno convinced him that the painter might surpass the writer in giving a true picture of religious austerity. Concluding a spirited description of this "animated mummy," Shelley demanded: "Why write books against religion, when one may hang up such pictures?"

For six days (November 14–19) their road wound around and over mountains and ravines. Following the valley of the Metaurus through scenery that was "exceedingly beautiful," they passed along a road made by the Consul Æmilius, and through an ancient tunnel in which the Roman chisel-marks were still plainly discernible. Spoleto, with the large castle that had dominated it from Roman times and the high aqueduct connecting two mountain tops, seemed to Shelley "the most romantic city I ever saw."

The falls of the Velino at Terni put Mary in mind of Sappho leaping from a rock and roused Shelley to one of his finest enthusiasms of description:

> Imagine a river sixty feet in breadth, with a vast volume of waters, the outlet of a great lake among the higher mountains, falling 300 feet into a sightless gulph of snow white vapour, which bursts up for ever and for ever, from a circle of black crags, and thence leaping downwards, made 5 or 6 other cataracts, each 50 or 100 feet high, which exhibit on a smaller scale and with beautiful and sublime variety the same appearances. . . . You

see the ever moving water stream down. It comes in thick and tawny folds, flaking off like solid snow gliding down a mountain. It does not seem hollow within, but without it is unequal, like the folding of linen thrown carelessly down; your eye follows it, and it is lost below; not in the black rocks which gird it around, but in its own foam and spray, in the cloud like vapours boiling up from below, which is not like rain, nor mist, nor spray, nor foam, but water, in a shape wholly unlike anything I ever saw before. It is as white as snow, but thick and impenetrable to the eye. The very imagination is bewildered in it.

Two days after witnessing this sight Mary wrote in her journal:

Friday, Nov. 20. — We travel all day the Campagna di Roma — a perfect solitude, yet picturesque, and relieved by shady dells. We see an immense hawk sailing in the air for prey. Enter Rome. A rainy evening. Doganas and cheating innkeepers. We at length get settled in a comfortable hotel.

Since they intended to return to Rome for two or three months at the end of February, the Shelleys remained there only a week (November 20–7) before resuming the journey to Naples. There were visits to St. Peter's, the Vatican, the Capitol, the Colosseum, the Forum, the Pantheon, and various other places of less note. The sight of galley slaves working among the ruins must have detracted somewhat from the pleasure of the scene. On November 22 they attended the opera, which Mary condemned as "the worst I ever saw." Shelley, who had been reading Plato's *Republic* on the journey, appears to have discontinued reading in favor of writing. Mary's journal for November 25 states: "Shelley begins the Tale of the Coliseum."

Shelley left Rome for Naples on November 27, a day ahead of the rest of the party, in order to secure lodgings into which they could move directly upon their arrival. Traveling *vetturino* with a Lombard merchant and a priest, he reached Naples on November 29, three days ahead of his family. Part of the journey lay through the most robber-infested district of Italy, and Shelley kept his pistol handy, but there were no incidents beyond the terror of the priest at sight of the pistol. All that Shelley thought fit to record of his journey was an impression of the wild beauty of the country and the barbarous ferocity of the inhabitants.

On entering Naples he was confirmed in his impression by witnessing an assassination:

A youth ran out of a shop pursued by a woman with a bludgeon, and a man armed with a knife. The man overtook him, and with one blow in the neck laid him dead in the road. On my expressing the emotions of horror and indignation which I felt, a Calabrian priest who travelled with me laughed heartily and attempted to quiz me as what the English call a flat. I never felt such an inclination to beat anyone. Heaven knows, I have little power, but he saw that I looked extremely displeased, and was silent.

The lodgings taken by Shelley were at No. 250 Riviera di Chiaia, in the better part of the city. Immediately in front of them were the Royal Gardens, in whose shaded walks Mary and Shelley often strolled, viewing Capri and Vesuvius across the blue waters of the bay. The weather was mildly warm and sunny and reminded Shelley of the best days of an English summer. Humanity in Naples might be base and degraded, but external nature provided a fine compensation. The scenery seemed "more delightful than any within the immediate reach of civilized man." About three weeks after his arrival Shelley concluded his first Neapolitan letter to Peacock by saying that his spirits were depressed and his health not good, but that he expected Naples to benefit him.

Though the climate and scenery of Naples continued to delight Shelley during January and February, his health did not greatly improve. An English surgeon diagnosed his illness as a disease of the liver and gained some temporary success by a treatment based upon mercury and Cheltenham salts. Some improvement was also produced by painful applications of caustic to his side. During a good part of the time he was confined to the house. Very likely it was on account of his health that Shelley bought carriage horses about the middle of February, by which the sightseeing was made much easier.

Externally, the life of Shelley's family in Naples consisted largely in sightseeing, described almost matchlessly in Shelley's letters to Peacock. The first sightseeing excursion was to Baiæ, on December 8. They took boat early on a fine, cloudless morning when the sea was so calm that the seaweed upon the floor of the bay could be seen with a startling distinctness that came back to Shelley when he wrote his "Ode to the West Wind." Through the intense heat and light of the early afternoon they traversed a part of the Bay of Pozzuoli, past lofty, rocky islets and enormous sea-caverns to the promontory of Misenum, where they disembarked to view the Elysian Fields, already made memorable for Shelley and Mary by the sixth book of Virgil's *Æneid*. They entered the Bay of Baiæ and coasted down the left shore, landing occasionally to inspect some of the picturesque ruins that line the bay. In the water under their boat (as a result of ancient seismic disturbances that had submerged a part of the shore) they could see the ruins of ancient Baiæ "standing like rocks in the transparent sea" — the "dim palaces and towers" Shelley was to describe later in "Ode to the West Wind."

On the same excursion they visited Lake Avernus, the cavern of the sibyl, a ruined temple of Pluto, and various ruins at Pozzuoli, where Shelley was reminded of a description in Petronius. "After seeing these things," Shelley wrote, "we returned by moonlight to Naples in our boat. What colours there were in the sky, what radiance in the evening star, and how the moon was encompassed by a light unknown to our regions!"

On December 16 there was another long day's excursion to Vesuvius. Shelley, Mary, and Claire took a carriage to Resina. From this point Mary and Shelley rode mules, and Claire, who had twice fallen from a horse at Bagni di Lucca, rode fearfully in a chair carried by four fierce-looking men. Past the hermitage of St. Salvador, where a rope-belted old hermit served them lunch, they wound up the mountain, crossing a vast stream of hardened lava, "an actual image of the waves of the sea, changed into hard black stone by enchantment." Over the rocks of lava and declivities of ashes they reached the summit, "an irregular plain, the most horrible chaos that can be imagined," of chasms, stones, cinders, and black, calcined boulders, with smoke and "liquid fire" issuing steadily from a central cone. They watched it in a sort of dreadful fascination until after nightfall, noting that one of the slow lava streams was about twenty feet broad and ten feet high. By daylight they could scarcely see the fire for the volumes of white sulphurous smoke in which the lava streams were enveloped, but in the dark, as masses cracked off from the main stream, they could see the fiery glow extending from top to bottom.

The return journey, at ten o'clock by torchlight, was something of a Gothic nightmare. Against the lurid background of the volcano they picked their way among boulders and ashes. The savage guides shouted and yelled or sang wild songs and eventually threatened to deposit Claire by the roadside. They were prevented only by Paolo's liberal promises of a beating. Shelley was attacked by one of his sudden seizures and had to be taken to the hermitage until his intense suffering was relieved. The "worst effect" of this, he added characteristically, "was spoiling the pleasure of Mary and Clare."

Shelley's memorable visit to the ruins of Pompeii occurred on December 22. His next letter to Peacock described at length temples, streets, dwellings, the forum, and the amphitheater. He did not limit himself, however, as in the two former excursions, to presenting a vivid and complete picture to the physical sense of a distant reader. Pompeii had been a Greek city, and Shelley was profoundly interested in the Greek manner of life. Viewing the modest but artistic dwellings, with their central open courts, the magnificent temples, and the theaters open to the sun and the stars, Shelley stood amazed at what Athens must have been, if this was only a small Greek city of about twenty thousand people:

> I now understand why the Greeks were such great poets; and, above all, I can account, it seems to me, for the harmony, the unity, the perfection, the uniform excellence, of all their works of art. They lived in a perpetual commerce with external nature and nourished themselves upon the spirit of its forms.

Shelley made a later visit to Pompeii in the company of Charles MacFarlane, a young English traveler of nineteen then sojourning in Naples. Only a few days before leaving Naples he had formed a chance acquaintance with MacFarlane in the Royal Bourbon Museum. The next day they made a visit together to Pompeii. The rapid journey from Naples, in a queer-looking *calesso* drawn by two black, spirited horses, brought the color into Shelley's cheeks and exhilarated his spirits. Later, after several hours among the ruins, they seated themselves on a lava rock by the sea, and Shelley fell silent. A look of such intense, unconscious melancholy descended upon him that MacFarlane was ever afterwards convinced it was the mood that produced "Stanzas Written in Dejection." On the return journey Shelley recovered his high spirits, joked with the Italian driver, and displayed great interest in a macaroni factory that they stopped to inspect. They were beset by beggars, for whom Shelley emptied his pockets of coins. "Poor creatures," MacFarlane commented; but Shelley responded; "Not a bit of it; they are happier than I — I dare say they are happier than you."

The longest of the excursions from Naples was to the ruins of another Greek city, Posidonia (Pæstum), sixty miles to the south. A part of the journey during the night lay along the shore and was lighted only by the breaking of the waves. Fifteen miles beyond Salerno a swollen stream had carried away the bridge and rendered the ferry unsafe, so that the last few miles had to be traversed on foot over a rough, marshy road. This left only two hours for contemplating the ruins. Shelley came away with the impression of "some half-remembered dream" of columns and walls and dark purple Apennines in the background, but it was enough for a rather detailed description to Peacock.

Between these longer excursions there were several visits to places of interest in Naples and near by — Herculaneum and the museum at Portici, Virgil's tomb and the Grotto of Pausilippo, and the Lago d'Agnano, with its tame wildfowl. On February 11 and again on February 14 they viewed the Caccia d'Ischieri, once (like the Lago d'Agnano) an active volcano, now a royal hunting preserve, in which they saw King Ferdinand in a shooting-box waiting for the wild boars to appear. At about the same date they saw the Grotto del Cane, where they refused to witness the usual exhibit of dogs being slowly asphyxiated by volcanic gas. On February 10 they went to Caserta. One visit to the opera (December 13) and two or three each to the Studii and the Royal Bourbon Museum apparently complete the record. The statues, particularly the ancient ones, Shelley admired greatly, but the Renaissance paintings he thought "sufficiently miserable," and overrated.

Both Shelley in his letters and Mary in her journal furnish remarkably meager information about their domestic life. They knew no one in Naples when they arrived, and they met practically no one except one or two casual fellow sightseers. Both Shelley and Mary read, of course, but hardly so much as usual. They read parts of Winkelmann's *History of Art* (in French) and two cantos of Dante's *Inferno* aloud to each other. Each read several books of Livy, and Madame de Staël's *Corinne*, and Shelley read a part and Mary all of Sismondi's *History of the Republics of the Middle Ages*. Shelley read separately in Euripides and in Plutarch's *Lives*, and Mary in Dante, Montaigne, Virgil's *Georgics*, *Adèle de Senanges*, and *History of the Two Viziera*.

Claire Clairmont is mentioned only once or twice in Shelley's letters, and once in Mary's journal, as ill on December 27; neither William Shelley nor his dead sister Clara is mentioned. One domestic occurrence ignored by Mary in her journal, but destined to have important consequences, was the loss of two servants, Paolo and Elise, who were discharged because they were about to become the parents of an illegitimate child. The Shelleys did what they could to protect Elise by insisting upon a marriage.

The loneliness of their private lives was probably an unfortunate circumstance for the Shelleys, considering the state of mind in which they had left Este. It was somewhat mitigated, however, by letters. Mary maintained a rather reserved and contracted correspondence with Mrs. Gisborne; Mrs. Hoppner sent some details about Byron and Allegra. Byron, she informed Mary, continued to live "dans une débauche affreuse" which would sooner or later ruin him. He would certainly never consent to Allegra's return to Claire.

Leigh Hunt wrote describing his new enterprise, *The Literary Pocketbook,* in which he had made bold to print Shelley's "Marianne's Dream," but without signature. With his usual sympathy, he must have guessed that Shelley felt the *Quarterly's* preliminary blasts more than he admitted. He warned Shelley that a more open assault was soon to be expected, and comforted him at the same time with the assurance that public disgust against the *Quarterly's* tactics was increasing every day. If Gifford and his allies continued their attacks, Hunt promised to "buckle on my old rusty armour, and give them such a carbonado as I know I am able to give, and they most capable of feeling." Shelley took note of this in his next letter by expressing the mistaken conviction that Southey was the anonymous *Quarterly* assailant and that he was animated by a deadly private hatred.

Peacock wrote about the general state of England, his own literary plans, his methodical, simple manner of life at Marlow, and his expectations of a lucrative position with the East India Company which would probably make it impossible to accept Shelley's invitation to Italy.

On February 27, 1819 Shelley appeared before a Neapolitan magistrate with a girl baby and two respectable witnesses, to perform one of the most puzzling acts of his entire career. He signed a statement that the child was Elena Adelaide Shelley and had been born to him and Mary on December 27, 1818. On the same day the child was baptized under that name and parentage at the parish of St. Joseph.

These statements could not possibly be true. Mary's journal shows that she could not have given birth to a baby at that time; Shelley's later letters to the Gisbornes contradict this account; and a later letter by Mary, while Elena was still alive, refers to Clara and William as her only children. To heighten the mystery, Mary's journal records that Claire was ill on the day recorded as Elena's birthday. In all subsequent journals and correspondence Shelley, Mary, and Claire maintained such a complete silence about Elena Adelaide that a conspiracy of concealment is perfectly obvious. Their only known confidants were the Gisbornes, who kept the secret. In such a mystery, if we are to discover the truth or the probable truth, the meager circumstances that survive must be weighed carefully against every possible theory of the child's parentage.

From Shelley's letters to the Gisbornes we know only that they were told of Elena as a "Neapolitan" and as a "ward." These two phrases, if taken as literally true, rule out the possibility of the child as either Shelley's daughter or Mary's, and might rule out any theory involving English parentage, unless "Neapolitan" means merely "born or living in Naples."

Unless we are to suppose that Shelley lied to the Gisbornes, we may therefore conclude at once that the mysterious "ward" was the child of Italian parents, adopted by Shelley under unknown circumstances, and named by him Elena Adelaide. Elena is the Italian form of Helen, the name under which Mary Shelley is presented in "Rosalind and Helen," the poem for which Shelley was writing his preface just at this time. Adelaide has no known Shelleyan significance unless it is a confused or disguised form of Adelina (Mowbray), heroine of the novel *Adelina Mowbray*, which so impressed Shelley just before his elopement with Harriet.

This supposition of adoption receives independent plausibility from other circumstances long antecedent to the incident. As a child and again as a youth Shelley had evinced a passion for adopting little girls. At Marlow, before the birth of Clara Shelley, he had in a way actually adopted Polly Rose. But Polly's parents were still living, and the birth of Shelley's own daughter, together with the decision of the Shelleys to leave England, had resulted in the return of Polly to her own home. Shortly afterwards Clara had died, and immediately Shelley begged Byron, in vain, to be allowed to keep Allegra. He had never been so lonely and desolate as in the three months following Clara's death. As late as December 1818 he was writing openly, in "Stanzas Written in Dejection," of his longing for "any other heart" that might share his emotions. He may well have supposed also that an adopted child would help cure Mary's melancholy. Such an adoption would have been the most natural consequence, not only of long predilection, but of the special circumstances at the time.

Granted an adoption, the method was from Shelley's point of view the most reasonable one. He expected to return to England. Adoption, while common enough in England on a *de facto* basis, had as yet no standing in statute law; the first statute giving legal status to adoption became law in 1819. Shelley had left England in 1818 fearing that his own natural children were no longer safe after the Lord Chancellor's decision. Since an adopted child would be far less secure, he did what many parents have since done for much less urgent reasons — he set up the legal background for establishing an adopted child as a natural child.

There was also, very probably, another reason for reticence. Mary Shelley evidently disapproved the adoption and co-operated only as far as it was unavoidable. She did not accompany Shelley with the child to the magistrate, as was usual in Naples. The child was not taken into her house, but was kept elsewhere; nor did Mary ever mention it before the servants. Otherwise the discharged servant Elise, who later told a distorted version of Elena's "birth," would never have asserted that the child was immediately sent away and that Mary never knew of its existence. Unless Mary did know of its existence Shelley could hardly have dared use her name in the birth certificate, or tell his story to the Gisbornes. She simply refused to be consoled for Clara by a nameless Italian substitute. This might well account for Elise's story of disagreements and harsh words to Mary from both Shelley and Claire at the time.

Another evidence (in spite of her resolute silence) that Mary knew all about Elena is to be found in her comment later when Elise and Paolo were telling a garbled version in order to damage Shelley. Mary then exclaimed: "They are as cunning as wicked." She could not have regarded their scheme as cunning unless she knew its real basis in fact; had she regarded their story as completely fabricated, it would have seemed to her, as to all subsequent commentators ignorant of the background, merely preposterous and clumsy.

While this explanation of Shelley's "Neapolitan ward" is wholly unproved, it fits every known circumstance and is logically the only possibility unless Shelley's account to the Gisbornes and Mary Shelley's denial of Elise's story were both guilty lies. In that case, however, Elena must have been his daughter by Claire, or Elise, or the servant Milly Shields, for they were the only women besides Mary with whom Shelley was in contact both at Naples and from seven to nine months earlier. The story told later by Elise would have been untold, or radically different, if either she or Milly had been the mother. But this story does incriminate Shelley and Claire, and since it is either true or a very cunning subversion of truth for the purpose of blackmail, it must be examined before any final solution of Elena's parentage is accepted.

In the summer of 1820 Elise Foggi told Mrs. Hoppner in Venice that while the Shelleys were in Naples Claire Clairmont had borne Shelley a child, that the child had been born in Claire's room and had been immediately spirited into a foundling hospital, and that Mary had been kept in entire ignorance both at the time and later. She added also that while in Naples, Mary was treated by both Shelley and Claire with neglect and positive unkindness. Mary Shelley wrote to Mrs. Hoppner a passionately earnest denial of Elise's story. Both statements are given in detail, in the circumstances of their occurrence, on pages 419–24 hereafter.

Against accepting Elise's story as true are her evident animus and Mary Shelley's denial. Mary's denial, in fact, completely disposes of the story, unless Mary was deliberately lying. Yet if Mary was lying, Shelley knew it, and she knew that Shelley was lying, and both knew that their lies to each other were perfectly transparent. They were both persons of unusual sincerity and integrity; there was no reason to lie passionately to each other when each would have known the other to be lying. It is doubtful if either could have made to the other such a bare-faced exposure of moral bankruptcy even if it had seemed needful, but to have done so for no reason at all seems incredible.

If we waive the question of Mary's veracity, Elise's story is at several points gravely in conflict with the natural probabilities. It is nearly, but not quite, impossible that Claire could have given birth to a child under the described conditions without Mary's knowledge at the time or shortly afterwards. It would have been mad for Shelley and Claire to *count on* succeeding with a plan that could only have succeeded by a miraculous accident. They would have planned instead to separate Mary and Claire for a month or two before the expected event, or they would have told Mary the truth, or that Claire was giving birth to a child whose father was *not* Shelley. Had they told Mary anything, her conduct could not have been as Elise described, nor could her subsequent letters on the subject to Shelley and Mrs. Hoppner have been as they were.

If Elena had been Claire's child, then surely Claire's journals and letters would have shown some interest in Naples while the child was still living there, or some emotional disturbance at the time of the child's death. Surely if the child was the child of Shelley and Claire, Shelley could not have made two public records unless Mary had previously been prepared and had consented to accept it as hers in order to protect Shelley and Claire. And in this case she would have felt obliged to co-operate more fully, and Shelley would hardly have put on her the unnecessary indignity of naming the child Elena. Moreover, Shelley would not have risked dismissing Elise and Paolo to become future blackmailers, nor would he have been likely to give Mrs. Gisborne, Mary's best friend, an account of the child which Mary could not corroborate. Least of all would Shelley, in recording the child's birth, have given the very day on which Claire was ill, when he could just as easily have given a less damning date.

Thus, even if we disregard statements by Shelley and Mary that would demolish Elise's story, her account is too innately unreasonable to be accepted as true. Byron regarded Elise as a dubious witness from the first, and Elise practically destroyed her own credibility two years later by writing to both Mary Shelley and Mrs. Hoppner denying that she had even told the story attributed to her. Therefore the only reconstruction of this hidden chapter in Shelley's life is the one which is consistent with the statements of both Shelley and Mary and also — independently of their statements — with all the known circumstances. Elena Adelaide Shelley was an unknown Neapolitan child, adopted by Shelley under necessarily mysterious circumstances, in strict accordance with his own long-standing proclivities, and in the added hope, unfortunately vain, of alleviating Mary's miserable condition.

Before coming to Naples the Shelleys had intended to return to Rome in the early spring. Their recent bitter experience with Clara had given them a dread of traveling in Italy with very young children. It was better to leave Elena in good hands at Naples and return in a few months for a longer sojourn. By February 19 they had already seen most of what was to be seen at Naples and were ready to carry out their original intention of returning to Rome. On February 27 Mary entered in her journal the one word: "Pack." While she was packing, Shelley was attending to the registering and christening of Elena Adelaide. Possibly she was already domiciled with a family living at Vico Canale, No. 45, where she was living at the time of her death. But tragic events were to prevent their return, and Shelley was never to see Elena Adelaide again.

Chapter XVIII

ON FEBRUARY 28, 1819, at two o'clock in the afternoon, Shelley's party set off for Rome, driving behind their own horses, as formerly. A new driver, named Vincenzo, supplied the place of the accomplished but unscrupulous Paolo. They slept the first night at Capua and tarried the second day at Gaeta, playing chess, strolling about the woods and seashore, and thinking thoughts of Cicero, who had once owned a villa on the very spot occupied by their inn. Three days later they reached Rome and, having secured lodgings, immediately set about exploring the city.

Through the remainder of March not a day passed without its record of sightseeing in the journals of Mary and Claire. Again and again, in sunlight, moonlight, or rain, they visited the Colosseum, with its weed-grown arena and broken arches overgrown with wild olive, myrtle, and fig. Next to the Colosseum Shelley was most impressed by the Baths of Caracalla. "Never was any desolation more sublime and lovely," he thought, than the high, straight walls of its six enormous chambers, their fissures sending forth vegetation, their floor now a level green in which elm trees had grown up. Through a crumbling stairway in one of the buttresses he ascended to the top, and from this viewpoint later described the scene to Peacock.

Often, in all lights and weathers, Shelley walked among the ruins of the Capitol and the Forum, which then stood in an open plain, with the modern city on one side. The Temple of Concord, with its eight granite columns, and the Arches of Septimius Severus and of Constantine were the objects of his almost daily admiration:

> I walk forth in the purple and golden light of an Italian evening, and return by star or moonlight, through this scene. The elms are just budding, and the warm spring winds bring unknown odours, all sweet from the country. I see the radiant Orion through the mighty columns of the temple of Concord, and the mellow fading light softens down the modern buildings of the Capitol, the only ones that interfere with the sublime desolation of the scene. . . . This walk is close to our lodging, and this is my evening walk.

By moonlight on March 9, "a beautiful and mild spring Evening," they entered the Pantheon, admired its perfect proportions and its sixteen fluted columns of polished yellow marble, and felt mildly critical that its perfect fitness should have been flawed by providing twelve niches for such trivial creatures as the gods. Temples, baths, tombs, and arches were all visited, sometimes with guide-book in hand.

But there was a modern city also, which had its attractions. Merely the fountains of Rome seemed to Shelley worth a long journey; he sent Peacock detailed descriptions of several of them. The palaces, churches, and gardens seemed superior to those of any other city. Yet St. Peter's, its greatest glory, proved disappointing. There were fine details, such as the colonnade, but even its loftiness failed somehow to seem emphatic. "Externally," Shelley pronounced, "it is inferior in architectural beauty to St. Paul's, though not wholly devoid of it; internally it exhibits littleness on a large scale, and is in every respect opposed to antique taste."

At various public and private buildings they saw a wealth of painting and statuary. Shelley's favorite statue, in the museum of the Capitol, was an Apollo leaning backward with feet crossed and head thrown up in the very act of being inspired to fresh music. Among the paintings of Guido Reni, Domenichino, Raphael, and Michelangelo, Shelley thought those of Raphael probably the finest in the world, but disliked those of Michelangelo as lacking "moral dignity and loveliness."

Best of all the pleasures of modern Rome, however, were the Gardens of the Villa Borghese, with their ilex and laurel shades, their fountains and statues. Here, beside a quiet pool, stood the ancient temple of Esculapius the Savior. Claire's comment repeated Shelley's sensations at Pompeii: "Here then I caught a glimpse of the ancients."

On March 12 the party heard Mass and a sermon at St. Peter's. "The Music of the Mass," Claire wrote, "is divine, and the voices of the Singing Boys sounded in this vast edifice like flutes. We saw the Pope Pius VII, a poor old man upon the brink of the Grave, and many Cardinals almost as old and trembling." The next day, as they were returning from a visit to the Baths of Caracalla, they again saw the Holy Father, who had descended from his carriage to walk. And about two weeks later (March 25) Claire wrote in her journal: "Fiesta of the Annunziata, Lady-day — Go to the church Maria Sopra Minerva. See the Pope and the Cardinals." The Emperor of Austria was expected to arrive in Rome on the afternoon of April 3. They went to the Ponte Molle to see the pavilion that was being prepared for his reception, and hoped to get tickets for some of the accompanying fiestas, but none was to be had.

Shelley's health had materially improved; life in Rome was less solitary and in all respects more pleasing than in Naples. "The Romans please me much," he informed Peacock, "especially the women: who though totally devoid of every kind of information or culture of the imagination or affections or understanding, and, in this respect a kind of gentle savages — yet contrive to be interesting."

The center of such social life as Shelley's party enjoyed in Rome was the salon of the Signora Marianna Candida Dionigi, an elderly Roman bluestocking who was rather uncharitably described by Mary to Mrs. Gisborne as "a painter and authoress, very old, very miserly, and very mean." Her *conversazioni* were attended by both Italians and foreigners and were visited by members of Shelley's party as often as two or three times a week. "In the Evening go to the Conversazione of the Signora Marianna Dionigi," Claire wrote in her journal on March 28, "where there is a Cardinal, and many proportionate Englishmen, who after having crossed their legs and said nothing the whole Evening, rose all up at once, made their bows and filed off."

All this amounted to less for Shelley than for Mary, who always depended more upon social life than Shelley did. Her journal entries still carried some slight suggestion of the stoical, clipped repression that had characterized them for three months after Clara's death, but her letters were now showing a more lively interest in the life about her. The change seems to have begun shortly before the departure from Naples, for Godwin, who had been alarmed at the state of mind shown in her earlier letters, was greatly pleased at a "vivifying principle" in her letter to him dated January 31. But Mary still suffered from low spirits. "God knows why," she wrote, "but I have suffered more from them, ten times over, than I ever did before I came to Italy. Evil thoughts will hang over me — but this is only now and then." In general, Mary was finding Rome a place of "perpetual enchantment," whose delights made her whole previous life seem almost blank by contrast. Under such influences, with both Shelley and Mary in improved health and spirits, the former morbid, unacknowledged strangeness that had followed Clara's death was apparently put aside.

Since March 19 Claire was again taking singing lessons, and Mary (March 24) had taken up drawing and painting. Shelley was spending a large part of his time writing the second and third acts of *Prometheus Unbound,* which were finished by April 6.

The month of April glided by much as March had done. After finishing the third act of *Prometheus Unbound* Shelley was probably taking a short rest from composition before beginning *The Cenci.* Attendance at the *conversazioni* of Signora Dionigi continued, a few new acquaintances were formed, calls were received and repaid from time to time. Godwin's friend Sir William Drummond, whom Shelley had admired as the author of *Academical Questions,* called on April 22. An extract from Mary's journal for the week following Easter, with bracketed entries from Claire's journal, will give a fair picture of the whole month:

Monday, April 12 — Drawing lesson. Draw in the Borghese Gardens. Visit the Signora Dionigi. [No lesson in music. Letter from Mrs. Hoppner concerning Mrs. Vavasour. Drive in the Borghese Gardens. In the Evening go to the conversazione of the Signora Dionigi. Music by two from Arpino. Mr. Davies and the Principessa Belvidera.]

Tuesday, April 13 — Draw in the Borghese Gardens. Signor Chiappa calls. Read Livy. In the evening Mr. Davies calls. [Arrange some little matters — Signor Chiappa call [sic]. Drive in the Borghese. Walk to the Campi D'oglio. In the Evening Mr. Davies calls.]

Wednesday, April 14 — Drawing lesson. Visit Monte Cavallo. Finish the 23rd book of Livy. Visit the Signora Dionigi. [A lesson in Music. Read S—'s translation of Plato's Symposium. Go to Monte Cavallo — Drive in the Borghese Gardens. In the Evening go to the Signora Marianna Dionigi.]

Thursday, April 15 — Draw all the morning in the Gardens Borghese. Walk to the Coliseum. Read "Huon de Bordeaux" and "Roman de la Chevalerie." [Practice, Read Plato's Symposium. Drive in the Borghese Gardens. In the Evening Visit the Signora Dionigi. Music by two from Arpino.]

Friday, April 16 — Paint; read Livy. Draw in the Borghese Gardens. The Neapolitan and his Sister walk about with us. After dinner, Shelley reads the first book of "Paradise Lost" to me.

Visit the Signora Dionigi. [Finish the Symposium of Plato —
Two Fanelli of Arpino call. In the Evening Practise.]

Saturday, April 17 — Drawing lesson. Read Metastasio. Shelley
reads "Paradise Lost" aloud. Visit the Signora Dionigi in the evening. [A lesson in Music. Read La Fleur des Batailles a history
of Chivalry — Drive in the Borghese Gardens.]

Sunday, April 18 — Draw. Signor Delicati comes. Afterwards ride
to the Vatican, and walk through it. In the evening, visit the
Signora Dionigi. [Read Regnes Lodbrog a history of Chivalry.
Go to the Vatican Meet there the two from Arpino. Drive in the
Borghese. In the Evening at the Conversazione of the Signora
Marianna. The two from Arpino called Fanelli two Irish Ladies
and Mr. Davies.]

On April 23, as Claire and Mary were driving in the Borghese
Gardens, they thought they recognized Miss Amelia Curran, the
daughter of Godwin's old friend and Shelley's Irish acquaintance,
John Philpot Curran. The next day they found that it was indeed Miss
Curran and left cards at her lodgings. This was the beginning of an
association that quickly ripened into friendship. The ladies exchanged calls frequently and visited various places together. Miss
Curran, who was an amateur painter, began portraits of Shelley,
Mary, William, and Claire. Her portraits of all but Shelley were completed, but that of Shelley was thrown aside as unsatisfactory, although it was resurrected and completed after the poet's death.

Shelley was again busy writing. Just when he began is uncertain,
but on May 14 Claire's journal mentions her reading of the manuscript history of the Cenci family that Mary had copied at Leghorn
almost a year before, and on the same day Mary wrote: "Shelley
writes his tragedy." On April 22 the party had visited the Colonna
Palace and had seen there the supposed portrait of Beatrice Cenci
by Guido. Later, on May 11, they had visited the old Casa Cenci, in
which the early action of Shelley's drama was to be laid. Conversations at the Signora Dionigi's salon convinced him that Italians, at
least, were still deeply interested in the story, and Guido's portrait
greatly stimulated his interest. He went briskly to work.

Probably on Elena's account the Shelleys had planned to return to
Naples late in May and remain there until winter. Mary believed that
the Roman air produced "cold, depression and even fever" in Shel-

ley, and the doctors recommended Naples. But Shelley's health again improved and the pleasant intimacy with Miss Curran developed, so that the last week of May found the family still in Rome. The Roman climate was well known to be dangerous in warm weather, and Clara's death was still a very recent memory, but it seems never to have occurred to either Shelley or Mary that there was any risk in the delay except for Shelley.

On May 25 William Shelley fell ill. At first his parents were not particularly alarmed: hitherto William had always enjoyed excellent health and spirits. The next day he was better, and he was soon pronounced convalescent. As the doctors were of the opinion that he suffered from the heat of the southern climate, his parents thought it unwise to take him still farther south, to Naples. Moreover, Mary Shelley was expecting another baby in November and was already under the care of a surgeon, Dr. Bell, who intended to be in Pisa or Florence at that time. Thus a new plan was formed, to leave Rome early in June for Lucca, spend the summer at the Baths of Lucca or the Baths of Pisa, and settle down for the winter in Pisa. A letter was dispatched to Mrs. Gisborne explaining the new plan and commissioning her to engage a servant.

It was too late, however, to save William. His convalescence was only temporary. Two days after Mary wrote to Mrs. Gisborne she wrote in her journal (June 2): "William becomes very ill in the evening," and Claire's journal adds: "Mr. Bell calls three times. — I sit up with Willy." The next day William was still very ill. Thereafter for some days there was no thought of keeping a journal. The occurrences of the intervening days are best told in two hurried letters that are tragically brief. On June 5 Mary wrote to Mrs. Gisborne:

> William is in the greatest danger — We do not quite despair yet we have the least possible reason to hope — Yesterday he was in the convulsions of death and he was saved from them — Yet we dare not must not hope —
>
> I will write as soon as any change takes place — The misery of these hours is beyond calculation — The hopes of my life are bound up in him —

For "sixty miserable, death-like hours" without once closing his eyes Shelley watched William's hopeless struggle for life, and emerged almost a wreck, all the great improvement that had taken place in his own health in the last month quite demolished.

On June 8 Shelley informed Peacock of the tragic outcome:

> Yesterday, after an illness of only a few days, my little William
> died. There was no hope from the moment of the attack. You
> will be kind enough to tell all my friends, so that I need not
> write to them. It is a great exertion to me to write this, and it
> seems to me as if, hunted by calamity as I have been, that I
> should never recover any cheerfulness again.

On June 10 the Shelleys and Claire left Rome for Leghorn. Several weeks later Shelley wrote Hogg: "I had been slowly recovering a certain degree of health until this event, which has left me in a very weak state, — and Mary bears it, as you may naturally imagine, worse than I do."

For months after William's death Mary's letters show her mood to have been predominantly hopeless and dead. She abandoned her journal and very likely much of her reading. In her letters she tried to keep her desolation in the background, but to no avail. "I no sooner take up my pen," she wrote to Miss Curran on June 27, "than my thoughts run away with me, and I cannot guide it except about *one* subject, and that I must avoid. . . . I never shall recover that blow; I feel it more now than at Rome, the thought never leaves me for a single moment; everything on earth has lost its interest to me."

To Marianne Hunt, two days later, it was the same: "We went from England comparatively prosperous and happy; I shall return broken hearted and miserable. I never know one moment's ease from the wretchedness and despair that possesses me. May you, my dear Marianne, never know what it is to lose two only and lovely children in one year — to watch their dying moments, and then at last to be left childless and for ever miserable. It is useless complaining and I shall therefore only write a short letter, for as all my thoughts are nothing but misery it is not kind to transmit them to you."

By August 4, Shelley's birthday, Mary had overcome her apathy sufficiently to resume her journal, but with one of the bitterest entries it ever received:

> Wednesday, August 4 — Leghorn (Mary) I begin my Journal on
> Shelley's birthday. We have now lived five years together; and
> if all the events of the five years were blotted out, I might be
> happy; but to have won, and then cruelly to have lost, the asso-
> ciations of four years is not an accident to which the human mind
> can bend without much suffering.

Finally William Godwin, whose opinions had great weight with Mary except on the one subject of Shelley, claimed the privilege of "a father and a philosopher" in speaking out plainly. He was bitterly disappointed, he wrote, to see one who was so far above the majority of her sex subject herself to "so inglorious a change," by joining a class of people who "sit with their arms crossed, a prey to apathy and languor, of no use to any earthly creature." "Remember, too," he concluded, "though at first your nearest connections may pity you in this state, yet that when they see you fixed in selfishness and ill humour and regardless of the happiness of every one else, they will finally cease to love you, and scarcely learn to endure you." This true but rather heavy-handed admonition might have done more good had it not been accompanied by a reminder that he and some others did not think any too highly of her husband's character. Also throughout the whole period of Mary's deepest depression Godwin did not scruple to add to it by laying his own renewed financial troubles at her feet.

After their arrival in Leghorn Shelley's family had remained there a week, seeing the Gisbornes frequently and making arrangements for a house. Since June 17 they had been living in a house called Villa Valsovano, about half-way between Leghorn and Montenero. The house stood at the end of a green lane in the middle of a cultivated field, where sun-browned, bare-legged peasants worked alternately with their cabbages and grapes and sang Rossini's music in competition with the more ancient and insistent noise of the cicalas and the creaking of a water-wheel supplying the irrigation ditches. At the top of the house was a small terrace, roofed and glazed, which Shelley took as his study. Here on the hottest days of a hot Italian summer Shelley wrote steadily on *The Cenci* or desisted for a while to watch some sudden summer squall sweep over the waters of the Mediterranean. It amused him to refer to this study as Scythrop's tower, in good-natured reference to Peacock's caricature in *Nightmare Abbey*.

Toward the end of August, Shelley gave Peacock the following description of a daily routine at Villa Valsovano, which differed very little from the one practiced at Marlow two years earlier: "I awaken usually at 7, read half an hour then get up, breakfast, after breakfast *ascend my tower* and read or write until two. Then we dine — after dinner I read Dante with Mary, gossip a little, eat grapes and figs, sometimes walk, though seldom, and at one half past five pay a visit to Mrs. Gisborne who reads Spanish with me until near seven. We then come for Mary, and stroll about till supper time." While Shelley was at work in his tower Mary spent the morning in writing and in reading Latin. Generally Mr. and Mrs. Gisborne called in the evening. They were almost the only callers.

The death of William had been a heavy blow to Shelley. "O that I could return to England!" he exclaimed. "How heavy a weight when misfortune is added to exile, and solitude, as if the measure were not full, heaped high on both." In England at least there were a few friends whose letters always assured him of a welcome back. But his health still demanded a warmer climate than England's, and there were also prudential reasons against his return. He had supposed all but one of his debts in Marlow settled by Longdill, his solicitor, but he now learned that there were several debts still unpaid, and he was not secure against an arrest for debt if he returned.

Not until July did Shelley feel equal, either in health or in spirits, to his usual program of reading and writing. Amelia Curran was instructed to see that a small pyramid of stone should be set up over William's grave in the English burying-ground at Rome, and Shelley wrote two stanzas of his unfinished poem "To William Shelley." About the streets of Rome he had heard workmen chanting a sad *ritornello*, importing that Rome could never be the same again. Byron had been moved by the same chant. It kept recurring to Shelley in his grief. At the top of his unfinished poem he wrote: "With what truth may I say —

Roma! Roma! Roma!
Non è piu come era prima!"

At times it must have seemed that Mary also would never be the same again — that she had withdrawn into a world of blank listlessness from which she was almost unwilling to emerge. In July he wrote the two unfinished poems entitled "To Mary Shelley," seeking to recall her to his need of her companionship:

My dearest Mary, wherefore hast thou gone,
And left me in this dreary world alone?
Thy form is here indeed — a lovely one —
But thou art fled, gone down the dreary road,
That leads to Sorrow's most obscure abode;
Thou sittest on the hearth of pale despair,
                                                where
For thine own sake I cannot follow thee.

The other is similar, and both recall the dejected poems of 1818.

By midsummer, however, Mary was forced to begin taking thought about the child whose birth was expected in October or November. Certain clothes and other necessities had to be purchased for her by friends in England, and plans had to be made for removing to Florence in time to have the attendance of Dr. Bell, almost the only available doctor whom she or Shelley trusted. Shelley pinned his hope of restoring Mary's normal spirits upon the birth of her child.

Matters might have been a bit more cheerful in Shelley's household if Godwin, after a quiescence of a year and a half, had not resumed his old nagging on financial affairs. There had been for some time a misunderstanding over Godwin's lease of his house in Skinner Street, which was not ended until 1822, but which in July 1819 had already brought Godwin into court as an anxious defendant. Shelley felt that he had discharged all his financial obligations to Godwin at the time he left England, but Godwin claimed otherwise. At about this time Shelley wrote to Godwin, after a year's silence, asking him to do what he could to alleviate Mary's terrible depression. The sequel is best stated in Shelley's indignant relation to Leigh Hunt:

> The *very* next letter, received yesterday, and addressed to her, called her husband (me) "a disgraceful and flagrant person," tried to persuade her that I was under great engagements to give him *more* money (after having given him £4700), and urged her if she ever wished a connection to continue between him and her to force me to get money for him. — He cannot persuade her that I am what I am not, nor place a shade of enmity between her and me — but he heaps on her misery, still misery. — I have not yet shown her the letter — but I must. I doubt whether I ought not to expose this solemn lie; for such, and not a man, is Godwin. But I shall, as is our custom, (I mean yours and mine), err on the side of patience and endurance.

Though the death of William was to both Shelley and Mary a heavier blow than the death of Clara, it did not, as Clara's death had done, produce a feeling of estrangement and injustice between them. Their mutual love and esteem remained even though they may have suspected that it might never again be quite what it had been before Clara's death. Shelley, moreover, had his work, in which he tried to obtain Mary's interest. *The Cenci*, which was completed in August, was the only one of his poems about which he consulted Mary constantly while it was in progress. There were also the daily conversations and readings with Mrs. Gisborne, whom both the Shelleys liked and praised more and more. Mrs. Gisborne taught Shelley enough Spanish to read the plays of Calderón, which he did with great enthusiasm, for a time almost forgetting his Greek.

The arrival of Charles Clairmont on September 4, consistent sponge as he was, added a new interest to the rather forlorn household. In his frugal, cheerful way Charles had probably been living partly on Shelley's bounty ever since Shelley in 1817 had declined to finance his marriage with the daughter of his French landlady. He was now on his way to Vienna, where he expected to earn a living by his linguistic ability. He lingered with the Shelleys until about November 10 — long enough to fall in love, again unsuccessfully, with another landlady's daughter. Charles had spent fifteen months in Spain and of course knew Spanish. He and Shelley, sometimes with Mrs. Gisborne, spent many evenings over Calderón. Shelley became quite proficient, and by the end of September had read twelve plays, some of which he was inclined to rank "among the grandest and most perfect productions of the human mind."

Shelley was having two hundred and fifty copies of *The Cenci* printed at Leghorn, where the work could be done more cheaply than in England and where he could correct the proofs himself. These were to be sent to England as a kind of advance edition, to be kept a strict secret even from the Olliers until the fate of Shelley's more ambitious design of a stage production was determined.

In July Peacock was given the task of procuring a stage production. Only Covent Garden was to be considered, since Shelley could think of no one except his favorite Miss O'Neill in the role of Beatrice. If accepted — and Shelley was inclined to think that the story was too compelling and too clearly and delicately handled to be rejected — it was on no account to be known as Shelley's. Eliza Westbrook alone, as Mary wrote to Miss Curran, would hire enough people to damn any play known to be Shelley's.

Peacock had some acquaintance at Covent Garden and procured a reading of the play by Harris, the manager. Harris's judgment was a bitter disappointment. He thought the story much too horrible for contemporary audiences; too objectionable, in fact, even for Miss O'Neill to read — but he would like to consider and would "gladly accept" a play by Shelley on a less offensive subject. Not until after it had been rejected by the theater did Shelley mention the play to Ollier except in one vague reference.

The first three acts of *Prometheus Unbound* were also ready for publication. "My 'Prometheus,' which has been long finished," Shelley wrote to Ollier on September 6, "is now being transcribed, and will soon be forwarded to you for publication. It is, in my judgment, of a higher character than anything I have yet attempted, and is perhaps less an imitation of anything that has gone before it." Two weeks later he sent the manuscript to Peacock, with instructions to withhold it from Ollier until he received further notice. Late in December Ollier received his instructions to publish *The Cenci* if it had been rejected by the theater and to begin printing *Prometheus Unbound* at once, with the additional fourth act that he would soon receive. "My 'Prometheus,' " Shelley concluded, "is the best thing I ever wrote." Both volumes appeared in the following year, *The Cenci* toward the end of March and the *Prometheus* in September. Ollier already had his instructions to send copies (and also copies of anything else Shelley published) to Hunt, Godwin, Hogg, Peacock, Keats, Thomas Moore, Horace Smith, and Byron.

The letters which the Shelleys received from England during the summer and autumn of 1819 were principally from Leigh Hunt. Probably because he realized the distress of his friends, Hunt formed a resolution of writing to them every Monday. Almost every letter contained some tactful indirect argument against indulging sorrow, and all were filled with amiable efforts to amuse and divert. "I wish in truth I knew how to amuse you just now, and that I were in Italy to try," he confessed to Mary. "I would walk about with Shelley wherever he pleased . . . I should be merry or quiet, chat, read, or impudently play and sing you Italian airs all the evening." As far as these things could be done in letters Hunt endeavored to do them. He discussed points of literature and art, quoted, gossiped about the opera and about common friends, and made a special point of saying encouraging things to Shelley about the rise of his reputation.

Despite Hunt's encouragement, there was little in the public prints about Shelley, either for or against. Hunt himself had published in the *Examiner* of May 9 a glowing tribute to *Rosalind and Helen*. The London *Chronicle*, the *Commercial Chronicle*, the *New Times*, and the *Gentleman's Magazine* had published practically identical reviews of *Rosalind and Helen* in June, bitterly condemning it as an effort "to bring a poetic sanction to the basest passions of the human heart." *Blackwood's Edinburgh Magazine* for June condemned its "strange perversion of moral principle," but expressed confidence that a "highly gifted man" who could write such undeniably beautiful poetry would soon outgrow his faults of opinion and take his proper place among the greatest living poets. None of these reviews, except his own, did Hunt call to Shelley's attention, nor is there any evidence that Shelley ever saw them.

To each of his friend's encouragements Shelley paid some particular notice in his letters. All the little reminders of how the Shelleys were missed — at the opera, or during a discussion when someone would be sure to say: "What would Shelley say?" or "If Mary were only here now" — all of Hoggs's accounts of his pleasure in reading Greek and his long Sunday rambles with Peacock, Coulson, or Hunt, when someone would deplore Shelley's absence, occasionally came together in Shelley's mind to form a brief, intense nostalgia. "Social enjoyment," he assured Peacock, "in some form or other, is the alpha and the omega of existence. All that I see in Italy — and from my tower window I now see the magnificent peaks of the Apennine half enclosing the plain — is nothing — it dwindles to smoke in the mind, when I think of some familiar forms of scenery little perhaps in themselves over which old remembrances have thrown a delightful colour. How we prize what we despised when present!"

Such feelings were probably intensified by the fact that both Byron and the Hoppners were now acting as if they had never known the Shelleys. In spite of pressing entreaties from Claire and Mary, not a line had reached them from Venice since March. As late as October 18 the Shelleys did not know the residence of either Byron or Allegra.

Hunt said nothing about the political situation in England, and Peacock was for a while too busy with his new duties at the East India Company to write; but Hogg gave Shelley a brief account of the trial of Richard Carlile for publishing Paine's *Age of Reason.* Hunt's *Examiner,* which now arrived regularly (though two months late) and Cobbett's *Political Register* gave much fuller information. Shelley also read *Galignani's Messenger,* a Paris newspaper in English.

From all these sources it appeared that England had gradually reached a serious crisis that might easily produce a revolution. By the autumn of 1819 it seemed to many that the inevitable explosion was fully prepared and needed only a match to set it off. On August 16, 1819, at a large reform meeting that had assembled outside the city of Manchester, an attempt was made to arrest the speaker in the midst of his crowded audience. A panic ensued during which the militia lost their heads and charged the crowd of workingmen. At least nine persons were killed and four hundred and eighteen were injured. The country rang with alarm as an official inquiry white-washed the local authorities. It was moved in Parliament to appoint a commission to inquire into the state of the country. Public journals did not disguise their apprehension that the country was on the verge of revolution.

Shelley heard of the Manchester Massacre, as it was called, early in September, and boiled with indignation. "The tyrants here, as in the French Revolution, have first shed blood," he exclaimed to Pea-cock. "May their execrable lessons not be learnt with equal docility!" But though such disturbances seemed clearly enough to be "the distant thunder of a terrible storm," Shelley did not expect the storm to break until the financial situation grew worse. By the last week in September he had completed a poem on the crisis, *The Masque of Anarchy*, which he sent to Hunt to be inserted in the *Examiner*.

Like the triumphs or masques of Petrarch, which he had recently been reading, the poem is in the nature of a vision into which both real persons and abstractions are introduced. Its language and im-agery are studiously plain, almost stark, as became direct appeal to the common people rather than to "the more select class of poetical readers" to whom he addressed *Prometheus Unbound*.

Shelley describes Anarchy, riding a white horse splashed with blood, seconded by Murder, Fraud, and Hypocrisy (Lords Castle-reagh, Eldon, and Sidmouth) and applauded by bishops, lawyers, peers, and spies, trampling down the workers of England. Ahead of the ghostly procession flees a maniac maid whose name is Hope, but who seems more like Despair. Just as she is about to be ridden down, the Spirit of Liberty arises and scatters the persecutors, while a voice which seems to be the voice of Nature herself urges the people to

> "Rise like Lions after slumber
> In unvanquishable number,
> Shake your chains to earth like dew,
> Which in sleep had fallen on you —
> Ye are many — they are few."

This voice describes their present slavery in plain terms that no laborer could misunderstand — undernourishment, exploitation, and a fraudulent currency — evils to which even savages and wild beasts are superior. It then pictures the freedom to which they are entitled

— clothes, fire, food, and decent living, Wisdom, Justice, Peace, and Love, in which the virtues flourish and Science and Poetry lead mankind forward. Let the laborers assemble and announce their determination to be free. If the tyrants invoke violence, let them; their hired soldiers, being human after all, will finally cease slaughtering from exhaustion and shame. Firm resolution will always achieve freedom by superior moral strength, but not by violence and revenge.

During the autumn Shelley wrote six other poems equally vigorous and simple. His desire was to publish them for the direct inspiration of the common people in the revolution that he thought was approaching. None of them was published until after his death. "In those days of prosecution for libel," Mrs. Shelley wrote later, "they could not be printed." Perhaps Leigh Hunt quietly suppressed them, as he did *The Masque of Anarchy* until 1832, because he feared they would damage Shelley more than they would advance his ideas. The *Prometheus* volume, however, contained his "Ode, before the Spaniards Had Recovered Their Liberty," and his "Ode to Liberty," both of which reflect Shelley's strong political excitement in terms sufficiently general to escape prosecution.

Quietly, and somewhat painfully for Shelley, dully and miserably for Mary, June wore into July, and the months of August and September passed by. By August, Mary's dejection had given way to the resumption of her regular reading and writing, but she expected never to be happy again, and she looked forward to her approaching confinement with apprehension, because one child only was "a fearful risk on whom all one's hope and joy is placed."

Her first literary effort since William's death, an unpublished story entitled "Matilda," was written mainly in August and is to a large extent a revelation of Mary's state of mind at the time. According to its recent discoverer, Professor Elizabeth Nitchie, Matilda (clearly Mary) "expresses a sense of estrangement from, even of physical repulsion toward, one whom she had deeply loved, a realization of her own selfish, petulant, and unreasoning absorption in her grief, and an acknowledgment that the man she loved, concealing or at least setting aside his own trouble, was unfailingly unselfish and kind — although, she felt, he did not love her." Shelley's two poems addressed to Mary in July show clearly enough that Mary was mistaken in the last point, if she really felt it to be true.

Shelley, depressed and ailing, was almost helpless in the face of

Mary's melancholy. He knew now that there was a wall between himself and Mary that not even their mutual love and confidence could
surmount. He had his work, however, and before the end of the
autumn he had been considerably restored in health and spirits.
Probably because of the danger to Mary of a journey to Naples and
the danger to Elena of a journey from Naples, nothing appears to
have been done about Elena Adelaide Shelley.

Dr. Bell was now in Florence. He had attended Mary in Rome and
it was much desired that her child should be born under his care.
On September 23 Shelley and Charles Clairmont went to Florence
to engage apartments there for six months, and on the 30th Shelley's
party left Leghorn for Florence, which they reached after two days'
slow and easy travel.

The journey to Florence was broken by a one-day stop at Pisa,
where the Shelleys made an acquaintance destined to be of great
value to them and to Claire as long as they remained in Italy. In Ireland many years earlier Mary's mother had been the much-loved
teacher of a young girl who later became Lady Mountcashell. Afterwards Lady Mountcashell had entertained Godwin in Ireland and
had ever since been in sporadic correspondence with him and the
second Mrs. Godwin. She was a woman of extraordinary mind and
appearance. In the early days Godwin had described her as a stern
democrat, a republican of unusual understanding and good nature,
but rather liable to caricature an account of the combination of these
qualities with a handsome countenance and a tall, brawny figure
most oddly and carelessly clothed. She had separated from her husband, and when the Shelleys met her had been living for many years
in a free-love union with Mr. George William Tighe, the son of an
Irish M.P. and a cousin of Mary Tighe, the author of *Psyche*. For
eight years "Mr. and Mrs. Mason," as they called themselves, had
been living a life of quiet, decent retirement in Italy, devoted to each
other and to their two daughters. They were both held in general
respect by all who knew them.

Mrs. Mason already knew all about the Shelleys from her correspondence with the Godwins. She welcomed them — and particularly
Mary — with a warmth that must have been very heartening to people
who had already spent a year and a half in Italy without forming more
than one friendship that had any roots in the country itself. Thereafter she was in constant correspondence with them when not in
their company, and from the first her advice and opinions were always sound and sensible. Almost immediately she helped guide Shel-

ley toward far better medical treatment than he had previously received. She dropped a wise, matter-of-fact observation to Mary that nursing mothers could not indulge melancholy without risking their children's health; she wrote letters to smooth Charles Clairmont's way in Vienna, and she became the best friend, except Shelley himself, that Claire Clairmont ever had.

Chapter XIX

DURING THE YEAR 1819 Shelley wrote so much of his best and most characteristic poetry that it has often been called his *annus mirabilis*. His best work was to such a remarkable degree the essence of the man himself that it would be impossible to understand him without glancing, even though briefly, at the nature of these works, particularly his *Prometheus Unbound*.

Even in childhood Shelley had shown an unconscious tendency toward a Promethean type of hero. More recently he had developed a great admiration for the sublime majesty of Æschylus. In his *Prometheus Unbound*, however, Æschylus had reconciled Prometheus and Jove by a compromise, and this Shelley could not endure. He was not unwilling to tolerate specific abuses indefinitely provided that the *principle* of resistance to tyranny was kept alive, but to surrender the principle, as the Æschylean solution seemed to imply, was to Shelley a surrender of the whole cause of freedom.

Since entering Italy he had been revolving in his mind a treatment of the old myth which should exalt, rather than compromise, the spirit of liberty. The first act of his drama, written at Este before the death of Clara, had made a splendid beginning. He had shown in the sufferings of Prometheus the awful torment of the human mind under the oppression of tyranny. Going beyond Æschylus, he had described the worst of these tortures as rising within the human mind, perverted by evil into providing its own bane. He had shown that even in the darkest hours of human fate slight vestiges of mortal decencies and nobilities must persist and give to tortured humanity valid grounds for hope as long as it will not surrender to the tyranny of evil. And by using Prometheus' self-controlled renunciation of hatred and revenge as the starting-point of his liberation, he had emphasized the typically Shelleyan (and Christian!) doctrine that man achieves freedom from evil only when he can rise above the feeling of revenge, which is in itself a self-perpetuating evil.

After this noble beginning the poem had been laid aside, with both Shelley and Prometheus chained to their respective solitudes of suffering. Rome and the spring, however, with improving health and a calm mind, restored to Shelley the mood and inspiration which his subject demanded. In Rome good and bad seemed timeless. On the same day he might pass the Arch of Constantine "loaded with reliefs of captives in every attitude of humiliation and slavery" and the Square of St. Peter's with its three hundred fettered criminals at work under guard, hoeing out weeds against the coming visit of the Austrian Emperor. Everywhere were the ruins of magnificence "by which expression is overpowered, which words cannot convey." And all this destruction, Shelley thought, was due to Christianity, that pernicious and rapid perversion of perhaps the greatest human hope. In the midst of the ruins of Græco-Roman civilization sat the Pope, a living symbol to Shelley, "a poor old man," in Claire's phrase, "upon the brink of the Grave, and many Cardinals almost as old and trembling." Jove, or God, a false deity substituted for a fair one by man's own mind, seemed almost palpable in his viceroy; his blighting power and his inherent weakness were visible to the physical eye.

In this general environment Shelley could not have chosen a better spot in which to do his writing than the lonely heights of the Baths of Caracalla. Here, as we learn from the Preface, the second and third acts were written, among flowery glades and blossoming thickets. He must have worked rapidly and enthusiastically, for March 13 is mentioned in both journals as apparently the first visit to the Baths of Caracalla, and on April 6 he informed Peacock that the two acts were "just finished."

It is in fact spring that dominates the second act, furnishing not only much of the physical imagery and the enthusiasm, but also something of the motivation. For, as Shelley had already made clear in the first act, there were deep human impulses, inscrutable and undying, which when once awakened could overcome the world of evil as victoriously as spring swept over the ruins of winter. The same imagery underlies his "Ode to the West Wind," published in the same volume, only there the seasons are reversed and the west wind of autumn is the symbolic destroyer of the old order, at the same time sowing seeds of the new which spring will quicken into a new birth.

In the second act Asia, who had been separated from Prometheus since the triumph of Jove, sets out on the journey which eventually reunites them. Accompanied by her sister nymph, Panthea, she wanders far over a spring landscape, obeying numerous voices heard first in a dream and then in various aspects of nature, which urge her to "follow, follow." What she is following would therefore seem to be both an innate human instinct and a vernal impulse from all nature. Both the fable and the lyrics emphasize Shelley's conviction that one

322

must follow both far and deep, beyond all the usual bounds of experience, before reaching, as Asia does, the Cave of Demogorgon.

Here Asia, like all humanity, seeks an answer to the riddle of evil — what is its source in the innate nature of things, beyond its existence in the mind of individual man? Demogorgon, a formless darkness in the innermost recesses of thought and space, answers evasively and somewhat at length, but his answer amounts to this: that God is the source of good and Jove the source of evil, but that Jove is not really the all-powerful ruler he seems, because he *is* evil and is hence a slave himself, and because he has never mastered the human will, which survives in the resistance of Prometheus. Both here and elsewhere Shelley makes it plain that Jove owes his seeming power to Prometheus, who never gave him power over the will. The power of evil, therefore, originates in the human mind and is terminable by the human will. But whence evil derives its very existence (as distinguished from its power) Demogorgon is unable to state in language comprehensible to mortal ears — "the deep truth is imageless."

Knowing now that the hour of Prometheus' liberation is at hand, Asia hastens toward her reunion with him. Her appearance undergoes a significant change, and Panthea notices that she has become as insupportably bright and beautiful as she was reported to have been during her first happy union with Prometheus, before evil fell upon the world with Jove's domination. Voices in the air sing a song addressing Asia in terms that establish her identity with Shelley's earlier conception of Intellectual Beauty, or, as he now called it, slightly modified, Love. She is the Life of Life, so intolerably beautiful that she is never seen except partially veiled:

> Fair are others: none beholds thee,
>   But thy voice sounds low and tender
> Like the fairest, for it folds thee
>   From the sight, that liquid splendour,
> And all feel, yet see thee never,
> As I feel now, lost for ever!
>
> Lamp of Earth! where'er thou movest
>   Its dim shapes are clad with brightness,
> And the souls of whom thou lovest
>   Walk upon the winds with lightness,
> Till they fail, as I am failing,
> Dizzy, lost, yet unbewailing!

Shelley repeats this identification by having Prometheus address her, on their reunion, as

> . . . thou light of life,
> Shadow of beauty unbeheld. . . .

Thus Shelley emphasizes his belief that the human mind can experience Love, or complete sympathy, only when in the shadow of intellectual beauty, and only when it can refuse to compromise with evil and can at the same time pity rather than hate its minions.

Meanwhile Jove is dethroned by Demogorgon, and in the moment of his fall realizes that he has never been complete monarch, because he has never subdued the human will. Too late he perceives that the real monarch of the world is Prometheus, "gentle, and just, and dreadless." The fact that Demogorgon at this moment identifies himself as Eternity is a clue to the motivation, so alien to dramatic convention and yet so typically Shelleyan. The apparent tyranny of evil, Shelley believed, exists only by permission of the human mind, which keeps this tyranny forever insecure by preserving the freedom of the will. "It is the will," he had argued with Byron in "Julian and Maddalo," "that thus enchains us to permitted ill." The actual overthrow of the tyranny when the human mind ceases to help perpetuate it by hatred and revenge is as inevitable as the spring and demands no particular cause. It *must* happen in the nature of things, and the time is not important because the event is sure — hence Eternity is the fitting agent of the overthrow, as earlier, to Asia, Eternity was the ultimate source of truth.

With the overthrow of Jove, Prometheus is freed and united to Asia. Prometheus then paints a glowing picture of the peaceful, retired life that he and Asia will lead henceforth, hearing echoes of the human world as "veil by veil, evil and error fall" before the mind's gradually widening perception of Beauty, through

> . . . Painting, Sculpture, and rapt Poesy,
> And arts, tho' unimagined, yet to be.

Already a great change has taken place everywhere. Men and women have dropped their evil masks, and what once seemed ugly or poisonous throughout the whole of nature now seems harmless and beautiful. Men no longer fawn, or trample on virtue, or submit their wills to tyranny by becoming its fearful tools, or talk the false hypocritical lies that had formerly corrupted human relationships. Women are at last "frank, beautiful, and kind,"

From custom's evil taint exempt and pure;
Speaking the wisdom once they could not think,
Looking emotions once they feared to feel. . . .

The authority of kings and priests with all their vast paraphernalia of tyranny and corruption is now "but an astonishment,"

And those foul shapes, abhorred by god and man, —
Which, under many a name and many a form
Strange, savage, ghastly, dark and execrable,
Were Jupiter, the tyrant of the world;
And which the nations, panic-stricken, served
With blood, and hearts broken by long hope, and love
Dragged to his altars soiled and garlandless,
And slain amid men's unreclaiming tears,
Flattering the thing they feared, which fear was hate, —
Frown, mouldering fast, o'er their abandoned shrines:
The painted veil, by those who were, called life,
Which mimicked, as with colours idly spread,
All men believed or hoped, is torn aside;
The loathsome mask has fallen, the Man remains, —
Sceptreless, free, uncircumscribed, — but man:
Equal, unclassed, tribeless, and nationless,
Exempt from awe, worship, degree, the King
Over himself; just, gentle, wise: but man
Passionless? no: yet free from guilt or pain,
Which were, for his will made, or suffered them,
Nor yet exempt, tho' ruling them like slaves,
From chance, and death, and mutability,
The clogs of that which else might oversoar·
The loftiest star of unascended heaven,
Pinnacled dim in the intense inane.

His great poem had been brought to a natural and inspiring conclusion. But Shelley had thought too long and too intently upon it to leave it so. Several months later, in the autumn and early winter, he added a fourth act, in which he repeated his conception of the liberated human spirit and the means by which the liberation had been achieved and could be preserved. Man, "one harmonious soul of many a soul," subjects his own evil passions; "All things confess his strength," and Nature's last secrets vanish before his intelligence

325

and will. Then Demogorgon reappears and summons in succession
the Earth, the Moon, even all creatures beyond the solar system, the
dead, the elemental genii of the mind, and the spirits of all living
creatures. They gather as a vast, all-inclusive audience to hear his
last word on how human freedom is won and kept:

> Gentleness, Virtue, Wisdom, and Endurance,
> These are the seals of that most firm assurance
>   Which bars the pit over Destruction's strength;
> And if, with infirm hand, Eternity,
> Mother of many acts and hours, should free
>   The serpent that would clasp her with his length;
> These are the spells by which to re-assume
> An empire o'er the disentangled doom.
>
> To suffer woes which Hope thinks infinite;
> To forgive wrongs darker than death or night;
>   To defy Power, which seems omnipotent;
> To love, and bear; to hope till Hope creates
> From its own wreck the thing it contemplates:
>   Neither to change, nor falter, nor repent;
> This, like thy glory, Titan! is to be
> Good, great and joyous, beautiful and free;
> This is alone Life, Joy, Empire and Victory!

This poem has far greater intellectual integrity than most critics
have granted it. Mrs. Shelley led the way to underestimation when
she stated in her note to the poem that "The prominent feature of
Shelley's theory of the destiny of the human species was, that evil
is not inherent in the system of the creation, but an accident that
might be expelled." Nowhere in his published works or in his letters
do we find any similar statement, and it is certainly not true of
Prometheus Unbound. In the first act (lines 293–4) Prometheus is
quoted as pronouncing evil and good "both infinite as is the universe." When in the third act Jove describes himself as sinking to
ruin "twisted in inextricable fight," Shelley is repeating an image
far more elaborately developed in *Laon and Cythna,* which he definitely explained was to typify the constantly repeated, never ceasing
struggle of the two opposing principles. And Demogorgon's last
words, in the conclusion of the drama, clearly envisage the possibility
of Jove's return to power.

Nor does Shelley minimize the power of evil. Nowhere is this power more truly seen, especially in its deadly effect upon the mind, than in *Prometheus Unbound*. Shelley's letters also show the same consciousness. Shelley did not view the liberation of humanity from its age-old oppressions as something to be lightly or quickly won. It was to be a "slow, gradual, silent change," as he had earlier made clear in the Preface to *Laon and Cythna*. In his opinion excessive expectations were sure to create dangerous reactions by underestimating the real power of evil. Still earlier he had realized that a great change must first be produced in men's habits of thought. The poem, therefore, is not only consistent in its philosophy; it is even moderate. Surely the faith that there is an inextinguishable spark within the human spirit is intellectually as respectable as the contrary belief, when neither is capable of absolute proof by the ordinary laws of reason.

A comparison between *Prometheus Unbound* and *Queen Mab* shows how greatly many of Shelley's ideas had changed in the seven years' interval, while others remained essentially the same. Vegetarianism, once an important gospel, was now no longer worth a word. On the evils of marriage Shelley was also silent in *Prometheus Unbound*, though he showed later in *Epipsychidion* some residue from his earlier ideas. Christ, who had been sneered at as an impostor in *Queen Mab*, becomes a misunderstood Promethean sufferer. In both poems hatred and revenge, hypocrisy, fear, custom, and faith (meaning theological faith) are compound causes and results of evil; and in both poems these forces are closely linked with kingcraft, priestcraft, and warcraft. The significant difference is that in *Prometheus Unbound* evil is far more powerfully realized as a subtle perversion of thought than in *Queen Mab*. A note to *Queen Mab* practically denies the freedom of the will, which is asserted in the text, whereas *Prometheus Unbound* makes freedom of the will the one quality that bulwarks humanity against an eternity of oppression.

Here, perhaps, lies the clue to one of the greatest differences between the two poems, the substitution of Love for Necessity. Necessity left no place for freedom of the will and was an impersonal force without sympathy or variation. Since 1816 Shelley had been steadily working toward a more sympathetic, less mechanistic belief, which he had first expressed in his "Hymn to Intellectual Beauty." In *Prometheus Unbound* the phrase "intellectual beauty" does not occur, but the word "love," meaning universal sympathy, is endowed with all its functions, to which has been added a nearer sense of sympathy not perceptible in Shelley's idea of intellectual beauty. Thereafter Shelley's god is Love.

The intellectual depth, subtlety, and unity of the poem may be accounted for by the steady growth of an extraordinarily fine mind, but the sudden lyrical splendor is practically unexplainable. Very likely Shelley learned something from the choral passages in the many Greek dramas that he studied in 1818 and 1819. Greek lyrics, however, differ so radically from English lyrics in metrical basis that any suggestions Shelley may have received from them involved total reconstruction in English. Shelley may also have adapted other stanzas found in his wide reading in English poetry and even in the poems that occur in Gothic novels, but if so, they have never yet been discovered. It is quite possible that some of his thirty-six different verse forms were suggested directly by music rather than by poetry. He was a fairly constant patron of the opera, and *Prometheus Unbound* at times suggests the opera rather than the drama. The poem contains cumulative effects of changing rhythms far commoner to music than to poetry. Such a source of inspiration, like the Greek choruses, would be transposed almost beyond recognition when turned into English poetry. But these are all vague guesses. There seems to be no adequate explanation of the lyrical richness of *Prometheus Unbound* other than a sudden flowering of pure lyric genius.

The reason why *Prometheus Unbound* has from the first been so commonly misunderstood lies in the boldness and originality of the imagery. Had the contemporary critics been entirely without other prejudices they would still have misunderstood and underestimated the poem on this ground. Except for William Blake, who was disregarded, no English poet since Milton had ventured far beyond the narrow bounds of subject matter and expression that were perhaps best stated by Dr. Johnson in his *Rasselas*. The efforts of Wordsworth and Coleridge to expand these limits had been comparatively modest and had dealt with material rather than expression, except for Wordsworth's theory of poetic diction, with which even Coleridge disagreed. Even so, they had aroused misunderstanding and resentment.

Shelley was fully aware of his imaginative daring and did not expect *Prometheus Unbound* to sell more than twenty copies. When his own friends considered it too wild and perplexed with imagery he clung to his opinion that it was his best and most original poem.

328

He was quite aware also that the originality was largely a matter of the imagery. He explained in the Preface that many of his images were "drawn from the operations of the human mind, or those external actions by which they are expressed." Such imagery, he added, was unusual in modern poetry except in Dante and Shakespeare, but abounded in Greek poetry, from which he professed to have borrowed it.

Mary Shelley also noted the peculiar nature of Shelley's imagery, and sought to throw some light upon it in her note on the poem. She insisted that the poem was not vague, but subtle; it required a mind "as subtle and penetrating" as Shelley's own to understand all its finer shades of meaning. It was obviously as a partial clue to this subtlety that she commented upon his unusual imagery, the source of which she attributed to Sophocles. To her its essence seemed to be an effort "to gift the mechanism of the material universe with a soul and a voice, and to bestow such also on the most delicate and abstract emotions and thoughts of the mind."

In personifying "the mechanism of the material universe" Shelley provides elaborate and puzzling descriptions of the moon and the earth in the fourth act, which sound like apocalyptic visions but are in reality only visualized images of these bodies as they would appear to the physical senses if scientific knowledge and speculation about them were all combined into physical, visible entities. In imagery "drawn from the operations of the human mind" Shelley presents again and again mental phenomena in terms of the physical, physical phenomena in terms of the mental, and even fuses matter and spirit in the same image.

The first of these types is not so unusual, though there have been few if any English poets who employed it so consistently as Shelley. Thus in *Prometheus Unbound* the soul is a judgment-throne, the heart a vine, the mind a sun or an ocean, thought a cavern, and all manner of thoughts and emotions are endowed with objective existence. The second and more unusual category illustrates even more clearly what Shelley meant by "imagery . . . drawn from the operations of the human mind." He likens the descent of spring to the advent of thought or the "memory of a dream"; feet are "sandalled with calm"; and the physical avalanche, accumulated flake by flake, is likened to an accumulation in "heaven-defying minds,"

> As thought by thought is piled, till some great truth
> Is loosened, and the nations echo round.

If Mary Shelley and Leigh Hunt, who best understood Shelley's poetry, ever understood more than vaguely what Shelley was about, with his imagery and symbolism, they remained strangely reticent. That contemporary reviewers, even those without a hostile bias, could understand it was not to be expected. *Blackwood's Edinburgh Magazine* passed the point without comment, but the *London Magazine and Monthly Critical and Dramatic Review* was obliged to qualify an extraordinarily enthusiastic admiration of the poem by calling it "a vast wilderness of beauty" and admitting that the dialogue between Asia and Demogorgon was obscure and metaphysical.

The *Literary Gazette*, the *Monthly Review*, and the *Quarterly Review*, however, concentrated a fierce attack upon the poem's alleged obscurity. Their protestations in turn that it was "inflexibly unintelligible," "only *nonsense*, pure, unmixed *nonsense*," and "*drivelling prose run mad*" must be discounted by their own uncanny ability to understand its danger to conservative theories of church and state. Nevertheless they devoted columns to demonstrating the intellectual anarchy of Shelley's style. "An' these extracts do not entitle the author to a cell, clean straw . . . a strait waistcoat, and phlebotomy," raged the *Literary Gazette*, "there is no madness in scribbling" — and proceeded to instance numerous examples of the "Babylonish jargon which is found in every wearisome page of this tissue of insufferable buffoonery." The *Quarterly* paraded specimens of "all the absurdities here accumulated, in defiance of common sense, and even of grammar," and asserted roundly that the whole volume contained "not one original image of nature, one simple expression of human feeling, or one new association of appearances of the moral with those of the material world."

Mary Shelley and Leigh Hunt had more than once tried to forestall such criticism as this by urging Shelley to write more concretely. Leigh Hunt made a partial reply to the *Quarterly*, but for a century after *Prometheus Unbound* none of Shelley's friends or admirers ever demonstrated the real integrity of his imagery and symbolism. Shelley's self-justification was unconscious and appears only incidentally in his "Defence of Poetry," a year later: "The jury which sits in judgment upon a poet . . . must be composed of his peers; it must be impanelled by time from the selectest of the wise of many generations."

Prometheus Unbound is the first public expression of a decided change in Shelley's philosophy. He had never in his life fully accepted reality for what it seemed to be. As a boy he had sought in various ways to escape its dullness and oppression. As a youth he had vowed war against some of its aspects, and as a young man he had vigorously prosecuted this warfare. His rationalistic reading at that time never suggested to him to doubt the nature of reality, nor did he feel any psychological need for such doubt while there was a hope of victory. When he first came into contact with Berkeley's doctrine of immateriality he rejected it. But the disastrous consequences of his first marriage must have convinced him that he could not conquer on the battlefield he had originally chosen. A revolution must first be accomplished in men's minds.

At about the same time he became a convert to Berkeley and projected his idea of an Intellectual Beauty whose real essence was never perceived, whose mere shadow was only inconstantly apprehended. Why might not life itself and all the phenomena commonly assumed to be real be after all only distorted shadows of reality? Plato, now his favorite philosopher, so argued in *The Republic,* in his wonderful image of the cave. In Plato and the Neo-Platonists, for whom he had now largely abandoned the rationalist mentors of his youth, he found abundant encouragement for the new tack which the circumstances of life forced upon his invincible optimism and sense of rectitude. Perhaps the forces that had checked him were really, like the ungodly, "not so." Perhaps life itself was merely a shadow of the mind, and the mind only a shadow of the Eternal Mind. "You know," he wrote to Peacock shortly after finishing the first act of *Prometheus Unbound,* "I always seek in what I see the manifestation of something beyond the present and tangible object."

Prometheus Unbound is full of this feeling. It is the *mind* of man that is invincible. A revolution in the mind of Prometheus, by which he abjures hatred and revenge, calls into action inscrutable and invincible forces that act automatically once they are released. Evil is a "loathsome mask" upon reality and falls "veil by veil" — veils being almost always with Shelley a symbol of the concealment of truth. Asia's beauty is "unveiled" to Panthea after they leave the cave of Demogorgon; life itself is a veil upon reality. Disappointment and personal misfortune had finally combined with philosophic influence to develop in Shelley a new conception of reality that could recognize fully the strength of evil while perceiving that it was not forever invincible, because it rested upon a distortion of truth.

A few months later, in time to include it in the *Prometheus* volume, Shelley wrote "The Sensitive Plant" with a wistfully beautiful conclusion in which he plainly stated his new philosophy:

> . . . but in this life
> Of error, ignorance, and strife,
> Where nothing is, but all things seem,
> And we the shadows of the dream,
>
> It is a modest creed, and yet
> Pleasant if one considers it,
> To own that death itself must be
> Like all the rest, a mockery.
>
> That garden sweet, that lady fair,
> And all sweet shapes and odours there,
> In truth have never pass'd away:
> 'Tis we, 'tis ours, are changed! not they.
>
> For love, and beauty, and delight,
> There is no death nor change; their might
> Exceeds our organs, which endure
> No light, being themselves obscure.

To a certain extent this new philosophy may have been an escape from an untenable position. But it was a re-forming of the lines rather than a retreat. To view freedom only *sub specie æternitatis* and omit to promote it in the here and now was to impoverish the will by which alone freedom could be called into being. And so the same volume in which he declared his new position also showed that he would not utterly abandon the old. It contained his "Ode, Written October 1819, Before the Spaniards Had Recovered Their Liberty" and his "Ode to Liberty," both of which show that Shelley's warfare against oppression had not entirely abandoned the old *Queen Mab* spirit.

While *Prometheus Unbound* was yet unfinished, Shelley was already writing his *Philosophical View of Reform,* designed as a practical contribution to the reform movement. One of the ideas urged earnestly in that work was that every true patriot should feel the necessity of doing everything in his power to keep alive the love of freedom and justice in the common people. At the same time he was himself writing a letter intended as a public protest against the conviction of Richard Carlile, and also six poems in a radically different, popular style, describing the state of England in 1819 and appealing to the English to resist their oppressors (like Prometheus) with an invincible and hateless passive resistance.

Before Shelley resumed *Prometheus* to add the fourth act he had produced *The Cenci*, written rapidly between May 14 and August 8, 1819. Both volumes were published in 1820, *The Cenci* in March or April and *Prometheus Unbound* probably in August.

For some time Shelley had been interested in the horrible Renaissance story of Count Francesco Cenci and his heroic daughter. No criminal or degenerate of Shelley's extensive youthful reading in the school of horror could have equaled the historical truth of the Cenci story, the full enormity of which is abated in Shelley's manuscript source and was further abated in his drama. Moreover, it was a story well suited to the thought that inspired *Prometheus Unbound*. Here was an apparently indubitable historical example of wickedness in alliance with the church against virtue. Shelley was from the first enthusiastic about its dramatic possibilities, but he considered that he was "too metaphysical and abstract — too fond of the theoretical and the ideal, to succeed as a tragedian." Mary, he thought, could do it better. It was only in Mary's default that he undertook the task himself.

How Count Cenci, old in years and in wickedness, rejoiced publicly at the death of his sons and sought to crown his villainy with the debauchery of his daughter; how Beatrice, surrounded by wickedness and cowardice, is raped by her father and sets about planning and executing his destruction; how inexorably she is forced to the scaffold by the guardians of righteousness, and how bravely she resists, is a story too well known to need detailed summary. Deeply moved himself, and noting that after two hundred years the Romans were still stirred by the story, Shelley concluded that it was a tragic theme suited to the English stage.

The essentially tragic nature of the story as Shelley retold it may well be doubted. If we waive the fact that the character of Count Cenci is too monstrous to be credible to many readers, still tragedy cannot exist without adequate, acceptable motive. Count Cenci committed violent incest upon his daughter not from lust, a dramatic motive comprehensible enough, but from a deep, unexplained hatred and a love of evil for its own sake. Beatrice is motivated by revenge, the tragic flaw in her character. "Revenge, retaliation, atonement," Shelley asserted in his Preface, "are pernicious mistakes. If Beatrice had thought in this manner she would have been wiser and better; but she would never have been a tragic character." Revenge was indeed to Shelley the great tragic flaw in human society, but it was not necessarily so in the conventions of drama. Yet in writing the drama

Shelley is so sympathetic with his heroine that he can scarcely tolerate his own notion of revenge as a part of her character. Her real
motive for the murder is self-protection and an almost religious mission to rid her family and the world of a dangerous monster. It is only
by a narrow margin that she escapes the dramatic fault of being
a flawless character.

Structurally the play is far less suitable to the theater than Shelley
supposed. It lacks consistent progression, and in one important detail it lacks unity. Most of the theatrical and dramatic effectiveness is
concentrated in two groups of three scenes each, in which Shelley
could profit from the previous examples of Shakespeare's *Macbeth*
and Webster's *The White Devil*.

It matters little, however, that *The Cenci* is not a good acting play
and according to formal criteria is essentially melodrama rather than
tragedy. It is still great literature. The speeches and the pivotal
scenes are on a par with those of all but the very greatest English
tragedies. The emotional tone and the poetry are such as are never
associated with melodrama, but always with great tragedies. Count
Cenci and Beatrice are both really great character creations. The protests of several contemporary reviewers that the story should arouse
only righteous horror because of the incest motive were due partly
to special conditions not generally valid. Even in 1820 any unprejudiced reviewer could have seen, as some did, that Shelley handled
his difficult motive tactfully and without morbid exploitation.

Though Shelley did not agree with his wife's opinion that *The
Cenci* was "the finest thing he ever wrote," he felt some justifiable
pride in having written it without "diffuseness, a profusion of inap-
plicable imagery, vagueness, generality and as Hamlet says, *Words
— words*." It is indeed remarkable that a poem practically every line
of which is immediately clear to the average reader should have been
written between two acts of *Prometheus Unbound*. Such a fact speaks
volumes for the command of expression that Shelley had acquired at
the age of twenty-seven.

Nevertheless, except in style, Shelley was not nearly so far from
his characteristic bent in *The Cenci* as even Mary seems to have supposed. *Prometheus Unbound* embodied a conception of evil as a
human perversion of ideas that were originally good, such as Christ's
doctrines perverted and the ideals of the French Revolution betrayed.
The Cenci sets forth an historical example of similar perversions.
Beatrice was for Shelley the victim of an evil society and an evil religion.

It was not even necessary to go the full length of his historical source to emphasize sufficiently the evil of Count Cenci and the Pope; Shelley omitted Count Cenci's three convictions for sodomy and some of the Pope's cruelty and vindictiveness. Count Cenci, described in the manuscript source as an atheist, is endowed by Shelley with a peculiarly horrible piety. Living in virtual alliance with the Pope, who profits by occasionally fining him for his crimes, he also feels an alliance between his own interests and those of his God. Were they not both fathers? As one father to another he prays earnestly to his God to heap curses upon a rebellious daughter. Nothing could be stronger evidence than this curse of Shelley's idea of the extent to which an evil nature perverts ideas of good. Significantly, it was one of Shelley's favorite passages.

In this one respect *The Cenci* story offered Shelley greater scope for his ideas of evil than *Prometheus Unbound*. The latter provided no place for parental tyranny, a *bête noire* at least of Shelley's youthful reading and experience. But the Pope, even in Shelley's source, is motivated partly by a desire to uphold the principle of parental authority. Shelley expands this motive to the extent of making Count Cenci suppose it a valid bond of sympathy between his own wickedness and God. This is possible because Cenci's God is the wicked God of perverted human ideas, like Jove.

At the very time when Shelley was writing *Prometheus Unbound* and *The Cenci* he also wrote a part or all of his *Philosophical View of Reform*. Had this unfinished essay not remained unpublished until 1920 it might well have modified a distorted impression of Shelley's views and mental powers all but established by mistaken Victorian critics. A brief examination of its contents illustrates once more the unity of Shelley's activity and thought in 1819–20 and emphasizes both his optimism and its firm, practical, and temperate basis.

Shelley begins with a historical view of the fluctuations of freedom and reaction from the ancient Greek city-democracies to his own day, with rather particular attention to England since the Restoration and the Revolution of 1688. He then makes a rapid survey of the present state of the world, finding great promise in the new American democracy and in the fact that reaction had been unable to cancel all the gains of the French Revolution.

Against this optimistic view of the vitality of Freedom throughout history and its hopeful prospects in the face of present discouragements Shelley proceeds to examine the present state of England.

Practically everyone in England, he truthfully asserts, realizes the inevitability of a fundamental change in government, and most people except those with a vested interest in existing institutions hope for it.

Clearly and soberly Shelley explains how in his opinion England has arrived at this state of affairs. A much larger proportion of the people than ever before are now unrepresented in the government. A proportion of one vote to eight potential voters in 1641 had become one to twenty by 1688 and one to "many hundreds" by 1819. The House of Lords, which represented the privileged classes, also possessed great influence, as landed proprietors, over the election of the Commons.

Since 1688 the relative power and influence of the wealthy had enormously increased. The principal cause of this increase was the device of public credit first systematically applied by William III. The paper money issued by the government had so far exceeded its physical basis, with a resulting increase in prices, that an English workman must now work twenty hours to earn the same bare physical necessities he had formerly earned in eight.

One result of this — since a twenty-hour work-day could not be endured — was the hideous spectacle of child labor, which was ruining the future manhood of the nation. Another was the creation of a new aristocracy of speculators, government pensioners, bankers, and brokers, in addition to the old one based upon the land. Their wealth arose from no useful occupation, but from manipulations in the funds. The English laborer, who produced the country's real wealth, was now saddled with a new class of drones. Overworked, ill-clothed, and undernourished, steadily degenerating in physical, mental, and moral stamina, the British workman was now advised by a leading economist (Malthus) to improve his condition by refraining from almost the only pleasures and comforts left him — those of sexual gratification and parenthood. It was even suggested that the poor-laws might be invoked to enforce such a program.

This intolerable state of affairs could result only in violent revolution if the privileged classes would not yield to reform, or a more gradual, peaceful improvement if they showed reason. The reforms that must be achieved were simply the restoration of former liberties and improvements in government that would preserve them. Specific approaches to these ends were the abolition of the national debt, and of sinecures, tithes, and religious inequalities, the disband-

ing of the standing army, the extension of the jury system, and the
speeding-up of legal processes. Since the national debt had been
created by and for the privileged classes who now held its obligations, and since its interest was being paid mainly in taxes by the
workers, Shelley boldly advocated paying off the debt by a proportionate levy on all the physical property in the country, thus letting
the mortgagee foreclose upon himself.

In instituting these reforms Shelley was willing to proceed with
a caution that many of his critics will find surprising. The important
point was to reverse the trend of events without violence. To achieve
this he was willing to postpone or even forgo a great deal. He believed both in universal manhood suffrage and in suffrage for women,
but he thought England so far from ready for either that he wished
to relegate them to an indefinite future. Universal suffrage would
almost certainly stimulate an attempt to set up a republic, with re-
sultant violence and bloodshed. Extreme caution was necessary:
". . . let us be contented with a limited *beginning*, with any whatso-
ever opening . . . it is no matter how slow, gradual and cautious
be the change. . . ."

If Parliament (as Shelley feared) would not itself initiate the reforms, he was for universal suffrage with all its consequences, even
if it involved abolition of the existing government. An intelligent
privileged minority, he observed, will not stand out against a determined majority possessed of overwhelming force. For this reason it
was the duty of all true patriots sedulously to encourage, unify, and
inform the people.

But the privileged minority might be so ignorant and the people
already so brutalized and misled by demagogues that a reasonable
accommodation might already be impossible. In that case every
means of petition and passive resistance should be cultivated, even
to the extent of passively defying armed force. Soldiers faced by
either force or flight are likely to be mere instinctive tools of oppression, but soldiers faced firmly by non-resistant fellow country-
men will eventually make common cause with them. If such preliminary skirmishes should incline the oppressor to make concessions,

the people ought to be exhorted by everything ultimately dear
to them to pause until by the exercise of those rights which they
have regained they become fitted to demand more. It is better
that we gain what we demand by a process of negotiation which

would occupy twenty years, than that by communicating a sudden shock to the interests of those who are the depositaries and
dependents of power we should incur . . . civil war.

Only as the last possible resort could Shelley tolerate the idea of
armed insurrection. "If there had never been war, there could never
have been tyranny in the world." Armies, as in the case of the French
Revolution, were tools ready to hand for would-be tyrants; any war,
from whatever motive, extinguished reason and justice and might
soon lose its sense of direction. But the English people, without Reform, were tending surely toward complete moral and political degradation. To avoid such a destiny, and in default of all other reme-
dies, Shelley says firmly and reluctantly that the last recourse is
armed insurrection. Not even at this point should the idea of revenge
be tolerated. Here Shelley left his manuscript unfinished, just as he
was launching himself upon his favorite doctrine that revenge is
under all circumstances a suicidal policy.

Shelley's *Philosophical View of Reform* as he intended it for public utterance is in strict conformity with his private correspondence.
In November 1819 he wrote to Leigh Hunt:

The great thing to do is to hold the balance between popular
impatience and tyrannical obstinacy; to inculcate with fervour
both the right of resistance and the duty of forbearance. You
know my principles incite me to take all the good I can get in
politics, for ever aspiring to something more. I am one of those
whom nothing will fully satisfy, but who [is] ready to be partially satisfied [by] all that is practicable.

A truly unified view of Shelley in 1819–20 must confirm an impression made quite clear by his earlier life — namely, that his life was
extraordinarily dominated by the purpose he had first formulated
for himself as a schoolboy at Syon House Academy or Eton. It goes
farther and adds a harmony and thoughtful wisdom to that purpose
which the earlier Shelley lacked and which the world has not yet
sufficiently conceded to the mature Shelley. *Prometheus Unbound,*
so significantly different in several ways, flows from the same clear
source as *Queen Mab; The Cenci,* so brilliantly different in style and
and probably even in intention, is still closely linked to the *Prometheus Unbound. A Philosophical View of Reform* is a thoroughly
harmonious practical counterpart to the highly idealistic *Prometheus
Unbound* and is at the same time a quite logical culmination of Shel-

ley's earlier addresses to the Irish and of the Marlow pamphlets. In fact, *Prometheus Unbound, A Philosophical View of Reform,* and various other works of Shelley's maturity are clearly forecast by his letters of 1811 and 1812. The three superficially different works we have considered all converge with perfect harmony, from widely different angles, upon a few simple propositions that, taken together, constitute the essential Shelley.

These are that the present state of man and society is predominantly evil, that this condition can and must be improved, that the fault lies primarily in the distortions of truth in the human mind and only secondarily in the institutions produced by the distortion, that the complete remedy lies far in the future and in an emancipation of the mind, and that it is the practical duty of all right-thinking people never to concede the principle that existing evils are permanent, while at the same time they must proceed toward reforming abuses with a full sense of the present power of evil. Over and above all these was a growing conviction that the so-called "realities" of life were mere illusions from the point of view of truth and Intellectual Beauty, even though they must still be dealt with on a practical plane of living as if they were genuine realities.

At the same time that Shelley was preaching these doctrines he was doing what he could to bring them into effect by addressing the "highly refined imaginations" of a "select class," the considerably less refined imaginations of the practical reformers, and even the English working classes, each within its own vocabulary and intellectual range.

Chapter XX

On October 2, 1819 the Shelleys and Claire took possession of their apartment in Florence, in the Palazzo Marini, a lodging house kept by Madame Merveilleux du Plantis, a silly, quick-tempered woman with a rather attractive daughter named Louise. Charles Clairmont, who had accompanied the party to Florence, was soon in love with Louise. But, in Shelley's phrase, Louise, "Not so fair but I fear as cold as the snowy Florimel in Spenser," was "in and out of love with Charles as the winds happen to blow."

Charles was on the point of leaving for Vienna. Claire settled down at once to her singing lessons. The Shelleys knew no one in Florence, and the Masons and Gisbornes, who had been somewhat acquainted there in earlier years, were now able to produce only one letter of introduction between them. Mary's condition also confined the party somewhat closely to home. Accordingly the first weeks at Florence were rather lonely ones.

Shelley went several times to the art galleries. One of the chief advantages he hoped from Italy was to achieve a better notion of ideal beauty as suggested by ancient and modern sculpture. Mary recorded later that Shelley spent several hours daily in the Florentine galleries, but her contemporary journal mentions only three or four such visits, and Shelley's uneven notes on his observations hardly suggest a much greater number. Occasionally he dropped into Delesert's reading rooms, to read the English papers.

One day in early October Lord Dillon, an English visitor in Florence, observed a rather delicate-looking young man in Delesert's reading rooms pouring intently over the *Quarterly*. Suddenly the reader burst into hysterical, uncontrollable laughter and hastily left the room. The reader was Shelley, and the *Quarterly* was the number for April 1819, containing the review of *The Revolt of Islam* now known to have been written by John Taylor Coleridge. Shelley concealed his hurt as best he could by comparing the conclusion to the bombastic first act of an opera: "It describes the result of my battle with their Omnipotent God; his pulling me under the sea by the hair of my head, like Pharaoh; my calling out like the devil who was *game* to the last; swearing and cursing in all comic and horrid oaths,

like a French postillion on Mont Cenis; entreating everybody to
drown themselves; pretending not to be drowned myself when I *am*
drowned and, lastly, *being* drowned." It seemed to amuse Shelley particularly that the *Quarterly* proclaimed that his "chariot-wheels" were
broken. He suggested that Ollier publish a solemn denial, as coming
from Mr. Charters, of Bond Street, the injured chariot-maker.

All this was merely pretending that he was not hurt; he had been
expecting this blow for some time, and preparing himself for it. In
the same letters in which he made light of it to Ollier he made it the
principal subject of remark. He began a letter of remonstrance to the
editor of the *Quarterly*, and he deeply appreciated the *Examiner's*
reply to the *Quarterly*. No periodical in England, unless it was the
Edinburgh Review, spoke with anything like the authority of the
Quarterly. Its lead was sure to be followed by practically all conservative or timid-minded reviewers. To be damned by the *Quarterly*
just as he was publishing two volumes that far surpassed his previous
work was a heavy misfortune for a poet with a strong sense of mission.

The *Quarterly's* excommunication was indeed only a little less thorough than the famous one read aloud by Mr. Shandy. Eleven pages
were devoted to demonstrating the dullness, obscurity, and moral
delinquency of the poem. The reviewer claimed to know that Shelley's private history and character afforded a disgusting and convincing corroboration of the strictures he had just passed on the
poem. With an appearance of sincerity he admitted the occasional
presence of real beauty in the poem and quoted five stanzas in proof
of it, but "As a whole, it is insupportably dull, and laboriously obscure; its absurdities are not of the kind which provoke laughter, the
story is almost wholly devoid of interest, and very meagre. . . ."
Having thus repudiated its own admission of beauty, the *Quarterly*
launches a stern moral indictment:

> As far as in him lay, he has loosened the hold of our protecting
> laws, and sapped the principles of our venerable polity; he has
> invaded the purity and chilled the unsuspecting ardour of our
> fireside intimacies; he has slandered, ridiculed and blasphemed
> our holy religion. . . .

The *Monthly Review* had also condemned the poem on the same
general grounds:

> It is lamentable, indeed to see the waste of so much capability
> of better things. . . . The author has many poetical talents, but
> he does not seem to have rendered a just account of a single one.

There is no evidence that Shelley ever knew of the attack in the
Monthly Review. Fortunately when he received the *Quarterly* article
it was accompanied by Leigh Hunt's reply to it. Hunt had indeed
kept his promise to buckle on his "rusty old armour" in Shelley's defense. He exposed the hypocrisy of the *Quarterly* in dragging forth
the suppressed *Laon and Cythna* in order to condemn alleged immorality which according to its own theories should have been left
in oblivion; he analyzed several passages in the *Quarterly* to demonstrate the weakness or unfairness of its conclusions; and he entered
upon a bold and spirited defense of Shelley's principles and personal
character as compared with those of his reviewers. Against the reviewer's assertion that Shelley was "shamefully dissolute in his conduct" Hunt opposed a detailed account of Shelley's daily life at Marlow, as he himself had seen it while Shelley was writing *The Revolt
of Islam*. While Hunt's method in the main was calmly expository, he
made no attempt to conceal his feelings, and such expressions as
"half-sighted and whole-clawed meanness" and "Heavy and swelling, and soft with venom, it creeps . . . like a skulking toad" show
a hearty willingness to meet the enemy on his own ground.

At about the same time Shelley received further encouragement
in *Blackwood's Edinburgh Magazine* for January 1819. *Blackwood's*
was indeed a Tory magazine, in some ways as conservative or reactionary as the *Quarterly* itself and far more reckless. Its treatment
of Keats was a shade more brutal even than the *Quarterly's*. It was
already involved in a fierce crusade against the "Cockney School of
Poetry," with which Shelley was known to be closely affiliated by personal ties. Being as reckless as they were clever, *Blackwood's* reviewers cared little about following the lead of the *Quarterly*.

It was a particularly fortunate accident for Shelley that *Blackwood's* sent the book to Thomas De Quincey for review. De Quincey
had not met Shelley at Keswick in 1812, but he knew of him from
common friends there. He was by temperament and experience far
better equipped than most of his contemporaries to review Shelley
intelligently. Though he declined writing the review, he read and
admired the book and furnished John Wilson with some of his opinions. Wilson, ever an adept at using other men's ideas, wrote a review
that was probably based on De Quincey's opinions.

In this review *Blackwood's* yielded nothing to the *Quarterly* in condemning Shelley's opinions. "A pernicious system of opinion," it began, "concerning man and his moral government, a superficial audac-
ity of unbelief, an overflowing abundance of uncharitableness toward

almost the whole of his race, and a disagreeable measure of assurance and self-conceit . . . in the character of any one person might, at first sight, be considered as more than sufficient to render that one person utterly and entirely contemptible." Mr. Shelley, it admitted, was such a person. But Mr. Shelley, though "weak and worthless" as a philosopher, was "strong, nervous, and original" as a poet; he was far superior to the other Cockneys; he had a strong genius that placed him already "near to the great creative masters" of the age. In this spirit the reviewer proceeded to describe the poem at length, dealing out equally generous praise of the poetry and condemnation of the principles.

The concluding sentences of the review not only reaffirm *Blackwood's* belief in Shelley's genius as a poet, but give a clear hint of the policy of temptation that the magazine maintained toward Shelley as long as there seemed any possibility of "converting" him:

> Mr. Shelly [*sic*] has displayed his possession of a mind intensely poetical, and of an exuberance of poetic language, perpetually strong and perpetually varied. In spite, moreover, of a certain perversion in all his modes of thinking, which, unless he gets rid of it, will ever prevent him from being acceptable to any considerable or respectable body of readers, he has displayed many glimpses of right understanding and generous feeling, which must save him from the unmingled condemnation even of the most rigorous judges. His destiny is entirely in his own hands; if he acts wisely, it cannot fail to be a glorious one; if he continues to pervert his talents, by making them the instruments of a base sophistry, their splendour will only contribute to render his disgrace the more conspicuous. . . . He has it in his power to select better companions [than Hunt and Keats]; and if he does so, he may very securely promise himself abundance of better praise.

In its second review *Blackwood's* praised *Rosalind and Helen* highly, with frequent excerpts of beauties, but expressed deep concern over the "monstrous perversity" of the author. It reiterated its faith in his ultimate triumph — only to be achieved, however, by abandoning his vices. "His fame will yet be a glorious plant if he do not blast its expanding leaves by the suicidal chillings of immorality."

In September, however, *Blackwood's* reached the crest of its quixotic effort to save wayward genius from its own perversity. It ferreted out for favorable review a copy of *Alastor*, published the year before *Blackwood's* was established, and announced that it did so in

order to give its readers an idea of the progress already achieved by
"a mind destined, in our opinion, under due discipline and self-
management, to achieve great things in poetry." In conclusion *Blackwood's* turned upon the *Quarterly* a long and spirited rebuke for its
review of *The Revolt of Islam*. Such reviewing, it roundly asserted,
was both infamous and stupid; a mere comparison of the reviewer's
prose with Shelley's poetry made one think of "a dunce rating a man
of genius." The *Quarterly's* praise of one passage in Shelley's poem
was denounced as a mere hypocritical dodge which should expose
the reviewer to the scorn and contempt of all true lovers of genius.
Both Shelley and the *Quarterly* reviewer are assured that England
will pardon much to genius, but will not pardon a dishonest attempt
to obscure genius. And "It is not in the power of all the critics alive
to blind one true lover of poetry to the splendour of Mr. Shelley's
genius."

This persistent and extraordinary wooing of Shelley by the most
powerful monthly of the day was a more significant thing than either
Shelley or his biographers realized. It was clear evidence that a genius like Shelley's could not be wasted, no matter how dull or antagonistic the majority of the reviewers might be. It showed also that
in 1819, before his best works were published, it was possible for
Shelley to achieve a fairly general recognition as a great poet. Shelley
was really yielding to a persecution complex in the letters in which
he spoke of his case as if it were hopeless. Had the two volumes then
in press been as free from his political, religious, and moral theories
as the *Alastor* volume, the story might have been different.

Mary's fourth and last child was born on the morning of November
12, 1819. The next day Shelley wrote to Leigh Hunt: "Yesterday
morning Mary brought me a little boy. She suffered only about two
hours' pain, and is now so well that it seems a wonder that she stays
in bed. The babe is also quite well, and has begun to suck. You
may imagine that this is a great relief and a great comfort to me
amongst all my misfortunes past present and to come. . . . Poor
Mary begins (for the first time) to look a little consoled. For we have
spent as you may imagine a miserable five months." A few days later,
in announcing the event to Miss Curran, Shelley reported that Mary
was "exceedingly well."

Young Percy Florence, as he was christened, was such a fine,
healthy child that it seemed absurd to worry about him, yet Mary
had been through too much not to worry. Though her spirits and

energy were now much improved, some morbid feelings still lingered in her letters. At length Mrs. Mason interjected a plain, sensible warning: "I am very sorry to find that you still suffer from low spirits. I was in hopes the little boy would have been the best remedy for that. Words of consolation are but empty sounds, for to time alone it belongs to wear out the tears of affliction. However, a woman who gives milk should make every exertion to be cheerful, on account of the child she nourishes."

There were other more substantial worries for the Shelleys in Florence. On October 19 Godwin was ordered by the court to pay several years' back rent for a property he had believed rent-free — an indeterminate sum of between £600 and £2,000. He expected Shelley to rescue him again, and Shelley, whose affairs were too much involved to assume the burden without borrowing, thought he might have to return to England to settle the matter. At no time since Shelley had come to Italy could Godwin's troubles have been so inconvenient, for Shelley had just rendered himself doubly helpless by becoming involved in the straitened finances of the Gisbornes.

The Gisbornes had been living on a small income a part or all of which was invested in the funds of the English government. Somewhat alarmed at the possible insecurity or future inadequacy of his investments, Mr. Gisborne had recently taken a journey to England to look into the situation and had returned after the Shelleys left Leghorn for Florence. Shelley was tireless in urging him to withdraw his money from the public funds as quickly as possible; he thought the English government in every way too shaky to maintain the interest on its bonds.

Why not make Henry Reveley's steam engine a source of income? Already in England, in New York, and even in Italy the first steamboats were beginning a revolution of water transport. The Shelley who as a freshman had dreamed of balloons over Africa and who a few years later had lent his enthusiasm to the Tremadoc Embankment dreamed another dream of progress. There seemed no reason why Henry Reveley should not build a steamboat to ply between Leghorn, Genoa, and Marseille. A few days before the Shelleys left Leghorn Mary's journal states (September 22): "Shelley reads Calderón and talks about the steam engine." On the day after the Shelleys left, a contract was signed for the fitting and launching of the boat. Henry and his assistant were going ahead with the engine, but were handicapped by lack of cash.

Mrs. Gisborne had already advanced all she could — a hundred and forty crowns. Shelley's financial assistance must have been arranged shortly before he left Leghorn. Its total extent is uncertain, but he furnished a hundred pounds on December 7 and another hundred on December 23. Shelley's letters to the Gisbornes were full of eager inquiries about the steamboat; Mrs. Gisborne's answers communicated Henry's eagerness and energy, while Henry's occasional letters describing his boat or giving a vivid account of casting the engine cylinders sustained and increased Shelley's enthusiasm.

The state of mind that had caused Shelley to write *The Masque of Anarchy* continued during the autumn and early winter of 1819. His sonnet "England in 1819" pictures a country with a mad and dying king, disgraceful princes, and heartless ministers, its people starved and assassinated, its religion meaningless, and its standing army dangerous to oppressor and oppressed alike.

As he wrote these poems Shelley was already coming to the defense of the oppressed. Hogg had recently sent him a brief account of the trial of Richard Carlile for blasphemy in publishing Palmer's *Principles of Nature* and Paine's *Age of Reason*. This was the second of Carlile's several martyrdoms at the hands of the law, and he received a very severe sentence. It was the Peter Finnerty case over again. Immediately Shelley dashed off a long letter to Leigh Hunt to be inserted in the *Examiner*.

"In the name of all we hope for in human nature what are the people of England about?" Shelley demanded. He held no brief for Carlile individually. He admitted that the defense might have been deficient in dignity and that the books for whose publication Carlile was sentenced might well contain offensive matter. The real points were that Carlile had been denied his constitutional right to a trial by a jury of his peers, that the terms of the indictment ("wicked, malicious," and blasphemous libel) were certainly unproved, and that Carlile's conviction was really a case of class oppression, which violated the principle of equal justice for all. How could a jury of orthodox churchmen be called peers of a man whose case their very orthodoxy forced them to prejudge? Why had the government not prosecuted the writings of Hume and Gibbon? Why had it not haled into court Sir William Drummond, William Godwin, and Jeremy Bentham, all of whom treated Christianity as "an exploded superstition"? Among the very men who prosecuted booksellers like Carlile were persons who Shelley said he could testify of his own knowledge were themselves deists. They cared little for religion except as a mask of worldly power. "In prosecuting Carlile they have used the superstition of the jury as their instrument for crushing a political enemy."

Under such conditions, with England trembling in the balance between despotism and free government, it seemed to Shelley that the case of Carlile forced every lover of freedom to speak out. But meanwhile Carlile was in prison, financially ruined. Let a good subscription be raised, not only to relieve Carlile, but to defeat the government's purpose of ruining him and thus damaging the cause of freedom in which he suffered. Shelley offered to deny himself some intended lessons in German and devote the money to Carlile's relief.

It is very probable that Shelley's "Peter Bell the Third," which was written within the same fortnight as the letter on Carlile, was not so completely a mere play of fanciful humor as it appears, though its origin was not very serious. Wordsworth's *Peter Bell: A Tale in Verse,* after lying nineteen years in manuscript, was published in 1819; but its publication was actually preceded by John Hamilton Reynolds's burlesque *Peter Bell: A Lyrical Ballad.*

The review of both poems in the *Examiner* for April 26 and May 3 furnished Shelley with the idea of creating a third Peter Bell. Shelley and everybody else knew that since about 1814 Wordsworth had been becoming duller. Shelley certainly thought Peter Bell a ridiculous product of nineteen years' incubation. He used to quote the poem, beginning with chuckles of amusement and reaching a point of almost uncontrollable laughter with the stanza beginning "It is a party in a parlour" and ending "All silent and all damned," which he used as a motto for "Peter Bell the Third." But Shelley also thought Wordsworth was a flatterer of tyrants.

In "Peter Bell the Third," beneath the odd Shelleyan horse-play and occasional cutting parody, is plainly to be seen not only Shelley's warning that a poet who deserts the cause of freedom must necessarily grow dull, having committed a sort of spiritual suicide, but his very plain conviction that Wordsworth was already growing dull for this reason.

It is a curious fact that *The Masque of Anarchy,* the letter on Carlile, and "Peter Bell the Third" were all sent to Leigh Hunt for publication within a few months of each other, and yet none was published until many years later. As late as April 5, 1820 Shelley complained to Hunt that he had not even acknowledged receipt of "Peter Bell the Third" and the letter on Richard Carlile. Hunt probably acted within the vague discretionary powers assigned him by

Shelley in suppressing these writings, but why did he do so? He had fearlessly published similar opinions of his own on all three subjects. Hardly any answer is possible except that Hunt believed that Shelley at this time had a real opportunity to win public recognition as a great poet, and that this opportunity should not be lost through relatively minor publications that were not sufficiently valuable to justify such a risk.

"I have deserted the odorous gardens of literature to journey across the great sandy desert of Politics," Shelley lightly informed the Gisbornes on November 6. He was, in fact, more excited over political matters than at any time since his first expedition to Ireland. Mrs. Mason, with a better notion than anyone else of the close connection between Shelley's health and his state of mind, wrote: "I am very sorry to hear such a bad account of Mr. Shelley, and fear that the interest he takes in the political state of England is very injurious to his health. I speak feelingly on this subject, as my nerves have never recovered the shake they got about twenty years ago on a similar occasion." Mrs. Gisborne was also concerned about Shelley's health: "Messere! I am not quite satisfied with the account of your health. What occasions the fixed pain in your side? You must move heaven and earth to get rid of it." The physicians in Florence thought his condition delicate enough to require forbidding his return to England during the winter.

The weather, too, was unfavorable. Florence was having one of its coldest and most disagreeable winters for many years. "Nothing," Shelley wrote to Tom Medwin, "reconciles me to the slightest indication of winter: much less such infernal cold as my nerves have been racked upon for the last ten days." At the same time Mary Shelley was writing to Mrs. Gisborne that Shelley's health, although better, still showed the effects of the cold in an "extreme nervous irritability."

Yet Shelley's health was not bad enough to prevent considerable activity. Besides the writing already discussed he wrote the fourth act of *Prometheus Unbound,* the "Ode to the West Wind," and several exquisite short lyrics.

As Mary recovered strength she occasionally accompanied Shelley on his frequent strolls in the Cascine Forest. Most of her time, however, was consumed by the needs of her rapidly growing baby. Claire was busy with her singing lessons and with reading Spanish, though she seems to have found more time for social life than either Shelley or Mary. Except for the lodgers in the house, the life of the Shelleys was almost as solitary as it had been at Villa Valsovano. Madame du Plantis, their landlady, they saw occasionally, and her rather winsome daughter, Louise, more often. They had a calling acquaintance with several English people – a Mr. and Mrs. Meadows, a Mr. and Mrs. Harding, and a Mr. Tomkins. Mr. Harding, a clergyman, christened young Percy Florence on January 25. Mr. Tomkins, an amateur portrait painter, sketched a portrait of Shelley on January 7 and 9.

A more familiar caller, on January 23, was Elise Foggi, who had come to Florence to live some time after leaving the Shelleys in Naples. As yet it was five or six months before she was to tell her damaging story to the Hoppners. The Shelleys received her and even recommended Paolo's employment by Henry Reveley.

Early in November, shortly before the birth of Percy Florence, a visitor came to Florence in whom the poet took an immediate interest. She was Miss Sophia Stacey, the ward of one of Shelley's favorite uncles, Mr. Robert Parker. Having spent three years with her guardian at Bath and Brighton, Miss Stacey was rather fond of social life. She had an excellent, well-trained voice, and some superficial interest in ideas and events; yet fundamentally, as her journal reveals, she was a simple, ingenuous English girl, with the touch of sentimentalism that was rather fashionable for young ladies at the time. Mr. Parker had told her enough about Shelley to stimulate her curiosity. Two days after her arrival in Florence she called at the Palazzo Marini and received the impression that the Shelleys often communicated, that "They see no company and live quite to themselves." On the next day (the day before Percy Florence was born) she and her companion moved to the same house, after which a considerable intimacy arose.

Sophia thought Shelley deliciously "mysterious" and "interesting" – his room was cluttered with Greek books; he always had a book under his arm or in his hand; and a little table with pen and ink stood always by his bed.

The romantic charm that Shelley had scarcely had opportunity to exercise since Hogg had observed its effect upon the young ladies of the Boinville-Newton circles claimed another delighted victim. Once (November 22) Shelley visited the Uffizi Gallery with Sophia Stacey and Mr. Tomkins and walked with them afterwards in the Cascine Forest. He helped her with her Italian. Mary Shelley soon grew strong enough to accompany Shelley to one of her tea parties and to walk with Shelley and Sophia in the Cascine (December 11). They were Sophia's guests for Christmas dinner.

Shelley took great delight in Sophia's singing. He particularly enjoyed hearing her sing *"Non temer, o madre amata"* and de Thierry's ballad "Why declare how much I love thee," often to her own accompaniment on the harp. His lyric "Thou art fair and few are fairer," which he entitled "To Sophia," was written for her to sing. Sometimes she asked him for a song or a poem. One of his most passionate lyrics, "Indian Serenade," was promised Sophia after hearing her sing on November 16, and was delivered next day. On December 28 he presented her with a copy of Leigh Hunt's *Literary Pocketbook* for 1819, in which he had written out three poems: "Good-night," "Love's Philosophy," and "Time Long Past." Two months after her departure from Florence, Shelley complied with one of her requests by sending her, in a postscript to one of Mary's letters, his lyric "On a Faded Violet."

Not all of these poems were originally written for Sophia, but there can be little doubt about the personal meaning of the following:

To ——

I fear thy kisses, gentle maiden,
   Thou needest not fear mine;
My spirit is too deeply laden
   Ever to burden thine.

I fear thy mien, thy tones, thy motion,
   Thou needest not fear mine;
Innocent is the heart's devotion
   With which I worship thine.

These lines show Shelley stating the same attitude he had formerly stated in letters to Elizabeth Hitchener and was soon to state again in poems to both Emilia Viviani and Jane Williams. If the ladies — or subsequent critics — misunderstood, it was scarcely for lack of a clear, tactful statement on Shelley's part. Certainly Shelley was charmed with the company of Sophia Stacey, but the beautiful lyrics that she inspired, but the beautiful lyrics that she inspired, and even, for the most part, the poem directly addressed to her, were not personal tributes, but tributes to the power of music. Some other lovely voice singing impassioned or sentimental lyrics would have done as well, as Claire Clairmont's had done before, at Marlow, and Jane Williams's was to do later.

Shelley continued to squire his attractive quasi-kinswoman about Florence until her departure for Rome, on December 29, bearing a letter from Shelley recommending her and her companion to the good graces of the Signora Dionigi.

Not long afterwards the Shelleys themselves began to talk seriously of departing for Pisa, though they had come to Florence to remain six months. Florence in January was so cold and rainy, and so socially cheerless, that there seemed no virtue in remaining. At eight o'clock on the morning of January 26 they set out, descending the Arno by boat to Empoli, thirty miles in five hours. Four hours more by carriage brought them to Pisa, in or near which city Shelley was to pass the rest of his life.

Chapter XXI

PISA IN 1820 was a sleepy, shrunken old city whose population in thirty years had decreased from 120,000 to 18,000. There were no great museums or art galleries and its best architecture was mainly Gothic, which Shelley rather despised in comparison with Greco-Roman remains. Only in his "Tower of Famine," describing the prison of Ugolino, and in "Evening: Ponte al Mare, Pisa," does the city of Pisa make any impression on Shelley's poetry. Nevertheless, he was attracted to its quiet peacefulness and expected to be greatly benefited by its mild climate and good water. The surrounding hills and neighboring forest, and the yellow Arno, flecked with foam from mountain freshets in spring or flashing like fire beneath a summer sunset, offered occasional thrills of natural beauty that compensated for the absence of the ruins of Rome or Naples and the art galleries of Florence.

On January 29 the family left their temporary quarters at the Tre Donzelle and moved into lodgings at Casa Frasi, Lung' Arno. But Shelley was "irritated to death for the want of a study," and in little more than a month (March 4) they moved to more commodious quarters on the top floor of the same building, where they remained till the middle of June.

Pisa was the home of one of the most distinguished physicians in Italy, Dr. Vaccà Berlinghieri, a man with a really international reputation who had the added merit, in Shelley's eyes, of being a political and philosophic radical. Here, too, lived the Masons, already good friends of the Shelleys. At Leghorn, distant only three and a half hours' travel, lived the Gisbornes. There were other English at Pisa, but to the Shelleys and Masons they seemed rather a dull lot. Only one of them, Walter Savage Landor, might have proved interesting, but he, unfortunately, was even more averse to English society than the Shelleys, who were merely indifferent. He declined to meet them, having recently contracted a strong prejudice against Shelley, based upon an account of Shelley's treatment of Harriet probably furnished him by Southey.

Among the rather odd collection of English people in Pisa was "the Reverend Colonel Finch," who had been for some time a flitting resident of several Italian cities and was occasionally in Pisa in 1820.

The Shelleys had met him before, at Signora Dionigi's, in Rome, and considered him a ridiculous bore. They bestowed the name of Calicot upon him from the character of that name in Moore's *The Fudge Family Abroad*. One day as Claire and Shelley were taking a walk they became aware of a grand commotion. A tall gentleman with an umbrella was chasing a blacksmith's boy, crying: "Seize him! Seize him!" The boy was cornered and his pursuer began calling loudly for the Governor. Shelley intervened to see that justice was done, but when Claire recognized the Reverend Colonel he allowed her to drag him away, preferring even the jeopardy of justice to the risk of being recognized by such a bore.

A much more violent encounter with a fellow Englishman that has been reported of Shelley in Pisa probably never happened at all. Medwin was told by Shelley of an assault by an English officer of the Portuguese army, supposedly as a result of the *Quarterly's* review of *The Revolt of Islam*. Overhearing Shelley call for his mail at the post office, this man, a tall, powerful fellow, exclaimed: "What! Are you that d—d atheist, Shelley?" — and straightway knocked him down. While Shelley lay stunned the man vanished. Mr. Tighe, or Mason, as he preferred to be called, traced him to his inn, whence he had also vanished, and Shelley and Mr. Mason followed him at once to Genoa, whence he had again vanished, this time without trace, like Shelley's previous assailants at Keswick and Tremadoc. Significantly enough, it can be proved from the journals of Shelley and Claire that Shelley never went from Pisa to Genoa.

In such society as Pisa afforded, the Shelleys went about very little. "I ought to tell you," Shelley warned Tom Medwin in inviting him to Pisa, "that we do not enter into society. The few people we see are those who suit us, — and I believe nobody but us. I find saloons and compliments too great bores; though I am of an extremely social disposition." Even from their correspondents the Shelleys were somewhat more isolated than usual. Sophia Stacey wrote several letters for a few months after the separation at Florence, but the correspondence with Amelia Curran had lapsed. Leigh Hunt, oppressed with his own worries, now wrote only infrequently, and Hogg, too lazy for much letter-writing, wrote only once to decline Shelley's warm invitation to visit him. One or two letters arrived from Horace Smith and Elizabeth Kent, but Peacock, full of India House business and immersed in matrimony, was more than usually lax in his correspondence.

A great part of the Shelleys' time was spent with the Masons. "She is everything that is amiable and wise," Shelley informed Leigh Hunt, "and he is very agreeable. You will think it my fate either to find or to imagine some lady of 45, very unprejudiced and philosophical, who has entered deeply into the best and selectest spirit of the age, with enchanting manners, and a disposition rather to like me, in every town that I inhabit. But certainly such this lady is."

Mrs. Mason not only possessed sound common sense, learning, and a humorously tolerant view of life; she was also a calm friend of freedom, though her greatest enthusiasm had died with Robert Emmet. With her reminiscences of the Irish revolt of '93 she set Mary and Claire reading the Irish pamphlets with which her library was still stocked. She remembered how, when Hardy had been acquitted of treason in 1794, she called at his shop to buy shoes of him that proved uncomfortable, and how she accused his lasts of being too aristocratic for her democratic feet. She could also touch lightly on the mildly scandalous details of Lady Oxford's Continental travels. Turning to the more immediate present she could tell of calling upon an old priest whose mistress had just died, and how sympathy gave way to laughter as she listened to his praise of her virtues — "una fresca donna di sessant' anni."

Mrs. Mason possessed a good library, and was quite at home reading the *Agamemnon* of Æschylus with Shelley. The Masons lived at Casa Silva, Via Mala Gonella. Almost every day for six months the Shelleys and Claire went there for tea, dinner, or an afternoon or morning call. Claire was especially attracted. She occasionally took it upon herself to straighten out the library and frequently went walking or driving with Laurette and Nerina, the Masons' attractive young daughters.

Shelley occasionally visited Leghorn, and the Gisbornes made at least two short visits to Pisa. Correspondence between the two families was frequent. But the Gisbornes were about to make a journey to England. The Shelleys tried hard, but in vain, to persuade Mrs. Gisborne to remain behind with them. On April 28 the Shelleys went to Leghorn to say good-by, and on May 2 the Gisbornes departed for England, having promised to keep a journal partly for the Shelleys' benefit.

In one matter in which the Gisbornes served Shelley's interests, letters have been either lost or destroyed. One or both of Shelley's visits to Leghorn in February and March seem to have been concerned with Elena Adelaide Shelley, still in Naples. Since the Shelleys feared to submit Percy Florence to the dangers of travel that had proved so fatal to Clara, some more permanent arrangement must be made for Elena than the one made in anticipation of an early return to Naples. In such a matter, Shelley's violation of Neapolitan law in making a false birth registration might well require the counsel of a lawyer. On March 8, two days after returning from Leghorn, Shelley wrote to the Gisbornes, arranging to put a hundred and fifty ducats in the hands of a lawyer to handle certain unspecified "expenses at Naples." The "expenses" could hardly have been for anyone except Elena Adelaide, a business which, for reasons which the Gisbornes evidently understood and approved, Shelley did not wish to manage from home. Probably Mary's attitude toward Elena was antagonistic, for Shelley asked the Gisbornes to address him on this matter as "Mr. Jones." It is just possible that Mary's antagonistic attitude, either expressed or unexpressed, is criticized in a cryptic line of Claire's journal for February 9, at a time when Mary's journal contains no entries from February 3 to 10: "A Greek author says 'A bad wife is like Winter in a house.' "

When the Shelleys moved to Pisa, Shelley was still suffering from the effects of the severe winter in Florence. This physical and mental depression, in a diminishing degree, continued in Pisa until the return of spring. From January 27 until June Claire's journal mentions no illness of Shelley's, and Mary's journal rather casually mentions Shelley as unwell only four times. Shelley's own view was more serious. To Medwin he wrote on April 16: "You will find me a wretched invalid unless a great change should take place"; and on May 1: "I have been seriously ill since I last wrote to you, but I am now recovering." But even in his own more serious view of his illness, the return of warm weather made Shelley describe his health as "materially better." He added: "I am on the whole greatly benefited by my residence in Italy, and, but for certain moral causes, should probably have been enabled to reinstate my system completely."

The wise and competent Vaccà evidently thought that Shelley's illness was at least partly nervous, and to some extent dependent on his state of mind. He "could only guess" at the cause, but he enjoined Shelley to abstain from all physicians and medicine, and trust to Nature. Warm baths and a still warmer climate than Pisa's seemed highly desirable. In the spring Shelley began taking the baths at the Baths of Pisa, with some slight benefit, and in June the family planned to go to the Baths of Lucca for the summer months. The hotter climate of southern Italy, however, was for the present out of the question, on account of the risk to young Percy Florence.

Godwin's situation was dragging on hopelessly. His letters were to be dreaded. It is not without significance that when Mary wrote in her journal for April 4: "Shelley ill," it was immediately preceded by "Letter from Papa." Letters from Elizabeth Kent and Leigh Hunt showed that Hunt's finances were again desperate, and Shelley was now too straitened himself to help. He did what he could by writing to Ollier about a debt of Hunt's that he had guaranteed shortly before leaving England.

Old debts of his own were cropping up in embarrassing profusion. Payment was due on the piano he had bought at Marlow on a deferred-payment plan negotiated through Vincent Novello. Two moneylenders of Bath, from whom Shelley had borrowed over five hundred pounds in 1817, demanded a large payment, reproached him for selling his furniture at Marlow and departing without leaving an address, and threatened legal action. Money was still owing to Madocks at Marlow, a debt which Shelley thought Longdill should pay but which that "insolent rascal" referred to Shelley through Peacock. The printers of *A Six Weeks' Tour*, and of *Alastor*, both pressed for payment.

Shelley was now living economically and well within his income, but it was impossible to meet these debts at the moment. He arranged for what slight payments he could, and wrote pacifying letters. Sir Timothy, hearing something of these difficulties, informed Whitton with a certain grim satisfaction: "It is not likely he will soon visit England with so many unwelcome guests to ask how he does by a gentle tap."

To financial worries were added increasing domestic discord between Mary and Claire. Mary's frequent low spirits sorted ill with Claire's vivacity and her critical attitude toward Mary's treatment of Shelley. Quite likely there were frequent little domestic clashes that both ladies were careful to omit from their journals. But, with all their reticence, two or three brief lapses tell a clear story. On June 8 Mary wrote: "A better day than most days, and good reason for it, though Shelley is not well. Clare away at Pugnano." On July 4 Claire's journal began:

> Heigho the Clare and the Ma
> Find something to fight about every day.

Both Mary and Claire were in somewhat worse health than usual, and Claire's nerves were not improved by the fact that there were fresh difficulties with Byron over Allegra. Since Allegra had visited her mother in 1818, Byron had given up miscellaneous profligacy and had settled down to his comparatively respectable liaison with the Countess Guiccioli. He had grown fonder and prouder of Allegra and had rejected the offer of an English lady to adopt her. Claire was uneasy and wished for another visit from Allegra. Byron's refusal, delivered through the Hoppners, was most decisive. He totally disapproved of the treatment of children in Shelley's family. "Have they *reared* one?" he harshly demanded. Certainly he would not allow Allegra to join them and "perish of Starvation, and green fruit, or be taught to believe that there is no Deity." He conceded only that Claire might see Allegra when there was "convenience of vicinity and access," and said that he was thinking of placing the child in a convent to be educated.

Claire spent a day in cogitation and then sent Byron a most emphatic protest against his plan. Sick and miserable as she was, she would forgo seeing Allegra, was "willing to undergo any affliction rather than her whole life should be spoilt by a convent education." What she felt about Byron as she wrote may be judged from her journal entry (May 1): "Write to my damned Brute," which she scratched through with belated prudence that might not have been exercised had she known that Byron was soon to characterize her to Hoppner as "a damned Bitch." Byron's answer to this letter is unknown, except inasmuch as it can be inferred from Claire's journal for May 19 — "Brutal letter from Albè" — and from Shelley's reply to it.

Drawn again into his trying role of mediator, Shelley wrote to mollify Byron and to beg him to express himself less harshly about Claire, adding:

I hope you know what my feelings, and those of Mary have ever been, about Allegra. Indeed, we are not yet cured of our affection for her; and whatever plans you and Clare agree upon, about her future life, remember that *we*, as friends to all parties, would be most happy to be instrumental to her welfare. I smiled at your protest about what you consider my creed. On the contrary, I think a regard to chastity is quite necessary, as things are, to a young female — that is, to her happiness — and at any time a good habit. As to Christianity — there I am vulnerable; though I should be as little inclined to teach a child disbelief, as belief, as a formal creed. You are misinformed, too, as to our system of

357

physical education; but I can guess the source of this mistake. I say all this, not to induce you to depart from your plan (nor would Clare consent to Allegra's residing with us for any length of time), but only to acquaint you with our feelings on the subject — which are, and must ever be, friendly to you, and yours.

Daily life during the first six months at Pisa was regular and uneventful. Mary's time was divided between her baby (who had a light attack of measles in March), her reading, and the Masons. Her journal records reading about thirty books — novels, memoirs, politics, and Latin. On one day, April 23, she wrote: "Read — I am sure I forget what." On April 1 she finished reading Machiavelli's *Life of Castruccio*, on which her own novel of *Valperga* is based, and in the latter part of the month she began writing her novel and wrote almost daily throughout May. At various times from March to June she also helped Shelley in his translation of Spinoza.

Claire had her music, and after March 16, dancing lessons also. She went about more than Mary, particularly with the Mason children, Laurette and Nerina, and kept up a correspondence with friends in Florence. She, too, was engaged in literary work, translating a French book and composing a work now lost, which she called "Letters from Italy." Her reading was if anything more extensive than Mary's, running to drama, dramatic history, and politics.

Shelley read (but apparently not so much as either Claire or Mary), wrote about half a dozen short poems and a number of letters, spent a good deal of time with the Masons, and from March 17 to April 8 devoted considerable time to translating Spinoza with Mary. Almost half the books read by Shelley during the first six months at Pisa were read aloud to Mary in the evening, probably after Claire had retired to her own room. A part of his comparative inaction Shelley explained to Hunt as due to the lack of a study previous to changing lodgings on March 14. The ill effect of the winter upon Shelley's vitality probably contributed more to his inaction. Possibly a still greater reason, on which both Mary and Claire were silent and on which Shelley affords a clue only in his letters to the Gisbornes, was the lack of "peace of mind" and "tranquillity."

Among the four poems known to have been written by Shelley in the first half of 1820 all but the "Ode to Liberty" may be thought of as connected with Mary's difficult state of mind. "The Sensitive Plant" presents a lovely lady whose presence causes a beautiful garden (and the sensitive plant in particular) to flourish, and whose absence blights it with foul decay. Her return, like that of the Maniac's lady in "Julian and Maddalo," is uncertain. She fills all the conditions of Intellectual Beauty visiting the garden of human life, in which the poet is the sensitive plant. But she also fills all the conditions of Shelley's own life when he felt himself abandoned by Mary — and she may just as well be both as one.

"A Vision of the Sea," written in April, is a strange, detailed picture of a shipwreck in which a mother and her child are finally left alone on a sinking ship whose cargo of tigers has been loosed by the storm. This may or may not reflect Shelley's view of Mary's withdrawal into herself. The 124-line fragment "Orpheus" presents the search for a lost Eurydice with almost autobiographical poignance:

> . . . so Orpheus, seized and torn
> By the sharp fangs of an insatiate grief,
> Mænad-like waved his lyre in the bright air,
> And wildly shrieked "Where she is, it is dark!"

Even the apparently playful little poem called "An Exhortation," dated 1819 when published by Mrs. Shelley, but "Pisa, April 1820" in Shelley's hand in the Harvard manuscript, contains the significant lines,

> Where light is, camelions change!
> Where love is not, poets do:
> Fame is love disguised: if few
> Find either, never think it strange
> That poets range.

In the absence of more objective data these poems, whose probable bearing upon Shelley's domestic life has hitherto been ignored, may easily be overemphasized. The surrounding circumstances indicate that they do reflect moments of dejection and unhappiness suggestive of the earlier crisis. But they do not indicate a fresh crisis so much as a considerably milder aftermath of the first one.

Though Mary was not what she had been before Clara's death, for Shelley she was still more than anyone else; and though Shelley had his moments of bitter disillusion, he also had hopes. He wore a ring with the motto "*Il buon tempo verrà*" (The good time will come) as a kind of symbol of his hope.

In one brief comment to Hunt at this time Shelley condensed much of the disillusion and continued faith that had gone into his poetry of the preceding year:

The system of society as it exists at present must be overthrown from the foundations with all its superstructure of
maxims and of forms before we shall find anything but disappointment in our intercourse with any but a few select spirits.
This remedy does not seem to be one of the easiest. But the
generous few are not the less held to tend with all their efforts
towards it. If faith is a virtue in any case it is so in politics rather
than religion; as having a power of producing a belief in that
which is at once a prophecy and a cause.

A strong inspiration to Shelley at this time, and also to Mary and
Claire, was the growth of the spirit of freedom in Spain. Each week
they eagerly scanned Galignani's Paris *Weekly Messenger* for news
of revolutionary progress. They exulted over the insurgent victories,
the restoration of the Constitution of 1812, and the abolition of the
Inquisition. Shelley even thought of a voyage to Spain.

Instead he wrote his lofty "Ode to Liberty." The poem begins with
a review of the history of Liberty somewhat similar to the one he was
making in prose at about the same time in his *Philosophical View of
Reform* and the one he was soon to make, with variations, in his
"Defence of Poetry." He then turns to the present prospects of Liberty in Europe, seeks to awaken "king-deluded" Germany, and urges
England to take her inspiration from Spain. The "Ode to Liberty"
seems in places to overleap Shelley's philosophic and æsthetic growth
of eight years and return to the vigorous direct radicalism of *Queen
Mab*. Kings and priests are excoriated in a way which unfriendly reviewers did not fail to note. But there was one significant, unnoted
difference from the old attitude. Shelley now considered the real
seat of oppression not primarily evil institutions, but the consent of
man's "own high will."

It is only in connection with the intense strength and unity of Shelley's poetry and prose of 1819 and 1820 that his nearest perfect
poem, "Ode to the West Wind," can be fully appreciated. Its description of himself as one "chained and bowed" by a "heavy weight
of hours" and suffering "in sore need" loses much of its sentimental
quality when seen as a keen realization of the disparity between the
tremendous things that must somehow be done and the inadequacy
of one mind and body to such a task. The poem is in fact a reaffirma-
tion of faith in spite of discouragement, a sustained invocation, concluding with a prayer for power and opportunity to carry out the
purposes resolved upon in childhood:

Drive my dead thoughts over the universe
Like withered leaves to quicken a new birth!
And, by the incantation of this verse,

Scatter, as from an unextinguished hearth
Ashes and sparks, my words among mankind!
Be through my lips to unawakened earth

The trumpet of a prophecy! O, Wind,
If Winter comes, can Spring be far behind?

Like *Prometheus Unbound*, this poem finds in the revolution of the seasons a semi-mystical assurance of social regeneration. Like *Prometheus Unbound* again, it was no sudden outburst, but a thoroughly natural and logical culmination of thoughts that had long been germinating. In March 1812 he had rebuked the pessimism of the Malthusians with the same analogy from nature. And in 1817, in two consecutive stanzas in *The Revolt of Islam* (IX, 21, 22), he had fully anticipated both the regenerative significance of autumn and spring in the "Ode to the West Wind" and the apostrophe to Spring which begins Act II of *Prometheus Unbound*.

During the first six months of 1820 Shelley devoted a little attention to the practical aspects of scattering his words among mankind. Besides seeking information about a publisher for his *Philosophical View of Reform* and his "popular songs," he gently chided Hunt for having completely ignored receipt of "Peter Bell the Third" and the letter on Carlile. He sent new poems to be published with *Prometheus Unbound* and arranged for Mr. Gisborne, who had heard it read, to read the proof after his arrival in London. It was his favorite poem, he said, and required fine ink, good paper, and especial care in printing, even though he realized it would not sell. He was comparatively indifferent about *The Cenci*, but he defended its fitness for the stage, and urged a new edition at once.

Shelley was becoming dissatisfied with his publisher. Though Ollier was generous as to royalties, allowing twenty per cent when Shelley would have accepted ten, he was dilatory and unenterprising. "I am afraid his demerits are very heavy," Shelley told Hunt; but at the same time he realized that he was practically in Ollier's power, since probably no other publisher would take over his books. There was really nothing to do, he concluded, except to "make the best of a bad business."

Prometheus Unbound was still in the press, but *The Cenci* appeared about the middle of March and received immediately far more critical attention than any previous work of Shelley's. Ten reviews appeared between March 19 and July 26, 1820. It did Shelley no good with the conservatives that the play was dedicated to Leigh Hunt and that the first notice it received was a brief note in the *Examiner* calling it "undoubtedly the greatest dramatic production of the day," followed by a full and enthusiastic review in Hunt's *Indicator* for July 19 and 26. The *Theatrical Inquisitor* for April also admired the play greatly, without reservation: "As a first dramatic effort 'The Cenci' is unparalleled for the beauty of every attribute with which drama can be endowed. . . ."

At the other extreme stood the *Literary Gazette,* a powerful weekly with a keen eye for impiety and immorality, both of which it professed to find in *The Cenci.* It began: "Of all the abominations which intellectual perversion, and poetical atheism, have produced in our times, this tragedy appears to us to be the most abominable." And without having once wandered from this theme it reached its conclusion: "We now most gladly take leave of this work; and sincerely hope, that should we continue our literary pursuits for fifty years, we shall never need again to look into one so stamped with pollution, impiousness, and infamy." Thus the *Literary Gazette* embarked upon an unintermittent, single-minded, pious, and unscrupulous effort to exterminate the Amalekite that lasted until after Shelley's death.

Mingled praise and blame, acknowledging Shelley's genius while emphasizing his "moral perversity," characterized the reviews in the *Monthly Magazine,* the *London Magazine and Monthly Critical and Dramatic Review,* the *New Monthly Magazine,* the *London Magazine,* and the *Edinburgh Monthly Review.* The *Edinburgh Monthly Review* commented upon a certain "foolish timidity" in reviewers who feared to do justice to Shelley's genius because of his "errors," and prophesied his great success "were he to choose and manage his themes with some decent measure of regard for the just opinions of the world."

An author less predisposed to consider himself the prey of hostile reviewers might have found more encouragement in the criticism of *The Cenci* than Shelley perceived. But Shelley was far more concerned with propagating the ideas which the reviewers generally assailed than in securing recognition of the "genius" which they gen-

erally admitted and praised. Yet when Ollier sent him some or all of
these reviews a few months later, his comment did not entirely ignore their more favorable elements, and he decided that in his next
drama, should he write one, he would profit by their criticisms of
The Cenci.

At this time Shelley's mind harked back to that first review in the
Quarterly, blasting him and his *Revolt of Islam.* It is now known to
have been written by John Taylor Coleridge, but Shelley suspected
that Southey was the author. On June 26 he wrote Southey a letter
confessing some doubt on the matter and asking Southey to deny
authorship. Thus began an interchange of criticisms and reproofs
between two former friends that lasted until September and altered
the opinions of neither. Southey denied authorship of the *Quarterly
Review* article, but seized upon the occasion to make a vigorous and
apparently well-meant criticism of Shelley's opinions and conduct.
Like the reviewers, he accused Shelley of debasing real genius by
devoting it to monstrous and pernicious ends, and he pointed to Shelley's own experience as proof that such doctrines and conduct lead
to unhappiness. Christian principles might have saved him and might
still save him. These admonitions, he warmly protested, were dictated neither by personal animosity nor by party spirit, but by a
genuine, sympathetic interest surviving from the old friendship at
Keswick.

Shelley replied that he could never think well of Christianity as
long as its effect seemed to be to transform men of amiable manners
and high accomplishments into men of the most un-Christlike violence and harshness. Southey himself had been so betrayed into a
presumptuously cruel condemnation of Shelley's private life. Most
solemnly Shelley protested that this accusation was false, that he
had been in no way responsible for Harriet's ruin, and that he could,
if he wished, tell a tale that would open Southey's eyes. As for the
calamities that Southey believed to be the fruit of his opinions, "The
immediate fruits of all new opinions are indeed calamity to the pro-
mulgators and professors; but we are the end of nothing, and it is
in acting well, in contempt of present advantage, that virtue consists."

Southey returned stoutly to the attack, insisting that Shelley was
morally responsible for Harriet's ruin, and pointing to orthodox
Christianity as the only proper guide. To this Shelley did not reply.
Two letters of Southey's written much later show that his view of
Shelley's character hardened with the years. "With all his genius (and

I think *most* highly of it)," he wrote to Sir Henry Taylor on February
28, 1830, "he was a base, bad man." The next day he amplified his
phrase thus: "I meant that he was a liar and a cheat . . . he paid no
regard to truth nor to any kind of moral obligation. It was mortifying to discover this, for I never saw a youth of whom I could have
hoped better things."

At about the time Shelley opened his correspondence with Southey
the Gisbornes, who had reached London on June 4, were listening to
some very positive opinions of Shelley from Godwin. He conceded
that Shelley had genius and some benevolence, but accused him of
immorality, instability, irresponsible enthusiasm, failure to fulfill a
solemn promise on which Godwin had depended, and of "a particular enmity against truth, so that he utters falsehoods and makes
exaggerations even when no end is to be answered by them." Mrs.
Godwin was even more bitter toward Mary, whom she considered
her greatest enemy in the world, and whose friends even, she regretfully stated through her husband, she preferred not to meet.
Against these, and the more temperate strictures of Samuel Taylor
Coleridge, it is to be presumed that the Gisbornes returned some
variant of the answer they gave their old friend Mr. Fenwick: "We
told him how much we admired S . . . and that there was not a person in the world that we preferred to him." Such conversation was
balanced, however, by that of the Hunts, which was always full of
Shelley's praise.

In Italy, meanwhile, the Shelleys were facing more tangible troubles than hostile opinion in England. On June 12 Shelley learned
that his discharged servant, Paolo, was threatening to spread slan-
derous stories about him among the English at Leghorn unless bought
off. The slander was the same one later repeated by Elise to the
Hoppners, namely, that Claire had borne Shelley an illegitimate
child in Naples. The one unexplained word "Paolo" in Mary's journal
shows that she understood perfectly well its significance. Shelley left
at once for Leghorn, and returned to move his whole family there on
June 15, to occupy the Gisbornes' vacant home, Casa Ricci. Three days
later Mary wrote to inform Mrs. Gisborne of the move, stating that
it had been necessary to consult a lawyer and that the partial cause
was that "most superlative rascal," Paolo, who had entered into "an
infamous conspiracy against us." "We have had a most infernal business with Paolo," Shelley wrote two weeks later, "whom, however,
we have succeeded in crushing."

The innocent cause of Paolo's attempted blackmail had died in
Naples on June 9, about a week before Paolo was disposed of, but
the Shelleys did not learn of it for several weeks. Shelley had written
to the Gisbornes on June 30:

> My poor Neapolitan, I hear has a severe fever of dentition. I
> suppose she will die and leave another memory to these which
> already torture me. I am waiting the next post with anxiety but
> without much hope. What remains to me? Domestic peace and
> fame? You will laugh when you hear me talk of the latter; indeed
> it is only a shadow. The seeking of a sympathy with the unborn
> and the unknown is a feeble mood of allaying the love within us;
> and even that is beyond the grasp of so weak an aspirant as I.
> Domestic peace I might have — I may have — if I see you I shall
> have — but have not, for Mary suffers dreadfully about the state
> of Godwin's circumstances. I am very nervous, but better in gen-
> eral health.

A postscript to this letter dated July 2, 1820 adds: "I have later
news of my Neapolitan. I have taken every possible precaution for
her, and hope that they will succeed. She is to come to us as soon as
she recovers." Soon, however, Shelley was writing in an undated letter to the Gisbornes: "My Neapolitan charge is dead. It seems as if the
destruction that is consuming me were as an atmosphere which wrapt
and *infected* everything connected with me." After these words no
member of the Shelley or Gisborne families ever wrote or spoke a
single word about Elena Adelaide Shelley that has survived. Her
death, like her life and her final illness, is entirely ignored in the journals and letters of both Mary and Claire.

Neither Mary nor Shelley mentioned the precise nature of Paolo's
"prodigious falsehoods" about "horrible crimes," nor had either mentioned Claire's name in this connection. Yet the Gisbornes knew
what they meant, and so they must have known the true story of
Elena, for Mrs. Gisborne remarked in her journal for August 28, 1820
that if Paolo made his charges public, *Claire's* reputation would be
damaged. It is also worth noting that their faith in Shelley and the
story he had previously told them remained unshaken by Paolo's
slanders.

The same letters that record the death of Elena and the villainy of
Paolo show that the Shelleys were in perhaps even greater distress
over Godwin's catastrophic finances. Godwin was begging with a
kind of tragic dignity to be at once relieved, or else allowed to face

his catastrophe without false hopes. "Do not let me be led into a fool's paradise. It is better to look my ruin full in the face at once than to be amused for ever with promises, at the same time that nothing is done." Shelley's old dream of being the means of preserving the world's greatest living apostle of truth had turned bitter when the means of preservation were no longer at hand and when the apostle himself was recognized as a domestic enemy and a financial vulture whose implacable demands even if granted seemed unlikely to promise a rescue. Yet Shelley, probably more on Mary's account now than on Godwin's, wished to do all he could.

Mary's state of mind was almost frantic, while Godwin was maintaining a bitter stoic silence. Then, on June 30, Godwin informed Mary that nothing could prevent his ruin unless £500 could be raised at once. Horace Smith had already paid Godwin £100 on Shelley's account, and the Shelleys wrote immediately to ask the Gisbornes, if they possibly could, to advance the remaining £400 against Shelley's enclosed note.

Shelley felt bitterly humiliated to be compelled to ask help from the Gisbornes under such circumstances. He knew that their own finances were not flourishing; he even doubted that the money, if obtained, would confer any real benefit on Godwin. He wrote to them, separately from Mary, to insist that no money should actually be paid over to Godwin until the papers of release were drawn up and signed, and to suggest that they write to him under cover to Mrs. Mason, "if you have any communications unfit for Mary's agitated mind."

The Gisbornes were either unable or unwilling to come to the rescue, and Godwin's miserable situation remained unchanged. Whatever frantic or stoical letters he wrote to the Shelleys during the next two months have been lost, but they resulted on August 7 in a long letter from Shelley in which he gave full reasons for the very firm stand he was resolved thenceforth to maintain.

In this letter Shelley reviewed his whole financial relationship with Godwin and stated at length why he both could not and should not yield to continued demands. His own finances, he asserted, had become more involved than even Mary knew. Any fresh drain upon his resources would involve him in personal peril. He owed nearly £2,000 to creditors, most of whom were importunate and some of whom were now threatening suit. Within a few years he had given Godwin between £4,000 and £5,000, procured largely from moneylenders at an actual cost of nearly four times the amount realized.

366

His credit with moneylenders was practically gone and his potential
fortune almost wrecked, yet Godwin had been benefited by the sacrifice no more than if the money had been thrown into the sea. He
denied, with one exception, ever promising Godwin anything, save
on condition of ability to pay. He promised still to do what he could,
but he could not produce the £400 that Godwin demanded.

Finally, Shelley insisted firmly that he would not allow Mary to be
further tormented by letters that almost seemed to be written with
that purpose:

> Mary is now giving suck to her infant, in whose life, after the
> frightful events of the last two years, her own seems wholly to
> be bound up. Your letters from their style and spirit (such is
> your erroneous notion of taste) never fail to produce an appall-
> ing effect on her frame. On one occasion agitation of mind pro-
> duced through her a disorder in the child, similar to that which
> destroyed our little girl two years ago. . . . On that occasion
> Mary at my request authorised me to intercept such letters or
> information as I might judge likely to disturb her mind. That
> discretion I have exercised with the letter to which this is a
> reply.

The Shelleys and Claire remained in the Gisbornes' home from
June 15 to August 5. Daily life there was even more uneventful than
at Pisa, for they knew few people at Leghorn, and Claire and Mary
were both in worse health than usual. For ten days after their arrival
Mary was "too much oppressed and too languid to do anything."
Soon afterwards, however, she was studying Greek with Shelley. As
for Shelley, he wrote Godwin on August 7: "I am tormented beyond
all expression by nephritic pains. . . . The surgeon here assured me
that my disease is nephritic, and adds, as my consolation, that it has
no tendency to shorten life."

Occasionally they took walks in the surrounding country or to the
seaside, sometimes with one another, sometimes with members of
the Ricci family, the Gisbornes' neighbors and landlords. Shelley and
Claire each made two or three short trips to Pisa. As usual, all three
read every day. Shelley read Euripides, the Greek romances, Lucretius (with Mary), and Forteguerri's *Ricciardetto* aloud. On July
14 he finished his translation of the Homeric "Hymn to Mercury."
Claire was still writing her "Letters from Italy" and was still endeavoring vainly to secure some satisfaction about Allegra.

A touch of humor was occasionally added to the predominantly dreary tone of existence by the presence of the Gisbornes' neighbors and servants. Mary pretended in her letters that the Signorina Appolonia Ricci was pining dreadfully for the absent Henry Reveley. The servants Giuseppe and Annunziata had just become the parents of a son for whom a lively christening party was given; Giuseppe insisted with ridiculous earnestness that he looked the very image of Mr. Gisborne.

If the Shelleys found private amusement in this circumstance, Giuseppe's turn came later. A sudden violent dispute having broken out between Giuseppe and Annunziata, Shelley endeavored in vain to compose the matter and in a pretended rage chased Giuseppe from the house with a pistol. With Shelley in close pursuit, threatening murder, Giuseppe darted round a corner and hid in the shrubbery while Shelley raced ahead. Shelley returned to the house to find the couple in the most amicable conversation, as if nothing had occurred. The air was sweet and heavy with many *"caro's"* and *"carissima's."* They denied, in fact, that anything had occurred, and with Mary's help half persuaded Shelley that the whole episode must have been an illusion.

Shelley had immediately taken over Henry Reveley's study. Thence, crowded by mysterious pieces of machinery — "Great screws, and cones, and wheels, and groovèd blocks" — he wrote his rhymed "Letter to Maria Gisborne" that touches so lightly upon the troubles by which he was surrounded and so gracefully upon his life with the Gisbornes and his absent friends in England. He pictured himself humorously as "plotting dark spells and devilish enginery" such as would "pump up oaths from clergymen" and grind "the gentle spirit of our meek reviews" into violent outbreaks — a "war of worms" of which he could remain heedless. Old pleasures with his friends thronged his mind to produce a delightful picture of former days with the Gisbornes. How they had enjoyed their country walks and frugal picnics together, their Spanish, and their talk of all the earth's business, and of poetry and liberty especially! Now that the Gisbornes were in London and would meet Shelley's old friends, he furnished a bright thumbnail sketch of what they should expect in each.

It was probably on the evening of June 22, just a week after this poem was written, that Mary and Shelley walked among the myrtle hedges near Casa Ricci and took a momentary joy in the flashing of the fireflies in the hedges and the singing of the skylarks overhead. Returning home, Shelley wrote his famous "To a Skylark."

There had been few times in Shelley's life when a symbol of joy could have been more welcome to him. From the first line of his poem the skylark is such a symbol — "Bird thou never wert." He is in fact a poet, a happy poet to whom the world will listen. Languor, which particularly oppressed both Shelley and Mary at the time, had no existence for this skylark-poet. Annoyance — a mild name for Shelley's importunate creditors — never came near him; he could love without feeling the sadness of too much love. More than Shelley and Mary he was a stranger to tears and a scorner of hate and fear — the hate of the reviewers and the fear of Paolo's slanders and of Godwin's impending ruin. In the end he is an example to his pane-gyrist:

> Teach me half the gladness
>   That thy brain must know,
> Such harmonious madness
>   From my lips would flow
> The world should listen then, as I am listening now.

All the shadows and miseries which surrounded Shelley as he wrote, and all his longing to surmount them, have their echoes in the poem.

The plan to spend the summer months at the Baths of Lucca had been abandoned when it was found necessary to go to Leghorn. But as the weather grew hotter at Leghorn it was decided to go for at least three months to the Baths of San Giuliano di Pisa, four miles above the city of Pisa. On July 30 Shelley took an apartment there which he described as "very pleasant and spacious," for a period of three months at a rental of forty sequins quarterly. And on August 5 the Shelleys and Claire left Leghorn and entered their new quarters, known as Casa Prinni. Two of Shelley's last actions before the removal were to write to Tom Medwin (July 20) insisting upon his promised visit, and to write to John Keats (July 30) offering sympathy and encouragement. Having just heard from Mr. Gisborne of Keats's pulmonary attack, he urged him warmly to conserve his health by spending the winter in Italy as the guest of the Shelleys. He added a word of encouragement and advice about poetry which Keats, in his illness and sensitiveness, may not have taken exactly as meant:

> I have lately read your "Endymion" again and ever with a new sense of the treasures of poetry it contains, though treasures

poured forth with indistinct profusion. This, people in general will not endure, and that is the cause of the comparatively few copies which have been sold. I feel persuaded that you are capable of the greatest things, so you but will.

Keats replied appreciatively on August 10, without definitely accepting the invitation. After some brief account of his health and his attitude toward his own poetry, he reminded Shelley of the latter's earlier advice to him to restrain his desire to publish and ventured to return the same advice, after reading *The Cenci.* He wished that Shelley would curb his impetuosity and "load every rift of your subject with ore." At the same time he confided to Charles Cowden Clarke that his sole motive in not accepting the invitation was a fear that in Shelley's company he could not remain a free agent.

Chapter XXII

THE BATHS OF PISA, or the Baths of San Giuliano (for they went under either name), were warm natural springs at the foot of the mountain of San Giuliano, four miles from Pisa. They were supposed to be particularly soothing for nervous ailments, and their hot summer climate suited Shelley exactly. Casa Prinni, the commodious house which Shelley had secured, was conveniently situated at the lower side of the square containing the little casino in which the life of the resort was centered. To the rear of the house a garden extended to a canal connecting the river Serchio with the Arno. Across the canal the low, flat fields, under frequent threat of inundation, were not a particularly inspiring view, but there were mountains close by, and in summer the neighboring slopes of Monte San Giuliano were covered with the bloom of myrtle.

On the evening of August 5 the Shelleys and Claire moved into their new quarters, where they were to remain until October 29. They were near enough to Pisa, Lucca, and even Leghorn for occasional callers, and to visit those places practically as often as they desired. Few days passed without some such visit, sometimes on pleasure, sometimes, in Shelley's case, on business. Mr. and Mrs. Mason came several times to visit them at the Baths, sometimes alone, and once or twice with the children. Also Madame Tantini, a Pisan lady in temporay residence at the Baths, exchanged occasional calls with the Shelleys. Claire remained at the Baths only until August 31, when she removed to Leghorn, apparently because she thought sea bathing might be more beneficial to her health.

There was little to do except walk, bathe, read, and write. The Shelleys and Claire enjoyed walking before breakfast or in the evening on the mountainside or along one of the several roads leading from the Baths. Occasionally they rode. Their one excursion to Lucca occupied two days (August 11 and 12) and was devoted by Mary and Claire to sightseeing, with some special attention to relics of Castruccio, on account of Mary's novel about him. Shelley left the others at Lucca and went on to climb Monte San Pellegrino alone, returning to the Baths on August 13 considerably fatigued, but inspired with the idea of his "Witch of Atlas," which he wrote during the three days following his return.

With the summer temperature, warm baths, and a life more in the open air Shelley's health improved notably. Only once does Mary record: "Shelley is not well." The recent death of Elena Adelaide, sad as it was for Shelley, may have terminated a strain in his life with Mary. Claire's absence removed an occasional domestic irritation, and Paolo Foggi seemed definitely silenced. Writing to Amelia Curran, Mary described their situation at the Baths as quite pleasant, and reported Percy Florence as thriving and Shelley as in improving health. "We go on in our old manner," she added, "with no change. I have had many changes for the worse — one might be for the better — but that is nearly impossible."

Going on "in the old manner," of course, meant regular reading and study and occasional writing. Mary was reading Greek, Lucretius, Virgil's *Georgics,* Boccaccio, a few books of travel and history, *Don Juan,* Keats's poems, and *Prometheus Unbound.* Shelley was reading alone Apollonius Rhodius, Plato's *Republic,* Herodotus, "Robertson's America," "Gillie's Greece," and "Ancient Metaphysics"; aloud he was reading *The Double Marriage, Love's Progress,* Boccaccio, and Keats's *Hyperion.*

Upon his return from Monte San Pellegrino Shelley immediately set about writing down the delightful poem "The Witch of Atlas," which he had imagined during his solitary expedition. Three days (August 14, 15, 16), as he playfully boasted to Mary in his introductory poem, were sufficient, though Wordsworth took nineteen years [actually twenty] in "dressing" Peter Bell.

Of late Mary had reasoned earnestly with Shelley that he should address his poems more to the average intelligence and so convince the world he was not the idle, reckless dreamer that he was supposed to be. She did not wish him to compromise with his principles, but merely to lay a broader foundation in the popular mind for their just reception. She also felt that Shelley's own mind and health might be greatly benefited if he could be convinced that his writings were not so totally scorned as he supposed. Better than most others Mary was in a position to understand that his protestations of indifference to the reviewers were too constant to mean anything except a despairing desire to be indifferent.

But Shelley, while reasonable and practical enough to begin planning "Charles I," was never the person to be diverted from his bent. "The Witch of Atlas" develops a delicately beautiful little semi-myth that seems almost Puckishly to desert the world of flesh and blood that Mary wished him to frequent. In a cavern of the Atlas Mountains, beside a secret fountain, dwelt this "lady-witch" whose insupportable beauty all men and creatures came to worship:

> For she was beautiful: her beauty made
>   The bright world dim, and everything beside
> Seemed like the fleeting image of a shade;
>   No thought of living spirit could abide,
> Which to her looks had ever been betrayed,
>   On any object in the world so wide,
> On any hope within the circling skies,
> But on her form, and in her inmost eyes.

Perceiving this, the Witch wove a subtle magic veil as "a shadow for the splendour of her love."

She was the mistress of many charms and spells, which Shelley described with a careful elaboration suggestive (like a number of specific details) of both Edmund Spenser and John Keats. At first she lived alone; later she created for herself a winged, sexless creature called Hermaphroditus, who propelled with its wings the magic boat in which she journeyed through mountain streams and austral oceans. Millions of her ministering spirits in the clouds built for her an imperial magic tent of vapor, light, and fire, whence she observed with pleasure or delight all that happened between the earth and the moon.

But her chief delight was to visit in sleep the spirits of human beings. To the most beautiful she offered a crystal bowl whose contents made them live thereafter under the control of some mighty power beyond them, and live on even after death. The less beautiful she would visit with strange dreams, wherein priests, kings, and soldiers would see themselves for the cheats they were, and timid lovers would overcome their timidity and yet take no harm from doing so. She was herself as ignorant of the love of the sexes as if she were a sexless bee, but later, Shelley says, she knew what love was.

The playful tone, the ottava rima, some of the setting, and the unfamiliar conception of a witch as beautiful and benevolent, all came apparently from Shelley's recent enthusiastic reading of Forteguerri's half-serious epic romance, *Ricciardetto*. The Witch herself is clearly Shelley's one and only goddess, Intellectual Beauty, transparently veiled in the cloudy, semi-mischievous magic of *Ricciardetto*. She is far more playful and youthful than in his other accounts of her, but otherwise her attributes are exactly the same. Like Asia and his first conception of Intellectual Beauty, her beauty is veiled because otherwise it would be insupportable. Like the Intellectual Beauty or Love of *Adonais,* she wields the world to her purposes, but only to the extent to which the reluctant mass is capable of being so molded.

In "Peter Bell the Third," written less than a year before "The Witch of Atlas," and in *Swellfoot the Tyrant,* written only a few days after "The Witch of Atlas," Shelley was unable, in spite of comparatively frivolous intentions, to avoid a serious undernote where his own theories of society were involved. No more was he able to do so in "The Witch of Atlas," the lightest and most elfish of all his poems. In the end he dwells lightly, but with unmistakable meaning, upon the old evils of human society that he could never put completely out of his mind.

Almost immediately Shelley turned from his Witch to a more familiar type of poetry. During the summer of 1820 the cause of freedom in Italy, never quite extinguished by the partial failure of the French Revolution, flared forth in a brilliant *ignis fatuus* that seemed at the time to be a true illumination. The success of the Spanish insurgents stimulated the Neapolitans. In July an incipient revolt broke out, which the soldiers of King Ferdinand refused to suppress. Most of the army went over to the revolution, and King Ferdinand was compelled to grant a constitution to Naples. In the sister Kingdom of Sicily (Naples and Sicily were then known as the Kingdom of the Two Sicilies) there was more violence, but the result was the same. Shelley wrote to Mary on July 30: "The soldiers resisted the people, and a terrible slaughter amounting, it is said, to four thousand men, ensued. The event however was as it should be — Sicily like Naples is free."

It was a false dawn, and Neapolitan freedom was to be bloodily extinguished by the Austrians within a few months. But while freedom still shone bright Shelley wrote his "Ode to Naples," which was finished on August 24. His earlier "Ode to Liberty" had been mainly an invocation; the "Ode to Naples" is an impassioned welcome. Yet the poet realized that liberty, like the Mohammedan's paradise, lay under the shadow of a sword. Already he saw a vision of the Austrian armies on the march, desolating the Alps, trampling beautiful cities into dust, and leaving only the fire-blackened fields behind them. The poem concludes with a moving invocation to Love to protect the spirit of freedom against brutish reaction and oppression.

On August 24, while Shelley was writing the "Ode to Naples," Mrs. Mason happened to be visiting the Shelleys. On that day also the near-by farmers brought their pigs to a local fair, held in the square of the village just beneath the Shelleys' windows. Undertaking to read his recent "Ode to Liberty" to Mrs. Mason, Shelley found himself riotously accompanied by the grunting of the pigs. Laughingly he compared them to the chorus of frogs in Aristophanes, and then in a spirit of burlesque he imagined a drama on the sordid trial of Queen Caroline in which the pigs should serve as chorus. So began, on October 24, his *Œdipus Tyrannus, or Swellfoot the Tyrant*.

For some time Shelley's letters had been showing a considerable interest in the trial of Queen Caroline for infidelity. His interest in political events at home had always been lively, and the coming trial was not only a political event, with the Whigs violently championing the Queen; it was also probably the most complete public display of dirty royal linen that England ever witnessed.

The Princess Caroline, separated from her royal husband, the Prince Regent, had long been traveling in Mediterranean countries with a fairly complete disregard of decorum. When the coronation of George IV was being planned, it was decided by the King and his Tory ministers to provide no place for her in the ceremonies. Caroline, who was no coward, returned to England to insist upon her royal position, and the ministers thereupon brought her to trial for infidelity. The Whigs, who hated her husband, took up her cause with alacrity. The country teemed with coarse cartoons and anonymous satires in verse and prose, some of which went beyond fifty editions. Ministers were mobbed, processions were formed, houses were stoned, and the notorious Italian witnesses that the ministers introduced were assaulted on landing. Abroad, wherever English newspapers and travelers went, it was incumbent on all good Englishmen to pronounce upon the Queen's virtue.

Mary Shelley was a strong partisan of Caroline. Shelley, this time not so warm as Mary, thought the charges probably exaggerated. His principal feeling, however, was one of disgust that "a vulgar cook-maid" should somehow become a symbol in the fight against oppression. Nevertheless, her enemies were worse than she, and were also the enemies of Freedom. Though he scorned her, he was technically on her side.

Within a week *Swellfoot* was completed and sent to Horace Smith in London, who had it printed as a pamphlet and published by J.

Johnson, 98 Cheapside, probably in December 1820. After only seven
copies had been sold, the Society for the Prevention of Vice threatened a prosecution, which the publisher averted by surrendering
all remaining copies.

Against a background of privation and oppression of the masses,
represented as a chorus of swine, Shelley presented the King's ministers seeking to ruin the Queen by pouring over her head the poisonous contents of a green bag full of perjured testimony. The Queen,
however, turned the tables by pouring the bag's contents over their
heads and riding forth in triumph on the Ionian Minotaur (John
Bull).

Written as a mere *jeu d'esprit*, it is in a sense the least Shelleyan of
all Shelley's mature poems. There is hardly an original device in it.
The green bag, the Rat, the Leech — in fact practically all of Shelley's characters — appear again and again in similar roles in the
numerous cartoons and other satires with which England was being
flooded. Even Shelley's old enemy Lord Eldon, satirized as Dakry
(Tear), is treated impersonally as the same sentimental wheedler
and weeper who appears in the contemporary satires. The similarities
are so general and so close that some of Shelley's characters may be
confidently identified from their parallel treatment in cartoons and
other anonymous satires.

But in another sense the poem is so peculiarly Shelleyan that no
one could possibly mistake it for one of the anonymous school to
which it otherwise belongs. Shelley could not debase his verse to
march *pari passu* with his subject, nor could he be boisterously,
coarsely humorous in the way that was natural to most of the pam-
phleteers. No one but Shelley would have been capable of writing
contemporary political satire in the grotesquely Gothic stage setting
that he employed. No more than in "Peter Bell" could he really
abandon himself to trifling upon a subject that was fundamentally
so serious for him. His attacks upon government spies, paper money,
corrupt courts, and the repression of the masses have an undernote
of suppressed earnestness that the mere partisans lacked. A serious
sense of impending revolution underlies the entire action and hints
that the author's jesting is almost consciously against the grain.

Claire Clairmont's unequal contest with Byron over the education
of Allegra still dragged on. On August 25 Byron wrote to Shelley a
short note declining further correspondence with Claire, "who merely
tries to be as irrational as she can be," and saying he preferred hear-

ing from Shelley. Shelley agreed that Claire's letters were probably childish and absurd. But after all, he reminded Byron, Claire's wish to see her child was natural, and she should be treated as indulgently as possible on account of her unhappiness and bad health. He politely declined to become Claire's means of communicating her sentiments to Byron, but suggested that for the present there was no need of Byron's doing more than sending news of Allegra at fairly regular intervals.

In the latter part of October Claire secured a position in the home of Dr. Bojti, who lived in Florence, opposite the Pitti Palace, and was one of the court physicians to the Grand Duke. Very likely she was a "paying guest" with light duties which somewhat reduced the pay. Probably Claire owed her new situation to the good offices of Mrs. Mason, who must have been aware of her occasional unhappiness in the same home with Mary. Shelley accompanied Claire to Florence and returned to the Baths on October 22 with Tom Medwin, whom he had picked up at Pisa on his return journey.

Medwin had been resident with the Shelleys less than a week when they were all compelled to leave the Baths and return to Pisa. Since the middle of October there had been constant rains. The Serchio rose steadily. On October 25 Mary wrote in her journal: "Rain all night. The banks of the Serchio break, and by dark all the baths are overflowed. Water four feet deep in our house." To the rear of the house the canal connecting the Arno and the Serchio overflowed. The water in the house rose to six feet. From an upper window the inmates watched the peasants driving their cattle from the plains below to the heights above the baths, and Shelley urged Medwin to do a sketch of the scene. Next morning they stepped from an upstairs window into a boat and after landing proceeded by carriage to Pisa.

Here, on October 29, the Shelleys and Medwin entered new lodgings, Palazzo Galetti, which Shelley described to Claire with some optimism as "sufficiently commodious":

> The rooms above [fourth floor], one of which is Medwin's room and the other my study (congratulate me on my seclusion) are delightfully pleasant, and to-day I shall be employed in arranging my books and gathering my papers about me. Mary has a very good room below, and there is plenty of space for the babe. I expect the water of Pisa to relieve me, if indeed the disease be what is conjectured.

Medwin did not find in his friend the hopeless invalid that Shelley had told him to expect. "His figure was emaciated, and somewhat bent, owing to near-sightedness and his being forced to lean over his books with his eyes almost touching them; his hair, still profuse, and curling naturally, was partially interspersed with grey; . . . but his appearance was youthful, and his countenance, whether grave or animated, strikingly intellectual. There was also a freshness and purity in his complexion that he never lost."

Shelley had probably forgotten that he had outgrown Medwin intellectually even while still at Eton, and it was too soon for him to reach his later conclusion that Medwin was, after all, a bore. He had recently criticized Medwin's mediocre poems with delicate tact and excessive respect; he was soon (November 10) to recommend one of them to Ollier as "a very elegant and classical composition." He and Medwin planned to begin at once the study of Arabic together, and by the middle of November the studies had begun.

Suddenly now the Shelleys were no longer the close friends with the Gisbornes that they had been. On their return to Leghorn the Gisbornes had reached Genoa by October 3, and proceeded straight to Leghorn without notifying the Shelleys, who had written to urge that they come immediately to the Baths of Pisa. When Shelley heard from Claire that they were in Leghorn he wrote to renew Mary's invitation. But he was puzzled and a little hurt: "We do not *quite* understand your silence; if you are less desirous to see us than we are to see you, you can send whatever letters or papers you may have brought us to Clare at Mrs. Mason's. . . ."

Still a strange silence from the Gisbornes. They were always negligent letter-writers, and it may be that their silence meant nothing. It may be, however, that they were somewhat offended by supposing that Shelley had mentioned their indebtedness to him as one of the reasons why he could not succor Godwin, and it seems certain that in London John Gisborne had been at least partly converted to Godwin's point of view on Shelley's financial obligations to Godwin. Finally, just before the Shelleys left the Baths, they received a call from Henry Reveley that threw Shelley into a real passion.

Henry came with a proposal of Mr. Gisborne's that the steamboat be abandoned and the engine used in an iron foundry. Otherwise four hundred crowns more would be needed to complete the boat. Shelley refused to invest any more money, and his indignation (as expressed to Claire) became so excessive that it indicates either additional unknown causes or else one of the sudden, irrational outbursts of which his earlier friends had sometimes been obliged to take note: "The Gisbornes are people totally without faith. — I think they are altogether the most filthy and odious animals with which I ever came in contact. — They do not visit Mary as they promised, and indeed if they did, I certainly should not stay in the house to receive them."

Later in the month Shelley's ire was still very much alive. "Henry Reveley," he informed Claire, "has been frequently at Pisa, and always dines with us, in spite of a conversation which I had with him, and which was intended to put an end to all intercourse between me and that base family. — I have not the heart to put my interdict in effect upon Henry, he is so very miserable, and such a whipped and trembling dog." By the beginning of December all intercourse with the Gisbornes had been broken off. Mary so informed Marianne Hunt, adding that it was not entirely "an affair of pelf," but that the Gisbornes had behaved with a folly and baseness that was extremely painful and disappointing. In a few months, however, the two families were again on friendly terms.

The Shelleys had heard seldom from their English friends during the autumn at the Baths, and continued to hear but seldom in the following winter at Pisa. Medwin said later that he never knew of an author who had less correspondence. The Hunts once or twice wrote letters that distressed Shelley by his inability to relieve Hunt in his deepening financial troubles. Horace Smith wrote that he intended to emigrate and was considering coming to Italy to be Shelley's neighbor.

Shelley still expected to be Keats's host and mentor in Italy, in spite of Keats's failure to accept his invitation. "If the *Hyperion* be not grand poetry," he assured Peacock, "none has been produced by our contemporaries." He also deeply sympathized with Keats as a victim of unjust criticism and wrote (but seems not to have sent) a letter to William Gifford in which he sought to persuade the *Quarterly Review* to deal more justly with him.

"Where is Keats now?" Shelley asked the Hunts at the time he was moving back to Pisa. "I am anxiously expecting him in Italy when I shall take care to bestow every possible attention on him. I consider his a most valuable life, and I am deeply interested in his safety. I intend to be the physician both of his body and his soul, to keep the one warm and to teach [the] other Greek and Spanish. I am aware indeed in part, that I am nourishing a rival who will far surpass [me;] and this is an additional motive and will be an added pleasure."

Soon, however, Shelley had a different patient to tend. Medwin's health, weakened by his long stay in India, broke down as a result of the hardships of his journey to Pisa. On November 5 he suffered a severe illness and was thereafter confined to his room for six weeks. Shelley nursed him as if he were a brother. "He applied my leeches, administered my medicines, and during six weeks that I was confined to my room, was assiduous and unintermitting in his affectionate care of me," Medwin testified later.

During his illness Medwin read all of Shelley's poetry and became an enthusiastic admirer of it. Shelley was surprised that anyone could admire his poems after what the reviews had said. He was, he said, "disgusted with writing, and were it not for an irresistible impulse, that predominates my better reason, should discontinue so doing."

Medwin fell easily into the reading habits of Shelley and Mary. While he was still ill he was soothed and delighted by Shelley's habit of reading aloud to him. "No one ever gave such emphasis to poetry. His voice, it is true, was a cracked soprano, but the variety of its tones, and the intensity of feeling which he displayed in the finest passages, produced an effect almost electric." Later Shelley translated aloud for him the *Prometheus* of Æschylus, "reading it as fluently as if it were written in French or Italian," often in extemporized blank verse.

Medwin had learned a little Spanish in India, and he and Shelley reveled in the "starry autos" of Calderón and also in his tragedy of *Cisma d'Inghilterra*. From Calderón they turned to Dante, and Shelley read the *Divine Comedy* aloud, lamenting at the time the inadequacy of English translations and showing Medwin a copy of his own exquisite translation from the 28th canto of the *Purgatory*. He also read with Medwin Cervantes's *Novelas,* which he deemed inferior, and Schiller's *Maid of Orleans,* which he admired for its bold treatment of Christianity as a mythology.

Naturally there was much talk of literature. Shelley expressed a great respect for Scott's novels and was an enthusiastic admirer of Manzoni's *I Promessi Sposi.* But he was no longer the indiscriminate reader of novels that he had been in his youth. Bad novels and bad verse, he now believed, should be avoided by a writer who desired purity in his own style. He was a constant reader of the older English dramatists, and particularly admired Webster's *The Duchess of Malfi.* The Latin poets he rather slighted, except Lucretius and Virgil, considering them poor copyists of the Greeks. He had lost much of his earlier interest in Tasso and Ariosto, but admired Petrarch intensely and frequently quoted his "Ode to Italy."

Milton was his idol among English poets. "So far, far above all other Poems indeed did he class the *Paradise Lost,* that he even thinks it a sacrilege to name it in speaking of any other Poem, and in his admiration of *Cain* said we had nothing like it since the *Paradise Regained* — a work which he frequently read and compared to the calm and tranquil beauty of an autumnal sunset, after the meridian glory and splendour of a summer's day."

He regarded contemporary English poetry with mixed feelings. Wordsworth was still a great poet to him, though a bad man; Byron had written some supremely great poetry and some that was bad; and "Moore's *Irish Melodies* were great favourites with him." But Campbell and Rogers were simply spoiled darlings of public taste; and the attempts of the Cockneys to write in a new poetic jargon falsely imitated from the Lakists were disgusting madness. From this criticism he did not exempt Leigh Hunt and the early poems of Keats, though he sang the praises of Keats's last volume and thought Hunt, in his *Indicator,* an excellent prose essayist.

It was Shelley's idea that a good library should consist of only a few well-chosen titles. "I'll give you my list," he told Medwin — "catalogue it can't be called: — The Greek Plays, Plato, Lord Bacon's Works, Shakespeare, The Old Dramatists, Milton, Goethe and Schiller, Dante, Petrarch and Boccaccio, and Machiavelli and Guicciardini, — not forgetting Calderon; and last, yet first, the Bible."

Like Hogg, Hunt, and Sophia Stacey before him, Medwin was deeply impressed with Shelley's studious habits. Never since leaving Oxford had Shelley ceased to be a more ardent student than he would probably have been had he remained:

> He was indeed ever engaged in composition or reading, scarcely allowing himself time for exercise or air; a book was his companion the first thing in the morning, the last thing at night. He told me he always read himself to sleep. Even when he walked on the *Argine,* his favourite winter walk, he read — sometimes through the streets, and generally had a book on the table by his side at dinner, if his temperate meal could be called one. . . . He was indeed an indefatigable Student. So little impression did that which contributes one of the main delights of ordinary mortals, make on him, that he sometimes asked, "Mary, have I dined?"

381

A few months later Edward Trelawny was to receive a similar impression: "He set to work on a book, or a pyramid of books, his eyes glistening with an energy as fierce as that of the most sordid gold-digger. . . ." At ten o'clock one morning Trelawny left Shelley standing in front of a mantelpiece, with a dictionary in hand, studying a German folio resting on the mantelpiece; returning at six in the evening he found Shelley in exactly the same position, fully believing that he had eaten the food that stood untouched on a tray at his elbow.

Shelley's studiousness was scarcely less impressive than his occasional melancholy and despondency. Few people, he told Medwin, had not been tempted at one time or another to commit suicide, adding that four of his friends had done so. Medwin thought, quite truly, that Shelley himself sometimes dwelt on the idea. Such moods, he added, were "most distressing to witness," they could not be dissipated, and they bowed Shelley to the earth in an utter "prostration of spirits." It was partly to help combat these moods with congenial society that Medwin urged his friends Lieutenant Edward Ellerker Williams and his common-law wife to come to Pisa.

Like all of Shelley's other friends who noticed these melancholy fits, Medwin was also conscious of Shelley's liveliness and playfulness at other times. "At times he was as sportive as his child, (with whom he would play by the hour upon the floor,) and his wit flowed in a continuous stream, — not that broad humour which is so much in vogue at the present day, but a genuine wit, classical I might say, and refined, that caused a smile rather than a laugh." He could be almost boisterously mirthful in deriding Wordsworth's *Peter Bell*, Elizabeth Hitchener's poetic enthusiasm for woman's rights, or Count Taafe's heavy-footed translation of Dante.

"So sensitive was he of external impressions," wrote Medwin, "so magnetic, that I have seen him, after threading the carnival crowd in the Lung' Arno Corsos, throw himself half-fainting into a chair, overpowered by the atmosphere of evil passions, as he used to say, in that sensual and unintellectual crowd." He was equally intense in his reaction to physical beauty. Many times he and Medwin watched a gorgeous Pisan sunset from their upper windows and saw the grim prison of the Torre del Fame turn to a bright gold. At such times Shelley seemed completely dead to his immediate surroundings in merging himself with the beauty of the scene. Returning to himself he would exclaim: "What a glorious world! There is, after all, something worth living for. This makes me retract the wish that I had never been born."

Soon it came Medwin's turn to be of benefit to Shelley's health. As the winter approached, Shelley's health grew worse. About the middle of November he "suffered horribly" from the pain in his side, now diagnosed by Dr. Vaccà as a kidney ailment. The spasms were so intense that Shelley rolled on the floor in agony, yet they seem to have been of such short duration as never to interfere for more than a day with his usual activities. Medwin (like Trelawny a few months later) suspected at least vaguely that there was some inter-relation between Shelley's mental and physical distress, and he also happened to have a rudimentary knowledge of hypnotism, or "animal magnetism," as it was then called. He consented to try its effect on Shelley.

The next attack occurred when Mary Shelley and another lady (Claire or Mrs. Mason) were present. No sooner had Medwin placed his hand on Shelley's forehead than the spasms ceased. Shelley fell into a deep state of somnambulism, with his eyes open. He followed Medwin to a couch at the other end of the room, answered questions in the same pitch and tone in which they were asked, and (during a second experiment) even improvised verses in Italian — all of which, after he was awakened, he denied having done. On December 15 Claire Clairmont saw one of these hypnotic experiments and heard Shelley beg not to be asked more questions, lest he should say what he ought not. Shelley became philosophically interested in the phenomenon and thought it a proof of the power of the mind under certain conditions to separate itself from the body.

Meanwhile Claire Clairmont had from the first been bored and discontented with her position in Florence. Within a fortnight Mary Shelley was writing in her journal (November 4): "Letters from —— complaining of dullness." She complained to Shelley about her health, about being neglected, and about the prospects of a cold winter in Florence. Friends returning to Pisa from Florence reported that Claire felt and looked wretched. Soon (November 21) she was back in Pisa, where she remained for a month, uncertain about seeking another situation, but in the end she returned to the Bojtis in Florence on December 23.

Claire's arrival in Pisa coincided almost exactly with a sudden enlargement of the Shelleys' circle of acquaintances. The first of these,

Professor Francesco Pacchiani, begins to appear in the journals of Mary and Claire during the last week in November. "Il Diavolo Pacchiani," as he was called, was a somewhat disreputable wreck of once brilliant prospects whom the Shelleys did not immediately recognize for quite what he was. He was a tall, thin man of fifty-one, dark almost as a Moor, with regular, strongly marked features, black eyes, and a recklessly witty tongue, of which both his friends and his enemies stood in awe. His stories, like his conduct, were occasionally dissolute. Some time previous to his acquaintance with the Shelleys he had been questioned in the streets as he was returning home with some gay companions and had given the watch an answer that passed into local tradition: "I am a public man, in a public street, with a public woman."

In his youth Pacchiani had become a canon at Prato. He still remained in orders and was confessor to the household of the Governor of Pisa, but he thought so meanly of the priesthood that he scoffingly called his beret his "Tartuffemestro," or "measure of hypocrisy." As a young man he had invented a new method of producing muriatic acid. His early experiments in chemistry and galvanism had attracted the attention of Volta, Cuvier, and Humboldt. As Professor of Physical Chemistry at the University of Pisa he neglected his duties and antagonized his colleagues. He was a poet also, and often quoted from a tragedy he said he had written, but which no one had ever seen. Yet he really was a man of extensive knowledge, original ideas, and great conversational powers. Mary Shelley, after ten days' acquaintance, described him as high-spirited, eloquent, a little eccentric, "the only Italian who has a heart and soul." Shelley, who had never heard Coleridge talk, thought Pacchiani might be his conversational equal.

Before the middle of December, however, Pacchiani had already revealed the "inquisitive and indelicate" side of his character; on December 14 Claire remarked in her journal that his conduct during an evening call was indecent. "Pacchiani is no great favourite of ours," Mary informed Mrs. Gisborne in January. "He disgusted Shelley by telling a dirty story." On December 23 he accompanied Claire on her return to Florence and remained absent from Pisa until the latter part of February, after which his calls upon the Shelleys practically ceased.

It was with Pacchiani that the improviser Tommaso Sgricci first visited the Shelleys, on December 1, 1820. Sgricci was at that time a young man of thirty-one who for seven years had been reciting his improvised poems in many of the principal cities of Italy. His vogue had continued after the attack upon the *improvvisatori* made by Giordani in 1816. He was especially able in improvising tragic scenes and even whole tragedies, reaching his greatest heights in passages of invective.

Mary Shelley mentioned with enthusiasm his advent into their circle: "We have further made the acquaintance of an Improvisor, a man of great talent, very well up in Greek and of an incomparable poetic mind. He improvises with admirable fervour and justice. His subject was the future destiny of Italy. . . ."

On December 20 Sgricci gave a public performance in the theater at Pisa. The pit was only half-filled, mostly with students, and the boxes were almost entirely empty, except for a few foreigners. Pisa was indifferent, partly because of ignorance, partly because Professor Rossini, Pacchiani's greatest enemy, industriously decried the improviser. The Shelleys, however, were enthusiastic. "A most wonderful and delightful exhibition," Mary wrote in her journal. "He poured forth a torrent of poetry clothed in the most beautiful language." Claire thought the performance "wonderfully fine" and virtually supernatural. A few days later Mary sent Marianne Hunt a glowingly enthusiastic detailed account of his performance. For nearly two months, until he left Pisa toward the end of January, Sgricci was a frequent caller at the Shelleys' lodgings.

For Mary, however, the most delightful of their new acquaintances was Prince Mavrocordato, who had also been introduced by Pacchiani. Having been compelled by the Turks to flee from Greece, Prince Mavrocordato was compiling a lexicon at Pisa while waiting for a better turn of events at home. His very appearance was romantic. His somewhat small size was balanced by huge mustachios and whiskers. His hair, over which he wore a turban, was bushy and jet black, his eyebrows thick and heavy. His head, large for his size, was finely modeled, and his large eyes, sparkling with intelligence and wit, carried also an impression of benevolence.

From his first advent on December 2 till his departure for Greece early in June he continued to see the Shelleys often. "Do you not envy my luck," Mary exulted to Mrs. Gisborne, "that, having begun Greek, an amiable, young, agreeable, and learned Greek Prince comes every morning to give me a lesson of an hour and a half?" Mary taught him English in return. Shelley played chess with him occasionally, and read *Paradise Lost* and the *Agamemnon* with him, but had little liking for his modern Greek accent or for his emendations and comments on the *Agamemnon*. Shelley gave him credit for the highest qualities of courage and conduct, and in 1822 dedicated his *Hellas* to him; but he could never fully like "our turbaned friend," as he called him. "I reproach my own savage disposition," he confessed to Claire, "that so agreeable, accomplished, and amiable a person is not more agreeable to me"; and when Mavrocordato departed for Greece: "He is a great loss to Mary, and *therefore* to me . . . but not otherwise."

From the autumn of 1820 Count Taafe was frequently in the Shelleys' company whenever they were in Pisa. The Shelleys, and a little later Byron, considered him a bore, but a good fellow. He fancied himself as a poet and was the author of several ridiculously banal occasional poems, besides a translation of Dante equipped with a two-volume Commentary. Shelley and his friends used to laugh secretly at the translation, but they regarded his Commentary with more respect.

In this new circle of acquaintances, in which the friendship with the Masons continued and that with the Gisbornes somewhat revived, life went on rather pleasantly through November, December, January, and into the next spring. A severe attack of ophthalmia, lasting from some time in December until about January 20, kept Shelley from all but the most necessary writing and reduced the time usually given to reading. There was much talk about literature, the trial of Queen Caroline, and the precarious future of the new Neapolitan revolution.

The greatest interest of Shelley's household, however, was in a suppression of liberty much nearer home. In Pisa, in the convent school of St. Anna, languished the beautiful and accomplished Teresa Emilia Viviani, to be kept there by a tyrannical father until released by an unwanted marriage.

Chapter XXIII

It was on the evening of November 29, 1820 that Claire Clairmont and Mary Shelley were taken by Professor Pacchiani to the Convent of St. Anna and there introduced to the beautiful Teresa Viviani. Pacchiani had been her tutor and confessor when she was still living at home in the Governor's palace, and he had formerly been one of the faculty of the convent school. Her elderly father, Niccolò Viviani, was not only the Governor of Pisa, but also head of one of the four civil and military districts under which the Grand Duchy of Tuscany was administered. Dignified and proud, with a quick temper, he carried an external air of hardness that was by no means proof against the domination of a wife thirty years his junior. When Teresa was sixteen years old, a bright and beautiful girl with a sensitive mind unusually eager for affection, her mother had easily prevailed upon Niccolò Viviani to place her and her sister in separate convent schools.

At the time Pacchiani told her story to the Shelleys, Teresa, or Emilia as they came to call her, was between nineteen and twenty years of age and had been a "prisoner" for nearly three years. That is, like most Italian girls who were educated, she had been in a convent school. To Shelley it seemed more a prison than the one from which he had rescued Harriet Westbrook. That she was there awaiting, like most Italian girls of the time, the conclusion of marriage arrangements in which she had no voice seemed peculiarly horrible to people whose views on marriage were those of Shelley, Mary, and Claire.

The heavily barred, curtainless windows of the conservatory, the high wall surrounding the garden, the large, echoing entrance hall, the cloisters, and the narrow, meager cells of the students did nothing to dispel the Shelleys' impression. Emilia herself did less, because she shared it. She was, in fact, much more a victim than the other students. She was of a higher social station than her companions and far above them in intellect and sensibility. In 1820 she had already written several poems, and a short prose rhapsody on Love that is quite in the same vein as the famous poem, *Epipsychidion*, that Shelley was soon to address to her. Add that Emilia was beautiful, with faultlessly regular Greek features, high forehead, profuse

387

black hair, and a clear white complexion that was almost pallid, and it is evident that at no time in his life except when he met the daughter of William Godwin and Mary Wollstonecraft had Shelley met anyone who upon early acquaintance was half so likely to send him into one of his intense idealizing enthusiasms.

For the next ten months, until Emilia's marriage, frequent letters passed between Emilia and Shelley, Mary, and Claire. During December, January, February, and March, Mary called upon Emilia weekly, sometimes with books and other gifts, and at least once to read Greek and Spanish with her. Claire, equally interested, undertook to teach Emilia English and corresponded regularly with her after returning to Florence. Shelley probably accompanied Mary on many of her visits, but there is slight record of his seeing her without Mary until after the Shelleys returned to the Baths of Pisa in May.

By a natural affinity of temperaments Emilia immediately struck the right chord for intensifying the new friendship. Medwin, accompanying Shelley and possibly Mary and Claire in an early visit to the convent, tells how she compared her own captive lot to that of a caged bird whose cage attracted her attention at the moment. Shelley remembered and echoed the sentiment in his *Epipsychidion* when he addressed her as "poor captive bird." In many of her letters thereafter the note of unhappy captivity was almost incessant.

These expressions occur more in letters to Mary than to Shelley, but one whole letter to Shelley (or all that is left of it, for it lacks a regular conclusion) is an agony of sensitiveness only to be matched by Shelley's characterization of himself in "Julian and Maddalo" as a single nerve for feeling "the else-unfelt oppressions of this earth":

My dear Friend,
   I am indeed unhappy! What a fate! I suffer heavily, and am the cause of a thousand griefs to others. O God! Were it not better that I should die? Then I should cease to suffer, or at least to make others suffer. Now I am the object of hatred to others and to myself. I afflict the most courteous and beloved persons. O my incomparable Friend, Angelic Creature did you ever suppose that I should be the cause of so much anguish to you? You see what a person you have come to know. Pardon me, my friend, pardon me! You are obliged to bear so many pains and anxieties on my account that your health even suffers through them. How remorse is torturing me! How many misfortunes have I caused! It would be better if you had never known me!

Thus Emilia was as sensitive to the misfortunes of others as to her own, and particularly to the agony which Shelley allowed her to perceive he felt over her sufferings. More than once she besought him to take care of his health. When she knew him to be suffering with ophthalmia she begged him to "rest from this long reading!" One of her letters to Shelley begins: "How are you? You must have suffered horribly from those spasms. May Heaven grant that they have now ceased!"

In these early letters, which constitute all but three or four of those extant, Emilia showed a deep sense of gratitude for the friendship of the Shelleys — for "tua famiglia," however, rather than for Shelley or Mary exclusively. Her warmest expressions of devotion were for Mary rather than Shelley. Shelley apparently realized that her affection for him was genuinely that of a sister. "Call me always, if you like, your Sister," she had written, ". . . and I too will always call you my dear brother." Once, after he had evidently expressed a feeling that his language might seem too ardent or familiar, she reassured him: "To show you that your familiarity does not displease, but on the contrary gratifies me, and in order that you should not take as a rebuke my treating you in any other way, I write to you in your own tone of confidence and sweet friendship."

With Latin intensity Emilia thought her new friends practically perfect and frankly said so. "You have much talent, my Mary, which, together with your virtue and your excellent heart, makes you one of the loveliest of God's or Nature's creatures." Shelley, as Emilia informed Mary, was really more than human. "His many misfortunes, his unjust persecutions, and his firm and innate virtue in the midst of these terrible and unmerited sorrows filled my heart with admiration and affection and made me think, and perhaps not untruly, that he is not a human creature; he has only a human exterior, but the interior is all divine." These words were written on the 14th of December, about a fortnight after her first meeting with Shelley.

Deeply stirred by Emilia's situation and rendered really ill at times by his sense of helplessness, Shelley sought unsuccessfully to effect her liberation. What chance had a foreigner, petitioning the Grand Duke, to frustrate the will of one of the four district governors of Tuscany? Nevertheless, Shelley drew up a petition, and sought Claire's aid in presenting it to the Grand Duchess. Since Dr. Bojti, at whose home Claire was living in Florence, was court physician, Claire came into occasional contact with ladies of the court.

The petition, if ever presented, came to nothing, as Emilia had predicted of a similar project that had been discussed more than two months earlier. At that time (December 12) Emilia had frankly stated that liberation, if it meant separation from the Shelleys, would be no blessing: "You say that my liberation will perhaps *divide* us. Oh, my Friend! My soul, my heart, can never be parted from my brother and from my dear sisters. . . . I do not love, nor shall I ever be able to love any thing or person so much as your family; for it I would abandon everything and should lose nothing. . . . I pray always to God to grant that I may live with you always. . . ."

No letters from the Shelleys or Claire to Emilia have been preserved. Shelley's letters to Claire after her return to Florence show the strength of his interest in Emilia without at all matching the ardor of Emilia's expressions, or of his own in his poems. "She continues to enchant me infinitely," he informed Claire on January 2. Two weeks later: "I am deeply interested in her destiny, and that interest can in no manner influence it." As a common-sense reassurance he added: "There is no reason that you should fear any mixture of that which you call *love*. My conception of Emilia's talents augments every day. Her moral nature is fine — but not above circumstances — yet I think her tender and true — which is always something. How many are only one of these things at a time!"

It seems to have been well understood that the affection was a Platonic one. But even so the situation cannot have been always entirely comfortable for Mary. She thought at first that Emilia had talent, if not genius, and she deeply sympathized with her in her troubles. Quite likely she was somewhat disgusted by Emilia's demonstrative affection for her; and probably no wife, however confident of her husband's fidelity, could have fully sympathized with Emilia's unrestrained adoration of Shelley. Otherwise Mary found much that was admirable in Emilia, and a strong sense of justice kept her assiduous in her efforts to render Emilia's position less miserable. This would hardly have been possible had she doubted the honesty of either Emilia or Shelley. Emilia noticed, and even jested about, a slight reserve in Mary's manner, but Shelley assured her it was "only the ashes that cover an affectionate heart."

Far otherwise was the effect of Emilia's emotional intensity upon Shelley. When Emilia, seeking to return some of the kindnesses she had received, sent a present of flowers, he began a poem, "To Emilia Viviani," in a vein of intense sentimental sympathy matching her letters. Another fragment, of uncertain date, begins:

> Thy gentle voice, Emilia dear,
>   At night seems hovering o'er mine.
> I feel thy trembling lips — I hear
>   The murmurs of thy voice divine. . . .

Not yet was Shelley's judgment sufficiently detached to suggest to him that Emilia was no better than a "slave" in her religious feelings and seemed totally uninterested in the great cause of freedom except her own. Except for a strong natural championship of the oppressed, one fact, and one fact only, now governed Shelley's feelings toward Emilia. In his essay "On Love" Shelley had written: "There is something within us which, from the instant that we live, more and more thirsts after its likeness," and he added his personal testimony: "With a spirit ill-fitted to sustain such proof, trembling and feeble through its tenderness, I have everywhere sought sympathy, and have found only repulse and disappointment."

Far more than anyone else had been, Emilia Viviani was the natural and almost perfect answer to Shelley's desire for complete and intense personal sympathy. The close spiritual kinship of Shelley and Emilia in this one particular is the personal foundation of Shelley's *Epipsychidion,* as the Dantean, Petrarchan, and Platonic conceptions of love are its intellectual basis.

Shelley's *Epipsychidion* was written very probably during the first two weeks of February 1821 and was sent to Ollier for limited publication on February 16. Only a hundred copies were to be printed, a large estimate, Shelley felt, for "the esoteric few," capable of judging rightly a poem "of so abstruse a nature." Its author's name was to be kept secret, "to avoid the malignity of those who turn sweet food into poison, transforming all they touch into the corruption of their own natures."

During the same spring Shelley characterized his spirits as being alternately depressed and seized by "almost supernatural elevation" — "I live, however, for certain intoxicating moments." In such a moment he must have written *Epipsychidion,* just as "Julian and Maddalo" is the product of the opposite extreme. In the later poem he recognized a perfect sympathy he had given up hope of finding, and in the earlier he recognized the loss of the most perfect sympathy he had then found. In both cases he exceeded himself, and very probably the facts, in his expression. Many lines written for *Epipsy-*

chidion and later rejected show that it began in a conversational, almost matter-of-fact mood very different from that of the completed poem.

For the intoxicating moment, however, the poem was in its main aspect literally and intensely true. Shelley's youthful vision of a complete sympathy seemed possible; after experience had almost demonstrated its impossibility it seemed actually present. The main purpose of *Epipsychidion* was to express this magnificent truth and to share it with the one person fully capable of sympathizing. Wiser now than when he had eloped with Mary under a similar domination, Shelley proposed an elopement with Emilia only in spirit, but he dwelt lovingly and at length upon their spiritual union on the Ionian island to which he wished to escape, as he said, from "the world," or reality. Even so, Shelley probably expected Mary, and possibly even Claire, to accompany them.

Had Shelley intended it, Emilia would not have eloped with him as Mary had done. She had made it as plain as possible in her letters that her affections were only sisterly and spiritual. On that point she and Shelley agreed, and understood each other perfectly. Each believed that there was nothing fleshly in their mutual attraction. Not for Emilia, probably, but for others, Shelley stated his denial of any such feeling:

> To whatsoe'er of dull mortality
> Is mine, remain a vestal sister still.

Had not Emilia described Love as "an essence eternal, spiritual, pure, celestial," with no wish but for virtue, and averse to illicit affections? The words, from her little essay "True Love," must have been before Shelley as he wrote, for he quoted a passage from the essay as a motto for his poem.

Some readers of Emilia's letters may feel, as Mary Shelley did, that they are excessive and emotionally unbalanced. Nevertheless, they are remarkably like many passages in Shelley's letters and poems. Mary's deficiency of sympathy with this side of Emilia was also a lack of sympathy for one of the most powerful springs in her husband's character. She recognized the phenomenon for what it was, or she would never have continued her friendship for Emilia for months after the writing of *Epipsychidion,* but she was innately incapable of the same feeling, and thought it slightly ridiculous. "Shelley's Italian Platonics" was her phrase for it shortly afterwards — an admirable critical phrase, yet a trifle scornful.

But the quality that Mary lacked and Emilia possessed was paramount at the moment and actually did produce more spiritual kinship while it reigned than Shelley ever felt for Mary or anyone else. No one can read Emilia's letters, and particularly her essay, taking them at face value, as Shelley did, and deny their utter kinship, almost identity, with a vital part of Shelley. Shelley's poem is the expression of the frustrated, impossible longing of a whole life, miraculously come true:

> I never thought before my death to see
> Youth's vision thus made perfect, Emily.
>
> .   .   .   .
>
> Spouse! Sister! Angel! Pilot of the Fate
> Whose course has been so starless! Oh too late
> Beloved! O too soon adored, by me!
> For in the fields of immortality
> My spirit should at first have worshipped thine.
> A divine presence in a place divine.
>
> .   .   .   .
>
> We — are we not formed, as notes of music are
> For one another, though dissimilar?

We need not pause over the initial somewhat sentimentalized sympathy with Emilia merely as beauty and innocence oppressed. Shelley would have done as much for anyone; his last essay of the sort had been to defend a blacksmith's apprentice from a gentleman with an umbrella, the irate Colonel Finch. The central point is spiritual affinity. From this everything else in the poem proceeds — the rehearsal of Shelley's spiritual history leading up to this overwhelming discovery, the outbursts of adoration, the attempted reconciliation of the discovery with the positions of Mary and Claire in Shelley's actual life, the escape from actual life in a purely ideal elopement, and the epilogue, again suggesting the non-physical quality of "true" Love.

For one brief, intense moment, Shelley had seen Intellectual Beauty in the flesh:

> Seraph of Heaven! too gentle to be human,
> Veiling beneath that radiant form of Woman
> All that is insupportable in thee
> Of light, and love, and immortality!
> Sweet Benediction in the eternal Curse!

> Veiled Glory of this lampless Universe!
> Thou Moon beyond the clouds! Thou living Form
> Among the Dead! Thou Star above the Storm!
> Thou Wonder, and thou Beauty, and thou Terror!

The difficulties which make *Epipsychidion* such a nightmare to the literalist all lie outside its relatively clear main significance. Shelley declared boldly (lines 148–59) his repudiation of the modern view that love should be limited strictly to one person, consigning all others, "though fair and wise," to "cold oblivion." This statement is followed by the famous passage beginning:

> True love in this differs from gold and clay,
> That to divide is not to take away.
> Love is like understanding, that grows bright,
> Gazing on many truths.

To take these declarations as a repetition of the anti-matrimonial thesis of *Queen Mab* is easy, but fallacious. It is the old position applied to ideal instead of physical love, and describes no more than the situation in which Shelley was living as he wrote. He was simply asserting a belief that to love Mary for her qualities and to love Emilia with a different kind of love for totally different qualities did not detract from either love. It could be nothing else without violating the clear logic of the poem's general meaning. Shelley's phrase "true love," like the word "witch" in "The Witch of Atlas," runs counter to conventional English usage, yet the poem itself is the clearest possible demonstration that by "true love" Shelley meant ideal love. In his mind as he wrote, if not actually before his eyes, was Emilia's little essay describing ideal love and calling it true love (*Il vera Amo*). He had implied the distinction between love and true love before when he wrote to Claire that he did not love Emilia "as you use the word love."

Epipsychidion is an important autobiographical document. That the poem is an idealized history of what Shelley was and had been we have Shelley's own word to John Gisborne. And in lines 319–20 of the poem we have his declared intention of being obscure in tracing a part of his own spiritual history. The definitely autobiographical section (lines 190–387) is in part too obscure for complete detailed analysis, but its main significance is clear enough. Shelley is simply tracing the whole history of his search for Intellectual Beauty and its human counterpart. Lines 190–255 merely elaborate the story already told in *Alastor,* "Hymn to Intellectual Beauty," and the prefatory poem to *The Revolt of Islam* — how in early youth he had devoted himself to the search for Intellectual Beauty, how for years he had followed this vision as unsuccessfully as the young poet in *Alastor.* To his various former accounts he adds that he listened to a voice which told him that the spirit he sought was beside him, but found instead "One whose voice was venomed melody" and whose touch was "as electric poison," who came near to being his spiritual death. This mysterious "One" may well be the Pandemian Venus (Earthly Love), whose opposite, the Uranian Venus (Heavenly or Ideal Love), was only another name with Shelley for Intellectual Beauty.

Shelley then turns to the "many mortal forms" in which he sought for "the shadow of that idol of my thought." One who "was true — oh! why not true to me?" was probably Harriet Grove. Several others are dismissed en masse with two or three vague, general phrases, until Shelley reaches one whom he compares with the Moon and who is undoubtedly Mary Shelley. Mary's advent into Shelley's life is hailed as enthusiastically as it was in the introductory poem to *The Revolt of Islam.* She resembled his Vision as the Moon resembled the Sun — that is, she was the reflection of his Vision, but without its warmth. As the Moon hid the night from its own darkness, Mary is described as having hidden Shelley until all was bright. Like Endymion in his subjection to the Moon, Shelley was laid asleep, "spirit and limb," "within a chaste, cold bed."

Since Shelley has given evidence again and again, both in the poem and out of it, that *Epipsychidion* is the history of spiritual, not physical love, this passage can only mean that his life with Mary was at first happy, a genuine "deliverance" from his sorrows, and that he was "asleep" to the fact that complete sympathy was lacking. The chasteness and coldness was spiritual and was not at first perceived because of the intense brightness of the intellectual light which Mary shed upon him. How intense Shelley felt this light to be is clear from letters to Hogg and Mary shortly after his elopement, acknowledging himself Mary's intellectual inferior. Before meeting apparently complete sympathy in Emilia, Shelley had come to a poignant realization of Mary's defective sympathies, and had made bitter record of it in "Julian and Maddalo."

An even more obscure passage follows Shelley's discovery that Mary did not completely embody his early vision:

What storms then shook the ocean of my sleep,
Blotting that Moon, whose pale and waning lips
Then shrank as in the sickness of eclipse;
And how my soul was as a lampless sea,
And who was then its Tempest; and when She,
The Planet of that hour, was quenched, what frost
Crept o'er those waters, till from coast to coast
The moving billows of my being fell
Into a death of ice, immovable; —
And then — what earthquakes made it gape and split,
The white Moon smiling all the while on it,
These words conceal; — If not, each word would be
The key of staunchless tears. Weep not for me!

This is professedly autobiography, and professedly cryptic. The period it describes must be subsequent to the summer of 1817, when Shelley wrote his introductory poem to *The Revolt of Islam,* his earlier spiritual autobiography. In that poem Mary was still his perfect "deliverance" and he was still "asleep," without then knowing it, to her inability to furnish the complete sympathy he sought. When Shelley awoke to this deficiency is made plain by "Julian and Maddalo." That poem, if any poem ever did, records a spiritual storm, and a storm in which Mary was "blotted." Also, like the present passage, it is autobiography that Shelley thought concealed. Shelley's life between 1817 and 1821 is too well known for the storms he described to have been anything except those following Clara Shelley's death and repeated possibly after the death of William Shelley. Under these blows, it is a known fact that Mary's spirits "shrank as in the sickness of eclipse," and Shelley's soul was often "as a lampless sea."

The identity of the Tempest and the Planet are not so certain, but Elena Adelaide Shelley, whose life was concealed just as Shelley says the truth behind these allusions is concealed, might well have been a Tempest in the life of Shelley and Mary. She alone was definitely "quenched," and her influence could most properly be limited to "that hour." The "frost" which at her death afflicted Shelley's spirits may be inferred from Shelley's words at the time: "It seems as if the destruction that is consuming me were as an atmosphere which wrapt and *infected* everything connected with me . . . An ounce of civet good apothecary to sweeten this dunghill of a world." Elena Ade-

laide fits into the pattern of the passage and of Shelley's life far better
than any other known person, even though she conforms rather badly
to the pattern set by Shelley's other Incarnate Sympathies.

The earthquakes that split the ice-pack of the poet's frozen spirit
were probably convulsions of the spirit which acted as liberating
forces. At any rate Emilia immediately appears, "Soft as an Incarna-
tion of the Sun," and Shelley hails her by name as

> . . . the Vision veiled from me
> So many years.

With Emilia's entrance Shelley's autobiographical accounts of his
search for Intellectual Beauty and its human personification come to
a triumphant end.

Emilia and Mary are then given complete dominion of the poet's
spirit as "twin Spheres of light." They are to rule with "alternate
sway" his day and night, and their influence is to be "equal, yet unlike." If Mary Shelley, an exclusive and possessive wife by nature,
resented Shelley's burning tributes to Emilia and their terribly frank
implications, here was a tribute which she could value more justly
than many subsequent critics have done. In the very ecstasy of recognizing his most perfect Incarnate Sympathy Shelley, for the first time
in his life, admitted the equal sway of his former ideal. The proposed partnership of Mary and Emilia in his life was little more than
an intensification of Emilia's own attitude. It was not Shelley alone,
but "tua famiglia," that she had protested her desire to follow to the
ends of the earth.

Quite in line with Emilia's words, Shelley invited Claire, undoubtedly the "Comet" of lines 368–73, to "float into our azure heaven
again." For Emilia, as for Shelley, Claire ("mia bella Chiara") was
a part of the circle, and Claire was the only person once a part of an
"azure heaven" including Emilia who could have been invited back
"again." Claire had not been alluded to in the preceding spiritual
autobiography, nor was she given equal dominion with Emilia and
Mary, but she was offered the loving sympathy of the three others.

The imaginary elopement of Shelley and Emilia, beautiful as it is,
throws the poem out of proportion, occupying nearly a third of its
six hundred and four lines. Its inconsistency with the rest of the poem
in its ignoring of Mary is obvious. This fact suggests that it was
added, like the fourth act of *Prometheus Unbound*, because Shelley
was too much absorbed in his poem to quit it and that he had per-

haps once intended to end the poem with lines 383–7, which complete the spiritual autobiography, and return to the opening lines of the poem.

By early May, Ollier had published anonymously a small edition of *Epipsychidion,* adding a hundred or more to Shelley's suggested one hundred copies. It did not pass quite unnoticed, as most of Shelley's editors and biographers have stated, but received three reviews. The Brighton *Gossip* on June 23 expressed high admiration for the poet's talents and closed the poem "with a pang of regret that his mind should be harassed and wasted" by such impracticable and unsocial ideas. Shortly afterwards (July 14) it published a longer article in which a gentleman of conventional taste dissected the poem for a sentimental girl who admired it, indulgently citing passages to show that its imagery was perfectly anarchic. There is no evidence that Shelley was aware of either of these notices or the one in *Blackwood's Magazine* the following February. The writer of this review was generously appreciative of the poem's "delicious beauty" in the parts not obscured by "impenetrable mysticism," but he took its object to be a defense of marrying one's sister, and evidently attributed it to Byron. The latter error was corrected in a footnote signed by Christopher North, who said that none but "the unfortunate Mr. Shelley" was capable of "wasting such poetry on such a theme."

Even as *Epipsychidion* was being written, Shelley was conscious of gossip about his relations with Emilia. In a town of eighteen thousand people an eccentric foreigner, a married man, too, does not without notice pay such particular attention to the beautiful young daughter of the Governor of the entire district. Some of the passages rejected from the completed poem refer to this local gossip. Whatever rumors existed continued throughout the spring and summer and until Emilia's marriage on September 8. If Mary Shelley knew of the rumors, which is probable, the knowledge made no difference in her consistently friendly treatment of Emilia. As early as May, however, even while continuing their friendship with Emilia, both Mary and Claire clearly regarded the connection as a misfortune.

On the day before sending *Epipsychidion* to his publisher Shelley wrote a letter to Peacock which showed that he had another literary enterprise also in mind. Some time earlier Shelley had received Peacock's essay, "The Four Ages of Poetry," arguing that poetry had outlived its usefulness. With Peacock's views of particular poets, especially Barry Cornwall, Shelley cordially agreed, but the attack upon poetry itself excited him to "a sacred rage," as he now informed Peacock. "I had the greatest possible desire to break a lance with you, within the lists of a magazine, in honour of my mistress Urania; but God willed that I should be too lazy." In fact, Shelley had already promised Ollier to write such a paper for his *Literary Miscellany;* and after some delay he dispatched on March 20 a manuscript complete in itself, but intended only as the first part of an essay in three installments. Before it could be published, however, the *Literary Miscellany* was discontinued; hence the other parts were never written.

Shelley's first concern in his "Defence of Poetry" is to inquire into the foundation and nature of poetry. Imagination, as distinguished from reason, is defined as mental action which synthesizes rather than analyzes; it is an active, creative agent as compared with reason, which is the mere instrument employed by the agent. Poetry is the "expression of the imagination." Thus Shelley laid a definite psychological foundation that is only implied in Sir Philip Sidney's *Apologie for Poetrie* and Wordsworth's famous Preface to *Lyrical Ballads*. Like Sidney, Shelley then proceeds to show the antiquity and universality of poetry, but where Sidney is most concerned to show by this means the power of poetry, Shelley's object is to suggest the nature and basis of that power.

To Shelley the poet is merely he who possesses most fully a recreative faculty born of imagination. "To be a poet is to apprehend the true and the beautiful, the good which exists in the relation . . . between existence and perception and . . . between perception and expression." Thus in the most elemental sense all artists are poets to the extent that they "imagine and express this indestructible order." So also were the early lawmakers, inventors, and religious teachers, for the same reason. Like Sidney, Shelley comments on the ancient identity of prophet and poet, and even carries the point further:

> For he [the poet] not only beholds intensely the present as it is, and discovers those laws according to which present things ought to be ordered, but he beholds the future in the present, and his thoughts are the germs of the flower and the fruit of latest time. . . . A poet participates in the eternal, the infinite, and the one. . . .

Shelley meets the moral objection to poetry expressed in Plato's *Republic* by asserting that it is based on a misunderstanding of the way in which poetry produces the moral improvement of humanity. Unlike ethical science, which acts didactically, poetry "acts in another and diviner manner" by awakening and enlarging the mind itself; it "lifts the veil from the hidden beauty of the world, and makes familiar objects be as if they were not familiar." Explaining clearly *how* poetry "lifts the veil," Shelley reveals not only the heart of his "defence," but also the guiding principle of his own conduct as a poet:

The great secret of morals is love; or a going out of our own nature, and an identification of ourselves with the beautiful which exists in thought, action, or person, not our own. A man, to be greatly good, must imagine intensely and comprehensively; he must put himself in the place of another and of many others; the pains and pleasures of his species must become his own. The great instrument of moral good is the imagination; and poetry administers to the effect by acting upon the cause. Poetry enlarges the circumference of the imagination by replenishing it with thoughts of ever new delight, which have the power of attracting and assimilating to their own nature all other thoughts, and which form new intervals and interstices whose void for ever craves fresh food. Poetry strengthens that faculty which is the organ of the moral nature of man, in the same manner as exercise strengthens a limb. A poet therefore would do ill to embody his own conceptions of right and wrong, which are usually those of his place and time, in his poetical creations, which participate in neither. By this assumption of the inferior office of interpreting the effect, in which perhaps after all he might acquit himself but imperfectly, he would resign the glory in a participation in the cause.

But Shelley was far from closing the argument with his dissent from the moral objection to poetry, the basis for his consistent aversion from "didactic" poetry. He devoted about a third of his essay to a survey of history designed to show that poetry, in its broader sense as the language of imagination, however expressed, has always attended every awakening of the human spirit. His greatest enthusiasm was lavished upon the Greeks; his least upon the Romans, whose "poetry" was to be found mainly in their laws and institutions. Even Christianity had once been a great imaginative or poetic movement and had eliminated the one great blot of Greek civilization — the servility of women. His own age seemed also an age of great poetry, and it must therefore be the beginning of another great awakening of the human spirit.

In his *Philosophical View of Reform,* a professedly practical treatise in which mere æsthetics had no place, Shelley developed precisely the same panoramic view of history as in the "Defence of Poetry" and lingered on the subject just as disproportionately. The two passages are quite similar. In the former he argued that great political and social awakenings were periodically inevitable and were always attended by a new life in the imaginative arts; he even felt confident that Germany was on the eve of such an awakening because her arts were already awake. His view of history was, in fact, dictated by a semi-mystical faith which linked it to his theory of poetry.

Proceeding to the second alleged fault of poetry, Peacock's argument that in the modern world it lacked utility, Shelley analyzed the real meaning of utility with a wisdom that is still insufficiently regarded. "Whatever strengthens and purifies the affections, enlarges the imagination, and adds spirit to sense," he earnestly contended, is more useful than whatever ministers merely to creature comforts, valuable as this lower form of utility might be. A narrowing view of utility had brought England to the verge of spiritual and even physical bankruptcy:

> We have more moral, political, and historical wisdom than we
> know how to reduce into practice; we have more scientific and
> economical knowledge than can be accommodated to the just
> distribution of the produce which it multiplies. . . . We want
> the creative faculty to imagine that which we know; we want
> the generous impulse to act that which we imagine; we want the
> poetry of life; our calculations have outrun conception; we have
> eaten more than we can digest. The cultivation of those sciences
> which have enlarged the limits of the empire of man over the
> external world, has, for want of the poetical faculty, propor-
> tionally circumscribed those of the internal world; and man,
> having enslaved the elements, remains himself a slave. To what
> but a cultivation of the mechanical arts in a degree dispropor-
> tioned to the presence of the creative faculty, which is the basis
> of all knowledge, is to be attributed the abuse of all invention
> for abridging and combining labour, to the exasperation of the
> inequality of mankind? From what other cause has it arisen that

these inventions which should have lightened, have added a weight to the curse imposed on Adam?

Up to this point Shelley's argument is finely idealistic, but also finely rational. His contention for the paramount utility and the vital necessity of poetry in society is skillfully and reasonably deduced from his distinction between imagination and reason. But his argument even when most rational carries also an overtone of mystical faith. In many of its passages it conforms to his own definition of poetry in the broader sense of the nobility and imagination of its "vitally metaphorical" language, appealing beyond reason to a transcendental, imaginative realization of the profound importance of poetry. "A poet participates in the eternal, the infinite, and the one"; poetry "acts in another and diviner manner"; poetry "acts in a divine and unapprehended manner." These phrases show clearly Shelley's sympathy with Plato's argument in the *Ion* that poetry contains something of the divine.

In the end Shelley absorbs Plato's view and makes it his own. "Poetry is indeed something divine. It is at once the centre and circumference of knowledge." Hence, "What were Virtue, Love, Patriotism, Friendship — what were the scenery of this beautiful Universe which we inhabit; what were our consolations on this side of the grave, and what were our aspirations beyond it, if Poetry did not ascend to bring light and fire from those eternal regions where the owl-winged faculty of calculation dare not ever soar?" At this point it is clearly to be seen that poetry is to Shelley simply the voice of Intellectual Beauty, that Intellectual Beauty is itself the sum of all true Imagination conceivable and inconceivable, that the individual human imagination flows from this fountain and back into it and is the nearest human contact with the Divine. It is this contact, in Shelley's view, that both stimulates Freedom and is stimulated by it.

Thenceforward, in a dozen repeated assertions whose appeal is more transcendental than rational, Shelley continually suggests the presence of divinity in poetry. It is "the interpenetration of a diviner nature through our own"; it "makes immortal all that is best and most beautiful in the world"; it "redeems from decay the visitations of the divinity in Man"; it "strips the veil of familiarity from the world, and lays bare the naked and sleeping beauty which is the spirit of its forms"; it "defeats the curse which binds us to be subjected to the accident of surrounding impressions"; it "creates for us a being

within our being" and "purges from our inward sight the film of familiarity which obscures from us the wonder of our being."

It is a consequence of the immortal element in poetry that even
the greatest poet cannot compose poetry to his own order. He is an
instrument through which poetry is produced, and an imperfect instrument at that. "The most glorious poetry that has ever been communicated to the world is probably a feeble shadow of the original
conception of the Poet." It is true of poetry in the narrower sense,
and even truer of the plastic and pictorial arts, that the mind is "incapable of accounting to itself for the origin, the gradations, or the
media of the process." The frequent recurrence of poetical power
makes of the poet a superior man, and it is "incontrovertible" that,
inasmuch as he is a poet, he is "the wisest, the happiest, and the best"
of mankind. In the intervals of inspiration the poet becomes a man
rather than a poet and may even be guilty of some of the sins that
have been charged against individual poets. He is partly a creature
of his own times, partaking of their limitations, and not always quite
conscious of what he is doing, or quite identical with his poetry. But
even so, he is by nature "more delicately organized than other men,"
and hence the cruder vices, such as "cruelty, envy, revenge, and
avarice," have seldom been charged against the conduct of poets.

At this point, after summarizing his essay, Shelley concludes with
the statement: "Poets are the unacknowledged legislators of the
world." So fully had he stressed the superrational element in poetry
that he completely ignored a point made by Wordsworth with which
he would certainly have agreed: namely, that a poet "must have
thought long and deeply." Such long, deep thought was for Shelley a
prerequisite to true inspiration, but by no means a substitute. In another respect also Shelley was closer to Wordsworth than he realized.
The older poet had written, but not published, his definition of the
Imagination as:

> . . . but another name for absolute power,
> And clearest insight, amplitude of mind,
> And Reason in her most exalted mood.

Shelley's "Defence of Poetry" is the very essence of his life and
thought. He had decided early in life that he had a paramount mission, and somewhat later that it could best be accomplished through
poetry. For years his reading and study had been constantly directed
to this end. As early as June 5, 1811 he had read, and recommended

403

to Elizabeth Hitchener, George Ensor's discussion of poetry in his
National Education (1811), which also regards poetry as the unacknowledged legislator of mankind. Politics and poetry had been allied
in his practice long before he so regarded them in his "Defence of
Poetry." He had stated the connection in his *Philosophical View of
Reform* and clearly implied it in *Prometheus Unbound* and the "Ode
to Liberty." More and more, poetry had become for Shelley a matter
of the inspiring imagination rather than of didactic reason, until
didactic poetry became one of his greatest abhorrences.

The distinction between the poet as a man and as the sometimes
divinely inspired mouthpiece of Intellectual Beauty appeared in his
letters as well as in this essay. His skylark, soaring into regions of
light and fire, foreshadowed not only the idea but even to a slight
degree the language of one of the passages in the "Defence of Poetry"
emphasizing the divine, superrational quality of poetry. The greatest
of all Shelley's shorter poems, the "Ode to the West Wind," was his
personal prayer that as a poet he might have his share in producing
one of the great human revolutions it was the function of poetry to
produce. The intensity of this desire (which is also suggested by the
conclusion of "To a Skylark") is the measure of his deep dejection as
he became convinced that his voice was failing to find an audience,
and it is a possible reason why in such poems as *Prometheus Unbound*
he turned deliberately to a more distant audience of the "highly refined imaginations" of the "more select" readers.

On January 19 Medwin's friends the Williamses had arrived at
Pisa, and they immediately became a part of the Shelleys' circle. Very
soon they were dining together, walking together, and visiting each
other several times a week. Lieutenant Edward Ellerker Williams
was a half-pay lieutenant in the Eighth Dragoons, in the army of the
East India Company. A year Shelley's junior, he had been briefly at
Eton in 1805, where Shelley may have seen him without recognizing
one of the most congenial of his future friends. His frank, lively
countenance and manly good sense and good taste appealed to Shelley from the start. He was himself a writer and a fairly clever painter
in water colors. His common-law wife, Jane, was sister of General
John Wheeler Cleveland, of the Madras Army. She had been deserted
by a husband with whom she was unhappy, and had subsequently
become the "wife" of Lieutenant Williams. When they reached Pisa
the Williamses had one child, Edward Medwin, almost a year old.
A second child, Rosalind, was born in Pisa on the 16th of March 1821.

Jane Williams was beautiful, sympathetic, and possessed of a pleasant singing voice. Her interests were quite domestic, and at first Shelley seems only to have tolerated her. "W[illiams] I like," Shelley informed Claire in May, "and I have got reconciled to Jane."

Edward Williams had been acquainted with Shelley only about two months when he sent his friend Edward Trelawny the following impression:

> Shelley is certainly a man of most astonishing genius, in appearance extraordinarily young, of manners mild and amiable, but withal full of life and fun. His wonderful command of language, and the ease with which he speaks on what are generally considered abstruse subjects, are striking; in short, his ordinary conversation is akin to poetry, for he sees things in the most singular and pleasing lights: if he wrote as he talks, he would be popular enough. Lord Byron and others think him by far the most imaginative poet of the day.

Some months later Williams entered in his journal the opinion that Shelley was one of the greatest living English poets, and would be the greatest "if he applied himself to human affections."

Except for the exciting episode of Emilia Viviani the spring of 1821 passed quietly enough for the Shelleys. On March 5 they moved to new lodgings, Casa Aulla. Mary was still studying Greek and writing *Valperga;* and Shelley and Mary both were reading, though somewhat less than formerly. After the departure of Medwin, Sgricci, and Pacchiani they still passed many more evenings with others than formerly. They were at home, as before, with the Masons. Henry Reveley called or dined occasionally, oblivious of the fact that Shelley no longer felt very cordial toward him. Count Taafe called frequently. So did Prince Mavrocordato, often with news of affairs in Greece.

Austrian proclamations and marching armies now clearly foretold the doom of Neapolitan liberty. Shelley viewed the gathering storm with a clear vision, but would not abate his faith in freedom. "I need not tell you," he informed Peacock, "how little chance there is that the new and undisciplined levies of Naples should stand against a superior force of veteran troops. But the birth of liberty in nations abounds in examples of a reversal of the ordinary laws of calculation." What if the Austrians were well disciplined and strong? Such considerations, "if the Spirit of Regeneration is abroad, are chaff before the storm, the very elements and events will fight against them, indignation and shameful repulse will burn after them to the valleys of the Alps." The Austrians would win if they marched straight to Naples without serious check, but one real defeat would ruin them, "for the good spirit of the World is out against them."

In Greece, however, freedom seemed prospering, as news arrived of local insurgent successes. On April 1 Mavrocordato called with news that made him "as gay as a caged eagle just free." Mary lost no time communicating it to Claire:

> Greece has declared its freedom! Prince Mavrocordato has made us expect this event for some weeks past. Yesterday he came *rayonnant de joie* — he had been ill for some days, but he forgot all his pains. Ipselanti, a Greek general in the service of Russia, has collected together 10,000 Greeks and entered Wallachia, declaring the liberty of his country. The Morea — Epirus — Servia are in revolt. Greece will most certainly be free. The worst part of this news to us is that our amiable prince will leave us — he will of course join his countrymen as soon as possible — never did man appear so happy — yet he sacrifices family — fortune — everything to the hope of freeing his country.

The same ardor overflowed into a note which she immediately dispatched to Mavrocordato's lodgings, offering to surrender the remaining Greek lessons due her to the great cause of Greek freedom. Mavrocordato accepted, with strong gratitude for her generous sentiments and for his happy association with her and her husband.

There were few letters from England that spring. Peacock wrote once or twice rather briefly and generally. Godwin (January 30) wrote Mary a long, tranquil letter in which, obedient to Shelley's stern warning, he omitted to attack Shelley and to complain about his financial situation, which was still the same.

Depressing news arrived from the Hunts. Leigh Hunt was in financial difficulties and had been ill for months. One of his children was seriously ill, and his brother John had just been imprisoned for a year for attacking the House of Commons in the *Examiner,* of which he was now, fortunately for Leigh, technically sole owner as well as printer. Overwork had driven Leigh Hunt into a nervous fever that compelled him to give up the *Indicator* and drop most of his writing for the *Examiner.* His wife wrote to the Shelleys in a tone of almost frantic desperation: "He is irritable beyond anything you ever saw in him, and nervous to a most fearful extent. Oh! how much I wish we could come over to you! I think of such a thing in a sunshiny moment, but the clouds soon gather, and the thoughts soon vanish. Ask Mr. Shelley, my dear Mr. Shelley, to *urge it to him.*" In spite of his consistent prudence in money matters since the previous summer, Shelley sent the Hunts money that he could hardly spare.

Horace Smith wrote to Shelley on April 3, primarily to announce that his proposed emigration to Italy would have to be deferred a few months. Almost incidentally he explained that Shelley's bankers had refused to turn over to him Shelley's quarterly allowance, insisting that the account had been stopped. This threw the Shelleys into a panic, but within two days Horace Smith wrote again to explain that it had been mainly a lawyer's muddle and was now cleared up.

During the first part of the spring Claire seemed much more contented than formerly with her position in Florence. Her duties were light, and she circulated almost gaily in society, either by herself or with Dr. and Madame Bojti. As summer approached, Claire began to think more and more of Allegra. To recover Allegra, she wrote in her journal on April 12, would be to "come back to the warmth of life after the stiffness of the grave." She wished the Shelleys to come to Florence to aid her in some wild scheme, evidently quite hazy in her own mind, of stealing Allegra and hiding her from Byron. Mary answered with sensible sympathy, agreeing with her strictures on Byron, but arguing that her fears for Allegra's health were without basis. She pointed out that Claire's scheme was utterly hopeless and, even if it could succeed, would very likely involve Byron and Shelley in a duel.

As usual, Shelley's health improved with the appearance of warmer weather. Dr. Vaccà recommended buying a saddle horse, but Shelley much preferred a boat, as less expensive in both care and money. Henry Reveley secured for him for a few pauls a small, flat-bottomed boat about ten feet long, a frail structure of lath and pitched canvas, of the type commonly used by hunters in the marshes, but regarded as quite unsafe among waves or rapid currents.

On April 16, after the boat had been fitted with rudder, mast, and sails, nothing would do but Shelley and Williams must sail it from Leghorn to Pisa through the canal by moonlight. Mrs. Gisborne flatly forbade any such undertaking unless Henry, an unusually good swimmer, accompanied them. It was well he did, for about halfway to Pisa Williams, reflecting small credit on his youthful years in the navy, stood up, lost his balance and overturned the boat by seizing the mast to steady himself. Williams could swim well enough to make shore. Henry, a much better swimmer, undertook the rescue of Shelley. As in the storm on Lake Leman in 1816, Shelley was quite calm and unafraid. "Never more comfortable in my life," he assured Henry; "do what you will with me." Once ashore Shelley fainted, but recovered while Henry was regaining and securing the boat. At a house near by they were hospitably received, fires were built up, dry clothes provided, and a good breakfast was cooked while their own clothes were drying. Before they set off on foot for Pisa, Shelley was quite merry over the adventure. The boat was refitted and was soon in constant use.

During the winter the Shelleys' curious estrangement from the Gisbornes had lost some of its sharpness. It had never interfered with the free use of the Gisbornes as purchasing and paying agents in Leghorn nor with Henry Reveley's frequent calls on the Shelleys. Though both Mary and Shelley no longer communicated personal information with the former fullness and affection, Mary did not cease to invite the Gisbornes to visit them. A new trip to England was now necessary for the Gisbornes. In late April (April 26–30) they visited the Shelleys for almost the last time.

Chapter XXIV

No DOUBT remembering the happy boating days on Lake Geneva, Shelley had written on May 4 to urge Byron to join him for the summer, taking care to mention that Claire was absent. But Byron was not yet quite ready to leave Ravenna. In his letters to Byron Shelley commented rather dejectedly on his own poems and their lack of success, but despite his altered opinion of Byron's character since the visit to Venice in 1818, his opinion of Byron as a poet was unchanged. With undiminished earnestness he repeated his old exhortations of 1816:

> I still feel impressed with the persuasion that you *ought* —
> and if there is prophecy in hope, that you *will* write a great and
> connected poem, which shall bear the same relation to this age
> as the "Iliad," the "Divina Commedia," and "Paradise Lost" did
> to theirs. . . . You know the enthusiasm of my admiration for
> what you have already done; but these are "disjecti membra
> poetae" to what you may do, and will never, like that, place
> your memory on a level with those great poets. Such is an am-
> bition (excuse the baseness of the word) alone worthy of you.

On May 8, 1821 the Shelleys returned to the Baths of Pisa for the summer months, and remained there until about the first of November. The summer and autumn passed quietly, in much the same calm, uneventful manner as the previous summer and autumn at the Baths. As Mary Shelley looked back upon this period she remembered it as "a pleasant summer, bright in all but Shelley's health and inconstant spirits; yet he enjoyed himself greatly, and became more and more attached to the part of the country where chance appeared to cast us."

Four miles away, at Pugnano, Edward Williams was writing his play, "The Promise; or A Year, A Month and A Day," and Jane Williams was bustling about among her pots and pans and cheerfully tending her two children. Almost every day the Shelleys and Williamses were in each other's company. The intervening distance was only an easy summer walk, or a still more delightful journey in Shelley's boat, by way of the canal joining the Serchio and the Arno. The

canal was full and deep, shaded by overhanging boughs and played
upon by multitudes of ephemera. During the heat of day its quiet
was emphasized by the almost unnoted hum of cicalas; in the evening fireflies gleamed fitfully in the bordering shrubbery and the
silence was occasionally broken by the cooing call of aziolas.

Jane Williams was as yet a person whom Shelley tolerated rather
than liked. Edward Williams, with his high spirits and high principles and his love of outdoor life, particularly boating, was far more
to Shelley's taste. Together they embarked on many a brief excursion
in the little canvas-covered sailboat. The flavor of these excursions
survives in one of Shelley's most pleasing unfinished poems of 1821,
"The Boat on the Serchio." The poem begins with a fine description
of early morning, when Shelley and Williams (Lionel and Melchior)
had intended to start on a trip to the sea. They arrive late; the boat is
"asleep on Serchio's stream"; and as they throw the ballast overboard and stow their food and other luggage they speculate light-
heartedly on what the boat is dreaming. Then:

> The chain is loosed, the sails are spread,
>   The living breath is fresh behind,
> As, with dews and sunrise fed,
>   Comes the laughing morning wind; —
> The sails are full, the boat makes head
> Against the Serchio's torrent fierce . . .

— and the two mariners are off on a voyage to the sea.

These and other verses suggest that Shelley's occasional fits of illness and depression were only brief interruptions of a season predominantly happy. Never before had Shelley's verse dwelt quite so
steadily upon the substantial comfortable details and even the light-
heartedness of life. Possibly his recent admiration of Keats's poems
had increased in his eyes the poetic value of earthy materials.

It was about April 19 that Shelley heard of the death of John Keats,
at Rome. On June 5 Shelley wrote to the Gisbornes that he had nearly
finished a poem on Keats's death and that it was "a highly wrought
piece of art, perhaps better in point of composition than anything I
have written." *Adonais* was finished by June 8 and was immediately
sent to London in a printed copy, in order to reduce the number of
errors in type-setting. Shelley also sent Byron a copy, admitting at
the same time that his praise of Keats as a poet, though genuine,
might be excessive:

410

. . . Yet I need not be told that I have been carried too far by
the enthusiasm of the moment; by my piety, and my indignation,
in panegyric. But if I have erred, I console myself by reflecting
that it is in defence of the weak — not in conjunction with the
powerful.

In general structure *Adonais* is quite simple. Twenty-two Spenser-
ian stanzas express not only the poet's desolation at the death of
Adonais, but the desolation of all the natural and imaginative forces
that he had made beautiful in his poetry. The next fifteen stanzas emphasize the same pity and sorrow as expressed by the Muse Urania
and by brother poets, ending with a typically Shelleyan curse upon
the assassin — a curse that renounces vengeance in the confidence
that self-knowledge is the worst possible punishment for such a
"noteless blot on a remembered name."

At this point (stanza xxxviii) the discovery is made that physical
death is not really the extinction of life for such as Adonais. From
the viewpoint of Eternity, physical life is itself a living death, and
actual life lies beyond. Adonais still lives as a part of the Nature
which he helped to make more lovely and as a part of that great
Spirit, Intellectual Beauty, or Love, which eternally shapes all forms
of life to its purposes, as far as they are capable of feeling its influence. The supposedly alive are seen to be really less alive than
Adonais. Rome, the sepulchre not only of Adonais, but of empires
and religions, is a visible proof that the only part of the past which
can never die is those spirits, like him, "Who waged contention with
their time's decay." The only ultimate reality to Shelley was Intellectual Beauty; human life was real and lasting only inasmuch as it
was identified with her. Thus he reached one of his highest points of
expression in the climax of *Adonais:*

> The One remains, the many change and pass;
> Heaven's light for ever shines, Earth's shadows fly;
> Life, like a dome of many-coloured glass,
> Stains the white radiance of Eternity.

In this brilliant image Shelley condensed almost the whole spirit of
Petrarch's *Triumphs.* Since 1818 Shelley had admired Petrarch as one
of the greatest poets. In his *Triumphs* Eternity is the only lasting perfection; earthly life, in the light of Eternity, is a procession of vain
shadows. Mary's journal for September 7, 1819, shows Shelley reading Petrarch's triumph of Death aloud. Here Petrarch states that

Death is called so only by the unwise, and that Laura, dead, is really alive, whereas her living lover is in truth dead. So thoroughly had Shelley made this idea his own that he expressed it in an image suggested by Shakespeare's *Macbeth* which at the same time expresses the significance of Petrarch's poem and of Shelley's own creed:

> Peace, peace! he is not dead, he doth not sleep —
> He hath awakened from the dream of life —
> 'Tis we, who, lost in stormy visions, keep
> With phantoms an unprofitable strife
> And in mad trance strike with our spirit's knife
> Invulnerable nothings. . . .

The three stanzas that conclude the poem transmute the author's personal despondency into something like ecstasy. Since his own earthly hopes were dead, why hesitate to join Adonais in an eternal Life?

The very essence of this Eternity is Intellectual Beauty, the One which remains steadfast in a universe of change and decay. In the fifty-fourth stanza Shelley gave impassioned utterance both of the power of Intellectual Beauty and of the manner in which it operates:

> That Light whose smile kindles the Universe,
> That Beauty in which all things work and move,
> That Benediction which the eclipsing Curse
> Of birth can quench not, that sustaining Love
> Which through the web of being blindly wove
> By man and beast and earth and air and sea,
> Burns bright or dim, as each are mirrors of
> The fire for which all thirst; now beams on me,
> Consuming the last clouds of cold mortality.

Possibly all of Shelley's championing of oppressed individuals was strengthened by his constant view of himself as a victim of persecution. In the case of Keats there is hardly room for doubt that this was particularly so. Making full allowance for Shelley's recently increased critical esteem, it is still difficult to think that he would have written *Adonais* had he not thought of Keats as assassinated by the reviewers. Shelley regarded himself as a similar victim. If he felt any natural impulse to fight back in his own behalf it must have been inhibited by his principle that revenge was one of the greatest of all human errors. In defending Keats, however, he was at the same time half-unconsciously defending himself. In the first draft of his Preface he linked his own wrongs from the reviewers with those of Keats and omitted his personal grievances only on the advice of Count Taafe. Among the brother poets who come to weep for Adonais Shelley disposes of Byron, Moore, and Hunt in not more than four lines each, but requires four stanzas to present his own impassioned self-portrait, as a "herd-abandoned deer, struck by the hunter's dart," one "who in another's fate now wept his own." Under such circumstances it was impossible to elegize Keats without elegizing himself. Once the amalgamation of Keats and Shelley is fairly complete, the classical "influences" from Bion and Moschus are dropped almost entirely. The poem gathers intensity and sweeps forward to its perfect conclusion in a manner characteristically Shelleyan.

Shelley frequently left the Baths to spend part of the day or evening in Pisa. He was often with the Masons at Casa Silva, and occasionally in Leghorn. Twice a week he called on Emilia Viviani. In the delays attending negotiations for her marriage, Danielli, the less fortunate of Emilia's two suitors, became almost frantic, and Shelley found himself cast in the odd role of pacifier. "Danielli almost frightens her to death," he wrote Claire, shortly after removing to the Baths, "and she handed him over to me to quiet and console. — It seems that I am worthy to take my degree of M.A. in the art of Love, for I have contrived to calm the despairing swain, much to the satisfaction of poor Emilia, who in that convent of hers sees everything as through a mist, ten times its natural size." Her marriage, Shelley informed Claire, would remove "a great and painful weight" from his mind, and yet Italian marriages were in his opinion so tyrannous that he "trembled" at her approaching fate.

On June 19 Claire Clairmont arrived in Pisa on a vacation that was to last until November 1. Most of this time she spent in Leghorn, taking the sea-baths, learning to swim, and exchanging calls with a number of Italian and Russian acquaintances. Her first visit to the Baths was signalized by a quarrel with Mary, insignificant in itself and soon mended, but interesting in the glimpse it affords of Shelley as a peacemaker: "I hear from you but seldom now you cease to correspond with Mary," Shelley wrote to Claire on June 22. ". . . I am trying to persuade Mary to ask your pardon. . . . In the meantime, as you were in the wrong you had better not ask hers, for that is unnecessary, but write to her — if you had been in the right you would have done so."

In Pisa and at the Baths the Shelleys continued most of their former associations. Count Taafe was a fairly frequent caller whose visits both amused and bored the Shelleys. Sending Mary a present of two guinea pigs, he accompanied them with a gallant note in which he wished to be a guinea pig himself in order to enjoy her company. "Mr. Taafe rides, writes, invites, complains, bows and apologizes," Shelley reported to Claire. "He would be a mortal bore if he came often." This was shortly after the removal to the Baths; Count Taafe did come fairly often thereafter, and Shelley thought enough of his literary judgment to request his criticism of *Adonais*.

Both Prince Mavrocordato and the Gisbornes were leaving Italy. The Prince was deeply immersed in his preparations and in revolutionary correspondence. He was unable to see the Shelleys as often as formerly, but he wrote Mary frequent letters in French, full of war news and respectful friendship. He sailed for Greece on June 26 after promising Mary to write whenever he could.

The Gisbornes, with some assistance from Mary and Shelley, had sold off most of their household goods by the end of July and were now ready to depart. Under the surface of his politeness, however, Shelley was still resentful. He reported to Claire that the Gisbornes were selling all their goods, "and mine too. I wonder how much they will have the face to offer me as the produce of the wreck of the steamboat." Yielding to repeated and seemingly cordial invitations from both Mary and Shelley, the Gisbornes came to the Baths on July 26 for a final visit of three days, after which Shelley accompanied them to Florence.

Shelley complained now that reading no longer held his attention, which could only be absorbed in writing poetry. Mary was busy trying vainly to finish writing *Valperga* (her novel on Castruccio) so that the Gisbornes could take the manuscript to England. Letters from England were few, and not encouraging. Godwin had been silent for months, but from Horace Smith the Shelleys at least knew that he had encountered no fresh disasters. He had sent Shelley his long forthcoming *Reply to Malthus*, which Shelley considered "victorious and decisive," although containing "decent interspersions of cant and sophistry."

Hogg wrote once about his Greek studies and pedestrian excursions, and two letters arrived from Leigh Hunt with further details of the misfortunes of his family and the *Examiner*. Both family and fortunes were now on the mend, however, and if the *Examiner* continued to recover its lost circulation Hunt had some hopes of joining the Shelleys in Italy. Peacock wrote that Shelley's old debts were still troublesome, and listed some of the more pressing ones. The Shelleys wished to settle these accounts. Since the spring of 1820 they had been economizing consistently in order to meet their financial obligations, which could only be reduced gradually.

There is no indication in Shelley's letters that he read any of the reviews of *The Cenci* that continued throughout 1821, or any of the seven reviews which *Prometheus Unbound* received in 1820 and 1821. In her journal for May 6 and also for May 7 Mary Shelley wrote the bare word "Reviews," without further detail. Shelley knew from Hunt that Hazlitt had attacked him in his essay on "Paradox and Commonplace" and that Hunt had remonstrated and threatened to attack Hazlitt if he continued. Shelley's letters consistently professed the indifference of a man who felt himself already sentenced to neglect or abuse. If he heard the current quip that *Prometheus Unbound* was well named because none would take the trouble to bind it, he probably accepted it as a true index of public opinion.

The later reviews of *The Cenci*, which had gone into a second edition in 1821, continued the same tone of mixed praise and censure that marked the 1820 reviews. *Prometheus Unbound* was reviewed in 1820 by the *London Magazine* (June), the *London Magazine and Monthly Critical and Dramatic Review* (September and October), the *Literary Gazette* (September 9), *Blackwood's Edinburgh Magazine* (September), and the *Lonsdale Magazine* (November); and in 1821 by the *Monthly Review* (February) and the *Quarterly Review* (October).

The inability of the reviewers to understand the style of *Prometheus Unbound* has been previously discussed, so that it only remains to summarize their general attitude toward the poem. Of the seven magazines, the *Literary Gazette*, *Monthly Review*, and *Quarterly* were almost entirely denunciatory. The *Literary Gazette* bitterly attacked the poem for its obscurity, pronouncing Shelley little better than a lunatic and the poem "a mélange of nonsense, cockneyism, poverty, and pedantry." The *Monthly Review* denounced it as "*nonsense, pure, unmixed nonsense.*" It also pronounced it impious, but nevertheless admitted Shelley's genius and "benevolent feeling, beautiful language, and powerful versification." To the *Quarterly* the poem was dull and unoriginal — "drivelling prose run mad." Its "total lack of meaning," however, did not prevent the reviewer's pronouncing it utterly impious and immoral. Somewhat more colorlessly and impartially the *Lonsdale Magazine* and *Provincial Repository* acknowledged Shelley's genius while condemning his principles. *Blackwood's Edinburgh Magazine* continued its policy of mixing stern criticism of Shelley's ideas with enthusiastic praise of his genius, and sought once more to win from his errors a poet "destined to leave a great name behind him."

Two of the reviews were enthusiastic almost without qualification. The *London Magazine,* somewhat briefly, praised *Prometheus Unbound* as "unsettled, irregular, magnificent," and the *London Magazine and Monthly Critical and Dramatic Review* gave it two full-sized reviews, the first praising "the extreme force and freshness" of the shorter poems and the second summarizing and copiously quoting from the title poem as "one of the most stupendous . . . works of modern poetry," "a vast wilderness of beauty." Few poems have received more extreme praise than Shelley's in this review, which apparently neither Shelley nor any of his biographers ever read. Another eulogistic review, written by Thomas Noon Talfourd for the *New Monthly Magazine* or the *Literary Gazette,* was rejected because the publisher thought the book seemed "full of Jacobinism and blasphemy."

Shelley was now receiving a considerable amount of general and incidental attention. American journals began to take notice of him by printing extracts from reviews and poems. An appreciative general article "On the Philosophy and Poetry of Shelley" appeared in the *London Magazine and Theatrical Inquisitor* for February 1821. The pious Quaker poet Bernard Barton published in 1820 his "Stanzas Addressed to Percy Bysshe Shelley," a dull, well-meant attempt to convert erring genius. Arthur Brooke (John Chalk Claris) printed an enthusiastic sonnet to Shelley in the *Examiner* for November 5, 1820, which was reprinted in the *Tickler* for April 1, 1821.

In the two years 1820 and 1821 Shelley received in all about thirty reviews and about forty brief incidental notices. Several journals quoted his poems independently of reviews, others published poems which were addressed to him, and one book was published about him. In 1822 this attention continued, with some slight abatement in both volume and favor. Granted that the *Quarterly* and possibly the *Literary Gazette* exerted more influence in condemning Shelley than any two friendly journals in his defense, the amount of favorable criticism and the recognition of Shelley's power and genius even by unfriendly critics offer a convincing demonstration that Shelley greatly underrated the impression he was beginning to make upon the reviewers. He prejudged the case against himself, and his judgment has been uncritically accepted as true by all subsequent critics and biographers. At this point, had he finished and published "Charles the First" instead of "The Witch of Atlas" it would have been possible for Shelley to have received far more general recognition.

The publication of *Adonais* late in 1821 undoubtedly helped swing the tide more strongly against Shelley. Instead of giving any wavering reviewer an opportunity for praise by presenting a non-controversial poem, Shelley threw down the gage of battle by assailing reviewers as the assassins of Keats. Rather significantly, only three journals reviewed *Adonais* in 1821. The liberal *Literary Chronicle and Weekly Review* reviewed it before it had been published, quoted almost all of it, and praised it as a poem of "transcendent merits" by a poet of "no ordinary genius." The *Literary Gazette* (December 8) scorned it as an unrelieved farrago of nonsense and impiety, quoting excerpts illustrating six different types of nonsense. But *Blackwood's Magazine*, which had been even more savage with Keats than the *Quarterly*, now abandoned its efforts to "save" Shelley and accepted his challenge. In the December issue it rained contempt and sarcasm upon him, quoted a whole column of his "absurdities," and offered two brutal parodies of *Adonais*. Having previously omitted to review *The Cenci*, it included in the same article a furious brief review of that poem as well.

Very probably the reviewers felt that *Adonais* should be treated as a declaration of war; Shelley, on the other hand, felt that his "least imperfect poem" was the final test of his ability to win public acceptance. "I am especially curious to hear the fate of 'Adonais,'" he wrote to Ollier on November 11. "I confess I should be surprised if *that* poem were born to an immortality of oblivion." Before he knew how the poem had been reviewed he wrote to Hunt (January 25, 1822): "My faculties are shaken to atoms, and torpid. I can write nothing; and if *Adonais* had no success, and excited no interest what incentive can I have to write?" Later in 1822 Leigh Hunt came strongly to Shelley's defense in four letters in the *Examiner* and in a favorable review of *Adonais*, but Shelley's tone of dejection had already been set by the earlier attacks.

In the spring of 1821 another circumstance occurred which further prejudiced Shelley's case with the reviewers. In 1819 the radical printer Richard Carlile had discovered *Queen Mab* and had asked and been refused permission to reprint it. He had respected Shelley's wishes, but his former employee William Clark was less scrupulous.

He brought out and advertised two slightly variant editions, and the notorious radical piratical publisher William Benbow anonymously brought out still another edition under a false New York imprint.

Shelley learned that *Queen Mab* was selling "by the thousands," and considered it rather a droll circumstance. He was nevertheless somewhat annoyed to be judged in 1821 by his comparatively crude artistic standards of 1813 and by beliefs which did not adequately represent him in 1821. It had been ruled in the case of Southey versus the piratical publishers of his *Wat Tyler* that books liable to conviction for blasphemy or sedition were not entitled to legal protection; hence it was impossible to suppress the piracy, though Horace Smith seems to have made some tentative efforts. Shelley contented himself with a letter in the *Examiner* disavowing and disapproving the publication, condemning the book as immature both artistically and philosophically, but reaffirming in general terms his opposition to social, political, and religious oppressions.

From this moment *Queen Mab* became an important weapon in the arsenal of British working-class radicalism. *John Bull's British Journal*, a radical weekly published by William Benbow, gave it a sympathetic review on March 11. The *London Magazine and Theatrical Inquisitor*, though only mildly radical, and not a workingman's magazine, reviewed it favorably in the March issue and prophesied that the author was meant to fulfill a high destiny. Within twenty years fourteen or more separate editions were issued by piratical radical publishers. The book took an honored place with Volney's *Ruins of Empire*, Palmer's *Principles of Nature*, Byron's *Cain*, and the works of Tom Paine in the little radical "libraries" constantly offered for sale.

In 1821 responsible authorities in England were far too nervous over the conditions of the country to ignore such a publication. William Clark was immediately indicted by the Society for the Prevention of Vice, that active and virtuously named association which genuine liberals like Sydney Smith regarded rather as a society for preserving aristocratic vices. Instead of awaiting his trial, selling the books meanwhile, the unheroic William Clark disgusted his fellow radicals by binding himself to good behavior in the interim, and publishing the anonymous *Reply to the Antimatrimonial Hypothesis and Supposed Atheism of Percy Bysshe Shelley, as Laid Down in Queen Mab* (1821), as a demonstration that his interest in *Queen Mab* was financial rather than propagandistic. At his trial on November 19, 1822 Clark made the most of this publication and of his willingness to surrender all copies of the offending book, but was nevertheless sentenced to four months' imprisonment.

Two conservative journals, the *Literary Gazette* for May 19 and the *Monthly Magazine* for June, vigorously denounced the poem; and the rather liberal *Literary Chronicle and Weekly Review* for June 2 reviewed the author, rather than the poem, as a striking example of perverted genius, powerful, but wicked. A reader of the review in the *Literary Gazette* sent in a short poem entitled "The Atheist," wondering why the author of such a line as "There is no God" should not immediately have been blasted by Heaven's lightnings "to his native hell." On the other side John Watson Dalby, in the *Literary Chronicle* for June 9, 1821, published two eight-line stanzas commenting sarcastically on the "clearest proofs" being offered that Shelley was either the devil or his equal. All this happened in the very year, 1821, when Southey, in the Preface to his *Vision of Judgement,* was urging public opinion to emphasize decency and order by suppressing the "Satanic School" for just such utterances as *Queen Mab.* Thus the piracy of *Queen Mab* was less "droll" than Shelley supposed.

Early in August a letter arrived from Byron, informing Shelley that the Countess Guiccioli's father and brother had been expelled from Ravenna for revolutionary sympathies and that she herself had fled to Florence. Byron requested Shelley to visit him, and as Shelley knew Byron himself would soon be leaving Ravenna, he must have thought at once of what would become of Allegra in her convent at Bagnacavallo. On the next day he set out to visit Byron.

Shelley reached Ravenna on August 6. On the very first evening Byron imparted some profoundly disturbing information. He showed Shelley a letter he had received from Mr. R. B. Hoppner eleven months before, detailing the scandalous charges brought against Shelley and Claire by Elise Foggi:

> . . . You must know then that at the time the Shelleys were here Clare was with child by Shelley: you may remember to have heard that she was constantly unwell, and under the care of a Physician, and I am uncharitable enough to believe that the quantity of medicine she then took was not for the mere purpose of restoring her health. I perceive too why she preferred remaining alone at Este, notwithstanding her fear of ghosts and robbers, to being here with the Shelleys. Be this as it may, they

proceeded from here to Naples, where one night Shelley was called up to see Clara who was very ill. His wife, naturally, thought it very strange that he should be sent for; but although she was not aware of the nature of the connexion between them, she had had sufficient proof of Shelley's indifference, and of Clara's hatred for her; besides as Shelley desired her to remain quiet she did not dare to interfere. A Mid-wife was sent for, and the worthy pair, who had made no preparation for the reception of the unfortunate being she was bringing into the world, bribed the woman to carry it to the Pietà, where the child was taken half an hour after its birth, being obliged likewise to purchase the physician's silence with a considerable sum. During all the time of her confinement Mrs. Shelley, who expressed great anxiety on her account, was not allowed to approach her, and these beasts, instead of requiting her uneasiness on Clara's account by at least a few expressions of kindness, have since increased in their hatred of her, behaving to her in the most brutal manner, and Clara doing everything she can to engage her husband to abandon her. Poor Mrs. Shelley, whatever suspicions she may entertain of the nature of their connexion, knows nothing of their adventure at Naples, and as the knowledge of it could only add to her misery, 'tis as well that she should not. This account we had from Elise, who passed here this summer with an English lady who spoke very highly of her. She likewise told us that Clara does not scruple to tell Mrs. Shelley she wishes her dead, and to say to Shelley in her presence that she wonders how he can live with such a creature.

The inconsistence of this story with the actual events it distorts has been previously discussed. But Byron for eleven months had believed that it was "just like them," even though Elise seemed to him a very shaky witness. Renewed contact with Shelley evidently made him ashamed of this judgment; he broke his promise to keep Hoppner's counsel, and laid the letter before Shelley. "Lord Byron," Shelley immediately informed Mary, "has also told me of a circumstance that shocks me exceedingly; because it exhibits a degree of desperate and wicked malice for which I am at a loss to account. When I hear such things my patience and my philosophy are put to a severe proof, whilst I refrain from seeking out some obscure hiding place where the countenance of man may never meet me more." After summarizing Hoppner's story as given above, he concluded:

420

As to what Reviews and the world says, I do not care a jot, but when persons who have known me are capable of conceiving of me — not that I have fallen into a great error and impudence, as would have been the living with Clare as my mistress — but that I have committed such unutterable crimes as destroying or abandoning a child, and that my own — imagine my despair of good, imagine how it is possible that one of so weak and sensitive a nature as mine can run further the gauntlet through this hellish society of men. *You* should write to the Hoppners a letter refuting the charge, in case you believe, and know, and can prove that it is false; stating the grounds and proofs of your belief. I need not dictate what you should say; nor, I hope, inspire you with warmth to rebut a charge, which you only can effectually rebut. If you will send the letter to me here, I will forward it to the Hoppners. Lord Byron is not up, I do not know the Hoppners' address, and I am anxious not to lose a post.

Two days later, before receiving Mary's reply to his former letter, Shelley wrote that he was determined to suppress this slander, "even if I am reduced to the disagreeable necessity of prosecuting Elise before the Tuscan tribunals."

Mary Shelley's reply to the first of these letters was prompt and passionate:

My dear Shelley,

Shocked beyond all measure as I was, I instantly wrote the enclosed. If the task be not too dreadful, pray copy it for me. I cannot.

Read that part of your letter which contains the accusation. I tried, but I could not write it. I think I could as soon have died. I send also Elise's last letter: enclose it or not as you think best.

I wrote to you with far different feelings last night, beloved friend. Our barque is indeed "tempest-tost"; but love me, as you have ever done, and God preserve my child to me, and our enemies shall not be too much for us. . . .

Pray get my letter to Mrs. Hoppner copied for a thousand reasons. Adieu, dearest! Take care of yourself — all yet is well. The shock for me is over, and I now despise the slander; but it must not pass uncontradicted. I sincerely thank Lord Byron for his kind unbelief.

Affectionately yours,
M. W. S.

The Countess Guiccioli, he assured Shelley, was very fond of Allegra, nor was he himself willing to depart for Switzerland and leave the child in an Italian convent.

At first Byron was undecided where he should go; he would have preferred Pisa, but Shelley was stopped from urging Pisa upon him by Claire's proximity. Within a week, however, he had decided on Pisa and commissioned the Shelleys to secure him a "large and magnificent house" there.

Before leaving Ravenna Shelley made a visit to Allegra. She was at first diffident, not having seen Shelley for three years; then, won over by the gold chain and basket of sweetmeats that he brought, she raced wildly about the place with him until he was exhausted, and concluded the romp by ringing the tocsin that usually summoned all the nuns from their beds. Nevertheless Shelley thought that the nuns had brought about a considerable improvement in her discipline. This, and the kindness with which she seemed to be treated, must have been an agreeable surprise for him, even though her prattle of saints, angels, and paradise made him fear for her intellectual development. Shelley asked her what he should say to her mother. "That I want a kiss and a beautiful dress," was the prompt answer. "And what kind of dress?" "All of silk and gold," was the reply. These messages were doubtless delivered, but not the message to Papa — "To make me a visit and bring *mammina* with him."

The wedding of Emilia Viviani to the more successful of her two suitors was now approaching, and both Shelley and Emilia were distressed. One wonders what hysterical words may have been said in some of the unrecorded scenes in which Shelley sought to reconcile the highly temperamental Emilia to a marriage that she did not desire and that he desired only as the lesser of two evils. Perhaps some such scene was overheard, or perhaps general rumor only was responsible for a temporary interdict on further visits from the Shelleys. "I beg you," Emilia wrote (probably in July), "to come no more to St. Anna, neither you, nor any of your family. My parents desire that I should henceforth see no one. Every attempt would be in vain; we should be humiliated without obtaining anything."

Emilia was married on September 8 to Luigi Biondi, rather than to the other suitor, Danielli, whose despair in May Emilia had asked Shelley to assist in calming. After her marriage she left Pisa to live with her husband's family at Pomerance, about sixty miles southeast of Pisa. The Shelleys seem not to have been invited to any of the wedding festivities, and the marriage is ignored by both Mary and Claire in their journals. A week later Shelley informed Byron of the marriage "after a great deal of tumult, etc.," and added that Emilia's brother-in-law watched her with great assiduity. "My convent friend . . ." he informed John Gisborne four months later, "is married, and I [am] in a sort of morbid quietness."

Some of the "tumult" took place in Shelley's own mind. Several of his shorter poems written in 1821 are probably to be connected with Emilia's wedding. An unfinished epithalamium of about thirty lines exists in three different versions, as if Shelley had tried to write a conventional, impersonal marriage ode and had given it up as a failure. A longer poem of 219 lines, "Ginevra," is the tragic story of a bride who stole forth from the marriage festivities to listen to the reproaches of her former lover and returned to her chamber to die quietly on her bed before the guests had left the house. The story is not of Shelley's invention; it had appeared in 1821 in *L'Osservatore Fiorentino;* but Shelley's poem about it could not have been written near the time of Emilia's wedding without being psychologically connected with that event. In "The Fugitives" Shelley attempted once more to realize the elopement he had proposed in *Epipsychidion.* It is a poem of rather spirited action, but falls far below the emotional intensity of *Epipsychidion.*

It was Shelley's belief that a poet was really two people, the poet and the man. The man could and did see that a union with Emilia was impossible and probably not even to be desired, that it was better for Emilia to marry Biondi. He had written Claire (April 29) that Emilia's marriage would remove "a great and painful weight" from his mind, and he had expressed to Mary (August 16) his desire to retire utterly from the world with Mary and their child. This was the man; the poet had proposed a purely imaginary elopement to Emilia. To the poet Emilia's marriage was another beautiful idealism shattered upon the rocks of reality. The intense idealizing fire of *Epipsychidion* still smoldered, even though much of its original heat had vanished, as it had risen, in the act of writing. To the poet Emilia's marriage could only have seemed, like the defection of Elizabeth Shelley nine years earlier, another addition to his poignant disillusions with life, a kind of death.

One realizes with a certain sympathetic comprehension that several brief, intense lyrics written by Shelley at about the time of Emilia's marriage are not merely the expressions of general melancholy that they have commonly seemed:

A LAMENT

O World! O life! O time!
On whose last steps I climb,
   Trembling at that where I had stood before;
When will return the glory of your prime?
      No more — Oh, never more!

Out of the day and night
A joy has taken flight:
   Fresh spring, and summer, and winter hoar,
Move my faint heart with grief, but with delight
      No more — Oh, never more!

REMEMBRANCE

Swifter far than Summer's flight,
Swifter far than youth's delight,
Swifter far than happy night,
   Art thou come and gone;
As the wood when leaves are shed,
As the night when sleep is fled,
As the heart when joy is dead,
   I am left lone, alone.

The swallow Summer comes again,
The owlet Night resumes her reign —
But the wild swan Youth is fain
   To fly with thee, false as thou.
My heart each day desires the morrow,
Sleep itself is turned to sorrow,
Vainly would my Winter borrow
   Sunny leaves from any bough.

Lilies for a bridal bed,
Roses for a matron's head,
Violets for a maiden dead,
   Pansies let *my* flowers be:
On the living grave I bear,
Scatter them without a tear,
Let no friend, however dear,
   Waste one hope, one fear for me.

428

TO ——

When passion's trance is overpast,
If tenderness and truth could last
Or live, whilst all wild feelings keep
Some mortal slumber, dark and deep,
I should not weep, I should not weep!

It were enough to feel, to see
Thy soft eyes gazing tenderly,
And dream the rest — and burn and be
The secret food of fires unseen,
Couldst thou but be as thou hast been.

After the slumber of the year
The woodland violets reappear;
All things revive in field or grove,
And sky and sea; but two, which move,
And form all others, life and love.

TO ——

Music, when soft voices die,
Vibrates in the memory;
Odours, when sweet violets sicken,
Live within the sense they quicken.

Rose leaves, when the rose is dead,
Are heaped for the belovèd's bed;
And so thy thoughts, when thou art gone,
Love itself shall slumber on.

There was no actual death or known melancholy event in 1821 which could have given definite occasion for these lyrics at that time — nothing except the marriage of Emilia. With this marriage a "soft voice" would die, to vibrate only in memory, and Emilia would be "gone" both physically and spiritually, leaving only the "thought" of her to brighten Love's slumbers. Its near approach *did* set, for the poet, a terminus to certain dreams, from which the awakening would be sad; a "maiden" *would* have died into a "matron," terminating a swift, beautiful interlude for the poet; a particular "joy" *had* "taken flight"; and for him, when Emilia's "passion's trance" of this marriage had "overpast," there *would* be an end of the "tenderness and truth" he had known in Emilia. "I knew a very interesting Italian lady last winter," Shelley wrote to Hogg on October 22, 1821, "but she is now married; which, to quote our friend Peacock, is you know, the same as being dead."

It seems a pity that the story of Shelley and Emilia does not end with these poems. Five days before her marriage Emilia had written to Shelley that she would be pleased to receive his letters if he wished to write after her marriage — "but please be very prudent in all your expressions." The bulk of her letter, however, concerned a very unusual request for money, apparently a considerable sum, with which to rescue a friend from distress. The details of this request and of its reception are unknown, except that Shelley was certainly in no position to grant it.

Thereafter, however, Mary Shelley's references to Emilia are tinged with a scorn and disgust which seem clearly connected with Emilia's request. A little later, some nine months after Emilia's marriage, Shelley expressed a similar revulsion in a letter to John Gisborne: "The *Epipsychidion* I cannot look at; the person whom it celebrates was a cloud instead of a Juno; and poor Ixion starts from the centaur that was the offspring of his own embrace." Giving definite point to this revulsion, Shelley asked his publisher to suppress all further sale of *Epipsychidion*.

One can only say that Mary and possibly Shelley thought that Emilia tried to obtain money from them for false or unworthy purposes, but whether or not such suspicions were just is another matter. It is possible that Mary was misled by a latent jealousy and that Shelley's revulsion was only a psychological phenomenon, similar to several other sudden revulsions in his affections. His idealization of Emilia may have crashed to earth simply as a result of its hyper-intensity. "I think one is always in love with something or other," Shelley concluded, in the same letter quoted above. "The error . . . consists in seeking in a mortal image the likeness of what is perhaps eternal."

Chapter XXV

THE SHELLEYS remained quietly at the Baths of Pisa until October 25, when they moved back into the city. Claire had arrived from Leghorn on October 9, and from October 11 to 30 was the guest of the Williamses at Pugnano. Almost every day the two families were together for at least a part of the time, either at the Baths or at Pugnano, at breakfast, at dinner, or in the evening. The days passed smoothly in walking, boating, or discussing.

Mary was busy copying her novel, and acquiring furniture for their house, for they were now fully decided to settle in Pisa and its neighborhood indefinitely. The fixity of this decision seems a little questionable, however; for soon Shelley wrote to Peacock inquiring about the possibilities of going to India in the employ of the East India Company, and at the same time was thinking of taking up an abode in Greece if the Greeks won their independence. Peacock replied congratulating Shelley on his "recent fixedness to one spot" and pointing out the practical impossibility of the Indian project.

The knowledge that Prince Mavrocordato was now fighting for Greek independence gave an additional fillip to Shelley's interest in that cause. Late in October a number of Greek revolutionaries, escaped from a recent defeat in Wallachia, passed through Pisa and were honorably treated by the government. Shelley was at that moment just finishing his *Hellas*, which he described as "a sort of imitation of the *Persæ* of Æschylus, full of lyrical poetry," "written without much care, in one of those few moments of enthusiasm which now seldom visit me." Edward Williams made the fair copy between November 6 and 10 and suggested the title.

In his Preface Shelley apologized for the thin and inaccurate "newspaper erudition" on which he was forced to rely for the factual basis of the poem. In truth, the obscure battles Shelley describes resemble those in the *Persæ* of Æschylus far more than they resemble any conflicts described by the historians of the modern Greek war of independence. Similarly Shelley's Greeks really belong to the world of Plato and the Greek historians and dramatists. "We are all Greeks," he asserted in his Preface. "Our laws, our literature, our religion, our arts, have their root in Greece. . . . The human form and the human mind attained to a perfection in Greece which has impressed its image on those faultless productions whose very fragments are the despair of modern art, and has propagated impulses which cannot cease, through a thousand channels of manifest or imperceptible operation, to ennoble and delight mankind until the extinction of the race."

Probably the only modern Greeks whom Shelley knew were Prince Mavrocordato, to whom *Hellas* was dedicated, and several of his relatives. To Shelley the modern Greek (as he said in his Preface) was "the descendant of those glorious beings whom the imagination almost refuses to figure to itself as belonging to our kind." He had seen more ignoble Greeks, no doubt, in the busy markets of Leghorn. Soon Edward Trelawny was to give him a view of the squalor and dirt of a Greek trading vessel, which he acknowledged reminded him more of Hell than of Hellas. Such revelations could never discourage a Shelley, for to him the Idea was more true than any factual representation of it limited to a particular time and place. The real Greece, as his chorus sang, was

> Based on the crystalline sea
> Of thought, and its eternity.

He had read Thomas Hope's *Anastasius* (1819), with its unflattering picture of the modern Greeks, as well as Byron's realistic comments on Greece in the notes to the second canto of *Childe Harold.* He probably knew, in one corner of his mind, more of the "facts" than Trelawny supposed, but regarded them as relatively insignificant. In his Preface he even admitted the inferiority of the modern Greeks. But what of that? As he had previously asserted of the French and Neapolitan revolutionists, their present lack of grandeur was only a temporary condition, a natural result of the very tyranny they were striving to overthrow.

Hence the outcome of this particular revolution seemed to Shelley not half so important as the fact of revolution itself. Freedom's losses were only temporary losses as long as the spirit itself survived. This was the doctrine of revolution as expounded in the parable of the Serpent and the Eagle in the first canto of *The Revolt of Islam,* the same doctrine that is implicit in Demogorgon's concluding speech in *Prometheus Unbound,* in *A Philosophical View of Reform,* in the "Defence of Poetry," and in Shelley's view of the contemporary Italian and Spanish revolutions.

Though he had written rapidly, in the midst of arranging for Byron's residence in Pisa and while still trying to keep warm the dying embers of "Charles the First," Shelley had a fondness for *Hellas* out of proportion to the care he had bestowed upon it. It represented the union of two of his greatest passions, liberty and Greece. He hoped that it would be published promptly, but Ollier was most irritatingly and uncommunicatively dilatory. It was published in the spring (probably March) of 1822, and received only one review, a very stupid and hostile one on June 30 in a shortlived London weekly entitled the *General Weekly Register of News, Literature, Law, Politics, and Commerce.*

The plot of *Hellas* is too slight to require more than passing notice. The Turkish Sultan, Mahmud, is oppressed with vague fears for the future of his rule; these are increased by the reports of land and sea battles brought to him by four successive messengers. He talks with an old and learned Jew named Ahasuerus, who is no other than the Wandering Jew of Shelley's youthful enthusiasm dignified and ennobled by all that Shelley had learned between 1811 and 1822. Through him Mahmud talks with the founder of his line and learns that its end is near.

Interspersing the thin action, a chorus of Christian slaves comments upon the struggle, not in its present aspects so much as *sub specie æternitatis.* Though the drama contains some fine passages of blank verse, it is in these choruses that it reaches a height showing that Shelley's poetic powers were not declining.

These choruses are more objective than most of Shelley's great lyrics and suggest Byron at his lyrical best almost as much as they do Shelley. It may not be without significance that when he was writing them Shelley was reading with extreme enthusiasm the third canto of Byron's *Don Juan,* containing "The Isles of Greece." Nothing could be more genuinely Shelleyan, however, than the underlying ideas of the drama or of some of the shorter choral passages. The semichorus in the first scene is an almost perfect summary of Shelley's philosophy of living. Though Hope, Truth, and Love may be obscured, it sings, they are never finally defeated or abolished — Liberty is the spark that preserves their life and beauty.

But Shelley had long since reached the conclusion that the time, space, and physical entities that environ living are not really the essence of living but only functions of thought. In *Hellas* he gave his final and most beautiful expression to this idea:

> . . . this Whole
> Of suns, and worlds, and men, and beasts, and flowers,
> With all the silent or tempestuous workings

By which they have been, are, or cease to be,
Is but a vision; all that it inherits
Are motes of a sick eye, bubbles, and dreams;
Thought is its cradle and its grave, nor less
The future and the past are idle shadows
Of thought's eternal flight — they have no being;
Nought is but that which feels itself to be.
. . . Thought
Alone, and its quick elements, Will, Passion,
Reason, Imagination, cannot die;
They are what that which they regard appears,
The stuff whence mutability can weave
All that it hath dominion o'er — worlds, worms,
Empires, and superstitions. What has thought
To do with time, or place, or circumstance?

Hellas is also Shelley's last utterance on another subject of lifelong interest — Christianity. The unfinished Prologue, the choruses, and the prose notes present a sympathetic view of Christ. In relation to Mohammedanism and the ancient pagan creed Shelley is even tolerant of Christianity; but in a universal aspect he still regards it as a monstrous perversion of Christ. "The sublime human character of Jesus Christ," he asserts in one of his notes on the poem, "was deformed by an imputed identification with a Power who tempted, betrayed, and punished the innocent beings who were called into existence by His sole will; and for the period of a thousand years the spirit of this most just, wise, and benevolent of men has been propitiated with myriads of hecatombs of those who approached the nearest to His innocence and wisdom, sacrified under every aggravation of atrocity and variety of torture."

By the end of November the Shelleys were comfortably settled in Pisa on the north side of the Lung' Arno, in the top floor of a house known as the Tre Palazzi di Chiesa. Their outlook was south, over open country toward the sea, rather than over the jumbled city streets that both Mary and Shelley found at times repulsive. They had installed their own furniture, bought with the savings of two years' economy, but they were still trying vainly to get possession of books and two desks that had been left behind in England. The Williamses had also furnished their own lodgings, in the same building on the floor beneath the Shelleys. Immediately opposite the Shelleys stood the Palazzo Lanfranchi, which Shelley had taken for Byron.

The Countess Guiccioli and Count Gamba, her brother, had already settled in Pisa. On November 1 Byron had arrived, bringing at least part of his household furnishings and menagerie in a train of eight wagons that Shelley had sent to him from Pisa. Claire had simultaneously departed for Florence, and had seen Byron probably for the last time as her carriage drew to the side of the road near Empoli to watch Byron's cortege pass toward Pisa.

A letter from Shelley to Peacock, written probably January 11, 1822, furnishes a picture of his daily life at Pisa in the autumn and early winter of 1821–2:

> I am still at Pisa, where I have at length fitted up some rooms at the top of a lofty palace that overlooks the city and the surrounding region; and have collected books and plants about me. . . . We live, as usual, tranquilly. I get up, or at least wake, early; read and write till two; dine; go to Lord B.'s, and ride, or play at Billiards, as the weather permits; and sacrifice the evening either to light books or whoever happens to drop in. Our furniture, which is very neat cost fewer shillings than that at Marlow did pounds sterling; and our windows are full of plants, which turn the sunny winter into spring. My health is better — my cares are lighter; and although nothing will cure the consumption of my purse, yet it drags on a sort of life in death, very like its master, and seems, like Fortunatus's, always empty yet never quite exhausted.

Mary saw Byron but seldom, as Byron's dinners were usually for men only. She saw the Countess Guiccioli rather frequently, however, and described her to Mrs. Gisborne as "a nice pretty girl without pretensions, good-hearted and amiable." To Shelley she was "a very pretty, sentimental, innocent, superficial Italian, who has sacrificed an immense fortune to live for Lord Byron; and who, if I know anything of my friend, of her, and of human nature will hereafter have plenty of leisure and opportunity to repent her rashness." The Williamses and Shelleys continued seeing each other as frequently as at the Baths. Shelley now thought Jane Williams "more amiable and beautiful than ever, and a sort of spirit of embodied peace in our circle of tempests." Occasionally one or both of the Shelleys called on the Masons at Casa Silva.

A Mrs. Beauclerc, a daughter of the Duchess of Leinster, who had been a neighbor of the Shelley family in Sussex, was spending the

winter in Pisa with her daughter. Shelley called on her somewhat unwillingly in late December, "after much solicitation," and was disgusted at her effusive reception of him. By spring, however, Mary's
journal shows that Mrs. Beauclerc was a fairly regular member of
the Shelley-Byron circle. Medwin had returned to Pisa on November
15, to something like his former intimacy with the Shelleys. With
Count Gamba, Count Taafe, Shelley, and Williams he was a regular
member of Byron's riding party and was already taking the occasionally inaccurate and gullible notes of Byron's conversation that
were later to bring down upon his head the wrath of Byron's friends.

The Hunts, delayed in England by bad weather and Mrs. Hunt's ill
health, were expected daily. With Mary's help the lower floor of Byron's palace had already been made ready for their reception. Between September and March Hunt wrote from various places to
Shelley explaining each new delay, but always enthusiastic about
the project of establishing a new liberal review in Italy with Byron's
and Shelley's co-operation: "What? Are there not three of us? And
ought we not to have as much strength and variety as possible? We
will divide the world between us, like the Triumvirate. . . ."

November passed in a succession of mild autumn days. On December 21 Mary reported to Mrs. Gisborne: "You will be glad to hear
that Shelley's health is much improved this winter; he is not quite
well, but he is much better. The air of Pisa is so mild and delightful,
and the exercise on horseback agrees with him particularly." Tom
Medwin, on his return to Pisa, "found him an altered man. His health
had sensibly improved, and he had shaken off much of that melancholy and depression to which he had been subject during the last
year."

Constantly the Shelley-Byron party of men dined together, rode
together, talked, and indulged in pistol practice. Shelley was an
awkward horseman, but he was better with a pistol, having a quicker
and firmer aim than Lord Byron. Conversation at the Palazzo Lanfranchi was lively and interesting. Occasionally the party was aug-
mented by some traveling friend of Byron's, as it was by Samuel
Rogers toward the end of April. Byron's talk, like his letters and
his *Don Juan,* was full of gay sharp flippancies and rapid changes
from grave to gay, and from the comic to the almost sublime. He
scoffed at nearly everything except freedom and religion.

Medwin, like Claire Clairmont, noted in Byron a basically super-
stitious attitude toward religion, and for that reason could not
quite agree with Shelley's opinion that Byron was to be compared

with Voltaire. Whenever Byron's talk turned upon subjects that to Shelley's finer sensibilities seemed gross and indelicate, Shelley would depart with scarcely concealed disgust. Shelley was also baffled and somewhat annoyed by Byron's constant flitting from subject to subject, his unwillingness to stick to the point and argue. Medwin, taking his unequal part in the conversation, was, like Taafe, occasionally the victim of a little mystification and leg-pulling; yet his comparison of Shelley and Byron shows that he was something more than the mere *seccatura* that Mary Shelley thought him: "There was something enchanting in his [Byron's] manner, his voice, his smile — a fascination in them; but on leaving him, I have often marvelled that I gained so little from him worth carrying away; whilst every word of Shelley's was almost oracular; his reasoning subtle and profound; his opinions, whatever they were, sincere and undisguised; whilst with Byron, such was his love of mystification, it was impossible to know when he was in earnest."

Edward Trelawny, taking part in similar gatherings a few months later, made a very similar comparison. In argument he found Byron quick, superficial, and shifty; Shelley acute, profound, and steady. Shelley "neither fled nor stood at bay, nor altered his course, but calmly went on with heart and mind intent on elevating his species. . . . His words were, 'I always go on until I am stopped, and I never am stopped.'"

Despite his opinion that *Don Juan* and *Cain* were almost super-natural achievements, and despite the charm of Byron's personal presence, Shelley had no illusions about the fundamental fickleness and instability of Byron's character. Nor did he hesitate to disagree with Byron on questions of literary opinion. When Byron showed him *The Deformed Transformed* Shelley stated frankly "that he liked it the least of all his works; that it smelt too strongly of *Faust;* and besides that there were two lines in it, word for word from Southey." Perhaps it was the last statement, rather than Shelley's lack of enthusiasm, that caused Byron to turn deathly pale and immediately throw the manuscript into the fire — only to reproduce it later.

Byron, on his part, had a high respect for Shelley's character and judgment. According to Medwin, he consulted Shelley on most of his personal and private affairs. He could be capricious, annoying, and rude with Shelley as with anyone; but despite his disagreement with most of Shelley's ideas of religion and society, he was compelled to respect and admire him. In answering occasional criticisms from his English correspondents Byron consistently defended Shelley against the current misunderstanding of his character.

As winter storms descended upon Pisa toward the end of December, Mary was seized with a "rheumatism of the head" from which she suffered severely. For several nights she was entirely deprived of sleep. Shelley also reported himself to Claire Clairmont as having "suffered considerably from pain and depression of spirits." But within less than a fortnight he was writing to Peacock: "My health is better — my cares are lighter," so that the letter to Claire may have been tinged by the always dissatisfied craving for sympathy to be found more in his letters to Claire than anywhere else except in his poetry.

Something of the same feeling crops out in an earlier letter to John Gisborne, in which Shelley expressed his extreme admiration for Antigone. "Some of us," he concluded, "have in a prior existence been in love with an Antigone, and that makes us find no full content in any mortal tie." In a fragmentary poem called "The Zucca," written in January 1822, this sentiment is more clearly expressed in the third stanza:

> I loved — oh no, I mean not one of ye,
>   Or any earthly one, though ye are dear
> As human heart to human heart may be: —
>   I loved I know not what — but this low sphere,
> And all that it contains, contains not thee,
>   Thou whom, seen nowhere, I feel everywhere,
> From Heaven and Earth, and all that in them are
> Veiled art thou, like a   star.

By 1822 Mary's journal had gradually drifted into more and more desultory mention of Shelley's reading and writing. Perhaps this tendency, which first becomes noticeable immediately after Clara Shelley's death in the autumn of 1818, is a sign on Mary's part (as his poems are on Shelley's) that the union of Shelley and Mary had lost some of its original sympathy. If so, it was only normal and seems to have been generally so considered by Shelley; he knew well enough that his ideal was not to be found in flesh and blood. But the unsatisfied craving still persisted, and he was even now beginning to see in Jane Williams some possibility of its fulfillment. Poems somewhat like those to Emilia Viviani were soon to follow.

Early in December two episodes occurred that brought passing excitement to the Shelley-Byron circle. On December 12 Medwin heard at a bookseller's a rumor that in Lucca a man was to be burned alive for stealing consecrated wafers from an altar. Shelley, out walking with the Williamses, heard the same rumor at the same time. They went immediately to Byron. Believing that the culprit was to be burned next day, Shelley was all for organizing a band to ride to Lucca and effect a rescue by force, to which Byron agreed, if it should be necessary. Meanwhile Taafe undertook to ride to Lucca to ascertain the truth of the rumor, and the others agreed to submit a written appeal to the Grand Duke, who was in Pisa at the time. The next day, however, news arrived that the thief had escaped from Lucca into the Tuscan dominions, where he had been arrested at Florence. The Grand Duke's officers, true to his reputation for humanity, consented to surrender him only on condition of his being tried according to Tuscan laws. He was eventually sent to the galleys.

On a lower floor of the same house with the Shelleys lived the Reverend Dr. Nott, who had once been subpreceptor to the Princess Charlotte and was said to have lost his position through abusing it for ambitious ends. Earlier, according to Medwin, he had earned the name of "Slip-knot" for his dexterity in evading matrimonial engagements. Every Sunday Dr. Nott held religious services for the benefit of the fourteen or fifteen English people who wished to attend. He gave Mary Shelley a personal and particular invitation, which she accepted, for three sermons.

These sermons, against atheism, were directed so pointedly at Mary Shelley that everyone felt that Shelley was being assailed through his wife. Shelley only laughed, even when Dr. Nott later referred to him at Mrs. Beauclerc's as a *"scelerato."* Not so Byron, who regarded the sermon as a shabby example of priestly malice. Dr. Nott, he said, had revised one of the Ten Commandments to read: "Thou shalt, Nott, bear false witness against thy neighbour." He wrote a nine-stanza satire, beginning: "Do you know Doctor Nott," which rehearsed various gossip at his expense and concluded:

> You may still preach and pray
> And from bishop sink into backbiter.

Shortly after this episode, a young Cornishman named Edward John Trelawny arrived in Pisa. He was already acquainted with the

Williamses and Medwin, having met them in Geneva in 1820. He had heard Medwin's praise of Shelley and had read and admired *Queen Mab* and *The Cenci*. Correspondence with Williams stimulated his desire to know both Shelley and Byron, so he set out for Pisa, planning to spend some time in its intellectual society and to hunt later. On January 14, 1822 he turned up at the Williamses' apartment in the Tre Palazzi.

Within a few minutes thereafter he became conscious that a young man in the darkened hallway beyond the open door was gazing upon him with a peculiar steadiness. It was Shelley; Mrs. Williams called him in and furnished the necessary introductions. Trelawny was astonished. He could hardly believe that this tall, thin, boyish-looking person could be the deadly enemy of church and state that reviews had pictured.

Jane Williams asked Shelley to read a little from the book he held in his hand, Calderón's *Mágico Prodigioso,* and Shelley complied in a manner that immediately assured Trelawny that he was in the presence of genius: "The masterly manner in which he analyzed the genius of the author, his lucid interpretation of the story, and the ease with which he translated into our language the most subtle and imaginative passages of the Spanish poet, were marvellous. . . ." After the reading Shelley vanished as silently as he had appeared, but reappeared almost immediately with Mary.

In the following days Trelawny soon became well acquainted with the Shelleys and Byron. From the first he was in their company almost every day. He was pleased with Mary's intellectual quality, and her engaging, alert, and witty conversation among her friends, even though he soon learned that she was often melancholy when alone. He greatly admired Shelley for his sincerity, his deep sympathies, and subtle intellectual penetration. He even admired Shelley's idealizing tendencies, though he often tried to bring the poet into closer touch with his own notion of the realities of life. Shelley listened considerately, and went his own way.

The Shelleys were perhaps a little longer making up their minds about Trelawny, though the mere physical impression was striking enough at first glance. This six-foot, black-haired, mustachioed, Moorish-looking Cornishman, with his overhanging eyebrows, monotonous, yet emphatic language, and quick smile, was plainly as unusual as his Oriental tales of blood and violence out of his own past. Some three weeks later Mary expressed to Mrs. Gisborne a piqued uncertainty which the association of many years perhaps did not entirely remove. Certainly he was clever, but how honest and truthful was he? Was he as generous as he was impetuous, and was he as honorable as he was independent and unconventional?

Even before Trelawny's arrival the Shelleys, the Williamses, and Byron had resolved to spend the summer on the Bay of Lerici, and Shelley and Williams were counting upon the help of Trelawny in building the boat which they were planning. The next day after his arrival Trelawny produced a model of an American schooner and was authorized to write at once to his friend Captain Roberts in Genoa, directing him to build a thirty-foot undecked boat on the same model. Mary and Jane listened to this fateful decision without enthusiasm, but without protest.

Byron at once decided to build a similar boat, but larger, and decked. Williams, however, was so much in love with a boat design he had brought with him from England that he ultimately prevailed against the judgment of both Trelawny and Roberts. During the months when the two boats were building, Shelley and Williams continued their naval exploits in the small boat that had already given them so much pleasure. Time and again they repaired with Trelawny to the banks of the Arno to sketch in the sand the lines and compartments of their larger boat; then with a chart of the Mediterranean spread before them they planned extended cruises. Byron stood by with a wicked smile and speculated on the amount of salvage Shelley's boat would fetch after *his* boat had rescued and towed it into port.

At this time Shelley also expressed a desire to learn to swim. After watching Trelawny perform a series of difficult aquatic feats he remarked wistfully: "Why can't I swim . . . ?" — upon which Trelawny proposed to give him a first lesson. Shelley shed his clothes briskly and plunged in, but made no effort to rise from the bottom of the pool. Upon rescuing him Trelawny found that he had regarded the prospect of death rather comfortably. "I always find the bottom of the well," he remarked, "and they say Truth lies there. In another minute I should have found it, and you would have found an empty shell. It is an easy way of getting rid of the body."

In his almost daily walks, rides, and meals with the Shelleys and Williamses Trelawny seemed scarcely conscious of a somewhat unusual emotional situation developing between Shelley, Mary, and Jane Williams. Yet by early January Shelley's admiration for Jane Williams had produced two poems, "To Jane: The Invitation," and

"To Jane: The Recollection," which show that it was to Jane, rather than Mary, that he now looked for his bright moments of spiritual sunshine. The two poems reflect Shelley's pleasure in a walk through the neighboring woods with Jane and Mary, apparently on January 2. It is Jane who is hailed as "best and brightest" and who is "ever fair and kind"; if Mary's presence is indicated at all it is only as the "envious wind" which "Blots one dear image out" and causes the poet to lament his lack of spiritual calm.

Shelley had found a secluded spot to which he loved to repair in order to compose in entire solitude. One fine spring morning when he had vanished in this direction Mary engaged Trelawny's assistance in finding him. After some fruitless searching Trelawny found an old man who had seen *"l'Inglese malincolico"* and undertook to guide the searcher. While Mary waited near the edge of the wood Trelawny and his guide plunged on until they reached a deep dark pool surrounded by stunted and twisted trees. Near by lay Shelley's hat, books, and papers. A few paces beyond, in the lee of a pine that had toppled over into the pool, sat the poet, gazing into the water in a mood of such abstraction or concentration that he had not noticed Trelawny's approach.

Trelawny reminded him that a "forsaken lady" was waiting at the entrance to the grove. Shelley jumped up and stuffed his books and papers into his jacket pockets. "Poor Mary!" he exclaimed in rueful contrition, "hers is a sad fate. Come along; she can't bear solitude, nor I society — the quick coupled with the dead." When they rejoined Mary she scolded Shelley affectionately as "a wild goose" with no sense of social obligations; then the party started back for Pisa in spirits as wild and high as Shelley's had been previously silent and abstracted.

Shelley had been working on a poem beside his fallen pine tree, and Trelawny picked up the manuscript. But it was such a frightful scrawl that he could read only two lines. With its smears, deletions, additions, and so forth, it reminded him of a marsh overgrown with bulrushes in which the blots appeared as wild ducks. When more fully drawn, the "rude sketch" later emerged as one of Shelley's most delicately beautiful fancies, the poem now known as "With a Guitar: To Jane."

The guitar had been purchased and presented when Horace Smith, about the end of January, had declined Shelley's request to buy for him in Paris a pedal harp to be presented to Jane. And when Jane sang to her guitar, Shelley was moved to another poem:

TO JANE

The keen stars were twinkling,
And the fair moon was rising among them,
          Dear Jane!
The guitar was tinkling,
But the notes were not sweet till you sung them
          Again.
As the moon's soft splendour
O'er the faint cold starlight of heaven
          Is thrown,
So your voice most tender
To the strings without soul had then given
          Its own.

The stars will awaken,
Though the moon sleep a full hour later,
          To-night;
No leaf will be shaken
Whilst the dews of your melody scatter
          Delight.
Though the sound overpowers,
Sing again, with your dear voice revealing
          A tone
Of some world far from ours,
Where music and moonlight and feeling
          Are one.

Jane Williams had learned from Medwin something of the art of hypnotizing and was able to use it in combating Shelley's occasional attacks of pain from his side. In a poem entitled "The Magnetic Lady to her Patient" Shelley gives a specimen of the soothing, sympathetic talk with which her "magnetic" ministrations were accompanied. In the second stanza Jane is made to say plainly: "I love thee not." At the same time she expresses deep pity that his case is so different from hers and Williams's in that Shelley's consolation in distress must come from a hand not his wife's. One cannot be certain that any such conversation actually happened except in Shelley's mind, but a later letter of Jane's shows that it could have happened. "You, I imagined," she wrote to Leigh Hunt, "as well as myself, had seen that the intercourse between Shelley and Mary was not as happy as it should have been."

In another poem, which Shelley sent to Edward Williams on January 26, he seems clearly to be speaking of Mary's objection to his intimacy with the Williamses. "The serpent is shut out from Paradise," he begins the first stanza, and concludes it:

> I, too, must seldom seek again
> Near happy friends a mitigated pain.

He expresses the despondency of spirits he felt in his "cold home" (the same phrase he had previously applied to his home with Harriet) and apologizes for the necessity of seeing his friends less often. The poem was sent to Edward Williams with a note requesting that it be shown to no one except Jane — and, on second thought, not even to her. The Williamses, seeing Mary's deficient sympathy and Shelley's excessive reaction to it, sympathized with both while condemning neither.

Shelley paid another strong tribute to Jane in the tenth stanza of "The Zucca," yet in the third stanza he quite clearly disposed of the question of love. This poem, which was written in January, is a fairly clear statement both of Shelley's sense of obligation to Jane and also of the fact that he was not in love with her:

> I loved — oh no, I mean not one of ye,
> Or any earthly one . . .

— which is but a slight variation from the passage from Saint Augustine that had been prefixed to *Alastor* six years before: "*Nondum amabam, et amare amabam, quærebam quid amarem, amans amare.*"

At the same time there were anxieties and irritations that were more tangible and were not at all exaggerated by a hopeless craving for perfect sympathy. Ollier had completely exhausted Shelley's patience by delays and indifference. On January 26 Shelley gave John Gisborne instructions to terminate the connection — "extract me from his clutches" — but Ollier, wishing to retain the business, made fair promises and delayed submitting an account. Shelley again insisted upon receiving his account from "this infinite thief," but Ollier again delayed, and the change to a new publisher remained unaccomplished.

Now that Horace Smith had left London, and Peacock was becoming more and more absorbed in East India Company affairs, it was to John and Maria Gisborne that the Shelleys turned to get their various London commissions executed. Eventually they were even able to prod Ollier into sending Shelley's books and Mary's desk, about which delays had been most irritating. Mr. Gisborne was a business man in whose judgment Shelley now seemed to have considerable confidence; the old miserable affair of Henry Reveley's steamboat was evidently forgiven.

He consulted Mr. Gisborne's opinion about employing a legal business agent to try to bring more order into his financial affairs than the unsatisfactory and exorbitant P. W. Longdill had accomplished. At this time Shelley expected to inherit an estate worth from £5,000 to £7,000 a year which was burdened with about £22,500 in debts (mostly Shelley's post-obits) and £10,000 devised to his sisters, besides an annual charge of "some hundreds a year" on his mother's jointure. The debts, Shelley thought, might by negotiation be reduced to £14,000 or £15,000.

Since early in 1820 the Shelleys had been living within their income, but with little to spare. Leigh Hunt's expenses in coming to Italy raised financial demands which Shelley could not meet alone. With considerable difficulty he got together £150 to send to Hunt on January 25. Byron had already paid the expenses of furnishing rooms to be assigned the Hunts, and it was for several reasons infinitely galling for Shelley to have to call upon him for more. Nevertheless, it was necessary, and Byron made no objection to advancing £250 on Shelley's security. Shelley promised £50 more of his own in the future.

On May 13 Hunt finally set sail from Plymouth. Long before this his various delays had assumed Odyssean proportions in the humorous point of view of Hogg, who wrote that "the meeting of Shelley and Old Hunt . . . might possibly take place about the close of the nineteenth century."

Claire Clairmont had returned to Florence upon Byron's first arrival at Pisa. But from the moment Byron left Ravenna her fears about Allegra had redoubled. Early in February she was pressing Shelley and Mary to help her do something about Allegra. Both the Masons urged vigorous steps, but Shelley, although extremely angry with Byron, clung to a policy of watchful waiting. Shelley urged her to keep as tranquil as possible and to come and spend the summer with him and Mary. He could offer little hope for improving Allegra's situation.

Meanwhile Claire was forming wild schemes. After her return to Florence she proposed a mad plan which evidently required kidnapping and a forged letter. It evoked one of Shelley's sternest admonitions. "I know not what to think of the state of your mind," he wrote, "or what to fear for you. Your late plan about Allegra seems to me in its present form, pregnant with irremediable infamy to all the actors in it except yourself; — in any form wherein *I* must actively co-operate, with inevitable destruction. I *would not* in any case make myself the party to a forged letter. I *could not* refuse Lord Byron's challenge; though that, however to be deprecated, would be the least in the series of mischiefs consequent upon my pestilent intervention in such a plan. I say this because I am shocked at the thoughtless violence of your designs, and I wish to put my sense of this madness in the strongest light."

In the case of both Claire and Leigh Hunt, Shelley stood in an awkward relationship to Byron. He had been the cause of Hunt's emigration, and even before Hunt arrived he had seen Byron vacillate again and again in his desire to set up a liberal journal of opinion. Strong pressure both direct and indirect had been put upon Byron. His friends had warned him not to cheapen himself by a public association with Leigh Hunt and Shelley. Byron's mixture of penuriousness and generosity made Shelley all the more uneasy about making financial arrangements with him, and yet his financial help was indispensable. It was an even greater strain to preserve friendly relations with Byron when he felt so keenly the harshness of Byron's treatment of Claire Clairmont and knew that he was suspicious of any suggestions about Allegra.

Matters reached the point where Shelley's dearest wish was to be able to separate himself from Byron without an open break — and yet Leigh Hunt's dependence rendered even this impossible. "It is of vital importance," Shelley wrote to Claire, "both to me and to yourself, to Allegra even, that I should put a period to my intimacy with L[ord] B[yron], and that without *éclat*. No sentiments of honour or justice restrain him (as I strongly suspect) from the basest insinuations, and the only mode in which I could effectually silence him I am reluctant (even if I had proof) to employ during my father's life." Some two months later he informed Claire that in his opinion "a great gulph" existed between him and Byron and that it must daily grow wider.

On Sunday afternoon, March 24, the whole Byron-Shelley circle was thrown into commotion. Byron's usual riding party, consisting of Lord Byron, Shelley, Trelawny, Captain Hay, Count Gamba, and Count Taafe, were returning toward Pisa, followed at a short dis-

tance by Mary Shelley and the Countess Guiccioli in a carriage. As
they neared one of the city gates a mounted dragoon (afterwards
identified as Sergeant-Major Masi) dashed through the riders and
seemed to brush insolently and defiantly against Taafe. Byron's party
(except Taafe, who remained prudently behind) put spurs to their
horses, stopped the man, and demanded an explanation. He was
half-drunk, however, and cursed them for *"maladetti Inglesi,"* announcing that he would arrest them. Whereupon Byron laughed:
"Arrest indeed!" and with Count Gamba rode on toward the gate.

Before the others could pass, the dragoon placed himself in the
gateway and called on the guard to stop them. Byron and Count
Gamba rode on, intending to arm themselves and return for the expected scuffle. The dragoon made a vicious saber-cut at Shelley, who
warded or dodged the blade but took a blow on the head from the
hilt and was knocked off his horse. The man cut at him again, but
Captain Hay warded the blow with his stick, only to receive a cut
across the nose when the saber cut through the stick.

After a few cuts and slashes at the empty air the man rode on into
Pisa. Here he met Byron returning to the scene with his sword-stick.
The dragoon put up his sword and begged Byron to do the same,
which Byron did only on being given his name, that he might require
satisfaction later. One of Byron's servants had caught Masi's bridle.
Byron ordered him to let go, and the dragoon immediately put his
horse to the gallop. By now, however, it was dusk, and Byron's servants, watching from his house, thought that another affray had taken
place and that Byron had been killed. As Masi passed, one of them
dashed out with a pitchfork and wounded him in the abdomen. He
fell from his horse and was carried to the hospital, where for several
days his recovery seemed doubtful. Vaccà, who attended him, believed and quoted his story that he would not have drawn his weapon
if one of the party had not struck him with a riding-whip, and Captain Hay privately admitted that Count Gamba had struck the man
with his whip.

Rumors immediately began to circulate. Some Englishmen had
placed themselves at the head of a peasant insurrection; Trelawny
had been killed and Byron mortally wounded. Taafe had assassinated
a dragoon and was being guarded against arrest by Byron's bull-
dogs; Lord Byron and all his servants, with four English gentlemen,
armed with stilettos and forty brace of pistols, had all been captured
after a desperate resistance.

Shelley received a message from a nervous lady, probably Mrs.

Beauclerc or Mrs. Mason, warning him that friends of the wounded man might assassinate him if he visited her home after nightfall. Taafe boasted so constantly of his valor that Jane Williams took to referring to him as False-Taafe. To Byron he even said: "My Lord, if you do not dare ride out today, I will alone." Needless to say, Byron regarded him with a bilious eye for some days thereafter; not until April 3 was he willing to shake hands with him.

Depositions were taken on all sides, from fifteen participants and witnesses. A commissioner arrived from Florence who interviewed Mary Shelley for six hours, the length of the interview, however, being due less to rigor than to politeness. No one of the witnesses could or would name Masi's assailant. The Pisan authorities arrested one of Byron's servants and one of Countess Guiccioli's. Both were perfectly innocent, but one of them unfortunately possessed a rather villainous look — "*quanto un assassino.*" This man was soon ordered released by the commissioner from Florence, but the relatively meek-visaged servant of the Countess Guiccioli was kept in solitary confinement for some time afterwards.

The Tuscan government, though liberally administered, had never regarded with enthusiasm the presence of such known Carbonari as the Gambas. It hinted that in view of the threats of vengeance Byron's party would be safer in another city. On April 9, therefore, Byron rented for himself and the Gambas a house in Montenero, about four miles from Leghorn, but did not himself take up residence there until about the end of May.

As Sergeant-Major Masi began to recover and the excitement died down, the Shelleys and Williamses turned again to their plans for a summer on the coast. An exploratory trip by Shelley and Williams early in February had shown that it would be extremely difficult to obtain suitable houses in or near Spezia. In the uncertainty of their situation it was decided that the Williamses and Claire (who was again visiting in Pisa) should make another trip to Spezia to attempt to find quarters there. They returned on April 25, having achieved nothing. During their absence, as Williams guessed from Shelley's face, disastrous news had reached the Shelleys.

Claire's worst fears had been realized. Allegra had been stricken with typhus fever in her convent school at Bagnacavallo and had died on April 19, at the age of five years and three months. The Shelleys and Claire had not even known of her illness, though she had been ill for weeks. Byron had known, but thought the danger past.

Under no circumstances, Shelley felt, could the news be broken to Claire when she was in the same neighborhood with Byron. Though there was only one house, unfurnished, to be rented near Spezia, it was better to go there in all haste and then break the news. This was Shelley's opinion; the others were doubtful. But Shelley was not to be denied; he was "like a torrent hurrying everything in its course."

Mary, Claire, and Trelawny went ahead on April 26. Shelley and Williams remained a day longer in Pisa to superintend the loading of the two boats that had been engaged to carry their furniture. Next day Shelley and Williams were at Lerici, straightening out customs difficulties about their furniture and seeking vainly for another house. Shelley wrote thence to Mary urging that she lose not a minute in securing Casa Magni, the one available house in San Terenzo. It was none too large for the Shelleys alone, but they contrived to allow the Williamses one of the three bedrooms, and the party settled down in one house as best they could.

It was now Shelley's task to break to Claire the news that had been for days such an oppressive secret among her friends. On May 2, a day after the Williamses were installed with the Shelleys, the two families were in a back room, planning how best to perform this sad duty. The door opened and Claire walked in. One look at their faces was enough to make her guess the truth.

In the first moments of bitterness and desolation she must have said to Shelley and Mary some of the things that are adumbrated in her journals and letters many years afterwards. She always regarded Byron as the murderer of her child. Mary and Shelley, by not falling in with her wild schemes of rescue, had been to some extent Byron's accomplices. Many years later, in a cryptic, bitter passage in one of her journals, Claire condemned Mary for calmly witnessing the execution of a child at Pisa, and afterwards shaking hands with the executioner.

Without consulting the others she wrote Byron a letter of searing denunciation. Byron sent it on to Shelley — this time, it is to be hoped, without his usual comments on Claire. The shock of his own grief softened Byron into an attitude temporarily more generous. He granted at once all of Claire's last requests — for a miniature of Allegra, a lock of her hair, and the right to see the body before it was shipped to England. He even agreed that she might dictate the funeral arrangements. But Claire was willing to leave this to Byron, and Shelley was even able to persuade her not to go to Leghorn to see Allegra's body.

After the first wild outbursts, during which Shelley feared she might lose her reason, Claire settled at first into a state of apparent bewilderment; then she called to her support a fortitude that was quite surprising. Within a week or two she had become far more tranquil and had returned to Florence, though she expected to come back to San Terenzo for the summer.

Chapter XXVI

THE GULF OF SPEZIA, which Shelley and Williams had selected for
their summer sailing, was at that time completely neglected by tourists. This considerable bay is divided by wooded rocky promontories
into numerous smaller ones, the most beautiful of which was the little
bay of San Terenzo, which was almost completely landlocked. Here
was the primitive hamlet of San Torenzo, not more than two hundred
yards distant from Casa Magni, the house Shelley had rented. The
surrounding scenery was lonely and romantic. Behind rose rocky foot-
hills, extending down to the beach; in front lay the blue, tideless
Mediterranean. Immediately behind Casa Magni rose a hill covered
by a young forest of chestnut and ilex trees.

Casa Magni was a two-story structure about twice as long as it was
deep, with the lower story projecting in front several feet beyond the
upper one, forming an open porch across the entire front of the
house. It looked almost as much like a large boat-house as like a residence. The ground floor was unpaved and fit only for storage purposes. The upper floor was reached by two stairways, one leading to
a large dining-room which occupied the entire center of the floor,
and another, in the right rear corner, leading to Mary's bedroom.
There were three bedrooms, each occupying a corner of the upper
floor. Shelley's room occupied the left front corner, separated by the
dining-room from the right front room occupied by Mary and Percy
Florence. The Williamses, with two children, had the rear room.
This whole story had once been whitewashed, but the walls were
now splotchy, the ceiling cracked, and the floor broken. There were
an outbuilding for cooking, and separate quarters for the servants.

Mary and Jane groaned and complained from the beginning, and
were with difficulty induced to stay. But there was nowhere else to
go, and they knew that Shelley and Williams had set their hearts on
a summer's boating in the bay.

The neighboring hamlet of San Terenzo was too small and poor
to be of any advantage as a source of supplies. Nearly four miles
away, on the other side of a little river, a limited amount of provisions
could be bought at Sarzana; Lerici, a mile away, could be reached by
following a rocky, winding footpath near the shore. The natives of
San Terenzo were so crude of speech and manners that Mary thought

them the most savage people she had seen in Italy. At night they gathered on the beach and the women danced among the waves while the men leaned against the rocks and joined them in a wild chorus. Once or twice Shelley and Trelawny joined them, much to Mary's disgust.

From the first Mary hated the place with an almost morbid intensity. She complained that the natives were wild and surly, that the living arrangements were extremely inconvenient, and that the Tuscan servants would soon leave — as some of them did. The Shelley and Williams servants quarreled among themselves "like cats and dogs." Jane Williams was dissatisfied also; she longed for her own pots and pans, which could not be unpacked now that the Williamses had been compelled to accept a room instead of a house of their own. Shelley, in turn, reproached Mary for her antagonism to a situation in which he felt his health and spirits better than ever before. The wise Mrs. Mason showed a true estimate of this situation when she wrote Shelley that she dreaded Claire's return to Casa Magni and wished the Williamses at least half a mile away.

Mary precipitated several painful domestic scenes that were witnessed by the Williamses and were later reported to Leigh Hunt by both Shelley and Jane Williams. Hunt considered them serious enough to produce a temporary coldness in his attitude toward Mary, yet nothing that a few words from an old friend might not easily smooth over. The Williamses, though unaware of Mary's subsequent private apologies to Shelley, seem not to have taken the situation very seriously.

Mary was really in a state of nervous and physical ill health for which the others possibly made insufficient allowance. She was expecting another baby in December, and her pregnancy was proceeding very unsatisfactorily. Her languor and irritability were extreme; she sometimes had alarming hysterical affections. After May 4 she wrote nothing in her journal until June 1.

Shelley confided to John Gisborne that the only flaw in his present happiness was "the want of those who can feel, and understand me. Whether from proximity and the continuity of domestic intercourse, Mary does not. . . . It is the curse of Tantalus that a person possessing such excellent powers and so pure a mind as hers, should not excite the sympathy indispensable to their application to domestic life."

Godwin's lawsuit had finally reached its miserable conclusion, though the Shelleys as yet did not know the result. Mrs. Godwin had

sent an alarming account to Mrs. Mason, requesting that she transmit
it to Mary. Instead, Mrs. Mason thought it best to send it to Shelley,
and Shelley wrote Mrs. Godwin a courteous letter explaining why
her news must for the present be withheld from Mary, and promising
such assistance to Godwin as seemed possible in his own circumstances. He wrote to Horace Smith, asking if the loan of £400 which
he had formerly offered Shelley for Godwin's benefit was still at his
disposal. This sum, added to Mary's expectations from her recent
novel, would just about make up the £900 Godwin was adjudged to
pay. But Horace Smith's £400 was no longer available. Moreover,
he was strongly of the opinion that Godwin should take advantage of
the Insolvency Act.

The end of the crisis was made clear by a letter from young William Godwin. In the long-drawn-out suit of Godwin's landlord for
disputed arrears of house rent, judgment had been given against
Godwin early in April. The Godwins had been evicted and had
moved to 195, the Strand. Here, with generous assistance from their
printers and stationers, they were able to continue in business, with
nothing to threaten them except the payment of rent in arrears,
which was not compulsory before October.

Despite worries and occasional fits of depression and pain, the winter and spring of 1821–2 were the happiest time of Shelley's life in
Italy. Certainly his health was better than ever before. For this his
outdoor life and his congenial association with the Williamses were
mainly responsible. Williams was a frank, manly, healthy-spirited
young man who far surpassed the rest of the Pisan circle in understanding Shelley and sympathizing with him. Jane, though intellectually somewhat shallow, possessed a sunshiny, affectionate disposition unfortunately in contrast with Mary's occasional moodiness and
self-absorption, pardonable as the latter was after the removal to
San Terenzo. Though Jane was also petulant on occasion, when her
domestic instincts were offended by the makeshifts of semi-commu-
nal housekeeping, she was more often bright and cheerful. In the
still, warm evenings, either on the water or along the rocky shores,
her guitar and her singing could create for the moment a brighter
world of thought and feeling than that with which they were otherwise surrounded.

There was a moment, probably in May, when Shelley and Jane
seem at least slightly to have overstepped the bounds of conventional
propriety. What this moment was is obscurely hinted at in two of

Shelley's last poems, "Lines Written in the Bay of Lerici," and "Lines: We Meet Not as We Parted." The first records a parting in the purple night from a "guardian angel" whose presence "made weak and tame All passions" and inspired thoughts the poet dared not speak. Whether the "guardian angel" was Jane Williams or Intellectual Beauty, or a combination of the two, is not clear. It does seem clear, however, that the poet dared not speak his thoughts to her. But the other poem, "We Meet Not as We Parted," appears to be a sequel, and clearly indicates that either by word or by action the poet did declare a feeling which he was forbidden to cherish.

If this was to Jane, as seems probable, it was the Jane of "The Keen Stars Were Twinkling," who lived in

> . . . some world far from ours
> Where music and moonlight and feeling
> Are one.

In the actual world Shelley lived too close to Jane to idealize her completely or to fall completely in love with her in any other sense. He realized that she was intellectually somewhat commonplace, and he was occasionally uncomfortably aware of her domestic discontents. Writing of these to Claire on May 29, he commented: "It is a pity that anyone so pretty and amicable could be so selfish — [But] don't tell her this. . . ." It seems to have been well understood by all the others that Shelley's devotion to Jane, even at its height, was limited. Her own exclusive love for Edward Williams was unquestioned even by Mary and was explicitly granted by Shelley.

For mundane living Shelley still undoubtedly preferred Edward Williams. Together they were having a glorious time, almost every day. At first Shelley's boat was not yet finished, and her delivery at San Terenzo was further delayed by heavy weather, so that for the first fortnight they were obliged to depend upon the little flat-bottomed skiff that had given them so much pleasure on the Arno and the Serchio. When the sea was relatively calm the small boat was adequate for inshore sailing or rowing, but more than once, when the waves were high, the sailors were drenched in launching or landing their craft. All the surroundings were magnificently grand and lonely. In heavy weather the seas boomed upon the beach like heavy artillery.

On May 12, as Williams and Shelley were walking upon the terrace after dinner, they noted a strange boat entering the bay. Slowly she took definite form as the long-expected *Don Juan*. At once they set off to Lerici to take possession and make a trial sail. Of the three men who were in charge of her they retained only one, a young English sailor named Charles Vivian. The boat was a strongly built, trim-looking, undecked craft, Torbay-rigged, twenty-four feet by eight, with a four-foot draught. To overcome her tendency to ride too high in the water two tons of iron ballast had been fixed in her keel. Though somewhat cranky in a breeze, she was fast for her size, and handled well.

Both Shelley and Williams were delighted with her. "The Don Juan is arrived," Shelley hastened to write to Trelawny, "and nothing can exceed the admiration she has excited. . . . Williams declares her to be perfect, and I participate in his enthusiasm, in as much as would be decent in a landsman. We have been out now several days, although we have sought in vain for an opportunity of trying her against the feluccas or other large craft in the bay; she passes the small ones as a comet might pass the dullest planet of the heavens." He begged Trelawny to express his warmest gratitude to Captain Roberts, the builder, and cheerfully promised early payment when informed that the cost had probably exceeded the original estimate of fifty pounds.

Scarcely an entry in Williams's journal of these days failed to record some sailing expedition within the confines of the bay. Shelley kept books and papers on board and did most of his writing there. Mary, who hated almost everything else about the neighborhood, felt more at ease in the boat than elsewhere. At times when they could not sail, Williams was busy making a small, light boat of reeds, to be carried on the *Don Juan* and used as a tender. Soon, between the straits of Porto Venere, they encountered the *Bolivar* as Trelawny and his crew were taking her from Genoa to Leghorn. Proudly they received her salute of six guns and raced alongside for a while, only to find that the larger vessel was also the speedier. "But I think we keep as good a wind," Williams boasted.

Trelawny made a short visit at Casa Magni and then sailed the *Bolivar* back to Leghorn. On a second visit about a week later Trelawny had a good opportunity to judge the *Don Juan* and the seamanship with which she was handled. Already her navigators were considering the Mediterranean too small a sphere of operations; they talked of the broad sea-room of the Atlantic. Shelley was still a most indifferent steersman. He had a book in his hand, as usual, and when Williams yelled: "Luff," he brought her into the wind's eye. He was promptly demoted by the skipper and told to attend the mainsheet.

On the next order: "Let go the mainsheet," the sheet was jammed and Shelley was almost swept overboard.

This did not affect Shelley's high spirits, nor were they depressed by Williams's disgust at his seamanship. Williams was actually a somewhat better sailor than Trelawny had expected to find, but was out of practice. The boy, Charles Vivian, was quick and handy. Nevertheless, Trelawny suggested that the boat needed also a Genoese sailor to help handle her in heavy weather. But Williams was as touchy about the boat's character as if she had been his wife — "as if we three seasoned salts were not enough to manage an open boat!"

About a fortnight before Trelawny's arrival Shelley had written to Claire, who was feeling ill and depressed, urging her to make a visit to Casa Magni. Claire had arrived about June 6 — a new Claire, no longer petulant and oppressed with forebodings, but vivacious and talkative.

Two or three days after Claire's arrival, during a spell of hot, sultry weather, Mary was threatened with a miscarriage. After a week of wretched health the miscarriage occurred on June 16. For seven hours she lay almost lifeless. Claire and Jane applied restoratives and stimulants while others sought frantically for ice and a doctor. The ice arrived first, but Claire and Jane were afraid to make use of it without a doctor's directions. When it looked as if nothing could save Mary's life, Shelley, who had read medical books and who had only recently acted as a doctor in some minor emergency of Jane's, took the responsibility of making Mary sit on ice. The doctor arrived only in time to commend Shelley's decision and to prescribe for Mary after the emergency was over. Thereafter her convalescence was slow, and her state of mind even more depressed and apprehensive than before.

In spite of his surface pleasure and his very obvious physical improvement Shelley had himself felt far more disturbed than he probably realized. A month before Mary's miscarriage, when he was compelled to repress his feelings in dealing with Byron about the death of Allegra, they had asserted themselves in a waking vision. As he was walking with Williams on the terrace in front of the house he had seen a naked child, like Allegra, rise up from the sea and clap its hands at him as if in joy. "There it is again — There!" he cried to Williams. He was so shaken that for some time he could not tell what he had seen, and it was with difficulty that Williams persuaded him that it was a trance and not reality.

Following Mary's miscarriage Shelley saw several visions. He met his own figure walking on the terrace, and the phantasm demanded of him: "How long do you mean to be content?" Another time, in the middle of the night, he screamed loudly and rushed into Mary's room. He continued to scream in spite of her efforts to waken him, until Mary, still almost too ill to walk, fled to the Williamses in a panic and collapsed at their door. Shelley was now awake and explained that he had had two visions. In the first the Williamses had appeared to him, mangled and battered, and had warned him that the sea was flooding the house and pounding it to pieces. Then he saw a vision of himself strangling Mary, and he had rushed into her room and had been awakened by her flight.

A strong subconscious tension seemed to be gripping almost everyone except Ned Williams. Even the unimaginative Jane was not exempt; she was sure she had seen Shelley walk across the terrace, followed a few minutes later by his phantasm.

This tension was certainly not seriously recognized, except by Mary. To the end Shelley considered the life at Casa Magni extraordinarily happy. "We drive along this delightful bay in the evening wind, under the summer moon, until earth appears another world. Jane brings her guitar, and if the past and the future could be obliterated, the present would content me so well that I could say with Faust to the passing moment, 'Remain, thou, thou art so beautiful.'" Shelley's last extant letter from Casa Magni concluded: ". . . My only regret is that the summer must ever pass, or that Mary has not the same predilection for this place that I have, which would induce me never to shift my quarters."

The subconscious apprehension which still dogged them was perhaps partly propitiated, for Shelley, by his unfinished "Triumph of Life." In the midst of his pleasure Shelley was writing his last long poem, a fragment which contains a powerful picture of human unhappiness and delusion. "My firm persuasion," he had written about five months earlier, "is that the mass of mankind, as things are arranged at present, are cruel, deceitful, and selfish, and always on the watch to surprise those few who are not. . . ." It is such a humanity that Shelley describes in the 547 lines of "The Triumph of Life" that he was able to write before he laid the poem aside for a supposedly temporary interruption.

Approximately the first half of the poem is devoted to the description of a weird and saddening triumphal procession, that of Life.

Millions of figures, young and old, dance madly and disgracefully before and after her chariot. Eventually they sink into the dust and the chariot passes over them. Along with the meaner captives of Life move great emperors, philosophers, and religious leaders — even Plato is there, and several of the fathers of the Christian church "who rose like shadows between man and God" until the eclipse they created was taken for the religion which it obscured. Only a few, like Christ and Socrates, were totally exempt from the vile bondage which Life imposed.

"Struck to the heart by this sad pageantry," the poet is addressed by one of the captives, who identifies himself as Rousseau. The remaining half of the fragment is devoted to Rousseau's story of how he became enslaved to Life after having once seen a brighter vision which is surely the Intellectual Beauty that Shelley had recently given a more definite form as the Witch of Atlas.

The cave and the fountain with which she is associated, the crystal glass which she offers to a few chosen spirits, the effects of its contents and of her presence, are all foreshadowed in the story of Shelley's beautiful Witch. Rousseau drank from her crystal glass; but soon a new vision came over him as the beautiful shape grew dim before his eyes. Still, as he moved along through the wilderness, he was conscious that the Shape kept its "obscure tenor" beside his path. After a while the new vision supplanted the former one; the triumphal car of Life swept across his way and he was caught up in her wild mob of singing, dancing sycophants. The grove grew dense with shadows, the earth gray with phantoms; soon from every form in the procession the beauty began slowly to wane. Weary of the madness, he dropped by the wayside where the poet later discovered him. Almost his last words before the fragment ends were: " 'Then what is life?' I cried. . . ."

Whether the answer, if any, was to be in Rousseau's words or Shelley's is uncertain. If Shelley's, one may suppose that the answer would conform to his previous answers that life was a dream, a shadow, a stain upon the "white radiance of Eternity," a "painted veil" mistakenly called life by those who think they live, a "loathsome mask" as long as the world is dominated by ignorance and error, a fair garden which at least to earthly eyes seemed abandoned by a celestial mistress until rank weeds flourished and the sensitive plants drooped. Entering it he called "the eclipsing Curse of birth"; leaving it he called lifting a veil from reality. He had stated in his essay "On the Devil and Devils" that "the most admirable tendencies to happiness and preservation are forever baffled by misery and decay," and in his "Essay on Christianity" that "some evil spirit has dominion in this imperfect world." To Trelawny he had characterized human life as "a perpetual torment to ourselves and to every living thing." Even as he was writing "The Triumph of Life" Shelley asked Trelawny to secure for him some prussic acid, stating that he had no present intention of suicide, but that a time might come when he would find life insupportable.

Certainly it is an unavoidable conclusion that when Shelley wrote "The Triumph of Life" he had a profound and almost morbid conviction of the pains and penalties of living. But it is a misconception of Shelley's character and writings to assume either that this was something new or that it negates his fundamental optimism. He held these same beliefs, and expressed them with equal poignance, in *Prometheus Unbound,* which asserts the perfectibility of the human spirit. Only a few months before "The Triumph of Life" he had written *Hellas,* which is anything but despondent. All of his associates regarded him as one whose view of human life was fundamentally optimistic.

It is very probable that both extremes owe a great deal to Shelley's conviction of persecution and to what modern psychologists would undoubtedly call a manic-depressive psychology — the violent fluctuations between depression and "almost supernatural elevation" which Shelley himself regarded as characteristic. One would be ill-advised to take either extreme for the whole outlook. According to his own testimony and that of most other witnesses, when Shelley wrote "The Triumph of Life" and desired to procure prussic acid he was in the best health he had felt for years and was finding his happiest enjoyment of life.

But fortunately one does not have to put one's own interpretation on an unfinished, highly intensified subjective poem to obtain Shelley's final opinion of the world and the possibility of its improvement. Only a few days before his death, while he was still composing "The Triumph of Life," he wrote in his last letter to Horace Smith:

> It seems to me that things have now arrived at such a crisis as requires every man plainly to utter his sentiments on the inefficacy of the existing religious, no less than political systems, for restraining and guiding mankind. Let us see the truth, whatever that may be. The destiny of man can scarcely be so degraded that he was born only to die — and if such should be the

case, delusions, especially the gross and preposterous ones of the existing religion, can scarcely be supposed to exalt it. If every man said what he thought, it could not subsist a day. But all, more or less, subdue themselves to the element that surrounds them, and contribute to the evils they lament by the hypocrisy that springs from them. . . .

England appears to be in a desperate condition, Ireland still worse; and no class of those who subsist on the public labour will be persuaded that *their* claims on it must be diminished. . . . I see little public virtue, and I foresee that the contest will be one of blood and gold. . . .

This is far from the rosy optimism with which Shelley had invaded Ireland ten years before. His sense of mission had suffered serious setbacks. He had found by experience that life cannot be lived in entire immunity from cross-currents that thwart or divert even the most determined will. He no longer felt obliged to take an immediate hand in events. But the liberation of the human mind, through which alone true freedom could be attained, was an object still to be pursued. He held it his duty and every man's duty to speak his mind against error. Whether or not he still wore the ring he had described to Peacock two years before, he had not renounced its motto: *"Il buon tempo verrà."*

On June 20 Shelley heard that the Hunts had arrived at Genoa. About the end of the month they sailed from Genoa to Leghorn, and as soon as the news reached Lerici Shelley and Williams prepared to join them. Shelley had grave doubts about Byron's constancy in the project for the *Liberal* and wished to be on hand promptly to see that everything was as propitious as possible at the start. In the spring he had done some translations from Goethe, Homer, and Calderón for the *Liberal,* but he was resolved to write little or nothing more for it, lest his unpopularity have a bad effect on the journal's circulation. He had already renounced in Hunt's favor any share in the profits.

Mary had wished to accompany Shelley to greet the Hunts, but she was still far too weak to do so. Weak and apprehensive as she was, she could hardly bear the thought of Shelley's departure. She sent a note to Leigh Hunt, begging him in hysterical terms not to accept Shelley's all too probable invitation to visit "this dungeon" where she thought of herself as chained. She called Shelley back several times, and wept bitterly when he finally stepped on board.

No such forebodings oppressed Shelley as he and Williams weighed anchor at two o'clock on July 1, made a short run over to Lerici to pick up Captain Roberts, and then laid their course for Leghorn. In seven and a half hours they had completed the run of forty-five or fifty miles. Next morning as they landed they encountered Count Gamba's group leaving the police office, having just been given short notice of exile from Tuscany. This was bad news for Shelley and the *Liberal,* for it meant that Byron's present household at Montenero was disagreeably upset and that Byron might accompany the Gambas into exile.

They met the Hunts, who welcomed them gladly. Marianne Hunt was seriously ill and was soon to be pronounced dying by the celebrated Vaccà, whom she outlived by many years. It did not help her state of mind or her husband's that Byron had welcomed her with almost insulting coldness and hauteur. Young Thornton Hunt, now a keen, quick lad of twelve, noticed that Shelley had changed greatly since the old days at Marlow; he was far stronger and healthier-looking; he had added some three or four inches to his chest measure; his voice was stronger; and his manner much more confident and downright.

On the morning of July 3 Shelley accompanied the Hunts to Pisa, and Byron returned to his Pisan residence. Getting the Hunts settled in their new quarters was less difficult than tying Byron down to a definite mode of operation for the *Liberal.* At first Byron said he did not wish to publish anything in it over his own name. He considered that the expulsion of the Gambas was also an attack upon himself, and talked of moving to America, to Genoa, Geneva, or Lucca. With Byron everything was confusion; with the Hunts everything was despair. Shelley's own state of mind was depressed by at least one semi-hysterical letter from Mary, urging his early return and saying that she was haunted by a feeling of impending disaster.

Gradually, under Shelley's tactful persistence, Byron came round to a definite agreement which was satisfactory. He offered for the first number the copyright of his *Vision of Judgment.* This was more than enough to start the journal, and when Shelley called on Mrs. Mason on July 7 before returning to Leghorn, he was in high spirits.

Williams had been waiting at Leghorn, impatient to return home, but unwilling to accept Shelley's permission to return ahead of him. On the morning of July 8 Shelley and Williams were busy buying supplies for the little colony at San Terenzo — food, milk for the children, and a hamper of wine to be presented to Signor Maglian, the friendly harbor master at Lerici. Trelawny accompanied Shelley first to a bank and then to a store, and at about one o'clock they boarded their respective boats, Trelawny with the intention of accompanying the *Don Juan* into the offing with the *Bolivar*.

The weather had been hot and unsettled. Captain Roberts, who did not quite like the look of it, suggested that they wait till next day. But Williams was impatient to be off, the wind was fair for Lerici, and Shelley was in high spirits to meet Williams's desire for a quick run before the wind. At the last minute Trelawny was prevented by the authorities from taking out the *Bolivar*, because he had not yet got his port clearance papers. Two Livornese feluccas left port at about the same time and in about the same direction. Roberts walked out to the end of the mole to watch the *Don Juan* out of sight; the *Bolivar* furled her sails as Trelawny watched the *Don Juan* through his glass. His Genoese mate remarked that a squall was coming up and that the *Don Juan* was too close inshore and carried too much sail.

About three o'clock Roberts saw the squall entering the bay and obtained permission to go up in the watch-tower and follow his friends with the glass. The *Don Juan* was then about ten miles out at sea, off Viareggio, and the crew were taking in sail. Then he lost sight of her in a swirl of fog and cloud and was unable to pick her up again. Trelawny, in the *Bolivar*, had lost sight of her a little earlier and had retired to his cabin and gone to sleep.

When Trelawny awoke at about half past six the sky had darkened, the sea was smooth and lead-colored, flat and quiet under the fitful gusts and raindrops that preceded a heavy squall. With a crash the storm broke, and for about twenty minutes the thunder roared and rain fell in thick sheets that obscured all vision to seaward. When the skies cleared there were still no ships to be seen in the offing. All the other boats that had put out ahead of the squall had returned; only the *Don Juan* was missing. No one on the feluccas that had returned to port would admit having seen the *Don Juan,* though Trelawny's mate saw on one of them an English-made oar which he thought might have belonged to the *Don Juan.*

The *Don Juan* was never seen again from shore after Captain Roberts lost sight of her in the fog and smother at about three o'clock. According to later information, however, two Livornese boats appear to have seen Shelley's craft shortly after Captain Roberts retired from his watch-tower. The captain of the first of these, doubting the ability of the *Don Juan* to weather the squall, offered to take the crew aboard, but was refused. Then, as a large wave broke over the little boat, he shouted: ". . . For God's sake reef your sails or you are lost." One of the gentlemen (supposed to be Williams) started to lower the sails but the other (supposedly Shelley) seized his arm and restrained him.

If this witness spoke the truth, the crew of a second vessel also saw the *Don Juan* but kept their own counsel, for when the boat was finally salvaged it was only too clear that she had sunk as the result of a collision. Her starboard timbers were broken, her gunwale was stove in, and both masts and bowsprit had broken off at the base. One large wave the next moment would have been sufficient to fill and sink her instantly.

It would appear, therefore, that Shelley's end came very quickly. He would not have had time, as when he faced drowning in the Channel in 1816, "to reflect and even to reason upon death," or to reach the conclusion then reached that "it was rather a thing of discomfort than horror to me." Byron had seen him resolve to drown rather than risk another's life on Lake Geneva. Trelawny, within the last few months, had been deeply impressed with his indifference both to the idea and to the physical discomfort of dying and had heard him speak of going down with the *Don Juan* like a piece of ballast in case she were wrecked. In poems, letters, and conversation he had shown for several years that he regarded death primarily as a release and an opportunity and that his desire to live was based mainly upon his personal obligations. "If I die tomorrow," he had remarked to Marianne Hunt on the previous day, "I have lived to be older than my father; I am ninety years of age." It seems certain that he died calmly, probably with little or no effort to save himself.

That night in Pisa Mrs. Mason dreamed that Shelley, whom she had seen looking so cheerful the day before, appeared before her, wearing a look of utter melancholy and speaking vague words of disaster. This dream soon merged into another, in which she thought that Percy Florence was dead. She awoke crying so bitterly that she wondered if the actual death of the child would have affected her so deeply.

Trelawny was now definitely alarmed. Another day of waiting produced no news. Thinking that Byron might have received some message from Shelley, Trelawny mounted his horse and rode to Pisa. Byron had heard nothing; he was visibly shaken by Trelawny's report. Trelawny then sent word to the *Bolivar* to cruise along the coast toward Viareggio and set out in the same direction himself, after dispatching a courier along the coast toward Nice. At Viareggio a punt, a water-keg, and some bottles had been washed up on the beach. With a sinking heart Trelawny recognized them as belonging to the *Don Juan*.

Yet there was still some room for hope. These articles might have been washed overboard or thrown out to lighten the boat, and the boat might have been driven across to Corsica. Or the boat's crew might have been rescued by some vessel outward bound. The search of the coastline was intensified; rewards were offered. Trelawny was indefatigable. But though the *Don Juan* had left Leghorn on July 8, it was July 18 before any further news was obtained.

Meanwhile Trelawny had been doing all he could to keep up the spirits of Mary, Jane, and Claire. On Monday, the 8th, they had received Ned Williams's letter written the preceding Saturday, saying that he at least would be back in San Terenzo by Tuesday at the latest, and probably Shelley with him. When no one appeared on Monday or Tuesday they supposed the *Don Juan* storm-bound in Leghorn. But Wednesday and Thursday provided fine sailing weather, and the waiters grew uneasy. Only a heavy sea on Friday prevented Jane's journeying to Leghorn to investigate. That day a letter arrived from Hunt to Shelley. Mary opened it, but was so agitated that it dropped from her hands. Jane picked it up and read: "Pray write to tell us how you got home, for they say that you had bad weather after you sailed on Monday, and we are anxious."

"Then it is all over," exclaimed Jane. But Mary, who had been dreading some vague calamity since Shelley's departure, refused to accept its apparent confirmation as final. She was far from well enough to travel, yet she insisted that they start at once for Leghorn to investigate. Passing through Lerici they were somewhat encouraged to learn that no wreck had been reported. Pisa lay on the route, and Mary determined to go by the Lanfranchi Palace to see if Hunt had any news. After four years of separation to greet an old friend with the desperate question: "Do you know anything of Shelley?" — the very thought was agony.

Hunt had gone to bed, but Byron and La Guiccioli saw her. They had no fresh news. Mary and Jane had been traveling since early morning and it was now midnight, but they refused all rest and set out for Leghorn, where they arrived between two and three o'clock in the morning. At six o'clock they found Captain Roberts at his inn and

learned all that he had to tell them. At nine o'clock they started back
to San Terenzo, and at Viareggio they saw and recognized the same
wreckage that Trelawny had seen earlier. Either here or at Leghorn
Trelawny joined them and accompanied them back to San Terenzo.
For five days there was no further news — only the whistle of the
sirocco, the sound of waves beneath the terrace, and the maddening,
half-savage jubilation of the villagers, making the most of a local
fiesta.

Trelawny returned to Leghorn on the 18th to see if anything more
could be done. While he was gone a letter arrived from Roberts which
he had expected and had left permission to open. Claire opened it
without telling the others — and learned that two bodies had been
cast up on the shore. She knew in her heart that Shelley and Williams
were dead, and she wrote to Leigh Hunt begging him to come and
break the news to Mary and Jane, since she was totally unable to
cope with the situation by herself.

Meanwhile Trelawny had heard that two bodies had been washed
up, one near Viareggio, the other three miles down the shore near
the Bocca Lericcio. He hurried to the scene. The first body, though
the exposed parts were fleshless, was undoubtedly Shelley's; the tall,
slight figure, the jacket, the volume of Sophocles in one pocket and
of Keats in the other, identified him. The second body was much
more mutilated, lacking not only most of the flesh, but most of the
clothes as well. But one of Williams's boots that Trelawny had
brought with him from San Terenzo matched the one boot left on the
body, and the black silk handkerchief around the neck was Williams's.

All doubt now at an end, Trelawny returned to Casa Magni, only
a few hours after Claire had dispatched her letter to Leigh Hunt.
His face must have borne his news, for the maid shrieked when he
entered the ground floor. Climbing the stairs, he entered unannounced the room where the ladies were sitting. No one spoke. Then
Mary, unwilling to accept the full implications of his silence, exclaimed: "Is there no hope?" Without answering, Trelawny left the
room and sent in the servant with the children. Later he returned
and won Mary's undying gratitude by attempting no useless consolation, but launching instead upon an eloquent eulogy. On the next
day, July 19, Trelawny took the whole household back to Pisa.

The rather difficult funeral arrangements were undertaken by Trelawny. Under the strict Italian quarantine laws both bodies had been

buried on the shore, with quicklime. Moving them was out of the question. They could be burned, but there was still a question as to whether the ashes could be carried across state boundaries. Several states were involved: Lucca, where Shelley's body had been cast up, Tuscany, where Williams's had been found, and Rome, where Shelley was to be buried by the side of William Shelley. Mr. W. Dawkins, the English minister at Florence, was very helpful in solving official difficulties. Permission was eventually obtained to burn the bodies where they lay and to transport the ashes.

On August 13 Trelawny placed on the *Bolivar* a sheet-iron furnace, fuel, and spices, and proceeded to the spot where Williams's body was buried. There he was met by a military guard, to assist him and also to see that the cremation did not violate the quarantine laws. Everything was made ready, and Byron and Hunt were notified to be present next morning. They drove out from Pisa and were joined by a Tuscan military guard. Wood was collected and piled up, the body was exhumed and placed in its iron box, the torch was applied, and for some time the fire burned furiously. As soon as they could approach the furnace, Williams's friends threw frankincense, salt, wine, and oil upon the body. By four o'clock in the afternoon (Byron and Trelawny having meanwhile taken a swim) the body had been reduced to ashes. The furnace was cooled in the sea, and Williams's ashes were placed in an oak box and given to Byron, who was to take them to Pisa, whence they were to accompany Jane Williams to England.

Next day, while the diggers sought for Shelley's body, Trelawny stood aside and thought what a desecration he was committing by this last necessary act of service to his friend. Why not leave him here with the sea in front and the wooded mountains behind him, in the midst of the solitude and natural grandeur that had given him such pleasure? Byron stood silent and thoughtful; Leigh Hunt had remained in the carriage, alone with his reflections. Trelawny had already spoken of Shelley's death as the loss of "all which made existence to me endurable." Quite possibly Byron was thinking, as he had written to Moore six days before: "There is thus another man gone, about whom the world was ill-naturedly, and ignorantly, and brutally mistaken" — a man "without exception," as he had previously written to Murray, "the *best* and least selfish man I ever knew." Hunt surely felt, as he did later, that for him the "land of sunshine" was now "smitten with darkness."

A dull thud announced the location of the body. The ceremony of the previous day was repeated. Heat-waves from the fire and the sun made the air visible and tremulous; the quicklime, the oil, and the salt made vari-colored flames above the corpse. The iron box was now white-hot and the contents were slowly turning to gray ashes. A few bits of bone remained unconsumed, and, strangely, the heart also. Of the English party only Trelawny had fortitude enough to face this final scene. It would appear that the military officer also turned away, for Trelawny found an opportunity to rescue Shelley's heart, unobserved, though he burned his hand in doing so. The ashes were placed in a box and carried on board the *Bolivar*, and the spectators and participants went their various ways.

Leigh Hunt begged Shelley's heart from Trelawny, and later resigned it to Mary, who carried it with her to her grave, nearly thirty years later. In some unknown manner Hunt also procured and kept a small fragment of Shelley's jawbone. The ashes were sent to Mr. Freeborn, the English consul at Rome, who was requested to hold them until Trelawny could arrive and make arrangements for their burial in the Protestant Cemetery, by the side of William Shelley.

Trelawny was unable to go to Rome until the following March, and meanwhile Mr. Freeborn grew uneasy over his custody of the ashes. Joseph Severn, who had remained in Rome after the death of Keats, did what he could to represent Mary Shelley's interests. The old Protestant Cemetery having been closed to further burials, Shelley was buried in the adjacent new cemetery on January 21, 1823. A kindly English priest, the Reverend Richard Burgess, D.D., defied criticism to read the burial service over an enemy of the church, miscalled an atheist. Eight people were present: General Sir George Cockburn, Sir Charles Sykes, Messrs. Kirkup, Westmacott, Scoles, and Severn, and two priests, the Reverend W. Cook and the Reverend Richard Burgess.

Trelawny reached Rome in March and was dissatisfied with the location of the grave. In the shadow of the pyramid of Caius Cestius, in a niche formed by two buttresses of the old Roman Wall, he purchased enough space for two tombs. He secured masons, built the tombs, removed Shelley's ashes, and planted a row of young poplars near the graves. The extra tomb was intended for himself, and was duly claimed for him nearly sixty years later.

When he first saw this spot, in 1818, Shelley had praised it as the most beautiful cemetery he had ever seen: "To see the sun shining on its bright grass, fresh . . . with the autumnal dews, and hear the whispering of the wind among the leaves of the trees which have overgrown the tomb of Cestius, and the soil which is stirring in the sun warm earth, and to mark the tombs, mostly of women and young people who were buried there, one might . . . desire the sleep they seem to sleep."

Within a little more than a year after Shelley's death all those most closely connected with him had scattered to different countries. Jane Williams, with her children, left Italy for England on September 17, 1822. In London she met and in 1827 "married" T. J. Hogg, with whom her union could not be legalized presumably because the legal husband from whom she had separated for Williams was probably still alive. Jane's close friendship with Mary was ruptured in 1827 by remarks of hers on Shelley and Mary which deeply wounded Mary; though the friendship was resumed, it was never the same afterwards. Jane survived Hogg by twenty-two years, and died in 1884, at the age of eighty-six.

Claire Clairmont left Italy only three days after Jane Williams. On September 20, with a light purse and a heavy heart, she quitted Florence to join her brother Charles in Vienna. For the rest of her long life in Austria, Germany, Russia, and Italy she worked hard tutoring children whom for the most part she disliked. Her circumstances were made somewhat easier by inheriting her legacy from Shelley when his will finally became operative in 1844 upon the death of Sir Timothy Shelley. She never lost her love for Shelley, her friendship for Trelawny, her hatred of Byron, or her connection — occasionally antagonistic, but predominantly affectionate — with Shelley's family. She died in Florence in 1879 at the age of eighty-one.

Mary Shelley remained in Italy until July 25, 1823, living with the Hunts, first in Pisa and then, for nearly a year, in Genoa. She was without hope, without money, and almost without friends. Byron was at first friendly with advice and offers of financial assistance. But he did not get on too well with Hunt, through whom much of Mary's business with him was carried on, and both Mary and Hunt considered that his attitude became more and more niggardly and ungenerous. Hunt did what little he could for Mary out of his great friendship for Shelley rather than on her own account, because he thought she had acted unworthily toward Shelley. Soon, however, a better feeling succeeded.

Hating England and loving Italy, Mary returned to England in 1823 in order to look after her son's interest. Sir Timothy Shelley finally made her an allowance, on condition that she publish no life of Shelley. For years Mary's life was devoted to her son, and she sub-sisted partly on her annuity and partly on her writings.

Long years of semi-poverty and financial dependence, together with a latent yearning for respectability, carried Mary in her later years far from the radicalism she had once held so enthusiastically in common with Shelley. In personal relations, however, she continued firmly loyal to the past — to her father, to the Hunts, to the increas-ingly contemptuous Trelawny, and to Claire, even though she some-times spoke of her with a tinge of bitterness. As soon as Percy Flor-ence came into his inheritance she saw to it that Hunt received an annuity for the rest of his life.

Percy Florence Shelley became the direct heir to the family title and estates upon the death of Charles Bysshe Shelley in 1826, and inherited them upon the death of Sir Timothy in 1844. Largely under his mother's manipulation he married Jane St. John, who was an en-thusiastic admirer of both Shelley and Mary. He was a passionate lover of amateur theatricals and also of yachting, the only taste in which he conspicuously resembled his father. He stood for Parlia-ment as a conservative, but he loyally aided Lady Shelley in her collection of the voluminous materials which have added so greatly to Shelleyan biography.

Sir Percy Florence died without issue and the title passed to the descendants of Shelley's younger brother, John. Shelley still has liv-ing descendants through Ianthe, who married Edward Jeffries Es-daile in 1837 and died in 1876, leaving two sons. Her grandson, Wil-liam Esdaile of Cothelstone House, near Taunton, owns a number of Shelley's early unpublished manuscripts.

On July 17, 1823, a week before Mary Shelley started back to Eng-land, Byron and Trelawny left Italy to take part in the Greek war of independence. One of Trelawny's last actions in Italy was to pro-vide Mary Shelley with enough money for her return to England. The *Liberal*, after four excellent issues, was a confessed failure. By-ron's indifference and the mighty artillery of concerted conservative criticism had been too much for it. Leigh Hunt remained in Italy two gloomy years and returned to England rather bitter against Byron's memory.

In less than a year after he landed in Greece, Byron lay dead at Missolonghi; but Trelawny remained, the hero of exploits both mar-tial and marital that equaled those of his youth. He lived longer than any of Shelley's other friends — long enough for a new series of rather discreditable adventures with wives and mistresses. Tough, positive, and vigorous, he continued to worship Shelley's memory and to scorn most of Shelley's friends except Hogg and Claire Clairmont. As an old man in his eighties he never missed his daily sea-baths, summer or winter. He died at the age of ninety-one, and his ashes were duly interred beside those of Shelley in Rome.

Chapter XXVII

How SHELLEY's aims throve or languished during his life has been
the theme of this book. Yet Shelley valued life so lightly as mere
physical activity and so highly as the expression of undying spiritual
values that for him a worthy life, as he said of Keats, becomes a portion of Intellectual Beauty, the only undying activity, and bears its
part in shaping to better ends the thoughts and deeds of unborn
generations. To what extent, and how, did Shelley attain this earthly
immortality?

Shelley's death was greeted with a short burst of the same factionalism — hatred from the Tories, championship from the radicals, and
a fairly generous desire for fair play from the liberals — which had
obscured his recognition during life. After the obituaries he might
have dropped at once out of public notice but for the verse-writers
and the *Liberal.*

The *Liberal,* with which Shelley's name was associated, was not
yet dead, and the abuse which the conservative press heaped upon it
included some posthumous abuse of Shelley. During 1822 seven
poems on Shelley's death were published, mostly by admirers. They
were all mediocre, but some of them asserted a strong conviction of
Shelley's greatness, and all of them, together with the conservative
abuse, helped keep Shelley's name alive until his poetry could be
more justly judged.

With a "Sonnet to Percy Shelley" in the *Literary Examiner* for
September 20, 1823, the immediate reaction to Shelley's death may
be said to have died away. Thenceforth his reputation becomes a
part of the ocean of human thought to which he contributed. Like
the waters of a distinctive stream, its color and current may be hazily
distinguished, as it seeks to amalgamate with the tides of opinion and
change that make up the complex character of what is called Victorian England. Eventually it is "borne darkly, fearfully afar" until
it merges indistinguishably with the elements of which it is a part.

For several years after Shelley's death he was but slightly noticed
by most people who expressed themselves publicly on literary matters. The publication of his *Posthumous Poems* in 1824 elicited ten
reviews and some incidental comment and quotation, but the book

471

was considered such a bad risk that it had to be guaranteed by B. W. Procter, T. F. Kelsall, and T. L. Beddoes, all ardent admirers of Shelley. Otherwise Shelley's name would have survived in the years 1823–30 chiefly because of his incidental connection with Byron and the *Liberal,* and because a small group of unliterary radical admirers considered him a prophet.

The year 1832 marks the crest of a much broader interest which had been gathering head for two years and which dwindled so rapidly during the next six years that again it seemed possible that Shelley might soon be forgotten. That this relapse creates an exaggerated impression, however, is shown by the fact that in 1834 two pirated editions of Shelley's "Works" appeared, and in 1836 still another appeared, and also the fourth edition of *The Beauties of Percy Bysshe Shelley.* In 1834 or 1835 Mary Shelley was offered six hundred pounds for an annotated edition of her husband's works. When this edition appeared in 1839, it received over twice the number of reviews that *Posthumous Poems* had received, and the volume and tone of other comment in that year made it practically impossible, for at least a generation, that Shelley's name would slip back into semi-obscurity.

The forces that brought about this increased interest in Shelley were, as usual, in part accidental and in part natural and inherent. The first growth of Shelley's fame owed a noticeable debt to his connection with Byron. For twenty years after his death nearly ten per cent of the attention to Shelley was stimulated by an original interest in Byron and the *Liberal.* This factor had no significance after 1832, but in the critical years when Shelley's reputation languished most it was an important sustaining element.

The gradual growth of liberalism was another accidental factor from which Shelley's reputation profited noticeably. It brought about a new toleration.and a genuine, though somewhat limited, appreciation and even enthusiasm. Such new liberal or radical-liberal periodicals as the *Westminster Review,* the *Athenæum,* the shortlived *Edinburgh Literary Journal,* the *Atlas,* the *Spectator,* the *Tatler,* and *Tait's Edinburgh Magazine* gave a distinctly more liberal tone to literary criticism. They were also, by and large, the periodicals most interested in Shelley for twenty years after his death.

Two of these journals, the *Westminster Review* and *Tait's Edinburgh Magazine,* were Benthamite organs and were considered somewhat radical. But the radicalism of the Benthamites was a utilitarian radicalism. There is a considerable difference between Shelley's condemnation of commerce, in *Queen Mab,* and the *Westminster Review's* ideal of solving social and economic difficulties by stimulating trade and sharing more fully with the working classes the profit that trade creates. Otherwise there should have been more articles about Shelley in the *Westminster Review,* whose coterie included several of Shelley's friends and admirers.

In the third and fourth decades of the century a new group of cheap journals arose, with the main purpose of furnishing educational matter for the working classes while avoiding all religious and political opinions in deference to the odious Newspaper Stamp Tax. These journals nevertheless evinced a peculiar interest in Shelley. Of his opinions they had little to say, except an occasional vague word of regret for his lack of Christianity. Their interest was largely in anecdotes, and in Shelley's romantic life. They quoted his poetry only occasionally, and never the more radical passages. Nevertheless this interest was considerable, especially in the early 1830's, and resulted in numerous little articles, particularly in the *Mirror.*

Side by side with these conservative workingmen's periodicals existed a vigorously radical labor journalism. Even before Shelley's death Richard Carlile had begun turning the interest of radicals toward Shelley, and William Clark, one of Carlile's clerks, had published a pirated edition of *Queen Mab.* Within ten years after Shelley's death Carlile and other members of his family had brought out five pirated editions of *Queen Mab,* besides buying and selling the remainder of Shelley's original edition. At the same time Carlile's *Republican* and *Lion* published articles and poems about Shelley. Eight of Carlile's radical friends, arrested in 1825 for continuing his activities during one of his numerous imprisonments, published from prison the *Newgate Magazine,* which within less than two years contained thirteen articles, quotations, and poems by or about Shelley.

Robert Owen, whom it is just possible Shelley may have known, was perhaps even more influential than Richard Carlile in spreading the knowledge of Shelley among English working-class radicals. The Owenites regarded Shelley's *Queen Mab* almost as a Bible. Shelley was indeed the patron saint of their periodical literature. Between 1826 and 1841 at least five Owenite periodicals flourished and made rather conspicuous use of quotations from Shelley and articles about him. The *Quarterly Review* (March 1840) and the *General Baptist Repository,* etc. (May 1839), charged that Owen derived much of his doctrine from Shelley. If, as has been claimed, Robert Owen was the founder of British socialism, it is possible for modern socialism to claim Shelley as a sort of foster-father.

Still another class of radicals who found strength in Shelley and helped to advance his fame were such men as Henry Hetherington, James Watson, W. J. Linton, and J. G. Holyoake. These men worked for the Chartist cause and fought for freedom of speech for the laboring man. Hetherington's *Poor Man's Guardian* (1831-5), "Published in Defiance of the Newspaper Stamp Tax," eventually compelled the government to cease prosecutions under that cloak. The *Poor Man's Guardian* carried more advertisements of *Queen Mab* than any other journal. The *Freethinkers' Information for the People,* edited by Hetherington and Watson apparently in 1836, contained short quotations from Shelley and an account of a visit to his grave.

Both Hetherington and his friend Watson brought out pirated editions of *Queen Mab.* For the first six months of 1839 W. J. Linton edited the *National, A Library for the People,* which in two months contained eleven Shelley items. Several of these men, led by Hetherington, forced an unwilling government in 1841 to convict Edward Moxon of blasphemous libel in publishing *Queen Mab,* thus compelling a relaxation of the government's policy of using this law only as a convenient whip for radicals.

Queen Mab was by long odds the most frequently printed, the most extensively advertised, and the most eagerly read of Shelley's works for at least twenty years after his death. Fourteen or more separate pirated editions circulated from hand to hand among British working-class radicals. Its vitality during that period was the largest single factor in the vitality of Shelley's reputation.

Meanwhile, through the years, Shelley's personal friends had been warm propagandists. In some of them Shelley had inspired almost a religious veneration that made of him something more than a mortal man. Emilia Viviani had expressed this feeling during Shelley's life, and it was echoed later by Mary Shelley, Claire Clairmont, Leigh Hunt, and Marianne Hunt. "My divine friend" Hunt had called him shortly after his death, adding: "I cannot help thinking of him as if he were alive as much as ever, so unearthly he always appeared to me, and so seraphical a King of the elements." Thirty-seven years later he described Shelley as "one of those great and rare spirits" who "approach divinity." Marianne Hunt thought she received supernatural visits from Shelley after his death, and Claire Clairmont wrote of him as an angelic, superhuman being. Mary Shelley described herself, in the preface to Hogg's biography of Shelley, as the "chosen mate of a celestial spirit . . . a priestess dedicated to his glorification."

Much of the service done to Shelley's reputation by these friends and missionaries cannot be detailed. Mary Shelley and Leigh Hunt both had extensive connections in literary and journalistic circles. Thornton Hunt continued this influence with a younger generation of journalists. Undoubtedly they were responsible for a personal influence far beyond the published record and beyond the evidence afforded by their extant letters.

Nearly every item published by this small group between 1822 and 1841 was of unusual importance. Medwin's *Conversations with Lord Byron* and memoir of Shelley presented Shelley to a large audience as Byron's moral and mental equal or superior, instead of the mere hanger-on he had been supposed by many to have been. Some years later Trelawny repeated and emphasized the same picture. Leigh Hunt defended Shelley against his early posthumous traducers, wrote tributes in prose and poetry, welcomed Shelley items in the various journals he edited, published *The Masque of Anarchy* with a valuable memoir, and encouraged his son Thornton to carry on the same tradition. Mary Shelley, though powerfully handicapped by her dependence on her embittered father-in-law, published *Posthumous Poems* in 1824 and the first complete editions in 1839 and 1840, with full semi-biographical notes that have ever since proved invaluable.

In life Shelley had come to despair of his ability to reach the popular mind directly. As in *Prometheus Unbound,* he had directed his "passion for reforming the world" more to "the highly refined imagination of the more select classes of poetical readers," hoping that it would eventually filter down to the popular mind through the minds of others. During the twenty years following his death this hope was not entirely fruitless.

One fine mind which listened while most others remained heedless was that of George Henry Lewes, later founder and editor of the *Contemporary Review.* As a young student in Germany Lewes wrote to Leigh Hunt in 1838 expressing his deep interest in Shelley, asking questions about him, and stating that he was writing a biographical and critical study of Shelley. The book was presumably written, since it was advertised as in the press, but it never appeared, nor is there any clue as to what became of it. Some of its ideas and values may have gone into the later work of William Michael Rossetti, whom Lewes is known to have helped in the preparation of his valuable *Memoir of Shelley* in 1869. Some of it may also have been preserved in the long enthusiastic and genuinely critical article which Lewes published in the *Westminster Review* for April 1841, hailing Shelley as one of the two great Englishmen of the nineteenth century, but the book itself remains a mystery.

Another mind such as Shelley had hoped to inspire was that of young Robert Browning. In the year 1826 Robert Browning, then a youth of fourteen, came across Benbow's pirated *Miscellaneous Poems* of Shelley (1826). He had never heard of the author before, but he so admired this volume that he immediately sought Shelley's other works. From that moment until his death in 1889 Browning was a great admirer of Shelley. Somewhere he obtained a copy of *Queen Mab;* for two years he became an atheist and a vegetarian. His first published volume, *Pauline* (1833), contained a long, passionate apostrophe to Shelley as the great "Sun-treader," first scorned and later ignored, who was too great and pure a spirit ever to die.

But Browning was a liberal rather than a radical. In his home environment and in his education he was a product of the new middle-class liberalism of which the Reform Bill of 1832 was a fairly typical product. After the first few years his appreciation of Shelley was primarily as a rare soul and a great voice of passion and human charity, but not as a radical prophet.

A more ephemeral example of Shelley's appeal to the more refined and superior type of reader is furnished by the Cambridge Apostles, who discovered Shelley in 1829, printed *Epipsychidion,* and debated the merits of Shelley versus Byron with Oxford undergraduates. They were interested primarily in Shelley's "pure poetry" and were said to have become later rather ashamed of their enthusiasm. Some of their Oxford antagonists admitted afterwards that they had not understood who Shelley was, and really thought they had been arguing about Shenstone.

It should not be supposed that the early posthumous reputation of Shelley was so smooth and regular a development as this survey may have indicated. Reputations do not arise so easily out of the confused sea of varying opinions which characterize every generation. Crosscurrents deflect and undertows retard at the same time that other currents accelerate. Throughout the whole period the reticence of many conservative journals and the constant note of apology common to most friendly criticism except that of the radicals (which was rather outside regular literary channels) indicate that the age continued a bit uncertain about Shelley.

In more than one genuinely enthusiastic appreciation Shelley was placed — as a climax — alongside Mrs. Hemans. The *Edinburgh Literary Gazette* of January 2, 1829, after sincerely praising Shelley's great poetic merit, asserted that it was less than that of Professor John Wilson. In 1830 the *British Magazine* remarked that Shelley was "gifted with powers almost equal to any poet who ever existed" — but the remark is a brief digression in an appreciation of the Reverend Mr. George Croly, who is dignified with a full sketch in a series on Popular Authors of the Nineteenth Century, from which Shelley is omitted. In January 1836 the *Edinburgh Review* could casually deprecate "the schoolboy popularity of Shelley," and in 1840 Ebenezer Elliott, in a "Defence of Modern Poetry," praised Keats and Byron while completely ignoring Shelley.

Every generation, like an individual, sees mainly what its own environment prepares it to see, and what it wishes to see. The white radiance of eternity, if it ever beats clearly upon any character, times its arrival in terms of light-years rather than of human generations, and too often finds its object either vanished or hopelessly discolored by the medium in which it has arrived. Certainly the first generation after Shelley saw him fully as much in terms of itself as in terms of the essential Shelley. His radicalism was too comprehensive for them. It was not an affair merely of literary expression, or of religion, or politics, or social or economic views, but an uneven combination of all five. It conformed badly to the tendency of most radicals to combine radicalism in one or more of these categories with conservatism in others.

This was true of Shelley's radical contemporaries and remained true after his death. To all of his admirers he was an object of imperfect sympathy. Most of Shelley's working-class radical admirers, like Richard Carlile, applauded his political and religious radicalism, rejected his social radicalism, and were completely uninterested in his radicalism of poetic technique. The Benthamites, interested mainly in economic and political reform, could not follow him beyond the inevitable divergence of their utilitarianism from his idealism. The loyal service of his personal friends was a loyalty much more to his personality than to his mission. The appreciation of the few "choice spirits" was predominantly æsthetic.

All, moreover, were affected by the growing security, comfort, and complacency of the times. After Chartism, working-class radicalism lost its vigor. The Benthamites relaxed comfortably in the arms of increasing material prosperity; Mary Shelley, growing yearly more conservative, became intent on reconciling Shelley to Victorianism; Leigh Hunt, in his *Autobiography,* could review his own stirring young manhood without the least spark of reminiscent fire; and Robert Browning, having begun as a Shelleyan atheist and vegetarian, could end as a typical æsthetic admirer.

The middle and later Victorian students of Shelley produced more than a dozen biographies, scores of editions, and hundreds of critical essays, many of them from the most distinguished critics of the age. Led at first by Lady Shelley, they collected and preserved priceless materials for later biography and criticism. Without distinguishing between editors, biographers, and critics, one needs only to call a list of distinguished names: Mrs. Angeli, Arnold, Bagehot, Bradley, Brailsford, Brooke, Browning, Clutton-Brock, Dowden, Forman, Garnett, Gosse, Hutton, Ingpen, Locock, Masson, P. E. More, Quiller-Couch, W. M. Rossetti, Salt, Sharp, Swinburne, Symonds, Francis Thompson, James Thomson, Todhunter, Wise, Woodberry, and Yeats. J. P. Anderson's bibliography appended to William Sharp's *Life of Shelley* (1887) contains over a hundred and fifty book titles in biography and criticism alone.

In 1886 a Shelley Society was formed, consisting of about four hundred members, among them Robert Browning, George Bernard Shaw, W. M. Rossetti, H. B. Forman, F. J. Furnivall, and T. J. Wise. For two years this society flourished and published volumes by or about Shelley, besides managing public productions of both *Hellas* and *The Cenci.* A number of papers were read at its meetings, including several distinctly able critical discussions.

By 1887 forty or fifty of Shelley's lyrics had been set to music, as well as all the choral part of *Hellas.* In 1892 the centenary of Shelley's birth was celebrated at Field Place and Oxford. Numerous books and articles were published, including George Edward Woodberry's scholarly edition of Shelley's poetical works. In 1894 Eton accepted a bust of Shelley (having declined to do so in 1870) — while Dr. Hornby still wished, *sotto voce,* that Shelley had gone to Harrow. Oxford accepted Sir Onslow Ford's sentimental sculpture and a part of Lady Shelley's accumulation of Shelleyana.

In 1922 the centenary of Shelley's death was even more extensively noticed, not only throughout the English-speaking world, but in most European countries. Again numerous books and articles were published, and *The Cenci* was produced on the stage in London and Prague. By this time it was a commonplace not to be questioned in either Europe or America that Shelley was one of the great English poets.

Still there was an interesting cautiousness or vagueness about much of the appreciation of Shelley by many of the Victorians. Some of them were definitely antagonistic, echoing Charles Lamb's earlier statement that "no one was ever the wiser or better for reading Shelley." Charles Kingsley vigorously accused Shelley of preaching "the worship of uncleanness as the last and highest ethical development of 'pure' humanity." "Yon man Shelley," said Thomas Carlyle, rudely interrupting a rhapsody by William Bell Scott, "was just a scoundrel, and ought to have been hangèd"; publicly he uttered: "Hear a Shelley filling the earth with inarticulate wail; like the infinite, inarticulate grief and weeping of forsaken infants." Tennyson, while granting Shelley's "splendid imagery and colour," found in his poetry "a sort of tenuity," and William Morris, a radical himself, charged that Shelley "had no eyes," and always floundered in narration.

One might discount most of these statements as random remarks if their counterparts did not present themselves so embarrassingly in some of the most impressive and fully considered critical essays of the age. Matthew Arnold's "beautiful and ineffectual angel, beating in the void his luminous wings in vain," was protested by Stopford Brooke in his Shelley Society inaugural address, but it remains to this day one of the most influential critical dicta on Shelley. Walter Bagehot's weighty essay is based upon the assumption that Shelley's actions were motivated by impulse rather than reason or principle; Browning expresses the belief that Shelley would eventually have turned to Christianity; and Francis Thompson makes of him an angelic creature of purely naïve and instinctive wisdom. With Thompson many an admirer has been glad to "peep over the wild mass of revolutionary metaphysics" and discover that Shelley was "to the last" an "enchanted child." To Leslie Stephen, who thought "the crude incoherence of his whole system too obvious to require exposition," a beautiful, iridescent mist above a muddy pool of Godwinism, Shelley's appeal to most readers seemed sentimentally pathetic — the poet and his readers were really weeping together over the "obstinate insubstantiality" of Shelley's hopes.

In America it was much the same. There was abundant appreciation of the Victorian type. The poetry of Edgar Allan Poe showed

479

some Shelleyan influences; that of his somewhat obscure predecessor
Thomas Holley Chivers showed more, including a poetic tribute to
Shelley. But in 1873 Emerson had hardly read Shelley and had never
cared for him, and about 1882 the president of Harvard University
hesitated to accept from Captain Silsbee the manuscript of Shelley's
"The Cloud." One of America's foremost critics, Paul Elmer More,
expressed a fair counterpart of Leslie Stephen's view by speaking of
Prometheus Unbound and *The Revolt of Islam* as a "kind of illusive,
yet rapturous, emanation of hope, devoid of specific content."

Such criticism owes much of its confusion both to the changed
times and to the half-apologetic attitude of Shelley's earlier liberal
admirers. The radical note, which had swelled so loud during the
Reform Bill and Chartist agitations, had died gradually without important issue. Thereafter there was no important great popular agitation in England for more than fifty years. Reminders of the old
radical admiration of Shelley cropped up only occasionally in the
writings of such men as H. N. Brailsford and H. S. Salt and in the
sarcasms of George Bernard Shaw.

As for Freedom, the facts seemed to support Tennyson's assurance
that Freedom was slowly broadening down from precedent to precedent. Were not the nineteenth-century French Revolutionists (whom
Mary Shelley even regarded with aversion) "the red fool-fury of the
Seine"? It was better for the middle and upper classes to make the precedents. England was steadily becoming stronger and richer, the
increased comforts of life were "broadening down" also, child labor
was being restricted, and public education was being extended. England was taking up the white man's burden with profitable resignation. Younger sons and discontented laborers knew where they could
go — or if not they could learn from a hundred novels that emigration
solved all difficulties. The fierce hopes and fears engendered by the
French Revolution and its aftermath belonged to a closed chapter
of human progress.

In this atmosphere one could appreciate Shelley a little more generously than the earlier liberals, and apologize a little less conspicuously and uneasily. But the fundamental attitude was the same.
Shelley was one of the great English poets; practically everyone
thought so now. Yet in everything that really mattered to *him* except
his purely personal emotions and his fine art, he was dead wrong.

Professor Dowden, Shelley's authorized biographer, could not be
independent of the dominant tendency of the age. His treatment of
Shelley is apologetically and sentimentally protective. To him Shel-

ley was great and good not because of, but in spite of, his major beliefs. He did not sufficiently perceive either the guiding purpose of Shelley's life or the strength of that purpose. This may explain why one so admirable in the collection and presentation of factual detail could be at the same time so glossily mediocre in his critical treatment of Shelley's ideas. Perhaps it is the same latent incongruity that prompted the opening paragraphs of Paul Elmer More's essay on Shelley (1909), in which he seeks to show, by very apposite quotations, that most criticism of Shelley is mealy-mouthed and straddling.

Undoubtedly a large part of Shelley's popularity for a hundred years has been based upon an evasion of the real Shelley. His lyrics were set to music, and his mission was set aside. His great lyrics were to him for the most part only tangential to the controlling purposes of his life, for which he reserved his greatest poetic energies. To most of his admirers these splendid lapses constitute his main glory, and his principal purpose in writing constitutes an utter failure which they are not quite frank enough to face squarely.

More than one poet has survived for generations on the basis of purely lyric poetry no greater than Shelley's, and Shelley could doubtless survive for several more generations on that basis alone. But it is yet too early to say that the vital radical force of Shelley, from which the early nineteenth-century reformers drew inspiration, is dead. To an appreciable extent it helped stimulate Young Germany in the abortive revolution of 1848, and the Italian patriots of the Risorgimento. Only a few years ago a group of Communists in a Milwaukee jail were reported to have attempted to convert fellow prisoners by reading *Queen Mab* aloud. We learn from the autobiography of Upton Sinclair, certainly one of the great radical voices of the age, that Shelley was one of the enthusiasms of his youth.

Karl Marx is reported to have said that, had Shelley lived, he would "always have been one of the advance-guard of socialism," but if he meant Marxian socialism, or communism, he was as badly mistaken as the later Browning in suggesting that Shelley would in the end have turned Christian.

Shelley was no communist; he feared the mob, and shuddered at the idea of progress based largely on class antagonism or material prosperity. Yet even in the Victorian era Henry M. Stanley once warned some members of the Shelley Society that they were ignorantly sponsoring a force which might eventually help overthow the social organization to which they adhered. Today, with Shelley's poems taught in thousands of class rooms, and with criticism gradually achieving a less distorted view of their intended significance, it is safe to say that hundreds of eager young minds will achieve, at least for a while, a deeper and more imaginatively sympathetic idealism than if Shelley had never lived.

It is true that no really significant organized radical movement since Shelley's day has yet achieved the moral idealism and the imaginative insight that would make a fully effective instrument of the greatest radical voice in poetry since Lucretius. But the mighty west wind to which he prayed has scattered and is scattering his ashes and sparks; and his voice is still heard as the trumpet of a prophecy.

Index

Index

Index

Index

Index

Index

Index

TYPE NOTE

The text of this book is set in Caledonia, a Linotype face which belongs to the family of printing types called "modern face" by printers — a term used to mark the change in style of type-letters that occurred about 1800. Caledonia borders on the general design of Scotch Modern, but is more freely drawn than that letter.

The book was composed by The Plimpton Press, Norwood, Massachusetts, and printed and bound by Vail-Ballou Press, Binghamton, New York. The typography and binding design are by W. A. Dwiggins.

WAD

808266

Iowa State University Library
Ames, Iowa 50010